COUNTRY MUSIC
Humorists and Comedians

COUNTRY MUSIC

MUSIC IN
AMERICAN LIFE

*A list of books in the series
appears at the end of this book.*

Humorists and Comedians

Loyal Jones

UNIVERSITY OF ILLINOIS PRESS
Urbana and Chicago

© 2008 by the Board of Trustees
of the University of Illinois
All rights reserved
Manufactured in the United States of America
C 5 4 3 2 1
♾ This book is printed on acid-free paper.

Library of Congress Cataloging-in-Publication Data
Jones, Loyal,
Country music humorists and comedians / Loyal Jones.
p. cm. — (Music in American life)
Includes bibliographical references and index.
ISBN 978-0-252-03369-8 (0-252-03369-8 : alk. paper)
1. Country musicians—United States—Biography—Dictionaries.
2. Comedians—United States—Biography—Dictionaries.
3. Humorists, American—Biography—Dictionaries.
I. Title.
ML102.C7.J66   2008
792.702'8092273—dc22 [B]   2008032919

This book is dedicated to those who made us laugh and to those whose burdens were lightened and whose lives were brightened by laughter.

CONTENTS

PREFACE AND ACKNOWLEDGMENTS

I began this book at the suggestion of the distinguished scholar Bill C. Malone, the author of *Country Music, USA*, and other important works. He pointed out that while there have been numerous scholarly books on country music, there has been no major work on the humor and humorists that have been an important part of country music entertainment. When I began to gather materials, I thought that this would not be a big book. That was about eight years ago, and since then it has evolved into an encyclopedia of country music humorists and comedians. I bring this work to a close with the knowledge that, even with diligence, I have missed a lot of persons and events related to country music humor.

All of the comedians and humorists included here are connected in some way to traditional, folk, old-time, country, gospel, or bluegrass music. I've edited out entries on interesting people who have assumed the country persona or employed country humor in some way but who were not music-related. Some whom I have included are only tenuously connected, but they have appeared in country music venues and have employed the same kind of humor that characterized those in my main category. I have included B-Western film sidekicks such as Smiley Burnette and Pat Buttram because they were part of country music shows during their careers. Overall, the ones included are varied, ranging from the most exaggerated rubes to some pretty sophisticated folks, even those admitting to high levels of education. This suits the variety of people who listen to country and related music. Some of these humorists will be familiar to most Americans, while others probably are known only at local musical venues or bluegrass festivals.

When I started this book, I was somewhat familiar with the subject, having grown up listening to broadcasts from WSM, Nashville; WNOX and WROL, Knoxville; WBT, Charlotte; WWNC, Asheville; WSB, Atlanta; and WLS and WJJD, Chicago, all of which beamed a lot of country music and comedy into my corner of North Carolina. Also, the singer-songwriter-humorist Billy Edd Wheeler and I have staged festivals of

Appalachian humor and published four books of decidedly rural Appalachian humor. In addition, I have published two biographies of musicians and a number of articles about country-related music. I have gotten acquainted with several country music promoters, humorists, and comedians, including John Lair, Bascom Lamar Lunsford, Grandpa Jones, Roni Stoneman, "Harmonica Joe" Troyan, Carl Hurley, "Old Joe" Clark, Pete Stamper, Bun Wilson, and Betty Lou York, in the course of my work. I have done some public speaking and entertaining, using country humor sometimes as the main thing or as a means of keeping the audience awake for other subjects.

I have also collected a pretty good library on country music, including six encyclopedias with many helpful facts and a lot of books and articles on comedians and humorists, as well as joke books and general books on humor and entertainment. I have scholar friends who have written on country music and who are well aware of the value of humor in this business. They have included Bill C. Malone, the late Charles K. Wolfe, Wayne W. Daniel, Bill Lightfoot, Robert Cogswell, and Ivan M. Tribe; I asked them and others for advice and for names of comedians. I later sent the list of those I had included to them for their input on the ones I had missed. I am grateful for their personal help and also for their contributions of articles, books, photographs, and other materials. There were many others whose work I have used or with whom I have discussed aspects of this project. I began interviewing as many comedians and humorists as I could, most of them by telephone, beginning with Grandpa Jones, Wade Mainer, Bill Carlisle, Jerry Clower, James "Sparky" Rucker, Beecher Kirby, Roni Stoneman, Melvin Goins, Tim O'Brien, Ron Thomason, John Hartford, Gary Mule Deer, Doug Green, Carl Hurley, "Old Joe" Clark, Pete Stamper, Randall Franks, and Betty Lou York (for a complete list of interviews, see Sources). I thank them for their time, their remembrances, and their insights into the value of humor in their careers and in the entertainment business.

I benefited from the resources in the Country Music Foundation Library in Nashville and from the help of staffers there: Ronnie Pugh, John Rumble, and Dawn Oberg. I would also like to acknowledge the Berea College Special Collections, which houses a huge Appalachian archive, and the John Lair and Renfro Valley Barn Dance Collections, staffed by Gerald Roberts, Steve Gowler, Shannan Wilson, and Harry Rice (Harry wrote the entry on Gene Cobb and sent me many materials and tips). I also want to thank Phillip Collins for sharing material he gathered on his father, Curley Collins, and on many other early musicians and comedians.

I have quoted a good many of those whom I have interviewed, either in the text of entries or for examples of stories and routines. To preserve the character of their speech, I have rendered them as I heard them speak, retaining some grammatical liberties. Punctuation of spoken English is always problematical, but I have used it as a means of clarifying the speaker's perceived intent. I have also compressed some of the longer quotes, editing out repetitive and irrelevant material from oral interviews without always using an ellipsis. Clarity in thought, opinion, or story was my main concern.

I have written extensively about some of the humorists because there was a lot of information about them. Entries on others are short because I couldn't find much information. In a few cases I had only a real name or a stage name, and thus they are not included. A few entertainers or their agents were not cooperative, and sufficient information was not otherwise available. It is my hope that knowledgeable readers will bring names and careers and information to light so they may be included in future editions.

I've had a wonderful time getting acquainted with these humorists and comedians who have brought delight to audiences across the country. Many of them came out of hard times and had little going for them except musical and verbal talent and quick, retentive, and creative minds. They deserve to be known and to have some record of their lives and achievements. I am gratified in presenting them here.

INTRODUCTION TO
COUNTRY MUSIC HUMOR

Country humor, as in the country bumpkin versus the city slicker, is an old theme in entertainment, coming down to us from oral tradition and literature through minstrel and medicine shows, vaudeville, repertory theater, and country music shows. The jokes and routines of this type of humor enable the rube to outsmart or out-retort the city slicker. The character of Jack (as in "Jack and the Beanstalk") in Old World folktales, coming to this country in the memories of our forebears, took on the modest country-boy manner in the New World, but Jack was always competent, and through intelligence, charm, luck, trickery, or magic, he triumphed over his adversaries. Country humor has a whole lot of Jack in it. Americans like stories about the underdog prevailing over the powerful, arrogant, or oversophisticated person.

Folklorists have commented on the usefulness of humor in helping us to understand our own identities and how our particular group differs from others. William Lightfoot credits William Hugh Jansen, an early folklorist, with showing the value of humor in delineating us from others. Jansen defined one type of humor as *esoteric* (about our own group) and another as *exoteric* (about other peoples' groups). "Jansen wrote that the esoteric factor 'stems from the group sense of belonging and serves to defend and strengthen that sense. . . .' Jansen went on to define the exoteric factor as 'what one group thinks of another and what it thinks that other group thinks it thinks.'"[1] An example of esoteric humor is a saying of the late governor Bert T. Combs of Kentucky, who came from the rural mountain end of the state: "You don't learn anything from the *second* kick of a mule." All rural people of his generation would instantly see the wisdom and logic of this statement. An example of an exoteric joke from the modest Appalachian perspective about Texans, known for their expansiveness in bragging, is this one:

> A southern mountain farmer is showing his small hillside farm to a Texas cousin, who has gotten rich in the oil and banking "bidness." The Texan wants to know

how many acres he has. When told that he has thirty acres, the Texan says, "I can get in my pickup and drive all day, and I'll still be on my ranch." The mountain farmer replies, "Yeah, I used to have a pickup truck like that."

In the rube–city slicker jokes, the city slicker assumes that he is better educated, more sophisticated, smarter, and has better manners than the rube, but the joke is constructed so that the rube comes out ahead, thus making rural people feel better about themselves as a group.

> A city fellow in a big car drives up to a farmer standing next to his fence and asks, "How far to Nashville?" The farmer says he doesn't know. The man says, "How far to Birmingham?" The farmer doesn't know. The city slicker says, "You don't know much, do you?" The farmer says, "No, but I ain't lost."

Sometimes the jokes highlight the differences between one group that is seen as needy in some way and another that has assumed the role of benefactor. Many missionaries were sent by churches to the South, especially to Appalachia, in the first half of the twentieth century, even though the local people saw themselves as religious already. There is a cycle of these "missionary" stories in which the two parties don't seem to be communicating on one level and yet are doing so on another. Here's one:

> An evangelist arrives in Kentucky and heads up a back road to try to save somebody. He sees an old man sitting on his front porch, jumps out, and yells, "Brother, are you lost?" The old man says, "No, I've lived here all my life." The evangelist says, "I mean have you found Jesus?" Mountaineer: "Well, I live so far back up this holler I don't get much news, so I hadn't heard that He was lost. The Bible says He's up in heaven until the Second Coming." Evangelist: "I want to know if you are a member of the Christian band?" Mountaineer: "No, but there is a Bill Christian lives about five miles on up the road." Evangelist: "Look, I'm trying to find out if you're ready for the Judgment Day." Mountaineer: "When is it?" Evangelist: "It may be next week, or it may be next month. We don't know about these things." Mountaineer: "Well, when you find out, you let me know, 'cause the old woman will want to go both days."

This type of humor is similar to the old "Arkansas Traveler" routine that was standard with some of the early country music comedians. Q: "Where does this road go?" A: "I've lived here all my life, and I ain't seen it go nowhere." Q: "How far to Little Rock?" A: "I don't know, but there's a big rock down there in my spring." This type of humor was common in minstrel and vaudeville shows, and it serves the function of making country people or other marginal folk feel better about themselves when they have to deal with people who feel superior to them.

In country comedy, there are numerous jokes and routines that let country people make fun of city or educated folks in an oblique way and thus get back at them for perceived haughtiness. One such joke is about the country boy enrolling in college. He walks across the campus, meets an English professor, and asks, "Where's the library at?" The professor says, "Here, we don't end sentences with prepositions." The country boy says, "Okay, where's the library at, Jackass?"

SOURCES OF COUNTRY HUMOR

Folk Sources

Jokes are the most popular and universal form of folklore. They seem to come out of nowhere, they keep coming, and all of us have heard or told them. Old ones are constantly being adapted to fit new issues, groups, or situations. Many jokes have come down from Old World sources, sometimes as shortened versions of folktales going back to Chaucer's time. Most of the early country music entertainers grew up in rural areas where the oral tradition was strong, and thus they had a rich repertoire of humorous stories from this tradition.

Minstrel Shows

Minstrel shows, as we mainly think of them, began with white people dressing up and blackening their faces to present their interpretation of the speech, song, dance, and humor of plantation blacks. However, such routines were based to some extent on performances of song, dance, and spoken humor by black people, who also appeared in early minstrel shows. Others were extrapolated from informal performances by black people. The image of blacks presented by whites in minstrel shows, however, was romantic, comical, and racist, distorted by the prejudices of the time and by theatrical requirements. Apparently, the first such minstrel performance by a white person dressed as a black person was by Thomas D. Rice in 1828 doing a solo song-and-dance act in blackface that he called "Jim Crow." According to Constance Rourke, "Rice had heard an old crippled Negro hostler singing in a stable yard as he rubbed down horses, and had seen him dancing an odd limping dance as he worked—'rockin' de heel.' Rice studied the dance and learned the song with its refrain—

> wheel about, turn about,
>   do jis so,
> An' ebery time I wheel about
>   I jump Jim Crow."

Rice was a hit with audiences, and soon he was doing other impersonations of black people—dandies from river towns, boatmen, and workers on plantations—with plantation melodies and slave dances. "Rice enjoyed a popularity in the '30s and '40s which was unmatched by any other American comedian of his time."[2]

Daniel Emmett, an Irishman from the backwoods, organized The Virginia Minstrels, a troupe that became famous in blackface minstrelsy, giving its first public performance in 1843. Edwin Christy's Minstrels got together in 1846, with some of their songs written by Stephen Foster. Other troupes followed, using Christy's three-part format: In the first, the company paraded in and took chairs in a semicircle, where the interlocutor elicited jokes from the "end men," and the troupe "walked around" in review. The second part was called the "olio," a hodgepodge or medley of music and other material in front of the curtain. Last was a burlesque performance of a play or opera. Minstrel shows flourished from 1850 to 1870 and then declined, partly because of the rise of vaudeville.

An example of minstrel humor that showed up in country comedy was the "Good and Bad" routine done in several variations by minstrel performers such as Billy Golden and Joe Heins, as well as Len Spencer. The piece was first published by Charley White in his *New Book of Black Wit and Darky Conversations* (1856). Archie Campbell did the routine on "Hee Haw" and in other venues.[3] Here is the routine, quite different in content from the earlier versions but with the same good/bad idea, as performed by Archie Campbell and Ralph Emery:

> Ralph: How's things in Bull's Gap?
> Archie: Well, I wish I could laugh more, but I'll tell you, I'm feeling pretty bad today. I guess you heard my great-uncle died.
> R: Oh, Archie, that's bad.
> A: No, that's good.
> R: That's good? How come?
> A: Well, you see, I was his favorite nephew, and when he died he left me fifty thousand dollars.
> R: Ho ho, that is good.
> A: No, that's bad, Ralph.
> R: Oh, that's bad. How come?
> A: Well, the income tax people got ahold of me, and when they got through with that fifty thousand dollars, I didn't have but twenty-five thousand left.
> R: Oh, they'll do it every time; that is bad, Archie.
> A: No, that's good.
> R: That's good?
> A: I still had enough to do something I'd wanted to do all my life, so I took that twenty-five thousand, and I bought me an airplane and learned to fly.
> R: Oh, I'll bet you really enjoyed that; that is good.
> A: No, that's bad.
> R: That's bad? How come?
> A: Well, I was out flyin' the other day, doin' a little stunt flyin', you know. And I was flyin' upside down, and I fell out of that thing.
> R: Fell out? That is bad, Arch.
> A: No, that's good.
> R: That's good? How come?
> A: Well, I got a little closer to the ground and looked right under me, and there was a great big soft haystack.

R: Oh, well, it turned out all right; that's good.

A: No, that's bad.

R: That's bad? How come?

A: Well, I got a little closer, and I saw there was a pitchfork stickin' in that haystack aimed right at me.

R: A pitchfork? Look out, that is bad.

A: No, that's good.

R: That's good? How come?

A: I missed the pitchfork.

R: Oh, well, it all worked out; that is good.

A: No, that's bad.

R: That's bad?

A: I missed the haystack too.

R: Oh, well, that, that's bad.

A: No, that's good.

R: That's good?

A: Yeah. You see, I bounced around there for awhile, an' the ambulance came and took me to the hospital.

R: Well, that's bad.

A: No, that's good.

R: That's good?

A: Yeah, you see, when I got to the hospital, I, uh . . . this girl takin' care of me, you know, pretty little thing, and I took a turn for the nurse; I fell in love with the nurse.

R: You fell in love with the nurse?

A: Yeah.

R: Mm hmm, that's good.

A: No, that's bad.

R: That's bad? How come, Arch?

A: Well, my wife came in one day, and she saw me kissin' the nurse, and she said to me, she said, "If that's the way you're goin' to act, I'll just pack my clothes and go back to mama."

R: Oh, well, that's good, Arch.

A: You're dadburned right that's good.[4]

The minstrel tradition developed great comic routines, many of them, as Robert Cogswell has shown, from traditional sources. Here are excerpts from a routine that is based on hunting tales that came from Old World folktales but with variants in American folklore called "Andy Goes a-Hunting" (the "2" indicates a second, unidentified comedian):

A. I went out huntin' one day with a rifle an' got fifty birds with one shot an' never touched a bird.

2. How come?

A. Well, de birds were sittin' side by side on a limb, an' I upped an' aimed right down the limb an' fired, an' the bullet went right straight down de limb where de birds were sittin', an' it opened up a crack an' caught dem by de toes before dey could fly away, an' all I had t' do was just go up dere an' pick 'em off de limb an' put 'em in my sack. Dat's how I got fifty birds without hittin' a one of 'em.

2. Dat's right. When you tell one, you tell a good one. . . .

A. Oh, man, dat ain't nothin' atall. A few years ago I went out huntin' by a big river, an' I looked up an' saw some ducks. Just as I was goin' t' shoot some ducks I heard sumpin' right down at my feet. I looked down an' dere was a big snake. I didn't know what t' do, an' all of a sudden dere was some quail landed nearby, an' I didn't know whether t' shoot de ducks, de quail, or de snake. An' den I looked up an' dere was a bear right by de other side of me.

2. Hmm.

A. I was in terrible shape.

2. Dat's a terrible predicament.

A. Oh, it 'uz worse dan dat. Just as I's wonderin' what t' do de gun exploded, de bullet killed de ducks, dey fell down on de quail an' killed dem, an' den de barrel flew off an' killed de snake, an' de other barrel killed de bear, and de gun kicked me back in de river, an' I come up wit a pocket full o' fish.[5]

The tall tale is as American as apple pie, but as the above example shows, it did not originate here. Constance Rourke traces it to the fairy- or folktales of Europe, through New England, and on into the frontier with all its excesses. Such humor was recycled into minstrel and later country music comedy routines, with the dialect changing to fit new participants.

The best-remembered blackface minstrel act associated with country music was Lasses and Honey, introduced by two Texans, Lee Roy "Lasses" White and Lee Davis "Honey" Wilds. They had earlier done a blackface comedy act in vaudeville circuits. In 1932, George D. Hay invited them to re-create their minstrel act on Friday nights over Nashville's WSM. Their comedy and song parodies were so well received, partly because of the great popularity of "Amos 'n' Andy," that they became regulars on the "Grand Ole Opry" in 1934. White soon moved to Hollywood to pursue a career as an actor, and Wilds also left but was back at the "Opry" in 1939 with a new act, based on the old one, called Jamup and Honey. He and other partners—Tom Woods and Bunny Biggs—played Jamup and Honey at the "Opry" until 1953. Wilds was one of the first "Opry" performers to take a tent show on the road. In 1953, Jamup and Honey went to WNOX and the "Mid-day Merry-Go-Round." Here, because of changing attitudes about racial matters, they abandoned blackface and did the same routines as whiteface comedy until 1957, when the act broke up.

Medicine Shows

While the minstrel shows generally played in towns and larger cities, the medicine shows set up mostly in the small towns and hamlets. The late Fred Smith, who did comedy with Red Rector as Red and Fred on Knoxville radio stations and who performed more recently at the Comedy Barn at Pigeon Forge, Tennessee, remembered the medicine shows that came to rural Madison County, North Carolina:

> I was just a child when the old medicine shows came. They'd set up, build their own stage. The first one I ever saw came to Mars Hill, and they worked every night for two weeks, and it would get larger every night. They had good shows, see. They had good music, and they'd have an amateur show. They'd pack them in because there wasn't no other entertainment back then. The finale would be on Saturday night, and everybody would come to see it. We'd walk miles to see that show. They had some funny stuff. They'd sell Big Chief Tonic. All it was was some bitters and alcohol. They'd make it in tubs, and they had their own labels, and they'd bottle it. The so-called doctor, he done his pitch—it'd cure anything. He'd say, "Take a spoonful before meals." Well, that alcohol in there would whet the appetite of these little old women. He sold that stuff, had these old boys that would run out into the crowd with armfuls of that stuff, and one would come back and say, "Sold out, Sweet Doc, sold out!" and he'd give them some more.
>
> I got a lot of my material from seeing those old shows.[6]

Brooks McNamara, who has written much about early American entertainment, said of the medicine shows, "[A] special sense of mystery and glamour surrounds the medicine showman—the itinerant patent medicine seller whose free performances were an important part of small town life." Such shows, he wrote, appeared in America as early as 1600, but "it was not until about 1850 that the idea of selling medicine between the acts of a free show resulted in the rapid growth of proprietary medicine companies, many of which sent advertising units on the road after the Civil War." Money-making companies, such as the Kickapoo Indian Medicine Company and Hamlin's Wizard Oil, soon found competition from groups such as Fred Smith described, who mixed their concoctions in a hotel-room bathtub or sometimes in a washtub on the spot. Many of the shows were simple affairs with the "pitchman" offering music and comedy alone or with a partner or a small band that included one or more comedians. Some sold medicine out of a satchel, some out of a wagon, and there were big-time shows that McNamara described:

> In addition to the pitchman who sold remedies, more elaborate shows carried an entire cast of performers and musicians, as well as a more-or-less completely equipped tent theater. Some large medicine show companies, in fact, were capable of mounting several hours of entertainment with a dozen or more acts as well as a half-dozen intervals during which the showman could sell his products.[7]

At the turn of the twentieth century the shows were traveling to most of the rural areas of the country. However, by the 1920s the number of shows had declined, partly because of new laws concerning the bottling and sale of alcohol, but also because of the rising importance of the automobile, moving-picture shows, radio, recordings, and other forms of entertainment. The rural audience was no longer as starved for amusement as it had been.

In 1979, Glenn Hinson, a folklorist from the University of North Carolina, with support from the North Carolina Arts Council, mounted a tent show called "Free Show Tonight," featuring many old-time musicians and comedians who had performed in medicine shows, with Roy Acuff (in one performance), Homer "Pappy" Sherrill, DeWitt "Snuffy" Jenkins, Julian "Greasy" Medlin, and others. Paul Wagner Productions of New York made a documentary film about it. In 1983, Hinson took his show, with additional medicine-show veterans, to the American Place Theater in New York as the "Vi-Ton-Ka Medicine Show," with Doc Fred F. Bloodgood as the pitchman.

Here is a comedy routine from the show by Pappy Sherrill and Snuffy Jenkins, both North Carolinians operating from Chapin, South Carolina:

> Snuffy: I want to ask you something, here. Do you know Old Man Brown?
>
> Pappy: Lord have mercy, as many Browns as there are in New York City. Is he in here?
>
> Snuffy: No, he ain't here. He may be dead for all I know.
>
> Pappy: Oh, man, don't say that. What about Old Man Brown?
>
> Snuffy: He got a little black pig, or had one.
>
> Pappy: Had a pig. What about the pig?
>
> Snuffy: He took it down there in the brain patch and blowed its cabbage out.
>
> Pappy: That sounds wrong. You mean he went to the cabbage patch and blowed his brains out. You got it backward.
>
> Snuffy: Well, whatever it was, anyhow the pig's dead. He took it down there and stuck him in a barrel of hot water and pulled him out and scraped all his feathers off.
>
> Pappy: No, no, you've done gone wrong. He scraped all the hair off the pig.
>
> Snuffy: He cleaned the pig.
>
> Pappy: He cleaned the pig.
>
> Snuffy: He took it up there to the smokehouse and divided it.
>
> Pappy: He's done dressed the hog and cut it in two?
>
> Snuffy: Yeah, and he hung one side of it on one side of the smokehouse and the other over here. And along about four o'clock the next morning, some lowdown good-for-nothing-dog-stealing Democrat come there and stole half of that hog.
>
> Pappy: Wait a minute! You've gone too darned far. You are throwing off on Democrats here in New York City, and it's full of 'em. Don't you know good and well that these people don't appreciate that at all?
>
> Snuffy: Well, it was a Democrat got the hog. I don't know which half he got, but he got half of the hog and took off with it.
>
> Pappy: How do you know it was a Democrat?
>
> Snuffy: If it'd been a Republican, he'd a got the whole hog![8]

Pappy Sherrill explained the comedy that he had been involved in over the years, usually with Snuffy Jenkins and Greasy Medlin:

> See, a *single* is a man that gets up by himself and does a comedy routine in front of an audience. Then when you have comedians doing *doubles*, they work together, back and forward; both of them would be comedians together. With *three*, you have the comedians working together, and I'd be the straight man.
>
> Snuffy wore the big britches, and the shoes he wore were on opposite feet. Greasy had a big pair of pants on and old shoes with paint on them. Snuffy and Greasy did a lot of work that we called *doubles*. Then we did a lot of work where we had to use a straight man to lead them up to what's happening, to throw in little things to carry it on, and I was the straight man. I was natural on stage [didn't dress up].[9]

The pitch from the "Doc" to sell his medicine was also part of the entertainment of medicine shows. The language was florid, stilted, with alliteration and other euphonious tricks, and of course it exaggerated the effectiveness of the product, including the purging from the patient of six-foot-long tapeworms.

Many of the early country music performers got their start in medicine shows, among them Fiddlin' John Carson, Riley Puckett, Clayton McMichen, Gid Tanner, Fate Norris, Tom Ashley, Gene Autry, Jimmie Rodgers, Roy Acuff, Bob Wills, and Hank Williams. It was a fine place to learn showmanship before an appreciative audience, to practice one's music, and to learn comedy routines that later would enhance their entertainment shows.

Early radio had many patent-medicine sponsors. A slew of radio entertainers in the 1920s and 1930s hawked Crazy Water Crystals (from a mineral spring in Texas) to facilitate proper elimination. Others sold Black Draught for those whose bowels needed more rigorous stimulation, or Carter's Little Liver Pills for vague ailments. Announcers earnestly promoted potions, such as Wine of Cardui, to deal with "female problems." Patent medicines gave a great boost to early country music and comedy.

Vaudeville

American vaudeville was popular theater that presented musical, dancing, acrobatic, juggling, and magic acts, comedy, and humorous skits at a dazzling pace. Such acts began in saloons and other places where people gathered, but by the 1880s vaudeville had become big business in elaborate theaters in leading cities, beginning with Keith's New Theater and later the Bijou in Boston, the Palace and other theaters in New York City, and smaller ones in other cities. Vaudeville in the beginning was a decidedly urban form of entertainment, although country entertainers were later added to appeal to audiences in smaller cities and towns. Vaudeville humor largely consisted of jokes and routines pared down to their bare essentials. The long rural stories about hunting and other drawn-out adventures didn't work here. The new jokes got right to it. Examples:

>Q: How's your wife?
>A: Compared to what?

Or,

>Q: Is he afraid of work?
>A: No, he can lie down beside it and go to sleep.

The comic monologue was another popular form in vaudeville; it featured incongruity, surprising diversions, wit, and charm. It became the standard form for television and comedy-club stand-up comedians from the "Ed Sullivan Show" to the Blue Collar Comedy Tour. Vaudeville was clean family entertainment with strict rules as to what subjects, or even words, could be used. A big change has come about from that time to modern stand-up comedy.

Stars who became famous through vaudeville in major cities included W. C. Fields, Lillian Russell, the Cohan Family (including George M.), Sophie Tucker, Will Rogers, Lillian Russell, Harry Houdini, Mae West, the Marx Brothers, Eddie Cantor, and Fred Allen. Through vaudeville, show business for the first time offered an avenue to real money, certainly for theater owners but also for individual entertainers.

Even though vaudeville began in cities, rural people following the labor markets had moved there and thus enjoyed this new entertainment and described it and retold its jokes to the folks back home. Entrepreneurs eventually created traveling vaudeville shows—notably the Keith-Orpheum, Loews Bisbee circuits, and Sun Players—that toured smaller cities and towns to entertain rural audiences. Therefore, country people knew what vaudeville was all about. These new audiences led the circuits to include country entertainers and subjects. Among the country musicians and comedians who traveled with these shows were Uncle Dave Macon, Al Hopkins, Asa Martin, Jimmie Rodgers, the Weaver Brothers and Elviry, Lew Childre, Lennie Aleshire, Floyd Rutledge, and James "Goober" Buchanan.

Bill C. Malone points out that vaudeville was influential in the growth of songwriting as a profession. While the vaudeville shows did not get to all of the small towns, vaudeville sheet music circulated widely, as did jokes and comic routines.[10] Some of those connected with the shows made off with jokes and skits, sheet music, and scripts for comedy sketches that became the basis of a lot of early country-radio and road-show comedy. James "Goober" Buchanan, who played vaudeville before becoming a country music comedian, commented on the thievery of comic material in general:

>You know, comics are among the worst thieves for stealing material, and I plead guilty. And I have been copied myself a lot, too. If I ever heard a good skit or joke that I thought I could use in my routine, I used it. Generally I changed it or didn't use it where it might be in the other fellow's territory.
>
>   They say to be copied is the greatest compliment that can be paid you. . . . Every band from the "Opry" had to have a comic, and they stole from each other constantly, and you generally heard the same gags on several different shows.

Slim Watts . . . asked to go along with us to a show one night. . . . I took him along. Soon I learned that he was Cedric Rainwater, doing the same routine I had used on that show.[11]

It was fairly easy also for writers and publishing entrepreneurs to get ahold of scripts or to copy down and publish jokes and routines. Thomas W. Jackson wrote the popular *Slow Train through Arkansaw* and other books of rural humor. *McNally's Bulletin* featured skits, dialogues, monologues, and jokes written especially for vaudeville, and *Fun Master* published comedy material monthly. The early radio star Bradley Kincaid kept two large ring-binder notebooks of songs, poems, and humorous material that he could use on his radio shows and personal appearances. James Buchanan compiled his own comedy books that he passed on to Bun Wilson and Pete Stamper, comedians at the "Renfro Valley Barn Dance." Lonnie "Pap" Wilson, the "Grand Ole Opry" comedian, kept a notebook of jokes, and Archie Campbell published jokes and routines. Captain Stubby (Tom Fouts) of Chicago's WLS published several joke books. Such collections were precious to entertainers who were always looking for material.

Tent Repertory Theaters

There were several kinds of traveling shows other than the minstrel, medicine, and vaudeville shows that offered a great deal of humor. Some towns had erected buildings to accommodate traveling shows, and larger towns had stationary stock companies. However, the groups that hit the most rural areas were the tent repertory theaters, or "tent-rep shows." Billy Choate gives a firsthand account of these shows in his 1994 memoir, *Born in a Trunk . . . Just Outside the Center Door Fancy*. He claims that his grandfather was among the first to mount such a show in the 1880s, known as Choate's Comedians. Billy Choate's father spent his life with this show, and he himself traveled with it for many years before joining and eventually owning and running Bisbee's Comedians well into the television era, when mounting costs for the cast and crew of some thirty people finally shut them down in 1967.[12]

The tent-rep shows were sometimes called "Toby Shows" because many of their plays featured Toby, a red-wigged, freckled, clownishly garbed country bumpkin who was the foil of the evil, conniving urban characters that tried to take advantage of simple rural people. Choate thinks that Toby was born in the early 1920s as a set character, although the persona of the simple but honorable rube was a much older figure in dramatic productions. Billy Choate played Toby for years, and in fact he is still doing Toby in an annual re-creation of the tent-rep show in Wayne City, Illinois. Choate's Comedians and Bisbee's Comedians originated in southern Illinois and mainly played that state as well as western Tennessee and Kentucky. There were other such shows, however, that played the length and breadth of rural America. Choate has written that in the first part of the twentieth century there were over four hundred tent shows touring the country, employing more actors and other artists than Hollywood and Broadway combined. Among them, in addition to Choate's and Bisbee's Comedians, were the

Haverstock Players, Murphy's Comedians, Billy Plumlee's Stock Company, Billy Ter-rill's Comedians, the Frank Smith Players, the Neil and Caroline Schaffner Players, and Ray Zarlington's Comedians. They specialized in comic plays and melodramas, usually written by tent-rep people. These plays almost always contrasted scheming city folks with simple country people. In between the acts of such plays were all sorts of other entertainment, comedians, musicians, jugglers, magicians, and an aftershow act that might include all of the above as well as a chorus line.[13]

Among the country comedians who came out of tent-rep shows were Lawrence "Boob" Brasfield, his wife Neva, and his brother, Rod Brasfield. Rod became the comic partner of Minnie Pearl at the "Grand Ole Opry" and was one of the best rube comedians in the business. In 1954, Boob and Neva joined the "Ozark Jubilee" in Springfield, Missouri, over KWTO and the ABC television network, as Uncle Cyp and Aunt Sap. All three Brassfields had been dramatic actors as well as comedians, and Lawrence had owned a circle-stock company in Gadsen, Alabama, for a time. Billy Choate considered Boob Brasfield to be one of the best comedians he had ever seen because of his acting abilities and superb timing.[14]

Country Music and Country Comedy

The place where country humor really found a home was in the early country music industry. When radio and the ability to satisfactorily record music came about in the 1920s, a whole new industry was born. With radio barn-dance shows that went on for hours, there was a need to provide variety, and comedy lightened the program after tragic ballads and mournful love songs. Comedy flourished in the personal appearances of radio entertainers in theaters, schools, and courthouses to which the whole family came. Because of this family factor, the humor had to be relatively clean, although subtle references to male-female relations or bathroom (or outhouse) matters titillated all but the most pious and sanctimonious.

The people who have sought their fortunes in towns and cities tend to look down upon those who have chosen to remain in rural areas. Many who have recently moved to town and prospered and who still have rural kin are confident in their belief that they have improved their worth as people, and they may indulge in jokes that reflect negatively on their rustic cousins. In country music comedy, the rube became more specifically the "hillbilly." The understanding was that the city slicker was more so-phisticated, better educated, better dressed, had better grammar and values than the simple rural character, but a lot of the humor that satisfied country audiences came when the rube turned the tables on the city slicker and came out ahead in the dialogue. Here is a story from the Mississippi Baptist preacher (and picker and singer) Will D. Campbell that illustrates how this kind of humor works:

> A country fellow comes to town and sees a bunch of men digging a great big hole in the middle of town. He stops and watches a while, and when the mayor comes out to check on the workers' progress, he asks, "What are you going to put in that hole?"

The mayor says, condescendingly and dismissively, "We're going to round up all the sons-a-bitches in town and put them in there."

The country fellow says, "Who's goin' to cover 'em up?"

Bill C. Malone, in his book, *Don't Get Above Your Raisin': Country Music and the Southern Working Class*, devotes a whole chapter to the humor of country music. He writes:

> Country music's reputation for crying-in-your-beer songs obscures the fact that humor has always been a staple of country entertainment, just as it has been a survival mechanism for southern rural folk culture. Its presence reminds us that although often fraught with sorrow and pain, the world of country music is also a world of laughter. Country humor at its best asserted the humanity of working people's lives, exposed the hypocrisies that lay around them, brought the pompous and mighty down to size, served as a painless way of calling up bittersweet memories of the past, eased the pain of lives that were often hard and lonely, and of course, added the healing balm of laughter to spirits in need of relief. Humor served as a populistic defense mechanism in southern folk culture, attacking pretension and sham and striving to keep people from becoming too self-important—admonishing them with the unspoken command not to get above their raising.[15]

The early country musicians and comedians were well aware that their status was not very high in comparison with urban elites. They were in many ways like the newly immigrated foreigners, such as the Irish who inspired Pat-and-Mike jokes that were soon told all over the country, illustrating how slow these newcomers were in understanding the ways of the new country. This kind of humor appealed to the emerging country entertainers and their audiences. In the Irish, they saw a people whose ineptitude exceeded their own. Some employed racial jokes to the same effect. However, a major motif in country comedy was the "underdog" joke, which elevated country people at the expense of those who thought they were better than them.

Country comedy, born with the radio and recording industry, was most welcome in the personal-appearance tours. Initially radio entertainment was primarily musical, but as the barn-dance shows grew to fill a whole evening, and when road shows went out to put on an evening of entertainment, the family audience expected more than just music. Wade Mainer, who hosted early radio shows, commented on comedy as a part of the entertainment program:

> When we began to make personal appearances we didn't have comedy. What we did, we went out and sang and played for the people. Then I got to thinking, maybe we needed some comedy in our outfit, and we got to doing stand-up comedy—just tell jokes, or maybe I'd come in the back door hollering and going on and disturbing the people, telling them that they shouldn't start the show until I got there. We'd stand up there and tell jokes backward and forward.
>
> I realized that comedy was essential with kids and all. Back then they brought their families. They brought kids, girlfriends, and all. The kids would really go for the humor. The old people did too, 'cause there wasn't much of it during the

Depression. I think the people really wanted something to entertain them—maybe to get their minds from some of their hardships that they went through. Back then they'd come out to see you. They'd sit and talk with you.[16]

Doc Williams, the sixty-some-year veteran of Wheeling's "Mountaineer Jamboree," also talked about the importance of comedy and how he balanced his shows in the early days of the "Jamboree":

> Humor at that time had a very important function in curing people up and making them feel good. They'd come out of those shows and be smiling from ear to ear— just having a ball. I played the same towns for twenty-five years. Smoky [Pleacher] would go with me, and Hiram Hayseed [Shorty Godwin] went some, too. They always knew they would see a comedian. I plugged that very heavily and always a girl singer, and that combination gave us entry into their homes. By having a girl, we could mix in with the family. We were always welcome, and the comedian was always funny, even when he left the stage. He'd keep everybody cheered up.
>
> The early "Jamboree" featured comedy skits with the whole cast. We would rehearse those things three or four days before the show. And on the radio you'd hear people laughing for five minutes. You wouldn't know what was happening. They'd come to see what was going on.[17]

Bill Bolick, from Hickory, North Carolina, who was famous with his brother Earl as the Blue Sky Boys, told of his early introduction to comedy:

> When we started in Asheville, none of us knew much about comedy, or anything else. We put a show together, mostly by Lute [Isenhour]. I was playing a kind of rube comedian. . . . I think we all realized that we had to have comedy in our shows. . . . None of us had any experience on the stage to amount to anything, except getting up there and playing and singing. That was the first time I was connected with comedy in any way. I think we put most of it together, maybe from older jokes, maybe from medicine shows we'd seen. . . .
>
> In 1938 . . . in Atlanta, most of the acts there used rube comedians. Earl and I played comedy then. Earl played most of it. Uncle Josh [a character played by Earl] wasn't blackface. He wore a beard, rimless glasses, kind of long sideburns, real loose sloppy pants, and big shoes that he wore on opposite feet. He was very comical-looking. In order not to use rube comedy, which was too common, we hit upon having him as an old man.[18]

Captain Stubby (Tom Fouts), whose band was known as the Buccaneers on the "National Barn Dance" and the "Boone County Jamboree," was another who thought that humor lifts our spirits when we have troubles. He said, "A lot of comedians came out of the Depression—hard times. I don't know what there was about it, but we used to make humor to bolster ourselves up, and we made fun of our problems."[19] Doyle Lawson, the head of the Bluegrass band Quicksilver, also mentioned the value of diverting people from their personal problems. He said, "Comedy is just a form of entertainment. You want to have a well-rounded program. Comedy is a way to relieve people of their daily stresses, take their minds off their problems."[20] Charlie Louvin, who worked at some pretty bad jobs as a young man, commented that music also serves the same purpose: "I know that music is a great release if you have a job you can't stand, but that you have to keep. Music can give you a night away from thinking of that job, or thinking of your problems, or your dim future, whatever that problem might be. I think that music can even soothe the beast." Louvin went on to stress the need for comedy:

> When you do a two-hour show, you can't just sing the whole two hours. A joke here and a joke there helps. Me and my brother Ira created an act that we called "Sal Skinner." Sal Skinner was a whole lot like Minnie Pearl, but she was from "Financial Flats." That was a good act. I would tell a joke once in a while. Not a whole lot of our humor came out of our life in Alabama. We didn't find a whole lot amusing in Alabama. There wasn't much comedy in the cotton fields.[21]

The late Jim McReynolds, of Jim and Jesse and the Virginia Boys, had this to say about comedy with bluegrass music:

> Bluegrass bands would always have a comedian on the program. We always tried to have a little fun on stage, try to put a little humor into the program. It seems like it works better if you can put the audience in a good mood. If you could make them laugh and have a good time, I always felt that you were ahead. One of the more famous comedians that worked with us was Chick Stripling. He was one of the funniest guys I've ever seen on stage. We'd always do about fifteen minutes of comedy in our programs.[22]

Betty Lou York, a comedian at the "Renfro Valley Barn Dance," summed up thoughts about comedy as a diversion from daily problems by saying, "Everybody wants to laugh. They want to have a good time, and they want to forget their problems. It seems that no matter where you go or what kind of organization, or party, or banquet, they want to laugh and have a good time."[23]

Beecher "Bashful Brother Oswald" Kirby said it strongly for comedy: "I think humor's the main thing with everybody. If you can make them laugh, you've got them."[24]

CENTERS OF COUNTRY MUSIC COMEDY

When the business of country music grew out of phonograph recordings, radio, and personal appearances, comedy continued to be an important component. Following are several places where comedy emerged and flourished along with country music as a part of entertainment aimed primarily at country people.

The Recording Industry

Cylinder recordings that became available in the waning years of the nineteenth century were not satisfactory acoustically, but they enjoyed some popularity, and they attracted comedians to record, such as Arthur Collins with his monologue "The Preacher and the Bear." Cal Stewart, with his "Uncle Josh" stories about rural life, was perhaps the best-known of the period.

It was not until the development of the disc recorder in 1921 that music could be recorded and played back somewhat satisfactorily. This development, and later the invention of the electronic microphone, brought the recording industry into its own in the 1920s. The promise of markets for records among black and white folk sent talent scouts into the hinterlands to record those who had heretofore been only amateur musicians. Although most early recordings had been of classical musicians, the efforts of the early scouts brought two additional categories—"race" and "hillbilly" recordings—to the public. Soon, aspiring musicians sought out the record companies at their home offices in New York and other cities, or wherever they had temporarily set up shop to record folk musicians. Eventually, however, the record companies saw that recordings of humorous songs and skits about country happenings would also sell records. The Georgia Skillet Lickers recorded skits on Columbia, "A Corn Licker Still in Georgia," "The Medicine Show," and "Kickapoo Joy Juice"; Bascom Lamar Lunsford recorded "Speaking the Truth" (a sermon parody written by the nineteenth-century humorist William P. Brannon) and "A Stump Speech in the Tenth District," also on Columbia; and Buell Kazee recorded "A Mountain Boy Makes His First Record" on Brunswick and "Election Day in Kentucky," parts 1 and 2, on Vocalion.

Radio

In 1920, the new medium of radio came on the scene, the earliest station being KDKA in Pittsburgh; by 1924 there were some six hundred stations in the United States. The early receivers required headphones, but when speakers were perfected, radio surpassed disc recordings in quality of sound. There was no technology for playing records on the radio, so station managers hustled to find talent to fill the new medium. Most of the stations were sponsored by companies as a goodwill gesture, giving out weather and agricultural predictions and advice. Examples were Chicago's WLS ("World's Largest Store"), set up by Sears and Roebuck, and Nashville's WSM, owned by the National Life and Accident Insurance Company. Not much thought was given in the beginning to radio's potential for selling products.

Following are radio stations or other venues with programs that included a lot of country humor.

WLS, Chicago, and the "National Barn Dance"

Sears-Roebuck aimed WLS, starting in 1923, at giving helpful advice, livestock prices, and weather reports to farmers. Music in the beginning was mainly provided by a staff organist. However, the station came up with a barn-dance program that aired first in April 1924. The standard story described the boisterous music of Tommy Dandurand's fiddle band, augmented by cowbells, that shocked listening Sears officials, who would have cancelled the show forthwith had not letters poured in from enthusiastic listeners.

John Lair and His Cumberland Ridge Runners stage a barn dance in this publicity shot for the WLS "National Barn Dance." Photo by Theatrical Chicago, courtesy of the John Lair Collection, Southern Appalachian Archives, Berea College.

George D. Hay, a Memphis newspaperman who had first observed and embraced country music and dance in the Ozarks, was hired as the announcer for the program that became the "National Barn Dance."

Bradley Kincaid was the first big star of this new show aimed mainly at rural people. He first sang on WLS as part of a quartet while he was attending the YMCA College in Chicago. On hearing that Kincaid sang the old ballads he had learned as a child in the foothills of the Kentucky Cumberlands, the musical director, Don Malin, asked him to sing some of these songs on the "National Barn Dance." Kincaid's rendition of "Barbara Allen" inspired bushels of mail and requests to sing the old ballad every Saturday night after he had become a regular.

Soon, an additional way of making money from radio occurred to musicians—the personal-appearance show. Avid listeners wanted to see those whom they regularly listened to and actually watch them perform. Early WLS entertainers announced that they would appear in schools and theaters near Chicago, and they were well received. Seeing possibilities, the station formed the WLS Artist Bureau. When asked to be part of the venture, Bradley Kincaid was skeptical. He remembered asking, "What would I do? They said, 'Well, you can think up a couple of jokes to tell and sing four or five songs.'" So he agreed; his first show was at a theater in Peoria. When he arrived in town, Bradley saw a line of people all around the block. Curious, he innocently went over to ask what was going on and found, to his complete surprise, that they were there to see him. Kincaid's later longtime traveling partner Grandpa Jones remembered Bradley telling him that he was so scared doing this first show that he was unable to move, and his feet went to sleep! But, of course, he and other musicians soon gained confidence in entertaining live audiences.

It became apparent to these entertainers, as it had to earlier minstrel and vaudeville players, that one could not simply sing or play music all evening. A program needed variety, and it also had to entertain a family audience. The minstrels, medicine-show entertainers, and vaudevillians had found that humor was a surefire way to lift a sagging program. When WLS's "National Barn Dance" moved into the Eighth Street Theater to accommodate a larger audience, there was need for variety in the radio show as well, for it eventually grew to over five hours each Saturday night. By this time, "The Prairie Farmer," a midwestern agricultural magazine, had purchased WLS and imposed a strict morality code on the family-oriented show. As an example, Lulu Belle and Scotty Wiseman, who had acquired rights to Bascom Lamar Lunsford's "Good Old Mountain Dew," were not allowed to sing it on WLS, although they recorded their version.

John Lair came to WLS in the late 1920s and became its musical director and librarian. He was soon adept at writing radio scripts and inserting humor throughout. He dressed his "girls" and "boys," the Coon Creek Girls, the Cumberland Ridge Runners, and Lulu Belle and Scotty, in country costumes. Jim Gaskin, the master of ceremonies and fiddler at the "Renfro Valley Barn Dance," related how Homer "Slim" Miller came to Lair's house to audition as fiddler for the Cumberland Ridge Runners, "one eye looking to the left, one to the right, a big awkward-looking fellow, who said, 'Are you the feller that wants a fiddler?' Mr. Lair said he fell back on the bed laughing, and said, 'You're hired. I hope to hell you can play the fiddle.'"[25] Thus, Miller, who was a mime-like comedian, was destined to dress up in baggy britches and porkpie hat and be funny while playing the fiddle. Lair, an authority on folksongs, scouted up many humorous ones for his programs and wrote other comic songs, such as "Winkin' at Me," "Keep Them Cold Icy Fingers offa Me," and "I Love Molasses."

Myrtle Cooper, who became Lulu Belle Wiseman, described how her comedy happened:

> George Biggar hired me for the show. They introduced me as Red Foley's old girl-friend, who lived in Kentucky [and who had] heard him on the radio and had rode the bus and come all the way to Chicago because I wanted to be on the radio too. John Lair, the program manager, had an idea of how I should dress (Mother Hubbard Dress, dime-store braid with red ribbon, and pointy shoes) and the character

I would play and gave me the name of Lulu Belle. I didn't care. I liked it better than Myrtle. I'd sing "How Can I Sing When He's Winkin' at Me," and I'd use a mirror to put a spotlight on someone in the audience, maybe a bald-headed man. That went over real big.

Red got married, so George Biggar said, "You and Scott [Wiseman] work up an act."[26]

Lulu Belle and Scotty became a very important act with good picking and singing but with a lot of comedy that appealed to a wide audience. They stayed on in Chicago after others, like Lair and his entertainers, had left, although they also did stints at WLW in Cincinnati. Scotty played five-string banjo, Lulu Belle played guitar, and they did serious songs as well as novelty and comic songs. Lulu Belle was the quintessentially innocent country girl to Scotty's more dignified straight man. They were enormously popular and in demand for personal appearances. In 1936, a *Radio Digest* poll named Lulu Belle as the most popular radio entertainer in America.

Tom Fouts, who played as Captain Stubby with His Buccaneers, also spoke of comedy at WLS and its importance as entertainment and its rewards to the entertainer:

> We did country, rural, humor, and I've always stuck to that, mostly something about growing up on the farm in hard times, about how poor we were. How poor? My mother would give us beans for breakfast, water for lunch, and we'd swell up for supper! A lot of humorists came out of the Depression. We used humor to bolster ourselves up, and we laughed at our problems. We'd make fun of the city slicker who came out on the farm, which is funny to farm people.
>
> Well, I think humor is very important. I think being a humorist is the most rewarding thing a person can do, because you are before people when they're having a lot of fun, and it's great standing up there seeing five hundred people holding their sides, laughing. It's a great way to make a living.[27]

George Gobel, later a comedian and comic actor on radio, movies, and television, began his career as a child star on the "National Barn Dance," performing there for a decade. The Hoosier Hot Shots joined WLS and the "National Barn Dance" in 1933. Their act included zany antics and raucous music on a variety of horns, stringed instruments, and other strange, unidentifiable soundmakers. Pat Buttram, the Alabama comedian who later was a sidekick in Gene Autry movies and was also a regular on the TV show "Green Acres," did rube comedy on the "Barn Dance." Gene Autry brought the versatile comedian-composer-musician Lester Alvin "Smiley" Burnette to the "Barn Dance" before they left for Hollywood to star in many movies and television shows.

WSM, Nashville, and the "Grand Ole Opry"

WSM went on the air in September 1925 and hired George D. Hay away from WLS to serve as announcer and manager. In November, Hay invited Uncle Jimmy Thompson to play his fiddle over the air, and the mail response encouraged him to start a regular barn-dance program in December. Early performers, in addition to Uncle Jimmy

The cast of WSM's "Grand Ole Opry" in 1935. Courtesy of Charles K. Wolfe.

Thompson, were Dr. Humphrey Bate, Uncle Dave Macon, Deford Bailey, and several string bands that Hay colorfully renamed the Gully Jumpers, the Fruit Jar Drinkers, and the like. Photographs of these groups from the period show them dressed to promote the country image and rustic humor. Uncle Dave Macon, with vaudeville experience, was the consummate entertainer whom Beecher "Oswald" Kirby called "a one-man show." He was funny with his antics, such as twirling his banjo and jumping around without missing a beat, singing comic songs and telling jokes. Yet he could be serious with his expert banjo picking, rendering of old hymns or songs with a social message, and his comments on religion.

A popular comedy act on WSM was Lasses and Honey (Lee Roy "Lasses" White and Lee Davis "Honey" Wilds) from the blackface minstrel and vaudeville stage. They soon moved to the "Opry" show at a time when "Amos 'n' Andy" was popular on the radio, and this was a factor in their popularity. White left the show for Hollywood in the mid-1930s, and Wilds continued the act as Jamup and Honey with other partners, Tom Woods and Bunny Biggs, after he also did work in Hollywood.

Another early comedy act on the "Opry" was the team of Sarie and Sallie (Edna Wilson and Margaret Waters), sisters who dressed up in old-fashioned long dresses as country women. When Roy Acuff came to the "Opry," he brought humor that he had learned in his medicine-show experience as well as that which he used with his "Crazy Tennesseans" at the "Mid-day Merry-Go-Round" show at WNOX in Knoxville. The banjoist and dobroist Beecher Kirby commented:

We did a lot of our stuff vaudeville style. It was the main influence, usually with a jokester and a straight man. Roy was the straight man, and he let us do the comedy. At one time or another all of us were comedians, Pap Wilson, Joe Zinkan, and Jess Easterday. I enjoyed being a comedian. Humor was the main thing.[28]

Rachel Veach also joined the group as "Cousin" Rachel, posing as Beecher Kirby's sister, and he became "Bashful Brother Oswald" to give Rachel cover as a single woman traveling with men. She blacked out her front teeth and did comedy with Oswald.

Robert Lunn, who had traveled widely with vaudeville circuits, specialized in a form of humorous songs called the "Talking Blues" when he was on the "Opry." Another interesting comedian was Ramblin' Tommy Scott, a Georgia medicine-show performer who appropriated the title of "Doc" to sell Vim-Herb Tonic and Herb-O-Lac. On the "Opry," he did a ventriloquist act with his dummy, Luke McLuke.

The best-remembered comedians of the "Grand Ole Opry" were Minnie Pearl, Rod Brasfield, "Whitey" Ford as the "Duke of Paducah," "Cousin Jody" (James Clell Summey), Lonnie "Pap" Wilson, Grandpa Jones, and later Jerry Clower. Like the "National Barn Dance," the "Opry" soon had traveling shows. Tent shows, pioneered by Jamup and Honey, were adopted by such stars as Roy Acuff, Bill Monroe, and Bradley Kincaid in the early 1940s. Comedy was an integral part of these shows as well as on the "Opry" itself. Several acts would sometimes travel together, leading to the larger "package" shows of later years. Douglas B. Green has pointed out that the package shows began to hire several bands or stars and one major comedian such as Minnie Pearl, Rod Brasfield, or Whitey Ford to provide comedy, and this led to a decline in comedians among the regular bands.[29]

Another popular duo doing comedy and song parodies on the "Opry" was Lonzo and Oscar (Rollin and John Sullivan, also with Lloyd George, Dave Hooten, and others as Lonzo), who at first provided comedy for Eddy Arnold's band before going on their own with a big hit, "I'm My Own Grandpa." The Louvin Brothers, Ira and Charlie, did comedy also and wrote and performed comic songs. Ira did an act in which he dressed up as a country girl, "Sal Skinner."

Lewis Marshall "Grandpa" Jones and David "Stringbean" Akeman were pals on and off the "Opry" stage. Both were banjoists, storytellers, and engaging entertainers, later to become regulars on "Hee Haw." Grandpa, a serious musician, singer, and composer, commented that he did not do much comedy for a long time: "I guess it was about 1935, after I was with Bradley Kincaid. I started doing some gags on stage to take up a little time." His success as a comedian often overshadowed his skill as a singer and instrumentalist. Jim McReynolds stated that "Grandpa has been there so long, and they love him so, that he could tell his jokes backward and still be funny."[30]

Cincinnati's WLW and Other Stations

When John Lair left WLS with most of his group and went to Cincinnati's WLW, the nation's first fifty-thousand-watt station, in addition to Slim Miller, he added other

The cast of WLW's "Midwestern Hayride," ca. 1948. Courtesy of the John Lair Collection, Southern Appalachian Archives, Berea College.

comedians to his cast, namely Whitey Ford, who became the "Duke of Paducah," and Margaret Lilly, a vaudevillian who became A'nt Idy, a sassy country woman. Soon A'nt Idy had a son in the person of Lair's hefty nephew, Harry Mullins, as Little Clifford, and later a henpecked husband, Uncle Juney, played by Danny Duncan. Lair also organized The Coon Creek Girls, who sang and also provided comedy. Lair had a genius for mixing sentimental and nostalgic songs about home and family, seasons and holidays, with hoedowns and clean country humor. His programs were backward-looking, and he once said that his simple criterion was to ask if his long-departed parents would have liked the song or routine. Lair's "Renfro Valley Barn Dance" was at first broadcast on WLW, which for a time went to the super power of five hundred thousand watts and was carried by the NBC Red and Blue networks. Lair also developed a Friday-night show, "Plantation Party," earlier aired at WLS in Chicago, and he developed the "Pinex Merrymakers" and other daily shows that were broadcast over WCKY and the Mutual Network.

Just before Lair moved his show to Renfro Valley, Kentucky, in 1939, WLW developed its own show, the "Boone County Jamboree," later to become the "Midwestern Hayride." The station hired George Biggar away from WLS to develop their new country program. Among the entertainers hired were Hank Penny, who did comedy,

Grandpa Jones, Merle Travis, the Delmore Brothers, Homer and Jethro (Henry Haynes and Kenneth Burns), Curly Fox and Texas Ruby, and Lulu Belle and Scotty.

Knoxville's WNOX and WROL

A man named Stuart Adcock started a small radio statio, WNAV, in Knoxville in 1921 that was part of the People's Telephone and Telegraph Company. It had a power of fifty watts. It was later sold to the Sterchi Brothers Furniture Company, and Adcock bought another station in 1927 that became WROL. Since Sterchi was a major distributor of Vocalion Records, the store was instrumental in getting Vocalion to record the musicians who played around Knoxville and eastern Tennessee. About 1926, the station changed its call letters to WNOX and its power to one hundred watts. The influential close-harmony duet, Mac and Bob (Lester McFarland and Robert Gardner), played over WNOX to an appreciative audience and also recorded over two hundred numbers for Vocalion at the Sterchi studios, before the duo moved on to Chicago's WLS.[31]

Some believe that if WNOX had had a stronger signal than the one thousand watts it was assigned in 1931 (later ten thousand), it would have made Knoxville the capitol

Red and Fred. Red Rector (derby) and Fred Smith (silly hat) clown with the band at Knoxville's WBIR-TV, ca. 1960. Other members, L-R: Claude Boone, Dan Bailey, Bud Brewster, and Willie G. Brewster. Courtesy of the Museum of Appalachia.

of country music because so many talented musicians worked there over the years. In 1935 the station was bought by the E. W. Scripps Company, which also owned the *Knoxville News-Sentinel*. Already performing on the station in addition to Mac and Bob were the Tennessee Ramblers; Archie Campbell, from nearby Bulls Gap, playing a character called "Grandpappy"; and Roy Acuff and His Crazy Tennesseans. In 1936, the program manager, Richard Westergaard, hired Lowell Blanchard, a young announcer just graduated from the University of Illinois, to develop programs that would appeal to a rural audience, "'to become a hillbilly . . . bring us hillbilly performers. Entertain with them as one of them.'"[32]

Like John Lair earlier, Blanchard had ideas about how shows should be staged and what kind of music and humor would appeal, and he set out to build not only a radio audience but a studio one as well. He helped develop new acts, routines, and costumes, extended the length of their noontime program, and attracted audiences to the broadcasts.

Blanchard named his new show the "Mid-day Merry-Go-Round." Tony Musco, a piano player, remembered that "Lowell Blanchard was the one that got the program together. It was his idea, and he worked on it, he produced, got the talent and every-thing." Blanchard also started a new Saturday-evening show, the "WNOX Carnival," in 1936, using his same noontime entertainers. The "Carnival" later became the "Tennessee Barn Dance."

Acuff and his group soon left WNOX for WROL and later moved on to WSM in Nashville. Another act that Blanchard hired and coached was the Stringdusters, (Kenneth and Aytchie Burns, Homer Haynes, and Charlie Hagaman). Out of this group came the talented comedy duo Homer and Jethro (Kenneth Burns and Homer Haynes). Both were already skilled musicians, but Lowell Blanchard gave them their stage names, taught them about show business, wrote some of their comedy routines, and polished them as entertainers.

Blanchard sought to build up the comedy part of the shows and made Archie Campbell his primary comedian. He helped Campbell develop his Grandpappy character more fully and wrote scripts and jokes that Campbell and he would perform on stage. Grandpappy became a big hit and inspired a lot of mail. Campbell briefly left WNOX for stations in Bristol and Chattanooga before World War II, but after service in the navy, he was welcomed back to WNOX. In 1949 he accepted a much higher salary at WROL and helped them to create their "Country Playhouse" and "Dinner Bell" programs that gave real competition to WNOX. When television came along, it was WROL that got the first permit, and Archie Campbell became popular also on TV. He played both TV and radio there until 1956, when he left for the "Grand Ole Opry."

Another comedian and dancer who played over WNOX was Charles Elza, a former miner from Harlan County, Kentucky, who played as "Kentucky Slim." Ivan Tribe wrote that Elza and his fellow coal miner Cas Walker had come together to Knoxville to seek their fortunes. Walker invested in a grocery store and eventually owned a chain of supermarkets, and he enthusiastically sold groceries over WROL and WBIR, organizing various groups of musicians to entertain between commercials. Elza played on Walker's programs but also was on WNOX with the Tennessee Ramblers and Carl Story. He eventually went to the "Renfro Valley Barn Dance" and also traveled with Flatt and Scruggs, the Stanley Brothers, and Hylo Brown. Kentucky Slim, also know as "Little Darlin'," earlier did blackface comedy but later used similar routines in whiteface. He had learned some dance steps, including one he became famous for, the "Pork Chop," from a black ex-vaudevillian in Harlan named Peg Leg Jones. Slim weighed 275 pounds, and so part of his charm was his agile dance steps that belied his weight. Blanchard wrote routines for Slim and served as his straight man.[33]

In September 1936, Pee Wee King and his band moved from WHAS in Louisville to join the "Merry-Go-Round." With him came Monk and Sam (Charlie Henson and Sam Johnson). William Smyth describes them as being "full-time comedians" at WNOX, doing "a variety of comic rural characters, including the female, Sophronia Apple." Sam did an "old man" act, and they also did comedy songs, accompanying themselves on banjo and guitar.[34]

One of the best-remembered comics on WNOX was "Jumping" Bill Carlisle. He and his brother Cliff joined the "Merry-Go-Round" in 1939. Bill created a character called Hotshot Elmer, with the help of Lowell Blanchard. Carlisle did a lot of onstage antics, such as jumping incredibly high while he was singing. "Sunshine Slim" Sweet, a regular on the show, said, "Hotshot Elmer was one of the funniest comedians I've ever seen in my life. He sat on a bunch of duck eggs for a couple of weeks one time and hatched out some ducks! He could stand flat-footed and jump on the stage at WNOX, and that stage must have been five feet high!"[35] Fred Smith, later a regular on the show, told of Carlisle doing antics on the street, like catching a bus and telling passengers that he had been fired, resulting in their calling the station to protest. Carlisle's comment on his humor was, "Well, it's a good thing they've got such a thing as humor, 'cause I can't sing. So I just go along with the humor."[36] When Carlisle left WNOX, he quit doing Hotshot Elmer, although he continued telling jokes and also doing his jumping act at the "Grand Ole Opry."

William Smyth quotes Bill Carlisle talking about a comic gag involving Molly O'Day (Dixie Lee Williamson). Carlisle was supposed to box O'Day while they were both blindfolded, but her husband, Lynn Davis, would come on and "beat the tar out of me," as Carlisle reported. "When they took the blindfolds off between rounds, Molly would be sitting in the corner pantin' like she was worn out." Carlisle also wrestled a midget called "Little Robert" on stage.[37]

In 1940, Cousin Emmy Carver, one of the most talented entertainers ever, performed over WNOX while she was also appearing over WHAS in Louisville.

Others who played comedy on WNOX in the 1940s were Red and Fred (William Eugene "Red" Rector and Fred Smith), both from rural Madison County, North Carolina.

After service in World War II, many of the old performers returned to WNOX, but other talent had to be recruited to replace those who didn't. Among the other notable comics who did time at the station was Max Terhune, a magician and ventriloquist who usually worked with a dummy by the name of Elmer Sneezeweed. He was later to become an accomplished actor playing "sidekick" roles in Western movies. The Louvin Brothers joined WNOX after the war, doing their comic routines along with their superb singing.

The Knoxville television personality Bill Landry, who did two episodes of his WBIR-TV "Heartland" series about early Knoxville radio, commented on the importance of this radio show:

> In the world of country music there were no schools that trained musicians, unless you consider the "Mid-day Merry-Go-Round." For more than twenty-five years, this modest radio show might well have been called the Academy of Country Music. It produced more stars than any other single source. . . . Roy Acuff, Archie Campbell, Chet Atkins, the Carter Sisters [and Maybelle], Martha Carson, Kitty Wells, Homer and Jethro, Red Rector, and Carl Story, to name a few.

The late Red Rector commented on the popularity of the show: "At one time I heard folks say that out in the country you could walk down a country road from noon until one o'clock, and every house would have it on. You could walk for a mile and not miss one tune."[38]

William Smyth contrasted the music and comedy on Knoxville's competing stations, WNOX and WROL. Cas Walker's shows on WROL were spontaneous affairs where the entertainers, mostly local rural folks, could do pretty much what they wanted to, with Cas selling groceries and making political comments in between. Walker, who sometimes exaggerated his country ways as well as the quality of his wares, often could be humorous himself. Sam Venable, a *Knoxville News-Sentinel* writer, told of one funny incident. In early black-and-white television, it was important to spray any glossy or chromed surface with a dulling spray, produced by DuPont, or else it would show up as black on screen. One day, after spraying all bright objects, a technician set the spray can in the middle of Walker's groceries that he was going to advertise. "Cas started down the line, shilling coffee, bread, meat, and other foodstuffs, when his gnarled fingers stopped. Cas picked up that can, turned it over and said, 'Neighbors. We got this DuPont dullin' spray. I can't remember what we're asking for it, but I know we sold a carload of it last week at the North Central store.'"[39]

At WNOX, Lowell Blanchard tightly scripted the shows, developed the comedy, and coached the performers. As Smyth concluded, "On the WNOX shows comedy and/or levity were kings. The shows were laced with jokes and gags, many, if not most, masterminded by Lowell Blanchard. The country-comedy format of the shows helped to develop some of the most popular rural comedians of our time: eventually to bring respect and recognition to country humor at the national level."[40]

Wheeling's WWVA and the "Jamboree"

WWVA was West Virginia's first radio station, licensed in 1926 with fifty watts of power (increasing to five thousand in 1929 and fifty thousand in 1942). As Ivan Tribe has pointed out in his book, *Mountaineer Jamboree: Country Music in West Virginia*, the station was slow in promoting country music, but by 1928, the songs of Jimmie Rodgers were becoming popular, and the station's musicians, the Sparkling Four, heretofore doing popular and Hawaiian music, had requests for yodeling and other Rodgers-like numbers. Apparently the station had a Saturday-evening "Jamboree" program even before it established its live-audience show at the Capitol Theater in April 1933. "The World's Original WWVA Jamboree" (later the "Wheeling Jamboree" and then "Jamboree USA") continued to broadcast from various locations until recent years, although it discontinued its live-audience shows during World War II and occasionally other times because of floods. The increase to fifty thousand watts in 1942 brought its shows to a wide radio audience that included the mid-Atlantic states, New England, and a large portion of Canada.[41]

The versatile musician and comedian Grandpa Jones came to WWVA in 1936, where he performed with the Rhythm Rangers. He left shortly thereafter but played the "Jamboree" again in 1941–42 and 1945. Another outstanding entertainer who also came to the "Jamboree" in 1936 was "Cousin Emmy" Carver, like Grandpa, from

The Cast of the WWVA "Jamboree," 1949. Courtesy of Doc Williams.

Kentucky. Grandpa credited her with teaching him to play the banjo in her dynamic frailing style. Cousin Emmy was a complete package of entertainment, playing multiple instruments and in tricky ways. She was a sight to see with her platinum hair, oversized mouth, and energetic ways.

Ivan Tribe wrote that WWVA "allowed generous space for rural comedy." Other comedians listed by Tribe include the yodeler Smiley Sutter (Anthony Slater), who was best known as the country clown Crazy Elmer; Henry "Hiram Hayseed" Godwin; Charles "Smoky" Pleacher, who could do a variety of voices in skits or comical songs; "Dapper Dan" Martin; "Lazy Jim" Day, a Kentuckian who became famous for his "Singing News"; Cy Sneezeweed; Ray "Quarantine" Brown; and "Doctor" Lew Childre, with his trained dog Mr. Pooch.[42]

Doc Williams (Andrew John Smik Jr.), who played more than sixty-five years on the "Jamboree," beginning in 1937, spoke at length of his road tours, his comedians, and the place of comedy in his groups:

> The area I traveled was from Wheeling to the Northeast, and north close to one thousand miles to Ontario and right up to the Arctic Circle. From 1941 WWVA beamed in that direction, and you could hear it a thousand miles away. I traveled all through there. Henry Godwin, "Hiram Hayseed," was with me. We did rube comedy. We took those old blackface comedy skits that were done in medicine shows, and we adapted them to a white audience in whiteface as rube comedy. Oh man, they loved it. We [also] used vaudeville and minstrel jokes.
>
> Later on there was Sleepy Jeffers, just a teenager, who worked with the Fiddling Farmers . . . [and who] later became a comedian. One of the best and funniest comedians I ever had was Smoky Pleacher. He worked with me for ten years. There was Smoky Davis from East Tennessee. He was funny as all get-out. Smoky and Henry [Hiram Hayseed] did blackface. They were a comedy team when I came here. Hiram knew all these things [routines]. Another comedian was Hamilton Fincher. I called him "Rawhide." He was my first comedian. James "Froggy" Cortez, he was my second comedian. He did a rube type comedy.
>
> I always tried to be the straightest man I could be. I never stole my comedians' lines to be funny. I always tried to set up my comedians to be as funny as they could be. My interest in comedy started with "World's Tonic," the medicine show I saw in my hometown in Pennsylvania. I saw these comedians, and I never forgot them. So when I went into show business, I decided I'm always going to have a comedian in my group, and I did from the moment I arrived.[43]

The "Renfro Valley Barn Dance"

The "Renfro Valley Barn Dance" was created by John Lair in Cincinnati and was first broadcast from the Cincinnati Music Hall over WLW on October 9, 1937. The station, with the super power of five hundred thousand watts from 1934 to 1939, could be heard from Texas to New England, and Lair's personal-appearance shows traveled widely.

Cast of the "Renfro Valley Barn Dance," ca. 1940. Courtesy of the John Lair Collection, Southern Appalachian Archives, Berea College.

Lair was a nostalgic person who thought fondly of the old ways that were rapidly changing. He also saw the anomaly of talented rural folk being attracted to big cities like Chicago and Cincinnati to perform over the new medium of radio for other folks mostly back in rural areas. Reflecting on this, he conceived the idea of a barn-dance show back home in Kentucky, with mostly local singers, musicians, and funny people who would entertain city folks who might like to travel to a rural place such as they remembered from childhood or had heard described to them by parents and grandparents. While he was still in Chicago, Lair had composed "Take Me Back to Renfro Valley," a nostalgic song with a haunting tune that became a theme song for Renfro Valley shows. Here are two verses:

> I was born in Renfro Valley,
> But I drifted far away.
> I've been back to see the old home
> And my friends of other days.
> Gone were old familiar faces,
> All the friends I used to know.
> Things have changed in Renfro Valley,
> Since the days of long ago.
>
> Take me back to Renfro Valley
> When I'm free from earthly care.

> Lay me down by Dad and Mother,
> Let me sleep forever there.
> When it's springtime in the mountains,
> And the dogwood blossoms blow,
> We'll be back in Renfro Valley,
> As in days of long ago.

John Lair planned to set his show in Renfro Valley, a beautiful area just north of Mount Vernon. His grandfather had owned a farm there, where Lair grew up attending the log Red Bud School that later would be the site of his "Monday Night in Renfro Valley" and "Sunday Morning Getherin'" programs.

After he was established in Cincinnati, Lair entered into a partnership with Red Foley, Red's brother, C. V. "Cotton" Foley (natives of Berea, Kentucky), and Benjamin "Whitey" Ford to purchase land in Renfro Valley, build a barn, and produce a barn dance. In the meantime, until their facility was built, Lair broadcast the "Renfro Valley Barn Dance" over WLW with audiences in the Cincinnati Music Hall in 1937 and Dayton's Memorial Hall in 1938. He moved the show to Renfro Valley in 1939.

Lair's Renfro Valley cast included Red Foley; Slim Miller (Lair's first comedian); the Coon Creek Girls; Whitey Ford (the Duke of Paducah); Margaret Lilly (A'nt Idy); Harry Mullins (Little Clifford); Danny Duncan (Uncle Junie); Jerry Byrd; the Drifting Pioneers (Merle Travis, Sleepy Marlin, and Walter and Bill Brown); Shug Fisher and Hugh Cross; and the Range Riders (Guy Blakeman, Jerry Behrens, and Roland Gaines, later renamed the Mountain Rangers).

The Renfro Valley barn was barely finished for the opening show on November 4, 1939. Lair had kept his affiliation with WLW, but to broadcast the show required running a telephone line into the valley and to the barn, and it had not yet been fully completed. The resourceful engineer hooked onto the telephone line and pulled the wire through the window and hooked it up to the sound system just minutes before the show began, and several boys had to hold the wire off the ground during the broadcast. To prove to skeptics that the program was actually coming from a barn in Kentucky, Lair offered to send a photograph of the barn. He received over 250,000 requests, showing the vast appeal of his broadcasting idea.[44]

In addition to the "Renfro Valley Barn Dance," Lair also created "Monday Night in Renfro Valley," beginning August 5, 1940, using most of his "Barn Dance" entertainers but with a somewhat different format, broadcasting over WLW from the Red Bud School without a live audience. These programs also had comedy, either A'nt Idy and Little Clifford, sometimes with Lair as straight man, or the song parodies of Homer and Jethro.[45]

In 1941, Lair arranged to broadcast his shows over WHAS in Louisville. Lair started his Sunday-morning "Renfro Valley Getherin'" program in 1943 with backing from Louisville's Ballard Mills. This show tended to be thematic, based on holidays, seasons, or nostalgic themes like home, patriotism, and mother.

The main comedy for the shows was provided by the Duke of Paducah and A'nt Idy, Little Clifford, and Uncle Junie. Shug Fisher, who had learned comedy in medicine and "Toby" shows, also did comedy as a part of his musical pairing with Hugh Cross, and the Coon Creek Girls provided a great deal of comedy with their innocent country-girl personas. Slim Miller also became an important part of the Renfro Valley band as an admired fiddler and rustic comic. The current "Barn Dance" emcee and musician Jim Gaskin commented on Miller: "He told few jokes—very few words. His comedy was facial expressions and little mannerisms. He had a trick that he pulled with his hat, with a fishing line and pulley. He'd sail his hat out over the audience, and it would come back to him. He was so funny-looking you couldn't look at him without laughing."[46]

Other comedians were Shorty Hobbs and Little Eller; Granny Harper (Flora Mae Williams), a real Kentucky character; and Manuel "Old Joe" Clark, a banjoist and comedian who had done blackface in medicine shows, played Knoxville's "Mid-day Merry-Go-Round,"and also had done comedy with Bill Monroe's Bluegrass Boys. Pete Stamper came from western Kentucky in 1952 to edit the *Renfro Valley Bugle* and to be a member of the "Barn Dance" cast. Originally a musician, he developed several comedy routines. Gabe Tucker was invited by Lair to join the show as a comedian and emcee after his vaudeville tent blew away in a storm. Gene Cobb, who had done blackface and tabloid musical shows, was hired as an emcee and comedian. Other comedy acts included Si, Fanny (about whom little is known), and Abner (a mule); Monk and Sam (Charlie Henson and Sam Johnson); Luke McNeely (with the comedic name of "Luke Warmwater"); Judge Ray Corns, an authentic circuit judge who did a ventriloquist act and stand-up comedy mostly spoofing relatives, lawyers, and judges; James "Goober" Buchanan, another medicine-show and vaudeville musician and stand-up comedian who commuted from Nashville to Renfro Valley; Billy "Bun" Wilson, a Tennessean who learned comedy from Goober Buchanan and had traveled with the "Philip Morris Show"; and Betty Lou York, a Kentuckian who lived for years in Ohio and had gotten her start as a comedian with a weight-loss club, developing some of her routines around the problems of being overweight.

The "Barn Dance" went off the air in 1957, a victim of the new age of television, but it continues as a stage show. In 1968, J. Hal Smith of Nashville and partners bought the show and grounds from Lair. However, Lair, unhappy with the staging of the shows, formed a partnership and bought the property back. In 1989, Ralph Gabbard, Glenn Pennington, and others bought the complex and formed Renfro Valley Entertainment, Inc. In the early 1990s, the restaurant magnate Warren W. Rosenthal joined the corporation and put up the money for a state-of-the-art auditorium, a replica of an early-times town with gift and record shops, a restaurant, and so on. Two shows, the "Renfro Valley Barn Dance" and the "Renfro Valley Jamboree," are staged over long weekends in season, both of which feature comedy. Jim Gaskin, a singer and fiddler who had played off and on at the "Barn Dance," was hired as principal emcee. He is a gifted straight man, and he also does comedy himself. Terry Clark joined his father,

Old Joe Clark, to do comedy as well as music, until his father's death. Jerry Isaacs, "the Chicken Man," has been popular on the shows doing the "Red Hen Boogie" in a red suit imitating a chicken. The "Sunday Morning Getherin'" also continues, and various festivals—harvest, Christmas, fiddle, and gospel—draw people to the valley. On Saturday afternoons, Pete Stamper, Bun Wilson, and Betty Lou York do thirty minutes of comedy in the old Renfro Valley barn. The new barn also features main-stream country performers from Nashville and elsewhere in special concerts. Among the comedians who have performed there are the late Jerry Clower, Mike Snider, Etta May, and Carl Hurley.

Harry Rice, at Berea College, who archived Renfro Valley recordings and papers, has pointed out that Lair did not only include comedy acts on his programs but wrote humor into all appropriate aspects of his entertainment.[47] Pete Stamper commented, "Lair thrived on comedy and novelty." Jim Gaskin added, "He had a good sense of comedy and knew what would work. We've always had a creative bunch of people here. He'd get an idea and work it out with the comedians."[48] Stamper commented on the value of humor in country entertainment: "On a scale of one to ten, it is five or more. I know you can get by without it, but when you take it away, you've taken the foundation of country music. They come for the music, but you also give them something they didn't expect. That's what makes them go away talking about it, more satisfied."[49]

In 2000, the Rosenthal Family Partnership donated the Renfro Valley Entertain-ment Complex debt-free to the nonprofit board of the recently built Kentucky Music Hall of Fame and Museum just up the road. In 2005, the board sold the entertainment complex to Don and Vera Evans, Kentucky natives who are longtime fans of the "Renfro Valley Barn Dance." Don Evans stated, "My family and I are passionate about Renfro Valley and are committed to preserving, maintaining, and enhancing the sixty-five-year tradition that has established Renfro Valley as one of the premiere entertainment centers in the state of Kentucky and the southeastern United States."[50]

Atlanta's WSB and WGST

Atlanta was an important transportation center, with eight railroad lines by the turn of the twentieth century and important north-south highways. It was also a center for textile mills and other sources of employment that attracted migrants from the hinterlands to swell the population to two hundred thousand by the time of the city's first radio station.

Wayne Daniel, in his book *Pickin' on Peachtree: A History of Country Music in Atlanta, Georgia*, wrote about the talent and resources of music and humor that the migrants flocking to Atlanta brought with them. He also pointed out the importance of Atlanta's Old Time Fiddlers Convention in preparing performers and audiences for the age of radio. He noted that WSB and the other stations that attracted droves of accomplished musicians made it possible for Atlanta to became a regional recording center.[51]

Pop Eckler and His Young'uns pose for a publicity shot for the WSB "Barn Dance," late 1930s. L-R: Pop Eckler, Tex Foreman, Kay Woods, Ruey "Curley" Collins, and Red Murphy. Courtesy of Phillip G. Collins.

WSB, the South's first radio station, went on the air on March 15, 1922, as an adjunct of the *Atlanta Journal*, powered by one hundred watts (five hundred watts by June, and eventually fifty thousand watts by 1937) and with a broadcasting schedule of three or four hours a day. Daniel's research shows that Fiddlin' John Carson was the first of the traditional musicians to appear on WSB. The date was March 23, 1922, making him the first such musician to play over any radio station. Carson, a colorful and eccentric fiddler and singer, born just after the Civil War in the hills of northern Georgia's Fannin County, had been making music in the Atlanta area for nearly forty years. He had won the Old Time Fiddler's contest seven times and had played at rallies for various politicians, including Governor Eugene Talmadge. He was invited to play on WSB numerous times and later performed with his daughter, Moonshine Kate (Rosa Lee Carson). The audience was as much entertained by their antics as by their music.

WSB also featured touring artists and vaudeville troupers who were doing shows in Atlanta. In 1927, Sears-Roebuck, which had opened its big mail-order plant in Atlanta the previous year, arranged to have Edgar Bill, the musical director at WLS (then owned by Sears-Roebuck), bring some of his entertainers to Atlanta to broadcast a week-long sampling on its "National Barn Dance."

In 1927, WSB joined the National Broadcasting Company, which committed them to airing network shows, thus cutting down on the time previously given to local and regional entertainers.[52] Two main shows attracted musicians and comedians to WSB. The "Cross Roads Follies," Monday through Friday, beginning in 1936, featured Pop Eckler and His Barn Dance Gang (later Pop Eckler and His Young'uns) and other groups. Eckler's band supplied comedy by the band members Curley Collins, Slim Clere, and Tex Forman. Red Murphy did a dancing act. The "WSB Barn Dance" began in 1940 as a Saturday-night show, with John Lair acting as program consultant. The show was broadcast from such locations as the Erlanger Theater and other places in the city and also eventually from high schools and other buildings elsewhere in Georgia. Since the "WSB Barn Dance" was managed (from afar) by John Lair, there was a hefty amount of comedy. Those noted for their comedy were Hank Penny; a character known as Aunt Sarrie; Jack Baggett, whose stage name was Oscar McGooney; Bill Carlisle, with his character Hotshot Elmer; Ivy Peterson, who did comedy as Herman Horsehair Buggfuzz; Cynthia May Carver (Cousin Emmy); and James Wilson "Chick" Stripling, a comedian, buck dancer, and fiddler.[53]

Atlanta had stations other than WSB that featured hillbilly music and comedy, although some had short tenure or changing call letters. The notable ones were WDBE, WATL, and WGST, the latter being the most important for country entertainment even though it started out as an educational arm of Georgia Tech and had a power of only a thousand watts. Their most important singing group was the Blue Sky Boys (Earl and Bill Bolick), who performed music and comedy over WGST intermittently between 1936 and 1948, with four years off for service in World War II. Bill Bolick reported in an interview that none of them knew much about comedy at the time but that he and his fellow band member Lute Isenhower developed their comedy:

> I was playing a kind of a rube character. There was always comedy. Most of the shows were about half comedy. We played as the Crazy Hickory Nuts [since Crazy Water Crystals sponsored their show]. I think we realized that there would have to be some comedy in our shows. That was the first time I was connected to comedy in any way. I think Lute put most of it together, maybe from older jokes, maybe from medicine shows he'd seen.[54]

Since Earl did not want to do emcee work, he agreed to be the comedian. So he created his "Uncle Josh" character. In the notes to their *Blue Sky Boys on Radio*, vol. 1, Bill remembered:

> On our stage shows, he blacked his front teeth, wore an old crumpled hat, eyeglasses without lenses, and attached gray sideburns and a goatee. Our mother had made him a long slit-tail coat. He wore large brogan shoes, each on the wrong foot. . . .

The name Uncle Josh just seemed to fit the character we were trying to create. The comedy of Uncle Josh was very spontaneous and none of our radio programs were rehearsed. . . . As for comedy on our stage shows . . . the people expected more than singing and playing, especially in the thirties. Your radio performances brought people out to see you but the comedy was the influence that brought people out when you made a return engagement. . . . This attendance, I feel, was due to the fact that we presented an entertaining program and comedy had a great deal to do with it.[55]

As a recording center, Atlanta attracted talent from well beyond Georgia. Jimmie Rodgers, the Carter Family, the Delmore Brothers, Pop Stoneman, Bascom Lamar Lunsford, Burnett and Rutherford, and Mainer's Mountaineers all recorded there. From the standpoint of comedy, the best known recordings were for Columbia in 1927 with the Georgia entertainers the Skillet Lickers (then including Gid Tanner, Riley Puckett, Clayton McMichen, and Fate Norris). In addition to their dynamic instrumental and vocal renditions, they were innovators in the recorded comedy skits "A Corn Licker Still in Georgia" and "A Fiddler's Convention in Georgia," playing on the familiar stereotype of the hillbilly as moonshiner and the popularity of the Atlanta Old Time Fiddlers Convention. These recordings were as popular as their musical ones. Other narrative records made in Atlanta in 1928 were Ernest Stoneman and Uncle Eck Dunford doing "My First Bicycle Ride," "The Taffy-Pulling Party," and "The Savingest Man on Earth." Stoneman's band, including Uncle Eck, had already done a narrative recording, "Old Time Corn Shucking Party," for Victor at Ralph Peer's famous Bristol sessions in 1927, inspired by the Skillet Lickers' success with such recordings. In 1930, Bascom Lamar Lunsford, who had recorded in Atlanta for OKeh in 1924, did two narrative humorous records for Columbia, "Speaking the Truth" (a sermon parody) and "A Stump Speech in the Tenth District," with the Skillet Lickers playing at the beginning and the end.

Atlanta had its share of comic entertainers, those who thought of themselves as comedians and those who just entertained with a great spirit of energy and fun.

Springfield, Missouri, and the "Ozark Jubilee"

The first and, many say, the most successful televised country music show in the country, the "Ozark Jubilee," was created by Ely E. "Si" Simon, from his job as promoter of the radio station KWTO in Springfield, Missouri. Originally he had organized a local TV show in 1953 on KYTV, but Simon had bigger fish to fry. He recruited Red Foley away from the "Grand Ole Opry" to serve as permanent host, then went to New York and sold ABC-TV on the idea of a weekly show of country music. The first network show went on the air on July 17, 1954. The show launched or accelerated the careers of such performers as Porter Wagoner, Brenda Lee, Bobby Lord, Ferlin Husky, Billy Walker, Carl Smith, Jean Shepherd, Hawkshaw Hawkins, and Lew Childre. The other show regulars who stayed in Springfield were also an entertaining lot: Tommy Soseby, Slim Wilson, Norma Jean (Beasler), the Tall Timber Band, and the square dance teams the Promenaders, the Tadpoles, the Wagonwheelers, and the Ozark Sashayers. It also featured many well-known guest stars. The show ran for nearly six years on ABC with varying times of one hour, ninety minutes, and thirty minutes, changing its name along the way to "Country Music Jubilee" and "Jubilee, USA." It ended on September 24, 1960.

Many who performed on the show credited its success, beyond the salesmanship of Si Simon, to the talents of Red Foley as the host and talented singer. Foley was also a good straight man for comedy and was a master of timing. The "Jubilee" had a talented lineup of comedians: Uncle Cyp and Aunt Sap (Lawrence and Neva Brasfield), Lennie Ayleshire and Floyd "Goo Goo" Rutledge, Lew Childre, and Pete Stamper.

Cyp Brasfield, also known as "Boob," was a veteran—along with his brother, the "Grand Ole Opry" star Rod Brasfield—of Bisbee's Dramatic Shows and various other tent-repertory theaters that toured the country in the early twentieth century, and for a time he headed a stock company. In addition to being a great comedian, Cyp also wrote numerous comedy skits that were used by other comedians, including Rod Brasfield and Minnie Pearl. Aunt Sap (Neva Inez Grevi Brasfield) was also a veteran of traveling dramatic and comedy shows. Pete Stamper remembered in an interview that "Cyp and Sap were a fine act, as fine an act as you'd find anyplace."[56] They delighted audiences throughout the tenure of the "Jubilee" television show.

Lennie Aleshire and Goo Goo Rutledge provided zany comedy and music from weird instruments made out of such materials as brooms, dresser drawers, and bottles. Although Lennie had lost all but one finger on his left hand in an accident, he played several instruments, cowbells tied to his hands and feet. Lennie and Goo Goo were an important part of the "Jubilee" show. Leroy Van Dyke remembered, "Lenny and Goo Goo were two of the funniest there was—and they were absolutely pro, right down the line. You could take 'em anywhere and they'd tear the crowd up.[57]

Lew Childre came to the "Jubilee" in 1959. He had finished premedical studies at the University of Alabama and had performed in a medicine show. Therefore, he performed as "Doctor" Lew Childre, playing the Hawaiian guitar.

Pete Stamper, after doing comedy at Renfro Valley for several years, was discouraged and about ready to give up show business and to go back to western Kentucky and try his fortunes in the coal mines. Then, Betty Cummins, Red Foley's daughter, told Pete that her father was heading to Springfield to headline a new show and might need a comedian. She invited Pete to go along with her and her husband to Nashville to visit Red before he left. When Pete asked Red if he might find a place for him on the show, Red informed him that he had already hired Ferlin Husky as a comedian-singer. However, Red asked Pete to go ahead and show him what he could do, and he liked his act. Red invited him to come to Springfield, and he talked the station managers into hiring Pete. As it turned out, Ferlin Husky didn't do his "Simon Crum" act except occasionally, and so Pete became a regular comedian on the show.

Luke McNeeley, with his comedic persona "Luke Warmwater," entertained "Jubilee" audiences, and George Clinton "Shug" Fisher, with the help of the guitarist and singer Slim Wilson as straight man, also did comedy.

The "Jubilee" also featured guest comedians. The best known were the comedian-singer-composer-actor Smiley Burnette and Fran Allison and her puppets, Coo-Coo and Ollie.

"Hee Haw"

"Hee Haw," launched on CBS-TV and later syndicated, ran from 1969 to 1992 as a country version of Dan Rowan and Dick Martin's popular "Laugh-In" show. It was created by the Canadians John Aylesworth and Frank Peppiatt and produced by Sam Lovullo. The hosts were Roy Clark and Buck Owens, introducing a large cast of well-known comedians, including Minnie Pearl, Grandpa Jones, Archie Campbell, Roni Stoneman, Stringbean Akeman, George Lindsey, Gordie Tapp, and others who became famous on the show, such as Roy Clark, Junior Samples, Lulu Roman, Gailard Sartain, Gunilla Hutton, Marianne Gordon, Misty Rowe, and Mike Snider. It also included a long line of top personalities in country music, singing straight but also getting involved in the comedy. A variety of non-country celebrities also appeared, such as Ray Charles, Mickey Mantle, Vic Damone, Dizzy Dean, Oral Roberts, Ernest Borgnine, Alan King, Ed McMahon, Ethel Merman, Henny Youngman, Doc Severinsen, Sammy Davis Jr., Senator Robert Byrd, Willard Scott, and Minnesota Fats. The show ran on CBS from June 15, 1969, to February 23, 1971, and it ran in syndication from September 18, 1971, to May 30, 1992, a total of twenty-four years.

It was a popular show, "merely foolish," as Grandpa Jones described it, but the producer Sam Lovullo confessed in his book, *Life in the Kornfield: My Twenty-five Years at "Hee Haw,"* that he thought he had made a colossal career blunder when he saw the critiques of the initial shows. However, the negative comments from the New York and California critics only made the largely country-oriented audience curious, and so they made sure to check out "Hee Haw." They liked it; it brought them country comedy from talented comedians and music from their favorite country music stars.

Some of the writers of the show, such as Archie Campbell and Pat Buttram, had played comedy at such venues as the "Mid-day Merry-Go-Round" in Knoxville and the "National Barn Dance" in Chicago, using scripts inspired by minstrel shows and vaudeville, and they brought this experience along with them. The other writers had access to joke books, radio scripts, and other sources of comedy, some of which had not been heard on radio or television for a generation. When country audiences heard this humor, it reminded them of earlier comedy, or it spoke in some way to them as country people. But, of course, small-town and city people enjoyed it, too. It was like a festival where you could go and suspend reality and just enjoy yourself for a brief time before returning to the cares of life. The show gained high ratings. Lovullo explained its success in this way, "'Hee Haw' was the 'Grand Ole Opry' of television, with a little bit of something for everybody."[58]

Other Comedy Venues

There were numerous other radio stations that featured comedy. Many of the musical and comedic stars went from one station to another, mainly in their quest for new territory where they could do personal-appearance shows, the main way that they made money. When working for low-power stations, the artists found that after a year or so, interest in their personal appearances waned, and so they moved on to other stations whose audiences had not heard or seen them. The best hope, of course, was to get to one of the fifty-thousand-watt stations where they could be heard over a large portion of the country and thus could have practically unlimited audiences for their traveling shows. Grandpa Jones, for example, started his career on three small stations in Akron, Ohio, then joined "Bashful Joe" Troyan on Cleveland's WTAM before he and Joe joined Bradley Kincaid on Boston's WBZ and Hartford's WTIC, giving them opportunities to do personal appearances all over New England. In 1937, Grandpa went on his own to play over and do personal appearances from WWVA in Wheeling; WTIC in Hartford, Connecticut; WMMN in Fairmont, West Virginia; WLW in Cincinnati; WSM in Nashville; WARL in Arlington, Virginia; WRVA and the "Old Dominion Barn Dance" in Richmond, Virginia; and then back to WSM and the "Grand Ole Opry" as well as "Hee Haw."

Other stations that featured comedy and attracted some of the best-known stars of the time were WWNC in Asheville, North Carolina; WBT in Charlotte (WBT-TV did a syndicated show with the musical talents of the Briarhoppers and Arthur "Guitar Boogie" Smith and His Crackerjacks, with comedy by his brother Ralph); WCHS in Charleston, West Virginia; WCYB in Bristol, Virginia; WDJB in Roanoke; WRVA in Richmond (the "Old Dominion Barn Dance"); WSPA in Spartanburg, South Carolina; WHO in Des Moines (the "Iowa Barn Dance Frolic"); KWKH in Shreveport (the "Louisiana Hayride"); and many others.

THE DECLINE OF COUNTRY HUMOR

As Douglas Green has pointed out in a fine chapter on comedy in his book, *Country Roots: The Origins of Country Music*, the star system and package shows boosted some comedians to national prominence, such as Minnie Pearl, Rod Brasfield, Grandpa Jones, and the Duke of Paducah, but they made the comedian in each band unnecessary. Nowadays, promoters of the big country-music stars who play large arenas usually don't bother with comedy at all. It is harder now to communicate country humor to younger people whose experiences, lifestyles, and tastes have been shaped to a great degree by television sitcoms, modern movies, pop or neo-country music videos, and the Internet.

Most of the barn dance shows are now gone from the air. The "Grand Ole Opry" comedy stars—Minnie Pearl, Rod Brasfield, Whitey Ford, and Jerry Clower—have come and gone, and so far they have not been replaced by regular comedians, although musicians such as Mike Snider, Riders in the Sky, and Little Jimmy Dickens provide some humor. Also, the "Opry" has comic guest stars such as Bubba Bechtol and Chonda Pierce. Bechtol has done some two hundred performances at the "Opry" as a regular guest, but he says that under the organization's new rules, an entertainer will not be invited to join as a member unless he or she has a major record contract with big sales. Few comedians or humorists have such contracts and high-level sales, and the big-time comedians, such as Jeff Foxworthy and his partners in the recent phenomenon, the Blue Collar Comedy Tour, are probably not interested in being bound by Opry membership.

The decline of comedy at the "Grand Ole Opry" parallels the changes in the Nashville country music scene. A main concern of the studios is to get their stars accepted by a wider range of listeners, and so a more mainstream image is projected. Fewer of the younger performers are "country" in the sense of the term covering the rural working class. The big hat, boots, and jeans suggest a background that they may not have. Of course, making such an assumption is problematical. No artistic field should be limited to a certain class of people, but there are many who feel that calling the music of some entertainers "country" is laughable, especially when it is presented in Hollywood or New York City in designer clothing or tuxedos, with smoke, pulsating lights, and other showbiz trappings. Bill C. Malone had made a strong point in writing that when country music—the functional poetry of the common people—loses its connection with ordinary working people, it will have lost its moorings and will be something else.

The people who make up modern audiences have changed also. Since most of them are no longer country, they don't always identify with the country image except in a pejorative way. If they see comedy at all, it is on Comedy Central or at comedy clubs. At bluegrass festivals and country music venues today, many Baby Boomers who may have a desire to relate to their or their parents' or grandparents' country roots really appreciate the music. However, they may have problems with the old type of comedy. It embarrasses them. This separation of the comedy from what was considered "authentic" or "genuine" in the music started in the 1960s, some authorities think, when the college people discovered folk, bluegrass, or sometimes country music. When groups such as the Stanley Brothers or Flatt and Scruggs did comedy routines, there were sometimes interrupting calls for them to "sing something." The music was perceived as authentic and something positive to relate to, but the comedy was thought to be outdated and corny, or worse, racist or sexist.

Ron Thomason, whose Dry Branch Fire Squad performs for many college audiences, disagrees with the idea that it was the college crowd that killed country comedy;

he thinks that it was the upwardly mobile people in general who were offended. Some of the performers, always alert to what would or would not sell, dropped the comedy. Ralph Stanley, who did comedy with his brother Carter in the old days, or later with members of his band, seemed uneasy discussing comedy in an interview. He said, "You know that comedy left this music years ago." When pressed, however, he admitted that he and his brother Carter had often done the old "Arkansas Traveler" routine, and he had more recently done it with his son and grandson. Finally, he commented, "Used to be everybody had a comedian, and everybody just quit having one."[59] In a later conversation, after the tremendous success of the movie and CD *O Brother, Where Art Thou?* and the *Down from the Mountain* concerts and video, Ralph Stanley seemed more at ease with the place of comedy in bluegrass music.[60]

A good many of the current bluegrass bands still do comedy. Doyle Lawson admits that there is not so much comedy nowadays in bluegrass, but adds, "In my case, I always try to keep my presentations light. I do a lot of ad-libbing." He also does some of the old routines with a member of the band as the butt of the humor, and he and his band even do a parody on the kind of showy groups that are common in gospel music. Ron Thomason does a lot of humor for reasons not usually mentioned. He describes his purpose:

> The reason I started this band, I wanted to do some things that I felt very strongly needed to be done, and one of those was to educate people. I try to educate people who are listening to this music and are not part of an agrarian society. There's only about 3 ½ percent of American society still a part of the agricultural society, but this music they're listening to comes out of an agricultural and working-class ethnic culture. What I'm trying to do is give people the tools they need to understand our songs. . . . There's a lot of information to give, and I'm just trying to present it in a way that is humorous, and light, and informative. So I've always seen my role as, first, I've got to educate them, and then I can present what we do.[61]

Mike Snider, a veteran of "Hee Haw" and a member of the "Grand Ole Opry" since 1990, mainly as a singer and super banjo picker with a fine string band, does comedy in his shows. He has talked with great appreciation for what he learned about comedy from the old "Hee Haw" cast, mainly Grandpa Jones, Gordy Tapp, and George Lindsey. He commented on humor's effect on an audience: "It's like they're coming to get a fix. I think that's what is neat about humor. It sucks you in, gets your attention, and you are escaping the things that stress you. It's a healer. It sure is. I enjoy doing it."[62]

As country humor, with its ingrained prudishness, has declined, along with the restrained comedy of such as Jack Benny and Bob Hope, a more audacious and unrestrained humor has risen to replace it in comedy clubs and on Comedy Central, and it has few restrictions on subject matter.

A newer form of country humor is part of this new age of humor. It is the "redneck" (and later "blue-collar") humor made famous by Jeff Foxworthy, who was named Comedian of the Year three times by *Music City News* readers and achieved superstar status with albums selling more than eight million and his own TV comedy show. Redneck-type jokes have been around for years as Appalachian or hillbilly jokes. They have negative and demeaning aspects and deal in rural stereotypes having to do with ignorance, incest, violence, drunkenness, and poverty. There seem to be no limits on what is said about this particular group. Nor, the writer Anne Shelby points out, is this type of humor limited to jokes. Several of the TV sitcoms have incorporated humorous jibes at people who are southerners, Appalachians, live in trailers, or who are just poor or uneducated. Thus, there are some differences between the old rube humor and redneck humor in that rube comedy was usually performed by real country people just a jump ahead of hard times themselves, mostly to other rural people. Foxworthy, however, is more urban than country, and his audiences for the most part are not country and not poor. In rube comedy the rube usually was elevated above those who assumed they were better than he was. In redneck comedy, the redneck is the butt of the joke. There is no good side to this humor from the standpoint of the redneck, except as it reinforces an in-your-face, I-don't-give-a-damn persona that is popular in country music and comedy clubs nowadays. While the comedian may be intelligent and inventive, the butt of the jokes is not graced with any of the admirable qualities that an older country music and comedy reflected.

The Kentucky writer Gurney Norman has an explanation for the changes in country music and comedy:

> It has to do with post–World War II affluence and the rise of the middle class. Minnie Pearl, Rod Brasfield, Stringbean, and Grandpa Jones were the voices for those who came out of the Depression. They grew up in dirt-poor hard times. There is a kind of survival humor that goes with being on the thin edge of survival. Every ethnic group has found the humor to cope with this kind of stress. To me, the important thing here is, who is your audience? Minnie Pearl's audience was a local, regional, rural, unprivileged segment of society. They were on the cultural margin. They created a community that allowed the roughest little old country boy and girl to feel pride in a show-business hero. They prevailed; they defined the "Grand Ole Opry" up through the Korean War. Hank Williams, for example, never became polished in any sophisticated way.
>
> Now the present generation is characterized by Jeff Foxworthy and Garth Brooks. I've watched their audiences. They are an affluent, post–Vietnam War, post-Reagan bunch of people whose personal and family issues are not survival. They are looking to be entertained and amused and to be involved by a screaming, jumping, clapping behavior that is a post-Vietnam, rock-and-roll, Elvis, the Grateful Dead phenomenon. They have to have social confidence to get up and show off like that. There is a social confidence that Garth Brooks and them have, and they define the present rootless media culture, although it has roots reaching back into the old place-based culture. Basically, though, the audience for Garth Brooks is urban and suburban, pretty much young professional white folks, although this is not to say that this is the limit of his appeal. I think the same thing can be said for Jeff

Foxworthy. I don't think Jeff Foxworthy addresses the audience that is the subject of his jokes. He's not telling his jokes to the people that his jokes are on. And that's the big difference between his humor and the earlier country humor.[63]

Anne Shelby also discusses how those with country roots have made it in the big world, and how redneck jokes serve their needs:

> Some of the people who enjoy redneck jokes the most are those, who when called on it, defend themselves by producing their own "redneck credentials." They grew up on a farm. Their parents still live there. . . . For this group the redneck joke works both ways. That's why they like it so much. It establishes a tenuous connection to the culture that is the subject of the joke, a connection that they, like Jeff Foxworthy, feel gives them the right to tell it. But more important, the joke functions to put distance between the teller and the subject. For this group the joke says, "Look at me, how far I've come, what good taste I have. I used to be a redneck. But I'm not anymore."

Shelby goes on to say, "For the larger society, redneck jokes and other forms of Appalachian stereotypes serve the important function of providing a scapegoat for racism and incest. We aren't racists. We aren't perverts, the jokes say. There they are, over there. It ain't us. It's them." However, Shelby points to a hopeful sign: "Foxworthy's incest jokes draw audible moans and objections from the audience. Here what we recognize is not a reflection of ourselves [as rural people] but an old stereotype, and a vicious and inaccurate one at that."[64]

The southern cultural historian Bill C. Malone, whose latest book, *Don't Get Above Your Raisin': Country Music and the Southern Working Class*, laments the great changes that have come about in country music and also its humor, gave a thoughtful answer to the question of who is the audience for the more demeaning redneck or blue-collar humor of today:

> I frankly don't know who the audience for this kind of humor is. Some of the fans may be folks who already have stereotypical perceptions of working people. Others may be the children or, more likely, the grandchildren of rural working folk who've grown up in town and who can distance themselves from real rednecks and still have fun at their expense. The putdowns of the liberals, gays, the handicapped, and others is probably a cultural product of the Civil Rights and other revolutions that came along in the sixties and challenged the old social hierarchies that had long held sway in the South and elsewhere (I'm speaking of machismo and white supremacy, among other things). White males, particularly, have been under siege since the sixties, and they've expressed their fears in the political arena and on the comedy stage. They've finally discovered, I think, that anti-black humor is unacceptable, so comedians like Larry the Cable Guy vent their spleen against other outsiders in the society.[65]

Another authoritative voice on redneck humor is Randall Franks, the Georgia fiddler, humorist, gospel and bluegrass singer, and television actor (he portrayed Officer

Randy Goode in the series "In the Heat of the Night"). He comments on the changing nature of the term "redneck":

I don't know how many people out there would really consider themselves a redneck. There was a time that the word was used as a demeaning term, but somewhere in the 1970s, for those who wished to cling to a new definition, it became a term describing rural or blue-collar individualists who wanted to follow the beat of their own drum. They do not care what others think of their actions; they do what they want to do in life no matter what they face. Of course, with the success of Jeff Foxworthy, the redneck term found its prominence in mainstream society and became the target of endless one-line jokes. City folks would have attached this term to the Dukes in the original "Dukes of Hazzard" TV series, but in reality, they [the Dukes] were close to country comedians of old. They always did what was morally right. They never used foul language. The comedy was close to the old ways despite the fact that it came from Hollywood. The characters were caricatures of Southern stereotypes.

There are folks who do have a "redneck" background, however, and the concept of the Blue Collar Tour rings more true to this audience because so many were raised in a blue-collar household and possibly share some of the experiences that are covered by the four entertainers. While there is some good stuff in there, unfortunately you have to endure some jokes that would have made Minnie Pearl and most of her audiences blush. It is sad to think that the kings and queens of country comedy could hit the stage in a big city concert like this one, starting life anew as it were, and they'd probably find their routines falling on deaf ears.[66]

It should be noted that Foxworthy has said that he will do no more redneck joke books and that he wants to move on to other subjects. However, in his and Bill Engvall's recent Blue Collar Comedy Tour, with its highly successful three-year run and resulting feature-length film by the same name, bestseller VHS and DVD versions, a soundtrack CD, and other recordings, the redneck jokes are prominent. In fact, the jokes have morphed beyond the redneck theme with the other two performers in this venture, Larry the Cable Guy and Ron White. They are veterans of the comedy-club circuit with in-your-face, politically incorrect personas who venture into bad-taste subjects that make the redneck jokes of Foxworthy seem tame indeed. Larry the Cable Guy personifies a worst-case rural stereotype and makes fun of political enemies on the left, including political-correctness but also gays, women, and even the physically handicapped. Ron White is somewhat more urbane with his glass of Scotch and cigar or cigarette, but his is a blunt bad-boy demeanor and nothing much is too indelicate for his humor. These latter-day comedians and the Blue Collar Comedy Tour itself highlight the great changes that have occurred between modern entertainment and the basic religiously inspired values and manners of most earlier country people. It is true that rural people within their gender and age groups always talked about almost everything, but there was a manners system that discouraged such in mixed groups. Country people were known for their restraint and for their sense of modesty. Such modesty and restraint have withered in the modern electronic-entertainment world.

There are those who have positive words for Jeff Foxworthy and his redneck humor. Rick Bragg, a Pulitzer Prize–winning writer from Alabama who has written numerous stories about the rural South for the *New York Times* and other papers, has stated that he thinks Foxworthy has keen insight into the humorous side of southerners. He acknowledges that people outside the South may like his redneck humor because it fits the stereotypes that they carry in their heads but claims that Foxworthy is popular also among southerners who love to laugh at themselves.[67]

T. Bubba Bechtol's humor should be noted in connection with redneck humor. He says that he has always avoided the negative redneck jokes that emphasize incest and such and goes on to explain his "Bubba" humor: "My whole thing is about being Southern and being proud of it. I come from the Dave Gardner/Lewis Grizzard school of thought. To me the difference between the redneck and Bubba is that anybody can be a Bubba."[68]

Melvin Goins, who played comedy with the Stanley Brothers and has headed his own bands, feels strongly that people still like to laugh and have fun and that the smart entertainer will offer up at least a bit of humor as he presents his or her other gifts. The music of country has changed. Yet the fact that we now speak freely of a "traditional" branch of this music suggests that there is a segment that wants to hold on to some vestige of rural, working-class identity. That part of country will probably always have some humor that reflects the values of this group. Comedy is more sophisticated today because the general audience is more sophisticated, but some performers have a strong desire to hold onto the rusticity of the comedy that has been a strong partner to country music.

The Geezinslaw Brothers (Sam Allred and Raymond "Son" Smith), veterans of the "Arthur Godfrey Show," do hilarious comic songs, such as "Help, I'm White and I Can't Get Down," and Allred is one of the great humorous storytellers with some pretty sophisticated twists in a country manner. Mel Tillis tells jokes and uses his stuttering as part of his comic act. Mike Snider is good at adapting old jokes to current situations, and he writes, seeks, and sings humorous songs. Many bluegrass acts include comedy still. Doyle Lawson of Quicksilver and Ron Thomason of the Dry Branch Fire Squad do humor, ranging from uptown to backwater country. The Moron Brothers (Michael Carr and Michael Hammond), who do comedy and music, are much in demand at bluegrass festivals and other venues. James "Sparky" Rucker, a black folk and blues singer, guitarist, and storyteller, testifies that humor is a bridge he uses to reach white audiences who may be uneasy with him.

There is also a lot of comedy in the country music centers. The "Renfro Valley Barn Dance" still reflects the influence of John Lair in its programming of comedians. The theaters at Branson, Missouri, Pigeon Forge, Tennessee, and Myrtle Beach, South Carolina, offer a great deal of comedy; Pigeon Forge even has the Comedy Barn. At

Branson, the Bald Knobbers have a balanced musical-comedy show, as do the Presleys. Jim Stafford, who stays away from the country-boy image, does a lot of comedy along with his picking and singing. These entertainers have found, like their predecessors in the radio personal-appearance show, that a good evening's entertainment must be varied to appeal to a variety of people. Comedy is still a proven ingredient.

Notes

1. William E. Lightfoot, "Esoteric and Exoteric Dimensions of Appalachian Folk Humor," in *Curing the Cross-Eyed Mule: Appalachian Mountain Humor,* ed. Loyal Jones and Billy Edd Wheeler (Little Rock, Ark.: August House, 1989), 189–90.

2. Constance Rourke, *American Humor: A Study of the National Character* (Garden City, N.Y.: Doubleday, 1953), 81–85.

3. Robert G. Cogswell, "Jokes in Blackface: A Discographic Folklore Study," Ph.D. dissertation, Indiana University, 1984, 850–54; Norm Cohen, Liner notes to *Minstrels and Tunesmiths: The Commercial Roots of Commercial Early Country Music* (LP-109; Los Angeles: John Edwards Memorial Foundation, 1981), 31.

4. Cohen, Liner notes to *Minstrels and Tunesmiths,* 31.

5. Cogswell, "Jokes in Blackface," 714–15.

6. Author's interview with Fred Smith, Pigeon Forge, Tennessee, September 15, 1996.

7. Brooks McNamara, "The Medicine Show," *Festival of American Folklife Program Book* (Washington, D.C.: Smithsonian Institution, 1979), 15–16.

8. From a recording sent to author by James Buchanan in 1998.

9. Author's telephone interview with Homer Sherrill, November 8, 1996.

10. Bill C. Malone, *Country Music, USA,* rev. ed. (Austin: University of Texas Press, 1985), 9.

11. Autobiographical material sent to author by James Buchanan, 1996.

12. Billy "Toby" Choate, *Born in a Trunk. . . Just Outside the Center Door Fancy* (Kearney, Neb.: Morris Publishers, 1996).

13. Ibid.

14. Ibid., 174–89; author's telephone interview with Billy Choate, September 4, 2002.

15. Bill C. Malone, *Don't Get above Your Raisin': Country Music and the Southern Working Class* (Urbana: University of Illinois Press, 2002), 172.

16. Author's telephone interview with Wade Mainer, November 9, 1996.

17. Author's telephone interview with Doc Williams, December 20, 1996.

18. Author's telephone interview with Bill Bolick, December 16, 1996.

19. Author's telephone interview with Tom Fouts, January 20, 1996.

20. Author's interview with Doyle Lawson, Clinton, Tenn., October 13, 1996.

21. Author's telephone interview with Charlie Louvin, November 15, 1996.

22. Author's telephone interview with Jim McReynolds, November 11, 1996.

23. Author's telephone interview with Betty York, December 21, 1996.

24. Author's telephone interview with Beecher Kirby, October 16, 1996.

25. Author's interview with Jim Gaskin, Renfro Valley, Ky., November 16, 1996.

26. Interview with Lulu Belle Wiseman by Marshall Dial, Spruce Pine, N.C., July 1986.

27. Author's telephone interview with Tom Fouts, January 20, 1996.

28. Author's telephone interview with Beecher Kirby, October 16, 1996.

29. Douglas B. Green, *Country Roots: The Origins of Country Music* (New York: Hawthorn Books, 1976), 80.

30. Author's interview with Louis Marshall Jones, Clinton, Tenn., October 12, 1996; author's telephone interview with Jim McReynolds, Nashville, Tenn., November 11, 1996.

31. William Jensen Smyth, *Traditional Humor on Knoxville Radio Entertainment Shows* (Ann Arbor, Mich.: UMI Dissertation Services, 1987), 38.

32. Quoted in ibid., 43.

33. Ivan Tribe, "Kentucky Slim: Comedian in Medicine Shows, Old-Time, and Bluegrass Music," *Bluegrass Unlimited* 16.5 (November 1981): 20–21.

34. Smyth, *Traditional Humor on Knoxville Radio*, 51–52.

35. Author's interview with Sunshine Slim Sweet, Norris, Tenn., October 12, 1996.

36. Author's interview with Bill Carlisle, Norris, Tenn., October 12, 1996.

37. Smyth, *Traditional Humor on Knoxville Radio*, 58, 78.

38. Bill Landry, *The Heartland Series*, vol. 14 (video, WBIR-TV, Knoxville).

39. Author's interview with Sam Venable, Norris, Tenn., November 11, 1998; Sam Venable, "There Wasn't Much Middle of the Road about Cas Walker," *Knoxville News-Sentinel*, September 29, 1998, A2.

40. Willie J. Smyth, "Early Knoxville Radio (1921–41)," *John Edwards Memorial Foundation Quarterly* 67–68 (Fall/Winter 1982): 114.

41. Ivan M. Tribe, *Mountaineer Jamboree: Country Music in West Virginia* (Lexington: University Press of Kentucky, 1984), 42–44.

42. Ibid., 47–52.

43. Author's telephone interview with Doc Williams, December 17, 1996.

44. Author's telephone interview with Ann Lair Henderson, February 12, 2008.

45. Harry S. Rice, "Renfro Valley on the Radio," *Journal of Country Music* 19.2 (1997): 20–21.

46. Author's interview with Jim Gaskin, Renfro Valley, Ky., November 16, 1996.

47. Rice, "Renfro Valley on the Radio," 18–20.

48. Author's interview with Jim Gaskin, Renfro Valley, Ky., November 16, 1996.

49. Author's interview with Pete Stamper, Renfro Valley, Ky., April 16, 1998.

50. *Renfro Valley Bugle* 61.2 (February 2005).

51. Wayne W. Daniel, *Pickin' on Peachtree: A History of Country Music in Atlanta, Georgia* (Urbana: University of Illinois Press, 1990), 15–44.

52. Ibid., 63–66.

53. Ibid., 127–51, 172–204.

54. Author's telephone interview with Bill Bolick, December 16, 1996.

55. Bill Bolick, Liner notes to *Blue Sky Boys on Radio*, vol. 1 (Roanoke: Copper Creek Recordings, 1993).

56. Author's interview with Pete Stamper, Renfro Valley, Ky., April 16, 1998.

57. Reta Spears-Stewart, *Remembering the Ozark Jubilee* (Springfield, Mo.: Stewart, Dilbeck, and White Productions, 1993), 88–90.

58. Sam Lovullo and Marc Eliot, *Life in the Kornfield: My Twenty-five Years at "Hee Haw"* (New York: Boulevard Books, 1996), back cover.

59. Author's telephone interview with Ralph Stanley, January 2, 1997.

60. Author's brief interview with Ralph Stanley, Clinton, Tenn., October 11, 2002.

61. Author's telephone interview with Ron Thomason, January 14, 1997.

62. Author's telephone interview with Mike Snider, December 17, 1996; author's interview with Mike Snider, Clinton, Tenn., October 11, 2002.

63. Author's telephone interview with Gurney Norman, August 30, 1999.

64. Anne Shelby, "The 'R' Word: What's So Funny (and Not So Funny) about Redneck Jokes," in *Confronting Appalachian Stereotypes: Backtalk from an American Region*, ed. Dwight B. Billings, Gurney Norman, and Katherine Ledford (Lexington: University Press of Kentucky, 1999), 156–57.

65. Author's email correspondence with Bill C. Malone, January 14, 2007.

66. Author's email correspondence with Randall Franks, December 30, 2006.

67. Author's telephone interview with Rick Bragg, October 14, 2003.

68. Author's telephone interview with Terryl Bechtol, December 11, 2002.

ENCYCLOPEDIA
of Humorists and Comedians

ROY ACUFF

Born Roy Claxton Acuff, September 15, 1903,
Maynardville, Tennessee; died Nashville, Tennessee,
November 23, 1992

Roy Acuff was the undisputed king of country music in his time, as a fiddler, bandleader, superb singer, music publisher, and reigning arbiter of musical taste for the "Grand Ole Opry." He soaked up folk humor along with ballads and fiddle tunes as he grew up in rural Union County, Tennessee. Acuff learned the value of comedy early on in his travels with Doc Hauer's Medicine Show in 1932, where he played blackface and rube comedy. He also learned to balance his fiddle bow, or fiddle, or both, on his chin, to do tricks with a yo-yo, to imitate train whistles, and generally to become an all-around entertainer. When he formed his band in Knoxville in 1933, he took on the musicians Lonnie Wilson and Beecher Kirby, who became adept at comedy. Then Rachel Veach joined the group, billed as "Bashful Brother Oswald's sister," dressed in quaint costumes with a blacked-out front tooth. Kirby reported:

> I started doing comedy with Roy in Knoxville. We did a lot of stuff vaudeville style. It was the main influence, usually with a jokester and a straight man. Roy had been on a medicine show. He played music and then came on stage with another guy. I think his name was [Tom] Ashley. With us Roy was the straight man, and he let us do the comedy. At one time or another all of us was comedians: Pap Wilson, Joe Zinkan, Jess Easterday, and me. All us boys dressed in comedy stuff except on a hymn. Then we took off our hats and sang like we were in church.

Charlie Collins, who joined Acuff's band in 1966 and who, after Acuff's death, continued playing with Brother Oswald on the "Grand Ole Opry," added, "Roy would tell a joke once in a while himself. I went with him one time over to Bailey, North Carolina, four or five years before he died, and he did some of the old medicine-show things. Some of the other old medicine-show people were there that night, and we did a regular medicine-show routine, the old-time way. I was privileged to be on the stage with him."

Acuff was invited to play a fifteen-minute segment of the "Grand Ole Opry" in 1938 as a fiddler to fill in for Arthur Smith, who was on the road. His singing of "The Great Speckled Bird" brought an invitation to be a regular member. He commented that as a fiddler he was deplorable, so nervous that he played as much behind the bridge as in front of it, and that it was "The Great Speckled Bird" and not "Turkey Buzzard" that generated the flood of mail that got him a job at the "Opry," where he became the quintessential country singer. He also became a recording star and, with Fred Rose, established the important music publishing house of Acuff-Rose. Even though he became wealthy and influential in the business of country music, he never lost his rural modesty. He enjoyed clowning with his fiddle and displaying his yo-yo skills, as well as playing straight man to Minnie Pearl and other comedians on the "Opry." He seemed to delight in spoofing himself and his success in his appearances on "Hee Haw."

He was married to Mildred Louise Douglas, and they had one son, Roy Jr., a singer, guitarist, and drummer.

(With credit to Elizabeth Schlappi, *Roy Acuff: The Smoky Mountain Boy* [Gretna, La.: Pelican Publishing Co., 1978]).

SHEILA KAY ADAMS

Born March 18, 1953, Greeneville, Tennessee

Although Sheila Adams was born in a Tennessee hospital, her mother said they didn't stay there long enough for it to count. Sheila grew up in the rural community of Sodom in Madison County, North Carolina, a county that Bascom Lamar Lunsford called "the last stand of the natural people." Presbyterian missionaries had disdained the name of Sodom and had it officially changed to Revere. However, the natives ignored this legality and insisted that they were from Sodom. Adams descends from and is related to numerous musicians, ballad singers, jokesters, and tellers of traditional folktales. She is a superb banjo artist and a ballad singer, songwriter, novelist, and gifted storyteller and humorist. She learned most of her ballads from her great-aunt Dellie Norton and

Sheila Kay Adams. Photo by Tim Barnwell, courtesy of Sheila Kay Adams.

her stories, riddles, and jokes from her father, Ervin Adams, the balladeer Cas Wallin, Inez Chandler, and other relatives.

After graduating from Mars Hill College and teaching North Carolina history for seventeen years in the Madison County schools, Adams now performs at festivals, teachers' workshops, and other venues, including workshops in storytelling, ballad singing, and banjo playing, and she occasionally is a visiting teacher in colleges, such as at Carleton College in Northfield, Minnesota. She has also toured with the "Sisters of the South" production in the United States as well as two tours in England. She appeared in and was the voice and singing coach for the Hollywood film *Songcatcher.* Her latest CD is *Sheila Kay Adams Live! at the International Storytelling Festival* (2007). She has three more CDs available: *My Dearest Dear, Whatever Happened to John Parish's Boy?* from a live performance of stories, and *All the Other Fine Things*, a studio recording of ballads, fiddle tunes, and shape-note hymns that is sort of a soundtrack for her novel, *My Old True Love* (Ballantine, 2005). Based on a true family story, the novel was a finalist for the Southeastern Booksellers Association 2004 Book of the Year Award. Earlier she published *Come Go Home with Me*, a collection of stories (University of North Carolina Press, 1995). She is working on a second novel, due out in 2009. She continues to travel extensively with her neat clawhammer banjo-picking, her songs and ballads, and her humorous stories. She and her husband, Jim Taylor, have made recordings of Civil War–era songs and tunes. Log on to www.sheilakayadams.com.

Adams can speak at length about her special brand of humor. In Sodom, where she grew up, she saw a strong feminine force in what was nominally a patriarchal society. The women were the primary carriers of the old ballads, including several rare bawdy ones, and they passed them on orally to their children and grandchildren. She saw a love of language and turns of phrase with double meanings in the jokes, the riddles, and the sayings that were in the oral tradition. She saw also a lot of humor in the subtle rivalry of the sexes, with men in their group telling jokes and stories that exaggerated their male prowess and the women, in their group, telling those that ridiculed such prowess. "I have to be careful onstage about what I tell, but there's a difference between the off-color humor and vulgarity. My father had this off-color, suggestive humor, with several ways of interpreting it, but it was not vulgar." Adams went on to say that the vulgar stuff was not told in mixed company but in separate gender groups. As a storyteller, Adams uses subtle suggestive material that gets a laugh with voice inflection or a knowing look, along with a well-turned phrase, but she avoids material that might offend.

Adams has three children by previous marriages, Melanie Rice and Hart and Andrew Barnhill, and she is a recent grandmother. She has been married since 1993 to Jim Taylor, a musician, singer, and hammered dulcimer maker. They live in Mars Hill, not too far from Sodom.

Here is one of Sheila's favorite stories, learned from the late notable ballad singer, Cas Wallin. It indicates how attached she and her relations are to their native county:

> *This fellow died and was walking down the Road of Eternity, and there was the Gates of Heaven, and St. Peter was out front with his big book. St. Peter ran down the list, and there was this fellow's name. He said, "My friend, you've made it into Heaven." Fellow looked kind of dazed, and St. Peter took pity on him. He looks down the Road to Eternity, didn't see anybody else coming, and said, "Well, since you're the only one who's showed up, I'll just give you a private tour." So they walked down the street. Everywhere there's beautiful music, wonderful mowed meadows as far as they could see. St. Peter puts his arm around him and says, "My friend, we're walking on the Streets of Gold. Over there you see that river—that's the River of Milk and Honey. There in the distance are the Crystal*

Mountains." This fellow started to relax a little bit. He began to notice people laughing and running through the meadows, picking flowers.

But around the curve in the distance are these people that don't look too happy. He gets closer, and he sees that they have shackles around their ankles, and they are all chained together. He turns to St. Peter and says, "I figured that everybody would be happy to be here in Heaven. What's the matter with them over there? They don't look none too happy." St. Peter brings his hands up to shade his eyes and looks at that crowd of folks. He gives a wave of his hand and says, "Oh, don't pay any attention to them. They're from Madison County, North Carolina, and if we didn't keep them chained together that way, they'd try to go home on the weekends!"

DAVID "STRINGBEAN" AKEMAN

*Born June 17, 1915, Annville, Kentucky; died
Goodlettsville, Tennessee, November 10, 1973*

David Akeman grew up in a family of eight children with a father who picked the five-string banjo. He got into show business in the middle of the Great Depression (after serving in the Civilian Conservation Corps) by winning a talent show sponsored by Asa Martin, who had a show on Lexington's WLAP. A fine banjo player and singer,

Akeman joined Martin's band and played with him and others in Lexington from 1935 to 1938. Martin was responsible for the "Stringbean" nickname. Struggling to remember Akeman's name when introducing him, Martin referred to him as "this tall stringbean of a fellow," a common expression for a long, lanky person. Martin, a good straight man, talked him into doing comedy.

For three years, beginning in 1935, Akeman was a member of Charlie Monroe's Kentucky Partners, and he later joined Bill Monroe's Bluegrass Boys, from 1942–45, playing clawhammer, or two-finger-picking style, banjo in those pre–Earl Scruggs days of what was to become bluegrass music. He became a member of the "Grand Ole Opry" in 1942 and for a time headed his own band, String Bean and His Kentucky Wonders (named after a popular pole bean). He later teamed up with the superb entertainer Lew Childre for three years, doing the "Opry" and tent shows, where he became a student of the old master entertainer Uncle Dave Macon,

David "Stringbean" Akeman.
Courtesy of Charles K. Wolfe.

learning from Macon's vast repertory of banjo tunes and songs. By then he had perfected his hillbilly comic persona, with a costume that put his waistline somewhere
between his knees and his hips, consisting of a long-waisted striped shirt, short-legged
pants, and a funny hat. A few daubs of paint on his eyebrows highlighted his mournful clown face. His comedy was distinctive, but so were his banjo style and singing, in
which he featured much of the traditional banjo music of an earlier time. His favorite
garment when he wasn't on stage was a pair of overalls. James Roberts, who traveled
and played music with him, reported an encounter where String asked how he liked
his new overalls. James replied that he liked them, and then String said, "Ever' time I
buy a new Cadillac, I get me two or three new pairs of overalls."

Stringbean recorded numerous EPs and LPs for Starday, beginning in 1960, and
albums for Cullman and Nugget, the most popular being *Barnyard Banjo Picking* (Cullman, 1960) and *Salute to Uncle Dave Macon* (Starday, 1966). Highland Music also
released a recording, *Stringbean: Front Porch Funnies* in 1993 (KS-4-476).

Akeman was ideal for television, and he was invited to play the "Ozark Jubilee,"
the "Merv Griffin Show," the "Grand Ole Opry Syndicated Show," the "Porter Wagoner" syndicated show, the "Flat and Scruggs" syndicated show, the "Bill Anderson"
syndicated show, and of course, "Hee Haw," which he joined in 1969, playing comedy
almost exclusively.

David Akeman and his wife Estelle (Stanfil) were murdered in 1973 by John and
Doug Brown, who waited for them to return from an "Opry" performance acting
on a rumor that Stringbean carried or stashed in his rural house huge sums of cash.
The Browns were apprehended, indicted, and convicted of the murders and are now
in prison. Louis "Grandpa" Jones, who found the bodies of his longtime friends and
neighbors, did two benefit performances for the children of Jackson County, Kentucky, to honor his friend "String" and unveiled a memorial statue to him in Annville,
Kentucky.

Here is some Stringbean humor:

Your left eye must have a wonderful personality.
Why?
Because your right eye is always looking at it.

If I was as drunk as you are I'd shoot myself.
If you were as drunk as I am you couldn't hit yourself.

I run ten miles this morning to whip a man.
Well, did you run back?
No, they carried me back.

LENNIE ALESHIRE. *See Lennie and Goo Goo*

SAMUEL MORRIS ALLRED. *See Geezinslaw Brothers*

BILL ANDERSON

Born November 1, 1937, Columbia, South Carolina

Although James William Anderson III, a member of the "Grand Ole Opry" since 1961, is best known as a songwriter, singer, and television host, his sense of humor has been ever present in his concerts and his interviews with performers on TNN's "Opry Backstage," when it was a popular part of the televised portion of the "Opry." In 1993 he published a memoir, *I Hope You're Living as High on the Hog as the Pig You Turned Out to Be* (Longstreet Press), in which he recounts humorous incidents he has encountered as a country singer, as well as those told to him by other performers. Prominent are stories about the prejudices against entertainers, particularly country musicians, and the power of humor in striking back and thus keeping a bit of dignity and self-respect. He also relates other stories about shows that went flat and how the only recourse from complete deflation was humor.

Graduating from the University of Georgia with a degree in journalism, Anderson worked briefly as a reporter at the *Atlanta Constitution* and then as a disc jockey. He had been writing songs since he was in high school, and when Ray Price took his "City Lights" to number one on *Billboard's* country charts in 1958, Anderson signed with Decca. He became a regular on the "Grand Ole Opry" in 1961. His biggest success came in the 1960s and early 1970s as a songwriter and performer when his songs were regularly high on the country charts, including "Mama Sang a Song," "I Get the Fever," "Once a Day," "My Life," "For Loving You," and "Sometimes."

Anderson has also been host or producer of television shows, including "You Can Be a Star" (TNN), the quiz show "Fandango" (TNN), and the game show "The Better Sex" (ABC). He has received more than fifty BMI songwriter awards and some fifteen awards from trade magazines. He still regularly performs and serves as host on the "Grand Ole Opry."

His recordings include *A Lot of Things Different* (Varese-Saraband Records, 2000) and *Bill Anderson: Twelve Classics* (Varese-Saraband, 2002).

Here are some excerpts from *I Hope You Are Living as High on the Hog as the Pig You Turned Out to Be*, with permission:

> *Musicians can be unmerciful toward other musicians about the instruments they play. The punch lines are all the same, only the instrument changes depending on who's telling the story. For some reason, however, accordion players and banjo players seem to take the brunt of most jokes.*

For example: "Do you know the difference between an accordion and a trampoline?"
"No, what?"
"You take off your shoes when you jump on a trampoline!"
Or:
"Do you know what you call ten banjos lying on the bottom of the Mississippi River?"
"What?"
"A good start."
Or:
"Do you know the epitome of optimism? That's an accordion player with a beeper!"
Something you'll never hear at a recording session:
"That's a banjo player's Porsche parked out back!"
Or:
"Porter Wagoner's definition of a gentleman: A man who can play an accordion but doesn't."

VIRGIL ANDERSON

Born June 14, 1902, Palace, Kentucky;
died May 30, 1997, Monticello, Kentucky

Bobby Fulcher, the director of the Tennessee State Parks Folklife Programs who recorded Virgil Anderson extensively in 1977 and 1979, said this about him as a musician and all-around entertainer in 1980:

> Perhaps the most distinctive living master of old-time banjo, Virgil Anderson, at age eighty-five is an amazing source of vitality, wit, and extraordinary musical skill. The two LPs featuring Virgil's music demonstrate his superb technical ability to pick delicate melodies, chord creatively, knock out syncopated dance tunes, utilize novel effects, and freely improvise. Virgil continues to learn new songs and to perform with enthusiasm and uninhibited abandon.

Virgil Anderson's father Maynard was a banjo picker who was mostly in the lumber and barrel stave business and thus traveled around to where the jobs were. Virgil took up the banjo also. He commented, "I don't know how I learned to play the banjer. I was too young. I can't remember. When I come to myself, I was a-knockin' it down the line."

At age ten, Virgil was pressed into service as a water boy for the work crews that his father supervised at various logging camps and lumber and stave mills. His father also ordered him to pick the banjo while the men were working or taking their dinner breaks. It was a rough environment among rough men, and from them Virgil learned a lot of his jokes, tales, and witticisms and told colorful stories about them. He talked at length of those who had influenced his music:

I copied after other people when I was about seventeen or eighteen. I started playing with colored folks, Cuge Bertram and Cooney Bertram and Andy from Three Forks of the Wolf River, around Pall Mall, Tennessee. I played there a sight. Cuge and Cooney, they played chord music. The most of the old-time music was just noted out, but when I got in with them Bertram boys, they played by chord a whole lot. Course, they played the banjer and fiddle some by note, but they played a whole lot by chord. I picked up a whole lot of that. I thought a sight of 'em. You get into playin' music, you naturally like each other.

Virgil Anderson at eighteen. Courtesy of the Virgil Anderson family and Bobby Fulcher.

Fulcher credits the Bertrams with converting Virgil to "a fuller, more sophisticated 'chord music' with a blues touch, and he was no longer satisfied with just 'noting out' the simple dance tunes his father played. The blues and the Bertrams' chord music, infused in a variety of songs and tunes of both black and white origin, became Virgil's love."

Virgil married Mabel Troxell in 1923. She came out of a musical family and also played the banjo. A lot of Virgil's humor was aimed at Mabel in a loving way. In later years, when folklorists and musicians trudged to their farm, which Virgil had named Wildcat Rock City, Mabel was a gracious hostess and a great cook.

Virgil joined up with Clyde Troxell and John Sharp in 1931 to form the Kentucky Wildcats, and they entertained timber workers at towns in Kentucky and Tennessee, but they never made recordings. Virgil moved his growing family to Wildcat Rock City in 1937. It was in a remote part of Wayne County, Kentucky, on the Little South Fork of the Cumberland River, now designated as Wild River. Their house could be reached only by a swinging bridge.

Three of the Anderson boys, Hershel, Willard, and Dillard, played music. As Virgil said, "I raised my boys on summer rabbits, poke sallet, borrowed meal, and good music." Willard commented, "I was a good-sized boy before I realized there was people who *didn't* play music." All three performed in bands in Kentucky, Ohio, and Indiana. One daughter, Annabelle, played the harmonica.

Virgil's humor was sly and playful. He had a lot of pat phrases, recitations, and monologues that he would do at concerts or to various interviewers. A lot of his humor was traditional, but some was someone else's invention that stayed in his mind, and he made up a lot himself. He savored the language and sly hidden meanings. Here are a few examples:

My daddy tried to raise me right. There's three things he always teached me against: that's lyin', drinkin', and stealin'. Said never steal more than you can carry, never drink more than you can hold, and when it comes to lyin', just tell it a dozen different ways before you lie about it.

I've trained my wife Mabel in the truth. When she dies they'll say, "There lies a body of truth," because none of it never did come out.

And my daddy teached me to never be afraid of work. I've never been afraid of a job in my life. I've laid down a many of a time right around work and gone to sleep. I don't dread it at all.

I've been thinking about retiring. I'm trying to rent the farm out to Mabel.

Virgil enjoyed himself, his music, and humor. He was truly a wonderful, amusing, and entertaining person.

Virgil's music can be found on *Virgil Anderson . . . On the Tennessee Line* (County LP 777), *Five Miles from Town: Music of the Cumberland Plateau* (County LP 787), and *Music of Tennessee: Recorded Live at the 1981 Brandywine Music Festival* (Heritage-Galax 042). In addition to his performance at the Brandywine Festival, Virgil also performed at the National Folk Festival, at Carnegie Hall (he looked the place over and said, "This is the best place I ever have seen to store fodder"), at the Berea College Celebration of Traditional Music, and he was a featured performer on the Cumberland Music Tour in 1988, produced by Bobby Fulcher and Robert Cogswell, the Tennessee state folklorist, that played in such cities as Montgomery and Huntsville, Alabama; Knoxville, Tennessee; Asheville, North Carolina; Washington, D.C.; and New York City.

Virgil Anderson died at the age of ninety-eight, and Mabel followed in 2006.

(With credit to Bobby Fulcher, Liner notes to *Virgil Anderson . . . On the Tennessee Line*, and *The Cumberland Music Tour* (Nashville: Tennessee Arts Commission Folk Arts Program, 1988).

Here is one of Virgil's stories:

This Methodist preacher got lost on Cumberland Mountain. Well, he took a path, come to a little log cabin. A woman come out. He said, "I'm lost. Can you tell me which way to go?" She said, "You go out here about a hill-and-a-half and come to a bear pen, and you turn left there. That'll take you over yonder somewheres." He seen right then that he was into it. He said, "You got any converts around here?" She said, "No, I don't think so, but John hunts varmints, and he skins them and nails their hides up on the back wall. You can go look." He said, "I see you're livin' in darkness." She said, "Yeah, but John's a-goin' to put me a window in over there." He said, "Where's your husband?" She said, "He's out huntin'." He said, "My land! Out huntin' on the Sabbath Day? Don't he know that there's goin' to be a Judgment Day?" She said, "Yes, but if you see him, don't tell him. He takes a gallon of liquor and tears up ever' big day there is. Don't tell him. He's mean, and he'll tear that Judgment Day all to pieces!"

ANDY ANDREWS

Born May 22, 1959, Birmingham, Alabama

Andy Andrews is a comedian, motivational speaker, college-circuit entertainer, television celebrity, writer, and he usually adds "fisherman" to this list. Although most of his performances are on college campuses, cruise ships, at conventions, and at places like Caesar's Tahoe, he appeared on TNN numerous times, has appeared in country music venues, and his video for children was produced by Opryland USA. He fits the role of country comedian, but he has other concerns, such as good parenting in any culture. Andrews is a writer who contributes to *Country America* magazine and has published books, including *Storms of Perfection* (Lightning Crown, vol. 1 [1992], vol. 2 [1994], vol. 3 [1996], and vol. 4 [1997]), with letters from famous people who succeeded despite rejection early in their lives. *Andy Andrews' Tales from Sawyerton Springs* (Lightning

Andy Andrews. Courtesy of Robert D. Smith, First Image, Inc.

Crown, 1995) is a collection of his stories published in *Country America* magazine. *The Traveler's Gift* (Thomas Nelson, 2002) shows Andy's interest in projects that appear to be failures but in the end are triumphs. After fifty-one rejections, this book was accepted by Thomas Nelson Publishers and went through three printings in six months and was an ABC's "Good Morning America" book-club selection in 2003. Andy has produced four recordings of humorous and motivational material, *Storms of Perfection, Burn the Boats, Give Me the Bat*, and *Andy Andrews Live at Caesar's Tahoe* (www.AndyAndrews .com or PO Box 17321, Nashville, TN 37217).

Andrews's comedy was first presented to an audience in a Pizza Hut, when friends dared him to perform. The manager liked it well enough to put his pizza bill on the house. His success as a comedian encouraged him to drop out of veterinary school at Auburn University and go on tour as a stand-up comic. His clean show caught the attention of Paul Harvey, who featured him in one of his radio shows. He was noticed enough to be invited to perform for Presidents Reagan and Ford and at theaters in Las Vegas, Lake Tahoe, Reno, and Atlantic City. He has toured with such stars as Kenny Rogers, Cher, Randy Travis, and Garth Brooks, and he joined Bob Hope on USO tours. Andrews was voted Comedian of the Year for two years and also Entertainer of the Year by the National Association of Campus Activities.

The following material is used by permission from *Andy Andrews Live at Caesar's Tahoe:*

I'm not even married yet, but I know one day I'm going to be a good father, and I know that I will because I've watched you guys for so long in malls with your own kids, I'm going to know what to say. The things my parents said are still ringing in my ears. So what I've done, I have compiled the fifty most famous parental sayings . . . and I'm going to try to do them in less than ninety seconds:

"You'd better change your tune pretty quick, or you're out of here. I mean it. Is that understood? Don't shake your head at me. I can't hear your head rattle. Don't mumble. You act as if the world owes you a living. You got a chip on your shoulder. You're not going anywhere looking like that. You're crazy if you think you are. If you think you are, just try me. I don't know what's wrong with you. I never saw a kid like you. Other kids don't pull stuff like that. I wasn't like that. What kind of an example do you think you are for your brothers and sisters? Sit up straight. Don't slouch. Would you like a spanking? If you'd like a spanking, just tell me now. We'll get this thing over with. You're cruisin' for a brusin'. I'm your father. As long as you live in my house, you'll do as I say do. You think the rules don't apply to you? I'm here to tell you that they do. Are you blind? Watch what you're doing. You walk around here like you're in a daze. Somethin' better change and change fast. You're drivin' your mother to an early grave. This is a family vacation. You're goin' to have fun whether you like it or not. Take some responsibility. Pull your own weight. You can't expect other people to pick up after you. And don't ask me for money. What do you think, I'm made out of money? Do you think I have a tree that grows money? You better wake up, and I don't mean maybe. You act like this when you're away from us? We've given you everything we possibly could. Food on the table. Roof over your head. Things we never had when we were your age. You treat us like we don't exist. That's no excuse. If he jumped off a cliff, would you jump off a cliff too? You're grounded. I'm not goin' to put up with this for another minute. You're crazy if you think I am. If you think I am, just try me. Don't look at me that way. Look at me when I talk to you. Don't make me say this again!"

A'NT IDY AND LITTLE CLIFFORD

*Margaret Lillie, born ca. 1900, Missouri (one source
    says Oklahoma); died May 26, 1942, Berea,
    Kentucky*
*Harry Mullins, born January 8, 1917, Rockcastle
    County, Kentucky; died August 17, 1978, Renfro
    Valley, Kentucky*

Just before John Lair left WLS in Chicago for WLW in Cincinnati, he wrote to Margaret Lillie to invite her to join one of his shows at WLW. Later he was to bring her to the "Renfro Valley Barn Dance." Lillie was described by Bill Sachs of *Billboard* as a

Uncle Junie, Little Clifford, and A'nt Idy. Courtesy of the John Lair Collection, Southern Appalachian Archives, Berea College.

"ninety-pound ball of fire." Lillie and her first husband, George Hall, had worked the Sun and Western tabloid tent circuits, mainly playing to oil workers in Oklahoma. She was half Cherokee and the niece of Pawnee Bill Lillie, who worked with Buffalo Bill Cody as a scout and later with his Wild West Show. Sachs described her as a "cross between a miniature Minnie Pearl and a rowdy, dynamic Beatrice Lillie." He also thought that she was "one of the most accomplished comediennes ever to trod the maples." After her husband died, Lillie operated a tavern in the Missouri Ozarks, but the team of the Weaver Brothers and Elviry recruited her to join them in their show that played vaudeville houses, and she became a hit. Lair caught one of their shows and was determined to get her in his own show.

On the "Renfro Valley Barn Dance," Lair teamed her with his cousin, Harry Mullins, a hefty man, over six feet tall, dressed up as a little boy in contrast to the diminutive A'nt Idy. Idy and Little Clifford began working the show in Cincinnati in 1937, played it for a year in Dayton's Memorial Auditorium, and then accompanied the show when it moved to the new barn at Renfro Valley in 1939. The duo was the most publicized of the many comedians who played the "Barn Dance." There were numerous pictures of them in comic poses, for example one of the hulking Little Clifford attempting to mount a tiny Shetland pony (from the wrong side) held by A'nt Idy, who is shaking her finger as she gives instructions. Norma Mullins, Harry's widow, remembers that they would come on stage and A'nt Idy would do a routine and tell jokes, while Little Clifford wailed and cried for his bottle. A'nt Idy would then produce a huge bottle of milk for him. Sometimes Clifford would pull a red wagon. In addition to the "Barn Dance," they traveled with personal-appearance tours.

Eventually, another comedian, Danny Duncan, was added as Uncle Juney (or Junie). He was an ex-vaudevillian who was known to Lair from his days in Cincinnati. Lair's daughter, Ann Lair Henderson, remembers that Little Clifford was allowed to choose his daddy from several prospects, and he chose Duncan.

The act was cut short by the death of A'nt Idy in 1942. At the time she was married to Jack Steven Chapman, and they had a daughter, Carolyn. Margaret Chapman was buried in Branson, Missouri. Harry Mullins left comedy but remained with the "Renfro Valley Barn Dance" for a number of years as ticket taker and booking agent for the road shows, and he later worked for the state highway department. He had been married to Velcie Boggs of Louisa, Kentucky, who died after giving birth to a son, Clyde Lair Mullins. In 1953 he married Norma Coffey, who had grown up at Renfro Valley and worked as a singer and guitarist with the Coon Creek Girls in 1946–47. They had a son, James. Norma Mullins has been the postmaster at Renfro Valley for more than twenty years.

No further information could be found on Danny Duncan.

ARKIE THE ARKANSAS WOODCHOPPER

Born Luther William Ossenbrink, March 2, 1906,
Knobnoster, Missouri; died June 23, 1981

Ossenbrink was a central figure at the WLS "National Barn Dance" from 1929 until the program was terminated in 1969. He was a singer, square-dance caller, and more a humorist than a comedian, although he played up a rustic image as the "Country Boy from the Ozarks," a bit of a fiction, since he was born far north of the Ozark Mountains. However, he knew country ways, and his humor incorporated farming, hunting, fishing, and other such activities.

Ossenbrink got into radio over KMBC in Kansas City, Missouri. In 1929 he was invited to join the "National Barn Dance." He had learned to play the fiddle and guitar for square dances when he was quite young, and at dances he learned the calls that went with them. He was a winning instrumentalist and singer, but he also did monologues and skits that played up his country humor.

Arkie toured with the WLS traveling shows, sometimes with a square-dance group.

His few recordings on Columbia and ARC included songs and dance calls. In 1940, the M. M. Cole Company issued a book of his songs and dance calls.

Luther Ossenbrink was married to the former Vera Firth.

UNCLE RUFE ARMSTRONG AND NORMA FRANCIS "PETUNIA" ARMSTRONG

Rufe Armstrong, born 1903, New Bern, North
Carolina; death date and place unknown
Norma Francis Armstrong, birth and death dates
and places unknown

Uncle Rufe Armstrong headed a band called the Coon Hunters for several years on WMMN in Fairmont, West Virginia. His wife Norma did comedy as "Petunia." Rufe had played vaudeville theaters with the Keith, Orpheum, and Interstate circuits, doing blackface comedy. His Uncle Rufe character probably was born when he organized the Coon Hunters and played on WMMN and other stations in the region. Norma, described in the WMMN *Family Album* of 1941 as born in Jacksonville (no state given), "had quit school in the eleventh grade to join the WSM 'Grand Ole Opry' road show." It further stated that "she started out as a toe dancer [ballet?] in her earlier years, but grew so tall that she turned to eccentric dancing." She is described also as being featured as an "eccentric character." Before coming with Uncle Rufe to WMMN, she had done comedy in "many road shows from various radio stations." It is unknown when she and Rufe met and wed.

Other members of the Coon Hunters were Bill Kirby, who was also the announcer; Earl Sampson, "the World's Biggest Little Fiddler"; and Mary Elizabeth Minner. The WMMN publication bragged that the station had received 375,000 letters in 1940 and that their entertainers did personal appearances before four hundred thousand people each year.

CLARENCE "TOM" ASHLEY

Born September 29, 1895, Bristol, Tennessee;
died June 2, 1967, Mountain City, Tennessee

Born Clarence Earl McCurry, Ashley was raised by his maternal grandfather, Enoch Ashley, and he later adopted his grandfather's surname. A versatile comedian, he was also an accomplished performer vocally and on the banjo and guitar. He started performing in medicine shows as a blackface comedian and musician in 1911, first with Doc White Cloud's show and later with Doc Hauer's show at the time it employed the young Roy Acuff. Although he performed with such bands as the Carolina Tar Heels (with Doc Walsh and Garley Foster), Byrd Moore and His Hotshots, and the Blue Ridge Entertainers, Ashley continued to perform intermittently in medicine and tent shows into the 1940s. Later he traveled as a comedian with Charlie Monroe and the Kentucky Partners and also the Stanley Brothers.

Ashley is best known today for his recordings, first in 1928 on Victor with the Carolina Tar Heels. He then recorded with Byrd Moore and His Hot Shots on Columbia. He recorded again in 1931 for Victor with a band called the Haywood County (N.C.) Ramblers and also with the Blue Ridge Mountain Entertainers (including Clarence Green, Walter Davis, and Gwen Foster). He recorded individually on 78 rpm records that were influential in the folk revival, and he and Gwen Foster recorded several sides for the ARC record group. Rediscovered and encouraged in the 1960s by the folklorist Ralph Rinzler, Ashley did several more recordings available from Smithsonian Folkways as *Original Folkways Recordings of Doc Watson and Clarence Ashley, 1960–1962* (SFW400299, 1994). Ashley joined with Doc Watson and the fiddler Fred Price in 1961 to play festivals, colleges, and other venues that arose from the folk revival.

RANDY ATCHER

Born Randall Ignatius Atcher, Tip Top, Kentucky,
   December 7, 1918; died October 9, 2002,
   Louisville, Kentucky

Randy Atcher was born into a musical family. His father played fiddle, his mother played piano, and all six boys played stringed instruments. Randy grew up in West Point, near Louisville. In 1933, his older brother Bob, a student at the University of Kentucky, began a radio program, singing mountain ballads over the university station, and that led to a job at WHAS. Randy became his partner. Later, the brothers sang together at WJJD and WBM in Chicago. In 1937, Randy became a member of Uncle Henry Warren's Kentucky Mountaineers. Then he joined Sunshine Sue and Her Rock Creek Rangers, and even though Randy was basically a singer and instrumentalist, he played rube comedy with Sunshine Sue when they were at WHAS in 1938–39, and then at WMOX in St. Louis. His rube character was Lemuel Q. Splutterfuss, who sported a long-haired wig, fancy little hat, and baggy britches. He remembered doing the cracked-voiced hillbilly before Pat Buttram did it.

Randy attended Western Kentucky Teachers' College (now Western Kentucky University) at Bowling Green. From 1942–46 he served with the Army Air Corps in the South Pacific and was discharged as a captain. He returned to WHAS with a group called the Swinging Cowboys in 1947. In 1950, when WHAS-TV went on the air, Randy was asked to head up a children's birthday program called "T-Bar-V Ranch." He

Randy Atcher. Courtesy of
Randy Atcher.

was also a star on the "Old Kentucky Barn Dance" on WHAS radio. In 1951 he added the "Hayloft Hoedown" to WHAS-TV. The program was on for nineteen and a half years, and "T-Bar-V Ranch" continued until 1971.

Randy wrote songs for these programs and in all has written over three hundred numbers, some of which he recorded on MGM Records, and some are published by Acuff-Rose.

After the demise of the "T-Bar-V Ranch" and the "Hayloft Hoedown," Randy went to Channel 32 in Louisville to head a hoedown show there for thirteen weeks. Afterward, the hoedown group played at different venues throughout the area. Randy made a variety of personal appearances throughout the years, including a Western-themed show at the Speed Museum in Louisville, with a trio. This group, High Wide and Handsome, including Randy, his son Mark, and Shorty Chesser, performed all over the region, including appearances at the WHAS Crusade for Children, a fund raiser created by the late Barry Bingham Sr., then owner of WHAS.

Randy's first wife, Daphne, died in 1977, and he and his second wife, Betty, lived in Louisville. They had six children and several grandchildren between them. For many years he was a narrator for the American Printing House for the Blind, reading materials commissioned by the Library of Congress for the visually handicapped. He also did regular appearances at the WHAS Crusade for Children. Randy Atcher died of cancer at a hospice in Louisville.

(With credit to Wade Hall and Greg Swem, *A Song in Native Pastures: Randy Atcher's Life in Country Music* [Louisville: Harmony House Publishers, 2002].)

A Lemuel Q. Splutterfuss story:

I had this cousin who moved to a house in Chicago where he said they had a room for everything. He said they had one room where you didn't do nothin' but cook, another where you didn't do nothin' but eat, another one they called the livin' room, and you just set around in there, and there was a room where you just slept.

But it was that other little room that got him. It was all white inside. It had a spring in there, and it had lids on it. He said it had toilet water in it, but that ever' time he'd lean over to put some of that toilet water on his head, the lid would fall down and knock him in the head. They got it fixed, though. They took them lids off, and they framed grandpaw's picture with one of them, and his mama's usin' the other'n for a biscuit board.

CHET ATKINS

Born Chester Burton Atkins, June 20, 1924, Luttrell,
Tennessee; died June 30, 2001, Nashville, Tennessee

Chet Atkins, who was known as "Mr. Guitar," recorded more than seventy-five albums featuring his consummately tasteful and precise guitar picking, with nearly eighty million copies sold. He was also the head of RCA's Nashville division and produced records for such country stars as Hank Williams, the Everly Brothers, Jim Reeves, Dolly Parton, Don Gibson, and Charley Pride. He is credited with helping to create the "Nashville Sound" to counteract the decline in country music brought on by the rock-and-roll revolution. Coming from eastern Tennessee, he also had a love of the rural humor of the countryside as well as the country music comedy that he first encountered at the "Mid-day Merry-Go-Round" on WNOX in Knoxville while he was working with Bill Carlisle, Archie Campbell, and others. Kenneth "Jethro" Burns, of the Homer and Jethro comedy-musical act, became his brother-in-law, and they shared a rich repertoire of country comedy, as well as some pretty sophisticated humor.

Chet's father James was a teacher of the shape-note system of hymn singing that was a part of the popular singing conventions that were held at courthouses and schools all over the South and utilized songbooks published by Stamps-Baxter, James D. Vaughn, and other companies. Chet remembered and told his father's favorite story about a man dying and going to Heaven. On being admitted, he sees a man tied to a stake and asks St. Peter about it. St. Peter says, "Oh, there's a shape-note singing this weekend in East Tennessee, and if we didn't do that, he'd go." The songwriter Billy Edd Wheeler, a longtime friend, remembered that Atkins used a lot of vaudeville material and some written by Lowell Blanchard at WNOX. If a car backfired during one of his concerts, Chet would yell, "Shoot him in the leg. That coat belongs to me!" Atkins loved to tell the story about him and Jethro Burns going to the ballet and afterward he asks Jethro what he thought of it. "I liked it, the lights, the scenery, the music, but all through the thing the dancers walked around on tippy-toes. Why don't they just get taller dancers?"

Atkins's modesty was legendary, and this too led to humor. He told a story (several versions) about hiring a fishing boat for some relaxation in between gigs. On board, he spies an old guitar, picks it up, and plays. When they debark, the boat owner observes, "You're pretty good, but you're no Chet Atkins." Polishing his glasses he tells the audience that he has just bought bifocals. Then he tells about observing a dog through them: "While I was admiring the big one, the little one peed on my shoe."

Chet Atkins eventually wound up in Nashville at the "Grand Ole Opry." However, he also played at WPTF in Raleigh, WLW in Cincinnati, WLS in Chicago, and KWTO in Springfield. At the "Opry," he first played fiddle for the Carter Sisters and

Maybelle, but it was his guitar picking as well as his administrative abilities and ear for talent that made him the youngest member of the Country Music Hall of Fame in 1973. His recordings are mostly on RCA except for two on Columbia (with Jerry Reed and Mark Knopfler) and *Galloping Guitar* on the Bear Family label.

Chet Atkins died in 2001 after a long battle with colon and brain cancer. Most of the television networks and major publications did stories about him. He was eulogized by Garrison Keillor on "A Prairie Home Companion," a show that Chet had played many times. Keillor and other friends remembered his gentle and modest humor during his difficult illness. He was married to Leona Johnson, and they had a daughter, Merle.

> *Chet: This duck walks into a bar, jumps up on the counter, and says, "You got any corn?"*
>
> *The bartender says, "No, we don't have any corn, and furthermore, we don't serve ducks, so get out!"*
>
> *The next day the duck comes back, jumps up on the counter and says, "You got any corn?"*
>
> *The bartender says, "I told you we don't have any corn, you flat-footed idiot, and ducks are not welcome here. If you come back in here, I'm goin' to nail your feet to the counter."*
>
> *The next day, the duck comes back in, says, "You got any nails?"*
>
> *The bartender says, "No, I don't have any nails. This ain't no hardware store."*
>
> *The duck says, "You got any corn?"*

AUNT BUNIE. *See Sarie and Sally*

AUSTIN LOUNGE LIZARDS

> *Tom Pittman, born May 19, 1948, Charleston,*
> *South Carolina*
> *Hank Card, born March 31, 1955, Caldwell, Kansas*
> *Conrad Deisler, born October 19, 1955, Oakland,*
> *California*
> *Boo Resnick, born June 11, 1950, Detroit, Michigan*
> *Eamon McLoughlin, born Bromley, Kent, U.K.,*
> *August 27, 1975*

Bill C. Malone, author of *Country Music, USA,* and other scholarly works on country music and comedy, says of the Austin Lounge Lizards' performances, "It's straight musicianship. They approach every song seriously, in that sense, and they play beautifully. They can create about any style." Then Malone reflects on their humor. "While they're playing the music seriously, they're poking fun at social conventions, religious hypocrisy, and political shenanigans. They're irreverent, I think, in a good sense, and

Austin Lounge Lizards. L-R: Eamon McLoughlin, Boo Resnick, Hank Card, Conrad Deisler, and Tom Pittman. Courtesy of Jill McGuckin.

they're politically liberal. They don't make fun of the music, but they use the music to poke holes in sham and hypocrisy. Mostly they just let the music speak for itself."

Since the Austin Lounge Lizards deal in social satire, they are different from most country comedians and humorists. Comedy deals in the belief that the human condition is flawed and that we can't do a lot about it, except to make fun of our foibles and failures and thus make ourselves feel better. Satire, in contrast, is predicated on the belief that human nature and society can be changed and that poking fun at our problems and social condition will give us some pleasure but also shame us into doing better. The Lizards are also different from most country humorists in that they are pretty sophisticated, intellectually and educationally. As they put it, members have included "Ivy Leaguers, recovering lawyers, former students of philosophy, history, music, and affiliations of similar dubious usefulness."

The Lizards came into being through the friendship of Hank Card and Conrad Deisler when they were undergraduates at Princeton University and later law students at the University of Texas. In Austin they got involved in the music scene, picking up Tom Pittman, Boo Resnick, and others to form the original Austin Lounge Lizards. They started out like the usual string band, but being overeducated and creative, they began composing satirical songs to comment on the subject of life in Texas, a rich field for comedy, and eventually the whole country, although they sometimes drag in references from beyond our borders. They can do almost all kinds of music. They are basically bluegrass but do pop, western swing, folk, honky tonk, country, a bit of jazz, and *conjunto*. They do wonderful harmonies. Their music and humor have been aptly described as "unplugged sardonic." As Bill Malone commented, they are serious about their music, but then so are they serious about their satire.

As of this writing, the group is composed of Tom Pittman, Hank Card, Conrad Deisler, Robert "Boo" Resnick, and Eamon McLoughlin, but it has included also Richard Bowden, Lex Browning, Michael Stevens, Tom Ellis, Tim Wilson, Kirk Williams, and others. Hank Card, with help of Kristen Nelson Card, Conrad Deisler, and Tom Pittman, writes a lot of the songs. He sings lead, plays lead and rhythm guitar, and is also an administrative-law judge. Conrad Deisler also writes songs and plays guitar and shies away from the practice of law. Tom Pittman, the philosophy major, is another writer of songs but also plays banjo, pedal steel, and sings harmony. Boo Resnick, a veteran of Austin rock and country bands, is the bass player, sings lead and harmony, and helps out on songwriting. The newest member, Eamon McLoughlin, a native of London, England, plays fiddle and mandolin and joins in on harmony singing.

The Lizards' satire is apt to go in any direction. They abhor political correctness, mindless trends and fashions, and the inanity and hypocrisy of politicians. They also make fun of popular music, songs about Texas, syrupy love songs, and other embarrassments of the music business. They even wrote "Stupid Texas Song," and here's one of the choruses:

> One more stupid song about Texas, for miles and miles it rambles on,
> Biggest egos, biggest hair, biggest liars anywhere, let's sing another
>   stupid Texas song.

Another unlikely song brings Rasputin, the mad and powerful Russian monk, into the modern world to deal with his health problems in an HMO (he's been poisoned, riddled with bullets, and thrown in the river), and he's directed to "please take a seat until your number comes up." Another song that strikes closer to this writer's North Carolinian heart is "Asheville/Crashville," which comments on the "growth" epidemic caused by people moving to the most beautiful and desirable spots and thus ruining them:

> Have you seen the Smokies lately?
> Demolition has improved them greatly.
> We've got plenty of room to spare,
> So we've been building everywhere!

The Austin Lounge Lizards released *Never an Adult Moment* in 2000 on Sugar Hill, and in 2002 *Strange Noises in the Night*. These and other recordings can be obtained from www.austinloungelizards.com.

WENDY BAGWELL

Born Wendell Lee Bagwell, May 16, 1925; died June 13, 1996, Hiram, Georgia

Wendy Bagwell headed the Sunliters, a popular southern gospel group, the first such group to perform at Carnegie Hall and to tour Europe. Bagwell was also a humorist, and his story about the Sunliters unwittingly accepting an invitation to perform in an eastern Kentucky snake-handling church, released in 1970 as *Here Come the Rattlesnakes*, propelled the Sunliters to the top of the gospel world.

Not much is available on Bagwell's early life. He graduated from West Fulton High School in Atlanta and served a hitch in the Marine Corps. He formed Wendy Bagwell and the Sunliters in 1953. The original members were Bagwell, Jerri Morrison, and Georgia Jones. Sandy Garvin replaced Jones for a few years and then was replaced in 1961 by the sixteen-year-old Jan Buckner. This final three played together for thirty-three years and made around forty albums.

Their first popular recording was not a gospel song but a sentimental one, "Pearl Buttons." *Here Come the Rattlesnakes*, with this comedy routine plus gospel numbers, was their most popular recording, selling to date more than two million copies. This recording got them interviews and invitations from all over the country. They eventually performed at Carnegie Hall and other important gathering places throughout the country, Europe, and South Africa. As a humorist, Bagwell did other routines, such as "10-4 on the Cotton Top," "Ole Ralph Ben-

Wendy Bagwell. Courtesy of the Georgia Music Hall of Fame Archives.

nett's Volkswagon," "Three German Police Dogs and One Yellow Cat," "Me, Old Ronnie, and the Monkey," "They All Wore Wigs," and "Wendy's Interview." The last one is about an interview he grants to a young reporter by phone; she shows up in a skimpy miniskirt with her tape recorder in what looks like an overnight bag. His motel room is in plain sight of bathers around the pool, and the humor comes from his anguish in trying to figure out how to make the bathers believe that this is just an interview. Wendy was a talented storyteller, and his tales were all funny.

For a time, Bagwell became the spokesperson for Stanback Headache Powders in their television advertising campaign.

A good number of Wendy Bagwell and the Sunliters musical recordings are still available in the form of used LPs and reprocessed CDs. Some of the popular ones are: *Timeless, Roll away the Stone, I Feel Like Singing, Tell It Again,* and *Wendy Bagwell Collection.* Bagwell also did a book entitled *Laugh and a Half.*

The Sunliters were presented the Southern Gospel Music Association's Pioneer Award and also an Album of the Year Award. In addition, they were installed in Southern Gospel Music Association's Hall of Fame. Wendy was named Comedian of the Year by *Record World,* and he was posthumously inducted into the Christian Music Awards Hall of Fame.

The Sunliters were a tight group, and they worked together for a long time. When Wendy Bagwell died of a brain aneurysm, his fellow performers, who often served as his "straight men" for over three decades, commented on their affection and admiration for him. Jerri Morris said, "He was such an energetic person, always positive and upbeat. . . . Wendy was my rose. He was precious. There will never be another like Wendy." Jan Buckner added, "He was loved because he was 'just Wendy' all of the time, whether he felt good or not. . . . He was tremendously funny—but I think people didn't realize how good a singer he was." His wife Melba reported that "he sometimes got criticized for making light of situations [but he'd say] 'Why, God's children are the only ones in the world who have a right to smile and laugh. . . . We've got something to be happy about.'"

Wendy and Melba were married fifty years; they had a son, Ronnie, two daughters, Wendy Cerkovnik and Rita McDuffie, and three grandchildren.

(With credit to Joseph R. Johnson, Georgia Music Hall of Fame, and "Wendy Bagwell: Thoughts from His Family And Friends," *Gospel Voice* 9.9 [September 1996]: 22–24.)

BILLY BAKER

Born March 12, 1949, Harlingen, Texas

Billy Baker abandoned a college scholarship eighteen hours shy of graduation after being bitten by the clown bug while he was working at Silver Dollar City in Branson, Missouri. He enrolled at the Ringling Brothers Barnum and Bailey Clown College, graduated as valedictorian, and then happily served as a circus clown with the Greatest Show on Earth for seven years. Afterward he went to Hollywood for eight years to write and do comedy and television commercials before moving to Tennessee to perform at Dollywood as the featured musical/comedy star attraction from 1984 to 1995. In 1992 he served as an ensemble member of "Hee Haw" the last year it was on the air. Baker opened his own show in Gatlinburg in 1996. This show, based in the old movie theater, was called "Hillbilly Hoedown," but eventually, after complaints from some patrons about the use of the word "hillbilly," he changed the name to "Ole Smoky Hoedown" and moved it into a new five-hundred-seat theater at nearby Pigeon Forge, complete with three hundred thousand dollars yearly rent. Coming up with some twenty-five thousand dollars a month keeps his creative and gastric juices flowing.

Baker plays many characters, but his main one is Elwood Smooch, whom he created at Silver Dollar City and played at Dollywood. He's a rube clown with oversized patched pants bouncing on suspenders, long clown shoes, red shirt, cap turned askew, missing teeth, and a rubbery face. He also plays Chlorine, a bag lady; Uncle Mildew, who at ninety-three is billed as the world's oldest stand-up comedian; and Elwood Presley, who impersonates the King of Rock and Roll with some great footwork. Baker has assembled a diverse and talented group of entertainers for his shows, and he frequently has special guest clowns and others whom he has worked with in the past. There is a lot of music, and Baker sheds his comic personas to appear on stage as himself doing such great hymns as "Peace in the Valley," "Wings of a Dove," "Amazing Grace," and "Precious Lord, Take My Hand."

Billy Baker as Elwood Smooch. Courtesy of Billy Baker.

In 2001, Baker was inducted into the International Clown Hall of Fame in Milwaukee. He believes he is the only member who is connected to country music shows. He has recently issued a DVD of his "Ole Smoky Hoedown" and also a CD of his original songs, *Billy Jim Baker: Contrary to Ordinary* (Ole Smoky Hoedown, 2135 Parkway, Pigeon Forge, TN 37863; www.olesmokyhoedown.com).

Billy married a fellow Ringling Brothers clown, Dolly, and they have a daughter, Katie, who has worked in the theater as a performer. Billy and Dolly are now divorced but remain friends.

Following is a stanza from Baker's song, "Contrary to Ordinary":

When I die, forget the tombstone on my grave.
Give me a guitar and all the songs we always played.
Don't send a preacher down or a fancy epitaph,
Simply say that I loved to live, and lord did I love to laugh.

BASHFUL BROTHER OSWALD. *See Beecher Ray Kirby*

JAMES TERRYL "T. BUBBA" BECHTOL

Born, May 1, 1945, Biloxi, Mississippi

T. Bubba Bechtol was fortunate in getting a job when he was a late teenager as a driver for Brother Dave Gardner, the popular southern comedian of the late 1950s and 1960s, when he visited Biloxi. Brother Dave became his greatest influence, Bechtol says, because "he gave me permission to be southern." Coming from the Mississippi Gulf Coast and from a poor family, Bechtol had a case of inferiority that afflicts a lot of southerners. He remembered Gardner's advice: "You can't go through life with two catcher's mitts on. Ever' now and then you've got to throw something back." Bechtol has been doing that for a number of years, and he has been paid pretty well to do it. His comic persona is that of T. Bubba, who, he is careful to explain, is not a redneck but rather a descendent of rednecks:

> The difference between a Bubba and a Redneck is that anybody can be a Bubba; Bubba is the number one nickname in America. Bubba might be a descendent of a redneck, but he's done gone to college, got him a little education, and he might be president of the local bank, but he still hunts and fishes on weekends and likes to cook outside, especially if he can make it dangerous. He might have a camouflaged canoe hid out back and a Cadillac Escalade. He's not a redneck at work but he might be on weekends.

T. Bubba Bechtol. Photo by Senor McGuire, courtesy of Top Billing.

Bechtol grew up in a family of three brothers and one sister and a single mother who worked in a garment factory. They didn't have electricity until he was in his teens, and they told stories for entertainment. His grandfather and four uncles were Baptist ministers, and he helped them with their tent revivals and learned a lot about delivering a message and about humor, too. Thus he was receptive to Brother Dave Gardner's style and advice. He grew up in Fountainbleu, Mississippi. He graduated from Perkinston Junior College, Wiggins, Mississippi, and then went on to the University of Southern Mississippi, where he said he met Jack Daniel's and cheerleaders. When it came time to declare a major, he was stumped. When asked what he wanted to be, he replied, "rich." His advisor then told him that if that was what he wanted he might as well drop out and go find something that he believed in and that people would pay money for. So he became a businessman importing and selling tanning beds—and got rich. He then became a professional speaker, entertaining after dinner mostly but also giving talks at meetings of organizations and corporations. Eventually he became a speech coach.

Bechtol got involved with the Jaycees and became their national president in 1979. He was also a city councilman in Pensacola Beach, Florida. When Ronald Reagan ran for president, he invited Bechtol to help with his campaign as a fund-raiser, and when Reagan was elected, he brought Bechtol to the White House as an aide. Reagan encouraged him to run for Congress in his district. He won in the primary but lost the election in 1982, so he went back to professional speaking for the next twenty years, and he sees this experience as being very important to him as a comedian/humorist. He is the past president of the Alabama Speakers Association and the Freedom Foundation of Valley Forge.

Bechtol's comedic career blossomed when the popular columnist and speaker Lewis Grizzard, who was another role model, became too ill to perform, and he was hired to fill Grizzard's commitments. His public speaking career then came in handy. He points out that a stand-up comedian usually has a thirty-minute routine, and if it doesn't fit a particular audience, he dies on stage. Bechtol says he has ten hours of material he can rifle through to find what will fit a particular audience if what he had planned doesn't work. He describes his humor as observational rather than narrative. In comedy, with today's sophisticated audiences, he says you have to be funny in the first fifteen seconds to keep their attention. He thinks the long stories, such as Jerry Clower did, will just not work with a lot of the younger audiences or on TV.

He still feels the influence of his Baptist grandfather and uncles and prides himself in doing a clean show, at least in comparison to much of today's humor. However, he targets religious groups along with others. Example: "Baptists don't believe in pre-marital sex because it might lead to dancing. We don't even believe in synchronized swimming." He remembers something his grandfather told him that has been helpful to his career: "Terryl, people will forget what you say and what you do, but people will never forget how you make them feel." Bubba's audiences go away feeling good, and that has made him a popular entertainer. His Bubbas of America Club has over three hundred thousand members.

His first appearance on the "Grand Ole Opry" came in 1998, and he has since appeared nearly two hundred times and is a regular guest. He has made many appearances with country music stars, including Brooks and Dunn, Phil Vasser, Vince Gill, Billy Currington, George Jones, and Merle Haggard. He has made television appearances on the former Nashville Network, "The Today Show," and "A Current Affair." He has performed at the White House twice, at big-time football bowl games, and he has been written about in *Forbes*, *Country Weekly*, *Time*, and *Newsweek*. He has the following recordings available: *Bill Ain't No Bubba* (Southern Tracks), *Bubba Unclogged* (MCA), *Prime Time Bubba* (video), and a book, *Buddha Was a Bubba*. For more information or to join Bubbas of America, write to 339 Panferio Drive, Pensacola Beach, FL 32561, call 1-850-916-3537, or email TBubba@tbubba.com.

Bubba Bechtol married Tarsha Ramich in 2001, and they live in Pensacola Beach.

T. Bubba: One day God said, "Let's take half the hair off Bubba's head and blow it out his nose and ears!"

I just got married recently. Her name is Bubbalicious. My first wife's name was Plaintiff! I'm going bald, but Bubbalicious thinks it's sexy. I say, "I don't know about that. If you had a dog and all its hair fell out, would you pet it? I don't think so."

MARGARET BELL. *See Bonnie Lou and Buster*

LOWELL BLANCHARD

Born November 15, 1910, Palmer, Illinois;
died February 19, 1969, Knoxville, Tennessee

Richard Lowell Blanchard was one of the premier shapers of early country music entertainment while he was writer, producer, and master of ceremonies at Knoxville's WNOX "Mid-day Merry-Go-Round" and "Tennessee Barn Dance" from 1936 to 1964. He coached and wrote material for such comedians as Archie Campbell, Red Rector and Fred Smith, Kentucky Slim (Charles Elza), Homer and Jethro, and Bill Carlisle. He also was the composer of several country songs, such as "I Heard My Mother Weeping."

Blanchard graduated from the Morrisville, Illinois, High School and earned a B.S. degree in dramatics and broadcasting from the University of Illinois in 1933. He found work as a salesman and announcer at a radio station in Des Moines and later at WXYZ in Detroit. When the Scripps Company, owner of the *Knoxville News-Sentinel*, bought WNOX in 1935, the new manager, Richard Westergaard, who had known Blanchard in Des Moines, invited the young announcer to join the Knoxville station. Blanchard, who was good at regional dialects, was instructed to present himself as a hillbilly and "Bring us hillbilly performers. Entertain with them as one of them." WNOX already had two shows characterized as "hillbilly," Roy Acuff and His Crazy Tennesseans and Archie Campbell, who was then mainly singing with a backup band and doing a little comedy.

Blanchard became the emcee and producer of the Crazy Tennesseans' noontime show. He had a lot of ideas about successful entertaining. He thought that such a radio show should be longer and should be seen as well as heard. He expanded it to an hour and a quarter and moved it to various locations to accommodate the expanding live audiences. Blanchard ran advertisements in the *News-Sentinel* promising "new costumes, new acts, a better show . . . to give the visible as well as the radio audience a more professional show." Archie Campbell was added to the noon show doing his "Grandpappy" act. Blanchard was a great believer in the value of comedy as a part of entertainment. He and Campbell developed dialogue pieces that they performed together. Blanchard proved to be a "perfect straight man," as Archie put it, "with that great gift of being able to lead a comic into the right situations." He had brought with him and continued to collect joke books to help with the comedy. Grandpappy became very popular, and soon they began to receive a large volume of mail as well as gifts from all over their listening area.

Lowell Blanchard. Courtesy of the *Knoxville News-Sentinel.*

Roy Acuff and his band soon left for WROL and then the "Grand Ole Opry," but Blanchard recruited other performers to replace them, and he coached them for a live audience, which was to serve them well in later personal appearances. Among them were Pee Wee King, whose band was to become the Golden West Cowboys, including the comedy team of Monk and Sam (Charles Hansen and Sam Johnson) and the Stringdusters (Kenneth Burns and Henry Haynes), whom Blanchard coached into becoming the comedy team of Homer and Jethro. Burns remembered that Blanchard "knew all the stuff I wanted to know. . . . Really, I give him credit for everything I've ever done." Even though Blanchard emphasized hillbilly music and had even developed a "mountain accent," he understood the need for variety in entertainment, and he hired other groups such as the Dixieland Swingsters, well-trained musicians who did many recordings and traveled as a dance band. Blanchard also brought Charlie Monroe and his band, Carl Story and His Rambling Mountaineers, Eddie Hill and His Mountain Boys, Johnny Wright and Jack Anglin, Bill Carlisle, and later Chet Atkins and the Carter Sisters and Mother Maybelle to WNOX. He also established a booking agency and arranged personal appearances for his talent.

Bill Carlisle, with Blanchard's help, created a character called Hotshot Elmer, a dynamo of energy that earned him the title of Jumping Bill. He could jump flat-footed onto a five-foot-high stage, jump over a straight chair, and leap high in the air while playing and singing. He also wrestled onstage with a midget and did other antics. He was with the show for thirteen years.

As William Smyth has noted in his dissertation about the humor in Knoxville's radio entertainment, in Blanchard's shows, "comedy and/or levity were kings." Smythe goes on to say, "The shows were laced with jokes and gags, many, if not most, masterminded by Lowell Blanchard. The country-comedy format of the shows helped to develop some of the most popular rural comedians of our time: eventually to bring respect and recognition to country humor at a national level." Indeed, many of those who performed under Blanchard's direction at WNOX went on to other venues and higher fame: Archie Campbell, Bill Carlisle, the Carter Sisters and Mother Maybelle, Chet Atkins, Homer and Jethro, and many others. Some have speculated that with Blanchard's skills as talent scout, producer of shows, and talented emcee, if WNOX had possessed fifty thousand watts of power (rather than ten thousand), Knoxville could well have become the country music capital rather than Nashville.

Lowell Blanchard married Sally Irene Marshall. Their children are Lowell Jr., Arthur, Rebecca, and Sally. Blanchard died of heart failure in 1968 and rests in Greenwood Cemetery in Knoxville.

(With credit to William Jensen Smyth, "Traditional Humor of Knoxville Country Radio Entertainment Shows" [Ph.D. dissertation, University of California at Los Angeles, 1987].)

RED BLANCHARD

Born Donald Francis Blanchard, July 24, 1919,
Pittsville, Wisconsin; died February 24, 1980,
Largo, Florida

Red Blanchard performed on the "National Barn Dance" from 1931 until it closed down in 1969, except for military service. His parents, William and May Blanchard, were apparently not musical, but young Red became fascinated with the "Blue Yodeler" Jimmie Rodgers and bought a guitar as an early teenager. He was also intrigued by cowboy performers, such as Will Rogers on vaudeville stages and other traveling shows, and he learned rope tricks. He could also sing and yodel. In 1930, when he was just sixteen, he followed two older brothers who had moved to Milwaukee, and there he got on radio at WISN. He called himself the "Texas Yodeler." He later joined Rube Tronson's Texas Cowboys, and they moved to the "National Barn Dance" in 1931.

The Texas Cowboys were an upbeat band that employed guitar, fiddle, accordion, banjo, clarinet, and drums. Red sang and played guitar, fiddle, banjo, and also wind instruments. There is little information about his comedy in this period before World War II. At WLS, Red met Lucille Overstake, one of the Three Little Maids, who later took the name of Jennie Lou Carson as an individual performer. They were married in 1934 but soon divorced, admitting complete incompatibility.

When World War II involved the United States, Red enlisted in the army on March 4, 1942. He served four years, half of this in the South Pacific as a member of a combat entertainment team. It is reported that he entertained a million soldiers and was awarded six battle stars. Comedy became an important part of his act with these army tours. Red returned to WLS and the "National Barn Dance" in 1946 with the Sage Raiders, a band that included Dolph Hewitt, Don White (Whytsell), and Ray Klein. It was during his four years with the Sage Riders and afterward that Red developed into the comedian that Jethro Burns was to call "the funniest comedian I ever saw."

Also in 1946, Red met and married Marcella Ebert, nicknamed "Sally," one of the square dancers at the "Barn Dance." Like other comedians of his time, he made Sally the butt of many of his on-air jokes, but she appeared to accept this cheerfully as part of show business. They reared three children: Donald Jr., Donna Colleen, and Laura Lee.

Red left the Sage Riders after four years to become a solo comedian and musician, but he served in other roles at WLS as announcer, emcee, and comedian who could lighten up a show with quips and jokes. He hosted the "Red Blanchard Show" and the Saturday "Merry-Go-Round" and was the emcee and performer on the "Smile-a-While" program with guests such as Dolph Hewitt, Arkie the Arkansas Woodchopper, Karl Davis, and Bob Atcher. He also appeared on the Armed Forces Radio Services program. He published joke books and did personal appearances and columns for "The Prairie Farmer" and "Wallace's Farmer." When the "National Barn Dance" was canceled by WLS in 1959, it was moved under the leadership of Dolph Hewitt to WGN, where it became "The WGN Barn Dance." Red went with it, and he was also featured on the syndicated television version that began in 1963. He stayed with the show until it closed in 1969. During his first year at WGN, Red commuted from Mason City, Iowa, where he was part-owner of a radio station, flying his own plane back and forth.

Red also wrote songs and recorded on Columbia, Dot, Kahill, Kapp, and Evergreen. He also recorded for M. M. Cole with the Trail Dusters (actually the Sage Riders). His most popular recorded numbers were "Open the Door, Richard," on Dot, and "Those Oklahoma Hills," a duet with Dolph Hewitt on Kahill.

After the demise of the "Barn Dance," Blanchard continued a strenuous performing schedule, with as many as 250 engagements a year, including after-dinner speeches, country music shows, and county fairs. During and after the WGN days, he and his old associate Dolph Hewitt with Harry Campbell bought and operated several radio stations in St. Charles, Dixon, and Ottowa, Illinois, and Mason City and Cedar Falls, Iowa.

Blanchard received many honors during his career. WLS staged "Red Blanchard Day," and his hometown of Pittsville elected him Honorary Mayor, Chief of the Fire

Department, and Chief of Police. This event was broadcast over WLS's "Dinner Bell" program, hosted by Harold Safford. The Blanchards retired to Florida, and Red died there in 1980.

Here is one of Red's routines, remembered by David Wylie:

> George Washington was not born in Virginia. He was born in Texas, and he chopped down a cactus, and his father said "George, did you chop down that cactus?" He said, "Yes, Dad, I cannot tell a lie." His father said, "If you cannot tell a lie, we'd better get out of Texas." They moved to Mount Vernon. When George and Martha got married, they went to Mount Vernon in a covered wagon. Martha didn't look so good. That's why he covered the wagon. After the Revolutionary War was over, George settled down at Mount Vernon, and a bunch of people came and said, "George, we're going to get together and have a government. We're going to have two parties—Republicans and Democrats—and we're going to let the people vote to decide which party they want to mess things up."
>
> Back at the beginning of the Revolutionary War, Paul Revere was sitting at home one night, and somebody knocked on the door and said "Paul, the British are coming!" He said, "Don't bother me now, I'm listening to the "Barn Dance." Paul Revere said to his neighbor, Lady Godiva, "You ride off in one direction and warn the people that the British are coming, and I'll ride off in the other direction and tell them." When Lady Godiva rode by, a lot of people came out because you don't see that many white horses. Paul Revere rode to one house and knocked on the door, and a lady answered. He said, "Tell your husband that the British are coming." She said, "I don't have a husband." Paul said, "To heck with the British!"

With credit to David Wylie, Debbie Gray, and Harry Rice, who provided information.

ROY BLOUNT JR.

Born October 4, 1941, Indianapolis, Indiana

Roy Blount has had to overcome the fact that he was born north of the Ohio River, but he has gone on to become the foremost living example of and authority on southern humor. The Blounts moved to Decatur, Georgia, when Roy was eighteen months old, and he grew up there. Since his father was from the Florida Panhandle and his mother from Mississippi, he has the right accent for his trade as a southern humorist, refined, though, if you ignore the dirty words, because Roy is educated. Blount was always interested in sports, and he won a Grantland Rice sportswriting fellowship to Vanderbilt and then got a Woodrow Wilson Fellowship to Harvard for a master's degree in English. He has published numerous books, including the hefty *Roy Blount's Book of Southern Humor*, an anthology with several references to humorists connected to country music. In a funny introduction, he approaches obliquely, or circularly, the subject of the nature of southern humor, leaving it largely at-large. He makes one good point, however; when asked by a northerner if southerners laugh at different things than northerners, he says, "Yes, northerners."

After serving in the army and two years as a reporter, columnist, and editorial writer for the *Atlanta Journal*, Blount landed a job with *Sports Illustrated* from 1968 to 1975. He interviewed and wrote about the greats in the business world, as well as about other things, but with a fine comic flair. His descriptions of his encounters, such as observing a Wilt Chamberlain telephone conversation, were hilarious and became fodder for his developing career as a humorist. In 1968 he became a freelance writer and published articles in the *Atlantic Monthly* before becoming one of its contributing editors. He also wrote for the *New Yorker, Esquire, Harper's Bazaar, Spy, Rolling Stone, Playboy, Vanity Fair, National Geographic,* and other high-rye publications, doing regular columns for eleven and writing articles, essays, and verse for more than a hundred. He has been on Garrison Keillor's "A Prairie Home Companion" a number of times, memorably for some of the annual joke shows, and appears as a regular panelist on National Public Radio's "Wait, Wait . . . Don't Tell Me." He has also been on the major TV evening and morning talk shows and has had his own one-man show off Broadway at the American Place Theater. He has written a movie, *Larger Than Life,* starring Bill Murray and an elephant (Blount hinted that neither star paid much attention to his script).

Blount is well known for his wacky but funny poems that have appeared in classy magazines and several anthologies. He writes about normal things in an abnormal way, like chickens, dogs, cats, and food: ham, oysters, grits, beans, grease, okra, barbecue sauce, catfish, and onions. One poem is about broccoli: "The neighborhood stores are all out of broccoli, / Loccoli" (that's it).

Blount's journalism has taken him all over the South and nation to interview interesting people, including country musicians and humorists. He has written a number of songs, naturally in a humorous vein, and he is a member of a rock band, the Rock Bottom Remainders, that also includes Stephen King, Dave Barry, and Amy Tan, and he has vocalized with them, although he admits to being musically challenged. In fact, back when there were all these government and foundation self-help programs, he claims to have written a proposal for ramps to get musically handicapped people like himself up on pitch. Among the over 150 selections for his *Roy Blount's Book of Southern Humor* are funny routines, stories, and songs by musicians and humorists such as Jerry Clower, B. B. King, Louis Armstrong, Garrison Keillor, Memphis Minnie, Jerry Lee Lewis, Blind Blake, Brother Dave Gardner, Billy Joe Shaver, Jelly Roll Morton, Kinky Friedman, Billy Edd Wheeler, Bessie Smith, Roger Miller, Hank Williams, Willie Nelson, and John Prine. So Roy Blount has gleaned in the vineyard of country and related music and humor.

He has written a bunch of books: *About Three Bricks Shy of a Load* (1974), *Crackers* (about President Carter and his kinfolk down in Georgia; 1980), *One Fell Soup* (1982), *What Men Don't Tell Women* (1984), *Not Exactly What I Had in Mind* (1985), *It Grows on You* (1986), *Soupsongs/Webster's Ark* (1987), *Now, Where Were We?* (1988), *About Three*

Bricks Shy . . . and the Load Filled Up (1989), *First Hubby* (a novel; 1990), *Camels Are Easy, Comedy's Hard* (1991), *If Only You Knew How Much I Smell You* (with Valerie Shaff; 1998), *Be Sweet* (a memoir; 1998), *I Am a Puppy, Hear Me Yap* (with Valerie Shaff; 2000), *Am I Pig Enough for You Yet?* (with Valerie Shaff; 2001), and a biography, *Robert E. Lee* (2003). Blount has also released audiotapes: *Not Exactly What I Had in Mind* (1986), *Now, Where Were We?* (1989), and *A Mystery, a Murder, and a Marriage* (with Garrison Keillor; 2001).

The following excerpt is from Blount's *One Fell Soup: Or, I'm Just a Bug on the Windshield of Life* (Penguin Books, 1985), with permission:

> *Which First, Chicken or Egg?*
>
> *I say, the chicken. If an egg were first, the chances are that Adam, Eve, one of the beasts of the field, even one of the beasts of the air, whatever was around then, would have broken and/ or eaten (I mean eaten and/or broken) it. We have no way of knowing how many projected species were nipped off because they made the mistake of starting out as eggs. I assume that the chicken was first, and that it evaded destruction long enough to lay several dozen eggs. This is just elementary Darwinism. Also, if the egg came first, then what fertilized it? In point of fact, the egg must have come third.*

BLUE SKY BOYS

William A. Bolick, born October 28, 1917,
Hickory, North Carolina
Earl A. Bolick, born, November 16, 1919,
Hickory, North Carolina; died Suwanee, Georgia,
April 19, 1998

The Blue Sky Boys were known mostly for their beautiful duet harmony, now called the "brother duet" style of singing. However, they also did comedy as a part of their entertainment. Bill got into music with a friend, Lute Isenhour, a banjo player. In 1935, Lute and Bill, with the fiddler Homer Sherrill and his brother Arthur Sherrill, got a job at WWNC in Asheville, a thousand-watt station, as the Crazy Hickory Nuts (sponsored by Crazy Water Crystals). After a while, they got a dozen or so invitations to do personal appearances. Bill spoke of those days:

> We put a show together, mostly by Lute, and I was playing kind of a rube comedian. There was always comedy in the show. Most of the shows were at least half comedy. I think we all realized that there would have to be comedy in our shows, and starting there, we began working on comedy. But none of us had any experience on the stage to amount to anything, except getting up there and playing and singing. That was the first time I was connected with comedy in any way. I think Lute put most of it together, maybe from old jokes from medicine shows he'd seen.

They were at WWNC for only a short time as the Crazy Hickory Nuts. Later in 1935, Bill, his brother Earl, and Homer Sherrill played again at WWNC as the Good Coffee Boys, sponsored by JFG Coffee. In 1936, Crazy Water Crystals invited them to WGST in Atlanta, another thousand-watt station operated by Georgia Tech, where they played as the Blue Ridge Hillbillies. There on personal appearances, Earl and Bill did blackface comedy. They did several stints at WGST, returning home to North Carolina between times. Bill spoke of their early comedy in Atlanta: "Earl and I played blackface. Homer was the straight man. He pulled the jokes with us. We got our material mostly from jokes we'd heard at medicine shows that came through in the early thirties about a mile from home." Bill spoke of the rube comedy that was coming into Atlanta, which was less messy than blackface. To differentiate themselves from rube comedy, Earl created the old-man persona of Uncle Josh, who did ad-lib comedy with the announcer during the radio shows or performed at personal appearances. During these shows, most of the comedy fell to Earl as Uncle Josh. When Homer Sherrill left them, Curley Parker and his brother Ruel, who played fiddle, performed with them and sometimes sang an additional harmony part. In 1936, the Blue Sky Boys began their recording career by cutting ten numbers for RCA's Bluebird. They eventually did 124 numbers for Bluebird.

The Bolicks interrupted their careers for five years to serve in World War II, Bill in an automatic weapons battalion and Earl in the paratroopers. They returned to WGST in 1946 for nearly two years and later did shorter stints at stations in Raleigh, North Carolina; Greenville, South Carolina; Bristol, Tennessee; Rome, Georgia; and Shreveport, Louisiana. Because Earl wanted to get out of show business, the brothers ceased performing in 1951, although they got together for a few concert appearances and recorded again for Starday and Capitol. Several reissues have been produced by RCA

Earl Bolick as Uncle Josh.
Courtesy of Bill Bolick.

Camden, County, Provencia, Rounder, Blue Tone, and Copper Creek. Some of the Uncle Josh comedy is on the Rounder recording of a University of Illinois concert and on *Blue Sky Boys on Radio*, vol. 1.

After ending their singing career, Bill attended Lenoir-Rhyne College and went to work for the U.S. Postal Service. He is now retired and living in Hickory. Earl moved to Atlanta and worked for Lockheed Aircraft. He died in April 1998.

Among their available recordings are *The Blue Sky Boys* (County, 1976), *The Blue Sky Boys in Concert* (Rounder, 1989), and *Blue Sky Boys on Radio*, vol. 1 (Copper Creek, 1993).

From a radio broadcast, Atlanta, circa 1936:

> *Bill: Uncle Josh, are you feeling pretty good as usual?*
> *Uncle Josh: You know it. I've been writin' some more poetry.*
> *Bill: When are you going to read some of it for the folks?*
> *Uncle Josh: Well, I don't know. I've got one I wrote here about Uncle Josh.*
> *Bill: One about Uncle Josh. Is that all you have?*
> *Uncle Josh: Well, what else do you want me to write about?*
> *The meanest man upon this land,*
> *Can whup a bear with either hand,*
> *Uncle Josh.*
> *Bill: That's enough, Uncle Josh. That's enough.*

BILL AND EARL BOLICK. *See Blue Sky Boys*

JOHNNY BOND

Born June 1, 1915, Enville, Oklahoma;
died, June 12, 1978, California

Cyrus Whitfield "Johnny" Bond was a singer-songwriter, guitarist, movie actor, and comedian; he wrote and performed humorous monologues, skits, and novelty songs.

As a boy, Bond was influenced by the recordings of Jimmie Rodgers and Vernon Dahlhart and began performing as a singer and guitarist while still in high school. After graduation, he moved to Oklahoma City, where he played with various groups while attending the University of Oklahoma. Subsequently he, Jimmy Wakely, and Scotty Harrell formed a trio that played over WKY and WVOO and toured Oklahoma. After appearing in a Roy Rogers film, *Saga of Death Valley*, in 1939, the trio (with Dick Reinhart replacing Harrell) moved to Hollywood where they were hired by Gene Autry for his CBS "Melody Ranch" radio show. Bond remained with "Melody Ranch" until the show closed in 1956, but he also did bit parts (usually musical) in thirty-eight motion pictures starring Gene Autry, Tex Ritter, Charles Starrett, Johnny Mack Brown, and his old trio partner, Jimmy Wakely. In addition, he was a regular on "Hollywood Barn Dance" and a writer and performer on the TV show "Town Hall Party" from 1953–61. Bond and Tex Ritter were partners in the music publishing business, and he wrote Ritter's biography.

Bond wrote over five hundred songs, including "I Wonder Where You Are Tonight," "Cimarron," "Tomorrow Never Comes," "Divorce Me COD," and "Those Gone and Left Me Blues." He recorded for OKeh, Columbia, Republic, Starday, Harmony, Capitol, Shasta, and CMH.

Cowgirlboy Germany released material after his death. Bond had five Top Ten hits in addition to his recorded humorous material, and his imaginative and humorous routines were part of his shows.

The following recordings are currently available: *Johnny Bond: Best of Comedy* (Richmond NS-2195, 1985); *Live It Up and Laugh It Up* (Starday, 1962).

Excerpt from *Johnny Bond: Best of Comedy*, with permission:

> *Johnny Bond as Hotel Clerk: Oh me, it's that darned gorilla again. Looks like he's got a woman with him.*
> *Gorilla: How do you do. I'm Mr. Nazrat. We'd like the bridal suite.*
> *Bond: The bridal suite?*
> *Gorilla: Certainly. This is my bride, Mrs. Nazrat. She's a baboon.*
> *Bond: You're a baboon?*
> *Baboon: Well, I ain't no monkey's uncle.*
> *Bond: Oh well, you can register here, Mr. . . .*
> *Gorilla: Nazrat. The name's Nazrat?*
> *Bond: Nazrat?*
> *Gorilla: Yeah, that's Tarzan spelled backwards.*
> *Bond: Oh, yeah, now I get it. Here's the key and there's the stairway, right over there.*
> *Gorilla: Oh, we don't need no stairway. We'll just climb up the side of the building, won't we dear?*
> *Baboon: Anything you say, darling.*
> *Bond: Goodnight, Mr. Nazrat, Tarzan, that is.*
> *Well, everything went well the rest of the night, but the next morning, Mr. Nazrat and his bride . . . they come down early.*
> *Gorilla: Clerk, my wife and I are checking out early. I'd like my bill, please.*
> *Bond: All right, hmm . . . bridal suite, that'll be ten dollars for the room and ten dollars for the meals. You owe me twenty dollars.*
> *Gorilla: Meals? We didn't eat any meals here.*
> *Bond: That was your hard luck, Mister. This hotel's on the American plan. They was here for you.*
> *Gorilla: Oh, is that so? Okay, here's ten dollars. I'm charging you ten dollars for making love to my wife.*
> *Bond: What are you talking about? I never made love to your wife!*
> *Gorilla: That's your hard luck, Mister. She was there for you!*

BONNIE LOU AND BUSTER

Margaret Bell, born June 4, 1927, Etowah,
   North Carolina
Hubert R. Moore, born October 28, 1919,
   Bybee, Tennessee; died January 13, 1996,
   Pigeon Forge, Tennessee

In addition to their Appalachian-influenced variety of traditional, bluegrass, and country music, this husband-and-wife team played hillbilly comedy, with Buster doing
"Humphammer," a character who has been described as "brash but bumbling."

Buster first got into show business with Eddie Hill at Knoxville's WNOX prior
to World War II, and he also worked for a short time with Carl Story at WWNC in
Asheville before being drafted. It was in Asheville that he met Margaret Bell, also
an aspiring musician, and they were married after he returned from service. Buster
rejoined Story's Rambling Mountaineers but soon left for Knoxville's WROL to lead
the Dixie Partners, including Ray Adkins and Wiley Morris. Substituting for Wiley
Morris when he was unable to perform, Margaret was so well received by the radio
audience that she became a regular on the show and was renamed Bonnie Lou. Bonnie Lou and Buster played also over stations in Greenville, South Carolina; Raleigh,
North Carolina; and Bristol, Tennessee. Bonnie Lou's brother Lloyd, Art Wooten, and

Bonnie Lou and Buster with Lloyd Bell (R). Courtesy of Bonnie Lou Moore.

Carl Butler joined them while they were in Raleigh. Lloyd, along with Homer Harris, went with them to Johnson City, Tennessee, to do television shows over WJHL-TV. They remained in Johnson City for nearly a decade, working part of this time for Jim Walter, the housing manufacturer, eventually appearing in "The Jim Walter Jubilee," a syndicated show. During this period, they recorded four sides for Mercury and did a gospel album for Waterfall Records.

For twenty-one years, beginning in 1972, Bonnie Lou and Buster presented the "Smoky Mountain Hayride" at the Pigeon Forge Coliseum during the summer tourist season. With a talented band, they played a variety of Appalachian, country, bluegrass, and gospel music. Buster continued to do his Humphammer comic character. They also recorded several country and gospel albums, sometimes including Bonnie Lou's brother Lloyd Bell, mainly for sale at their shows. Buster died in Pigeon Forge of a heart attack on January 13, 1996. Bonnie now lives in Morristown, Tennessee.

This skit was performed by Buster and Lloyd Bell:

> *Humphammer: Don't make a big to-do over me, just treat me like you would any other great banjo picker. . . . I looked up my family tree, and they're still in it.*
>
> *Lloyd: Humphammer, did you come from a large family?*
>
> *H.: Yep, big family, and they were so poor they couldn't buy me any clothes. They had to let out the hem of my diaper.*
>
> *L.: What have you been doing lately, Humphammer?*
>
> *H.: Well, today I went horseback riding.*
>
> *L.: Horseback riding?*
>
> *H.: Yep, the horse got back two hours before I did. I stopped at a gas station, and there was a man putting gas in his car, and he let it run over. His little dog jumped down out of the car and started lapping up that gas. All of a sudden, he started running around that car, around and around, then he just dropped over.*
>
> *L.: Dead?*
>
> *H.: No, he was out of gas!*

CLAUDE BOONE

Born February 18, 1916, Yancey County,
North Carolina

Claude Boone has been a comedian as well as a guitar and bass player in various groups, including those headed by Cliff Carlisle, Eddie Hill, and Carl Story. His first radio job as a teenager was with Cliff Carlisle's band on WWNC in Asheville. Boone also worked with Leon Scott as Scott and Boone, the Elk Mountain Boys, and they cut ten sides for the Decca label. Boone played and sang with Cliff on his Bluebird and Decca recordings. He stayed with Carlisle until 1938, when Carlisle moved to Charleston, West

Claude Boone. Courtesy of the Museum of Appalachia Archives.

Virginia. Boone then joined Carl Story's Rambling Mountaineers, and he credits himself for getting Story to move from WWNC to WNOX in Knoxville. Later he worked with Eddie Hill, who was also at the "Merry-Go-Round," where he did some comedy with Buster Moore. In addition to playing bass and guitar and singing bass in the quartet of Story's Rambling Mountaineers, Boone did comedy as a character named Homeless Homer. He was part of Story's group when they played at WCYB in Bristol and WAYS in Charlotte. He was also with Story in 1957 when they first recorded with bluegrass instrumentation, adding banjo and dobro to the band. Boone's bass singing also helped define the sound that earned Story the title "Father of Bluegrass Gospel." He is on recordings that Story made for Mercury, Columbia, and Starday.

While still working with Carl Story, Boone became part of "Cas Walker's Show" on WBIR-TV in Knoxville and was with the show for two decades.

Retired in Strawberry Plains, Tennessee, a community near Knoxville, Boone still entertains occasionally.

CHRIS BOUCHILLON

Born Christopher Allen Bouchillon, August 21, 1893,
Oconee County, South Carolina; died September
1968, West Palm Beach, Florida

Chris Bouchillon is remembered as the man who popularized a new style of music and comedy, "the talking blues." Charles Wolfe has written that few people know much about its origins, but Bouchillon had considerable success with his Columbia recording "Talking Blues" and "Hannah," which sold some ninety thousand copies. "The Medicine Show" and "Born in Hard Luck" disc sold forty thousand copies, which was considered to be good in the late 1920s. He became known as "the original Talking Blues Man." Numerous others have performed his "Original Talking Blues" or other compositions on the theme, including Lonnie Glosson, Robert Lunn, Woody Guthrie, Bob Dylan, Snuffy Jenkins and Pappy Sherrill, and the New Lost City Ramblers. Bouchillon has been called one of the foremost wits of the South. His most famous recording started like this:

> If you want to get to Heaven let me tell you how to do it,
> Grease your feet in a little mutton suet.
> Fan right out of the devil's hand,
> And slide right into the Promised Land.
> Go easy
> Make it easy
> Go greasy.

Bouchillon was born in the western mountains of South Carolina near the Georgia line. His father, John, a banjo player, moved the family to Greenville, where he and later his sons got jobs in a foundry. He also formed a string band when his sons Chris, Charley, and Uris were old enough to play music. They took several prizes at popular fiddle contests, and at these events they heard about recordings that other musicians were making in Atlanta. When they too decided to make recordings in 1925, for some reason their father did not go along. They recorded four sides as the Bouchillon Trio, but only one number was released. They recorded "The Talking Blues" in 1926 as the Greenville Trio. Charles Wolfe reports that Frank Walker, who directed the recording session, claimed that Bouchillon at first sang the song but that he asked him to recite or chant it over guitar accompaniment. However, Wolfe also reports that others said that Bouchillon had chanted it at earlier venues. His chanting style has been called the root of present-day rap music. The song is from the point of view of a lazy black man—"Ain't no use in me workin' so hard, / I got a woman in the white folks' yard"—indicating that it may have come from the blackface minstrel tradition. The group also recorded "Hannah" at this 1926 session, with Chris doing the vocals. The song was about an errant lover begging his sweetheart to open the door. It was later rewritten and recorded by Mel Tillis as "Honey (Won't You Open That Door)." This version went to number one with Ricky Skaggs. The recording of "Hannah" that the Bouchillons made was so popular that they were called back for other recordings. They did the "New Talking Blues" with "Blind Heck" on the B-side and another song that has also survived in country music, "Born in Hard Luck" (with "The Medicine Show" on the flip side). It was a song that was popular during the Great Depression when a lot of people felt that they had been born in hard luck:

> Now, people, I'm a goin' to tell you what a hard luck man I really am.
> You know, I was born in hard luck,
> I was born in the last month in the year,
> In the last week in the month,
> In the last day in the week.
> In the last hour in the day,
> In the last minute in the hour,
> In the last second in the minute,
> And to tell you the truth, now,
> I like not to have got here at all.

Although Bouchillon and his brothers sold a lot of records, they never really capitalized on their popularity, according to Charles Wolfe, but mainly played local venues and never used radio to open the way for personal appearances. Chris also recorded with his second wife, Ethel. In 1986, Old Homestead Records released an LP, *Chris Bouchillon: The Original Talking Blues Man* (OHC-181), with old numbers he had recorded for Columbia.

During his later years, Bouchillon ran a dry-cleaning shop in Greenville, and then he and Ethel retired to Florida. He died in 1968, and Ethel died in 1980.

(With credit to Charles Wolfe, Liner notes to *Chris Bouchillon: The Original Talking Blues Man* [Old Homestead Records, 1986]).

DON BOWMAN

Born August 26, 1937, Lubbock, Texas

Don Bowman's skill in writing and singing song parodies has been ranked with that of Homer and Jethro and Sheb Wooley. As a comedian, he won the *Billboard* Comedian of the Year Award in 1966.

Bowman began show business as a local disc jockey after picking cotton. He attended Texas Tech and then headed for the West Coast for a job as a DJ in San Diego. From there he followed radio jobs in San Francisco, Minneapolis–St. Paul, and then Nashville (WKDA). In Nashville his talent at songwriting, music, and comedy came to the attention of Chet Atkins, who signed him for RCA. He billed himself as the world's worst country singer and guitarist, but his first single, *Make Me a Star,* nevertheless made the Top Fifteen. Some of his songs were hits for other artists, such as "Just as You Are" (cowritten with Waylon Jennings) for Bobby Bare (number one) and later for Barbara Mandrell. His "Wildwood Weed," written with Jim Stafford, was a pop Top Ten for Stafford. His own parodies and comic songs included "Giddyup Donut" (a parody on Red Sovine's "Giddy-Up Go"), "A Coward at the Alamo," "Hillbillies in a Haunted House" (recorded by the Austin Lounge Lizards), "Hillbillies in Las Vegas," "Frieda on the Freeway," and "Poor Old Ugly Gladys Brown." He did eleven albums with RCA, and his final one was on Lone Star in 1979, *Still Fighting Mental Health.*

"BOOB" AND NEVA BRASFIELD

Lawrence N. Brasfield, born in the late 1880s,
  Smithville, Mississippi; died September 6, 1966,
  Raymondville, Texas
Neva Inez Greevi Brasfield, born March 3, 1914,
  Luther, Michigan; date and place of death
  unknown

"Boob" Brasfield and his wife Neva were veterans of tent shows that played all over the United States, mainly Bisbee's Dramatic Shows, one of many that toured the country in the late 1800s and early 1900s. They did both dramatic and comedic roles. Boob was the older brother of Rod Brasfield, who also worked for Bisbee's and later became famous at the "Grand Ole Opry." Boob played comedy long before Rod tried his hand at it, specializing in playing the Toby character. The singer Bobby Lord, a fellow entertainer on the "Ozark Jubilee," and others reported that he wrote comedy for several other comedians of the time and wrote most of the skits that Rod and Minnie Pearl did on the "Opry." Their fellow comedian Billy Choate wrote that the Brasfield brothers got their love of comedy from their mother Nonnie, who "was always telling jokes and had a big infectious laugh." Neva Brasfield also said that Boob got his abil-

Lawrence and Neva Brasfield. Reprinted with permission of the Museum of Repertoire Americana, Midwest Old Threshers, Mount Pleasant, Iowa.

ity from his mother, who was never on stage but "could mimic anything or anybody." Neva Greevi attended Quachita Baptist University from 1902 to 1903, and it is not clear how she got into dramatics and comedy.

The Brasfields became part of the first big country music television show, the "Ozark Jubilee," on ABC from Springfield, Missouri, from 1955 to 1960. There they played Uncle Cyp and Aunt Sap, characters created by Rod Brasfield in his routines about the people in his supposed hometown of Hohenwald, Tennessee. The many people who played the "Jubilee" spoke enthusiastically about the writing and acting ability of Boob on this show.

Lawrence Brasfield died in 1966 and is buried in Raymondville, Texas. Date and place of Neva's death are unknown.

The following script was written by Brasfield for a broadcast of the Ozark Jubilee:

> *Sap (at phone): Hello, is this the _____ Piano Company? This is Aunt Sap Brasfield. Will you send a piano tuner over to tune our old piano? I'm entertaining the Rook Club here tonight, and some of them always want to sing. . . . Hurry, won't you? Thanks, goodbye.*
> *I would have a sick headache at a time like this. Central, give me Dr. Brown's office. Hello, Dr. Brown. I have a terrible headache, got company coming. Could you stop by and give me something for it? Thanks, Doctor.*
> *Pete Stamper: (knocks)*
> *Sap: Come in. (Pete enters)*
> *Pete: Did you send for a piano tuner?*
> *Sap: Thank goodness you got here. It's in the front room. Get to work on it.*
> *Pete: I'll fix it up all right. (exits)*
> *Cyp (enters): Hi Puddin'. Supper ready?*
> *Sap: You'll eat cold supper. I'm sick. My head is killing me.*
> *Cyp: Oh, Sweetheart. Can I go to town and get . . .*
> *Sap: No, you ain't going to town. You've been gone all day. I've already called the doctor. (exits)*
> *Cyp: Ain't that a mess. Shore as I get hungry, she gets sick. (Pete enters) Oh, that must be the doctor now. Hello, Doc, how is she?*
> *Pete: Bad shape.*
> *Cyp: Yeah, she ain't like she used to be.*
> *Pete: That old thing ain't worth fooling with. How long you had that old job?*
> *Cyp: Thirty-six years.*
> *Pete: Well, no wonder. Why not trade it off and get a new one?*
> *Cyp: That's a good idea. No, it ain't. I can't. I mean I won't.*
> *Pete: Yeah, you do get attached to 'em. You must have traded for it second-handed.*
> *Cyp: I never done it. I don't think so.*
> *Pete: Well, I examined that one thoroughly.*
> *Cyp: Tell me what's wrong.*
> *Pete: Well, under her lid she's got a wasp's nest. Her peddle wiggles. Her ivories are all gone. Her bellows leak. Did you ever leave her out in the rain?*

Cyp: Why?
Pete: She's all warped. But I'll do what I can do. Sandpaper her good and give
*   her a good coat of varnish, and she'll look like a new one.*
Cyp: Sandpaper? Varnish. Aunt Sap?
Pete: Who said anything about Aunt Sap?
Cyp: Ain't you the doctor?
Pete: Doctor? No, I'm the piano tuner.

ROD BRASFIELD

Born August 22, 1922, Smithfield, Mississippi;
died September 12, 1958, Martin, Tennessee

Rodney Leon Brasfield was the younger brother of Lawrence L. "Boob" Brasfield who, with his wife, Neva, had established reputations as actors and comedians with Bisbee's Dramatic Shows that toured the South in tents. It was natural for Rod to join his brother and sister-in-law at Bisbee's when he was about sixteen years old, working first as an errand boy but eventually doing bit parts and then dramatic roles. It was a decade later that he began doing comedy with Bisbee's Comedians.

Rod served a year in the army during World War II but was discharged because of a back injury, and he returned to Bisbee's Comedians, where George D. Hay saw him perform and invited him to the "Grand Ole Opry" in 1944. There he billed himself as "the Hohenwald Flash," after a town in Tennessee. To populate his adopted town of Hohenwald, Ivan Tribe credits Rod with creating the characters of Uncle Cyp and Aunt Sap, which Boob and Neva adopted as their comic characters for skits on the "Ozark Jubilee" from 1955 to 1960.

He was the ultimate rube comedian, with baggy pants, high-top shoes, ill-fitting coat, and silly hat. He did comedy with Red Foley as his straight man on the NBC portion of the "Opry" beginning in

Rod Brasfield. Reprinted with permission of the Museum of Repertoire Americana, Midwest Old Threshers, Mount Pleasant, Iowa.

1947, but he is best known for his comedy with Minnie Pearl, using the "doubles" technique where both cracked jokes with each other without a straight man. Brasfield, Minnie Pearl, and Whitey Ford, as the "Duke of Paducah," shared billing as the top comedians of the "Opry" for a number of years.

Many of Brasfield's "Opry" performances were transcribed, but *Rod's Trip to Chicago* on Hickory Records (1957) was his only commercial recording. He appeared during the 1950s in the Al Gannaway TV color productions that in effect restaged the "Opry" for Gannaway's cameras to present its best-known performers. Brasfield also appeared in two movies: *A Face in the Crowd*, starring Andy Griffith, and *Country Music Holiday* (both in 1957).

Rod Brasfield died of a heart attack in September 1958 while doing a show in Martin, Tennessee, and he was buried in his birthplace of Smithfield, Mississippi. He was inducted into the Country Music Hall of Fame in 1987, presented by his old partner Minnie Pearl. "I was so happy," she said later, "because if anybody ever belonged in the Country Music Hall of Fame, Rod does."

From a 1951 WSM broadcast:

> *Red Foley: It's the Hohenwald Heartthrob himself, Rod Brasfield.*
> *Rod: Howdy, Mr. Foley.*
> *Red: I'll be right with you as soon as I lay my guitar down.*
> *Rod: Right now, while you do that, I'm a goin' to give the weather report. "Fairer and warmer, follered by women in shorts, follered by men."*
> *Mr. Foley, tonight I am sad and jealous-hearted. I'm tellin' you I'm just plumb put-out. I am, I really am, 'cause my gal Susie has done started flirtin' around on me.*
> *Red: That's bad wrong. That's terrible. What makes you think such a terrible thing?*
> *Rod: Well, I called her up at her house, out there in Hohenwald last night, and I asked her what she was a doin'.*
> *Red: Yeah?*
> *Rod: She said, "I'm a settin' here at the radio with the lights turned out listenin' to one of them mystery radio programs, and I'm settin' on the edge of my chair with suspense." I said, "Well, that's all right to set on the edge of the chair with Mr. Suspense, but by Ned, you better not get up in his lap!"*

THE BRIARHOPPERS

Claude Casey, born September 13, 1912, Enoree,
*   South Carolina; died June 24, 1999, Augusta,*
*   Georgia*
Roy "Whitey" Grant, born April 7, 1916, Shelby,
*   North Carolina*
Shannon Grayson, born September 30, 1916,
*   Sunshine, North Carolina; died May 10, 1993,*
*   Indian Trail, North Carolina*

*Arvol Hogan, born July 24, 1911, Robbinsville, North
  Carolina; died September 12, 2003, Charlotte,
  North Carolina*

*Fred Kirby, born July 19, 1910, Charlotte, North
  Carolina; died April 22, 1996, Indian Trail, North
  Carolina*

*Hank Warren, born April 1, 1908, Mount Airy,
  North Carolina; died 1998, Pineville, North
  Carolina*

*Don White, born Waldon Whytsell, September 25,
  1909, Wolfe Creek, West Virginia; died March 6,
  2005, Matthews, North Carolina*

*Others who have played with the Briarhoppers: John
  McAlister, Clarence Etters, Jane Bartlett, Billie
  Burton, Jack Gillette, Thorpe Westerfield, Homer
  Drye, Bill Davis, Sam Poplin, Homer Christopher,
  Cecil Campbell, Arthur Smith, David Deese, and
  Dwight Moody*

In 1935, Charles Crutchfield, an announcer at WBT in Charlotte, North Carolina, assembled a band that became the Briarhoppers. Even though most of the original members moved on before long, there were always good musicians to replace them, and the Briarhoppers were the top act in Charlotte over WBT until 1951. Members of the band have continued to perform at special events and now claim to be the oldest continually performing band in the country.

Hank Warren, the fiddler for most of these years until age slowed him down, was the main comedian. He wore oversized pants, red wig, comical hat, painted freckles, a blacked-out tooth, and horn-rimmed glasses. He loved to change back into his street clothes and mingle with the audience at intermission to find out how well his comedy was going over. In addition to Warren, the rest of the band often did skits and contributed to the humor. Don White remembered that Johnny McAlister did a character named Pappy on the program. "After he left, I took over and did 'Pappy Briarhopper.' I did slapstick and told jokes. As for real comedy, I wasn't that good at it." Whitey Grant, who with Arvol Hogan sang as Whitey and Hogan, one of the best male duets in the business, told of the comedy they did: "Hogan and me and Claude Casey did a skit called 'Little Nell.' I was Little Nell, dressed like a woman, and it ended up with—it's a wonder we didn't get killed—with me running and jumping up in the air and Claude Casey would catch me. He was a pretty good-sized fellow, and I was little. That was the climax of that little skit." He went on to say:

> Hank Warren did most of our comedy. We were always amused by what Hank was
> going to do next. We had a lot of fun with the comedy. Humor is number one. I

The Briarhoppers. L-R: Fred Kirby, Roy "Whitey" Grant, Claude Casey, Arval Hogan, "Big Bill" Davis, and Hank Warren (kneeling), ca. 1948. Courtesy of Don White.

think a little comedy does wonders for everyone. I told an audience in Monroe last night, "We've reached the age now where we don't buy green bananas anymore. When we bend over to tie our shoe, we look around to see if there's anything else we can do while we're down there." Hank and Hogan and I did comedy, and Hank would do 90 percent of it. He would cut up with the fiddle, and the fiddle would talk back to him. He'd say, "What would you like to do for the folks tonight, Mr. Fiddle?" and the fiddle would say—you could hear it, "I'd like to recite a poem," and Hank would say, "You do. What would you like to say?" And the fiddle would say, "Mary had a little lamb. Its fleece was white as snow," and the audience would eat that up. He imitated sound on the fiddle. He was good on the fiddle. He one time teamed up with Rubinoff to play "Bile 'em Cabbage Down." Every act that came through town wanted to be on the Briarhoppers' show.

In recent years, the surviving members of the Briarhoppers have toured schools as a part of arts-council programs, have played the annual Bob Evans Farm Festival in

Ohio, the Celebration of Traditional Music at Berea College in Kentucky, and other festivals, and they have appeared on "A Prairie Home Companion."

They have recorded three albums for Old Homestead: *Early Radio* (1977); *Whitey and Hogan (with the Briarhoppers)*, vols. 1 (1981) and 2 (1984); and they recorded three albums for the Lamon label: *Hit's Briarhopper Time* (1980); *Hit's Briarhopper Time Again* (1983); and *Hit's Briarhopper Hymn Time* (1988).

In 2003, the Briarhoppers received the North Carolina Arts Council Folk Heritage Award, with three of the original band members in attendance: Whitey Grant (eighty-seven), Arvol Hogan (ninety-one), and Don White (ninety-three). Dwight Moody and David Deese joined them for their concert. This honor inspired Joe DePriest of the *Charlotte Observer* to do a long article on the Briarhoppers, with pictures, then and now (April 20, 2003). The group used to play several personal appearances a week. Joe De-priest quotes Roy Grant on the importance of the band and the entertainment they did: "Without music, traveling, and meeting good people, I think we'd be pushing up daisies now. We can't see or hear good, but we're happy. And we love getting together and trying to play. The power of music will do wonders for the soul." Roy Grant is the only surviving member of the original group. At ninety, he still has a fine sense of humor.

Here is Arvol Hogan's remembrance of a skit between Whitey Grant and Hank Warren:

> *Whitey: Hank, what does a man wear on his feet on a cold rainy day?*
> *Hank: I don't know.*
> *Whitey: It's a pair of overshoes. Now how many would two men wear?*
> *Hank: I don't know.*
> *Whitey: Two pairs of overshoes. Now, how many would three men wear?*
> *Hank: I don't know.*
> *Whitey: Three pairs of overshoes. Now, tell me the answer to this. It's not my father, it's not my mother, it's not my sister or brother, still it's a child of my father and mother. Who is it?*
> *Hank: Oh, boy, oh boy, I've got this one. It's four pairs of overshoes!*

"CACTUS" TOM BROOKS

Born William Thomas Brooks, March 4, 1910,
Louisville, Kentucky; died December 14, 1997,
Louisville, Kentucky

Tom Brooks came from a musical family of eight boys that included the well-known humorist Foster Brooks. Their mother was the first woman singer on WHAS when it started broadcasting in 1922, and the family quartet performed on WHAS for several years. But music was not the strong forte of Tom Brooks. Instead it was comedy, and he played it for many years at WHAS and elsewhere in Louisville.

Cactus Tom Brooks. Courtesy of Elizabeth Atcher.

After first working for Reynolds Metals in Louisville, he got a job as an announcer at WHAS. Reportedly, his tenure wasn't secure in that position, and when the station launched its weekly "Circle Star Ranch" program, they needed a comedian, preferably one of the "grandpappy" type that was popular elsewhere. Brooks took out his false teeth and became "Cactus Tom." Randy Atcher described Brooks's act: "It was mostly slapstick humor—Rod Brasfield kind of stuff. He told stories and jokes. He also did a little dance routine in bib overalls, plaid shirt, a big safety pin in the front of his cowboy hat."

When Randy Atcher launched his "T-Bar-V Ranch" television program in 1950 on WHAS, he asked Brooks to serve as cohost and continue his Cactus Tom character, except then he became more of a rodeo clown on the Western-oriented show, with painted face—"slapstick for children," as Atcher put it. Atcher went on to say, "It was a children's birthday show, and we had birthday cake. About once a week he'd fall face down in the birthday cake." "T-Bar-V Ranch" was on the air for more than twenty years, and some 153,000 children appeared on the show. Cactus Tom and Randy had held most of them on their laps to wish them a happy birthday. The show had many kinds of skits to entertain or excite the children. Atcher commented that Cactus Tom didn't always memorize his lines but that his improvisations and ad-libs were funnier than the script anyway.

Atcher also reported that Cactus Tom was known to drink a little too much, which could have caused problems for a family or children's show, but that it never affected his performance, and then he said that Cactus was such a beloved figure in Louisville that no policeman would have arrested him.

Brooks also teamed with Atcher for a show called "Cartoon Circus" on WHAS-TV, and they did many country music shows at Fontaine Ferry, an entertainment complex. Brooks also did yeoman service in an annual fund-raising event, the WHAS Crusade for Children. An editorial in the *Louisville Courier-Journal*, lamenting his death, gives us this final view of Brooks: "Cactus always danced a soft-shoe on the 'T-Bar-V' show, and as the dance wound down, he would race head-first into the camera lens, filling the screen with his painted face. And Cactus would greet every audience of screaming children with a high-pitched and drawn-out, 'HOWWWW-DEEE.'"

(With credit to Wade Hall and Greg Swem, *A Song in Native Pastures: Randy Atcher's Life in Country Music* [Louisville: Harmony House Publishers, 2002].)

RAY "QUARANTINE" BROWN

Date and place of birth and death unknown

Ray "Quarantine" Brown was a comedian with Frankie More and His Log Cabin Boys in 1936 at WWVA in Wheeling. He later went with Jake Taylor and His Railsplitters. It was Taylor who named Brown "the ugliest man on radio." It is not clear how he came by his nickname of "Quarantine," but perhaps the inference is that he was so ugly that he had to be quarantined. He worked for Doc Williams out of WWVA off and on but not on a regular basis. Doc remembers that he was from Kentucky or Tennessee and thinks that he died in Minnesota.

SLIM BRYANT

Born Thomas Hoyt Bryant, December 7, 1908,
Atlanta, Georgia

Slim Bryant is a progressive musician who, after taking up the guitar at eighteen, took music lessons and applied himself diligently in learning to read and play any kind of music. He became an innovative guitarist, flat-picking single-string melodies or doing percussive rhythm. However, for many years he was also adept at being a funny man. "I did comedy, you know, big britches, wide suspenders, blacked-out tooth, a funny hat, all that stuff." At six feet, three inches and weighing 174 pounds, he could cut a comic figure

Slim Bryant (L) with Clayton
McMichen. Courtesy of Juanita
McMichen Lynch.

in costume. During the years he was with Clayton "Pappy" McMichen, he did his part
of the comedy, about which he said, "When you went out on personal appearances with
an hour-and-a-half show playing music, comedy was a relief in the middle there."

Bryant joined the famed Georgia Skillet Lickers in 1931, but he soon went with
McMichen to form the Georgia Wildcats. McMichen wanted to play more progressive music than that played by the Skillet Lickers, and they moved their new band to
Louisville, where they played over WHAS and WAVE. They also played at WRVA in
Richmond, Virginia, for a time, but McMichen, ever restless and ambitious, wanted
to form a big band, and so he moved back to Louisville. Bryant, who renamed their
old band Slim Bryant and His Wildcats, stayed on in Virginia to help form the "Old
Dominion Barn Dance." In 1940, he moved his band to KDKA in Pittsburgh for
a twenty-two-year stay, almost half of that on television. In 1950, he had his own
Saturday-afternoon coast-to-coast radio show on NBC.

Bryant and McMichen did gigs together from time to time, aside from the bands
they were with. In 1933, they played at WLS in Chicago in connection with the World's
Fair that year. McMichen, who was invited by Jimmie Rodgers to join him for the
1932 Victor recording sessions in Camden, New Jersey, and New York City, brought

Bryant along. Rodgers, needing new songs, quickly accepted and recorded Bryant's "Mother the Queen of My Heart." Bryant played on all those recordings.

Bryant composed more than two hundred additional songs, including "If You'll Let Me Be Your Little Sweetheart" and "Yum Yum Blues." The NBC Music Thesaurus Library holds 278 of his band's recorded numbers, including forty of his own compositions. He recorded for Majestic, MGM, Decca, and Lion. His composition "Eeny Meeny Dixie Deeny" made *Billboard's* Top Ten in 1947.

After retiring from KDKA, Bryant became a writer of jingles for Chevrolet, Westinghouse, U.S. Steel, Alcoa, and other companies. He also has a guitar studio and gift shop in Pittsburgh. In 1997, he was inducted into America's Old Time Country Music Hall of Fame in Anita, Iowa, and has a prominent exhibit in their Pioneer Music Museum. Recently, Merle Haggard invited Slim to play on one of his shows, and the audience gave him a standing ovation. At ninety-seven, Slim wrote, "I am fairly good, fairly good. About halfway between *absolutely* and *positively*."

> *Pappy McMichen: Now listen, It's not my sister, not my brother, and yet is the child of my father and mother. Who is it?*
> *Slim: Gosh, I don't know.*
> *Pappy: It's me.*
> *Slim: I'll pull that on Loppy [his brother Loppy Bryant, the bass player].*
> *Slim: It's not my sister, not my brother, and yet it's the child of my father and mother. Who is it?*
> *Loppy: It's you.*
> *Slim: No, it's Pappy.*

JAMES GILBERT "GOOBER" BUCHANAN

Born June 17, 1907, Hillsdale, Kentucky;
died June 16, 2008, Bowling Green, Kentucky

James "Goober" Buchanan had a part in every play in his high school, and thus he grew fond of entertaining people. In 1936 he was hired by the Willard White Minstrels as his first professional job, doing blackface skits, and he also worked for medicine shows in his early career. Later on, he and his band, the Kentuckians, joined the Field Shows from WLS, Chicago, traveling through the Midwest, where he played a character called "Grandpa Snazzy." After two years, he and his band went to WDZ in Tuscola, Illinois, and there he played Grandpa Fudley, mainly telling funny stories. Like many other entertainers, he went from station to station: WDOD and WAPO in Chattanooga (1939), WDZ in Tuscola (1940), WIBX in Indianapolis (1940), WHOP in Hopkinsville, Kentucky (1940–42), WPAD in Paducah, Kentucky (1942), WDEF in Chattanooga (1942), and WSM in Nashville and tours with the Jamup and Honey Tent Show (1942).

James "Goober" Buchanan.
Courtesy of James Buchanan.

Buchanan got the name "Goober" while working with Roy Cross and the Radio Rangers at WDOD in Chattanooga in 1938 in a program called "The Playhouse." Cross didn't like Buchanan's grandpa act and encouraged him to do a Toby-like country-boy act. He got Billy Wade, a comedian at the Playhouse, to tutor Buchanan in the new character. Buchanan remembered, "The first show we played was down in the peanut section of Georgia, and the kids in the front row went to yelling 'Goober' to me. Roy said, 'That's a good name,' and I became Goober."

He was in the army in 1942 and 1943 and then returned to Nashville's WSIX from 1943–48. Other stations he worked from were: WVLN in Olney, Illinois (1948–50), WLAC in Nashville (1950), and WVLN in Olney again (1950). He joined the Sun Players in Des Moines, Iowa (1950–51), worked for Bill Monroe, and then joined the Slout Comedians (1952), Sun Players (1952–53), and for two winters the Circle Stock Theater. "We did tent shows in the summer and then old opera houses in the winter where we put on three-act plays. We had about ten actors. It was mostly comic. They all had a Toby character in them, sometimes a Suzy too. I did stand-up comedy. I didn't just pull one-liners. I've done that, but generally I'd weave it into a story."

Buchanan continued with his band but also did promotion work for WSIX and WSIX-TV in Nashville in 1953 and 1954, worked as a salesman (1954–56), then went back on the road with Benny Martin in 1956 and Porter Wagoner in 1957 for four and a half years. During most of this time, he also headed and did comedy with the Kentuckians. "I had just a regular hillbilly band. I sang comic songs, like 'The Preacher and the Bear,' 'The Little Shirt That Mother Made for Me,' things like that. I used to tour with Bill Carlisle. I played bass some for him. I play guitar, mandolin, tenor banjo, drums, whatever they need. Did Dixieland. My wife is a ragtime piano player." Buchanan also toured with Jim Reeves, Ernest Tubb, Jimmy C. Newman, Billy Grammer, Elton Britt, Homer and Jethro, and Audrey Williams.

He tried to retire several times, but opportunity called. He commuted from Nashville to the "Renfro Valley Barn Dance" to do comedy for fifteen years. He noted that this was his best experience as an entertainer. He joined Doc McConnell's Echoes of Tennessee storytelling group and toured the state as a storyteller performing and giving workshops. He also performed at the Wild Horse Saloon in Nashville. In 1983, Buchanan and his wife, Lila Mae ("The best ragtime piano player I ever heard"), were part of the cast for a re-creation of an old-time medicine show, *The Vi-Ton-Ka Medicine Show*, at the American Place Theater off Broadway.

Buchanan reminisced that he had learned early in the business the important ingredients that every good show should have: "It should have a sigh, a romantic song; a cry, a tear-jerker, a sad song; and plenty of laughs."

Buchanan and Lila Mae moved to a retirement village in Bowling Green, Kentucky, in the late 1990s. Lila Mae died a few years later. Goober remains active, entertaining people at the village, and in 2006, he published *The Original Goober: The Life and Times of James G. Buchanan*, with Ruth White (Madision, Tenn.: Nova Press). In 2006, at the age of ninety-nine, Goober traveled to Murfreesboro, Tennessee, to receive the Trailblazer Award presented by the Board of Directors of Uncle Dave Macon Days.

(With credit to Wayne W. Daniel, "Goober Buchanan," *Old Time Country* 9.3–4 [Fall/Winter 1993–94]: 12–17.)

From a Goober Buchanan monologue:

Well, I went out to a party last night. I'm tellin' you, I had me a ball. It was one of these gay nineties parties, where the men were all gay and the women were all ninety. Pretty interestin' people there, though. There was one set of newlyweds. There was an old man that had married a teenage gal, and she was goin' on eighteen, and I think he was goin' on Benzedrene. That's the way of these old timers. They're allus looking for greener pastures, and then when they finally find them, they're too old to climb the fence.

I met a gal there at the party. Oh, I'm telling you, she was a swell looker. She was one of those sweater girls, looked like one of these old-fashioned bureaus with the top drawer pulled out. That gal could take a shower and get neither foot wet. . . . She had slacks on. I don't like slacks, though. You can't tell whether its a woman walking down the street, or a man with cantaloupes in his hip pockets. . . . I told her I'd like to have some old-fashioned lovin', and she introduced me to her grandma. I said goodbye to her.

I went down the street where they were havin' a dance. Oh, man, it was crowded in there. They's dancing cheek to cheek in ever' direction. Most of 'em was doin' this new twist dance. I ain't seen so much action since I put Feen-a-Mint in the candy bowl. That twist dance, I think that's somethin' they learned watchin' a Scotchman in front of a pay toilet. . . . I heard two old boys, one was braggin' about a new baby he had at home, I think. He said, "Oh, that kid of mine, he's got muscles like a wrestler, a great big barrel chest, and bawls like a bull." The other'n said, "He has?" And he said, "No, he does!"

SMILEY BURNETTE

Born Lester Alvin Burnette, March 8, 1911,
Summum, Illinois; died February 17, 1967,
California

Smiley Burnett was the son of Church of Christ ministers. His fame came mostly as the hapless sidekick of Gene Autry, Roy Rogers, and Charles Starrett, riding a white horse with a ring drawn around its left eye. Behind his comic character, however, was the talented composer of more than four hundred songs and a musician on numerous instruments. He began entertaining as a child with the musical saw, and in high school he organized his first band. After graduation, he worked at several kinds of jobs before

Smiley Burnette.

he landed one as an announcer and musician on the hundred-watt radio station WDZ in Tuscola, Illinois, sponsored by a furniture store. He was, in fact, the sole staff of the station from morning to night. As the entertainer as well as announcer and engineer, he learned hundreds of songs and learned to play a dozen instruments.

In 1933, Gene Autry was in nearby Champaign to do a show and indicated that he needed an accordion player for his band. He was directed to Burnette, and Autry hired him to appear with him on WLS's "National Barn Dance." This program gave him national recognition. Burnette and Autry became great friends, and he went with Autry to California, where both had singing parts in the Ken Maynard movie *In Old Santa Fe.* They made a good impression and were signed to do a twelve-part serial, *The Phantom Empire.* Not sure that movies offered much promise compared to radio and personal appearances, they went to Louisville's WHAS, but by the next year they were back in California, where Autry made fifty-seven movies with Burnette as his sidekick, Frog Millhouse, a moniker coming from a voice trick that went from high falsetto to bullfrog bass. There had been movie sidekicks before him, but Burnette's comic persona became the standard for sidekicks following him, with a lot of the elements of the country rube who fumbled, bumbled, and fell down. But he always had endearing qualities of unquestioned loyalty to his white-hatted partner, and in Frog's case, great musical talent. He composed many of the songs for the Autry films, including "Riding down the Canyon," cowritten with Autry. However, he was under personal contract to Autry, meaning that all royalties went to Autry. Within years, he was almost as popular as Autry and was the only cowboy comic to be among the Top Ten Western stars. In all, he made as many as 350 movies, with Autry, Roy Rogers, Sunset Carson, and Charles Starrett, but he also had his own series. Most of the films were with Republic and Columbia Studios. He also had two syndicated radio shows and played the role of railroad engineer on the popular CBS-TV series "Petticoat Junction."

Among the songs Burnette composed were "It's My Lazy Day," "Ridin' down the Canyon," "Call of the Canyon," "Song of the Range," and "Hominy Grits." His songs were recorded by Bing Crosby, Red Foley, Dean Martin, Vaughn Monroe, George Morgan, Ferlin Husky, and Riders of the Purple Sage. In 1971 he was made a member of the Songwriters Hall of Fame in Nashville. He recorded for Capitol, Abbott, Conquerer, Bullet, and Cricket. Burnette made appearances at the "Ozark Jubilee," the "Grand Ole Opry," and the "Louisiana Hayride," and he also loved to do fairs and rodeos.

Smiley was married to the former Dallas McConnell, a newspaper writer, and they had four adopted children, Linda, Steven, Caroline, and Brian. Dallas died in 1977.

(With credit to David Rothel, *Those Great Cowboy Sidekicks* [Madison, N.C.: Empire Publishing, 2001], 13–47.)

Excerpt from the "Smiley Burnette Show" from Hollywood, date unknown:

> *Joe Slattery, emcee: And now, here he is, that panhandle Poe, the sagebrush Shakespeare, Smiley Burnett.*
>
> *Smiley: Howdy doodle, Joe. Of all the Gloomy Gusses around the place, what's the matter with you?*
>
> *Joe: I'm gloomy, all right. I'm glad you came in. You know about six months ago, you told me to give coal oil to my cow that had colic.*
>
> *Smiley: Yeah.*
>
> *Joe: I did. You know, that cow died.*
>
> *Smiley: Now, that's funny. My cow died too! Listen, this moniker you give me about Poe. Was he a poet too?*
>
> *Joe: Oh, he was a poet too. I understand that you've got some poetry?*
>
> *Smiley: Oh yes, today I'm a poet, Joe. I've writ, wrote . . . I mean, I've got some poems. Here's one. Quiet, please, listen to this:*
>
> *I'm not a beauty, you see.*
> *There are others more handsome than me.*
> *But my face I don't mind it,*
> *For I am behind it.*
> *It's the people in front that scare me.*
>
> *Oh me [in frog voice]. Now, here's another one:*
> *There once was a feller named Hall*
> *Who fell in the spring in the fall.*
> *T'would have been a sad thing,*
> *If he'd died in the spring,*
> *But he didn't, he died in the fall.*

PAT BUTTRAM

*Born June 19, 1915, Addison, Alabama; died January
8, 1994, Los Angeles, California*

Pat Buttram is best remembered for his role as the conniving rube Mr. Haney, with
the falsetto break in his voice in the long-running TV series "Green Acres." Before
that, however, he flourished on the WLS "National Barn Dance" in Chicago as a rube
comedian and traveled on road shows with Gene Autry, before Autry left for Hollywood. Eventually Buttram wound up in California also, and beginning in 1948 he made

seventeen films with Autry. Buttram's wife, Sheila
Ryan, was one of Autry's leading ladies. He took
his role as a comic sidekick seriously and studied
comedy from the old master, Buster Keaton, especially the old clown trick of getting laughs by falling down. Sidekicking wasn't easy. He was almost
killed when a cannon blew up on the set, and he
didn't get along too well with horses, commenting
that they were hard in the middle and dangerous
on both ends.

He was also on Autry's "Melody Ranch" radio
shows for fifteen years and in eighty episodes of
"The Gene Autry Show" on television. Another
job Buttram had was writing speeches for Autry,
who in later years was in demand as a prominent
Los Angeles businessman, and he and Autry were
close friends.

Born in rural Alabama, Buttram parlayed his
southern dialect and country ways, or at least his
ability to imitate them, into a successful career as a

Pat Buttram.

radio comedian and comic actor. In his later years, he did stand-up comedy and after-
dinner speeches around Hollywood with a wit compared to that of Will Rogers. He
joined the writing staff of "Hee Haw" in 1969 and wrote scripts for seventeen episodes
while it was on CBS. He was also an occasional guest as a comedian during the years
of syndication. After he retired in 1980, Buttram returned to Alabama for a year, but
then moved back to California.

Buttram's ranch house in the San Fernando Valley, filled with books, Civil War
relics, and antiques, belied his stage persona as the simple country boy. His nephew,
the Reverend Mac Buttram, verified that he was a far more sophisticated man than his
TV and movie roles would indicate. He died of kidney failure in the UCLA Medical
Center in 1994.

(With credit to David Rothel, *Those Great Cowboy Sidekicks* [Madison, N.C.: Empire Publishing, 2001], 107–15.)

Here is an excerpt from a "National Barn Dance" show in 1943:

> *Emcee: We're glad to welcome the Winston County Flash, folks, Pat Buttram. . . . Haven't you put on some weight since I was gone?*
>
> *Pat: No, I just put on my winter underwear.*
>
> *Emcee: There have been a lot of changes in the last ten years. You know, I was just looking over a newspaper of ten years ago. One headline said, "Hitler Wants Peace."*
>
> *Pat: Well, he sure took the long way round to get it, didn't he.*
>
> *Emcee: Another story in the same newspaper said, "The German army and navy had sworn to die for Hitler."*
>
> *Pat: Well, he's making them keep their word on that part, all right.*
>
> *Emcee: And prices were different too, Pat. Just think, ten years ago, haircuts were only thirty-five cents. Now they're seventy-five cents and a dollar.*
>
> *Pat: Yeah, well, you was lucky, Joe, you got all of your haircuts when they was still thirty-five cents. . . . Well, Joe, I hate to rush off, but I've got to beat it. We're having a big fall picnic tomorrow. It's the last one this year, and I got charged with the tennis tournament.*
>
> *Emcee: Oh yes, I'm in that tournament too. Now don't forget that.*
>
> *Pat: Oh, I won't. I've got the schedule all made out. You see, the very best players will play in the morning, and then the poorer players will play in the afternoon, and the worst players will play along toward evening.*
>
> *Emcee: Well, what time do I play?*
>
> *Pat: Ah, here's your flashlight.*

CACKLE SISTERS. *See Dezurick Sisters*

ARCHIE CAMPBELL

Born November 7, 1914, Bulls Gap, Tennessee;
died August 29, 1987, Knoxville, Tennessee

After two years at Mars Hill College during the Great Depression, Archie Campbell had a lean time of it wandering the South as minstrel and sign painter before landing a job at Knoxville's WNOX in 1936. There he sang on a daily afternoon show and on the Saturday "Farm and Home Hour" with Roy Acuff and His Crazy Tennesseeans. In 1936, the announcer Lowell Blanchard came to WNOX to put more emphasis on country music, and he saw the need for comedy to add variety. Under his tutelage, Archie developed a character called "Grandpappy" who was a hit with listeners.

Archie later had his own shows at Bristol's WOPI and at Chattanooga's WDOD before spending two years in the navy in World War II. He then rejoined the WNOX "Mid-day Merry-Go-Round." However, in 1949, he went to the rival station WROL in a show called "Country Playhouse," which became the city's first country music television show.

In 1958, Archie joined the "Grand Ole Opry" as a comedian on the "Prince Albert Show." There he shed his Grandpappy character and did comedy mostly in street clothes, one of the first country comedians to do so. In addition to radio, he did concerts and made comedy records for RCA, including *Trouble in the Amen Corner, The Cockfight,* and *Rinderceller,* a spoonerism version of the fairy tale "Cinderella." Spoonerisms, a transposition of word sounds, became his trademark.

In 1969, Archie was named Comedian of the Year by *Music City News* and was hired as a writer-comedian for "Hee Haw," which first aired in June of that year. He helped to recruit other comedians for the show. Some of the routines and characters that he developed were inspired by earlier skits that he and Lowell Blanchard had created at WNOX in Knoxville. It was Archie who came up with the "Where, Oh, Where Are You Tonight?" routine that involved regulars as well as guests on the show and became a weekly feature. During the time he was on "Hee Haw," Archie also had a comedy show in Pigeon Forge, which later became Hee Haw Village. Archie was also an avid painter, and he produced paintings of nostalgic landscapes and log cabins and such that were sold as prints at his many venues and at the annual Tennessee Homecoming at Norris.

Archie and his wife, Mary Elizabeth (Lewis), had two sons: Steve, a Nashville art teacher, and Phil, also a comedian who was a regular on "Hee Haw" in its last years and a partner with his father in Hee Haw Village in Pigeon Forge.

Archie Campbell died of heart failure in a Knoxville hospital in 1987.

Here are three of Archie's stories:

A traveling salesman stopped at a country store and saw a man playing checkers with a dog. After watching for a while, he said, "That's the smartest dog I ever saw." The man said, "Oh, he ain't so smart. I beat him three out of five times."

There are some real ugly people up there in Bulls Gap. We had a beauty contest one time, and nobody won. My cousin was married to the ugliest woman I ever saw, but he took her everywhere he went. I asked him why, and he said, "I'd rather take her with me than have to kiss her goodbye."

A mother caught her daughter and a boy hugging each other on the front porch, and she said, "What is the meaning of this?" Her daughter said, "Come back in about fifteen minutes and I ought to know something by then."

SARAH OPHELIA COLLEY CANNON. *See Minnie Pearl*

JUDY CANOVA

Born Juliette Canova, November 20, 1916,
Jacksonville, Florida; died August 5, 1983,
Hollywood, California

Judy Canova was born into the relatively affluent family of a cotton-broker father and a concert-singing mother, but she chose to become a female rube comedienne, and nationally she was as well known as Minnie Pearl. She was a strong and versatile singer also, beginning on radio at the age of twelve.

When Judy's father died, her mother encouraged her and her brother and sister, Leon and Diane, to get into the entertainment field. They formed a trio called Anne, Judy, and Zeke, Three Georgia Crackers. When they moved on to New York City in 1930, their hillbilly act of comedy, dance, and songs (with yodels) at places like the Village Barn and Jimmy Kelly's was impressive enough to get them into vaudeville and radio and a part in the Broadway show *Calling All Stars*. After more radio work, visits to Hollywood for small film roles, and a tour of England, they had a Broadway show called *Yodel Boy* that drew attention to Judy's talents.

Thereafter, Judy developed a solo act with song, dance, jokes, and yodels that got her small film roles and a place in the 1936 *Ziegfield Follies*. She also continued with the Canovas, and they appeared on several radio shows and were included in NBC's experimental television broadcasts in 1939.

Judy went back to Hollywood in 1940 and got a starring role in *Scatterbrain*, a Republic Studios picture. She became this studio's only female star in a string of pictures stretching into the mid-1950s, featuring her as the simple country girl up against urban deviousness, with plenty of song and comedy

Judy Canova.

and a yodel or two thrown in. For ten years, beginning in 1943, she also headed "The Judy Canova Show," with some eighteen million radio listeners, and its popularity kept it in the Top Ten. She also recorded for the "Melody Roundup" radio programs for the armed forces and appeared on television in "The Cavalcade of Stars" and "The Colgate Comedy Hour."

Canova recorded for Mercury, OKeh, Varsity, Coronet, Sterling, RCA, and other labels. She had a hit in 1947 with "No Letter Today," paired with "Never Trust a Man."

Judy Canova proved the enduring appeal of the rustic hero or heroine up against the wiles of sophisticated city folks.

The following is from a 1940s "Melody Roundup" program with guest John Wayne, produced by the Special Services Division of the War Department:

> *Canova: Well, John, are you goin' to marry me or not?*
> *Wayne: Shucks, Judy, I ain't the marryin' kind. . . .*
> *Canova: You've just gotta get hitched with me.*
> *Wayne: Well, I can't do it, Judy. Have your folks ever been to Hollywood?*
> *Canova: Hollywood? Listen, John, my folks live so far back in the hills, they*
> *   think a hillbilly's a city feller.*
> *Wayne: Well, Judy, I wish you'd try to get over this marriage idea. You couldn't*
> *   live the life I live. Why, I have a big mansion with forty rooms and fifteen*
> *   baths.*
> *Canova: Baths? What's them?*
> *Wayne: Well, it's kind of hard to explain, but you remember the time your*
> *   brother Zeke fell in the creek?*
> *Canova: Yeah, he got all wet, he did.*
> *Wayne: Well, city folk do that on purpose.*

CAPTAIN STUBBY AND THE BUCCANEERS

Born Tom C. Fouts, November 24, 1918, near
*   Galveston, Indiana; died May 24, 2004,*
*   Kokomo, Indiana*

Tom Fouts's mother got him started in comedy and song at the age of five by involving him in entertainment shows that she organized locally. "She taught me songs and played the piano for me and taught me two or three little jokes to tell, and that started me. Boy, I got to liking that applause and laughter." Fouts grew up on the farm and went to school in the town of Young America. "I did comedy all the way through high school, and I had a little band. We played mostly hokey instruments. I played a washboard, and we had a jug player. We kind of modeled ourselves after the Hoosier Hot Shots. We had a lady teacher who played the accordion with us and kind of held us together, and we had a harmonica player. Nobody could afford instruments. This was the depths of the Depression, so you had to make do with what you had."

Fouts's brand of humor came early in his career:

> We did country rural humor, and I've always stuck to that. I mostly do comedy about growing up on the farm and hard times, about how poor we were. How poor? My mother would give us beans for breakfast, water for lunch, and we'd swell up for supper. We used to make humor to bolster ourselves up, and we laughed at our problems. We'd make fun of the city slicker who comes to the country—the mistakes

he makes out on the farm, which is funny to rural people. I think humor is very important in entertainment. It breaks up the show, is a great part of the show. It's great standing up there seeing five thousand people holding their sides laughing. I get a high out of that. It is a great way to make a living.

During a year at Indiana Central College, Fouts joined up with the clarinetist Jerry Richards from Freeport, Illinois, to form another band. In 1938 Fouts and Richards joined a group called the Hoosier Ramblers, and they played on WDAN in Danville, Illinois, for Semi-Solid Buttermilk Products. By 1940, the group, now called the Semi-Solid Ramblers, was being broadcast over a fifteen-station syndicate that included the powerful WLS in Chicago. In 1940, the group was hired by WLW's program director George Biggar in Cincinnati, where they had a daily program, "Time to Shine," and also appeared on the "Boone County Jamboree" on Saturday nights. There the group became the Boone County Buccaneers and finally Captain Stubby and the Buccaneers. Fouts, being short, had the nickname of Stubby. In addition to Fouts, with his horn-equipped washboard, the band included Jerry Richards on clarinet; Dwight "Tiny" (sometimes "Slim") Stokes from Frankfort, Indiana, on bass; Curley Myers from Frankfort, Indiana, on guitar; and Tony Walberg from Cincinnati on accordion.

Captain Stubby.
Courtesy of Tom Fouts.

While he was in Cincinnati, Fouts did a Roto-Rooter commercial in a froggy voice—"and away go your troubles down the drain"—that became the longest-running jingle in advertising history.

In 1944, the whole band auditioned to join the U.S. Navy Entertainment Section; except for Curley Myers, who didn't pass the physical, they were accepted. Myers's place was taken by Sonny Fleming from Paducah, Kentucky, who was already in the navy. They did a program called "Meet the Navy" over WLS and the ABC Network and toured naval bases in the continental United States, Alaska, Guam, and Okinawa.

After the war, the band members thought they might do all right in the New York nightclub circuit, and they did, but they all missed the Midwest. George Biggar, then at WLS, was glad to hire them to be part of the "National Barn Dance" and other WLS shows. They arrived just as the "National Barn Dance" began broadcasting over a newly organized sixty-eight-station hookup in March 1949. There they performed until the show ended in 1960, also making personal appearances all over the Midwest.

The Buccaneers played for a time on the "WGN Barn Dance" and became regulars on the A-TV program "Polka Go-Round."

Captain Stubby and the Buccaneers recorded for Decca, Majestic, Mercury, Columbia, Rondo, and Stephany. Even though the band played as "the Buccaneers" for fifty years, its members changed over the years. When Tony Walberg was killed in an automobile accident in 1952, his place was taken by Pete Kaye, and when Sonny Fleming died, he was replaced by Ralph "Rusty" Gill.

In the 1960s, when members of the band decided to retire, Captain Stubby was not ready to hang it up. He was a writer and did comedy on Don McNeil's "Breakfast Club" on ABC and did an hour-long morning program on WLS with Charles Homer Bill. He and his wife Lou moved back to the farm in Young America, Indiana, in 1973, but he continued to do many after-dinner speeches, with a lot of humor about farming, and he did humorous monologues on two syndicated radio shows. He also wrote a humorous column for several farm magazines, including the *Prairie Farmer*, published four joke books, and released nine comedy tapes (available from Captain Stubby, Box 100, Young America, IN 46998). Captain Stubby and his wife, Eva Lou (Sittitt), whom he married in 1940, had three children: Tom, Connie, and Dan.

(With credit to Wayne W. Daniel, "King of the Gizmo: Captain Stubby," *Journal of Country Music* 15.3 [1993]: 8–10.)

From Captain Stubby's *Country Humor No. 4*, with permission:

> *I love folks when they get up in years a little bit. They kind of tell you like it is, and they're a lot of fun. We've got Aunt Maude over there. Wonderful lady—never did get married—ninety-two years old. I asked her one time, I said, "Aunt Maude, how come you never did get married?" "Well," she said, "I'd rather want something all my life and never have it, than to have something all my life and never want it!" I couldn't argue with that.*
>
> *That was a lady who did everything for herself. She paid her own taxes, bought her own groceries, got her own driver's license—everything. She even made out her own funeral arrangements. She was out of the room one day, and it was laying on her desk there, and I happened to look at it. I saw she had all women pallbearers. She came back in the room, and I said, "Aunt Maude, I see you've got down all women pallbearers. How come no men?" She said, "They never took me out when I am living, and they ain't going to take me out when I'm dead!"*

BILL CARLISLE

Born December 19, 1908, Wakefield, Kentucky;
died March 17, 2003, Goodlettsville, Tennessee

Bill Carlisle was a genuine comic character. He was also a good musician, singer, and songwriter. He had plenty of practice growing up in western Kentucky during Sunday singing sessions with his mother, father, four brothers, and two sisters. He got into show business by joining his older brother Cliff, a dobro player and singer of bluesy-yodeling songs in the style of Jimmie Rodgers. They had a daily show in Louisville at WLAP Radio (now located in Lexington) and a Saturday-night "Carlisle Jamboree." They went from Louisville to stations in Charlotte, North Carolina; Greenville and Columbia, South Carolina; Charleston, West Virginia; Atlanta; and Knoxville.

Bill and Cliff had done some comedy all along. Cliff said of Bill, "He was a natural comedian. If he made a mistake on the guitar, he'd do the same thing over again, and grin like he's done it a purpose." However, it was not until he got to Knoxville that Bill gave full vent to comedy. There, at WNOX's "Mid-day Merry-Go-Round," with the help of the emcee and program director Lowell Blanchard, he created his alter ego, Hotshot Elmer. He said of Blanchard, "Lowell Blanchard was one of the best emcees and straight men that ever hit the stage. He wrote a lot of my material. We'd advertise our show as 'Hotshot Elmer and Little Red Riding Hood,' and we'd act it out. The next time we'd go to something else." When asked how he became "Jumping" Bill Carlisle, he explained, "When I started doing Hotshot Elmer, we'd do a mock fight. I'd run around the stage, me and my brother would, and I could jump over a chair backwards and forward." Sunshine Slim Sweet, a fellow performer, reported that Carlisle could stand flat-footed and jump up onto a five-foot-high stage. Later, while playing and singing, he would jump straight up into the air, pulling his legs up against his body to give the impression that

Bill Carlisle.
Courtesy of Bill Carlisle.

he was jumping higher than he actually was, and all the while not missing a beat. Slim Sweet also reported that Bill once sat on a nest of eggs for two weeks and hatched out some ducks! The comedian Fred Smith reported that Bill would go into the street and do crazy things, like getting on a bus and making a big fuss, claiming that WNOX had just fired him, causing sympathetic fans to call the station to protest. James Roberts, another performer at WNOX, said that when they went into a restaurant, Bill took a handful of toothpicks. When asked why, he replied, "My father-in-law's in the timber business, and I'm trying to drive up the price of lumber."

Bill and Cliff recorded together and separately through the years, for Gennett, the ARC group of companies, Victor, Decca, King, Columbia, and Mercury, and Bill also recorded for Bluebird and Hickory. Together, the brothers' biggest hit was "I Saw a Rainbow at Midnight" (King, 1946). Bill wrote and recorded novelty and humorous songs, which were high on the charts, including "Too Old to Cut the Mustard"

(Mercury, 1951), "No Help Wanted" (Mercury, 1952), "Knothole," and "Taint Nice" (Mercury, 1952).

The Carlisles were invited to the "Grand Ole Opry" in 1953, mainly because of their hit recordings. Cliff shortly went into partial retirement, but Bill continued with a band known as the Carlisles, eventually joined by his daughter Sheila and son Bill. The last lineup of the Carlisles was Bill, Bill Jr., and the talented guitarist George Riddle. Bill continued performing on the "Opry," despite serious illness, until shortly before his death by stroke, still singing, cracking jokes, and doing routines with George Riddle as his straight man.

> *Bill: There's a pickpocket in the house, sure enough. Now, hold on to your pocketbooks. I ain't worried myself. I've got a trap set for him. I've got the bottoms of my pockets cut out. He gets in there, I'll know it.*
>
> *Last Saturday night there was one at the "Opry." I was salamandering up and down the aisle, with my trap a-settin'. First thing I knew, I felt a hand easin' down in my pocket. You know what I done? I just reached down in the other pocket and shook hands with him! It looked like it surprised him to meet me there.*

MIKE CARR. *See Moron Brothers*

RODNEY CARRINGTON

Born October 19, 1968, Longview, Texas

Rodney Carrington is a comedian and singer whose first five CDs have sold over a million copies to fans who have flocked to his performances across the country for the past fifteen years. He got into comedy, like several other young comedians, by overcoming his basic shyness and taking the stage for an open-mic session at a comedy club. He discovered that he could make people laugh, and he thought it would be a way to have some fun and make some money while he was auditioning to be an actor. His national comedy tours haven't left much time for acting.

Since he was born in and grew up in Texas, Carrington uses a great deal of East Texas humor and dresses like a cowboy, or at least a cowboy singer. However, his music came after he was fairly well established as a comedian. He bought a pawn-shop guitar, learned three chords, and took it on stage with him. He sang a few country songs but then began writing songs about amusing topics that are not usually discussed in mixed company. He commented to one writer, "A song for me is really just a joke with music."

His comedy overall is definitely naughty. For example, he sometimes includes among the stage props two inflatable phalluses. He is also politically incorrect, making fun of our pretenses and posturing. His humor is more reflective of the comedy-club circuit than of the country music stage. One writer said in regard to his comedy, "It darned sure ain't always pretty, but it's darned sure real, and it's a whole lotta fun."

While Carrington's humor may offend some, he has a huge following. His first three CDs were all on the comedy charts. *Morning Wood* (2000) was number one and remained in the Top Three for forty-three weeks; *Live: C'Mon Laugh* (2001) was also number one. *Hangin' With Rodney* (1998) was also on the charts. His last two albums on Columbia are *Nut Sack* (2003) and *Rodney Carrington: Greatest Hits* (2004).

In September 2004 Rodney opened in an ABC comedy show, "Rodney," about a family man from Tulsa who quits his blue-collar job to follow his dream of becoming a stand-up comedian.

Carrington makes his home in Tulsa, Oklahoma, with his wife, whom he takes out on dates, and three boys, with whom he does outdoor things. He also plays some golf.

Rodney Carrington. Photo by Dean Dixon, courtesy of Julie Goldstein and Publicity Plus.

JOE CARTER

Born Joe Dougherty Carter, February 27, 1927,
Scott County, Virginia; died March 2, 2005,
Scott County, Virginia

Joe Carter was the only son and youngest child of A. P. and Sara Carter of the original Carter Family. He was five months old when his parents took him to Bristol to record for Ralph Peer in the legendary "Bristol Sessions." He traveled as young boy with the family to Del Rio, Texas, and later San Antonio when they played over and made transcriptions for XERA and other border stations. As a teenager he played and sang with the family when they were at WBT in Charlotte. Yet he chose not to continue in the entertainment business, partly because of the separation of A. P. and Sara and the split-up of the Carter Family. Joe went into the construction business, as superintendent of crews that built homes, schools, and churches. However, he had grown up with good stories and learned a lot more during his service in the Pacific as a sailor in World War II. In later years, he helped his sister Janette in running the annual Carter Family Festival as well as the Saturday-night gatherings of musicians at the old Carter store. He also began to perform again as a guitarist and singer, but also as a humorous storyteller.

In 1975, before he retired from construction work, he built the huge barn now called the Carter Fold on the old Carter homestead. Under the direction of Janette and her son, Dale Jett, and in later years her daughter, Rita Forrester (Janette died in 2006), the Carter Fold presents some of the best of Appalachian folk, country, and bluegrass music every Saturday night. Joe became a valued part of the lineup, providing comic relief amid sometimes tragic or sad songs. His specialty was the imitation of animals. He liked to tell hunting stories, such as when he says he took his dog into the woods and trailed what Joe assumes to be a coon but turns out to be a sow with pigs. Joe told of the ensuing fight with all the sound effects. He told another about his dog pursuing a raccoon down into a hole in the ground. Joe reported that the coon chewed off his dog's front feet and thereafter he used him to punch holes in the ground for tobacco plants. He also imitated horses, cattle, chickens, jackasses, hummingbirds, and goldfish (the way they purse their lips).

Joe explained how he learned such an art: "There was a boy—Dewey Hensley—I learned a lot from, lived up on the mountain. You could name anything, and he would make the sound of it. I started doing that sort of thing here, and it went over good, especially with the kids. They really liked that." He went on to say that the old folks loved it too: "It would remind them of an old hog or whatever. They would crack up." He also went out with Janette for a few appearances, such as at the annual Tennessee Homecoming at the Museum of Appalachia in Norris.

Joe Carter lived near Maces Spring, Virginia. He was married to Nancy Keller, and they had three daughters, Connie, Lisa, and Benita. Joe died from cancer of the liver.

Here is one of Joe's stories from his navy experience:

> When we were shipping out to go overseas, the water got really rough. We were all just out of boot training and, man, you talk about a seasick bunch, including me! We'd had spaghetti for supper, and it was all over the deck and walls, and the toilets were full. I went up on the top deck and hung my head over the rail, and I was getting rid of mine. The captain came by, and he said, "What's the matter, sailor, you got a weak stomach?" I said, "No, sir, I'm throwin' mine just as far as anybody!"

CYNTHIA MAY CARVER ("COUSIN EMMY")

Born 1903, Lamb, Kentucky; died April 11, 1980,
Sherman Oaks, California

Cynthia May Carver was one of the best all-around entertainers ever to grace a stage. She played all of the standard country instruments and nearly a dozen more as well, including the handsaw and an inflated rubber glove. Although she was not a comedian as such, in the early days she dressed as the simple country girl in a gingham dress, thick white cotton stockings that bagged at the knees, and high-topped black shoes. Her performances were rousing and amusing, and she laid on the country talk. Mac Atcheson, a member of her band, was quoted as saying about her, "When she'd do a show she'd pack the house twice every night, at these little school houses. Ah, she was a showman that wouldn't wait. . . . She was a real character."

Born the youngest of eight children in a tenant family in southern Kentucky, she allegedly learned to read from the Sears-Roebuck catalog. Indeed, she had only about two years of formal education. However, she grew up hearing the old traditional ballads, string music, and other rural lore from her relatives. On the strength of her musical talent, she escaped the tobacco fields to join two of her cousins, Noble and Warner Carver, who had organized a band that recorded in the early twenties. Cynthia played for a time with her cousins on WHB in Kansas City, and then she returned to Kentucky in 1935 to perform with Frankie More's Log Cabin Boys over WHAS in Louisville.

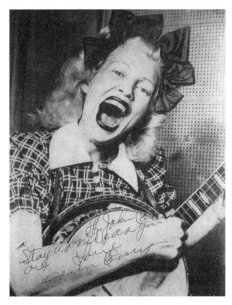

As an entertainer, Cousin Emmy was a dynamo, with her platinum hair and huge toothy smile. Mike Seeger described her as the most high-energy entertainer he'd ever seen. She later became one of the first women to head her own band. As an instrumentalist, she became the first woman to win the National Old Fiddler's contest in Louisville, but her best instrument was the banjo. In 1937 she joined the "Mountaineer Jamboree" in Wheeling, where she met Grandpa Jones and taught him her frailing banjo style. By 1938, she was back at WHAS and

Cousin Emmy. Courtesy of John Cohen.

then moved to Atlanta for stints on WAGA and WSB in a show called "The Cross Roads Follies" as Cousin Emmy and Her Kinfolks. In 1941 she joined the "Mid-day Merry-Go-Round" at WNOX in Knoxville, and in 1941 she was at WMOX in St. Louis, a fifty-thousand-watt station that brought her talent to a wide audience in the Midwest. Her popularity inspired a *Time* magazine article in 1943, in which she explained her show: "First, I hits it up on my banjo, and I wow 'em. Then I do a number on my *guit*-ar and play the French harp and sing, all at the same time. Then somebody hollers, 'Let's see her yodel,' and I obliges. And then somebody hollers, 'Let's see her dance,' and I obliges." In 1944, she made a movie for Columbia, *Swing in the Saddle*. Also in 1944, she played at WAVE radio in Louisville and then in 1945 moved back to Atlanta for the WSB "Barn Dance."

In 1946, the folklorist Alan Lomax was so impressed by one of her performances that he arranged a contract with Decca records, where he introduced a collection of

78s entitled *Kentucky Mountain Ballads* (1947; later rereleased by Brunswick on two 45 rpm extended-play records). Her most popular recording was "Ruby," a song that later became a hit for the Osborne Brothers.

In 1955, she moved to the West Coast and appeared in another movie, *The Second Greatest Sex*. She then became a regular entertainer at Disneyland. In 1965, Mike Seeger and John Cohen, of the New Lost City Ramblers, persuaded her to go with them to the Newport Folk Festival, where she was a smash hit. This led to her being on Pete Seeger's television show "Rainbow Quest" (a video, *Rainbow Quest No. 18*, is available from Norman Ross Publishing, 330 W. Fifty-eighth Street, New York, NY 10019). She also toured with the New Lost City Ramblers in America as well as Europe. Afterward, she and the Ramblers cut an LP, *The New Lost City Ramblers and Cousin Emmy* (Folkways, 1968), and they played several festivals in the 1970s, including the American Folklife Festival in 1971. John Cohen remembered her as "coming on so strong you knew she was mocking herself and country ways, but she was always communicating something exciting."

(With credit to Wayne W. Daniel, "Cousin Emmy: A Popular Entertainer Country Music History Almost Forgot," *Bluegrass Unlimited* 20.4 [October 1985]: 64–68.)

Cousin Emmy: I ain't educated, but I'm sincere.
I don't know much about art, but it's mighty educational I reckon.
(Before playing "Turkey in the Straw" by slapping her cheeks while shaping the tune with her mouth.) You have to be a little off to do this. I feel just like an addled goose struck in the head with a wet corn cob.

JUNE CARTER CASH

Born June 23, 1929, Scott County, Virginia;
died May 15, 2003, Nashville, Tennessee

June Carter is the second of three daughters of Maybelle Addington Carter and Ezra Carter, A. P. Carter's brother. She performed with the original Carter Family beginning at age ten and soon developed into a country comedian, with her back-home accent, innocent but brash country girl manners, and sly flirtation. She went on, however, to become a multitalented artist as an instrumentalist on autoharp, banjo, guitar, and mandolin, a songwriter ("Ring of Fire" with Merle Kilgore), a student of acting with Elia Kazan at the Actors Studio in New York, and an actress and author. Her 1999 album *June Carter Cash* received positive reviews and won a Grammy for Best Traditional Folk Album.

As a comedian, June Carter had role models for her innocent "rubette" character, namely Minnie Pearl and Lulu Belle Wiseman. She was attractive, dressed in frilly and feminine dresses, and she let it be known that she had her eye out for a "feller." Yet she was the butt of jokes as a country innocent coming to town. Her exaggerated southwestern Virginia accent and her batting eyelashes carried the comedy. She also sang novelty and comic songs, such as "Plain Old Country Girl" and "Keep Them Cold Icy Fingers Off of Me." June Carter came up with a comic character, Aunt Polly Carter, that she played for a while, mostly on road shows. Aunt Polly wore a ladylike hat and pantaloons. However, June soon went back to just being herself. One writer described her as doing the rube version of "blacking-up" for the part; that is, getting into a hillbilly mode and exaggerating her backcountry ways.

Underneath the frivolity was a serious and religious person and an artist. She has been on numerous albums, has appeared in films (including *The Apostle* [1997], starring, written, and directed by Robert Duvall, whom she had met when she was a drama student in New York). She has also done television and has written a screenplay and two books, *Among My Klediments* (1979) and *From the Heart* (1987).

June Carter cut her show-business teeth on the Mexican border station XERA, built by Dr. John Romulus Brinkley and allowed for a time by the Mexican government to broadcast at five hundred thousand watts, heard all over the United States and Canada. Brinkley hired a lot of talent from his native Appalachia to attract the interest of gullible people for his questionable and sometimes lethal operations to cure male impotency and to sell patent medicines. The Carter Family became enormously popular over radio and through their recordings, and June became a vital part of their act, both as a singer and comedian.

When the original Carter Family broke up in 1943 after A. P. and Sara went their separate ways, June became a solo performer and then was a central figure in the new Carter Family, made up of Mother Maybelle and daughters Helen, June, and Anita. They traveled for a time with Elvis Presley and then sang at several radio stations, including Richmond's WRNL and WRVA and its "Old Dominion Barn Dance," WNOX and the "Mid-day Merry-Go-Round" in Knoxville, augmented by the then-timid fiddler and sometime guitar player Chet Atkins, and then moved on to Nashville and WSM's "Grand Ole Opry."

June Carter was married to and divorced from Carl Smith. Their daughter, Carlene Carter, is a well-known country singer. She was also divorced from Rip Nix. In 1968 she married Johnny Cash, after touring with him along with her mother and sisters and appearing on the "Johnny Cash Show." She is credited with helping Cash to overcome an addiction to pain pills and amphetamines. Cash had lavish praise for her as one who could "lift me when I was weak, encourage me when I was discouraged, and love me when I was alone, and unlovable." He also called her the "greatest woman I have ever known." June and Johnny had a son, John Carter Cash, now a record producer, guitarist, and songwriter.

Her last two CDs were *Press On* (Risk Records, 1999) and *Wildwood Flower* (Dualtone, 2003), both generously reviewed. There is a lot of footage of her doing comedy on Al Gannaway's videos *Memories of the Legends*, featuring Opry stars of the 1950s (Gannaway Productions, Inc., PO Box 1, Nashville, TN 37202).

June Carter Cash died of complications from open-heart surgery in a Nashville hospital in 2003.

June: I'm too sore to move. I've been riding horses. It's just been terrible. It's made me bow-legged. I'm just sore all over. There was plenty of room between me and the horse—blue sky and sunshine mostly. I had a real polite horse though. Ever' fence we come to, he always let me go over first. I ain't never goin' to ride a-straddle of no horse again. I'm a-goin' to ride sidesaddle. If I ride sidesaddle I can save a little place to set down on!

GARY CHAPMAN

Born August 19, 1958, Waurika, Oklahoma

Gary Chapman was expected to follow in his preacher father's footsteps, but that wasn't to be. However, he did become a gospel singer and a writer of gospel songs, and one of his albums, *The Light Inside*, was nominated for a Grammy. He went to

Nashville hoping to make it as a steel guitar player, but after half-starving for a year and a half, he was invited to join the Rambos, a gospel group. It was Dottie Rambo who encouraged his songwriting. The first performer to record one of his songs was Amy Grant with "Father's Eyes," which became a number one hit in 1979. He and Grant were married in 1982, and he became a guitarist in her band. He continued to write songs that were recorded by such diverse singers as Vanessa Williams, T. G. Shepherd, Kenny Rogers, Lee Greenwood, Barbara Mandrell, and Alabama.

Chapman won the Gospel Music Association's Male Vocalist of the Year Award in 1996. He has won several Dove Awards: Songwriter of the Year, 1982; Praise and Worship Album of the Year for *Songs from the Loft*, 1994; Male Vocalist of the Year, 1996; Inspirational Recorded Song of the Year for "Man after Your Own Heart," 1996; Special Event Album of the Year for *My Utmost for His Highest*, 1996; and Country Album of the Year for *Hymns from the Ryman*, 1998. He has also had Grammy nominations for each of three albums: *The Light*

Gary Chapman. Courtesy of Jennifer Bockman.

Inside, 1994; *Shelter*, 1997; and *This Gift*, 1998. He now has a total of eight Dove awards. A recent album is *Circles and Seasons*, which he recorded, produced, and engineered, performing all vocal parts and instruments.

Chapman's comedic skills rose to the surface in 1996 when he successfully auditioned for host of the TNN show "Prime Time Country." His potential as a host had been earlier noticed by TNN officials when he cohosted the Dove Awards for gospel music and when he developed and hosted a show called "Sam's Place—Music for the Spirit" at the Ryman Auditorium. Even though he describes himself as a quiet sort of person, Chapman rose to the challenge on "Prime Time Country" and developed funny startup monologues and showed a talent for one-liners. He also ended up doing things a "quiet sort of fellow" wouldn't ordinarily do, such as riding an enormous bull down the Las Vegas strip, skydiving, and grappling with a professional wrestler. These antics aren't so far out when you learn that Gary is a licensed helicopter pilot. He was also successful in a largely unscripted show in getting guests to show off their natural wit. Chapman's own comedy won him the Music City News Comedian of the Year Award in 1998. His modesty came through in his acceptance remarks: "I always thought this was the Jeff Foxworthy award. I thought they'd have to scrape his name off it."

With the purchase of TNN by CBS, "Prime Time Country" was canceled, as eventually were all the country music shows for which TNN had become distinctive. Chapman's marriage to Grant, which produced three children—Matt, Millie, and Sarah—also came to an end. However, Gary Chapman continues his career as a witty entertainer, singer, and successful songwriter. When Grandpa Jones died in 1998, Gary Chapman eulogized him with compassion and wit at a memorial service in the Grand Ole Opry House.

BOBBY CHEEK. *See Ernest and Elwood*

LEW CHILDRE

Born November 1, 1901, Opp, Alabama;
died December 3, 1961, Foley, Alabama

Bill C. Malone describes Lew Childre as a "complete" and "extraordinarily versatile entertainer" and as a "singer, instrumentalist, comedian, dancer." Childre, the son of a county judge, was encouraged by his father to study medicine. He graduated from the University of Alabama, where he learned just enough medicine to ease him into his "Dr. Lew" comedy act as a country doctor claiming to cure liver and lights (lung) diseases. He was helped along with this act by years touring with medicine shows. He also performed with a trained dog named Pooch. He sang, played the guitar with a steel bar in the Hawaiian style, and could simultaneously yodel and buck dance around the stage in an astonishing fashion. He had honed these skills in vaudeville and tent-repertory shows that traveled the South.

Childre was adept at improvising dialogue, reciting poetry, and ad-libbing advertisements. This made him a natural for radio, starting out at stations in Texas and Arkansas and then moving on to the big stations: WWL in New Orleans; XERA in Del Rio, Texas; WWVA in Wheeling, West Virginia; the NBC Blue Network; WAGA in Atlanta; and WSM in Nashville. He did few recordings except on radio transcriptions but recorded for Gennett in 1930 and for ARC in 1934. Just before he died, Starday released *Old Time Get-Together with Lew Childre* (1961), and Old Homestead released material from his radio transcriptions, *On the Air 1946, Vol. 1*, in 1983.

Childre joined the "Grand Ole Opry" in 1945 and there formed a partnership with another comedian and entertainer, David "Stringbean" Akeman. At the same time, he did radio transcriptions for several companies, such as Pepsi and General Foods. An avid fisherman, he also patented a fishing lure that made him some money. In 1959 he retired from the "Opry" because of ill health and died two years later.

BILLY "TOBY" CHOATE

Born March 17, 1923, Cambria, Illinois

Billy Charles Choate was literally born in the tent-repertory theater, one started by his grandfather in 1881 and continued by his father. He became an actor, musician, and comedian with the show when he was only a boy. After retiring his own tent-rep show in 1967, he continues to produce, direct, and act in an annual reproduction of the show in Wayne City, Illinois. He is also author of a 1994 book, *Born in a Trunk . . . Just Outside the Center Door Fancy*, that gives an insightful firsthand look at the tent-repertory shows that toured the country in the early part of the last century.

Although the tent-rep shows did some popular farce comedy, most of the plays—usually written by members of the repertory companies—were built around the Toby character and thus were popularly known as "Toby Shows." Toby is a country boy, innocent and ignorant of some things but pure of heart and usually the nemesis of the conniving city slicker who tries to hoodwink the good rural people in the play. Billy, who played Toby, was an accomplished comedian. Between acts, he did additional comedy, supplemented by dancers, musicians, jugglers, magicians, and the like. Usually the evening's entertainment included the After-Show, which featured more comedy, musical numbers, variety acts, and a chorus line. During this period, Choate worked with three of the great country comedians—Lawrence "Boob" Brasfield and his wife Neva, who left the show to play the "Ozark Jubilee," as Uncle Cyp and Aunt Sap, and Boob's brother Rod Brasfield, who later won fame as a comic partner of Minnie Pearl on the "Grand Ole Opry." Billy Choate worked continually with the family show, Choate's Comedians, until World War II. In the war, he served as an infantryman in Patton's Third Army in Germany, saw a lot of combat, and was awarded the Bronze Star for rescuing three wounded comrades during an artillery attack in which he was also wounded.

After the war, Choate joined Bisbee's Comedians and became its general manager in 1953. When the owner, Jess Bisbee, died of a heart attack, Billy Choate, like his grandfather and father, became the owner-manager of a tent-rep theater, which he operated until 1967. His show usually opened in western Tennessee, toured the larger cities of that portion of the state, and then moved on to towns in western Kentucky and Illinois. He and his wife Vera perform in his annual re-creation rep show, with Billy reprising his Toby roles of the past. The show features talent from Wayne City, including students at the local dance studio. Until recent years, Billy also took the show to Greenville, Kentucky, a stopping place for his old tent show.

James married Vera Thomason in 1946, and she became an actress and dancer in Bisbee's Comedians. They have two children, a daughter, Cherita, and a son, Welby.

Following is a Toby Show excerpt from Billy Choate's book, *Born in a Trunk:*

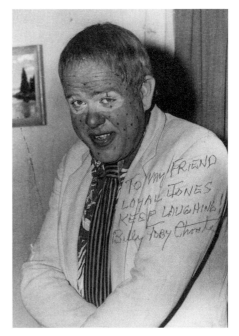

Billy "Toby" Choate. Photo by Lucy Reeder, courtesy of Billy Choate.

> Toby: *And Cousin Fud and his four kids were there. . . .*
> Susie: *He's got five kids, ain't he?*
> Toby: *No, they's only four. Elviry is one . . . (on his fingers) and his twins is two. . . . Oliver is three, and the half-witted one is four.*
> Susie: *You said the twins is two.*
> Toby: *Well, the twins is two.*
> Susie: *No, they ain't. The twins is three.*
> Toby: *All right then, the twins is three. Elviry is four, Oliver is five, and the half-witted one is six!*
> Susie: *Toby Tolliver, you said the two twins is three.*
> Toby: *That's what* you *said.*
> Susie: *I did not. Now listen, the first twin is one, the second twin is two. . . .*
> Toby: *Yeah, two and one is three.*
> Susie: *Elviry is four. . . .*
> Toby: *Four and three is . . . wait a minute, Susie, you got seven already and you ain't counted Oliver ner the half-witted one yet.*

MANUEL DEWEY "OLD JOE" CLARK

Born August 6, 1922, Erwin, Tennessee; died
February 20, 1998, Richmond, Kentucky

Manuel Clark got into show business as a high school student with a band that played at dances, cakewalks, candy pullings, and corn shuckings. This led to him and a friend, Oscar "Shorty" Sheehan, being hired by the blackface duo Pick and Pack (Pick Malone and Pat Padgett) to join their touring show. Calling themselves Sunshine and Stormy Weather, Clark and Sheehan entertained in blackface. Malone and Padgett were dismayed when Clark and Sheehan left the show to finish high school.

Old Joe Clark. Courtesy of Terry Clark.

Members of Clark's family worked for the Clinchfield Railroad, but in their spare time they played banjo and fiddle. Joe became proficient on the banjo and learned a large repertoire of the old ballads and folk songs. Radio was coming into its own when Clark was just a boy, and it had a great effect on him. He dreamed of being a radio announcer, but his musical talents led him into country music despite his religious parents' objections that it would lead him to "being just trash."

In about 1938, Charles Elza, known as "Kentucky Slim," talked Clark into joining Doc Hauer's Medicine Show, which had earlier made use of the talents of Roy Acuff. Kentucky Slim was a smash entertainer in the show, with his "Pork Chop" dance. Clark had been interested in dancing but lacked money to sign up for a tap-dancing class at his high school; instead he observed the classes from the hallway, memorizing the movements and practicing them later. Clark remembered, "Kentucky Slim taught me the greatest thing on earth. He taught me how to take my tap dancing and go into the buck-and-wing." Clark began doing intricate dance steps on stage as a part of his act. For the medicine show, Doc Hauer paid him $3.50 a week, and the whole cast slept in the back of a 1933 Dodge truck. During this tour Kentucky Slim helped him to create a character called Pappy Snodgrass, with Slim serving as straight man. By then he was known as Speedy Clark.

Clark credited Robert Porterfield, the founder of the famous Barter Theater in Abingdon, Virginia, with teaching him some things about vaudeville entertainment and giving him good advice. He and Shorty Sheehan did an hour's show at the Barter

Theater, and Clark remembered, "It tickled Robert Porterfield to death." However, he felt that their show was not right for the Barter Theater and suggested that they try Knoxville's "Mid-day Merry-Go-Round," where they played briefly before returning to Johnson City to form a band called the Prairie Cowboys, taking advantage of the current fad in western attire and music. The band was later renamed the Lonesome Pine Boys.

In 1942, Clark was hired by John Lair at the "Renfro Valley Barn Dance" to do the commercial announcements previously done by the departing Whitey Ford. This fulfilled his desire to be a radio announcer, but he also began to sing the old ballads in the style of Bradley Kincaid and Doc Hopkins. At the age of twenty, he had a clear, high voice and felt that he was on his way as an announcer and singer. However, Uncle Sam called, and he spent five years in the army as a military policeman in and after World War II, during which time he played bass fiddle in the noncommissioned officer club band. When he was discharged, Lair invited him back to the "Renfro Valley Barn Dance," but by then his voice had deepened, and he could no longer sing in his earlier style. Lair, always as inventive as he was parsimonious, made the maximum use of Clark's talents as announcer, singer, musician, and comedian.

Lair came up with the name of "Old Joe Clark," basing it on a Clay County, Kentucky, character of ill repute that he believed was the basis of the song of that title. He thought it would have name recognition. Since the "Barn Dance" was then a network radio show with expensive advertising, admen from the sponsors—Ballard and Ballard, Allis Chalmers, and Proctor and Gamble—got involved in creating a proper image through photographs and other promotional materials. Clark was not enthusiastic about his new moniker and character but less so with some of the costumes they came up with. He said, "It didn't look right. It was fake. Then one night I set down to a mirror and came up with one with the combat boots, little tiny glasses, and the chin beard. A man who owned the Mt. Vernon newspaper happened to be there to take pictures, and that sold Mr. Lair's first big commercial. The sponsors liked it, and that was the way it was." Joe's character was an irascible old man who ordered everybody around, said impertinent things, and told moderately ribald stories. He spat jokes and ad-libbed, teased someone in the band or the audience, did his combination tap and buck-and-wing dance, played the banjo in the old mountain styles, and sang a variety of songs. In addition, in those days, Lair had him perform under his old name of "Speedy" and do commercials under the pseudonym of "Bud Parker," although the radio audiences soon caught on to this deception.

In 1949, Joe left Renfro Valley to join Bill Monroe as a comedian with the Bluegrass Boys, touring for a year and a half. By late 1950, however, he was again at the "Renfro Valley Barn Dance" and stayed there for the rest of his career. He was still performing, although slowed down somewhat by emphysema, until illness led to surgery and his death in 1998 at the age of seventy-six. In his latter years he performed with his son, Terry, also a fine banjo player and singer, as his straight man.

Clark recorded for ARK, REM, Sun-Ray, and Renfro Valley Enterprises, as well as on his own labels. He appeared in two films, *Country Music on Broadway* and *The Renfro Valley Barn Dance*. The Old Joe Clark Bluegrass Festival continues at Renfro Valley, and a restaurant in the Renfro Valley village complex bears his name. In 2001, a statue of him, commissioned by Warren Rosenthal, who owned and rebuilt the Renfro Valley complex in the 1990s, was unveiled at the Renfro Valley Entertainment Center.

Thirty Years of Old Joe Clark is available on cassette (Terry Clark, 420 S. Dogwood Dr., Berea, KY 40403).

> *Emcee: I hear that a windstorm knocked your barn down.*
> *Joe: Yeah, it did.*
> *Emcee: What about your livestock?*
> *Joe: Well, we've got that billy goat in our bedroom.*
> *Emcee: But, what about the smell?*
> *Joe: Well, he'll just have to get used to it.*
>
> *Joe: I wouldn't fly in one of them airplanes.*
> *Emcee: You shouldn't be afraid. If it's not your time to go then you'll be all right.*
> *Joe: Yeah, but what if I'm up there and it's the pilot's time to go?*

ROY CLARK

Born April 15, 1933, Meherrin, Virginia

Roy Linwood Clark, an amply endowed talent—singer, comedian, actor, and musician on numerous instruments—got his start in a musical family. The Clark family moved various places as the father followed employment, settling eventually in Washington, D.C. An early whiz on the banjo, Clark won a banjo contest when he was sixteen, and he soon found part-time employment as a musician. By the late 1950s, he had played in bars and clubs, on shows with Grandpa Jones and Hank Williams, and had landed a spot in Jimmy Dean's band, then playing daily over radio and television in Washington. Dean fired him for habitual tardiness, but Clark appeared on Arthur Godfrey's "Talent Scouts" and went on to Connie B. Gay's "Town and Country Jubilee." Later he played with Marvin Rainwater, George Hamilton IV, and in Las Vegas he was hired to open for Wanda Jackson and to be a member of her band. He also played with Hank Penny in Las Vegas, where he became an avid student of Penny's comedic skills. In fact, Penny, who was rejected as a comedian on "Hee Haw" in favor of Clark, expressed some bitterness that Clark had worked with him just long enough to learn his act and material. Penny later apologized for making such a claim.

Clark recorded for Four Star, Coral, and Debbie, but it was with Capitol that he began to have success with *The Lightning Fingers of Roy Clark* in 1962. A single, "Tips of

My Fingers," was in the Top Ten and moved to the pop charts. Moving to Dot Records in 1968, Clark achieved a Top Ten as well as Top Twenty pop hit with "Yesterday When I Was Young." In 1969, he hit the Top Five with "I Never Picked Cotton" and the Top Ten with "Thank God and Greyhound." He had a number one hit in 1973 with "Come Live with Me." In 1976, he achieved Top Three with "If I Had to Do It Over Again." He had other instrumental and singing successes that were high on the charts.

Clark was hired as a musician and comedian on "Hee Haw" in 1968, and he became one of its hosts in 1969. His comment on the show: "'Hee Haw' may have set me back, but it sure set me up." It gave him a chance to develop his comedy by playing several comic characters: straight man to Archie Campbell; the sissy hotel clerk; Royella, who gave personal advice; a rube in the haystack with the "Hee Haw" Honeys; and a hillbilly in numerous skits.

Since the demise of "Hee Haw," Clark has remained a member of the "Grand Ole Opry" since 1987 and has a regular show in Branson, Missouri, at the Celebrity Theater (formerly the Roy Clark Celebrity Theater). He has also played the Las Vegas hotels and is the first country performer to be inducted into the Las Vegas Entertainers Hall of Fame. He has appeared with the Boston Pops Orchestra and played Carnegie Hall. He has appeared in television commercials and in acting roles (Cousin Roy and Big Mama on "The Beverly Hillbillies") and he has also acted in movies, including *Uphill All the Way* (1987), *Freeway* (1988), *Branson City Limits* (1994), and *Gordy* (1995). His Web site lists sixty available albums, including five released in 2005: *Bluegrass: It's about Me* (Varese), *The Best of Roy Clark* (Intersound), *Hymns from the Old Country Church* (Wonder Disc), and *The Very Best of Roy Clark* (Time Life). To date he has won twenty-five major awards, including three for comedy, twelve for instrumentalist or musician of the year, and three for entertainer of the year.

In recent years Clark has been involved in several business enterprises, such as ranching, real estate, and publishing. He has been awarded at least two honorary doctor's degrees, has donated a lot of money to charity, and has headed fund-raisers for programs that he supports. He is still active as an entertainer with a new band, Roy's Toys.

CLARENCE C. "SLIM" CLERE

Born July 11, 1914, Ashland, Kentucky;
died April 14, 2001, Charleston, West Virginia

Clarence Clifford Clere, whose father, grandfather, and great-grandfather (an Irish emigrant) were fiddlers, also aspired at an early age to play the fiddle. That instrument became his primary means of livelihood for most of his life. But since he was playing on radio stations, which led to personal appearances, somebody had to do comedy, and he was elected. His comedic stage name was Nimrod. "I used to be called a nitwit, then a halfwit, and later I lost the 'half' and the 'wit.' I used to be a stand-up comedian, but now I'm getting so old I have to sit down, and so I'm now a sit-down comedian."

Clere started his career in 1933, before he was twenty, on WSAZ in Huntington with a band called the Melody Boys. Their show was also broadcast over WOBU (later WCHS) in Charleston. Eventually, they moved to a new station, WCMI, in Ashland, Kentucky, playing its first program. He also worked with Riley Puckett and Bert Layne at WSAZ and at WIND in Gary, Indiana, in a band called the Mountaineer Fiddlers. "That's where I learned my comedy, from them. They were good. They knew how to put on a show. They taught me how to ad-lib and to do stand-up comedy." He then joined "The Cross Roads Follies" at WSB in Atlanta from 1936–38, playing with the Boys of Old Kaintuck and continuing his comedy, but in 1938 he came back to West Virginia, to Charleston and WCHS. "The only fault I had with it [WSB] was that the trips were so long—had to stay on the road all the time. I preferred to come back to the mountains. I like little dates—go out thirty or forty miles, put on your show, come back, and get a good night's rest." In 1940, he joined up with T. Texas Tyler (David L. Myrick) for the Slim and Tex duet. He and Tex also played at WOPI in Bristol, Virginia, and WBTH in Williamson, West Virginia.

Eventually, Clere went into the jukebox business in Charleston, and this business also enriched him as an entertainer because he learned every tune that interested him from the jukeboxes. He was later employed by the Charleston Library. He came out of retirement to play with various bands, but mostly he did solo acts, playing the fiddle and doing stand-up (or sit-down) comedy. He also wrote a humorous column for the *Charleston Gazette-Mail*. Slim Clere died in his eighty-sixth year, leaving a son, Robert, and a daughter, Judy Hass.

The following is from a *Gazette-Mail* column of September 15, 1999:

> *When Uncle Dude's son came home from the war, he made good his promise to get his mother some indoor plumbing. He had spent a lot of time in demolitions while in the service and was quite familiar with explosives, which would be a good way to dispose of the outhouse facility on the hill. Grandpa was goin' to miss this relaxin' "two-holer" that he had enjoyed so long. Not knowing that this was the fatal day, he took his newspaper and went to his retreat for his regular call of nature, not aware that his son had planted the destructive device to blow up his outhouse. Grandpa had just entered and was preparing to do what comes naturally. The blast went off and Grandpa went sailing through the air into a treehouse in the top of a large oak tree. He said later, "That's the first time I ever clum' out of a tree that I never clum' into."*

JERRY CLOWER

Born September 28, 1926, Amite County, Mississippi;
died August 24, 1998, Jackson, Mississippi

Jerry Clower was one of the best-known American comedians of the last half of the twentieth century through his performances on the "Grand Ole Opry," some two hundred personal appearances a year, syndicated radio and television shows, thirty albums, and four books. Growing up on a farm in Amite County, Mississippi, and joining a 4-H Club when he was nine, Clower aspired to be an agricultural extension agent working with 4-H Clubs, but he graduated from high school during World War II and joined the navy the next day. After service on an aircraft carrier in the Pacific and three battle stars, he attended a junior college on the GI Bill and then moved to Mississippi State University on a football scholarship.

Jerry Clower. Courtesy of Top Billing.

After graduating with an agriculture degree, Clower worked for the Agricultural Extension Service for a while and then joined the sales force of a fertilizer company. A storyteller all his life, Clower found that his stories were helpful in warming farmers up to his sales pitch. This led to his career as an entertainer. He explained:

> In 1970, I was asked to be on a panel at Texas Tech to talk about fertilizer. I got up and saw they were about half asleep, so I hollered about three times, told them some stories about the Ledbetters, folks I growed up with in Mississippi. There was a radio director there taping everything, and he sent it to MCA at Universal City, California. They [MCA executives] flew to Yazoo City, and thirty days later we had an album [*Jerry Clower from Yazoo City, Mississippi, Talkin'*].

Clower went on to say that he never intended to get into show business. "I just cut the album as a tongue-in-cheek venture to get rid of them, and it was number five on the *Billboard* charts worldwide." He added, "And MCA Records is the most prestigious company in the world, and this old G-rated comic has been on their label longer than any other artist." All of his recordings were on MCA.

He said that his stories came from real-life happenings: "As long as I travel, as long as I see people, I'll have a new story. I think I've proven that the funniest things in the world actually happened." The Ledbetters, for example, were people he actually knew.

After he told a few Lamar Ledbetter stories, the fans wouldn't let him move on. "So I had to add some brothers and sisters to the Ledbetter clan," he said, "but they are all real people." Of course, traditional rural stories are thrown in, sometimes attached to the Ledbetters.

Clower was definitely a southern rural comedian, but when asked how he went over with sophisticated eastern audiences, he said this:

> There's no more North, South, East, and West that we once knew. If you get a laugh in Birmingham, you'll get the same laugh in Boston. You have to tell them everything they need to know to understand the story—and that's where some comedians make a mistake. I don't just say, "We went coon huntin'." I say, "We went coon huntin', which is we got coon dogs, we take 'em into the woods. We turn 'em loose, and they start smellin' on the ground to see if a raccoon's been there, and if they smell 'em, the closer they get the louder they bark, and eventually he'll run up a tree." Then I go on with my coon huntin' story, and they'll laugh just like they do in Birmingham.

Clower joined the "Grand Ole Opry" in 1973, two years after his first MCA recording, which had a long tenure on the *Billboard* charts. Twenty-nine more MCA albums followed, including *Clower Power, Jerry Clower on the Road, Live from the Stage of the Grand Ole Opry, Jerry Clower's Greatest Hits* (certified gold), *The Mouth of the Mighty Mississippi, Fishin', Frogs, Dawgs, and Hawgs,* and *Live at Dollywood.* He also published four books: *Ain't God Good* and *Let the Hammer Down* (Waco, Tex.: Word); *Life Ever-laughter* (Nashville: Rutledge Hill Press); and *Stories from Home* (Oxford: University of Mississippi Press). He is also the subject of a documentary film, *Ain't God Good.* He was the cohost of a syndicated radio show, "Country Crossroads," and a syndicated television program, "Nashville on the Road." He received the Country Comic of the Year award from 1973 to 1981.

Clower was married to his childhood sweetheart, the former Homerline Wells, also of Amite County, and they had four children: Ray, Amy, Sue, and Katy.

A long-time Baptist deacon and Gideon Society member, Clower had some words about humor and Christianity: "Christian folks are supposed to be happy. You laugh, you giggle, and you grin. The Good News of the Gospel makes people happy. God don't expect folks to go around with their lips pooched out. Even if I wasn't a country comic, I'd be happy, looking forward to the blessed hope." Clower believed that people's religion ought to influence their relations with others. As examples, he was outspoken in his support of racial integration and harmony in the South and equal pay for women (although he poked fun at some women's libbers).

Here's a Jerry Clower story from *Jerry Clower's Greatest Hits,* with permission (MCA Records, 1979):

> *They called a deacons' meetin' at the East Fork church. Uncle Versie Ledbetter was up in years, and he didn't get to many of the deacons' meetin's no more, 'cause he thought that*

the young folks, them about fifty or sixty, could take care of the church's bid'ness. But he got word they's fixin' to spend some money, and he got Newgene, his grandson, to take him over to the church house in a mule and wagon for the deacons' meetin'.

And they got in a big discussion about buyin' a chandelier.

Man said, "I move you, Sir, a chandelier for the church." Another deacon said, "I second the motion." The moderator said, "Is there any discussion?" And Uncle Versie said, "Sir, I'd like to speak. I want all of you to know that if we buy a chandelier, they ain't nobody got enough education that when we order it from Sears and Roebuck that they could spell it. Then, if we ordered the chandelier, and it got here, there's nobody in our church that knows how to play it, and what I'm concerned about is we don't need to spend this money on no chandelier as bad as we need lights in the church!"

GENE COBB

Born 1891, Gordonsville, Tennessee;
died 1970, St. Louis, Missouri

Gene Cobb, blackface comedian, radio personality, and manager of tent shows for the "Renfro Valley Barn Dance," began his show-business career in Nashville in tabloid ("tab show") musical comedy when he was twenty-one. He also performed in minstrel troupes, including Neil O'Brien's Minstrels that played small-town theaters and movie houses in much of the South and some of the Midwest. He produced and managed his own tab shows as well as working for others.

Cobb's comedy specialty was the "wench" character Honey Gal, played as a single and with various partners as male counterparts in blackface dialogue comedy. In a 1925 newspaper interview, Cobb said that he based his character on "funny expressions, stories, and dialect" that he picked up from blacks he got to know while clerking in his brother's grocery store as a teenager in Nashville. His pairing with Jack Gray as Honey Gal and Smoke during the 1920s was his most successful act, artistically and financially. Cobb and Gray also had a bit of recording success with *Honey Gal and Smoke* on Gennett (6669), also released on Supertone (9383) and Champion (15627) as *Social Functions*. Cobb also made brief appearances on some of Emmett Miller's 1936 Bluebird recordings (6550/6577), using both his natural and "Honey Gal" voices.

The fading of small-time vaudeville brought about Cobb's move to radio in the late 1930s, first on WGY in Schenectady, New York, with Goff Link as Magnolia n' Sunflow'r, and then in St. Louis, where he did blackface comedy with Pat Daly on the KMOX "Old Fashioned Barn Dance" and other local radio shows.

In 1940, John Lair hired Cobb as comedian and manager of the "Renfro Valley Barn Dance" tent shows, where he proved to be as good a manager as a performer. He is not so well known as a Renfro Valley performer as others, however, because he spent most of his time on the road and was heard on the air mostly during season breaks in

Gene Cobb. Courtesy of the
John Lair Collection, Southern
Appalachian Archives, Berea
College.

late fall and early spring. Print advertising at Renfro
Valley billed him simply as Gene Cobb or Gene
"Nubbin" Cobb, the rube character he developed
when he came to Renfro Valley. The only evidence
of a "Nubbin" routine was captured in a photograph showing him reading "A Letter from Home"
in the vein of those done by David "Stringbean"
Akeman and others. In recordings he did dialogue
routines with other members of the cast in his role
as tent-show emcee. Some of these routines were
recycled from his old "Honey Gal" scripts. In 1947,
he briefly reprised Honey Gal on broadcast portions of the "Renfro Valley Barn Dance," working
with Kentucky Slim (Charles Elza) as Sugarfoot.

Cobb left Renfro Valley in 1948 and settled
in St. Louis. After several small-business ventures
failed, he ended up working as a dispatcher for the
St. Louis Police Department.

(This entry was written by Harry Rice, Berea
College sound archivist.)

Excerpt from a Honey Gal and Smoke routine
by Cobb and Jack Gray, issued by Gennett:

> Honey Gal: Then the lady started
>   servin' chicken?
> Smoke: That lady consulted me with
>   that chicken.
> HG: How'd she do dat?
> S: She brung the chicken out dere
>   and say she's goin' to try somethin'
>   new . . .
> HG: De lates' style?

S: Some society way uv servin' chicken.
HG: Yeah.
S: An' she said to de man over heah, said, "Wheah are you from?" De man
  said he's from New York. She give him de east wing of de chicken. An' den
  she come to de next man and said, "Wheah are you from?" De man say he's
  from California. She give him de west wing of de chicken.
HG: Dat's proper.
S: Yeah. Den she come to de nex' man and say, "Wheah are you from?" De man
  say he was from Canada. She give him de neck a' de chicken.
HG: Ke-rect.

S: Uh-huh. Den she come to me an' says, "Wheah are you from?"
HG: An' what did you say?
S: I says, "I'm from Alabama, but I-I don't want no chicken, ah, no."

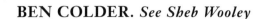

BEN COLDER. *See Sheb Wooley*

BONNIE COLLINS

Born June 9, 1915, Doddridge County, West Virginia

Bonnie Mae Starkey Collins is a storyteller, stand-up comedian, and entertainer, a favorite at folk and storytelling festivals. She came from a musical family and also learned to read music and to play various stringed instruments.

Collins's talent was first noticed when she was a cook in an elementary school. She was a writer of humorous poetry and was asked to involve children in poetry in an early childhood program. Soon she was entertaining groups of teachers, superintendents, and professors in West Virginia and elsewhere in the region.

By the 1960s Collins was kept busy at gatherings with her stand-up comedy and stories. She was especially popular at folk festivals, such as West Virginia's Vandalia Gathering and Jackson's Mill Jubilee and the Berea College Humor Festival. She has also served as a judge at the West Virginia Liars' Contest. Her stories, songs, and comedy are based on her own experiences and local tradition. She tells stories of love, murder and mayhem, and ghosts, and jokes about marriage, preachers, and corpses.

In 1980, Governor John D. Rockefeller IV gave her the Distinguished West Virginian Award. In 1990 she won the Charleston Cultural Center's Vandalia Award for her humorous stories and heritage talks in schools and elsewhere. In 1995, the state's longest-running Homecoming Reunion in Pinch (near Quick), West Virginia, gave her its Good Samaritan Award for "lifting people's spirit."

She quit the circuit when her husband Archie died, but at the urging of family and fans, she, in her eighties and with the help of a walker, returned to work.

Collins: I was brought up in a strict religious home. When we had a protracted meeting, the preacher would come and stay at our house for two weeks—until the vittles ran out or the meeting closed, whichever came first.

One time, we were running low on wood, and my mother, being polite, kept saying, "Stand back and let the preachers up to the fire." Well, I stood back and froze, and finally I went to bed and had a nightmare.

The next morning I came through the kitchen, and there's a preacher eating hotcakes like taking pills. He said, "How are you this morning, young lady?" And I said, "I'm fine, but I had this horrible dream last night. I dreamed I was in a hot place, and there was an old man with a pitchfork chasing me around."

He said, "Why, you know what that was? That was hell. Tell me, what was it like down there?"

I said, "Just like down here. They kept saying, 'Stand back and let the preachers up to the fire!'"

RUEY "CURLEY" COLLINS

Born July 28, 1915, Catlettsburg, Kentucky;
died October 27, 1986, Richmond, Virginia

Basically a fiddler and singer, Curley Collins was also a comedian and, according to his fellow fiddler Slim Clere, he was "the best I ever saw doing blackface comedy." When he was quite young, his father, Neal Collins, a banjo player, sat him down and ordered him to learn to play the five-string banjo. Before that day was over he had learned to play "Soldier's Joy," and he learned also the mandolin, guitar, and tenor banjo. The fiddle came later. He and his father and brother Ransome joined other musicians to play at picnics, private homes, and dances, where they were sometimes rewarded rather well by passing the hat. The Collins family owned a radio and phonograph, and young Ruey became familiar with the music that was played in the early days of radio and the recording industry. His father, Neil, was the composer of the banjo and fiddle tune "Breaking Up Ice in the Allegheny."

Ruey "Curley" Collins, in two roles.
Courtesy of Phillip G. Collins.

Ruey's professional life as a musician and comedian began in 1928 with the Mountain Melody Boys, a group from Catlettsburg, Kentucky, headed by the police chief, Dolpha Skaggs, on WSAZ in Huntington, West Virginia. It was with this group that Collins also became a blackface comedian. In the mid-1930s, he joined up with Tex Forman, Slim Clere, and Reedy Reed to form the Prairie Pals, who played over WCMI in Ashland, Kentucky. When Pop Eckler brought his WLW show "Happy Days in Dixie" to an Ashland theater, he so impressed Collins, Forman, and Reed that they joined his band. Eckler's "Happy Days" show was on the NBC network and was played over WSB in Atlanta. This led to their being invited to WSB, where they played as Pop Eckler and His Young'uns on the "Cross Roads Follies" and were booked out all over Georgia and adjoining states, even into Kentucky for personal appearances. To add to their income, they played over other Atlanta stations, WGST and WAGA, under a different band name.

Eckler also organized fiddling contests and bought a fiddle for Curley, who became so proficient on the instrument that he won the National Fiddlers' Contest in Atlanta in 1938, as well as lesser contests. The fiddle thus became his main instrument. It was probably during this time in Atlanta that Curley met Roy Rogers, who invited him to go with him to California, but he decided to stay with the Young'uns.

In late 1942, Collins and Eckler, along with Benny and Bud Kissinger, joined Scott's Exhibition Shows and performed their way to Wheeling, West Virginia, where they played over WWVA. Collins briefly played over WCHS in Charleston before getting a defense job and going into the army. When he was discharged, he joined Jack Gillette's Tennessee Ramblers, performing over WRVA in Richmond, Virginia, and later on the WWVA "Jamboree." About 1955, Curley with Benny Kissinger returned to Richmond to play on the "Old Dominion Barn Dance," where they were billed as stars of the show. Collins then worked for Automatic Electronic, a division of the General Telephone Company, until he retired in 1979. He and Kissinger continued to perform around Richmond until Collins's death in 1986, mainly on the "Virginia's Lil Ole Opry" in Mathews, Virginia, a show that they helped save from oblivion.

Collins made two commercial 78 rpm (four sides) recordings on Bullet in 1946, with Benny and Bud Kissinger and the Tennessee Ramblers. Included were two of his original compositions, "In the Same Old Way," sung by Benny, and "My Blue Eyed Baby," sung by Curley.

Collins was married to Hazel Maddix in 1935, and they had two children, Phillip and Ramona. He later married Carolyn Treadwell of the singing Treadwell Sisters in Atlanta, and they had one son, Cary Lee. After his return from World War II in 1945, he was married for a short time to Ruth Kazee, of Ashland, Kentucky, with one child, Linda. In 1949, he married Kathleen "Kaki" Williams, a fellow performer, in a well-publicized wedding on the stage of the "Old Dominion Barn Dance" with so many fans, including the governor, that the show had to be moved to a larger theater. From Curly and Kaki's thirty-seven-year marriage came three children: Rueyenne, Robin, and Randy.

(With thanks for material and photograph supplied by Curley's son, Phillip Collins, Lexington, Kentucky; and credit to Wayne W. Daniel, "Tex Forman and Curley Collins Remember Pop Eckler and His Young'uns" *John Edwards Memorial Foundation Quarterly* 6.59 [Fall 1980]: 133–39.)

COON CREEK GIRLS

Lily May Ledford, born March 17, 1917, Lombard,
 Kentucky; died July 14, 1985, Lexington, Kentucky
Charlotte "Rosie" Ledford, born August 15, 1916,
 Lombard, Kentucky; died July 24, 1976, DeLand,
 Florida
Esther "Violet" Koehler, born February 6, 1916,
 Wilton, Wisconsin; died October 4, 1973, Berea,
 Kentucky
Evelyn "Daisy" Lange, born July 7, 1919, St. Henry,
 Ohio
Minnie "Susie" Ledford, born October 10, 1923,
 Lombard, Kentucky; died July 22, 1987,
 Nicholasville, Kentucky

Billed as the first all-women radio string band, the Coon Creek Girls were organized by John Lair in 1937 in Cincinnati around the talents of Lily May Ledford, a regular on his previous shows on WLS in Chicago. They were enthusiastically received over WLW and WCKY in the Cincinnati area as part of Lair's "Renfro Valley Barn Dance." The band included Lily May, Charlotte Ledford, Evelyn Lange, and Esther Koehler. Since Lily had a flower name, Charlotte became "Rosie," Esther became "Violet," and Evelyn became "Daisy." They wanted to call themselves the Wildwood Flowers, but Lair thought they ought to have a quainter name: the Coon Creek Girls. They were an old-time band with fiddle, banjo, mandolin, and bass, playing folk songs and others learned from Lair and fellow performers.

They also did comedy. Their persona, directed by Lair, was of innocent country girls, dressed up in old-fashioned gingham dresses, with country accents. Lair wrote a lot of humorous material into the scripts that the Coon Creek Girls did. They also sang comic songs, such as "How Many Biscuits Can You Eat?"

They were among those invited by President and Mrs. Roosevelt in 1939 to entertain King George VI and Queen Elizabeth of England at the White House. Lily May, always a great storyteller, told about an incident that happened while they were rehearsing at the White House:

The Coon Creek Girls. L-R: Charlotte "Rosie" Ledford, Ester "Violet" Koehler, Lily May Ledford, and Evelyn "Daisy" Lang. Courtesy of the John Lair Collection, Southern Appalachian Archives, Berea College.

A gentleman came in and stood listening. He told me he also played the fiddle and wondered if I might fiddle a few tunes with him. He went somewhere and got a fiddle and came back. He said, "Just call me Cactus Jack." We went to another room and fiddled away for a while. He was pretty good. Later on, I found out that he was the vice president, Mr. John Nance Garner.

Lily May also remembered that the king looked pretty sour, but when they started playing "Sourwood Mountain," "I saw him start patting his foot, and I knew we had him."

When Lair's show moved to Renfro Valley, Kentucky, in 1939, Koehler and Lange left the group, and Minnie Ledford became "Black-Eyed Susie" and joined her sisters in the band. From Renfro Valley, the Girls went to the "Old Dominion Barn Dance" in Richmond, Virginia, and were part of Sunshine Sue's New York Broadway show.

Eventually, they dropped out of show business to raise families, but in 1968, Ralph Rinzler, of the Smithsonian Institution, persuaded them to play the Newport Folk Festival and the Smithsonian's American Folklife Festival in 1972.

In 1938, the original group recorded nine numbers for Vocalion. The three Ledfords did twenty-four additional numbers, released on Perfect, OKeh, Conqueror, and the Renfro Valley label. They later recorded a County LP, *Coon Creek Girls*, and Old Homestead reissued the early 78 rpm recordings in LP format as *Coon Creek Girls— Early Radio Favorites*.

In the 1970s, Mike Seeger persuaded Lily May to revive her career at college concerts and folk festivals. She also was artist-in-residence and taught workshops at Berea College in 1980. In 1983, she recorded an LP, *Banjo Picking Girl*, for Greenhays and appeared on TNN's show "Fire on the Mountain," hosted by David Holt.

Lily May died in 1985, before she was to receive that year's prestigious National Folk Heritage Fellowship Award. However, at the awards ceremony at the Ford Theater in Washington, D.C., three notable musicians—Carol Elizabeth Jones, Suzanne Thomas Edmondson, and Cathy Fink—re-created the spirit of the Coon Creek Girls for the occasion. In 1979 the New Coon Creek Girls band was formed at the "Renfro Valley Barn Dance" around the talents of Jan and Kelli Cummins, Vicki Simmons, and Betty Lin. This band celebrated the music of the original Coon Creek Girls for over twenty-five years. More than a dozen other women performed as part of the New Coon Creek Girls, including Dale Ann Bradley and Pam Perry.

Lily May's art lives on in the current performances of Sandy Harmon of Henderson, Kentucky, who portrays Lily May as a part of the Kentucky Humanities Council Chautauqua Series.

JUDGE RAY CORNS

Born March 19, 1934, Epworth, Kentucky

Although his profession as a lawyer, state official, and circuit judge suggests a serious demeanor, Ray Corns is a funny stand-up comedian, ventriloquist, and motivational speaker. For many years he has been a regular on the "Renfro Valley Barn Dance" and "Jamboree." Born in the mountains of Lewis County, Kentucky, Corns graduated from Berea College and the Samford University Law School. He has served in many Kentucky offices: as legal advisor to two governors, as commonwealth attorney, as juvenile judge, as chief legal counsel for the State Department of Education, and as a circuit judge in the capitol city of Frankfort. He has also been secretary of the Kentucky Justice Cabinet and commissioner of the state police. He is author of a textbook on public school law, a book entitled *Trial of Jesus of Nazareth*, a legal analysis, and he has written a syndicated column of humor called "The Corn Crib." Judge Corns's judgment that the state's system of financing public schools in Kentucky was unconstitutional brought about the Kentucky Educational Reform Act, which made Kentucky a pioneer in school reform and added a total to date of eight hundred million new dollars for education.

While he was a circuit judge in 1970, he traveled on weekends to Chicago to study ventriloquism with the noted ventriloquist Bob Falkner and honed this art as a regular comedian on the "Renfro Valley Barn Dance" and "Jamboree." His comic figure is named Cedric. He has also done stand-up comedy around the country and does many serious talks that are spiced with humor, much of it aimed at lawyers, judges, and the legal profession, but most of his stories have country characters involved.

From a cassette tape, *Are You Confused? Judge Ray Corns*, with permission:

> *A man who was an avid deer hunter decided on the first day of the season to try his hand at the sport again. His wife, who had never been deer hunting, insisted that he take her along, which he did reluctantly. He put her down in the valley where a little brook passed by, with a ford, and he trekked off to the mountainside to a grove of apple trees, where he thought the deer would more likely be passing by. No sooner was he settled in his place than he heard two shots in rapid succession from the valley down below. Thirty seconds later, a third shot, and wondering if his wife had had beginner's luck, he tore out of his hiding place and came down to the area where she was. She was holding a gun on a man, and this fellow had his hands in the air, and he was saying, "Yes, lady, I know he's your deer. You shot him. You can have him, but please, let me get the saddle off!"*

JAMES "FROGGIE" CORTEZ

Born December 5, 1914, Elwood City, Pennsylvania;
death date and place unknown

"Froggie" Cortez came from an Italian family of fifteen children, ten boys and five girls. He replaced Hamilton "Rawhide" Fincher as the principal comedian with Doc Williams's Border Riders on WWVA in Wheeling, West Virginia, and the "Mountaineer Jamboree." Doc Williams remembered, "He really started with me. I hired him in 1937, and that was his first professional job. He sang comedy songs, like 'Courtin' in the Rain.' He worked great in comedy skits. He was that type of comedian, not a great ad-libber of the Bob Hope kind. I used a lot of skits that came from blackface medicine shows, and we made them into rube comedy. He played in those." Froggie wore a rube costume, including an overlarge polka-dot shirt, suspenders, and a floppy hat pinned up in front.

Cortez stayed around WWVA for several years playing with various groups such as Jake Taylor and His Railsplitters in Fairmont, West Virginia, beginning in 1947. He eventually went back to his hometown area of Elmwood, Pennsylvania, and had his own band there. He was married to the former Nellie Lemmon of Kittanning, Pennsylvania, and they had a daughter, Mary Catherine, born in 1939.

JOHNNY COUNTERFIT

Born Ronald DeMoor, March 24, 1956,
Omaha, Nebraska

Ronald DeMoor discovered at the age of five that he was good at imitating people, and so he practiced by sticking his head close to the speaker of the family stereo as they played their favorite country stars and sang along with them—Johnny Cash, Hank Williams, Buck Owens, Merle Haggard, and others. His parents, Robert and Catherine, moved the family to Portland, Oregon, when Ron was three, but they took their love of country music with them. Ron and his twin brother Donald, and Dennis, Donna, and Cheryl grew up in Portland, and Ron graduated from Franklin High School in 1974. Earlier, he had learned to play the guitar, but his real passion was imitating the people he heard on the stereo and saw on television or in the movies—country stars of the day but also politicians, comedians, and actors. Later on, when "Hee Haw" came to television, it was his favorite show, and he studied the comedy of the old pros on the show. Archie Campbell became his favorite country comedian, and he did a rendition of Archie's "Rindercella" in the seventh grade.

After high school, Ron took jobs loading trucks at warehouses and driving a delivery truck, but he started going to local music clubs such as Nashville West. There he imitated Johnny Cash, and others. When he started doing his country music impressions at one particular club every Sunday night in the early 1980s, he drew a following. Then the owner of another club asked him to perform, and he decided that it was time to start charging for his act. At first he used his real name but soon decided he needed a stage name that protected his privacy and also indicated something about his act. Since his main thing was imitating Johnny Cash, he took the name Johnny and deduced that an imitation of "Cash" would be "Counterfit." So he's been Johnny Counterfit ever since. In the age of "lookalikes" he bought wigs and makeup and did Cash, as well as Elvis and others. From the beginning, though, he sprinkled his show with jokes and stories.

Johnny moved to Nashville in 1993 and did the Nashville Network shows "Country Music Family Reunion," "Music City Tonight," "Crook and Chase," "Prime Time Country," and "Opry Backstage." He made the first of many guest appearances on the "Grand Ole Opry" in 1994. He has continued to do clubs but also corporate meetings, county and state fairs, state electric co-op meetings, as well as his own Johnny Counterfit Show at auditoriums throughout the country. He has opened for, or performed with, such stars as George Jones, Merle Haggard, Charley Pride, Reba McEntire, Marty Stuart, and Ronnie McDowell. He has also performed in Branson, Missouri, theaters. His voiceovers for television and radio commercials have sold such products as Kentucky Fried Chicken, Heinz Steak Sauce, Alka-Seltzer, and Post Raisin Brand and have earned him a Silver Microphone Award. He was the voice of Rex, the main character in Disney's animated "Claymation Christmas Celebration," which earned an Emmy and is shown annually. He has appeared on ABC's "America's Funniest People" and is featured on the radio show "Salute to America," sponsored by the U.S. Department of the Interior.

Counterfit calls his impressions "exact and not exaggerations for comedic purposes." However, his audience gets plenty of comedy as he cracks jokes and employs the voices of Ronald Reagan, Bill Clinton, Jimmy Stewart, and John Wayne to tell stories or to recite humorous poems. Indeed, his impressions of the speaking and singing voices of his subjects are startlingly accurate. He even does Archie and Edith Bunker, including their ghastly theme song, which stretches the range of his voice. He commented, "I consider myself an actor, just acting a part." He does a lot of political humor in the voices of the politicians he is featuring, but he explains, "It's spread out evenly. I nail the Republicans as much as the Democrats. One thing you don't want to do as an entertainer is to make an audience member angry. I usually preface the political stuff with, 'Listen, this is just for fun. We're going to spread it around a bit, so don't get upset,' and they don't. I've never had a problem with that."

When asked whether he has performed at the "Opry" in recent years, Johnny replied,

> I have not performed there since the new management came in. Comedy is a lot more important than a lot of the industry people realize. People love to laugh and they need to laugh. The lack of comedians doesn't make any sense except that the people running many venues don't understand entertainment. All they understand is what they hear on the radio today, and if they don't hear it on the radio, they don't get it. That's a problem in the entire business today, the lack of knowledge of entertainment, that is, giving the audience what they want. The "Opry" is severely guilty of that. They're trying to turn it into something it was never intended to be. They don't have enough comedy now. Thank goodness for Branson and Pigeon Forge because they get it. This town [Nashville] is only concerned with record sales. Radio doesn't play very much comedy.

Johnny has three available recordings: two CDs, *Johnny Counterfit on Stage* and *John DeMoor*, in his own voice with orchestra, and *Live in Concert 2* on DVD and VHS (JC Productions, PO Box 292767, Nashville, TN 37229-2767; info@counterfit.com; 615-444-5711).

Johnny makes his home in Nashville with his wife, Karen, their daughter, Elise, and their son, John.

Johnny Counterfit's comedy employs innuendo, double entendre, and other tricks. Here he has John Wayne and Jimmy Stewart reciting a poem:

> *Wayne: All right, Pilgrims,*
> *Well, Mary had a pocket watch.*
> *She swallowed it one day.*
> *The doctor gave her castor oil,*

To pass the time away.
Stewart: The ah castor oil did not work,
    The time it-it-it did not pass.
    So, if you want to know the time of day,
(Much laughter)
    Just look up Mary's . . . uncle.
    He has a pocket watch too!

COUSIN EMMY. *See Cynthia May Carver*

COUSIN JODY. *See Clell Summey*

COUSIN WILBUR. *See Willie Egbert Wesbrooks*

COUZIN ELMER. *See Charlie Payne*

CRAZY ELMER. *See Smilie Sutter*

BETH CREMER. *See Shorty Hobbs and Little Eller*

SIMON CRUM. *See Ferlin Husky*

GEORGE DAUGHERTY

Born December 12, 1932, in Mannington,
    West Virginia

George Daugherty makes his living as a lawyer, but he has had time for other things as well. In addition to calling himself the Earl of Elkview, Daugherty claims he is a "psychoneuroimmunologist," which he translates as "a doctor of perpetual celebration." He further describes himself as "a minstrel who brings a message of love, peace, pride, heritage, and humor." Proud of his American, West Virginia, and Irish heritage, he has

George Daugherty.
Courtesy of George Daugherty.

toured in the United States, Ireland, England, and Germany, presenting more than a thousand shows reflecting patriotism, mountain humor, and his original humorous songs. He has also been involved in community theater in Charleston, appearing in such plays as *Dylan, The Field, Cat on a Hot Tin Roof, Little Mary Sunshine,* and *Oliver.* He produced and appeared in *A Touch of Ireland* with the Irish actor John B. Keane.

His partner in his traveling shows is the musician Buddy Griffin, and he sometimes adds other singers and musicians. Daugherty sings and plays the guitar and banjo, but his sure crowd-pleaser is "Danny Boy," performed on the handsaw. His comedy songs include "I'll Pump the Gas, Jimmy, You Run the World" (a tribute to President Carter's brother Billy); "It Takes a Snuff Dippin' Woman for a Baccer Chewin' Man"; and "Someone Rubbed Our Mayor the Wrong Way" (an ode to the forced closing of a massage parlor). He has two recordings, *The Relax Radio Show* and *The Irish Relax Radio Show*, both on the Braxton label (PO Drawer 100, Flatwoods, WV 26621).

Daugherty practices law in Elkview with his law partner and wife, Suzanne W. Daugherty. In recent months, he has performed at numerous gatherings of West Virginia activists protesting the practice of mountaintop removal in the strip mining of coal.

When I grew up in Elkview, we didn't have motorcycles that you see kids running around on today. We had no such thing up at Elkview. Back then you had to take a girlfriend home on a mule or pony from Wednesday-night prayer meeting or whatever. I had an elk myself.

One Wednesday night I talked this beautiful young lady into taking her home after prayer meeting. She jumped up behind me on the elk, put her arms around my waist, hands around my tummy, and I put my hands on the elk's antlers, and we were just flying up Elk River. All at once she said, "My hands are cold."

I never gave it a thought. I said, "Just put them down in my overall pockets." Lo and behold, I had forgotten that my mother had neglected to mend that hole in my right pocket. So, directly she said, "Well, what in the world is that?"

Thinking very quickly, like us boys up at Elkview do, I said, "That's my chewing tobacco."

She said, "You're just about out, ain't ye, buddy?"

LAZY JIM DAY

Born October 10, 1911, Short Creek, Kentucky; died September 5, 1959

Lazy Jim Day is best known for his "Singing News," which featured the refrain, "But I don't reckon that'll happen again in months and months and months" in the "talking blues" style originated by Chris Bouchillon. He came from a large farming family in Grayson County. His father, William Jesse Day, was a fiddler who called himself Baldy Bill, and son Jim got his start in music accompanying his father on the guitar and banjo at square dances. After about six years in the Short Creek School, young Jim worked on the farm and did odd jobs in the community. When his sister married a man from Mattoon, Illinois, Jim went there and got a job as janitor at the radio station WDZ in Tuscola. One snowy day, when an entertainer couldn't get to the studio, management put Jim on the air. He told humorous stories and got a good response from listeners. So he became an entertainer. He played a six-string banjo as well as guitar and had a pleasant singing voice and a wealth of stories.

It's unclear when he became "Lazy Jim" and started his Singing News. His daughter Leora speculates:

There are two versions of how he got his Lazy Jim name. One was, he may have been too lazy for farming, but I think it was because he spoke in a slow drawling style.

He was just a natural storyteller. I don't know when he started the Singing News, but when he got on radio he started to think, "What am I going to say?" And he started doing these stories with simple banjo riffs. Then people started saying, "You should sing about such-and-such that had happened." They started writing him and sending newspaper clippings or telling him funny stories that had happened in their family.

He moved on to WLW in Cincinnati, WHO in Des Moines, WSM in Nashville, and WWVA and the "Mountaineer Jamboree" in Wheeling. At WWVA he worked with Dusty Owens and Skeeter Bonn.

Day worked for a number of years at the "Grand Ole Opry" and traveled with "Opry" bands, including Little Jimmy Dickens's band. Although he had a great repertoire of jokes and stories, his main thing was the real and made-up news that he sang, always to the same beat and tune, usually with banjo accompaniment. Here is an example:

Well, I've got a little bit of singing news fixed up. I guess you-all heard about that big snake down South that like to have skeered everybody to death:

> *Listen everybody, here comes the singin' news,*
> *With just a little music to chase away the blues.*
> *This news is true, ever' line, says I.*
> *I bet you thirty cents you can't catch me in a*
> *   lie.*
> *A boy down in Florida went to the woods with*
> *   his father,*
> *To drag up some poles, one pole after another.*
> *He thought he saw a twelve-foot snake, I*
> *   couldn't a guessed how long,*
> *I wouldn't even a been there when the other*
> *   end come along.*
> *But I don't reckon that'll happen again in*
> *   months and months and months,*
> *And I don't reckon that'll happen again in*
> *   months and months and months.*

Lazy Jim Day. Courtesy of
Leora G. Day.

King Records included Lazy Jim Day on *Homespun Humor—Various Artists* (726) with "Jim Day's News," "Old Maid and the Burglar Man," "When I Worked on the Farm," "Tickled Her under Her Chin," and "Deck of Cards."

Day married Darlene Blankenship from Iowa, and they had four children: William Davis Day, of Waterloo, Iowa, who plays banjo and bass in bluegrass bands; Richard Jamison Day, also of Waterloo, who plays guitar and sings in bluegrass and contemporary Christian groups; Leora Day, who lives in Short Creek, Kentucky, and is a dancer and dance teacher; and Maurice Day, who died in his forties.

Lazy Jim Day died of a stomach aneurism while on a tour of the East Coast. He was forty-eight. He is buried at Short Creek, Kentucky.

Lazy Jim told the following story on "Town and Country Time," a program sponsored by the Army Recruiting Office and hosted by Jimmy Dean, probably in the mid-1950s:

Pap took off a load of terbaccer. It brought a lot more than he thought it would. He said, "I believe I'll just surprise the old lady." He's always nice to Ma. He got her a new outfit to wear to the county fair, a new hat and dress and a new pair of shoes, and he thought he'd better get him a new outfit—he was goin' to the fair with her. So he bought him a new outfit. He started home, and he come to the old covered bridge, down there by Old Man Hydriack DeWeese's hoglot there. He thought, "Now here will be a good place to put on my new outfit," and he took his old overalls off that he'd been workin' in the terbaccer in, and throwed 'em over in the creek. He reached under the spring seat to get his new suit, and it had slipped out of the wagon, had bounced out. He didn't know what to do. He thought, well, he'd just have to wring his overalls out and put them back on, and he went down to the edge of the water to git 'em, and they'd done floated away. He didn't know what to do. There he was, and he come back to the wagon and turned ever' sack of feed over, and his clothes just wasn't there. He just got upon the spring seat and picked up the lines and said, "Git up, Nell, I'll surprise the old lady anyhow!"

RONALD DEMOOR. *See Johnny Counterfit*

DEZURIK SISTERS

Mary Jane DeZurik, born February 1, 1917,
  Royalton, Minnesota; died September 3, 1981
Caroline DeZurik, born December 24, 1918,
  Royalton, Minnesota

The DeZurik Sisters were a dynamic and popular singing duet whose specialty was the yodel in all of its forms. Coming from a Dutch background, they combined Swiss- or European-style yodeling with what they had heard from Jimmie Rodgers. They have been described doing "Sky-high," "triple-tongue, machine-gun" yodels and "warbling, tweeting, and whistling their way through multiple octaves." Their big gun was a yodel that resembled chickens cackling, hence the nickname "the Cackle Sisters." They also imitated other animals and did bird calls. Their act got them a job with one of the nation's top producers of animal feed, the Ralston Purina Company, on their "Checkerboard Square" program from 1937 to 1941.

The DeZuriks's first job was at the top, the WLS "National Barn Dance," beginning in 1936. There they were advertised as "trick yodelers." They went on to the "Midwest Hayride" in 1941, and then in 1944 they arrived at the "Grand Ole Opry," performing on the Ralston Purina portion of the show. Actually, the Cackle Sisters commuted by train between Chicago and Nashville, appearing on both the "National Barn Dance" and the "Opry." Mary Jane retired in 1948, but her place was taken by her younger sister Lorraine. Another sister, Eva, also sometimes filled in when one or the other of the duo was incapacitated. Caroline and Lorraine finished out their careers in the 1950s at WLS. After their sister act ended, Caroline and her husband, Rusty Gill, continued to perform, for a time hosting a TV show in Chicago called "It's Polka Time."

The only recordings of the DeZurik Sisters were six 78 rpm sides in 1936 for the American Record Corporation, but transcriptions were made of their "Checkerboard Square" radio shows.

LITTLE JIMMY DICKENS

Born James Cecil Dickens, December 19, 1920,
Bolt, West Virginia

Little Jimmy Dickens is a first-rate showman, primarily a singer, but he loves telling jokes and doing one-liners, such as, "I'm Willie Nelson after taxes" (referring to his four-foot, eleven-inch stature). He is best known and loved for his humorous novelty songs "Take an Old Cold Tater (and Wait)," "Country Boy," "A-Sleepin' at the Foot of the Bed," "Out behind the Barn" (all Top Ten), "Hillbilly Fever" (Top Three) and "May the Bird of Paradise Fly up Your Nose" (number one, country).

Dickens got his start in show business at the Beckley station WJLS, moving from there to stations in Fairmont, Indianapolis, Cincinnati, and Topeka. He also toured for a time with the Philip Morris Country Music Show. He signed with Columbia Records in 1948, the year he also became a member of the "Grand Ole Opry." He later recorded for Decca and United Artists. He has recorded serious songs such as "The Violet and the Rose," "I've Got to See You One More Time," and "My Heart's Bouquet." The country music scholar Bill C. Malone thinks that Dickens is one of the great country singers.

Little Jimmy is more of a serious musician and singer than he is a comedian, and yet he has made much of his diminutive size in a variety of colorful suits by Nudie Cohen, and he can't resist telling jokes. One comedian accused him of being a shameless thief of jokes, mentioning that Jimmy once arrived late for a show and told the same jokes that he had just told, without getting much of a laugh. It is mostly his novelty songs that put him in the comedy category. Little Jimmy Dickens was inducted into the Country Music Hall of Fame in 1983.

The Bear Family released a CD boxed set, *Country Boy*, in 1997 and another boxed set, *Out behind the Barn*, in 1998. Other recordings available are *Columbia Historic Edition* (1984) and *Straight from the Heart (1949–59)* (Rounder, 1985). A video prepared by his wife, Mona, *Reflections of Little Jimmy Dickens*, is available from Tater Patch Productions (5010 Concord Rd., Brentwood, TN 37027).

> *Joke: My brother asked my mother if he could go to the bathroom, and this embarrassed her, so she said, "When you want to go to the bathroom, say 'I want to whisper,' and I'll know what you mean." So one day I was lying on the couch, and he came up and said, "I want to whisper." I said, "Right here in my ear." I'm glad he didn't want to carry on a long conversation.*

THE DILLARDS

*Douglas Flint Dillard, born March 6, 1937,
East St. Louis, Illinois*
*Rodney Adean Dillard, born May 18, 1942,
East St. Louis, Illinois*
*Mitchell Jayne, born July 5, 1928, Hammond,
Indiana*
*Roy Dean Webb, born March 28, 1937, Independence,
Missouri*

The Dillards became famous playing the mute but musical Darling Family on "The Andy Griffith Show." However, the core of the group, Doug and Rodney Dillard, have been involved in music all their lives. Their father, Homer, and older brother, Homer Jr., were living-room musicians, heavily influenced by the bluegrass tradition. The younger brothers joined a group in the late 1950s known as the Ozark Mountain Boys (with Doug on banjo and Rodney on bass) and appeared on the "Ozark Jubilee." They played with several other bluegrass bands in the St. Louis area, including one with John Hartford. They formed the Dillards in 1962 with the addition of Dean Webb on mandolin and Mitch Jayne on bass, and Rodney changing to guitar and dobro.

Comedy was a large part of the band's act, and Mitch Jayne soon became the primary humorist of the group. He had been a tail gunner on navy bombers in World War II, an Ozark one-room schoolteacher, and a radio announcer and disc jockey. He soon became the principal spokesman for the band. On their comedy, he commented:

> At the time we went to California, comedy had gone out of fashion in bluegrass. Since we had grown up on the comedy of Flatt and Scruggs, we knew that comedy always works. We'd make up stories from back home, 'cause we knew a bunch of interesting characters. I had always collected them. We were the only storytelling group in California, and it made us different. We told stories about coon hunting and moonshining, about townspeople—changed their names to protect them—real stories about little schoolhouse communities.
>
> Douglas was famous for just standing up there grinning like a possum eatin' sawbriers. Dean played the great stoneface, and when he said something it was acerbic and unexpected. Rodney and I did the comedy between us. Rodney played the youngest kid in the family whose stairs didn't go quite up to the top, but he always had the put-down line.

Rodney Dillard has commented that they always knew that humor was important as a way to make people like them and their music and that their humor was mostly from the Ozarks. However, he emphasized that they made an effort to maintain the dignity of Ozark people by usually making themselves the butt of their jokes.

In California, they played at the Ash Grove, got a contract with Electra, then a folk label, and made three albums: *Back Porch Bluegrass* (1963), *Live . . . Almost!* (1964), and *Pickin' and Fiddlin'* (1965). Their big break was doing six episodes of "The Andy Griffith Show" on CBS from 1963 to 1965. In the first episode, they have speaking roles, while in the rest they are mute. Nevertheless, they evoke much laughter as they create bedlam. Richard Kelly, in his book *The Andy Griffith Show*, wrote, "Their essential function in the show was to provide a comic menace to the town." Kelly also quotes the producer, Sheldon Leonard: "[T]hey did threaten. . . . But our feeling was that they were comedy menace rather than legitimate menace." The Darlings played the uncivilized hillbillies coming into contact with the relatively genteel folks of Mayberry, with each group trying to understand the other. Andy played a mediating role between the Darlings and the townspeople in much the same way that he was a buffer for inept Deputy Barney Fife. In the years following, Mitch Jayne assumed a role similar to Andy's between the band and its audiences, being their spokesman and also their interpreter, always with a great deal of humor.

Jayne also began a sideline writing career. His *Forest in the Wind* was published in 1966; *Old Fish Hawk* followed in 1969 and became a movie in 1980, and *Home Grown Stories and Home Fried Lies* was published in 2000. A novel, *Fiddler's Ghost*, was published by Wildstone Media in 2007. Jayne left the group in 1976 to return to Missouri and write for state newspapers and magazines, although he rejoins them for special concerts.

The Dillards were never a typical folk or bluegrass band, although they emphasized their folk roots to take advantage of the folk revival. They added drums and electric instruments, including a steel guitar and even an orchestra in recordings—much to the chagrin of true-blue bluegrass fans—and they experimented with country rock and pop. However, they continued to play traditional tunes and songs, along with more recent compositions by Bob Dylan and Paul McCartney. They got on the pop charts with a single, "It's About Time," and toured with Elton John.

After leaving Electra, the band made albums with Anthem, Poppy, Flying Fish, and Crystal Clear. *Live . . . Almost!* on Electra is probably the best album for a taste of their comedy.

Sibling rivalry and disagreement over musical styles eventually brought a split in the Dillards, with each brother going his own way with other bands. In recent years, however, Doug, Rodney, Dean, and Mitch have come together to reprise the old band with traditional bluegrass instruments and to play several festivals and gigs each year. They carried on comedy, with Mitch as the centerpiece until he finally retired after a Carnegie Hall concert in 2002. The old Ozark stories still brought a good response from their audiences.

Mitch Jayne: We were invited to the Newport Folk Festival and met Judy Collins, Joan Baez, and Bob Dylan. Joan sang a folk song we'd been singing since we'd been together ["Old Blue"], but she didn't sing it like we did. She sang it slow and sad. Rodney said, "Do you suppose we've been singing it wrong?" I don't believe Joan Baez felt the same way about dogs that we did in the Ozarks.

We had an old man back home who made good whiskey. He'd never gone to jail because people respected him for his good whiskey. He carried his own snake, because we were a religious folk, and you didn't drink unless you'd been snake-bit. We just had this one snake, and we just about wore him out! (This story inspired one of the Dillards' best-known songs, "Dooley.")

DUKE OF PADUCAH. *See Benjamin "Whitey" Ford*

ALBERT ELLIOT

Born January 6, 1934, Big Stone Gap, Virginia

When Albert Elliot worked with the Stanley Brothers as one of the Clinch Mountain Boys, Carter Stanley came up with the name of Towser Murphy for the comedic character he wanted him to play. Eliot joined the Stanleys in the latter part of the 1950s and went with them to Florida, where they played for over three years. Elliot did doubles comedy with another member of the band, Bill Napier, who played mandolin and guitar and whose comedic stage name was "Dad" Napier.

"We had a little thing we did on each show, a skit, and jokes, you know," Elliot related. "We took turn about. We were both dressed up as comedians. I wore a pair of bibbed overalls and an old-timey brimmed hat. Bill wore a checked shirt and a pair of pants too big for him with a great big latch pin in the front holding them up. We got our skits from a book that Carter had."

In Florida, the band settled around Live Oak, and they played on the "Suwannee River Jamboree" over local television, sponsored by Jim Walter Homes. They also traveled widely and recorded for Starday and later King Records. Elliot played mandolin and bass fiddle. He also had his own band, Albert Elliot and the Blue Ridge Partners. He worked for a year with Charlie Moore and the Dixie Partners, playing mandolin and singing harmony, and then in 1982 he did Friday- and Saturday-night shows at the "Grand Ole Opry" as a part of Charlie Louvin's band.

Elliot married his hometown sweetheart, Geneva Boggs, and in Big Stone Gap, Virginia, they raised six children: Albert Jr., Frankie Lee, Michael, Angela, Sheri, and Misty. He eventually left the entertainment business to work at the local public health department. He has been retired since 1983, but he volunteers as a driver of a transit bus for the senior citizens' center. He also still plays music and does comedy.

CHARLES ELZA. *See Kentucky Slim*

BILL ENGVALL

Born William Ray Engvall Jr., July 27, 1957,
Galveston, Texas

When Bill Engvall went off to Southwestern University in Georgetown, Texas, he planned to become a teacher. But he got a job at a bar and found that he could make customers laugh. He moved to Dallas and worked as an emcee at the Comedy Corner, which also included warming up the audience for the featured comedians. This gave him a chance to perfect his comedic skills. Engvall is no rube comic, even though he has a southern accent. He is from a new generation with a somewhat different sense of humor from that practiced by the older country comedians. Although he did not start off in Nashville, like many other country comedians, he has often been associated with country music venues and has performed with country singers.

After touring the comedy clubs for a year, he moved to Los Angeles to see if there was a place for him in TV and film. He shortly won the "Laff Off" competition in San Diego, and this opened the way for him in several TV shows, including the "Tonight Show" and the "Rosie O'Donnell Show," and he also appeared on and hosted "An Evening at the Improv." He was in the films *Split Image* and *Logan's Run* and played characters on "Designing Women," "Golden Palace," "Delta," and "The Jeff Foxworthy Show." He prefers stand-up comedy to film or video acting because of the intimate contact with a live audience. He relishes those who come up and tell him that his comedy made them feel better, made them forget their problems for a little while.

Even though Engvall is pretty sophisticated, he employs a lot of the old rural southern charm, being modest and telling stories that make him the butt of his humor, especially in his routines about being stupid. He has written a book reflecting this trait of laughing at oneself, *You Don't Have to Be Dumb to Be Stupid.* Two of his most popular routines are "Stupid People" and "Stupid Stuff." He also has an affinity for the world of animals and can be funny about that too, and his own children have provided grist for his mill.

In 1992 he won the American Comedy Award for Best Stand-up Comedian, and his 1996 Warner Brothers album, *Here's Your Sign*, sold over five hundred thousand copies and was number one on *Billboard's* comedy chart for fifteen straight weeks and for seventeen weeks on the country album Top Ten. He also teamed up with Travis Tritt for a video, also called *Here's Your Sign.* Two more recordings are *Dorkfish* (1998) and *Now, That's Awesome* (2000). In 2002 he recorded *Cheap Drunk: An Autobiography.* In 2002, *Here's Your Sign Reloaded* appeared, and in 2004, *A Decade of Laughs.* Beginning in 2000, Engvall did the Blue Collar Comedy Tour that lasted for three years with fellow comics Jeff Foxworthy, Ron White, and Larry the Cable Guy. This venue was so popular that it was made into a feature film in 2003, *Blue Collar Comedy Tour: The Movie*, with a soundtrack album. A television show, "Blue Collar TV," was launched on WB Channel in 2004. Another DVD, *Blue Collar Comedy Tour: One for the Road*, was released in 2006. *Delta Farce*, a movie with Larry the Cable Guy, was released in 2007, and *Bait Shop* was released in 2008.

Bill Engvall and his wife Gail have two children, Emily and Travis, and they live in Los Angeles.

ERNEST AND ELWOOD

Bobby M. Cheek, born March 29, 1943, Swain
  County, North Carolina
Edwin Bruce "Butch" Medford, born 1945, Canton,
  North Carolina

Butch Medford related how he and Bobby became a comedy act:

> We were up at Hoyt Mason's house at Bethel, having our big Saturday-night jam session. Hoyt's daddy, Tibb, said, "Bobby, why don't you make up some lies about Butch's barnyard animal noises?" We went upstairs and worked on it for about thirty minutes, came down, and did it for the crowd. Well, they laughed—two or three were down on the floor laughing.

Right after that, Bobby and Butch dressed up in old clothing when they did a benefit for a local fire department, with Butch reading a script that was pinned to Bobby's back for a humorous routine. This went over well, and they became Ernest (Butch) and Elwood (Bobby). They had been great fans of the comedy team of Lonzo and Oscar, and they used some of their routines and also specialized in doing similar harmonies with mandolin and guitar accompaniment.

Ernest and Elwood did local venues until their neighbor, the bluegrass banjo whiz Raymond Fairchild, suggested that if they were going to perform, they ought to get paid for it. That sounded good to them, and Fairchild promoted them to managers of the many bluegrass festivals that he worked. Soon they were traveling to the Northeast, Southeast, and Midwest. One of their most appreciative audiences is at the annual Tennessee Homecoming at the Museum of Appalachia at Norris, where they perform all day for three days on four stages. In addition to their comedy, Ernest imitates animal noises, and they do the great song parodies of Lonzo and Oscar. They have written or collected other comic songs as well, such as "The Grass Is Greener 'round the Septic Tank."

Ernest and Elwood (Bobby Cheek
and Edwin "Butch" Medford).
Courtesy of E & E Productions.

A few years ago, Bobby Cheek had a car wreck that damaged blood vessels to his
brain, which brought on a stroke. This misfortune sidelined their act for a time, but in
1996 they came back. He could no longer play the guitar, but he took up the tub bass,
and Butch switched from mandolin to guitar. They continue their zany humor, much
of which is ad-libbed. At a festival in Michigan, rife with gnats and mosquitoes, a gnat
flew down Butch's throat. He said, "Lord, Elwood, I've swallered a gnat!" Elwood said,
"Well, he'll have to walk down. We ain't got no water."

Butch works at a local company that makes pallets for cargo. Bobby is retired from
the Champion Paper Company in Canton. They have produced four tapes of their
comedy and music: *Ernest and Elwood: Twenty Years of Shooting the Bull* (1993), *Ernest
and Elwood with Rev. Bill Snyder* (1993), *Ernest and Elwood Tribute to Lonzo and Oscar*
(1995), and *Ernest and Elwood: Live in the Smoky Mountains* (1995), available from E &
E Productions, PO Box 1755, Canton, NC 28716.

> *Elwood: We went to see Uncle Warsaw here the other day. We went on Interstate
> 40 for about twenty miles.*

Ernest: Yeah, we cut off on Highway 209 and went through Bowlegged Valley there for about sixteen miles.

Elwood: Then we cut off on a little two-lane state road. It was called 116, and you go up there about six miles and turn left . . .

Ernest: On this little two-lane gravel road for one and a half miles and cut right on a loggin' road.

Elwood: Then when you get on that loggin' road across Betsy's Gap, and it comes down over there into a little trail . . .

Ernest: You hit this little foot trail, and you go up it for about six miles and cut off on this horse trail . . .

Elwood: And you go on that horse trail for three-quarters of a mile, and you come to a creek . . .

Ernest: And there hung a grapevine, and you've got to swing across the creek to get to Warsaw's side of the branch . . .

Elwood: And you swing across the creek on that grapevine . . .

Ernest: And Uncle Warsaw lives way on top of the hill up there.

Elwood: We went up there to Uncle Warsaw's house, and there was a note he'd pinned on the screen door. It said, "We'll be back in two days. We have gone to the country."

ETTA MAY

Born in Bald Knob, Arkansas, so she says, but she
refuses to give out personal information, including
a birth date

Etta May says she grew up in a farming family, the youngest of ten, the rest boys, and she claims her mother didn't realize she was a girl until she needed a training bra. Although she gives out some information about her husband, Delbert, and their children, a daughter and three sons, Rob, Skip, Ernie, and Tramp, they may not answer to these names.

Etta May talks of two incidents that started her thinking about doing something other than driving a school bus, which she did for a decade. The first was seeing Barbra Streisand in *Yentl*, about a girl who wanted to succeed in life and took steps, somewhat devious, to do it. The second had to do with a cousin who died of cancer but felt fulfilled because she had done a lot in her life. While Etta May was visiting the dying cousin in Los Angeles, she and her husband went to the Comedy Store on a night that featured an open microphone for new comics. She got up and told stories about her family and various happenings, and this led to a job at the Comedy Store in Las Vegas at a thousand dollars a week. Another version of her start as a comedian was that she was volunteering as a bingo caller, and the "ball sucker got stuck . . . with a roomful of angry Catholics." She started telling stories and kept them laughing all evening.

However she got her start, Etta May went on to become the Female Comic of the Year at the American Comedy Awards in 1999. She was also on "Jeff Foxworthy's Greats of Country Comedy" in 2000; "Showtime's Aspen Comedy Festival," hosted by Jerry Seinfeld; "The Fifteenth Anniversary of the Comedy Store," hosted by David Letterman; was featured in a Time-Warner video that was nationally distributed in 2002; and she was on the "Oprah Winfrey Show" in 1994. She has also appeared in several movies and TV sitcoms and was on two nationally syndicated radio shows, "Bob and Tom" and "Rick and Bubba," and had her own show, "Ask Etta," from 1995 to 2000, syndicated in the United States and Canada. She has a fan club of over forty thousand members.

Etta May. Photo by Zlozower, courtesy of Etta May.

Although she is from a rural area and dresses as a country woman (bandana on her head, 1960s horn-rimmed cat-eye glasses, polyester pants, and a frumpy sweater), not all of her comedy falls into the country category. For example, her jokes about gaining weight and raising children are universal concerns. She is irritated at how sophisticated executives in places like Los Angeles disparage people who come from rural or small-town places, and she has some pungent comebacks. She has been described as "Minnie Pearl with a migraine."

Etta May and her family now live in Lexington, Kentucky. She describes the "breathtaking scenery of Kentucky" and the people as friendly . . . with deep human feelings in contrast to the urbanites she had encountered living in Los Angeles. She commented, "In New York and LA, you *survive*. I feel like I'm *living* in Lexington." She now mostly does comedy clubs and conventions, such as Carl Hurley's Cavalcade of Comedy for Motorcoach Travelers at Renfro Valley, Kentucky. She also works comedy clubs for about twenty weeks of the year.

Etta May has three DVDs or videos available (*I'm Not White Trash . . . I'm Financially Challenged, The Evolution of Etta May,* and *Southern Fried Chicks*) and three CDs (*Life on a Pedestal, Not Another Pretty Face,* and *A Real Woman*). See www.ettamay.com for details.

Here are a couple of her comments:

You know you're getting fat when you sit in the bath tub and the water in the toilet rises.

My kids remind me of hemorrhoids. Every time I sit down, they start irritating me.

TOMMY FAILE

Born September 15, 1928, Lancaster, South Carolina;
died August 2, 1998, Gastonia, North Carolina

Tommy Faile was a singer, guitarist, fiddler, songwriter, and comedian. He was a longtime associate of Arthur "Guitar Boogie" Smith at WBT-TV in Charlotte, but earlier he had made music and played comedy with the venerable entertainers Dewitt "Snuffy" Jenkins and Homer "Pappy" Sherrill and their group, the Hired Hands, in Columbia, South Carolina.

Faile started comedy early in his career: "When I got into radio in 1946 with Snuffy Jenkins and Pappy Sherrill, we used to do little skits on the stage. We'd also do little plays at the end of every show. That's where I learned to do it." It was during the eighteen years with Arthur Smith and His Carolina Crackerjacks, however, that he became well known, since the show was syndicated to some sixty-five stations throughout the country. "I was a feature with Arthur Smith at WBT from the time television started. Actually, we were the first country group to do national television, on the 'Kate Smith Hour,' out of New York. We pioneered with the 'Arthur Smith Show' on WBT-TV." There Faile created a character called Cousin Fudd with material he had heard over the years, as well as some written by Smith's brother Ralph (see the Smith brothers). Among the comedy he and Ralph Smith did was something called "Counselors of the Airwaves." "We put on robes, and we had professors' hats, with a little tassel hanging down. People would send in problems, and every one of them would be signed So-and-So Bates, every kind of name you could imagine, but always the same last name. We'd give stupid answers. Ralph would write most of them."

Tommy Faile. Courtesy of Dorothy Morford.

Faile was Arthur Smith's featured solo singer. Smith was quoted in a *Charlotte Observer* article (August 8, 1998, by Don Huntley) calling Faile "one of the best male singers in country music." Smith went on to say, "I had only respect for Tommy. . . . He's morally one of the best men in the world. If he told you something, you could put that in the bank." After Arthur Smith and His Crackerjacks left WBT-TV, Faile had his own show on the station for seven years. He also continued to do show dates with Arthur Smith as lead singer and comedian.

Faile was a prolific songwriter, his best-known song being "Phantom Three-O-Nine," which sold a million and a half copies for Red Sovine. In more recent years, Faile worked as an announcer at local radio stations, most recently at WKNT in Rocky Mount. He also played at festivals in the Carolinas.

"Comedy was very important," Faile commented in 1996. "I have people stop me on the street to tell me what a memory it was to meet me. They'll say, 'We used to wake up every morning to your show, and we'd know what time it was by the things you did on the program.'"

Faile's last composition, played at his funeral, was "The Shirt." It came about, according to his friend Dorothy Morford, in this way: "He was down to a fiddler's convention in South Carolina, and he was to be one of the judges. He walked up to Pappy Sherrill and said, 'How are you feeling?' Pappy said, 'Well, I'm about ready for my last white shirt.' And Tommy said, 'That's just got to be a song.'"

JOHN HENRY FAULK

Born August 21, 1913, Austin, Texas;
died April 9, 1990, Austin, Texas

John Henry Faulk was a humorist, teacher, political activist, radio-show host, and a regular on television in the country comedy show "Hee Haw." The son of a sometime-socialist trial lawyer and judge, Faulk grew up with an affinity for liberal causes and a great love of the Bill of Rights, especially the First Amendment. His humor was in the style of Will Rogers, wielded as a lance to form an opening for serious ideas about American life, the government, and the foibles that beset society. Although his approach was rustic, delivered in a Texas twang, his ideas were sophisticated and intellectual.

Faulk graduated from the University of Texas, greatly influenced by the folklorist of the Southwest J. Frank Dobie. Dobie encouraged him to study black and white folk speech; Faulk earned his M.A. degree with a thesis in which he phonetically transcribed African American sermons. Faulk taught in the English department at the University of Texas, where he led students to deal with oral language directly rather than written versions of spoken speech, and his interest in folklore expanded from the black community to Texas folklore in general. His work among blacks, as well as the friendship with J. Frank Dobie, a pronounced liberal, led him to espouse unpopular political solutions to racial and other problems in America.

At first, a bad eye kept Faulk from enlisting in the army at the beginning of World War II, so he joined the Merchant Marine instead. However, by 1944 the army was willing to take him, and he enlisted and trained as a medic but wound up serving as an education officer.

Faulk's academic studies in folklore and the spoken language were helpful in developing his humor. After the war, he started out as an announcer-humorist on local Austin radio stations, creating such characters as Old Man Mosteller, Calvin Banks, Aunt Effie McDoo, and Congressman Guffaw. A master of dialect and mimicry, he made his characters believable but also very funny, yet there was a serious message underneath. His humor was satirical, playing off of current events, always with the intent of getting his audience to rethink their attitudes about basic principles and to make moral decisions.

Faulk's popularity on Austin radio led to his being hired to do a show on but had never been a member of the American Communist party, nor had he been involved in the activities that AWARE alleged. AWARE's blacklisting of performers had resulted in other performers, writers, and newscasters being fired and not being able to get work elsewhere.

With the famed lawyer Louis Nizer as his attorney, Faulk sued AWARE and its director for libel. Although CBS took a dim view of his suit and many friends advised him against it, Faulk was determined to have his day in court and to challenge the practice of blacklisting, which he thought was un-American. He was supported by such famous people as the actors Tony Randall and Kim Hunter and the newscasters Charles Collingwood and Edward R. Murrow.

The suit finally came to trial in 1962, and Faulk won a $3.5 million judgment, the largest that had ever been awarded in such a suit to that date. However, only seventy-five thousand dollars was ever paid, with most of it going to Faulk's attorneys. From the time he was fired until the conclusion of the trial, no network or radio station would hire him because of the blacklist. Nor did his vindication in the suit improve his employability, for by then he was seen as a controversial figure. He made his living by lecture tours, where he talked about the importance of the Bill of Rights and freedom of speech. Of the First Amendment, he said, "It puts every American citizen of every color, of whatever walk of life precisely on the same footing." One speech brought him a standing ovation from the students at William and Mary College. He also did a one-man show, staging the Texas characters he had created for radio to highlight his humor and satire.

In 1978, John Aylesworth, one of the creators of "Hee Haw," recommended to the producer Sam Lovullo that he hire Faulk. Lovullo had the courage to do so, and Faulk was on the show until 1981. Lovullo received some negative response from those who thought Faulk was too political in his humor. However, he and Faulk sat down and worked out historic and patriotic routines that were less offensive, and he kept Faulk on the show.

Faulk was married three times, to Holly Wood in 1940 (one child); to Lynne Smith in the late 1940s (two children); and to Elizabeth Peake in 1965 (one child). He died at seventy-seven in Austin, shortly after he retired from "Hee Haw."

(With credit to John Henry Faulk, *Fear on Trial* [Austin: University of Texas Press, 1983]).

Following is a bit of Faulk's satire on religious commercialism:

Calvin Banks, he invented a do-it-yourself baptismal kit. It was for shut-ins, and if you sent your money ahead of time, prepaid, Calvin would send you an autographed picture of Jesus Christ. His eyes would follow you everywhere you went in the room.

HAMILTON "RAWHIDE" FINCHER

*Born January 30, 1911, Anniston, Alabama;
died 1980s, Newcastle, Pennsylvania*

Hamilton Fincher grew up in Texas and Oklahoma, and he and his brother, Shorty Fincher, both musicians, drifted into radio work in the 1930s. They eventually took their band, the Cotton Pickers, to KQV in Pittsburgh, where Hamilton met and was hired by Doc Williams as a comedian with his Border Riders. Doc took his group to WWVA and the "Mountaineer Jamboree" in 1937. Shorty Fincher and the Cotton Pickers soon followed. As a comedian with Doc Williams, Hamilton became "Rawhide" Fincher. However, he suffered a major accident shortly thereafter that took him out of show business for several months. Doc Williams remembered, "The day after Christmas [1937], someone torched the apartment building he and three other members of my band were living in. Rawhide tried to get out a window onto a drainpipe, and he lost his hold and fell about twenty-five feet onto a sidewalk. He spent a while in the hospital." When he recovered, he continued his comedy with Doc's group, but he left after several months to rejoin Shorty, and they eventually moved to the Lancaster-York, Pennsylvania, area, where they ran a music park and played over radio as the Prairie Pals.

SHUG FISHER

*Born George Clinton Fisher Jr., September 26,
1907, Tabler, Oklahoma; died March 16, 1984,
California*

Shug Fisher—so named because his mother called him "Sugar" in the southern tradition but also to distinguish him from his father, for whom he was named—was a comedian and musician who played with a variety of entertainers and bands, a song composer, and he appeared in Roy Rogers movies and in television series.

Fisher got his interest in comedy from traveling shows, especially those with rube characters. He developed his own rube comedy and later added a stuttering act. He also made himself a hobbyhorse that he rode around stage and into the audience. Fisher's father had been an old-time fiddler, and he had learned to back him up on guitar. He also learned to play the fiddle, as well as mandolin and bass, and he was a singer as well. He saw that he would be more attractive as an entertainer by having comedic and musical abilities.

Fisher moved to California when he was eighteen and worked in the oil fields. His talent got him onto a program called the "Hollywood Breakfast Club," and later he was invited to join the Hollywood Hillbillies, headed by Tom Murray. Then he joined the Beverly Hill Billies, which included the versatile Stuart Hamblen, and soon he went with Hamblen and a group he had formed. After a brief time at the border station XERA, Hugh Cross invited Shug to go back east as a partner to join the WWVA "Mountaineer Jamboree" in Wheeling, West Virginia. They later went to WLW's "Boone County Jamboree," where they played for four years as the Radio Pals.

Fisher returned to California in 1941 to work for Lockheed Aircraft. In 1943, he joined the famous Sons of the Pioneers, playing the bass fiddle and doing comedy for their personal appearances. He went back and forth between Stuart Hamblen and the Pioneers. His work with the Pioneers led to an invitation from Roy Rogers to do movies, and he did sixteen with Rogers. He was also in additional films, including *The Man Who Shot Liberty Vallance* and *Cheyenne Autumn*. He had an early exposure to television on the "Ozark Jubilee" on ABC-TV. He later joined up with Ken Curtis, then a singer as well as actor, and they drifted into television series: "Ripcord," "The Beverly Hillbillies," and "Gunsmoke."

As a composer, he is remembered for "A Million Memories," "Cincinnati Lou," "Forgive and Forget," and "I'm Not Foolin' Now." He recorded with Hugh Cross and the Radio Pals in 1937 on Decca. He also recorded with the Sons of the Pioneers on RCA.

Shug Fisher was married to the former Peggy Summers.

BENJAMIN "WHITEY" FORD

Born May 12, 1901, Desoto, Missouri;
died June 20, 1986, Tennessee

Benjamin Francis Ford was born in Missouri but was reared by a grandmother in Little Rock, Arkansas. Though best known as a comedian, the "Duke of Paducah" was a musician on tenor banjo, mandolin, and harmonica who formed his own Dixieland jazz band in 1922 to play medicine shows, vaudeville, burlesque, and dramatic tent shows. He was a member of Otto Gray's Oklahoma Cowboys, credited as one of the first bands to play what became known as western swing. He was also an original member of the WLS "Show Boat" and "National Barn Dance," was emcee for Gene Autry's WLS radio show, was a writer, emcee, and comedian on the NBC "Plantation Party" radio show, was a founder and part-owner of the "Renfro Valley Barn Dance," and was a member of the "Grand Ole Opry" from 1942 until 1958. He became famous

Whitey Ford, the Duke of Pad-
ucah. Courtesy of the John Lair
Collection, Southern Appalachian
Archives, Berea College.

as the Duke of Paducah, a moniker he acquired while playing over KWK in St. Louis. He was from nowhere near Paducah, but that city made him an honorary citizen, mayor, and Paducahan-by-adoption. He was also honorary mayor of Paducah, Texas. He dressed up in a sporty, belted, and too-small suit and a derby or porkpie hat. His parting line, some variation of "I'm goin' to the wagon, folks. These shoes are killin' me," was known to millions of people.

Ford claimed to have 450,000 jokes that he had filed under numerous categories. This file was sold to the producers of "Hee Haw," and thus his gags lived on through the life of that show. He owned nearly five hundred joke and humor books published in the nineteenth and early twentieth centuries, including those of such humorists as Fred Allen, Milton Berle, Eddie Cantor, Henny Youngman, Sam Levenson, Irvin S. Cobb, and Opie Read, and these, along with some six hundred humorous radio scripts, are now in the Emory University Library in Atlanta. Ford had dug much of the humor for his routines and radio scripts from this impressive collection of American humor. He privately published one book, *Funnee*, in 1980, with the Duke of Paducah listed as the author. The Country Music Hall of Fame has his scrapbooks, some radio scripts, microfilm, and photos relating to his career.

After leaving the "Plantation Party" in 1942, Ford went overseas to entertain ser-vicemen. On returning, his agent booked him for three appearances on the "Grand Ole Opry." He was such a hit that he was invited to become a member, a term that lasted sixteen years. There, the Duke of Paducah was a comedic star ranking alongside Minnie Pearl and Rod Brasfield. After he retired from the "Opry," he continued to live on his chicken and cattle farm near Brentwood and became a popular after-dinner speaker on serious subjects (such as "You Can Lead a Happy Life?") with humorous underpinning, but he also continued to tickle audiences as a stand-up comedian. He cut an album of his humorous monologues for Starday in 1963 (*Button Shoes, Belly Laughs, and Monkey Business*). He owned two circuses and in later life re-created a side show, medicine show, and fair midway that resulted in another Starday album in 1963 (*At the Fair*). He also appeared in two movies, *Country Fair* and *Country Music on Broadway*.

The Duke was well respected as a responsible and thoughtful citizen who supported many charitable causes. He was an avid reader of religious history and philosophy, Emerson being his much-quoted favorite. He led a busy life in retirement, but a long battle with cancer eventually sent him to a nursing home, where it is said that he maintained a humorous demeanor until the end. He was inducted into the Country Music Hall of Fame posthumously in 1986.

Excerpts from one of the Duke's monologues:

Yes, sir, I'd shore like to be an explorer. I'd like to be one of them fellers that goes to the out-of-the-way places and digs up ancient ruins. Louie Buck is that kind of explorer. Last week he went over to the other side of town and dug up a date with an old ruin that looked like she had been buried for years. . . .

My wife is an explorer. Yeah, she goes through my pockets every night. Oh, that's the fattest globetrotter I ever seen! That woman has girdled the world, and you ain't never seen anything funnier with a girdle on—unless it's her. Looks like a rubber band around a watermelon. . . .

My wife went to one of them travel bureaus one time and said, "Me and my husband want to go to Europe, and I don't know if we want to take your A-tour, your B-tour, or your C-tour." The travel agent said, "Lady, if your husband is as big as you are, you better take our Detour. . . ."

On my last trip around the country I had more bad luck. I lost my hat in Hatsville, my coat in Coatsville, my gloves in Gloversville, and I lost my vest in Vest Virginia. Oh, boy! I sure am glad I didn't go through Pants-alvania.

Yes, friends, I'd like to be an explorer and travel o'er land and sea, but the only place I ever travel is back to the wagon, yelling, "These shoes are killing me!"

TEX FORMAN

Born September 13, 1915, Pargon, Kentucky

Trying to get Tex Forman's real name out of him isn't easy. When first asked, he said, "Pendoris Pigeon-Puss Pug-Nose Pot-Belly Texas-T Tokey-Top Side-Liner Dishwater-Hands Forman, 'Tex' for short." With persistence he admitted that he was born in eastern Kentucky as Otho Woodrow Forman. Like many other radio pioneers, Forman grew up in a musical family that bought and played popular phonograph records. However, the family also made music themselves, Tex learning the harmonica at an early age. He got his first guitar at twelve with three dollars borrowed from his cousin. It was a Sears-Roebuck Bradley Kincaid "Houn' Dog" guitar, and since Kincaid was at the time a popular singer on the WLS "National Barn Dance," perhaps this guitar steered him toward the life of an entertainer.

The Formans moved to Mansfield, Ohio, when Tex was sixteen, and there he got a job singing and playing harmonica and guitar over the radio station WMAN, but with no pay. He later teamed up with the fiddler Reedy Reed to play on street corners and in poolrooms, earning enough to buy a ten-dollar T-Model Ford. When Chief Black Hawk came through with his medicine show, he hired Forman and Reed to make music, and Forman also played blackface comedy.

In the early 1930s, Forman and Reed joined a band called the Prairie Pals that also included Ruey "Curley" Collins and Clarence "Slim" Clere, two other eastern Kentucky boys who were playing at a bar in Ashland, Kentucky, and doing a radio show over WSAZ in nearby Huntington, West Virginia. Forman developed a country rube act with the band.

Tex Forman.
Courtesy of Tex Forman.

Then Pop Eckler brought his popular WLW (Cincinnati) "Happy Days in Dixie" show to town and offered jobs to Forman, Collins, and Reed. "Happy Days" was broadcast over the NBC network and was heard over WSB in Atlanta. Impressed by the show, the WSB booking agent offered Eckler's band a job over WSB. They arrived in 1936 and joined the "Cross Roads Follies," first as Pop Eckler and His Barn Dance Gang and later Pop Eckler and His Young'uns, by then including the singer Kay Woods. Forman was billed as "chief comedian and all-round cut-up." He also played the guitar and sang Jimmie Rodgers songs, winning a yodeling contest in 1936.

Eckler, Tex remembers, was a master booker. The band traveled all over Georgia for shows, and Eckler organized fiddle contests that were popular. Eckler also rented the Atlanta Burlesque Theater and started a Saturday-night "Radio Jamboree," part of it aired over WSB from 1938 to 1940. The Young'uns also played over two other Atlanta stations, WGST and WAGA, although under other names, since they were under contract to WSB.

Tex was a popular showman as a guitarist, harmonica player, singer, yodeler, and rube comedian, quick with a quip on- and offstage. However, he did not make any commercial recordings. He left Atlanta in the early 1940s and returned to Mansfield, Ohio, where he became a bricklayer and house builder. In 1966, he moved back to Georgia, settling in Douglasville, where he built a house and rental apartments. He has continued to play music but says it is harder now to get a band together.

(With credit to Wayne W. Daniel, "Tex Forman and Curley Collins Remember Pop Eckler and His Young'uns," *John Edwards Memorial Foundation Quarterly* 6.59 [Fall 1980]: 133–39).

Some comments from Tex Forman:

> *I'm getting so forgetful now, the other night I went to go to bed. I throwed my pants in the bed and hung over a chair all night! Can't remember a thing.*
>
> *If you're going to call me, be careful what you say, 'cause I get mad awful easy on the phone. If you're going to give me a ring, put a diamond in it.*

JOE FORRESTER

Born Hickman County, Tennessee, March 21, 1919

Joe Forrester is the older brother of Howard "Howdy" Forrester, a fiddler with Bill Monroe, Roy Acuff, and other bands. There were four of these musical brothers, with Clyde and Clayton, whose father, grandfather, and uncle were contest-class fiddlers. Joe's first instrument was the harmonica, but he became a western swing guitarist and a bass player, and he also sang lead and harmony. He started doing comedy about 1938 as "Lespedeza" with Herald Goodman's Tennessee Valley Boys at the suggestion of Fiddling Arthur Smith, who was the most famous member of the group. For this role, Forrester dressed up in baggy pants, suspenders, a wig, and blacked-out teeth. Sometimes he dropped his pants to show off white cutoffs (later dyed red because the white pants looked too shockingly to the management like nothing at all). Initially, the Tennessee Valley Boys played over WSM and did personal appearances, but earnings were low, and in 1939 they moved to KVOO in Tulsa, where they started a barn-dance show called the "Saddle Mountain Roundup."

Joe, Howdy, and Howdy's new wife Wilene, renamed Sally Ann, also played on numerous other western stations until Joe was drafted in 1941. He served in the Fourth Infantry Division, landing at Utah Beach on D-Day. He advanced with his division through France, Belgium, Luxemburg, and into Germany. In the battle of the Hurtgen Forest, the Americans took heavy casualties, and after eight months of combat, Forrester was sent to the rear with combat fatigue and reassigned to Paris. He was discharged in 1945.

Howdy and Sally Ann had played with Bill Monroe and His Bluegrass Boys before the war, and when Howdy was discharged, he rejoined the Bluegrass Boys and Sally

Ann, and he procured a job for Joe as well. Monroe was interested in Joe's comedy and put him to playing the bass. However, Monroe thought that "Lespedeza" was too hard to pronounce, and Joe became "Josephus," doing comedy routines with Lester Flatt as the straight man. Incidentally, when Howdy rejoined the band and brought along Joe, they arrived the same month that Earl Scruggs joined in December 1945. Thus, Joe was with the band when, according to experts, real bluegrass music was formed.

After only a few months with the Bluegrass Boys, the three Forresters went to work with Art Davis and then joined Georgia Slim Rutland on the "Texas Roundup" at KRLD in Dallas. There they mostly played western swing music, with Joe doing his Josephus character for comedy. In 1949 the Forresters moved back to Nashville, where Howdy joined Roy Acuff's band, Sally Ann got a job with the Social Security Administration, and Joe worked at post offices in the Nashville area until he retired. Now in his eighties, he continues to play music. He lives in Hermitage, Tennessee.

(With credit to Murphy Henry, "Joe Forrester: Forgotten Bluegrass Boy," *Bluegrass Unlimited* 37.2 [August 2002]: 44–50).

BILL FOSTER

Born January 1, 1939, Chattanooga, Tennessee

Charles William Foster was born into a family of musicians, storytellers, and singers— Appalachian for several generations on his father's side, and his mother was seven-eighths Cherokee. His grandfather played in a North Georgia string band, and he passed along to his grandson jokes and one-liners he used on stage. Foster grew up in Soddy Daisy, Tennessee, among traditional musicians, and he described their special brand of humor as "Appalachian."

Foster started playing the banjo in his early teens, but mostly for fun. He eventually enrolled at the University of Chattanooga, then transferred to East Tennessee State University, where he studied English and importantly folklore, which gave him a chance to fully understand his cultural heritage. After graduation, he enrolled at the University of Alabama and earned a doctorate in English. He taught English at the University of Alabama and played in a band called Sour Mash. When he moved to North Alabama State University at Florence, he was asked to start a folk festival. He performed in it with his brother, just back from a tour in Vietnam, mainly doing Blue Sky Boys songs. Among others who performed at the festival were the McLain Family Band from Berea, Kentucky. Foster thought it was a great idea to have a family band, and when his brother moved away in the mid-1950s, he talked his wife Anne, daughter Melissa, and son Will into forming a family band. The Foster Family Bluegrass Band was so successful that they performed about forty-five weekends a year from 1957 to 1995, with son-in-law John Green joining them for the last several years. They did the usual bluegrass music but put their special twist on non-bluegrass songs. Bill was adept

Bill Foster.
Courtesy of Bill Foster.

equally with bluegrass banjo picking and with the old clawhammer style from his home community. In addition, he enlivened their concerts with jokes and one-liners. "The audience," he says, "likes to hear something funny between numbers."

Foster's sense of humor is heightened by his studies in folklore and literature. It is also grounded in his sense of Appalachian humor, which, he notes, "delights in word play." For example, he sometimes ended their concerts with, "We would like to say that in the eighteen years we have been performing, and all the audiences we've ever played for, this audience tonight—has been the most recent." He also liked to use fictitious song titles, such as "She Was Only a Moonshiner's Daughter, but We All Loved Her Still." Another type of humor, a bit different, is saying, "After this song, we're going be driving back home. Those of you who are in the habit of praying, pray for us, but if you're not in the habit, just leave us alone. We don't want you practicing on us!"

Bill Foster continues to teach English, and he still performs, sometimes solo, and sometimes with Anne, or he gets the band together for special events, such as the annual Tennessee Homecoming at the Museum of Appalachian at Norris.

Here is a Bill Foster story:

> My Grandpa was sort of a self-taught veterinarian. We were in Claude Stewart's store one day when someone came up and said, "Garland (my Grandpa's name), I've got a problem. My mule limps one day, and the next day he don't. I've tried everything, but I can't figure it out. What should I do?" Grandpa said, "The next day he don't limp, sell him!"

TOM C. FOUTS. *See Captain Stubby and the Buccaneers*

JEFF FOXWORTHY

Born September 6, 1958, Atlanta, Georgia

Jeff Foxworthy is undoubtedly one of the most popular comedians ever, with three albums that have sold over eight million copies and books that have also sold in the millions. His success was based primarily on the formulaic statement, "You might be a redneck if. . . ."

Foxworthy, however, is not a redneck, as the term is generally understood. He grew up in Atlanta in a middle-class home, graduated from Georgia Tech, and once worked for IBM. His redneck humor is somewhat different from the old rural humor, where entertainers of rural background told rural stories primarily to rural people. In redneck humor, someone who probably isn't a redneck tells stories about rednecks to people who also are not rednecks, or who take pride in having risen above such a designation. Redneck jokes have a harder, more negative edge than most of country comedy, reflecting formerly tabooed subjects such as incest and sexual looseness or perversion. However, Rick Bragg, the former *New York Times* reporter and a shrewd observer of southern ways, has defended the accuracy of Foxworthy's humor:

> A lot of people who listen to Foxworthy wind up nodding their heads, "Yeah, he's got that just right." The things he did when the Olympics came to Atlanta, he nailed so close to the bone, it was almost uncomfortable. The truth is, he got a lot of it right. The reason he was so popular among outsiders was he did reinforce the stereotypes . . . but he was also, though, popular among us southerners, laughing at ourselves.

Foxworthy recently commented that while he is known for redneck jokes, they take up no more than five or ten minutes of his show. The rest of his humor deals with sunnier and more acceptable subjects that were common in the older rube humor, and he has said that he will not do any more redneck books. While he still does redneck as a routine, he wants to be recognized also for his other humor, such as his caricatures of strange and probably fictional relatives, his comments on society in general, southern speech, comparison of California with the South, marriage, and family and baby humor.

His most popular album (triple platinum) is *You Might Be a Redneck . . .* (1994), but his second, *Games Rednecks Play* (1995) also went double platinum. His third album, *Crank It Up: The Music Album*, with the band Little Texas, came out in 1996. He is a multiple Grammy winner and has published eleven books, most of them on the redneck theme. In 1995, ABC-TV launched "The Jeff Foxworthy Show." It lasted only one year on ABC, but NBC-TV picked it up for the 1996 season. He also did an HBO

Jeff Foxworthy.

comedy special and two Showtime specials. Beginning in 2000, Foxworthy was coproducer of the Blue Collar Comedy Tour, with Bill Engvall, Ron White, and Larry the Cable Guy. The tour was so popular that it ran for three years to ninety cities and reportedly grossed fifteen million dollars. Warner Brothers released a feature-length movie in 2003, *The Blue Collar Comedy Tour: The*

Movie, which premiered on Comedy Central and was watched by more people than any other of their programs. It reportedly sold two and a half million copies in its DVD/VHS form. A soundtrack album was also released in 2003 and ranked in *Billboard's* Top Ten. "Blue Collar TV" was launched on WB Cable as a series. *Blue Collar Comedy: One for the Road* was another DVD, released in 2006.

Among his other recordings are *Greatest Hits* (1999), *Big Funny* (2000), *Best of Jeff Foxworthy* (2000), and *Have Your Loved Ones Spayed or Neutered* (2004).

Foxworthy lives in Atlanta with his wife Pamela (Gregg) and his two daughters, Jordan and Julianne. He continues do specials, to appear on television talk shows, to open for country artists such as Vince Gill, to host "The Foxworthy Countdown" of Top Twenty-five country hits that is syndicated to some 225 stations. His charity work is mainly concentrated on the Duke University Children's Hospital, of which he is honorary chairman and for which he has helped raise four million dollars in the last few years.

RANDALL FRANKS

Born November 21 in an undisclosed year,
Decatur, Georgia

Randall Franks is known as the Appalachian Ambassador of the Fiddle, playing tunes that came down from his fiddling great-uncle and great-grandfather. He is also proficient on the mandolin, guitar, and mountain dulcimer and is an award-winning bluegrass, gospel, and country singer and musician, television and movie actor, comedian, and humanitarian. He is a published writer and journalist and a promoter of bluegrass and gospel music.

As a child, Randall heard a variety of traditional fiddle music at family reunions and other gatherings, and he says that at the age of eight, he heard somebody play "The Orange Blossom Special," and this inspired him to learn to play the fiddle. He was later to study classical violin at the same time that he was learning tunes and fiddle techniques from veterans of the Georgia Old-Time Fiddlers' conventions, such as Gordon Tanner, son of Gid Tanner of Georgia Skillet Lickers fame; Cotton Carrier, the host of "WSB Barn Dance"; Anita Sorrels Wheeler Mathis, the onetime Georgia State fiddle champion; and Dallas Burrell.

While he was still in elementary school, Randall formed a bluegrass band, the Peachtree Pickers, that appeared on Atlanta television and were guests on "The Grand Ole Opry." The Father of Bluegrass, Bill Monroe, noticed the group and Randall's skill on the fiddle, and he invited Randall to join him on tour as a fiddler when Kenny Baker left his band. Randall jumped at the chance and toured for several months before returning to finish college. However, he had the rare opportunity to learn from the old master as well as from another member of Monroe's band, Tater Tate.

Randall was enrolled at Georgia State University in Atlanta, where he studied business administration and commercial music but also continued performing with his Peachtree Pickers. It was during this time that he led an effort to form the South Eastern Bluegrass Association (SEBA). Through SEBA, he also supported the creation of the International Bluegrass Music Association (IBMA), and he later appeared as a presenter on its annual awards ceremony.

After graduation, he became sales and promotions manager for MBM Records in Atlanta, where he discovered that bluegrass and gospel music were a hard sell to music distributors. This knowledge led him into a lifelong effort to promote bluegrass and gospel. He joined the Marksmen Quartet on five of their most successful recordings in the 1980s, and that group helped to form the Southern Gospel Music Guild. He joined the cast of WRFG's "Bluegrass Festival," a popular Atlanta bluegrass show, and hosted other shows on the station. He also served as host of "Sacred Sounds," which featured bluegrass gospel on WGFS in Covington, Georgia. During these years, he performed or recorded with some of the greats of bluegrass and gospel, including the "Grand Ole Opry" stars Jim and Jesse McReynolds.

Randall Franks. Photo by Terry Pennington/Catoosa County News, courtesy of Randall Franks.

As an actor, Franks played the role of Officer Randy Goode for five years on the popular television series "In the Heat of the Night," starring Carroll O'Connor on NBC, CBS, and in reruns on TNT and Turner South. He testifies that he learned a lot about comedy from O'Connor. Randall has also appeared in other movies, such as *Desperate for Love*, with Christian Slater; Hallmark Hall of Fame's *The Flamingo Rising*, with William Hurt; *Phoenix Falling*; *Firebase 9*; and *Blue Valley Songbird*, with Dolly Parton on Lifetime. Franks has used his celebrity status as a movie actor to promote old-time fiddling, bluegrass, and gospel music and several humanitarian and charitable works, such as serving as an honorary officer in the antidrug organization DARE.

Comedy came early in his career through his childhood gospel group, the Peachtree Pickers. He commented:

> I remember the first time I realized I could make people laugh. We were performing at Everett's Bluegrass Barn in Suwannee, Georgia. Just before we went on my glasses fell into the sink and broke. Without my glasses, I am as blind as a bat. I couldn't see my set list, I couldn't see to put the capo on my guitar, I couldn't see the faces in the audience. So I began playing the vision problem and throwing out

every country joke I knew, and the audience rolled in the aisles with laughter. I knew then that I wanted to make people laugh whenever I went on stage.

Franks did comedy with this group in their regular gigs and at appearances on the "Grand Ole Opry" and on the early cable "Country Kids TV Series." Later on, he gave credit to three persons who sharpened his comedic skills: the Georgia Music Hall of Fame member Cotton Carrier, the longtime host of the "WSB Barn Dance;" Carrier's wife, Jane; and the country humorist Doodle Thrower of Tallapoosa, Georgia. A mechanic by trade but also the bandleader of the Golden River Grass, Thrower had appeared at the National Folk Festival and the 1986 World's Fair in Knoxville. Franks played fiddle with Doodle's band and served as straight man for his humor. Randall said this of Doodle: "I watched him put crowds of any size or any socioeconomic background in the palm of his hands and make them laugh, cry, or simply come to their feet in elation. I learned a lot of comedy from him."

In 1994, Franks teamed up with "Doc" Tommy Scott, one of the last of the medicine show entertainers and a onetime "Grand Ole Opry" performer. He and Scott brought the Last Real Oldtime Medicine Show to the 1996 Atlanta Olympics, and he worked with Scott on his traveling show up into the twenty-first century. Franks hosted and narrated the PBS documentary on Scott, entitled "Still Ramblin'." He commented on this experience of working with Ramblin' Tommy Scott: "We had a great time bringing together some wonderful country comedy routines. We worked really well together. While this style is not what really sells to the standup audience of today, I am very proud of the classic feel that we created. 'Doc' Tommy Scott knows how to make an audience laugh, and he is tops when it comes to entertaining."

Randall Franks has made many recordings over the years, including fiddle tunes, and he has appeared on the recordings of other major performers. Among his available recordings are: *God's Children, Tunes and Tales from Tunnel Hill, Sacred Sounds of Appalachia*, and *Comedy Down Home* with "Doc" Tommy Scott, *Golden River Fiddlin'*, and others. (Available from Randall Franks Fan Club, PO Box 42, Tunnel Hill, GA 30755.)

Randall has always harbored a love of writing and has written articles for various music-related journals, such as *Bluegrass Unlimited* and *Precious Memories*. He also does a syndicated entertainment column, "Southern Style," for News Publishing Company of Georgia. He helped Tommy Scott with his autobiography that was published in 2007 as *Snake Oil, Superstars, and Me* (Katona Productions) and is also writing *Tales of the Gravelly Spur: Appalachian Reminiscing and Recipes*, including stories that his mother shared with him, some of his experiences in growing up with visits to his grandparents' farm, and also family recipes and humor. Earlier, he coauthored *Stirring Up Success with a Southern Flavor*, a cookbook with recipes from celebrities, as a fund-raising project for the Catoosa (Georgia) Learning Center.

Randy Franks lives in Ringgold, Georgia.

Here is a routine that he performed with "Doc" Tommy Scott:

Randall: Did I ever tell you about Uncle Elige and the automobile?

Tommy: No, did he buy one?

Randall: Well, he borrowed one from Uncle Cletus and took his boys on a trip.

Tommy: Lige Doolittle had some boys? I didn't know that.

Randall: He did. They was twin boys, two of 'em, sure was. Their names were Will Dolittle . . .

Tommy: Will Dolittle?

Randall: And Won't Do-a-Lot.

Tommy: And Won't-Do-a-Lot?

Randall: They went on this trip to the big city of Ellijay. Along the way, the boys kept seeing these great big signs on the side of the road.

Tommy: I love to read them signs on the side of the road.

Randall: Yeah, they're awful nice. Some of them are very pretty. But they said, "Take Ex-Lax and Feel Young."

Tommy: Take Ex-Lax?

Randall: Yeah, "Take Ex-Lax and Feel Young." Up the road a way, Uncle Elige pulled off and got him a Moon Pie and an RC and then went in, and the boys said, "We'd better try some of that," and they got 'em a great big box—said it tasted just like chocolate.

Tommy: I bet it did!

Randall: They took a bunch of it there, and after a while Uncle Elige turned to them and said, "Now, boys, do you feel any younger?" They said, "No." Little ways on up the road, he asked one more time, said, "Boys, you'all feelin' any younger? Well, maybe you ought to take some more of that stuff."

Tommy: They loved that chocolate.

Randall: Yeah, they did, they always did. Just before gettin' to Ellijay, he asked one more time, said, "Will, you feelin' any younger?" Will said "No." He said, "Won't, you feelin' any younger?" He said, "No, but I've just done a childish thing."

("Uncle Elige's Automobile," copyright 1999, Randall Franks/Peach Picked Publishing, BMI.)

KINKY FRIEDMAN

Born Richard Friedman, October 31, 1944, Chicago, Illinois

Kinky Friedman—comedian, country musician, bandleader, and mystery writer—was born a Chicago city boy, but the family soon moved to Austin, Texas, where his father was an education professor at the University of Texas. Later, the elder Friedman bought a ranch, Rio Duckworth, where he ran a summer camp for boys. Kinky created the fiction that he was born in Palestine, Texas, and thus could call himself "a Jew from Palestine." Friedman liked the idea of being a westerner. He said that cowboys and

Jews have one thing in common: they both wear their hats indoors. Friedman studied psychology at the University of Texas and while there headed a band, King Arthur and the Carrots. After graduating, he joined the Peace Corps and served three years in Borneo, where he commented that he was assigned to teach people to farm who had been farming for thousands of years.

Returning to the United States, Friedman organized another band, Kinky Friedman and His Texas Jewboys, a takeoff on Bob Wills's Texas Playboys, revealing his sardonic sense of humor. They headed to California in 1971, and shortly thereafter Friedman made a name for himself with a biting humor that was decidedly political, hitting at both the Left and the Right. Friedman was a child of the 1960s with its "let it all hang out" freedom of speech, and he was frequently ousted from stages for offensive language and searing commentary. Bill C. Malone described him as "colorful and outrageous." The *New York Times Book Review* called him "the world's funniest, bawdiest, and most politically incorrect country music singer." The California record moguls shied away from his antics, and so the band moved to Nashville, where they were guests on the "Grand Ole Opry," to the bewilderment of a portion of the audience as well as some in the music industry. However, Friedman had a real love of tradition and for country music and made friends in Nashville. There he and the band got a contract with Vanguard, which released their *Sold American* in 1973 with such cuts as "Ride 'em Jewboy." Later, with the help of Willie Nelson, Tompall Glaser, and Waylon Jennings, he recorded *Kinky Friedman* for ABC Records. It contained an example of his satiric sense of humor, aimed mostly at anti-Semites, "They Ain't Making Jews Like Jesus Anymore." In 1976, he and the band did *Lasso from El Paso* for Epic, featuring Bob Dylan and Eric Clapton. The band broke up in 1979, and Friedman's last recording was a solo act, *Under the Double Ego*, for Sunrise, in 1983.

In 1975 and 1976 Friedman and his band became part of Bob Dylan's Rolling Thunder Review tour. In 1979, Friedman moved to New York and appeared at the country music venue the Lone Star Café. In the 1980s, he turned his talents to mystery-novel writing. At last count he has turned out fifteen novels, featuring a Jewish private eye who was once a country music singer. His titles are intriguing: *Elvis, Jesus, and Coca-Cola* (1993); *Armadillos and Old Lace* (1994); *God Bless John Wayne* (1995); and *The Love Song of J. Edgar Hoover* (1996). He has also published other books, such as *Kinky Friedman's Guide to Texas Etiquette: Or How to Get to Heaven or Hell without Going through Dallas–Fort Worth*.

Friedman lives alone, except for a passel of dogs, cats, donkeys, and such, on his animal rescue ranch in the hill country of Texas near Medina, and he does a column for the *Texas Monthly*. Kinky ran full-swing for governor of Texas in 2006 as an independent with the slogan, "Why the Hell Not?" As the late Texas writer Mollie Ivins pointed out, he wouldn't have been the first country singer to be governor. With hard-hitting comments and his trademark humor, Kinky got a lot of publicity. However, with four strong competitors, he went down to defeat. He blamed the low voter turnout of 33 percent and, according to Jay Root in a blog, he commented, "The people didn't really speak. They mumbled." He also said he intends to continue to be politically involved and may even run for office again.

(With credit to Bill C. Malone and Bobbie Malone and their interview with Kinky Friedman, September 3, 1999.)

BROTHER DAVE GARDNER

*Born June 11, 1926, Jackson, Tennessee;
died September 22, 1983, Myrtle Beach,
South Carolina*

Dave Gardner, one of the best-known humorists of the third quarter of the twentieth century, entered show business as a drummer in a television show hosted by Wink Martindale in Memphis. It was on this show that he began telling jokes and developing his southern-boy routine that led him through honky-tonks and roadhouses and on to an appearance on the "Jack Parr Show" and a contract with NBC. His performances and later his recordings were enormously popular. Gardner, who had grown up poor, went on to live in a thirty-some-room Hollywood mansion and to own a yacht and a fleet of Cadillacs.

Although Gardner is remembered mostly as a comedian, he had considerable talent as a singer. In 1957, he recorded a pop song, "White Silver Sands," on the OJ label, with some success. This song got him a spot on the "Jack Parr Show," bringing in hundreds of letters. This response to Gardner won him a three-year contract with NBC. He was on the Parr show more than sixty times during this period. When Gardner took to the road, he had a band with trumpet, saxophone, piano, bass, and drums (which he usually played). He would open with an up-tempo number, such as "I'm Sitting on Top of the World," "When You're Smiling," or "White Silver Sands," sometimes adding zany lyrics and often singing in a falsetto. Since his main theme and devotion was the South, he also included "Dixie" or "Is It True What They Say about Dixie?"

Brother Dave used the intonations and vocal tricks of the southern country preacher in his comedy, addressing his audience as "Dear Hearts," "Friends," and "Children of Light," and he interjected such exclamations as "Rejoice," "Halleluiah," "Glory" (as Billy Graham would pronounce it), and "Joy to the World." His comedy was greatly enhanced by his ability to mimic people, male and female, and to use southern black and white dialects, and he went back and forth between these dialects regardless of whether his character was black or white. For example, his Georgia version of Shakespeare's *Julius Caesar* was introduced in a literary-sounding white voice, but the dialogue was part black and part white country dialect. Yet it all fit together and was funny. He did a similar thing with the biblical story of David, the humor mainly coming from the incongruity of southern scenes and accents with the ancient stories. He was also adept at sound effects and other vocal tricks. Roy Blount Jr. wrote that he wasn't a traditional storyteller like Jerry Clower but was a "far-out polyphonic spritzer, in the urban, jazzy, stoner tradition . . . of his contemporary Lenny Bruce."

Yet his main theme was the South and included laudatory comments about his native region and deprecatory ones about the North ("The only reason people live up North is they got jobs up there"). Another theme, as William E. Lightfoot has pointed out in a scholarly article, was his embrace of the rebellious and free lifestyle of the 1960s, to "promote a classless society of spiritual, yet prosperous, hedonists." He sprinkled his comedy with such "hippie" words as "groovin'," "swingin'," "cat," "man," and "kick" in sermon-like sets, saying things like, "I mean, all I want y'all to do is love one another." His message, reminding one of the flower children of the sixties, was strongly antiestablishment, with Eastern religious thought thrown in, promoting self-realization and a heightened awareness, eventually embracing the subject of drugs. T. Bubba Bechtol, another well-known southern humorist who was Gardner's driver as a teenager, said that Brother Dave was using marijuana before most folks had ever heard of it. His mysticism stressed enlightenment, expansion of awareness, and transcendence into some sort of togetherness for all, and there were numerous innuendos about sex. ("I believe women are smarter than men, because they have always possessed what we've been seeking [pause for laugh]. Yes, Dear Hearts, companionship.")

Gardner made many recordings: *Rejoice, Dear Hearts* (RCA Victor, 1959); *Kick Thy Own Self* (RCA Victor, 1960); *Ain't That Weird?* (RCA Victor, 1961; reissued on Camden, 1973); *Did You Ever?* (RCA Victor, 1962); *All Seriousness Aside* (RCA Victor, 1963); *The Best of Dave Gardner* (RCA Victor, 1963); *It's Bigger Than the Both of Us* (RCA Victor, 1963); *It Don't Make No Difference* (Capital, 1964); *It's All How You Look at "It"* (Capital, 1966); *Hip/ocracy* (Tower/Capital, 1966); and *Out Front* (Tonka, 1970).

The subject of drugs became a larger part of Gardner's humor as time went by. In performances for college audiences, for example, he said, "that's why I love to work for school audiences . . . because there's one thing I learned about higher learning, and that's to get high and learn! Get *on* the *kick!*" In 1962, Gardner was arrested in Atlanta for possession of amphetamines and other drugs. Perhaps related to his drug use, he became more erratic in the contradictory themes in his humor. As the 1960s unfolded, he became more conservative and reactionary, railing at Yankees, communists, and liberal politicians, as well as the hippies he had earlier found appealing. More troubling, he became more racist in his humor and turned on the very people from whom he had sprung—the poor—labeling them as "trash that don't want to work." Although his animosity toward disadvantaged people alienated some, it played well to others who had risen out of disadvantaged lives, perhaps assuring themselves that they had risen above blacks and hillbillies and other people that they viewed as unworthy. Gardner's message was that it is all right to prosper and feel superior to people who haven't had the gumption to get out of poverty. In this latter period, Gardner became friendly with members of the Ku Klux Klan, and Gardner's son stated once that the

Klan looked after him on the road. At the end, this comedian who had celebrated togetherness, patriotism, happiness, and love became cynical and negative. He also did prison time for tax evasion, which he blamed on his accountant, and he ended up doing small venues like the ones that began his career. He died of cancer.

T. Bubba Bechtol, who credits Gardner with making him aware of the strengths of southern culture and with his also becoming a southern humorist, says that he never heard any racist remarks from Gardner all the while he drove for him. He points out that Brother Dave's story about the segregationist Governor Ross Barnett of Mississippi dying and going to Heaven is at the expense of Barnett. When the governor gets to the Pearly Gates, a voice from inside says, "Who dat out dere? Come in heah!" The governor says, "Forgit it." Another story dealing with black dialect is really on Gardner. He sees an African American out in California and says, "O happy day, here's somebody to talk some trash with. I say, 'Yeah, man, how you is?' He say, 'Very well, thank you, and how are you?'"

(With credit to William E. Lightfoot, "Brother Dave Gardner," *Southern Quarterly* 34.3 [Spring 1996]: 81–93); and Roy Blount Jr., "Tennis-Shoe Tongue in His Head: How Brother Dave's Political Incorrectness Boomeranged," *Oxford American* 40 [Fifth Annual Music Issue, n.d.]: 205–7).

> *Brother Dave: I see this old man standing there, and I says, "Hey, Old Man, have you lived here all your life?" He says, "No, not yet."*

JIM GASKIN

Born September 27, 1937, Russell Springs, Kentucky;
died May 3, 2008, Danville, Kentucky

Jim Gaskin is a fourth-generation fiddler, a longtime emcee and musician at the "Renfro Valley Barn Dance," and a fine straight man to the comedians of that stage. Jim grew up in the small town of Russell Springs, and the family avidly listened to the broadcasts from Renfro Valley, some forty miles away, and he dreamed of someday playing at the "Renfro Valley Barn Dance." It took a long time for him to make it. His introduction to show business was with "Cowboy Jack" Alexander's band as a child, and with an Indian medicine showman who called himself Rabbit Foot. "He mixed his own medicine and sold it for a dollar a bottle, and it would cure anything from ingrown toenails to dandruff. You could rub it on or drink it, whatever." He also admits to playing blackface comedy in a minstrel show in those early days.

Gaskin got into radio playing fiddle for a band and later had his own band, the Cumberland Rangers, on WAIN in Columbia while he was in high school. He wrote John Lair and got an invitation to play at the "Renfro Valley Barn Dance." Lair liked the boy fiddler and invited him to be a part of the barn dance, but he didn't want the whole band. Jim declined, but occasionally played there.

After studying music at Lindsey Wilson College, he studied also at the Cleveland Institute of Radio/Electronics and Professional Academy of Broadcasting. He has worked on several radio stations in Kentucky: WKAY in Glasgow; WEZJ in Williamsburg; WRSL in Stanford; WRVK in Renfro Valley; WKXO in Berea; and WDFB in Danville. In 1961 he bought WIRV in Irvine, Kentucky. There he met the Kentucky entertainer Asa Martin, who had recorded many sides with Fiddling Doc Roberts and his son, James Roberts. He and Martin organized a new band, also called the Cumberland Rangers, with Gaskin playing fiddle and also singing, and they performed daily on WIRV. With the new interest in folk and early country music, the Rangers played many college campuses, special events, and folk festivals, including the National Folk Festival and the Smithsonian Institution's Folklife Festival.

Jim Gaskin.
Courtesy of Jim Gaskin.

Gaskin spoke of his main influence: "One of my best experiences was getting to know Blind Dick Burnett and Leonard Rutherford, and I guess Rutherford had more influence on my fiddling than anyone else, and I've got his fiddle." Burnett and Rutherford were among the first Kentuckians to record for a major label, Columbia, in the mid-1920s. Gaskin also played with many of the early radio and traveling-show entertainers, including Bill Monroe, Carl Story, Hylo Brown, and Jimmy Skinner.

Jim played off and on at the "Renfro Valley Barn Dance." "Mr. Lair and I had an understanding that if I wasn't playing somewhere else and I was there at 6:30, he'd put me on." But in 1979 he joined the "Barn Dance" as a regular, as emcee, performer, fiddler, straight man, and host. He was also cowriter and coproducer of the "Sunday Morning Getherin'." In 1990 he became the sole writer and producer of the "Getherin'" as well as emcee for the "Barn Dance," assuming the roles of John Lair, who died in 1985.

"I never really considered myself a comedian," Gaskin said. "I did get to know Slim Miller when I came to Renfro Valley in 1955, and I really admired him. After Slim died, I put together an outfit like he wore, and I did a few of the antics that he did on the 'Renfro Valley Barn Dance.' It's now a regular act. I've also been straight man to comedians like Old Joe Clark and Bun Wilson." He went on to talk about comedy:

Of course, comedy adds variety to a show, but it also gives the musicians a little rest. People need humor. It's been a rule that when times were tough, attendance was up. People needed relief. I know, growing up, seeing old medicine shows, country music shows. Everybody in town would remember those jokes and tell them to one another, with everybody knowing how they went, at the barbershop or poolroom, everywhere, for months after the show had been there. A joke is like a good song. People love to hear it over and over.

Following is a story told by Jim Gaskin:

> This man and his wife were operating a farm, and they needed a bull. The farmer read all the farm papers, and he saw one advertised that was way up in Wisconsin. He said, "Boy, that's a long way to go, but I'd like to see the bull. I don't want to drive that big truck all the way to Wisconsin." He told his wife, "I'll catch the bus up there, and if that bull suits me, I'll buy him, and I'll send you a telegram, and you and the hired hand can bring the truck and come get us." She said, "All right." Well, he went up there. He liked the bull, and he bought him, but he didn't take much extra cash with him. He went down to Western Union and wrote out the telegram the way he wanted it. The fellow read it, and he said, "That'll be eighteen dollars." The farmer looked in his pocket, and he said, "I ain't got that much money with me. Will you take a check?" He said, "No. We'll take credit cards." The farmer said, "I never had one in my life." He said, "Well, how much money have you got?" The farmer said, "I've just got a dollar. How much will that send?" He said, "One word."
>
> So, the farmer turned around and around two or three times, picked up another piece of paper and wrote the word "Comfortable" on it and said, "Send her that." The Western Union guy said, "My goodness, man, she ain't goin' to know what to do with that." He said, "Oh, yes, she will. She's a slow reader, and when she reads that, she'll read. 'Come-for-t'-bull.'"

GEEZINSLAW BROTHERS

Sam Morris Allred, born May 5, 1934, Austin, Texas
Raymond Dewayne Smith, born September 19, 1946,
   Bertram, Texas

Sam Allred started the Geezinslaw act with his partners Jerry Brown and Jody Meredith in Austin, Texas, in 1950, but he had to go into service, and when he returned, Brown had started a dance band and Meredith was otherwise involved. Allred heard about "Son" Smith, a seventeen-year-old high school student, liked him, and they began performing together in 1959, doing a combination of comedy and country music.

In 1961, while Sam was a student at the University of Texas, Arthur Godfrey came to Texas, staging shows to scout for talent. The Geezinslaws performed, Godfrey liked them, and he brought them to New York to appear regularly on his show from 1961 to 1970. When they were in New York, they did shows at such venues as the Latin Quarter and the Bitter End, Carnegie Hall, the "Tonight Show" (five times), the "Ed

The Geezinslaw Brothers.
Courtesy of Sam Allred.

Sullivan Show," and the "Jackie Gleason Show." Sam commented, "If we hadn't had comedy we'd never have gone to New York in the first place, because they didn't know what country music was. They considered us comedy rather than country music." Their comedy, as well as their good picking and singing, eventually took the Geezinslaw Brothers all over the country, from the Edgewater Beach Hotel to the Hollywood Bowl, to Las Vegas, Lake Tahoe, Canada, and Europe.

They began their recording career in 1963 for Columbia Records with an album, *The Kooky World of the Geezinslaw Brothers*, and then switched to Capital in 1966 for four albums: *Can You Believe*; *My Dirty Lowdown, Rotten, Cotton-pickin' Little Darlin'*; *Chubby (Please Take Your Love to Town)*; and *The Geezinslaws Are Alive (and Well)*. In 1979, Lonestar Records released *If You Think I'm Crazy*. The Geezinslaws were often in Nashville and were regulars on Ralph Emery's "Nashville Now" television program. Clips of these shows were released on a video in 1993 as *What a Crowd! What a Night!* by Shadetree Productions.

Over the years, the Geezinslaws have continued to tour and have appeared on "Austin City Limits," "The Texas Connection," "Nashville Now," and have never missed a Willie Nelson annual picnic. Their show consists of Sam playing mandolin and singing great duets, many of them also humorous, with Son, who plays guitar. Their best-known song is probably "Help, I'm White and I Can't Get Down." Their comedy is mostly Sam telling jokes and doing topical routines, while Son maintains a stony expression, never saying anything. One continuing joke is the celebrated Geezinslaws World Tour, which they announced on "Nashville Now" about 1980. Sam Allred reported recently that "the Geezinslaws World Tour is still going strong, and we're now a hundred and fifty miles from home."

The Geezinslaws currently have five CDs produced by Step One Records with music and a lavish amount of comedy: *The Geezinslaws* (1989), *The Geezinslaws World*

Tour (1990), *Geezinslaws, Feelin' Good, Gitten' Up, Gittin' Down* (1992), *The Geezinslaws, I Wish I Had a Job to Shove* (1994), and *The Geezinslaws, Blah . . . Blah . . . Blah* (1997).

The following story is from *The Geezinslaws: I Wish I Had a Job to Shove* (Step One Records, 1994), with permission:

> *Sam: A fellow walks into a Wanna Sack? store—you know why I call them a Wanna Sack? store? 'Cause you go in there and you buy about forty-five items, you carry 'em up there, stack 'em on the counter, they add it all up, you pay 'em, and then the clerk looks down for the longest time, and then looks up, says, "You wanna sack?" "Oh, no, I don't want a sack. Let me make six trips to the car with this stuff! Of course I want a sack!"—so a guy walks into the Wanna Sack? store. He had a two-by-four, said, "This is a holdup." The clerk said, "You don't understand, Sir. You don't hold up Wanna Sack? stores with a two-by-four." Whap! He hit the clerk right in the head with the two-by-four, and the clerk said, "Sir, you just don't understand, you don't rob stores with. . . ." Whap! he hit him again, knocked him right to his knees. So the clerk just reached up in the cash register and handed the guy the money, and as the guy was leaving, the clerk said, "Listen, mister, you better get yourself a gun. You're goin' to kill somebody with that damn board!"*

GEORGE GOBEL

Born May 20, 1919, Chicago, Illinois;
died February 24, 1991, Los Angeles, California

George Gobel first came to public notice at the age of thirteen on WLS's "National Barn Dance" as the Little Cowboy. He had an exceptional singing voice and did many solos, especially the popular cowboy numbers. He did stints at other radio stations—WMAQ in Chicago, WDOD in Chattanooga, and KMOX in St. Louis—but he was at WLS for a decade, giving him time to grow up, such as it was, and to develop a comedic sideline. He capitalized on his drawling understated delivery and diminutive size to develop an effective comic persona. He could get a long laugh just by standing at the mike with his oversized guitar and announcing an impossibly long and fictional song title. While he was at WLS, the American Record Corporation issued two of his recordings on the Conqueror label (78 rpm).

Gobel was inducted into the Army Air Corps in 1942, actually on the stage of the "National Barn Dance." After the war, he mostly abandoned his singing career and did stand-up comedy in Chicago venues. Along the way he acquired the title of "Lonesome George," no doubt from his dolesome and forlorn delivery. Migrating to California in the 1950s, he broke into television, first as a guest on such shows as "The Colgate Comedy Hour," "Who Said That," and the "Ted Mack Amateur Hour." In 1957–58 he hosted the "George Gobel Show." He appeared in two movies in 1956, *I Married a Woman* and *The Birds and the Bees*. He also appeared in episodes of "Death Valley Days" on television. Then followed several other movies in the 1970s and 1980s, including

George Gobel (R), with unidentified fellow performer. Courtesy of
Juanita McMichen Lynch.

'Twas the Night before Christmas, The Day It Came to Earth, Ellie, and Alice through the
Looking Glass.

In his last years, George Gobel made TV guest appearances and worked at clubs.
His comedy had become mainstream American, and yet in his delivery and demeanor,
there was still a lot of the old country comedy. He is buried in the San Fernando Mis-
sion Cemetery, where many other Hollywood greats lie.

FREDDIE "MUNROE" GOBLE

Born September 9, 1945, Auxier, Kentucky

Freddie Goble says he was born in L.A. and then adds with a laugh, "Lower Auxier, in
the hills of eastern Kentucky." A bridge engineer with the Kentucky Highway Department, he had played music and some comedy for many years. One day, the president

of the "Kentucky Opry," in Prestonsburg asked him if he knew anybody who could play comedy on the popular show. He allowed that he had done some comedy in high school as a character named Munroe. They proceeded to write up a skit, and Munroe was a hit with the audience. In spite of two heart attacks, three angioplasties, fourteen heart catheterizations, and a triple-bypass, he has been a regular on the show for more than a decade. He is as well prepared for adversity as one could be because of his irrepressible sense of humor.

Goble characterizes Munroe as a sort of Ernest T. Bass, the character on the "Andy Griffith Show." He is mostly based on a town character Goble once knew. "He was real quiet until he got about three beers in him, and then he became this other person. His eyes would get big and his expression change, and he was just as funny as a monkey. He was a great old guy, wouldn't hurt anybody, just said funny stuff." Munroe comes on stage with a red ball cap slanted sideways with a bird sitting on it, a red bow tie and red vest over a polka-dot shirt and baggy black pants. He usually works with the emcee to do little skits that involve his wife, Fairybell, and incorporate regional jokes.

Freddie "Munroe" Goble.
Courtesy of Fred Goble.

> Doctor: Munroe, ye wife don't look too good.
> Munroe: I know, Doc, but she's good to the kids, and they're kind of attached to her and all.
> Doctor: Has Fairybell been through menapause?
> Munroe: I don't think she has, Doc, but she's been to the Breaks of the Sandy.
> Doctor: Munroe, is she still on that banana-coconut diet I put her on, and has she lost any weight?
> Munroe: She ain't lost a pound, but you ought to see her climb a tree!
> Doc: You know, Munroe, I found a suppository in Fairybell's ear!
> Munroe: Now I think I know where she put her hearing aid!

WILLIAM HENRY "SHORTY" GODWIN.
See Hiram Hayseed

NORRIS GOFF. *See Lum and Abner*

MELVIN GOINS

Born December 30, 1933, Bramwell, West Virginia

Melvin Goins is a gifted singer, guitarist, and comedian who played with Ezra Cline's Lonesome Pine Fiddlers, Hylo Brown's Timberliners, the Stanley Brothers, and his brothers Ray and Conley in the Kentucky-based Bluegrass band, the Goins Brothers, and he now heads Windy Mountain.

Goins learned comedy from Ezra Cline, who played bass and did comedy with the Lonesome Pine Fiddlers. Melvin remembered, "In those days the bass player was always the comedian. So Ezra did most of the comedy. He went by the name of Cousin Ezra and did jokes with a straight man. He wore an old flop-billed hat, an old shirt, old pair of pants with the legs rolled up—always wore extra-big clothes. You just slipped them on over your other clothes. Sometimes they'd use makeup, black out their front teeth."

Melvin had played some comedy throughout his career but never as his main function until he joined the Stanley Brothers in January 1966, prior to Carter Stan-

Melvin Goins (polka-dot suit), with (L-R): Curley Ray Cline, Larry Sparks, and Ralph Stanley. Courtesy of Neil V. Rosenberg.

ley's death in December. He credits Carter Stanley with giving him the name of Big Wilbur, his comic character. "We were riding along one Sunday morning, me and Carter Stanley. We'd been up to Wheeling. We's coming through Ashland, Kentucky, and Carter pinned that name on me—Big Wilbur. He liked comedy a lot. He was a good straight man too. Carter was the straight man, and I was the comedian." Goins was the last of several good comedians who played with the Stanley Brothers.

With the Stanleys, Melvin played bass and did the comedy, although he was also a good guitarist and lead singer. As a comedian, he sometimes dressed up in a polka-dot suit, bow tie, and funny hat, although he had at least three different outfits. Tim O'Brien remembered that "Melvin had this box he carried around with his costumes and stuff in it. I'd ask, 'What's in there, Melvin?' and he'd say, 'That's my show. That's what makes the show.'" O'Brien also remembered Melvin's glibness in a monologue or dialogue: "He'll say a thousand words if he says two."

Melvin and Ray Goins had both played with the Lonesome Pine Fiddlers, and they first formed the Goins Brothers in 1953, with Ralph Meadows playing fiddle. They later rejoined Ezra Cline's group. In 1969, with the rise of bluegrass festivals, Melvin and Ray became the Goins Brothers again, including several now well-known blue-grass musicians, such as Art Stamper, Curley Lambert, John Keith, and their younger brother Conley Goins. Melvin continued to play comedy, and later on he formed the Shedhouse Trio as part of the band, and they did comedy songs. The Goinses recorded bluegrass albums for Rem, Rebel, and Old Homestead Records.

Ray Goins has dropped out of active entertainment, but Melvin and his new band Windy Mountain perform at festivals and at the governor's mansion in Frankfort (a show that was later released on Kentucky Educational Television stations). Melvin also does many school programs in eastern Kentucky, including his Big Wilbur act. He also is a Saturday-morning DJ for two Kentucky radio stations: "Top of the Morning Bluegrass" at WSKV in Stanton and "Big Sandy Bluegrass Time" at WSIP in Paints-ville. His imaginative advertisements make you want to run out and get biscuits and gravy at the Clay City Diner or buy a car down at Bunt Gross Used Cars, where "If it ain't right, they'll fix it." Melvin signed off on his Saturday-morning show on WSKV recently with, "Good-bye, neighbors, have a good weekend. Smile. The sun will be good for your teeth!"

Melvin Goins likes to talk about the value of humor: "Everybody wants to laugh. Say you and me have had a bad day, and we're kindly depressed. Somebody comes up and tells a little funny joke. Well, if we laugh for half a minute that gets our mind off our worries. It lifts our spirits. I love to see people laugh."

Melvin and his wife Willia live in Catlettsburg, Kentucky, and have one son, Greg-ory, and two daughters, Barbara and Billie Jo.

At this writing, Melvin Goins has been in bluegrass music for fifty-six years. He and Ray have gotten together again recently to do a DVD, *Masters of Bluegrass: The Goins Brothers, Part 1* (3541 Blue Ribbon Drive, Catlettsburg, KY 41129).

Carter Stanley: How do you feel tonight?
Big Wilbur: Just like a cross-cut saw.
Stanley: How's that?
Big Wilber: It'd take two good men to handle me!

Big Wilbur: Ralph, I stayed in a motel the other night in Clintwood, and this couple that had just got married took the room right next to me, and they ate candy all night!
Ralph Stanley: You mean they checked into a motel just to eat candy? How do you know they ate candy all night?
Big Wilbur: Well, the woman kept saying, "O, Henry! O Henry!"

GOOSE ISLAND RAMBLERS

K. Wendell Whitford, born February 27, 1913,
Albion, Wisconsin; died June 10, 2000,
Cottage Grove, Wisconsin
George Gilbertsen, born September 28, 1925,
Morningside Heights, Wisconsin
Bruce Bollerud, born October 8, 1934,
Hollandale, Wisconsin

Bill C. Malone wrote in *Don't Get above Your Raisin': Country Music and the Southern Working Class* that he had to move to Wisconsin to find "a survival of the kind of stage show that once characterized country music." He goes on to describe the Goose Island Ramblers, who "have delighted midwestern audiences with a marvelous blend of solid musicianship, a wide variety of songs, and zany stage humor." Malone describes their performances as "entertainment," with comedy and humorous songs an important ingredient. The group plays a variety of instruments and sings individually and in harmony. They do sentimental numbers like "Goin' Back to Old Virginny," "Dear Old Southern Home," "The Wreck of the Old '97," and "Faded Love." However, they specialize in novelty songs, and they have written some funny ones, such as "Norwegian War Chant," "The Hurley Hop," "The Beach at Waunakee" (a town in the middle of Wisconsin), and "There's No Norwegians in Dickeyville." They are adept at exaggerated German or Norwegian accents.

Wendy Whitford ("Uncle Windy"), the oldest of the group, learned fiddle from his grandfather, who was born in 1849, and tunes from Norwegian fiddlers and from his mother, who sang old songs as she did her housework. When radio came along in the 1920s, he tuned in to WLS in Chicago and heard singers such as Bradley Kincaid from Kentucky and westerners like Gene Autry. On good nights he could get WSM in Nashville, and thus his repertoire included southern songs. His day job was with the Oscar Meyer Packing Company, but he regularly played guitar and fiddle with several string bands, and one of those bands was the original Goose Island Ramblers.

The Goose Island Ramblers.
L-R: George Gilbertsen, Wendell
"Windy" Whitford, and Bruce
Bollerud. Courtesy of Bruce
Bollerud.

This name was resurrected in 1962 when Whitford, Gilbertsen, and Bollerud started playing together.

George Gilbertson, known as "Smoky George," started picking tunes on his brother's five-dollar guitar and playing the harmonica when he was seven, began playing in a school trio at nine, and at fourteen had a Saturday-night job in a tavern. He soon mastered the fiddle, mandolin, and Hawaiian guitar, and at sixteen he played in a six-piece dance band. He learned tunes and songs from the broadcasts of WLS and WSM. He commented that when he heard country fiddlers over these stations, "I realized that there was another way of playing besides violin. When I heard fiddle music, I got interested." When he joined the navy in World War II, he took his fiddle with him and played for his shipmates, and since he was a medic, for sick or wounded sailors in New Guinea, the Philippines, and China. Gilbertsen, who worked as a repairman for the city of Madison, has played with bands around Madison such as the Fox River Boys, the Badger Ramblers, and the Dakota Roundup.

Bruce Bollerud ("Loose Bruce the Goose"), the real Norwegian of the group, learned tunes from his grandfather, a fiddler, and his mother, who accompanied him on the piano. Young Bruce first learned to play the bandonian, a type of concertina, but as a teenager he switched to a piano accordion. Although he is by profession a special-education teacher, he has played with numerous bands in Madison, such as Gilbert Prestebroten's Rhythm Rascals, Emil Simpson's Nighthawks, and Roger Bright and Verne Meisner's polka bands. During the 1950s Bollerud started playing country and even rockabilly music with Dick Sherwood and the Johnson Brothers. With the Johnson Brothers he played Glen and Ann's Tavern, famous for its music, and it was there that the revived Goose Island Ramblers were formed.

The Ramblers played at Glen and Ann's Tavern for about twelve years to working-class people and university students. They also played other venues. Their greatest thrill was playing for the Masters series of concerts at Wolftrap Park, near Washington, D.C. Their performance was captured by Radio Smithsonian and syndicated over National Public Radio.

Bollerud commented on the importance of comedy in their entertainment: "It was very important in our show. Two things were going on: one, we were having a good time, entertaining ourselves, with things going back and forth amongst us; and two, we wanted to make the crowd happy. We have a lot of repartee back and forth between the audience and us. A lot of it was just spontaneous, but we had our little routines, but always with variations on them, as the crowd shouted up things." As an example, he describes a routine, "Mrs. Yonson, Turn Me Loose":

> It was a story about an old Scandinavian bachelor who had this woman, Mrs. Yonson, a love-starved widow, chasing after him. She keeps pursuing him, and he keeps trying to fend her off. He's worried that she's going to love him to death, because she's had four husbands already, and they all died. George would put on a wig and a bonnet and an apron, and as I was singing things he would respond to it, like in the line, "She says she'll cook dinner for me in my flat," and he's out there with his fiddle held like a frying pan tossing flapjacks in the air, and they get stuck on the ceiling, and he has to pry them off with his bow. There's another line, "She looks at me and she breathes heavily," and he grabs the mike and draws in a huge breath that makes a racket on the microphone. That's one we did a lot.

With "The Milwaukee Waltz," Bruce becomes progressively tipsy as he sings in a caricature of a German accent. In "The Norwegian War Chant," George dons a bucket with Viking horns on it that one of the university students constructed for him, another example of audience participation. When one of the band is verging on off-color humor, another will remind him that this is a "family place." Whereupon, he looks at the audience and says, "Yes, several families have been started right where you're sitting."

The Goose Island Ramblers disbanded in the mid-1970s, but they were regularly invited to do concerts. Wendy died in 2000. George has continued playing with local musicians, and his big thrill was playing on stage with Bill Monroe at his Bean Blossom Festival in 1992. Bruce plays with the Southern Wisconsin Fiddlers, featuring house-party music, and he is collecting such music for a book.

(With credit to Bill C. Malone and James P. Leary.)

JAMES GREGORY

Born May 6, 1946, Lithonia, Georgia

James Gregory is billed as the "Funniest Man in America," and not long into one of his performances, you are ready to believe it, as members of the audience roar, gasp, wheeze, hold their sides, and reel in their seats. In the first place, he has that comedic look, a big smile, and he's big—"fat" is a word he uses a lot—and he has a sly way of looking around at everybody under heavy lids right before or after a punch line, with that knowing conviction that he has you completely involved in his thing. Even the politically sensitive blue noses eventually give in and have a good time. Gregory has some fun with almost everything: death, funerals, wakes, car wrecks as a traditional southern way to go, yuppies, Californians, weight lifters, joggers, vegetarians and health naggers in general, food, global warming, and all sorts of activity that bugs some groups of people. He has a conservative view of current happenings, although he says he makes fun of right wingers when they deserve it.

Gregory didn't get into comedy right away. He graduated from Lithonia High School and then went to work for the U.S. Postal Service, transferred to the Defense Department, joined the Marine Corps, worked in accounting, then sold encyclopedias, pots and pans, and vacuum cleaners. This brought him to 1982, when the Punch Line Comedy Club opened in Atlanta. Gregory went on an amateur night, and his buddies dared him to take the mic. He made people laugh, came back to perform as often as they would allow, and eventually became an emcee in the club. In 1983 he decided to try to make a living at comedy, although he admitted nearly starving to death, but eventually comedy clubs and other venues opened in the major cities, and he didn't turn down the little places with limited budgets. Eventually he began traveling all over

James Gregory. Courtesy of James Gregory, FMIA Marketing.

the United States. Comparing his political and social bent with what he observed up North and in California, he gathered a wealth of material for his comedy.

However, he doesn't think of himself as a country or southern comedian, although he appeared regularly on the Nashville Network, and he has opened for such acts as George Jones, Kenny Chesney, the Judds, Randy Travis, Reba McIntire, Dolly Parton, and Sawyer Brown. Also, he has a southern accent, and his comments on topics such as funerals and food have a definite southern slant. He says he just talks about everyday things that most people can relate to. He changes a few words or phrases when he goes up North to make sure the audience knows what he's talking about, but says he goes over well wherever he is. "You don't hear me go on stage and do things that are exclusive to the South," he says. "I don't talk about grits or pickup trucks, rednecks, coon dogs, bird hunting, or make fun of Yankees." He notes one difference between the South and New England on a subject he gets a lot of laughs about: "In New England they have a wake, and they have all these covered dishes *after* the body's been put in the cemetery. But us Baptists start eatin' the minute the person dies."

A great experience for Gregory was when he entertained the troops and sailors in the Middle East during the war in Afghanistan. They loved him. They all "got" his humor. Another triumph was being invited to the U.S. Comedy Arts Festival, sponsored by HBO, in Aspen, Colorado, in 1999. Here his humor won over a multitude of politically correct, sophisticated, reared-on-television young people (he was the oldest comedian there), and this resulted in a month's run at the Hudson Theater in Hollywood, where he charmed the liberals and others of that city.

He loves his job and has strong convictions about the worth of humor and how it helps us cope: "Humor is important in life. I don't know how people get by without it. People who don't have a sense of humor do not handle major problems well. They'll take a small problem and make it big. They get depressed worse than someone who has a sense of humor. Humor's a major thing in life."

Gregory has three CDs available: *The Funniest Man in America: James Gregory*, *The Legend Continues*, and *Grease, Gravy, and John Wayne's Mother* (FMIA Marketing, 800-548-FMIA).

Here is an excerpt on funerals from *The Legend Continues*, with permission:

People come to pay their respects. They stay one minute at the casket and three days in the kitchen. You know what they do? They stand around and gossip—about that food, who brought which dish, as if that was important at a time like this. There's a dead guy twelve feet away! Here's what you hear around the table. Somebody goes, "Well, I see Elizabeth brought that damned macaroni salad again. I knew she'd do it. I'll tell you one thing, if it'd been somebody on her side of the family, she'd a brought some kind of meat! Now, don't let this go no further, about a year ago when her sister's husband died—you know, he's the one got killed in a grain silo. What happened was that he dropped his Bic lighter down in there. I told him, 'I don't think I'd go in there for a Bic lighter.' He said, 'But I just bought that Bic this morning.' I said, 'Well, hell, jump! I thought it was an old Bic!' Well, he died, and that bein' her side of the family, hell, she baked a ham! Well, she said she baked it. She didn't bake that damned ham! It had pineapple rings and cherries on it. But I didn't want to say nothing. Get this now, I'm still talkin' about her side of the family. A few months later, her nineteen-year-old nephew died. Nobody knows why. He just died. I think it was a stab wound. When he died, she showed up over there with eight or nine pounds of Boar's Head roast beef. Get this. She also brings along four or five loaves of that high-dollar Jewish rye. That's just her showin' off, right there! There ain't no Jews in our family. Wouldn't nobody touch that bread. These were rural country people. They were scared of that bread! You could hear them in the kitchen talkin'. They'd be goin', 'They's black specks in that bread. Why, this bread ain't got no corners. How in the hell can I fix a sandwich? I got square meat and round bread. This is the worst funeral I've ever been to!'"

ANDY GRIFFITH

Born Andrew Samuel Griffith, June 1, 1926, Mount Airy, North Carolina

Andy Griffith entered the University of North Carolina intending to become a Moravian minister, but he majored in music and became involved in the Carolina Playmakers, a drama group. As an undergraduate, he began playing Sir Walter Raleigh in Paul Green's outdoor drama *The Lost Colony*, staged each summer at Manteo on the Outer Banks of North Carolina. He was in the show for seven years. With his country drawl and ways, Griffith became a sure entertainer, and after graduating from the university in 1949 and while teaching in the Goldsboro, North Carolina, high school, he worked up country routines for night clubs and other venues. His main monologue was "What It Was, Was Football," a country bumpkin's attempt to describe his first game without knowing anything whatever about football. A local record label released the monologue as a recording, and then Columbia Records picked it up and got Griffith a spot on the "Ed Sullivan Show" in 1954.

While he was doing the nightclub circuit, he read a copy of Mac Hyman's novel *No Time for Sergeants*, and when he heard it was headed for Broadway as a play, he wrote to Hyman to say that he thought he would be a natural as the main character, Will Stockdale. He invited Hyman to come to Atlanta to see his act. Hyman came, liked what he saw and heard, and recommended Griffith for the role. Andy's Will Stockdale was a hit on Broadway, and in 1957 he was cast as a country singer in the movie, *A Face in the Crowd*. The next year, he made the movie version of *No Time for Sergeants*. Also in 1958, he made *Onionhead*, and he was in the Broadway musical *Destry Rides Again*.

Griffin had other comedy monologues. These also played up the idea of an innocent and not-too-knowledgeable country boy attempting to describe his experience with sophisticated material such as Shakespeare's *Romeo and Juliet* and *Hamlet* and the ballet *Swan Lake*. But Griffith's tenure in country comedy, as such, was brief. By 1960 he was in Hollywood playing Andy Taylor, the genial and uncomplicated sheriff on the "Andy Griffith Show," set in the southern town of Mayberry, based on Andy's hometown of Mount Airy. It ran from October 3, 1960, until April 1, 1968, a total of 249 shows. It was one of the most successful television shows ever and is still going in reruns. As an example of the influence of the "Andy Griffith Show" on American culture, in 1981, Richard Kelly, a University of Tennessee professor, published a scholarly book, *The Andy Griffith Show*. Kelly explained that at first Griffith's Andy Taylor was a continuation of the comical persona of Will Stockdale, but when Don Knotts joined the cast as Andy's deputy, he realized that he should be the straight man to Barney. Thus, Kelly explained, the success of the show was this caring relationship between the impetuous, nervous, and sometimes officious deputy and the unflappable, decent, modest, and ultimately effective sheriff.

In addition to the "Andy Griffith Show," Griffith appeared in all 195 episodes of the crime drama "Matlock," which ran on NBC from 1986 to 1995, as a wily and humorous southern country lawyer.

In 1997, Griffith won a Grammy for *I Love to Tell the Story: Twenty-five Timeless Hymns*, which highlighted his singing talent and was sometimes featured on his TV series, as much for comedy as music. He can play the guitar and ukulele, and he knows a lot of songs. His closeness to country music was acknowledged in a recent appearance on the "Grand Ole Opry." His other awards include the Theatre World Award for *No Time for Sergeants* (1956); Outstanding TV Personality of the Year Award (1968); a Lifetime Achievement Award from the American Film Institute (1992); and induction into the Television Hall of Fame (1992).

Griffith married a university classmate, Barbara Bray Edwards, in 1949, but they separated in 1972. In 1983, he married Cindy Knight. He has two daughters, Dixie and Nan, and a son, Andrew Samuel Jr., who died in 1992.

LEWIS GRIZZARD

Born October 20, 1946, Fort Benning, Georgia; died
March 20, 1994, Atlanta, Georgia

Lewis Grizzard was one of the most successful humorists of all time. For more than twenty years he wrote humorous columns for the *Atlanta Journal-Constitution* and was syndicated in other newspapers. He authored over twenty bestselling books and had numerous recordings. He appeared on the major talk shows and played a character on "Designing Women" on CBS. He had his own television special, but he failed to get his own sitcom. However, this failure gave him an additional reason to promote the South. The California TV executives, after interviewing Grizzard, declared that he was "too southern" for a national show. "Too southern!" he yelled. "That is an oxymoron. There is no such thing as being too southern!"

Like many other humorists, Grizzard had his times of disappointment, anger, and sorrow. His father, an infantry captain, was a lifelong victim of his combat experiences in World War II and in Korea. A charming, gifted man, he became an alcoholic and abandoned his family when Lewis was six. His mother moved them to Moreland, Georgia, where Lewis's grandparents, "Daddy Bun" and "Mama Willie," and later a stepfather, provided some stability for the young boy. However, his disappointments later added fuel to his humor, and Moreland became the center of his life and of his humor. As other writers have said, it was his Mayberry, Lake Wobegon, and Hannibal.

Lewis Grizzard. Courtesy of Dedre Grizzard.

Grizzard attended local schools in Moreland and then graduated from the University of Georgia in Athens. He was a great fan of the Georgia Bulldogs, and this led to a job as sportswriter at age twenty-three at the *Atlanta Journal*, where he later became sports editor. He left Atlanta for a short while to become executive sports editor at the *Chicago Sun-Times.* He quipped, "I was a prisoner of war in Chicago for two years, where they have only two seasons, winter and the Fourth of July." No doubt, this time of exile heightened his love of the South, especially when he heard disparaging comments about his accent or aspects of southern culture. He came up with comic retorts about the differences between northerners and southerners. He claimed that Chicagoans would listen to his accent and then say something like, "Do you read?" and his response was, "Well, some of us southerners may be ignorant, but I ain't never seen no southerner paying to go into a reptile farm!" He said if he ever got back to Georgia, "I'm going to nail my feet to the ground" (this comment later was used in a book title).

He did get back to Georgia and a job with the *Atlanta Journal-Constitution*, where he began writing his famous humor column on an old manual typewriter. "When I write," he said, "I want to hear some noise." He flourished as a humorist during the 1980s and up until his death in 1994, with his columns in over 450 newspapers. These columns were fodder for eighteen books, some of which are still available, such as *The Wit and Wisdom of Lewis Grizzard; Life Is Like a Dogsled; Chili Dogs Always Bark at Night; I Took a Lickin' and Kept on Tickin' (and Now I Believe in Miracles)*, about heart surgery; *Southern by the Grace of God; It Wasn't Always Easy, but I Sure Had Fun: The Best of Lewis Grizzard;* and even a cookbook, *True Grits: Tall Tales and Recipes from the South.*

Grizzard also made several recordings, mostly on Southern Tracks Records. On cassette are *Alimony: The Bill You Get for the Thrill You Got; Lewis Grizzard—Let's Have a Party; Lewis Grizzard—Don't Believe I'da Told That; Lewis Grizzard—On the Road with . . .* ; and *From Moreland to Moscow.* On CD: *Addicted to Love; Best of Lewis Grizzard;* and *An Evening with Lewis Grizzard.*

Grizzard was a fan of country music and wrote about it and country musicians in his columns. He appeared on many country music venues, such as a "The Ralph Emery Show" and "Crook and Chase" on TNN. He was friend of such singers as Alan Jackson (they attended the same high school) and Brooks and Dunn, and he opened for Randy Travis in Las Vegas. He wrote country songs and had a contract with Sony as a singer-songwriter, although Sony did not release any of his recordings. Bad Boot Productions has released a CD of him performing his original songs, *Bulldog's Prayer: The Songs of Lewis Grizzard.* For more information on Lewis Grizzard or to purchase his recordings and books, log on to www.lewisgrizzard.com.

Lewis Grizzard's unsettled issues in his life, such as his disappointment with his father and the contradictions of southern life, were reflected in his writing and humor helped him to resolve some of them, but he harbored some anger. He had a sharp edge in his humor aimed toward women in general and toward gays and others who ruffled his conservative feathers. A congenital heart problem no doubt affected his outlook, although he wrote and spoke humorously about it. Roy Blount Jr., a fellow southern humorist, commented, "I thought that he got too angry and sometimes also too sentimental, but I actually liked him better when he was being sentimental, writing about his daddy." Indeed, after his father's death, Grizzard wrote *My Daddy Was a Pistol and I'm a Son of a Gun* (1986). It is a serious book in which he rises above his anger and disappointment with his father to do a remarkable portrait of him. He was fascinated with his father's ability to charm people into loaning him money, which he did not repay, to get good jobs but not hold them, to become the center of attention as a talker or singer anywhere there was a piano for him to play, but also how he failed his family. Yet Lewis believed that this war hero, who was himself a casualty of war, deserved a book. It became a catharsis for him and a national bestseller.

Grizzard had three open-heart surgeries. He almost died as a result of his third in 1993, and his doctors called it a miracle that he lived. He received fifty thousand letters from well-wishers, dying people offered their hearts for transplant, and church buses filled with parishioners drove by Emory Hospital flying get-well banners.

After three unsuccessful unions, he married Dedra Kyle, a native of Cleveland, Tennessee, in March 1994 and found happiness and contentment with her and her daughter, Jordan. Dedra took care of him during his convalescence, and he dedicated the book he wrote about it (*I Took a Lickin' and Kept on Tickin'*) to her. She commented on her last year with Lewis:

> That surgery where he almost died in 1993 did change him, and his doctor, Randy
> Martin, said to me that Lewis's life would really change. He got away from some

of his friends—hangers-on because of his fame and money—and he started to cling to the people he loved the most and who loved him, a small-knit group. He stayed home more. He drank a lot less and prayed a lot, watched movies, spent a lot more time on the front porch, thinking about the things that were really important in his life. He was grateful to be given a year to reflect and be thankful. Roy Blount was right, that last year he wrote a lot of sentimental columns.

In the southern tradition, his mother had always admonished him to "be sweet," and he turned to this theme in his last days and called on his readers to be sweet, kind, tolerant forgiving, tender, and slow to anger.

Lewis Grizzard died after a fourth open-heart surgery in 1994.

The South Carolina actor Bill Oberst now performs a tribute to him, entitled *Lewis Grizzard: In His Own Words*. The show was written by Dedra Grizzard and Lewis's manager, Steve Enoch. In the first part of the show, Oberst performs some of Grizzard's best material, and then in the last part, he pays tribute to him. The play has been well received throughout the South, and it was scheduled for the 2004 Spoleto Festival in Charleston, South Carolina.

The following is from a live performance:

> *Went down to see my mother the other day. I started to leave, and Mama said, "Where you goin'?" I said, "Mama, I've got to go to New York City." She said, "You wearin' clean underdrawers?" I said, "Mama, why do you ask me a question like that? I'm a grown man." She said, "You might be in a wreck." I said, "Mama, if I see a big truck comin' at me, I ain't goin' to have no clean underdrawers anyway!"*
>
> *Do you really think doctors care? I go out here and I get run over by a semi haulin' hogs, okay? They take me to the emergency room . . . not one but two doctors standin' over me, and one says, "Doctor, this man's in bad shape." The other says, "Yeah, but ain't his underdrawers clean?"*
>
> *I had open heart surgery—wrote a book about it,* They Tore My Heart Out and Stomped That Sucker Flat. *. . . . I'm goin' to tell you something . . . I don't like doctors much. I really don't. It ain't nothing personal, but we know how much money you make. You drive 'em big ol' Mercedes cars, you live in those big ol' houses. . . . But you're too cheap to put new magazines in your office! Did you ever notice that? I walk into my doctor's office and pick up* Time *magazine, and Roosevelt's on the cover!*

STEVE HALL AND SHOTGUN RED

Born December 1, 1954, Sheldon, Iowa

Steve Hall was a musician trying to get a break in 1982 when he wandered into a hobby shop and spied a big-mouthed, mustachioed puppet. On a whim, he paid forty dollars for it, and that led to his success in show business. "Shotgun Red" became a part of Hall's band and act, and after the band won the Minnesota Battle of the Bands

Steve Hall with Shotgun Red.
Courtesy of Steve Hall.

contest, he went to Nashville and eventually wound up on Ralph Emery's "Nashville Now" on the newly formed cable company TNN. He later played "Hee Haw" and the "Grand Ole Opry," and the Shotgun Red Band became the main entertainment on the General Jackson Showboat that plies the waters of the Cumberland River from its dock at Opryland, now Opry Mills.

Steve Hall grew up in a close, fun-loving family that moved around Iowa, following the elder Hall's jobs. His father was a country music fan and played everything from Bob Wills to Little Jimmie Dickens. Steve began playing snare drums in a rock band called the Electric Funeral, but he also learned the guitar. He later joined several country bands and first got on television in Duluth, Minnesota, with the "Tim Patterson Show Featuring Linda Lou." In 1976, he started his own band, Southbound '76. After he bought his ventriloquist's puppet, he fitted him out with a cowboy hat and used him as the emcee for his band. A publicist for the Minnesota Battle of the Bands contest, which his band won in 1983, was fascinated with Red and encouraged Hall to go to Nashville and get on Ralph Emery's TV show. Thinking the publicist had procured an invitation from Emery for an appearance, Hall and Red showed up only to find that there was no invitation. However, he took Red out of his case in front of a troop of Cub Scouts who were in the audience, and they went wild. Emery, who had gone to a station break, rushed over to see what the fuss was about, and he was captivated by Red's charm and wit. Steve and Red were brought on stage, and Emery invited them to audition for his "Nashville Now" show that was to help inaugurate the Nashville Network. They remained on the show for a decade.

Until the end of 2002, Hall and Red worked on the General Jackson Showboat in summertime and did fairs and festivals the rest of the year. Hall is a talented singer and guitarist, as well as a humorist. A great deal of his band's program consists of impressions of other distinctive singers, such as George Jones, Merle Haggard, Ronnie Milsap, and Johnny Cash, whom they do very convincingly. Between numbers, Steve and Shotgun Red do humorous jokes and routines. Hall says that a lot of his comedy comes from members of the audience who come up after the show to give him material. Steve Hall has a video, *Will the Real Shotgun Red Please Stand Up* (1-800-822-8522; www.shotgunred.com), that provides a great deal of Hall's comedy as well as good music from the Shotgun Red Band. Hall and Shotgun Red were nominated ten times for the *Music City News* Country Comedy Act of the Year and have been in the Top Five of the funniest people in country music.

Steve and his wife Daisy have three children—Jimmie, Steve Jr., and Angela—and three grandchildren, Megan, Kayla, and Pete. Steve Hall's main philanthropic cause is an annual benefit show in his hometown of Brainard, Minnesota, for several charities.

Following is a comic routine between Ralph Emery and Red:

> Ralph: What did you do before you were a singer?
> Red: Raised three-legged chickens.
> Ralph: Raised three-legged chickens? Oh, come on!
> Red: A standard chicken, now, is a four to eight mile bird. These three-legged chickens can run seventy-five miles an hour, Ralph.
> Ralph: There is no such thing as a three-legged chicken.
> Red: Yes, there is. We raise them because I like the drumstick, my wife likes the drumstick, and my boy likes to have a drumstick.
> Ralph: I see. What does it taste like?
> Red: I don't know. We never have caught one of those little boogers!

MIKE HAMMONDS. *See Moron Brothers*

GRANNY HARPER

Born Flora Bell Walters in 1873, Jessamine County, Kentucky; died April 19, 1961, Nicholasville, Kentucky

Granny Harper is best remembered as a piping-voiced singer, comedian, fiddler, pianist, harmonica and banjo player, and dancer at the "Renfro Valley Barn Dance" in its heyday in the 1940s as a CBS network show. Before that, during the Great Depression, she was a Lexington street entertainer and later a performer on Asa Martin's "Morning Roundup" on WLAP. She also did appearances at Lexington's Opera House. John Lair brought her to the "Barn Dance" shortly after he moved it to Renfro Valley in 1939. She remained on the show until 1958, when she was eighty-five years old.

Flora had an accident resulting in a broken back when she was young that left her permanently stooped and humpbacked and four feet tall. She used her unusual build to enhance her comic personality. At the "Renfro Valley Barn Dance," she was billed as the "Clamor Girl," in contrast to some of their really good-looking performers, such as Linda Parker and Lily May Ledford, but she was also called the "gayliest" girl

on the show. Lair claimed that she could "execute the fastest jig in seven counties." She dressed in old-fashioned clothing, such as long dresses and a sunbonnet, and smoked a corncob pipe. In addition to some appearances on Lair's early-morning radio show, Granny was a regular at the Saturday-night "Barn Dance" and also went out with the Renfro Valley tent shows. Here's how John Lair introduced her in 1953:

Granny plays the fiddle and harmonica (she says it's a "french harp"), dances, and sings with the best of them. Age has made her voice high-pitched and liable to waiver a bit on the high notes, but it has not dimmed her smile or slowed her nimble feet. You'll take to Granny the minute you see her.

Granny Harper. Courtesy of the John Lair Collection, Southern Appalachian Archives, Berea College.

Granny was married to James Williams, and they made their home near Camp Nelson, Kentucky. They are buried in the Maple Grove Cemetery in Nicholasville, Kentucky.

RODNEY HARRIS

Born 1938, Dion, Kentucky

Rodney Harris was a comedian for a good many years while also serving in the air force and running several business interests. He grew up listening to Knoxville's "Mid-day Merry-Go-Round" on WNOX and the comedy groups there led by Lowell Blanchard, the inspired program director.

Harris did a few gigs as a comic before joining the air force in 1960. Thus, his interest in comedy led him to seek out opportunities to entertain in clubs near his duty stations in Texas, New England, and New York. His comedy was country. "I used a kind of Will Rogers type of humor—a monologue, one-liners, and barnyard jokes. You couldn't do anything off-color in those days. It was basically vaudeville stuff. I took jokes and reworked them for what I needed."

After he got out of the air force, he purchased a truck stop near Renfro Valley, met Pete Stamper, a comedian at the "Renfro Valley Barn Dance," and was invited to do several guest appearances there. Later he moved to Providence, Rhode Island, for business reasons. While there he did theatrical work with the Trinity Repertory Theater. Later in the 1960s, he worked with Jim Ed Brown and Helen Cornelius and Faron Young, doing a comedic warmup show for them. He also did a few shows with Grandpa Jones and package shows with several stars where he entertained while the stage and bands were changed between acts. He was part owner of a show called "Country Time Review" out of Wheeling, West Virginia, with Johnny Dollar, Van Treavor, and Penny DeHaven. In Wheeling, he did several guest appearances on WWVA's "Mountaineer Jamboree." He also did a guest spot on the "Grand Ole Opry." Harris did two 45 rpm recordings on the Natural Sound Label and one on Federated Artists.

In the 1970s, Harris quit comedy for newspaper, radio, and television work. He also did hot-air-balloon promotions before he and his wife Jennifer founded Jen-Rod Artist Directions, an artist management and development firm in Centerville, Tennessee.

Harris sees humor as very important in entertainment and life:

> Humor is a necessity of life. It's also an escape. In laughing, the only thing you can do is laugh. It's difficult to think about anything else except what you are laughing about.
>
> Comedy in the early days of country music was a part of the entertainment cycle. Music is great, but you also need the value of laughter. You can't leave them on the down side with sad songs. You put them on the up side with laughter. A lot of my comedy was done to prepare the audience for the singers, to get them in a good mood.

When asked why he got out of comedy, Harris quickly said, "Because everybody laughed at me."

JOHN HARTFORD

Born John Cowan Harford, December 30, 1937,
New York, New York; died June 4, 2001, Madison,
Tennessee

John Hartford is known as a singer-songwriter, superb musician, humorist, dancer, collector, scholar, riverboat pilot, and television host. He is perhaps best known for his composition "Gentle on My Mind." Hartford was a sure country entertainer who turned away from a career in Hollywood to pursue his love of old-time music and river lore.

Although Hartford was born in New York City, his father, a physician, soon moved the family to St. Louis, where young John grew up in a river culture that included paddlewheel craft and all sorts of music. By the time he was thirteen he was playing the banjo and fiddle. He gained a special love of the bluegrass music of Lester Flatt and Earl Scruggs, but he also loved the clawhammer banjo style of David "Stringbean" Akeman. In high school, he headed a bluegrass band that imitated the sounds of Bill Monroe, Flatt and Scruggs, and Reno and Smiley.

Hartford dropped out of St. Louis University to work as a deckhand on boats and to play with bands in the area. He moved to Nashville in 1965 to do session work and to try to sell his songs. He went to work for the Glaser Brothers as a songwriter and soon had an RCA contract with recordings produced by Chet Atkins, who added the "t" to his name. His first album, *John Hartford Looks at Life* (1966), didn't do too well, but his second, *Earthwords and Music* (1967), contained "Gentle on my Mind," the single of which went Top Sixty. Other singers covered his song, first Glen Campbell (a gold album), then Dean Martin (pop Top Three), Patti Page, Aretha Franklin, and Floyd Kramer. There were about 295 recordings of the song, and it won Hartford two Grammys.

It was then that CBS offered him a role in a TV drama, but he turned them down, opting to do his own thing. However, he did become a writer and performer on the "Smothers Brothers Comedy Hour" on CBS and was a fixture on the "Glen Campbell Goodtime Hour."

On comedy, Hartford said:

John Hartford. Photo by McGuire, courtesy of Keith Case and Associates.

Its real purpose is to liven the show. I have a tendency to play fiddle tunes that not everybody likes. About the time they may say, "This guy's getting boring," I tell them a joke.

You know, it's funny about people who tell jokes: they're considered to be at the low end of the entertainment scale. However, if you can tell a good joke and really get someone to laugh, you can go from the bottom to the top faster than you can with any other form of entertainment.

I don't believe in playing down to an audience. Country people are not stupid. I have a story that is very sophisticated, something that actually happened to me. A young lady came up to me, looked me right in the eye, and just as serious as she could, she said, "When you go back up there, would you sing something I know, so I can tell if you're any good or not." That gets a laugh.

Hartford earned his riverboat pilot's license in 1969, and for a dozen years he worked every summer about ten days a month out of Peoria, Illinois, on the *Julia*

Belle Swain. The boat carried passengers, and Hartford was part of the entertainment as well as pilot. He wrote and performed in a show for TNN, "Banjos, Fiddles, and Riverboats."

In 1971, he teamed up with the folk guitarist and singer Norman Blake, the fiddler Vassar Clements, and the dobroist Tut Taylor to make some remarkable music on the bluegrass festival circuit. Hartford has appeared on the albums of many other artists but has an impressive list of his own, sometimes with other well-known artists as guests. His Flying Fish albums are notable, among them *Tennessee Jubilee* (1975, with Lester Flatt and Benny Martin), *Mark Twang* (1976, a Grammy winner), *Gum Tree Canoe* (1984), and *Oh My, How Time Does Fly* (1988). Also important is *Aero Plain* (Rounder, 1997).

One writer described Hartford's act as an "unhurried and homespun mix of bluegrass, folk, and vaudeville." In addition to his performing, he had a profound appreciation of the folk music of this country. He befriended such people as Elmer Byrd, the West Virginia banjo player and singer, and produced his albums. He also did meticulous research on the late Blind Bill Haley, a legendary Kentucky fiddler, collected recordings of his music, and produced a recording for others to enjoy. John Hartford battled cancer for a decade while continuing his maverick career. At the end, he invited his musical friends to come to his house on the Cumberland River to play during his last week.

Introducing his first CD, Hartford said:

> *Now, this recording sounds a little strange. It's real quiet, and it may bother you a little, but I have a tape to go along with it that has some hisses and clicks and background noise, and if you play it along with the CD, it will sound real natural.*

GEORGE DEWEY HAY

Born November 9, 1895, Attica, Indiana;
died May 8, 1968, Virginia Beach, Virginia

George D. Hay was known widely as the founder, announcer, and promoter of the "Grand Ole Opry." Since the show appeared on radio along with "Grand Opera," Hay chose to differentiate the two kinds of music by naming his show in this way. Hay was a major force in the creation of the country music industry.

Hay started his career on the *Memphis Commercial Appeal* as a municipal court reporter. He had a humorous bent, and related to his court beat, he began a column called "Howdy Judge" that purported to be conversations between a white judge and various black malefactors. This column, published as a collection in 1926 under the same title, earned the young reporter the title of the "Solemn Old Judge." He also became an announcer for WMC, owned by the newspaper, and editor of the paper's radio news and schedules. He was enthusiastic about his radio work. He wrote scripts, served as announcer, and introduced his shows by blowing on a wooden whistle that sounded like a steamboat whistle, the same one that he later used on the "Grand Ole Opry." His success at WMC brought him to the attention of the Sears-Roebuck executives who launched WLS (World's Largest Store) in Chicago, and they invited him in 1924 to become an announcer there. The "National Barn Dance" was the creation of Edgar L. Bill, a WLS executive, who pressed Hay into service as one of the announcers for the show. It became popular, the first show to do a program of mostly old-time music, and it lasted from 1924 to 1960. Hay reported that he had attended a hoedown party in the Ozarks when he was there doing a story as a newspaper reporter and that the "Barn Dance" was the first use of radio to present the kind of music and dance that he had observed and admired. As evidence of his success as an announcer for this and other programs at WLS, he was voted the "most popular announcer" in a *Radio Digest* poll in 1924.

Later on, executives at WSM, formed by the National Life and Accident Insurance Company in Nashville, were looking for a director, and they took note of the *Radio Digest* honor and offered Hay the job. He moved to Nashville in November 1925. He decided to create in Nashville the same kind of show that he had worked with at WLS. Eva Thompson Jones, who worked at WSM, told Hay about her uncle, a fiddler, born in 1848, who had a vast repertoire of tunes. Hay invited Uncle Jimmy Thompson to audition; pleased with his playing, he scheduled him for November 25, 1925, to play some fiddle tunes over the air. The response through telephone calls, telegrams, and letters was enthusiastic, and Hay made ready to have a regular program of what he called "folk music" every Saturday night. Uncle Dave Macon, Sid Harkreader, and Dr. Humphrey Bate and his band had already been playing over WSM prior to Hay's arrival, and they were among those who joined Uncle Jimmy for the "Barn Dance" show that was to be renamed the "Grand Ole Opry" in 1927.

Hay had a humorous bent, and he dressed up his entertainers, who had heretofore usually worn suits and ties, in overalls or other countrified clothing and named or renamed them with colorful rustic names. Dr. Bate's band became the Possum Hunters, the Binckley Brothers band became the Dixie Clodhoppers, and there were also the Fruit Jar Drinkers and the Gulley Jumpers. Hay had a wonderful vocal flair and introduced his performers in a colorful fashion, usually with a standard identificaton tag, such as "Uncle Dave Macon, the Dixie Dewdrop," and "DeFord Bailey, the harmonica wizard." Although he invited a good many individual comedians to his stage, he also encouraged the use of comedians in individual bands, such as Roy Acuff's. However, he did not serve as a straight man to them. He hired Edna Wilson and Margaret Walters, who portrayed the comical country women Sarie and Sally. He encouraged Uncle Dave Macon's comedy and antics, although he and WSM executives were nervous about what topics the old man might bring up when he'd had a drink or two. Hay also imported the veteran minstrel, vaudeville, and tent-theater comedians Lee Davis Wilds and LeRoy

White to WSM and eventually the "Opry" to do blackface comedy as Lasses and Honey. Wilds later performed at the "Opry" with other partners as Jamup and Honey. When Minnie Pearl joined the "Opry" in 1940, she reported that she was scared and nervous but that Hay reassured her by saying, "Just love them, and they'll love you back." She valued this as her best advice. The other best-remembered comedians, Rod Brasfield and Whitey Ford as the Duke of Paducah, joined the cast later. Hay hugely enjoyed comedy and those who could deliver it, and he was a shrewd judge of humor, although, apparently, he didn't write comedy scripts or rehearse comedians in the manner of John Lair at Renfro Valley or Lowell Blanchard in Knoxville. However, his "Howdy Judge" columns were written in dialogue style and in the manner of vaudeville skits, and according to the writer Charles K. Wolfe, Hay performed some of them with a partner in the early days of the "Opry."

It was as a publicist and promotor that Hay excelled. Wolfe called him a "public relations genius." As director of the station and all of its programs, Hay saw an opportunity to create a show that would attract a huge audience, especially in the rural South. In newspaper articles and publicity releases, he emphasized the term "folk music." This term was somewhat a misnomer, since most of the performers played a variety of music, including folk, minstrel, Tin Pan Alley favorites, and increasingly, recently composed numbers. His concept of the music changed as he went forward, but he tied it to traditional moral values that were preserved in the music and in the lifestyles of rural people. Radio was a national fascination in these early years, and the "Opry" was particularly popular throughout the South and in other rural areas.

With the popularity of the "Opry" as a radio show, it also became a live stage show at various locations in the city, most notably in the Ryman Auditorium. Personal-appearance shows became a major part of the operation, and later there were tent and package shows that traveled far and wide. Hay was a colorful part of these shows.

As Charles Wolfe has noted, Hay was not a good manager, and so professional managers were hired to run the "Opry," bringing their own ideas. Thus, Hay began to lose influence. About 1936, he suffered a nervous breakdown and was gone from the station for many months, although he was back in 1938 and worked on a half-hour portion of the show that was broadcast over the NBC network. He was also involved in promoting and starring in the film *Grand Ole Opry*, in 1940. In 1945, he published a book, *A Story of the Grand Ole Opry*. He hosted an "Opry" show in Carnegie Hall in 1947. For a time, he edited *Pickin' and Singin' News* in Nashville, and he unsuccessfully promoted two syndicated radio shows. In the meantime, the "Grand Ole Opry" was changing, as was country music, and apparently Hay was no longer consulted about the direction of the station or his beloved show. Disillusioned, he eventually moved to Virginia Beach, Virginia, where he died at the age of seventy-two.

(With credit to Charles K. Wolfe, *A Good-Natured Riot: The Birth of the Grand Ole Opry* [Nashville: Country Music Foundation Press and Vanderbilt University Press, 1999].)

HIRAM HAYSEED

Born William Henry Godwin, South Georgia, 1889;
died 1959, Wheeling, West Virginia

Hiram Hayseed, born in Georgia but reared in the Texas cotton country, was a comic character created by William Henry "Shorty" Godwin. Godwin was a musician and

William Henry Godwin as Hiram Hayseed. Courtesy of Doc Williams.

comedian who had played in vaudeville under the name of the Texas Cotton Picker and recorded two sides for Columbia in 1929—"Good Old Turnip Greens" and "Jimbo Jambo Land"—under his real name. He also worked with Otto Gray's Oklahoma Cowboys. He later performed over radio stations in Cincinnati with a group called the Fiddling Farmers, headed by Mark Jeffers. With the Fiddling Farmers, Godwin and Sleepy Jeffers did an act they called "Sleepy and Shorty, the Happy Hoedowners."

The Fiddling Farmers moved to the WWVA "Mountaineer Jamboree" in Wheeling in 1937, where Godwin started doing his Hiram Hayseed character as a regular thing. For fourteen years he worked with Doc Williams at WWVA doing road shows throughout West Virginia, Pennsylvania, and the East. Doc Williams remembered, "Hiram basically did the old blackface comedy skits, but of course we did them whiteface. We took those old blackface comedy skits that were done in the medicine shows, and we adapted them for white audiences in whiteface as rube comedy. Oh, man, they loved it! I was the straight man."

Godwin recorded several numbers for Wheeling Records (Box 902, Wheeling, WV 26003), some of which are still available on cassette.

(With credit to Ivan Tribe and Doc Williams.)

THE HIRED HANDS

DeWitt "Snuffy" Jenkins, born October 27, 1908,
Harris, North Carolina; died April 30, 1990
Homer "Pappy" Sherrill, born March 23, 1919,
Sherrill's Ford, North Carolina; died November
30, 2001, Chapin, South Carolina
Julian "Greasy" Medlin, born September 18, 1910,
Pontiac, South Carolina; died July 5, 1982,
Columbia, South Carolina

Snuffy Jenkins is perhaps the best known of the Hired Hands, who entertained out of Columbia, South Carolina, mainly because of the influence his three-finger banjo picking had on Earl Scruggs and bluegrass music. He was also a funny comedian. Homer Sherrill, a superb fiddler and straight man, had long played with Snuffy in various bands. Julian Medlin, a medicine-show veteran blackface comedian, ragtime banjoist, guitarist, and singer, joined them later.

Snuffy Jenkins entered professional music with a brother and cousin on WBT, Charlotte, in 1934. In 1936, he joined J. E. Mainer and His Mountaineers at WSPA, Spartanburg, South Carolina, and then WIS in Columbia. Jenkins appeared on some of Mainer's Bluebird recordings. When Mainer left the station, Byron Parker took over the band and called it Byron Parker and His Hillbillies (also Mountaineers). Parker, an Iowan, had earlier worked with the Monroe Brothers and was a gifted announcer. Wade Mainer commented, "He could sell a bushel of rotten apples even if there was only one good one in it." The band included Verle Jenkins; George Morris, who did blackface comedy; Leonard Stokes, guitar and mandolin; Clyde Robbins, guitar; and Jenkins, banjo and comedy. Although Jenkins did the old clawhammer and two-finger style of banjo, he also excelled in the rarer three-finger style, which was taken to new complexity by Earl Scruggs, Don Reno, and others.

Homer Sherrill joined them as fiddler in 1939. He had taken up the fiddle at the age of seven and was playing on the radio by the time he was a teenager. His first real job was with the East Hickory String Band over WBT, Charlotte. The band became the Crazy Hickory Nuts (advertising their sponsor, Crazy Water Crystals). The band later moved to WWNC, Asheville, and then to WSGS, Atlanta. Sherrill had also played with Wade Mainer, the Blue Sky Boys, and the Morris Brothers. He has a wonderful old-time fiddle style and is a fine harmony singer and straight man.

The band played over WIS but did the "kerosene circuit" of schools before they were wired for electricity. When Byron Parker died of a heart attack at thirty-seven in 1948, Jenkins and Sherrill took over the band and changed its name to the Hired Hands, as a tribute to Parker, who had dubbed himself "the Old Hired Hand." They

The Hired Hands. L-R: Snuffy Jenkins, Greasy Medlin, and Pappy Sherrill.
Courtesy of Homer Sherrill.

invited Julian Medlin to join them as a comedian and musician. Other musicians also
played with the band, including Harold and Randy Lucas.

Julian Medley was born a decade after the turn of the twentieth century at the end
of the minstrel-show era, when medicine shows were still common and employed many
entertainers. Medlin had mostly played blackface in medicine shows, and he may have
played other types of shows in his early days. He was adept at ragtime tenor banjo and
the guitar, and he sang novelty songs with a commanding flair. The folklorist Glenn
Hinson proclaimed his version of "Step It Up and Go" to be one of the best by a white
entertainer ever. In the 1930s, Medlin did a stint with Fisher Henley's Aristocratic
Pigs over WBT Charlotte, with many schoolhouse performances. His career is vague
between those days and the 1950s, when he abandoned blackface. With the Hired
Hands, he still blackened the lower part of his face and kept the white lips and a line
drawn down across his eyelids in the manner of clowns. His appearance was also that
of a tramp. His repertoire remained much the same as in the medicine shows. He loved
to perform, and when he was not touring with the Hired Hands, he did comedy and
music at a pizza parlor in Columbia.

Jenkins and Sherrill valued comedy, and even before Medlin joined them, they
hired an old vaudevillian and comedy stage showman, Billy F. Jones, to write material

for them. It ranged from gags to full-blown skits in which all members of the band would take a part. Medlin also coached Sherrill and Jenkins on comedic styles, and he contributed many of their gags and skits. Sherrill explained their comedy:

> You can do singles or doubles, and sometimes you had a third man, a straight man, to bring up a point for the comedy to carry out. I was the straight man. Snuffy wore those big britches, and big shoes on the wrong feet, and a pointed hat. Greasy had big pants and shoes with paint on them. So, Snuffy and Greasy were funny-looking anyway. They did a lot of what we called doubles, where both were comedians. We had an act called "The Three O'Clock Train," and I was the straight character that led them up to what was happening.
>
> Comedy gets everybody in a happy mood, but you can't go too long with comedy. It's got to be quick and get to the point. When you get good laughs, don't keep on. If you keep running on and on, it wears out and won't work. We did it as a finale, and they looked forward to it.

By 1953, WIS Radio was also WIS-TV, and the Hired Hands adapted to the new medium. Sherrill commented, however, that television was a different medium in that it was mainly visual. In radio, audiences flocked to personal appearances to see what the performers looked like, but with television you already knew. Soon, though, bluegrass and old-time music festivals sprang up over the country, and the Hired Hands were invited as a surviving bridge between old-time and bluegrass. Their comedy appealed to festival groups because not a lot of it had survived in modern musical venues.

In 1979, the Hired Hands, along with other surviving medicine-show performers, were invited by the University of North Carolina folklorist Glenn Hinson to stage an old-time medicine "Free Show." It was performed first in the hamlet of Bailey, North Carolina, and then North Carolina Public Television produced "Free Show Tonight," narrated by the old medicine showman Roy Acuff, which aired over PBS. The show was staged again at the Smithsonian Institution, where the performers were interviewed for the archives. Finally, in 1983, *Free Show* played at the American Place Theater in New York City. The Hired Hands' comedy was a central part of each show.

The Hired Hands did relatively few recordings: *Carolina Bluegrass* (Folk-Lyric, 1962, later reissued by Arhoolie); *Thirty-three Years of Pickin' and Pluckin'* (Rounder, 1972); *Crazy Water Barn Dance* (Rounder, 1976); *Something Special* (Old Homestead, 1989); and in 2000, Old Homestead released early recordings of *Byron Parker and His Mountaineers*. Snuffy Jenkins also appears on Mike Seeger's Folkways release *American Banjo Scruggs Style*.

Snuffy and Greasy used this routine often:

> *Greasy: I've been all over Columbia and South Carolina, and there's too much propaganda goin' 'round.*
> *Snuffy: Too much what?*
> *Greasy: Too much propaganda goin' 'round. You know what propaganda is?*
> *Snuffy: Sure I know what propaganda is.*

Greasy: What is propaganda?

Snuffy: Propaganda is . . . uh. . . . You know what it is.

Greasy: Sure I know what it is.

Snuffy: And all the folk out there know what it is, so what's the use of my tellin' you?

Greasy: I knowed you didn't know what propaganda is. He ain't got a bit of sense.

Snuffy: Wha'd' you say it is?

Greasy: Propaganda is a lot of stuff goin' 'round that ain't so.

Snuffy: No, that ain't no sich a what-ya-may-call-it.

Greasy: Shore it is.

Snuffy: No, it ain't.

Greasy: Well, what is it?

Snuffy: You a married man, ain't ya?

Greasy: Married man! Ha, ha, you don't think rheumatism causes me to look like this, do you? Sure, I'm married.

Snuffy: How long you been married?

Greasy: How long? Forty-five years.

Snuffy: You got any children?

Greasy: No, I ain't got any of them things. Ain't got nary a one.

Snuffy: That's what I call propaganda. You see, yore wife is a proper goose, but you ain't a proper gander!

SHORTY HOBBS AND LITTLE ELLER

*Roy Hobbs, born January 27, 1912, Wolfe County,
Kentucky; died June 1973*

*Beth Jane Cremer, born ca. 1922, Detroit, Michigan;
death date and place unknown*

Shorty Hobbs and Beth Cremer Ward were best known as the comedy team of Shorty Hobbs and Little Eller at the "Renfro Valley Barn Dance." Hobbs being short and Little Eller being well over six feet tall, they were visually a comic pair.

Before his career as a comedian, Hobbs performed and recorded with Asa Martin as Martin and Hobbs, playing mandolin and doing the first recording of Asa's composition "Hot Corn, Cold Corn."

Beth Cremer grew up with a desire to be in front of the public. When she was about twelve and five-foot-eight, she thought maybe she could be a model. At five-foot-ten and real skinny, she thought she would be suitable as a dress mannequin. When she kept growing, she became so self-conscious that her mother took her out of school, gave her a guitar, and took her to dancing lessons. The dance teacher looked her up and down and suggested that she be a comedian. This was taken as an insult. Later, though, when she danced before groups, she found she could make them laugh, and so she

Shorty Hobbs and "Little Eller"
Long. Courtesy of the John Lair
Collection, Southern Appalachian
Archives, Berea College.

began to see ways she could make use of her unusual height. She performed at garden
and women's clubs. In 1939, Cremer entered the Michigan State Talent Contest and
won a trip to New York for the World's Fair, and she was also a guest at the Michigan
State Fair. This brought an invitation to audition for WLS radio in Chicago. There
she went out with the road shows, now with the name of Ella Long, and one act was
with Salty Holmes, who danced with a life-sized rag doll. Holmes would dance off
stage and, for his encore, discard his doll, sweep the limp Ella onto the stage, dance
around with her arms and legs flopping, and then drop her on stage. When she got
up and walked off, the audience was incredulous, and the act was a great success.

Beth and her mother listened to the "Renfro Valley Barn Dance" on the radio and
liked it, and her mother encouraged her to go to Kentucky and audition. She caught
the bus, and when she arrived at Renfro Valley, a busload of teachers had also just
arrived, and John Lair was lining up impromptu entertainment for them. He invited

her to do a dance to the Hawaiian-guitar accompaniment of Jerry Byrd. Thus she became a member of the Renfro Valley cast. Lair saw the comic possibility of five-foot-two Shorty Hobbs and the six-foot-four Ella. He changed her name to Little Eller, and they worked up an act. Actually Eller knew only four or five songs, but she soon learned more. She would dance around, flinging her arms this way and that and kicking over Shorty's head, while they sang and he played the mandolin. Then they would leap-frog over each other. They were a successful comic team on the "Renfro Valley Barn Dance" and in its road shows. Little Eller left Renfro Valley once to join the Olsson and Johnson *Hell's-a'Poppin'* show, which was touring the country, but she yearned for Renfro Valley and returned.

Eller met the fiddler Smokey Ward at Renfro Valley, and they soon married. They opened the Bellyachers Restaurant in nearby Mount Vernon but later worked with Pee Wee King. They also did television shows in Louisville and Dayton. She and Smokey had one child, Danny, before they divorced. She later married Dan White, and they retired to St. Petersburg, Florida.

This writer was unable to find additional information about Shorty Hobbs.

(With credit to the late Reuben Powell, of the Renfro Valley Tape Club, for his interview with Little Eller, January 16, 1969.)

SALTY HOLMES

Born Floyd Holmes, 1910, Glasgow, Kentucky;
death date and place unknown

Salty Holmes was a vaudeville comedian known for his "talking blues" harmonica who later got into country music and comedy with the Prairie Ramblers at WLS and the "National Barn Dance" in Chicago from 1932–47. There he also teamed up with Ella Long (Beth Cremer), who was six feet, four inches tall. Holmes would dance around the stage with a life-sized rag doll and then skip off stage, and for an encore, he would discard his doll, grab Ella, and dance back with Ella's arms and legs flapping around, then drop her on stage. The audience thought she was the doll, and when she got up and walked off, it brought the house down. Holmes also worked at stations in Knoxville and Nashville as well as WLW in Cincinnati. He eventually went to Hollywood and made movies with Charles Starrett and Tex Ritter and later appeared on the "Andy Griffith Show" on CBS. He recorded for Columbia, Decca, London, and Four Star. His best-known numbers were "Mama Blues" and "I Found My Mama." He retired to Anderson, Indiana.

DAVID HOLT

Born October 15, 1946, Garland, Texas

A four-time Grammy-winning entertainer, musician, humorist, storyteller, folksong collector, and radio and television host, David Holt has dedicated a large part of his life to performing, preserving, and promoting traditional American music and story-telling. He has hosted TNN's "Fire on the Moun-tain," "Celebration Express," and "American Music Shop," National Public Radio's "Riverwalk: Classic Jazz from the Landing" from San Antonio, and the PBS series "Folkways." He was a frequent guest on "Hee Haw," "Nashville Now," and the "Grand Ole Opry" and has traveled to Nepal, Thailand, South America, and Africa as a cultural ambassador spon-sored by the U.S. Department of State.

Humor and storytelling are a large part of his performances. He sees humor as a way to involve the audience in what he is doing. He learned this from a master. "Jethro Burns was on 'Fire on the Mountain,' and he said, 'If you're going to be funny in your show, you need to make people laugh in the first five seconds.' I said, 'You're barely out on stage,' and he said, 'That's right, you do it on the way to the mic.' Jethro's point was that humor is

David Holt. Courtesy of High Windy Productions.

the elixir that loosens everybody up in the audience." Holt went on to say, "I think humor has more power to bring people in to you than anything. It boosts people up and gives them a reason to care about you."

A graduate of the University of California at Santa Barbara, Holt founded and directed the Appalachian Music Program at Warren Wilson College in Swannanoa, North Carolina, which brought traditional musicians and storytellers to class and sent students out to find, interview, and record additional folks. This program resulted from his own experience of seeking out and recording traditional people, beginning with the cowboy singer Carl T. Sprague in Texas. On a trip to the Appalachian Mountains, he discovered, as the English folksong collector Cecil J. Sharp had much earlier, "a people who sang as naturally as they talked." They also told humorous stories and long folktales and played numerous instruments. One such person was Dellie Norton of Madison County, North Carolina, who sang ancient British ballads that had been passed down from both sides of her family. Dellie became a surrogate grandmother to Holt and to his students.

Holt also learned to play all the stringed instruments in the traditional styles. He had already learned from his father to produce rhythm on the spoons and bones, and he remains the only artist to have played a paper bag on the "Grand Ole Opry" stage.

Holt is coauthor, with Bill Mooney, of two books on storytelling—*Ready-to-Tell Tales* (1994) and *The Storyteller's Guide* (1996). He has numerous recordings of his music and stories: *I Got a Bullfrog: Folksongs for the Fun of It; Grandfather's Greatest Hits* (with Chet Atkins, Doc Watson, and Duane Eddy), nominated for a Grammy; *Stellaluna* (winner of two Grammys); *Why the Dog Chases the Cat: Great Animal Stories; Mostly Ghostly Stories; The Hairyman;* and *Tallybone* (the last two won the American Library Association's Notable Recording designation), all on the High Windy label. He also has videos: *The Hogaphone and Other Stories, Folk Rhythms,* and *Old Time Banjo I, II, III* (Homespun Tapes). In 2002 David won two more Grammys for *Legacy,* which presents Doc Watson's inspiring story in three CD collections of songs and interviews, and a live concert recording. His latest recordings are: *Live and Kickin' at the National Storytelling Festival* (2003), *Let it Slide,* and *David Holt and the Lightning Bolts* (2006). David can also be seen in the film *O Brother, Where Art Thou?* For information on David Holt's books and recordings, go to www.davidholt.com.

David Holt lives in Fairview, North Carolina, with his wife, Virginia Callaway, and their son Zeb. They grieve for a daughter, Sara Jane, who was killed in an automobile accident in 1989.

Following is a short version of a story that David Holt told at a festival of Appalachian Humor at Berea College:

> *Leroy Teets came in from the navy with this brand-new Harley-Davidson motorcycle. They said it had a headlight as big as a dinner plate.*
>
> *They said, "What is that old thing, Leroy? Why, you can't take that on these old mountain roads." Leroy said, "I can take it anywhere in the county!"*
>
> *Old Jeeter Ledford walked up and said, "I'll bet you five dollars that you can't ride it up to the top of High Windy."*
>
> *Old Leroy pulled five dollars out of his pocket and threw it on the ground. Then Old Leroy started up the motorcycle—vroom, vroom, vroom. Now High Windy is a long, tall mountain. There's no road nor no trail to the top, just rocks, sticks, leaves, and trees all the way to the top. So Old Leroy had to have it at full throttle and hold on for everything he was worth just to stay on.*
>
> *Now, they forgot about old Rhubarb Golightly, who lived a way up on the top of High Windy. Rhubarb was a man that didn't like people. He hadn't been to town for seven years and didn't care if he ever went again. He just lived on top of High Windy with his little wife, Samantha, and did all his own chores and grew all his own food. So, that day, after old Rhubarb had finished his big old dinner of biscuits and sowbelly gravy, skunk cabbage, poke sallet, jar-bean pie, with possum sauce, and two mouth-shrinking dill pickles, he went out on the front porch to take his ease.*
>
> *Just then he heard something coming up through there—vroom, vroooom. He jumped up. He'd never heard man nor bear make a sound like that—vroom, vroooom! Then he*

saw it coming, that headlight just a-flashing. There were dogs a-runnin', sticks a-flyin', and chickens a'goin'!

He said, "Samantha, bring me my gun!" She brings him his big old gun, and he levels that thing and goes bang, bang, bang, and that motorcycle goes flying one way and Leroy goes flying another!

She says, "Did you kill it, Honey?"

He says, "I don't know, but whatever that thing was, I made it turn that boy loose!"

HOMER AND JETHRO

*Kenneth C. "Jethro" Burns, born March 10, 1920,
Conasauga, Tennessee; died February 4, 1989,
Evanston, Illinois
Henry Doyle "Homer" Haynes, born July 27, 1920,
Knoxville, Tennessee; died August 7, 1971,
Lansing, Illinois*

Homer and Jethro were one of the best-known and most popular radio comedy duets in the business, and they were superb musicians as well, creating some imaginative parodies of popular songs. They began their radio career at WNOX in Knoxville on the "Mid-day Merry-Go-Round," then went on to the "Renfro Valley Barn Dance," WLW's "Plantation Party," and WLS's "National Barn Dance." All the while they played every personal-appearance venue there was, and their success took them eventually to the theaters of Las Vegas and to guest spots on network television shows.

Burns and Haynes were not quite teenagers in 1932 when they met at a talent contest at WNOX, young Burns playing with his brother Aychie and Haynes with another group. Lowell Blanchard, the program director of the station, formed members of the two groups into the "String Dusters" as a house band. Jethro remembers that they were fired every time a new band came to town and rehired when it moved on. In between, they played at stations in Chattanooga and Bristol. Neither Burns nor Haynes were particularly interested in "hillbilly" music, but it was a job. Blanchard was a master at selling the new concept of country music, and he was also good at writing comedy scripts. He wrote several for Burns and Haynes and gave them the name of Homer and Jethro.

In 1939, Homer and Jethro traded their fellow band members out of their interest in an ancient Lincoln, with no heater and bad brakes, and went for an audition for the "Renfro Valley Barn Dance." The owner, John Lair, started them at twenty-five dollars a week but shortly raised them to fifty. These city boys were bored in the tiny town of Mount Vernon, but they were soon doing a two-hour morning broadcast, a Monday-evening show, and the Saturday-night "Barn Dance," as well as doing personal appearances. During this time, they also received invitations to do guest spots on WLW's "Plantation Party" and the WLS "National Barn Dance."

Homer and Jethro (Henry Haynes and Kenneth Burns), ca. 1939. Courtesy of the John Lair Collection, Southern Appalachian Archives, Berea College.

The duo's act was broken up by World War II. Homer was drafted into the medical corps, and he was attached to General Patton's Third Army in Europe, seeing frontline action in France, Belgium, Luxemburg, Austria, and Germany. Jethro wound up in the Thirty-seventh Infantry Division and combat in the Pacific—Guadalcanal, New Georgia, Bougainville, and Russell Island—before getting a place in the relative safety of the regimental band.

After the war, Homer and Jethro decided not to go back to their job at Renfro Valley. They went instead to Cincinnati and were hired at WLW. Among their fellow performers at the station were Chet Atkins and two good-looking women billed as the Johnson Sisters. Jethro married Louise Johnson, and Chet married Leona. In Cincinnati, Homer and Jethro did five recordings for King Records, including their version of Frank Sinatra's hit "Five Minutes More" as well as "Rye Whiskey," "Over the Rainbow," and "I Feel Old Age Coming On." They tried a tent show in the summer of 1947, and after it went broke they headed back to Knoxville for another stint at the "Mid-day Merry-Go-Round." In 1949, they signed with RCA Victor and were encouraged to try song parodies. This resulted in "Baby It's Cold Outside" (Top Ten) and "Tennessee Border No. 2" (Top Fifteen). They did several other recordings for RCA, including, "How Much Is That Hound Dog in the Window?" (Top Three), "Hernando's Hideaway" (Top Fifteen, their most successful parody), "The Battle of Kookamonga" (1959 Grammy for best comedy performance), and the following LPs, *Homer and Jethro at the Comedy Club* (1960), *Homer and Jethro at the Convention* (1963), and *The Best of Homer and Jethro* (1967).

After a brief stay at KWTO in Springfield, Missouri, the Indiana State Fair, and a hotel act with Spike Jones in St. Louis, Washington, D.C., and New Orleans, the duo arrived in Chicago, where they did guest spots on the WLS "National Barn Dance" and Don McNeil's "Breakfast Club" for two years. The WLS Artists Bureau booked them for personal appearances over most of the Midwest. They also did several Las Vegas gigs and even the Village Barn in Greenwich Village. They were guests on major television-network variety shows and did successful ads for Kellogg's Corn Flakes. The pair had long since abandoned their hillbilly costumes and demeanor; they appeared now in street clothes and sometimes tuxedos.

In 1970, Homer and Jethro teamed with Chet Atkins to form the Nashville String Band and did several RCA albums: *Down Home, Identified, Strung Up, The Bandit,* and *The World's Greatest Melodies.*

Homer died of a heart attack in 1971, sending Jethro into a slump for a time. He rallied and continued to make music, sometimes with his brother-in-law Chet Atkins and others, playing country, bluegrass, and jazz in much admired styles. He was a guest on numerous television shows, including the "Tonight Show" and "Nashville Now." He and Ken Edison wrote two books on mandolin techniques, *Jethro Burns' Book,* vols. 1 and 2. Jethro Burns continued to perform until he died of cancer in 1989.

(With credit to Henry "Homer" Haynes and Kenneth "Jethro" Burns, "From Moonshine to Martinis," *Journal of Country Music* 15.2 [1993]: 4–5, 15.3 [1993]: 3–4, and 16.1 [1994]: 3–5.)

Here are some one- and two-liners from Homer and Jethro:

> *Our music is a cross between country and rock. We call it crock.*
> *We don't do political jokes. We're afraid they'll get elected.*
> *I was born with a banjo on my knee, which made it very uncomfortable for my mother.*
> *You can drive your wife crazy. Don't talk in your sleep, just smile.*
> *Most country singers sing through their nose. This way they can sing 'em and smell 'em at the same time.*
> *I asked a guy, "Did you see our last TV show?" His answer—"I certainly hope so."*
> *Remember, it's better to be a bachelor than a bachelor's son.*
> *Watching the girls on "Hee Haw" is like watching an Amtrak train. You love to hear the whistle even if you know you ain't gonna make the trip!*

HOOSIER HOT SHOTS

*Kenneth "Rudy" Trietsch, born September 13, 1903,
Acadia, Indiana; died September 17, 1987, Studio
City, California*

*Paul "Hezzie" Trietsch, born April 11, 1905, Acadia,
Indiana; died April 27, 1980, Ventura, California*

*Frank Kettering, born January 1, 1909, Monmouth,
Illinois; died June 1973*

*Charles "Gabe" Ward, born November 26, 1904,
Knightstown, Indiana; died January 14, 1992*

From the 1930s to the 1970s, the question, "Are you ready, Hezzie?" was a familiar herald to another assault on musical taste by the popular quartet of musical pranksters known as the Hoosier Hot Shots. The band was built around the talents and wild imaginations of Kenneth and Paul Trietsch, rural Indiana farm boys who, with their three brothers and father, had played a vaudeville circuit with Ezra Buzzington's Rube Band. Ken played tuba and guitar, and Paul took to such instruments as the washboard and cowbells stolen from the family herd. The Trietsches joined with Charles "Gabe" Ward, another Hoosier, with the Buzzington group. Ward played saxophone and clarinet, fife, and harmonica. The trio, sensing in 1931 that vaudeville was on the skids, got a job in radio at WOWO in Fort Wayne, Indiana, and there became the Hoosier Hot Shots. In 1933, they moved to Chicago's WLS "National Barn Dance," where they were joined by Frank Kettering, who had also played with the Buzzington group. He became the group's songwriter, musical arranger, and bass player.

The Hoosier Hot Shots were encouraged at WLS for their zany humor as well as their cacophonous music on unorthodox instruments, and there they became a popular group. They had their own daytime programs and appeared on the Saturday-night "National Barn Dance." They also appeared all over the Midwest at fairs, festivals, schools, and theaters. Their show included comic novelty songs, such as "I Like Bananas (Because They Have No Bones)" and "From the Indies to the Andes in His Undies."

They soon came to the attention of record companies and made over a hundred discs for ARC, Decca, OKeh, and Vocalion. They were number three on the country charts in 1944 with "She Broke My Heart in Three Places," which crossed to become number twenty-five on the pop charts. In 1946 their "Someday You'll Want Me to Want You" and "Sioux City Sue" were respectively number three and two on the country charts, and "Someday" reached number thirteen on the pop charts.

The Hot Shots also made movies: *Mountain Music*, with Bob Burns and Martha Raye; *Old Monterey*, starring Gene Autry and Smiley Burnett; *The National Barn Dance*; and twenty others, some with Ken Curtis and usually with other musical stars.

During World War II the Hot Shots entertained troops in USO shows overseas and at home. When Frank Kettering left to join the armed forces, his place was taken by Gil Taylor from Alabama. In 1946, the boys left the "Barn Dance" for the West Coast to be closer to movie making and recording, and they continued to entertain there and also in the nightclubs of Las Vegas. During 1950–51 they had their own show on the Mutual radio network. In the age of television they appeared on several network shows. The group broke up when Paul Treitsch died in 1980. Ken Treitsch died in 1987. Gabe Ward carried on for a time as a solo act, master of ceremonies, and comedian.

The Hoosier Hot Shots had several imitators, the best known being Spike Jones and His City Slickers.

(With credit to Wayne W. Daniel, "Are You Ready, Hezzie? And Other Harmonious High Jinks of Those Hilarious Hoosier Hot Shots"; in *Nostalgia Digest and Radio Guide* [October–November 1996]: 26–30.)

CARL HURLEY

Born March 23, 1941, East Bernstadt, Kentucky

Carl Hurley tells his audience, "I'm not a country comedian. I'm a comedian who's from the country." Hurley grew up in a two-room cabin built by his father in Laurel County, Kentucky, and among a family of storytellers. He attended local schools and worked his way through Eastern Kentucky University. After earning a doctorate from the University of Missouri at Columbia, he returned to Kentucky and spent three years in the State Department of Education and then taught for eight years in the education department at Eastern Kentucky University.

His ability to enliven speeches with humor from his native roots made him a popular conference and after-dinner speaker. Soon he was traveling widely to entertain audiences. In 1982 he decided, with the urging of his agent, Mike McKinney, to go full-time as a humorist and motivational speaker, billing himself as "America's Funniest Professor." He explained, "I got out of teaching because my job was to stamp out ignorance, but I looked around and ignorance was gaining on me." His humor is definitely of the country variety, like saying his wife first saw him when he was slopping the hogs, and she said, "He just stood out from the crowd." Since

Carl Hurley. Courtesy of McKinney Associates.

then, he has traveled all over the country doing stand-up comedy, convention keynote addresses, seminars, workshops, entertainment for motor-coach travelers, and has appeared on Kentucky Educational Television, the Nashville Network, the Odyssey and Family Channels, Bill Gaither videos, and on the stage at Renfro Valley. He is an honorary member of the "Renfro Valley Barn Dance."

In about 150 appearances each year, he brings traditional humor from his rural background but creates a lot of it from family and living situations, preaching the importance of laughter, especially in the confusion brought about by rapid change and the likelihood of miscommunication and misunderstanding. His personal hope is that he will be strong enough to laugh in the face of adversity, and he hopes this kind of humor strikes a sympathetic chord with members of his audience: "We all eventually develop some medical problem that can give us concern, but one of the ways we will survive is being strong enough to laugh." He goes on to say, "I cannot imagine a life without humor. I think we were given humor for a purpose. The Lord created the world and everything, and he looked down and said, 'Have mercy! This is going to be stressful, and I better give them something to help them cope.' And he gave us humor."

In talking about his humor, Hurley says, "The first thing I ask myself is, 'Is that story funny?' and then, 'What point does it make?' It doesn't necessarily have to make a point, but if it does, it makes it a little better." He adds, "The best compliment I can receive is someone coming up to me and saying, 'That was real funny, and there was a good message there also.'"

In 2004, Hurley served as master of ceremonies for the induction of new members into the Kentucky Music Hall of Fame, including his fellow Kentuckians Ricky Skaggs, J. D. Crow, the Coon Creek Girls, Boots Randolph, Billy Vaughn, Jerry Chesnut, and Howard and Vestal Goodman. He shared the stage with Dwight Yoakam, Montgomer/ Gentry, Kevin Richardson, and Brian Littrell.

Hurley has recorded thirteen humor tapes, some available also as CDs, videos, or DVDs, and has written a book, *We Weren't Poor—We Just Didn't Have Any Money* (available from McKinney Associates, Box 5162, Louisville, KY, 40255-0162; 1-800-955-4746; or www.carlhurley.com).

Carl and his wife Angela, a college teacher, live in Lexington, Kentucky. They have two children, Lori and Chad.

Here is a story from Carl Hurley's *We Weren't Poor—We Just Didn't Have Any Money*, with permission:

> *Cousin Eldean and I fished from early morning to almost dusk. We caught one little fish, eight inches long.*
>
> *On the way home, Eldean drove, and I pondered.*
>
> *"Eldean," I said, "if you figure all the money we spent today—for the food, our fishing license, the bait, tackle, boat rental, gasoline and everything—that little old fish cost us about a hundred dollars apiece."*
>
> *Eldean thought a minute. "At that rate," he said, "just be glad we didn't catch two."*

FERLIN HUSKY

Born December 3, 1927, Flat River, Missouri

Ferlin Husky (at first spelled Huskey) is his real name, although he has used other professional ones, such as Tex Terry and Terry Preston, and he also performs as Simon Crum, a comic rube character. He has had many records that made the charts and has been in eighteen motion pictures.

Husky grew up on a Missouri farm, where he learned to play the guitar early on and to sing in church and at other functions. He spent five years in the merchant marines during World War II and was on an army transport that landed troops on D-Day. In 1947, he worked with Smiley Burnett at KXLW in St. Louis and then moved to California to become a DJ at KBIS in Bakersfield, at the same time entertaining oil workers and farm laborers at Rainbow Gardens, a dance hall. In 1951, he replaced Tennessee Ernie Ford on Cliffie Stone's TV show, "Hometown Jamboree." He also did a lot of honky-tonk singing and is credited with being a pioneer shaper of the Bakersfield Sound. He recorded with the 4-Star label and then with Capitol.

In 1953, he created his rube alter-ego character, Simon Crum, whom one writer compared to Andy Kaufman, the stand-up and television comedian described as a "pop-cultural prankster." Simon Crum is the irrepressible bumpkin, described by Husky as being a smart hillbilly who knew what was going on in the world. Simon could do Lum and Abner impersonations and even a recognizable Kitty Wells. On the radio, Husky and Simon would sometimes do a conversation with one another. Simon's voice and accent were based on interesting characters that Husky had known in the Ozarks. In 1955 Simon did a single, "Cuz You're So Sweet," that went to the Top Five. "You Pushed Me Too Far" was Top Fifteen in 1967, and in 1958, "Country Music Is Here to Stay" was number two.

Husky is credited with being the first star to appear on the "Grand Ole Opry" using drums and also the first to record in Nashville with backup singers. He appeared on the "Kraft TV Theater" in a dramatic role, and he made his first movie, *Mr. Rock and Roll*, the same year. He followed the next year with *Country Music Holiday* with Zsa Zsa Gabor and Faron Young. Although his movie career did not flourish, he was in an additional sixteen films. He was a tireless promoter with a charming gift of gab, and he appeared on many talk shows, including the "Ed Sullivan Show," the "Steve Allen Show," the "Rosemary Clooney Show," and as guest host of the "Arthur Godfrey Show." As time went on, Simon Crum was summoned on stage less and less. Husky's life was fraught with divorce and the loss of a son. He had a bout with alcoholism and survived heart bypass operations. He rebuilt his life with remarriage and a new family and has persevered in the entertainment business. He built a theater and museum in Myrtle Beach that was not successful, but he continued to perform at the "Grand Ole Opry" and has played in various theaters in Branson, Missouri.

Husky's best-known recordings as a singer were "Wings of a Dove," which was number one in 1960; "Timber, I'm Falling," number thirteen in 1964; "Once," number four in 1967; and "Just For You," number four in 1968, all on Capitol. He switched to ABC Records in 1972 and released a long string of singles, with three in the Top Forty. He has also recorded with Cachet and Audiograph and did a video at MCA. During the 1990s and into this century, a number of record companies—Curb, Pair, CEMA, Jasmine (UK), Capitol, Pickwick, ABC, MCA, and Music Mill Entertainment—have released recordings of his earlier work and live performances.

RED INGLE

Born Ernest Jansen Ingle, November 7, 1906, Toledo,
  Ohio; died September 7, 1965, Santa Barbara,
  California

Red Ingle, by many accounts, was one of the most talented entertainers of the twentieth century as a musician, singer, comedian, composer, arranger, bandleader, cartoonist, caricaturist, and writer of comedic gags and routines. Beyond that, he loved to fly airplanes and make things, including hand-tooled saddles. As a child he studied the violin at the urging of his mother and even got tips from the famed violinist Fritz Kreisler, a family friend of his father's employer. Young Ingle was also impressed by the fiddlers he heard in rural Ohio and learned their tunes. Some of his comic publicity photos show him holding the fiddle under his chin as a classical violinist and down on his arm like a country fiddler. He could play in either style. He also mastered the saxophone and the clarinet. He was later to satirize or parody almost every form of music—classical, country, pop, and traditional.

Ingle began playing in dance bands while he was in high school and then was admitted to the Toledo American College of Music. He was talented enough to get jobs with various orchestras while he was a student, and when he married Edwina Alice Smith in 1926, he dropped out of school and became a full-time musician with dance bands in Kentucky, Detroit, Cincinnati, and Kansas City. He worked with many talented musicians during this time, including Bix Beiderbecke, Hoagy Carmichael, Frankie Laine, and Ted Weems. Ingle joined the Ted Weems Orchestra in 1931 and began doing vocals and comedy. The band worked for a time in New York on the Jack Benny radio show and in Chicago with Fibber McGee and Molly, and Red played comedic roles in skits with both shows. He was also a vocalist, along with Perry Como and Marilyn Maxwell, on a quiz show hosted by the young Gary Moore.

In 1941, Red went with the Weems band to California, but by this time America was gearing up for World War II. Ingle had learned to fly during a summer job in Florida, and he sought a job with the Civil Aeronautics Administration (CAA), where he trained pilots in Santa Monica. He was shortly promoted to a job in Washington,

D.C., as director of CAA publications. In 1943, he sought a commission in the Army Air Corps, but he failed the visual test. He and his family, now including a son Don, returned to California, where he worked in bands and acted in radio shows.

In 1943 Ingle joined up with Spike Jones and His City Slickers, where his comedic skills were quickly put to work. One source credits Ingle with having a profound influence on the visual aspects of the band with his stage-setting caricatures, outrageous costumes, vocal abilities, and comedic behavior. He was with the City Slickers for nearly three years, and during that time they appeared in Paramount's *Bring on the Girls.* Ingle was prominent in several numbers they recorded and performed, arranged by Ingle's bandmate Joseph Howard "Country" Washburne, notably "Cocktails for Two," the old vaudeville favorite "Chloe," "Liebestrom," and "Glow Worm." Ingle's and Wasburne's talents moved Jones into his highly successful "music depreciation" career.

Ingle left Jones in 1946, reportedly over money matters. He did bit parts in California on the "Phil Harris–Alice Faye Show" and appeared with the Los Angeles and San Francisco light opera companies but had time for flying airplanes and for tooling saddles. Then he was summoned by his old pal Country Washburne, who, with Foster Carling, had written "hillbilly" parodies of popular songs that they sent to Capitol Records. When they got a contract, Ingle put together a band that became Red Ingle and the Natural Seven, including the country musicians Noel Boggs on steel guitar, Art Wenzel on accordion, and Herman "the Hermit" Snyder on banjo. Various other musicians did duty with the Natural Seven as well. Ingle, Carling, and Washburne worked up inspired arrangements of the songs for their first recording session. The number that gave Ingle's career a major boost was the parody on the Nacio Herb Brown and Arthur Freed hit "Temptation," which they recorded as "Tim-Tayshun." As they were rehearsing, Jo Stafford came into the studio, loved the song, and volunteered to sing on the recording under the pseudonym of Cinderella G. Stump. It became a big hit in 1947—number two on *Billboard's* most-played jukebox song in its category.

The success of the recording caused other record companies to rush out "hillbilly" parodies with artists such as Dorothy Shay, and Capitol put pressure on Ingle and his writing team to come up with additional material. Ingle also molded the Natural Seven into a touring band to play clubs and thus take advantage of his popularity. The group played California and then was at New York City's Village Barn for most of 1949, while also appearing on radio and fledgling television. They continued recording for Capitol, with such numbers as "Pearly Maude" (a takeoff on "Jole Blon"), "Cigareetes, Whusky, and Wild Wild Women," "Serutan Yob," and "Comin' round the Mountain March." The players in his Natural Seven changed over the years and included fine musicians as well as his son Don. His female singing partners in these years were Karen Tedder, Illean Martin, June Foray, and Mimi Laurie.

After a tour of the British Isles in 1961 with his band pared down as the Frantic Four, Ingle's group cut two more numbers for Capitol, but neither was released. Tired of touring, Ingle looked for other opportunities and rejoined the Ted Weems Orchestra as a featured performer. In 1956, he reformed the Natural Seven for another tour, played briefly with the Eddy Howard Orchestra, and in declining health retired to Santa Barbara and opened a saddle shop. He died of an internal hemorrhage at the age of fifty-eight.

The best of Red Ingle's recorded music is available on a CD, *Tim-Tayshun* (1997; www.bear-family.de).

(With credit to Dave Samuelson, Liner notes to *Tim-Tayshun*.)

JERRY ISAACS

Born April 25, 1943, Somerset, Kentucky

Jerry Isaacs is best known as the "Chicken Man," dressed up in a red suit with tail feathers and chicken feet, singing and dancing to the Louvin Brothers' "Red Hen Boogie" as a member of Kentucky's "Renfro Valley Barn Dance." He remembers getting laughs in school as a small boy doing "Old MacDonald Had a Farm," complete with realistic farm-animal sounds. Since then he has perfected such imitations, and his shrill cluck and cackle together with his dance to the "Red Hen Boogie" always bring appreciative applause.

Isaacs has performed at the "Renfro Valley Barn Dance" and on an excursion train that takes tourists to the Big South Fork National Recreation Area in southern Kentucky. He has been on television programs in Lexington, Kentucky, and one of his performances was picked up by NBC News in 1990. After that, he was on ABC's "Good Morning, America," and this brought a call from "America's Funniest People," also on ABC, where he appeared in January 1991. These appearances made him a local celebrity. His latest appearance on a national television show was on the "Tonight Show with Jay Leno" in 2004.

Although his chicken act is his best, Isaacs has also played as Elmer Spudbuster on the "Renfro Valley" show, wearing a straw hat, glasses with a false nose, checkered pants, red shirt, and long white shoes. As Elmer he plays the harmonica and tells jokes and sometimes does a routine with the emcee as straight man. He credits the longtime Renfro Valley comedian Pete Stamper with helping him with his comedy. Later Stamper found a huge imitation egg, which he pulls across the stage in a wagon after Isaacs has performed his chicken act.

Jerry Isaacs lives in Somerset, Kentucky, with his wife Betty Ruth and stepson Michael.

LUTE ISENHOUR

Born ca. 1913, Taylorsville, North Carolina;
died 1970, probably Clayton, North Carolina

Lute Isenhour was a three-finger banjo picker, guitarist, jokester, and singer who worked with Homer "Pappy" Sherrill, Arthur Sherrill, and the guitarist Olen Benfield in the East Hickory String Band. The band became the Crazy Hickory Nuts when Crazy Water Crystals hired them to promote their product over WBT in Charlotte and WWNC in Asheville. Bill Bolick (later to perform with his brother Earl as the Blue Sky Boys) had been singing and playing informally with Isenhour since Bolick was in high school, and Bolick replaced Olen Benfield when the band moved to Asheville. He and Isenhour sang duets on the radio and personal-appearance shows and did comedy. Bolick credited Isenhour with putting together the comedy acts for their personal appearances. He related that Isenhour had a vast repertoire of early country songs that may have been learned from recordings, and he thinks that the comedy shows Isenhour created were from traditional jokes he knew as well as routines that he had learned from medicine shows.

After the band broke up, Isenhour, then married with children, went back to the textile business, where he had been before his short professional career. He worked at textile mills in the North Carolina towns of Murphy, Hickory, and finally in Clayton, where he was superintendent of a mill.

COTTON IVY

Born Lamarse Howard Ivy, May 15, 1930,
Decatur County, Tennessee

Cotton Ivy bills himself as "the Commissioner of Country." This makes sense, because he was once Tennessee commissioner of agriculture, and he is a master of country humor. Since his first name is Lamarse (La-már-see), he was glad that his blonde head earned him the nickname of "Cotton." Young Ivy grew up on a tenant farm among colorful people in western Tennessee and absorbed the many stories and expressive language of the place. After graduating from the University of Tennessee, he taught high school vocational agriculture and served as basketball and football coach. Later on he worked for American Cyanamid, visiting farmers and speaking to farm groups about his company's animal-health products. Like Jerry Clower, who sold fertilizer for Mississippi Chemicals, Ivy employed country humor to entertain his farm customers. After serving two terms (1985–88) in the state legislature ("the greatest place in the world for finding humor"), he was appointed commissioner of agriculture in 1989.

Ivy reported that when Jerry Clower first started out as a professional humorist, he went to hear him. He said to his wife, "I can do that," and she responded, "You and a million other idiots *think* you can do that!" But Cotton knew he could. His confidence came from his years of entertaining farm groups all over Tennessee and in nearby states using a fictional place he created: "Ty Whop," Tennessee, populated by some interesting folks that he wove his stories around. He had learned a lot by trial and error:

Cotton Ivy. Courtesy of Cotton Ivy.

I'd tell a story, and if they laughed, I'd leave it in, and if they didn't, I'd take it out.

I made a great mistake in the beginning. Jerry Clower dressed up in a red suit, and Speck Rhodes in a plaid one, and I wanted to be Speck Rhodes. I got me a suit, put a cotton ball on it—fancy. I got one orange and white, and I experimented with denim. I'd appear for three or four hundred dollars at civic functions to do an hour of humor. Then I learned that I could put on a regular suit and tie and do the same thing and double my money!

He sought out the Nashville agent Tandy Rice of Top Billing International, who managed Clower, and Rice agreed to book him at half the price Clower was getting and a money-back guarantee. This was fine, for as Ivy said, "I'd performed for thirty-five or forty dollars on the back of a truck, fronting for many country bands." Rice reported that he never returned a dime for any of Cotton Ivy's performances. The arrangement worked out fine, and as Clower's fortunes improved, so did Ivy's. He was later managed by McKinney Associates of Louisville, but he takes pride in saying, "I've never signed with an agent. I always shook hands with them and said, 'You book me, and when I don't suit you or you don't suit me, we'll part company as friends." He went on to explain, "You don't need someone to tell you you can't go duck hunting, or can't visit your kids." So he filled dates that he wanted to fill, and turned down the others.

Ivy met the Reverend Grady Nutt when he and Nutt tried out for "Hee Haw" on the same day. Nutt became a regular on the show, and Ivy went to Branson, Missouri, to perform for a summer in the Hee Haw Theater. Episodes of his performances taped in Branson and others taped in Nashville were part of several broadcast "Hee Haw" shows. He was on TNN's "Nashville Now" seventy-five times and on the "Ralph Emery Show," "Opry Backstage," and the "Grand Ole Opry" several times.

Ivy met the well-known humorist Carl Hurley when they both entertained the Pork Producers of South Carolina. When Grady Nutt died in an airplane crash, Ivy encouraged Hurley, then a college professor, to go full-time as a comedian and introduced him to his agent, Mike McKinney. Cotton Ivy has done eight straight years of Hurley's Calvacade of Comedy for Motorcoach Travelers.

Another funny man that Ivy had a hand in promoting is the "Grand Ole Opry" and "Hee Haw" star Mike Snider. Ivy hired Snider as a banjo picker to travel with him when he campaigned for the state legislature. At that time Snider picked, and very well, but he wouldn't talk. Ivy said, "Mike, after three numbers, all that bluegrass sounds alike. You need to do some talking and tell jokes between numbers." Ivy helped Snider prepare material. When he was elected to the legislature, he enticed Snider, a West Tennessee farmer, to come to Nashville where he would find him a job grading hogs. His offer was never fulfilled because Snider got on "Hee Haw" and the "Grand Ole Opry," where he is now the main source of humor.

Ivy has done commercials for the DeKalb and Pioneer seed companies, plus multiple others. He is a member of many farm-related organizations, including the Tennessee Farm Bureau, and has been president of the Southern Association of State Departments of Agriculture and the Southern United States Trade Association. He has also served on the board of trustees of the University of Tennessee and the board of regents for the State University and Community College System, has been a member and officer of numerous other state organizations, and he has won many honors. He is a Gideon and a man of faith.

Cotton Ivy released a humor tape, *Cotton-Pickin Good: The Comedy of Cotton Ivy* (1-800-955-4746). He is also co-author, with Roy Herron, of *Tennessee Political Humor: Some of These Jokes You Voted For* (Knoxville: University of Tennessee Press, 2000).

He and his wife Pat have four sons and five grandsons, four great-grandsons, and one granddaughter. The Ivys live at Decaturville, Tennessee. Cotton reports that he is now retired and talking to bird dogs and Sunday schools these days.

Following is a story he sometimes tells:

A fellow about my age came up to me the other night and said, "Cotton, I've been meaning to ask you a question—me and my wife was talkin' about it the other night—was it you or your brother who was killed in the war?" I said, "It was bound to have been me, 'cause my brother never was in the army." He said, "I told my wife that!"

JAMUP AND HONEY. *See Lee Roy White and Lee Davis Wilds*

SLEEPY JEFFERS

Born George I. Jeffers, February 15, 1922, Norma,
Tennessee; died 1992, Charleston, West Virginia

Sleepy Jeffers grew up in a musical family that eventually, under the leadership of the father, William M. Jeffers Sr., became the Fiddlin' Farmers, broadcasting over WKRC in Cincinnati. His nickname came from the stage names they selected for the band members (including Shorty Godwin, another comedian), "Sleepy," "Slick," "Slim," and "Shorty." After several years in Cincinnati, the band moved to WWVA in Wheeling, West Virginia, then to stations in Fairmont, Clarksburg, and Charleston, West Virginia. In addition to his fiddling, Sleepy created the comic character Little Willie, an overgrown kid with a sailor hat, big sash bowtie, and short pants. He and Shorty Godwin also did a comedy act called "Sleepy and Shorty, the Happy Hoedowners."

Sleepy enlisted in the Marine Corps in 1942 for a four-year tour, including landing with the Second Marine Division on Saipan and Okinawa.

Afterward, Jeffers took a job as a disc jockey at WTIP in Charleston and toured with the Davis Twins, Honey and Sonny. He eventually married Honey (Maxine). She and her twin brother had started their radio career in 1940 over WWVA. In 1949, Sleepy and the Davis Twins were invited to join the road show of the Bailes Brothers, who were popular on the "Louisiana Hayride" in Shreveport. That lasted for about a year, and then they returned to West Virginia.

Jeffers went back to his job at WTIP in Charleston and remained there for a total of thirteen years. He and the Davis Twins also were part of the station's "Magic Valley Jamboree," and they did personal appearances, with him playing Little Willie. In the early 1960s, he and the Davis Twins joined the "Buddy Starcher Show" at the NBC affiliate WCHS-TV in Charleston, with Jeffers again playing Little Willie. It was a popular show with many personal appearances. When Starcher left the show, Jeffers took over, and it became the "Sleepy Jeffers Show." He also hosted a children's show. Before the "Sleepy Jeffers Show" went off the air in 1973, a victim of NBC's "Today Show," Sleepy and Honey's daughter "Little Linda" was also a part of the cast (they also had a son, Randy Lynn). Jeffers later did thirty-nine weekly programs at WHTN-TV in Huntington.

DEWITT "SNUFFY" JENKINS. *See the Hired Hands*

GRANDPA JONES

*Born Louis Marshall Jones, October 20, 1913,
Niagra, Kentucky; died February 19, 1998,
Nashville, Tennessee*

Grandpa Jones's wife Ramona remembers that Grandpa decided that he wanted to be in show business very early, in high school, when he found that he could make people laugh and then make them get very serious. He was a first-rate musician from an early age, and the comedy that he was most famous for came a little later, when he became "Grandpa" at the age of twenty-two. Appearing with Bradley Kincaid over WBZ in Boston, Bradley said that Grandpa sounded old and grumpy on the early-morning show, especially after a long drive back from a personal appearance. Kincaid reported, "Someone wrote in and asked, 'How old is that old man on the show?' So we started calling him 'Grandpa.'" Jones bought makeup and false whiskers for personal appearances. Eventually Kincaid purchased the ancient boots that Grandpa wore throughout his career.

Jones was born into a family of ten children on a tobacco farm in Kentucky, but when he was a teenager, the family moved to Akron, Ohio, for better opportunity. His mother was a ballad singer and his father was a fiddler, and young Jones became proficient as a singer and guitar player. When the Akron radio station WJW held a musical contest, he entered and won, earning a broadcasting spot, performing as the Young Singer of Old Songs.

Grandpa Jones.
Photo by Loyal Jones.

He later teamed up with Harmonica Joe Troyan, a mouth-harp whiz and comedian from Cleveland, and the two of them became part of the band for the "Lum and Abner" radio show. In the mid-1930s he and Troyan joined Bradley Kincaid on his popular radio show from WBZ, where Jones got his "Grandpa" moniker. "The first place we played was Walton, Massachusetts," he remembered. "We played three shows and never did get them all in. They were awful fine people up there. They'd ask us to come eat with them or put a pie in the back of our car."

He remembered starting to do comedy: "After I was with Bradley Kincaid, when I went to Wheeling [WWVA] in 1937, I started doing some gags on stage, to take up a little time." He stayed in West Virginia for about six years, at stations in Wheeling, Charleston, and Fairmont. At the Wheeling "Mountaineer Jamboree" he met a fellow

Kentuckian, Cousin Emmy Carver, who taught him to play the banjo in her dynamic frailing style, and it became his main instrument for the rest of his career. In fact, the banjo was a prominent feature of his music and comedy through years when banjos were scarce in country bands.

Jones then went to WLW in Cincinnati, where he, the Delmore Brothers, and Merle Travis formed the Brown's Ferry Four, a gospel quartet. He also started his recording career at King Records with two of his original compositions, "It's Raining Here This Morning" and "Eight More Miles to Louisville," along with "Rattler" and "Mountain Dew." These recordings brought him to the attention of a national audience. Military service interrupted his successful Cincinnati years, and he wound up as a military policeman in Germany in the last months of the European part of the war. There he and his fellow country musicians formed the Munich Mountaineers and played over Armed Forces Radio.

In 1946, Bradley Kincaid lined up an audition for him with Pee Wee King, a veteran of the "Grand Ole Opry," and Grandpa joined his band. He later played in Bradley Kincaid's tent shows out of Nashville. He married Ramona Riggins in 1946. She was a fiddler, mandolinist, and singer who had been on the "Old Dominion Barn Dance" in Richmond. They played with the Bailes Brothers and Lonzo and Oscar. On the tent-show circuit, he observed the art of popular comedians such as Minnie Pearl and Lazy Jim Day as he perfected his own comedy. He also remembered advice from Bradley Kincaid in terms of off-color material—it was acceptable only "if the wit exceeds the smut."

In 1949, Grandpa moved to the Washington area to play over WARL in Arlington. Then he and Ramona went to the "Old Domionion Barn Dance." In 1959, he returned to the "Opry" as a full member, and there he stayed.

Grandpa was in the cast of "Hee Haw" on its first broadcast, and he was a popular performer throughout the twenty-four years of the show. Grandpa, in his understated fashion, described the show as being "merely foolish." He was best known as a member of the listless Culhanes and for his "What's for Dinner, Grandpa?" spots. Jones, who loved to read poetry, wrote all of the rhymed inventories of victuals that answered the query. He also sang tenor in the "Hee Haw" quartet.

In 1978, Grandpa was elected to the Country Music Hall of Fame.

Grandpa balanced his comedy with serious songs, some of which he wrote, such as "Falling Leaves," about the shortness of our days. He also recorded a recitation, later to become a video, *The Christmas Guest*. He made records for King, RCA, Decca, CMH, MCA, and other labels. Little of his comedy, however, is on recordings. In 1984, the University of Tennessee Press published his autobiography (with Charles K. Wolfe), *Everybody's Grandpa: Fifty Years behind the Mike*. Charles Wolfe reported that Grandpa, not one to do things in a conventional way, started the book by sitting down at the typewriter and pecking out his story, then taping the pages together consecutively. He then rolled them up into a scroll and presented them to Wolfe.

Grandpa's friend John Hartford commented on his comedy: "Grandpa Jones, when he walks out on stage, he's brilliant. He's on many different levels. Some comedians are on only one or two levels. Grandpa made the context of his humor such that almost all he had to do was say something, period. The fact that he said it was funny." Grandpa Jones was indeed the consummate entertainer. At fairs and festivals such as the annual Tennessee Homecoming at Norris, when he performed, talk and activity stopped and eyes and ears were directed toward the stage. Ramona reported that people would request his jokes just as they did his songs. She also said that he was on the phone daily to his old friends Bill Carlisle and Stringbean Akeman, exchanging funny stories.

On January 3, 1998, after finishing his set on the second "Opry" show, Grandpa Jones suffered a massive stroke. He died on February 19. Surviving are his wife Ramona, daughters Eloise and Alissa, and son Mark. Marsha, an older daughter, died also in 1998.

So strong was Grandpa Jones's personality and art, two impersonators have done presentations of his music and humor: Robby Spencer of Bluff City, Tennessee, and Dr. David Hurt of Berea, Kentucky, who does a portrayal as a part of the Kentucky Humanities Council's Chautauqua series.

Grandpa was known for his one-liners. At the Tennessee Homecoming he approached Bill Foster, owner of a shiny gold-plated Gibson Mastertone banjo. "How do ye keep yer banjer so shiny?" he asked. "Mine looks like it's been plowed up."

On a bumpy plane ride, he remarked, "Tell that pilot if he sees a hole in the fence to get back on the road."

Ramona tells this story: "Grandpa had been in the hospital with a heart problem, and Stoney Cooper was in the hospital for an appendicitis operation. We were at the "Opry," and Wilma Lee [Stoney's wife] and Grandpa were talking to each other. Wilma Lee said, "We just got baskets of mail at the hospital for Stoney." Grandpa said, "Well, I got a little box full." Then he said, "Appendix operations always did draw better than heart trouble."

CLEDUS "T." JUDD

Born Barry Poole, December 18, 1964,
Crowe Springs, Georgia

Barry Poole graduated from hairstyling school, but before he got settled in that profession he entered an amateur show in Atlanta and won first prize doing his "Farm Boy Rap." This prompted a move to Nashville, where he got the idea of doing parodies of the hit songs of country music stars and becoming Cledus "T." Judd. Among the stars he has parodied are Tim McGraw ("Indian Outlaw," parodied as "Indian In-Laws"), Shania Twain ("Any Man of Mine" as "If Shania Was Mine"), Johnny Cash ("Jackson" as "Jackson [Alan, That Is],"), Charlie Daniels ("The Devil Went Down to Georgia" as "Cledus Went Down to Florida"), David Ball ("I've Got a Thinking Problem" as "Stinking Problem"), Alan Jackson ("Gone Country" as "Gone Funky"), and Tracy Lawrence ("Paint Me a Birmingham" as "Bake Me a Country Ham"). He says that the stars don't resent his parodies, and some have even appeared in his videos. Garth Brooks once asked when he might be a subject, and Cledus replied, "When you have a hit." He has summed up his job as "I take good country music and ruin it."

His persona is that of the overweight southern redneck. "The 'T' in my name stands for trouble, not tubby," he says. One of his videos is "Coronary Life," in which he collapses from a life of overeating with a cheeseburger still in his hand and is rushed to the hospital where the doctors remove a bucket of lard, a wedding cake, and other foodstuffs. He survives and fights off the grim reaper on his Stairmaster.

Judd has opened shows for such stars as Billy Ray Cyrus, Aaron Tippin, and Sammy Kershaw. In 2001–3, he traveled with Brooks and Dunn and has shared the stage with Shania Twain, Buck Owens, Alan Jackson, Vince Gill, and Toby Keith. Among his recordings are *Cledus "T." Judd* (Laughing Hyena, 1995); *I Stoled This Record* (Razor and Tie, 1996); *Did I Shave My Back for This?* (Razor and Tie, 1998); *Juddmental* (Sony, 1999); *Just Another Day in Parodies* and *Cledus Envy* (Sony, 2000); *Cledus Navidad* (Sony, 2002); and *A Six Pack of Judd* (Sony, 2003).

GARRISON KEILLOR

Born Gary Edward Keillor, August 7, 1942,
Anoka, Minnesota

Garrison Keillor is best known for his "Prairie Home Companion," heard on National Public Radio, but he has hosted other radio shows and is also a gifted writer for magazines such as the *New Yorker* and *Atlantic Monthly*. The Barnes and Noble Web site lists 128 titles (books and recordings) that he has written, narrated, or contributed to. While Keillor is a sophisticated and urbane man, most of his writings and radio monologues are about country and small-town folks, based on his kin and the other people he has known, as well as from his rich imagination. "A Prairie Home Companion" is his attempt to re-create entertainment like that of early radio.

His family was religiously fundamentalist, and a great deal of what he writes and talks about is religious piety. He has said that his novel, *Wobegon Boy*, was a revolt against piety. In fact, a great deal of his humor is directed at people who show off their piety or are inflated with self-importance. He admits to being an arrogant youth, but he has made up for it in his public persona by directing a lot of his humor at himself, pointing out his gangly frame and his unusual features and making a fetish of his and his neighbors' humility. He is called a genius by some for his ability to show the contradictory elements in human nature. His comments are palatable to most of his audience because they are imbedded in his droll humor.

Keillor graduated from Anoka High School and enrolled at the University of Minnesota, where he studied literature and got involved in the university radio station. After getting his B.A. in English in 1966, his dream of being a writer took him to New York briefly, but he returned to Minnesota and began writing stories that eventually appeared in the *New Yorker*. He conceived of "A Prairie Home Companion" while doing an article on the "Grand Ole Opry" for the *New Yorker*. "A Prairie Home Companion" opened on July 6, 1974, in the Macalester College auditorium, with an audience of an even dozen. It took the show several years to evolve and for his fictional Lake Wobegon to emerge as a community of interesting and funny people and as Keillor's "home town." It also took a long time for Keillor to find his true voice as a humorist and storyteller. Judith Yaross Lee, in her excellent book, *Garrison Keillor: A Voice of America*, describes the development of Keillor's comic poses, from the "Amateur [broadcaster] to the Shy Person, the Cracker-Barrel Philosopher/Preacher, the Witness, and the Exile," all reflecting a "becoming Midwestern reticence." Lee shows that a great deal of Keillor's charm is in his warm storytelling without a script but that his stories, with their many nuances, are carefully constructed.

"A Prairie Home Companion" became enormously popular, bringing a version of rural and small-town humor to a whole new audience—preppy, college-educated folk who would not have appreciated the old rube humor. Yet many who grew up country felt at home with the characters that Keillor made up, the stodgy, reticent, and modest Lutherans, the serious Catholics of Our Lady of Perpetual Responsibility church, the Norwegian bachelors, aspiring folk like himself who deal with the fear that they may be way down on the totem pole of ability. They aren't that different from the southern Baptists who try to out-humble one another, or Methodist competitors who piously admonish us to shape up and forsake sin. Keillor's choice in musicians—Chet Atkins, Robin and Linda Williams, Doc Watson, Johnny Gimbel, and the like—have made country music fans right at home, and Keillor's own singing, and the Hopeful Gospel Quartet, make the program sound kind of populistic and amateurish, like maybe we could join in, too. The Annual Joke Show, with guests like Roy Blount Jr., was a surefire hit, although its sexual frankness and four-letter words were way beyond the limits of early radio programs.

"News from Lake Wobegon—My Home Town" grew into the most popular part of the show, and Keillor became a national figure. However, his schedule—helping to write the show, preparing his monologue, and on the side writing novels and short stories—wore him down, and he discontinued "A Prairie Home Companion" in 1987, to the dismay of his many fans. He moved briefly to Denmark with his new wife Ulla Skaerved, but then settled in New York and in 1989 started a new program, "The American Radio Company of the Air," on American Public Radio, now Public Radio International. It was a success, but it just wasn't the same thing as his old show, and after four seasons, Keillor moved back to Minnesota and reprised "A Prairie Home Companion." It is still a very popular radio show disseminated by American Public

Media over PBS stations on Saturday evenings at six, usually with a repeat performance on Sunday afternoons. He moves his show around to American cities and often recruits local musicians, humorists, and other entertainers from those locations. In addition, he does another program, "The Writer's Almanac," reflecting his literary interest.

Keillor has continued to write novels and stories for magazines. They are usually set in Minnesota with some crafted and enlarged from his radio monologues and other parts of his radio programs. He has ten adult books in print and three for children. He also has joke books and CDs of his radio monologues and skits (prettygoodgoods.publicradio.org).

In 1994, Keillor was inducted into the Radio Hall of Fame. *A Prairie Home Companion: The Movie,* directed by Robert Altman, was released in 2006, starring Keillor, Meryl Streep, Lily Tomlin, Lindsay Lohan, and Kevin Kline.

Garrison Keillor was married to Mary C. Guntzel from 1965 to 1976, and they had one son. He married Ulla Skaerved in 1985, and they later divorced. He is currently married to Jenny Lind Nilsson, and they have a daughter.

(With credit to Judith Yaross Lee, *Garrison Keillor: A Voice of America* [Oxford: University of Mississippi Press, 1991].)

KENTUCKY SLIM

Born Charles Elza, April 4, 1912, Harlan County,
   Kentucky (some sources give Laurel County);
   died February 23, 1996, Knoxville, Tennessee

Charles Elza, a blackface and rube comedian known as Kentucky Slim and Little Darlin', famous for his Pork Chop dance, was a comedian at the "Mid-day Merry-Go-Round," the "Renfro Valley Barn Dance," and the "Grand Ole Opry," playing with Roy Acuff, Carl Story, Esco Hankins, Hylo Brown, Flatt and Scruggs, the Stanley Brothers, and others. He had picked up dance steps from a black ex-vaudevillian in Harlan, according to Ivan Tribe. Nearly seven feet tall and weighing 275 pounds, his finale, the Pork Chop dance, pleased and amazed his audience. Earl Scruggs and others spoke of his tap dance and how he was so light on his feet for such a big man.

Tribe reports that Elza had earlier worked in the coal mines with his fellow Harlan Countian Cas Walker, and they decided there must be a better way to make a living. They went to Knoxville, where Walker established a chain of grocery stores, using country music shows to promote his products. Slim went into entertainment and later worked on Walker's shows on WROL and WIVK for several years. He joined Doc Hauer's medicine show, where Roy Acuff also worked, and according to William Smyth, there he learned minstrelsy routines, skits, and jokes from Jake Tindall, a blackface comedian who had long been with Hauer. He and Tindall later worked with Acuff, but when the latter went to Nashville, Slim decided to stay in Knoxville.

Slim did more medicine-show work and then went with WNOX's "Mid-day Merry-Go-Round" and traveled with Esco Hankins and the Cope Brothers. He went to WOPI and WJHL in Bristol and played with Manuel "Speedy" Clark and his band. "Pop" Eckler hired Clark and Elza for his show at Atlanta's "WSB Barn Dance," but Slim soon returned to Knoxville to work again for Cas Walker. During World War II he became a partner with Clark at John Lair's "Renfro Valley Barn Dance," until Clark was drafted. He and Clark also did the Renfro Valley tent shows after the war.

In the 1950s Slim did comedy with Carl Story and his Rambling Mountaineers, gradually abandoning blackface because of changing attitudes and going to rube costumes and from black to country dialect. He then joined Lester Flatt and Earl Scruggs and the Foggy Mountain Boys, who were performing out of Raleigh, and went with them to the "Grand Ole Opry." They called him Little Darlin', a name preferred by Lester Flatt. Hylo Brown also called him Little Darlin' when he was part of his traveling band.

When his wife Mary died of cancer in 1957, Slim left entertainment and did factory work for a while before traveling with the Stanley Brothers out of Florida. He retired from traveling shows in 1963 and worked for the next decade or so as a house painter in the Knoxville area. He played the

Kentucky Slim. Courtesy of Terry Clark.

World's Fair when it was in Knoxville in 1982 and appeared at David's Music Barn on the Clinton highway. He occasionally performed at the Annual Tennessee Homecoming at the Museum of Appalachia near Norris.

Although Slim was primarily known as a comedian and dancer, he was also a singer, especially at the "Renfro Valley Barn Dance," where John Lair hired him primarily to sing the old sentimental songs that Lair loved, such as "The Blind Child," "The Convict and the Rose," "Girl in the Blue Velvet Band," "I'll Remember You Love in my Prayers," and "The Tragic Romance."

Elza was twice married. When he died at eighty-three, he left his second wife, Cora Gamm Rambo Elza, and two daughters, Bobbie Burchfield of Knoxville and Teresa Blanton of Williamson, West Virginia, and one son, Phillip, of Indianapolis.

(With credit to William Jensen Smyth, "Traditional Humor on Knoxville Country Radio Entertainment," Ph.D. dissertation, University of California at Los Angeles, 1987; and Ivan Tribe, "Kentucky Slim: Comedian in Medicine Shows, Old-Time, and Bluegrass Music," *Bluegrass Unlimited* 16.5 [November 1981]: 20–22.)

BEECHER RAY "PETE" KIRBY ("BASHFUL BROTHER OSWALD")

*Born December 26, 1911, near Pigeon Forge,
Tennessee; died October 17, 2002, Madison,
Tennessee*

"Pete" Kirby loved to play comedy with Roy Acuff's bands, first the Crazy Tennesseans and later the Smoky Mountain Boys, but he was also an important instrumentalist and singer with Acuff for fifty-four years. He played great clawhammer banjo (learned from his father), and his dobro sound was as distinctive as Acuff's voice on such signature numbers as "Wabash Cannonball," "Wreck on the Highway," and "Great Speckled Bird."

Before Kirby joined Acuff, he already had a colorful and varied work history: sawmill worker, bootlegger, barber, cotton-mill hand, fry cook, and beer-joint and burlesque-show musician. While playing joints in Chicago, he met Rudy Wakiki, who played the newly popular Hawaiian-style guitar, and Kirby bought himself a National steel guitar and learned to play in this style.

When Kirby came back to Tennessee, he got a job with Kern's Bakery in Knoxville but also began playing with local bands, including Roy Acuff's on a part-time basis. When Acuff was invited to join the "Grand Ole Opry," his dobro player Clell Summey decided to stay in Knoxville, so Acuff invited Kirby to join him in Nashville as a regular member of what became the Smoky Mountain Boys. His banjo, his dobro, and his braying laugh became a distinctive part of the show.

Pete Kirby (Bashful Brother
Oswald). Courtesy of
Manuel Clark.

"At one time or other, we all played comedy with Roy," Kirby remembered. "Pap Wilson, Joe Zinkan, and Jess Easterday. Roy was the straight man. I liked being a comedian. I'd like to go back and do it again. Humor was the main thing [in the early shows]. I think humor's the main thing with everybody. If you can make 'em laugh, you've got 'em. It's changed now. I don't guess they have time for comedy anymore."

Kirby got his "Bashful Brother Oswald" name because Roy hired Rachel Veach to sing and play banjo with the band, and there was criticism about his having a single woman traveling about the country with men. So Acuff began announcing them as "Bashful Brother Oswald and his sister Rachel."

A great admirer of Kirby's humor was John Hartford. "He's someone who works on many levels. Now Oswald may go out there and tell the same old jokes, but there's just something in the way he delivers them and the way he is that puts them on these other levels. I never get tired of hearing the same routine from him."

Kirby played on virtually all of Roy Acuff's recordings. He also appeared on several Starday records as a side musician, and Starday released *Bashful Brother Oswald* in 1962. He also appeared on the Nitty Gritty Dirt Band's *Will the Circle Be Unbroken* in 1972. Rounder Records released recordings of Oswald and his sideman Charlie Collins: *Brother Oswald* (1972) and *The Best of Oswald* (1995).

Pete Kirby married Lola Lee Letner in April 1936, and they had two children, Billy and Linda. Lola died in 1981, and in 1983 Pete married Euneta Orene Adams. They lived in Madison, Tennessee. After Roy Acuff died in 1992, Oswald and Charlie Collins continued to play music on the "Opry," and Brother Oswald was inducted into the "Opry" in his own right in 1995. He and Collins also played other venues, such as the annual Tennessee Homecoming in Norris. In 1994, he and Euneta published his personal story as told to Peggy and Mike McCloud, *Bashful Brother Oswald: That's the Truth If I Ever Told It*, with jokes and comments on Roy Acuff and other musicians. Beecher Kirby died in 2002 after a long illllness.

Here's a story from Brother Oswald:

> I bought my wife this brand-new car. She wanted me to ride into town with her. She come to this red light and drove right on through it. "Why did you do that?" I said. She said, "My brother always runs through red lights." We come to this second red light, and she ran right through it. I said, "Why did you do that?" She said, "I told you that my brother always does that." Pretty soon we came to a green light, and she slammed on her brakes and like to have throwed me through the windshield. I said, "Now why did you do that?" She said, "My brother might be comin' through!"

JOHN LAIR

Born July 1, 1894, Livingston, Kentucky; died
November 12, 1985, Renfro Valley, Kentucky

John Lee Lair was a Kentucky original, a one-in-a-million person who saw things that escaped others. He grew up in a traditional rural society, and he saw the strength and beauty of that culture and its music and stories that reflected humor and sentiments dear to the hearts of rural people. He instinctively knew that the values of rural culture would be important to the millions of people who had gone through tremendous change after World War I, especially those who had moved to the city.

Lair got a taste of show business in the army when he became part of a Special Services unit to entertain troops during World War I. He helped to write skits for a show that toured army bases called *Atta Boy*, parts of which were included in the *Ziegfield Follies*, where Lair met Broadway stars of the day. When he got home after service, he taught school, farmed for a while, then attended the Battle Creek Art Institute, where he developed cartooning skills that enabled him to sell cartoons to several periodicals.

John Lair. Courtesy of the John Lair Collection, Southern Appalachian Archives, Berea College.

Then he became an insurance-claims adjuster in Chicago, and when his fellow Kentuckian Bradley Kincaid became a star at WLS's "National Barn Dance," Lair approached him to see if he would like to use any of the many songs he had collected. Feeling that Kincaid was not sufficiently interested, he arranged with WLS to bring other talented Kentucky musicians to WLS to perform the kind of music that he knew so much about. Among them were Red Foley, Karl Davis, Harty Taylor, and Lily May Ledford. He also hired Slim Miller from Indiana, forming a band he called the Cumberland Ridge Runners, with Miller as fiddler and comedian and including Gene Ruppe and Hugh Cross.

In 1930, Lair was hired as WLS's program director and music librarian. He immediately saw the value of comedy in entertainment but also the need to make sure that the entertainers were having fun themselves, thus ensuring that the audience too had fun. The scripts Lair wrote had comedy throughout, not only with Slim Miller's clowning but also posing Myrtle Cooper as Scotty Wiseman's back-home sweetheart who has joined him in the city; they became Lulu Belle and Scotty. Lair himself was to become a gifted emcee, with a warm, sincere, and unassuming voice, and an artful straight man to numerous comedians.

Lair moved to Cincinnati in 1937, closer to his Kentucky pool of talent, where he produced the "Renfro Valley Barn Dance" over WLW and "Plantation Party" and "Pinex Merrymakers" on WCKY. He had been dreaming of a show set in an authentic rural community that would draw city people there, rather than doing city shows that drew country talent to the city. He planned to locate the show in Renfro Valley, Kentucky, where his people had lived for generations. He had already written a nostalgic theme song, "Take Me Back to Renfro Valley." His show began in Cincinnati while he and his partners, Whitey Ford, Red Foley, and C. V. Foley, acquired land and began work on the Renfro Valley barn. On November 4, 1939, the first show was broadcast from the new barn in Renfro Valley over WLW at first and then WHAS in Louisville. Sensing that the radio audience might not believe they were actually broadcasting from Renfro Valley, Lair offered to send a picture of the barn to anyone requesting it. He received 254,000 requests.

The "Renfro Valley Barn Dance" mainly featured Kentucky talent, sprinkled with plenty of comedy, with Lair working to make sure that the entertainers were having fun themselves. Through the years, Lair featured such comedians as Slim Miller, Whitey Ford (also a Renfro Valley partner), Granny Harper, A'nt Idy, Little Clifford, Shorty Hobbs and Eller Long, Gene Cobb, Kentucky Slim, Homer and Jethro, Old Joe Clark, Pete Stamper, Jerry Isaacs, and James "Goober" Buchanan. Lair was usually the straight man. He made sure the comedy was clean and suitable for the whole family. He commented on his criterion for taste: "My father and mother were both dead, but I'll tell you, every program I put on was aimed at their class of people. I tried to do something that they would have liked if they had been living."

Lair sold the "Barn Dance" to Hal Smith and other investors in 1968 but bought it back a few years later. After his death in 1985, his daughters continued the show for a time, and then it was bought by other investors, mainly Ralph Gabbard, Glenn Pennington, and later Warren Rosenthal, to be rebuilt into a modern music complex with a state-of-the-art auditorium, shops, and a restaurant. Rosenthal continued to operate the show after the deaths of Pennington and Gabbard, with shows in season Thursday through Sunday. The music was still mostly older-style country and featured the comedy of Pete Stamper, Old Joe Clark, Bun Wilson, and Betty Lou York. In 2000, Rosenthal donated the entire complex debt-free to the nonprofit board of the Kentucky Music Hall of Fame and Museum, located next to the entertainment complex. In 2005, the board decided to sell the complex to the Ohio businessman Don Evans (from nearby London, Kentucky) and his wife Vera, who were longtime fans of the "Renfro Valley Barn Dance." The Evanses promise to preserve and maintain the musical traditions established by Lair.

John Lair suffered a stroke while in Nashville for the Country Music Awards in 1982, at which he was an unsuccessful nominee for the Country Music Hall of Fame. His health declined after the stroke, and he died in 1985, a week after the forty-sixth anniversary of the opening of the "Renfro Valley Barn Dance" at his beloved valley. He was one of the pioneers inducted into the Kentucky Music Hall of Fame and Museum in 2002, and his influence is still strong at the "Barn Dance," especially in its country comedy.

LARRY THE CABLE GUY

Born Daniel Lawrence Whitney, February 17, 1963,
Pawnee City, Nebraska

On December 17, 2006, Larry the Cable Guy was profiled on "60 Minutes" by Bob Simon. After several clips of his bawdy and scatological humor, Simon revealed that Larry the Cable Guy is among the top-earning comedians. Thousands of jaws of "60 Minutes" fans must have dropped and questions remained unanswered as to how this could be. One answer soon became obvious: the producer of the Blue Collar Comedy Tour, J. P. Williams, had a "eureka!" moment and asked his own question, "Why should we play small comedy clubs, auditoriums, and theaters when we could be playing football stadiums, basketball arenas, and civic centers?" With the Blue Collar Comedy Tour, featuring Jeff Foxworthy, Bill Engvall, Ron White, and Larry the Cable Guy, it was possible to fill such places, and Larry was such a hit that he can now fill these arenas all by himself. The other questions remain largely unanswered, for he has taken country humor to new heights or, as some would say, depths.

Whitney has been stingy with accurate information about himself and is more likely to portray himself in the role of Larry the Cable Guy, giving fictitious information about this character. Dan Whitney mostly grew up in Nebraska, but the family moved to West Palm Beach, Florida, in 1979. Whitney's father was once involved in show business as a guitar player for the Everly Brothers, but he was also a preacher and became principal of the academy where Dan went to high school and where he was a member of the pep band. Dan got a fast-food job, like many teenagers, and later was a bellboy in a hotel, but he had a hankering to do stand-up comedy. His first appearance in a comedy club was in Blue Springs, Missouri. He eventually got into radio comedy, where he would call into the station posing as a fictional character. Larry the Cable Guy was one of these characters. This was good training for portraying different characters and eventually that of a working-class, country, anti-intellectual loudmouth. He appeared on radio shows in Omaha, Baltimore, Kansas City, Tulsa, and Orlando.

During the late 1980s and 1990s, Whitney did stand-up comedy as Dan Whitney, a fairly clean-cut fellow in a regular long-sleeved shirt and dress pants, with his real accent. He went on to "An Evening at the Improv" and "Comic Strip Live," was a guest on the nationally syndicated "Bob and Tom Show," and then was a regular on Jeff Foxworthy's "Country Countdown Show." Soon he had syndicated comedy spots in numerous markets across the country. His Larry the Cable Guy persona as we now know it was developed in these later years and especially after he joined Foxworthy, Bill Engvall, and Ron White on the Blue Collar Comedy Tour. No doubt he was influenced by Foxworthy and J. P. Williams. His exaggerated accent is now more southern than midwestern, although he is fond of some contemporary adjectives like "awesome" that no southern country person would utter. His main slogan, on much of his merchandise, is "Git-R-Done." His dress as Larry is old shirts with the sleeves torn off at the shoulders, work pants, and a duck-bill cap.

Larry's popularity went ballistic with his success on the Blue Collar Comedy Tour, which began in January 2000 and ran for three years in large gathering places across the country. This tour resulted in *The Blue Collar Comedy Tour: The Movie*, which premiered on Comedy Central to over five million viewers, and the DVD and VHS sold two and a half million copies. The soundtrack of the movie was in *Billboard's* Top Ten, and there are also CD and DVD versions of *Blue Collar Comedy Tour Rides Again*.

Larry's recordings include *Lord, I Apologize* (Hip-O Records, 2001), *A Very Larry Christmas* (Warner Bros., 2004), and *The Right to Bare Arms* (Warner Bros., 2005). He also has a lot of merchandise to sell (www.larrythecableguy.com). In 2006, he starred in a movie, *Larry the Cable Guy: Health Inspector*, was the voice of Mater the tow truck in the Disney/Pixar film *Cars*, and the voice of Ryder, a cat, in the Disney film *The Fox and the Hound II*.

Larry's humor is lowdown stuff with references to all the bodily or sexual functions, and he pokes barbs at liberals and those who rail against his humor. He even aims his humor at fat people, the handicapped, and others whom, we fear, a lot of people hold prejudices against that they would never themselves reveal in public. After one of his quips that is especially repugnant, though, Larry is apt to bow his head and say, "That ain't right. Lord, I apologize." He may then mumble a prayer having to do with the starving pygmies in Africa. He uses all of the four-letter words that once shocked people and that still do provoke laughter. Larry has many vocal critics, but he has a lot of defenders who seem to admire his view of the world. This vast audience is a puzzle. At really big bucks for a stadium show, they don't appear to be much like the country or blue-collar folk that came out to hear Minnie Pearl or Jerry Clower. But who are they? Working-class people who feel looked down upon by elites? Country people? Yuppies who have risen above their working-class roots and who measure themselves by Larry? Or are they people who just need someone to look down on? Bob Simon commented on "60 Minutes" that "Larry is not angry, he's not depressed, he's not paranoid. He's a happy, hard-working, supremely confident, happy-go-lucky funnyman." Larry seems to agree and to be content making people laugh as his way of making a (high) living. He says that elites, liberals, and politically correct gripers just need to lighten up. His philosophy of humor is pretty well summed up in another of his catch phrases: "I don't care who you are, that's funny right there."

Dan Whitney and his wife Cara have a son, Wyatt, born in 2006. They live in Orlando but also maintain a home in Lincoln, Nebraska.

LASSES AND HONEY. *See Lee Roy White and Lee Davis Wilds*

CHET LAUCK. *See Lum and Abner*

DOYLE LAWSON

Born April 20, 1944, Kingsport, Tennessee

Doyle Lawson is known for his virtuosity on the mandolin and for the great bluegrass and gospel singing of his band Quicksilver. He also keeps the old comedy alive in his performances. "I always try to keep my presentation light. I do a lot of ad-libbing. People ask me where I get that stuff. It just comes off the top of my head. It's both what I make up and what I remember. A lot of times I seize on the situation." An example of this is, "I played the banjo at first, but I quit that because it makes you walk funny." He reminisces about the earlier bands he listened to or played with that always had comedians. "Comedy was just a form of entertainment. You wanted to have a well-rounded program. Comedy was a way to relieve people of their daily stresses, take their minds off their problems." He waxes serious when he talks about the relationship between his heartfelt gospel music and comedy. "Bluegrass is the people's music, and they relate to the gospel music, which turns their thoughts to the more serious side of life, 'cause there is an eternity after life, but by using the comedy, you make them happy."

No one attending a Quicksilver concert would doubt Lawson's deep feeling for the gospel music his group presents, a devotion he inherited from his father, who sang shape-note gospel in quartets. He has had a pattern of alternating his bluegrass and gospel recordings and is known for presenting unaccompanied hymns in smooth, tight harmony. However, not even gospel groups escape his humor. Recognizing the ambiguities and conflicts between the music business and sincere faith, he does a hilarious parody on a gospel group. He explains it as follows: "The Kingsmen Quartet did a takeoff on bluegrass music, so I thought, 'Why not a takeoff on gospel?'" Perhaps because of his faith and his success in gospel music, he gets away with it. He reports that no one has ever complained about this spoof on gospel groups.

Lawson and his wife Suzanne have three children, Robert, Suzi, and Kristi.

Lawson: Down where we're from, when you get a little past the marrying age, they kind of write you off. This old boy, he kinda got past that age by a couple of decades. But one day, he noticed this lady in church, a little past it too, and he decided he'd go over and visit with her. He went over in the afternoon, and he got on one side of the porch swing, and she got on the other. He looked over and kind of grinned at her.

Well, next week he went back, same thing, went on for about a year. Second year rolled around, and he got about halfway across that swing to where he could grin at her and pat her hand. That went on for about a year. Third year, he was about all the way over, almost touching her shoulder. Fourth year the same thing. The fifth year, he got so he could hold her tight by the hand, with an adoring look in his eye.

One day she said, "You know, Albert, we ought to just get married." He looked at her and he said, "Law mercy, Gladys, who'd have us?"

HOMER LEDFORD

Born September 26, 1927, Ivy Point (later Ivyton and
*   now Alpine), Tennessee; died December 11, 2006,*
*   Winchester, Kentucky*

Homer Ledford was a superb craftsman of musical instruments—dulcimers, fiddles, banjos, guitars, mandolins—and partly growing out of his additional role as an entertainer, he made and played several other creations (a dulcitar, a dulcibro, a fiddlephone). He could also coax music out of a harmonica, a Jew's harp, and a handsaw. Tall and angular in a straw floater and Uncle Sam costume, he did a great One-Man Band, with banjo, cymbals on his knees, harmonica on a rack, and a folktoy doll tied to his thumb that danced wildly as he frailed the banjo. In addition, Ledford led an old-time bluegrass band called Cabin Creek.

Homer Ledford with musical saw.
Courtesy of Colista Ledford.

Homer was born the youngest of a family that included two brothers and a sister. He was fascinated with the music and the traditional musicians of East Tennessee, but the family was too poor to own musical instruments, except for an uncle who had ordered a guitar from Montgomery Ward. Homer acquired a pocketknife and began making instruments out of dynamite boxes and wire from screen doors. Eventually he made a playable fiddle out of maple with a hemlock top—with his pocket knife. One of his running jokes later on was to ask the audience if they'd like to see his shop, and then he would pull out his knife.

Homer left home at eighteen to enroll at the John C. Campbell Folk School in Brasstown, North Carolina. There he learned to use power tools and saw his first mountain dulcimers and began to make them. He studied at Berea College—where he was a woodcarver in the student labor program—and graduated from Eastern Kentucky University with a degree in Industrial Arts. He taught his skills in high school for a while, but his dulcimers and other custom-made instruments were soon so popular that he became a full-time instrument maker and repairman at his home in Winchester, Kentucky. The year of his death he reported that he had made 6,014 dulcimers, thirty-three guitars, 520 banjos, and thirty-six mandolins. His first mandolin, which he continued to play, was modeled from a picture of Bill Monroe with his F-5 Gibson. Homer's instruments are in the collections at the Smithsonian Institution.

Homer headed the Cabin Creek Band since 1976. It was nominally a bluegrass band, but its superb musicians and singers—Rollie Carpenter, L. C. Johnson, Pam Case, and Marvin Carroll—produced a wonderful old-time sound. They played festivals and other venues in the United States and performed also in Ireland and Equador. They had a weekly radio show over WSKV in Stanton, Kentucky, and later WMST in Mount Sterling. Homer appeared once on "Good Morning, America" and five times on the internationally syndicated "Woodsongs Old-Time Radio Hour." Homer was a natural wit, turning a phrase neatly to get a smile or a laugh as he made a point. He also told many of the rural jokes and stories he had heard in the region or from the early country music shows. He and members of his band bantered a lot and pulled jokes on one another onstage. The Cabin Creek Band continues to perform, partly as a tribute to Homer Ledford.

In 1984, the folklorist R. Gerald Alvey published a remarkable book about Homer, *Dulcimer Maker: The Craft of Homer Ledford* (University Press of Kentucky, 2003). In 1993, Timber Wolf Television produced a documentary, "Homer Ledford: Instrument Maker," that aired on Kentucky Educational Television. The Cabin Creek Band also has cassette recordings available that include Homer. In 2004, Homer published *See You Further Up the Creek: A Collection of Stories and Poems*, illustrated by his daughter, Cindy Lowy. Recordings and books are available from Colista Ledford, 125 Sunset Heights, Winchester, KY 40391.

At its 2006 winter commencement exercises, Eastern Kentucky University presented Homer with an honorary doctor's degree, posthumously.

Homer was married to the former Colista Spradlin, and they had four children: Mark, Cindy Fess, Julie Baker, and Mattie Lee Conkwright.

One of Homer's stories:

I'm from down in the hills of Tennessee. We'd have a revival for a week, and we'd have twelve or fifteen converts, and then on Sunday afternoon, weather permitting, or sometime not permitting, we'd have a baptizing, put 'em all under and get 'em fixed up just right. I lived right above the river. Well, one Sunday I went down there and the preacher, he was puttin' 'em under, boy.

Well, after he's about finished, he noticed that there was another one in line. As it turned out, it was an old drunk who had wandered in. He didn't know what was goin' on, but he thought he'd just be part of it, and the preacher grabs him and puts him under and brings him up and says, "Did you find Jesus?" He said, "No." So the preacher puts him under again, leaves him just a little bit longer, and brings him back up—he's spluttering a little bit—and the preacher says, "Did you find Jesus that time?" The drunk said "Nooo!" So he socks him under and leaves him about three minutes. He brings him back up, and he's spluttering and carrying on, and he asks, "Did you find Jesus this time?" He said, "Preacher, are you sure that this is the place where he fell in?"

LENNIE AND GOO GOO

Lennie Aleshire, born 1897, Springfield, Missouri;
    died 1987, Springfield, Missouri
Floyd Raymond Rutledge, born 1906, Springfield,
    Missouri; died 1970, Springfield, Missouri

Lennie Aleshire and Floyd Rutledge grew up together in Springfield playing traditional instruments such as guitars, fiddles, and harmonicas and also homemade instruments at church socials and other occasions, sometimes with the help of Lenny's sister Lyda. But tragedy struck Lennie when he was in his late teens. Working at a lumber mill, he sawed off all of the fingers on his left hand except for his little finger. This accident slowed him down only somewhat, for he was determined to go into show business.

Floyd Rutledge worked on the Springfield police force for a time but was let go when he showed a reluctance ever to arrest anyone. In about 1921, Floyd and Lennie joined the vaudeville act of the Weaver Brothers and Elviry based in Springfield. They toured with the troupe as Flash and Whistler in the Orpheum circuit of theaters around the country, including the Palace in New York City. Lennie was adept at keeping all of the musical instruments in tune.

After leaving the Weaver Brothers and Elviry, the pair teamed up for shows on KGBX in Springfield, Missouri. Then Lennie left to tour with Grandpa Jones during the 1940s, and they worked for a time at WWVA in Wheeling, West Virginia, and the "Mountaineer Jamboree." It was he, a talented tap dancer, who turned Grandpa

Lennie and Goo Goo (Lennie
Aleshire and Floyd Rutledge).
Courtesy of Pete Stamper.

and Ramona Jones on to playing tunes with cowbells strapped to their feet and hands.
Lennie made a variety of weird musical instruments out of such things as oil cans,
cigar boxes, broomsticks, and dresser drawers.

Back in Springfield, Lennie tuned pianos for a living, and Floyd drove a taxi, but
they returned to the entertainment business in the "Korn's-a-Krackin'" radio show on
KWTO. This show, with its musicians, comedians, and production crew, evolved into
the "Ozark Jubilee" radio show in 1953, and then became an ABC television show in
1955. Lennie and Goo Goo were part of the show until it folded in 1960. Rutledge
went back to driving taxis and Lennie to tuning pianos for a living. Both men remained
in Springfield and continued to perform at local functions until their deaths.

"LITTLE ROY" LEWIS

Born Roy M. Lewis Jr., February 24, 1942,
Lincolnton, Georgia

In the tradition of the South, when a boy is given the same name as his father, he is usually called "Little" So-and-So. Therefore, young Lewis got his nickname because he is a junior. He became a banjo virtuoso at an early age and won his first contest at the age of eight. He subsequently learned to play the guitar with great skill as well as the bass, autoharp, fiddle, and mandolin. And, of course, he sings and is part of the "First Family of Bluegrass Gospel," the Lewis Family. He is equally well known for his comedic talent and for his wild antics onstage, whether with his own family or invading the sets of other bluegrass bands to harass them while they attempt to play. Sometimes he dresses as a Georgia peanut or wears an E.T. mask, rolling up the britches leg of Buck White or tousling the hair or pouring popcorn on Sonny Osborne's head while they are performing. His energy and stage manner bring up the image of a tornado.

Little Roy grew up with gospel music. He began performing with his brothers and cousins at local gatherings, mostly church affairs. His hero was the great banjo player Don Reno, whom Roy first saw on Arthur Smith's syndicated television show. Earl Scruggs also was a musical influence.

By the time the Lewis Family got under way as a traveling gospel group, Little Roy became its youngest member at age nine. Originally, the group was the Lewis Brothers, with Esley, Wallace, and Tallmadge. When Esley went into service in 1951, Roy joined the group, and later Roy Senior also joined, Tallmadge left, and eventually the daughters, Nannie, Polly, and Janis, got involved. Later on, Wallace's son Travis and Janis's son Lewis Phillips were added. The group did weekly shows for a time over WJBF-TV in Augusta and after that yearly specials. They have recorded for Solid Rock, Canaan, Starday, and Riversong. The Lewis Family is in much demand at bluegrass festivals and special events, with Little Roy and his musical wizardry and comic antics as a major part of their appeal. The bluegrass musician Tim O'Brien puts Lewis's comedy into perspective in this age: "Little Roy Lewis is a guy that amazes me. His humor is very controversial among bluegrass people. It's very much a kind of throwback." He means that bluegrass fans, and especially bluegrass gospel fans, have gotten really serious about the music and have lost the ability to laugh at it or at themselves, but Lewis's comedy comes from an earlier time when comedy was always a part of the music. O'Brien concludes, "The more serious the subject matter, the greater the need for humor."

Little Roy has also had a solo recording history, starting in 1968 with *Golden Gospel Banjo* on Starday. This was followed by five albums on Canaan: *Gospel Banjo* (1972), *The Entertainer* (1977), *Super Pickin'* (1981), *The Heart of Dixie* (1984), and *The Best of Little Roy Lewis* (1985). Check www.thelewisfamilymusic.com.

Roy Lewis Jr. is married to the former Bonnie Reeves from Monroe, Louisiana, and they live in Lincolnton, Georgia, near the rest of the Lewis family.

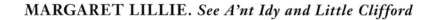

MARGARET LILLIE. *See A'nt Idy and Little Clifford*

LILLY BROTHERS

Mitchell Burt "B." Lilly, born December 15, 1921,
*   Clear Creek, West Virginia*
Charles Everett Lilly, born July 1, 1924, Clear Creek,
*   West Virginia*

The Lilly Brothers, with the fiddler Tex Logan and the banjoist Don Stover, are well known in bluegrass circles for popularizing that sound in New England, after beginning their career over local West Virginia radio stations in the "brother duet" tradition. They loved the songs of the brothers Callahan, Delmore, and Monroe and hastened to learn them, but they already had a rich repertoire of traditional music. Everett commented, "The Lilly Brothers were branded as bluegrass. We were actually American, folk, mountain, country singers. Bill and Charlie Monroe were also American, folk, country singers. We sang a form of country music that tells stories about things."

They played over WCHS, Charleston, in 1938 and then began playing over WKLS, Beckley, in 1939. By 1945, they were at WNOX in Knoxville. In 1948, they joined Red Belcher's band at WWVA's "Mountaineer Jamboree," where they first met Tex Logan. They went to Fairmont for a time and then returned home to Clear Creek. Everett then played with Flatt and Scruggs for a year and a half until Tex Logan persuaded him and "B" to join him in Boston, on the "Hayloft Jamboree" at WCOP.

In Boston the band began playing local nightclubs, the most important being a working-class bar called the Hillbilly Ranch. During the 1960s, with the folk revival, students from Harvard, the Massachusetts Institute of Technology, and other colleges in the area started coming to their club shows, forming a new audience for their emerging bluegrass sound. Soon they had an invitation to play a concert at Harvard. They didn't know what to expect. Everett described that night:

> When we went over there to play, we were full of surprises to them because we had a driving sound. When we went in, here they were settin' all over the floor. Nobody was settin' in seats. I guess they wanted to mix with us. We should have been happy about it, but it almost pissed us off. Everything we played or sang, they would just go wild. We thought, "What is this? Did they invite us over to poke fun at us? It turned out that those people thought we were just tops."
>
> We did comedy at Harvard, and it went over all right. I think humor is real important to everybody. To me, that's the kind of person you are [what you think is funny]. Are you going to get mad at a joke, or are you going to be a good fellow and go along with it? People can't just swell up and say, "I'm it! Don't say anything out of the way to me." Humor can take the wind out of someone's sail.

Some humor scholars have suggested that the college-educated people who joined the folk revival helped to kill country comedy, because while they loved the authenticity of the music and those who played it, they thought corny comedy was beneath them. Everett Lilly denied that this was the case with the comedy of the Lilly Brothers when they played for college students in New England.

Careful students of the older bands, the Lilly Brothers saw the need for complete entertainment, especially when they ventured out to schools and other venues, and so they developed comedy routines to lighten things. One part of their comedy was the contrast between their West Virginia dialect and that of Boston—for example, "Pa-a-r-r-k the ca-a-r-r" versus "Paik the cai." Everett likes to talk about comedy: "The Lilly Brothers had a lot of comedy in our act. Mostly we had somebody in the band to do comedy, usually the bass player. I was usually the straight man, but sometimes I dressed up too and told jokes. The comedy was always clean because we played schools. We wouldn't have dared do anything offensive to families. I played a character called 'Hillbilly Tex' at the Hillbilly Ranch. I pulled that on them at Harvard College. It worked for some, but some recognized me."

The Lilly Brothers influenced several young easterners to play bluegrass music, such as Peter Rowan. Several contacted them for lessons on various instruments, including Bill Keith. New England eventually had its own bluegrass tradition to a great degree because of the Lilly Brothers.

In 1970, Everett and Joann decided to take the rest of the family back to West Virginia after the death of their son Jiles in a traffic accident. "B" and his family also moved back but later returned to Boston. The brothers, with Don Stover and Tex Logan, occasionally did bluegrass festivals for a few years and even toured Japan. In recent years Everett has played with his sons Mark and Daniel. He and Daniel do the old comedy routines with some new material thrown in. Another son, Charles, played bass and did comedy with Johnny Russell until Russell's death in 2001. Charles died in an auto accident in 2006, along with the country star Billy Walker and his wife, as they were returning from an engagement.

"B" and his wife Joan still live in Boston. Their children are Floragale, Mitchell, Monty, Daphene, Joey, Shelly, Cindy, Michael, and Jody. Everett and Joan live in Clear Creek. Their other children are Everett Allen, Tennis, Diana, La Verne, and Karen.

The Lilly Brothers did many recordings, some of which are still available, including *Folksongs from the Southern Mountains* (Folkways, 1961), *Bluegrass Breakdown* (Prestige and Rounder, 1964), *Early Recordings* (County, 1970; re-released by Rebel as a CD), and *What Will I Leave Behind* (County, 1973). Everett also appears on the 1951 Flatt and Scruggs Columbia recordings singing tenor and playing mandolin.

Here are some excerpts of Lilly humor performed by Everett and his son Daniel at the Celebration of Traditional Music at Berea College in 1997:

> *Daniel: We're from Beckley, West Virginia. We drove down here, and just before we got out of West Virginia, a state trooper pulled us over. He done had half the ticket wrote out*

before he got up beside the van. He said, "You's speedin', Buddy." I said, "Yeah, I's just tryin' to get there." He said, "Well, you're gettin' a ticket." A little old fly kept buzzin' around his face while he's writin' out that ticket. I said, "Officer, that's one of them ol' geetchee flies." He said, "What on earth is a geetchee fly?" I said, "Are you from West Virginia?" He said, "Yeah." I said, "You ought to know what a geetchee fly is." He said, "Well I don't. You tell me." I said, "Well, Officer, it's just one of them ol' flies on the farm that flies around a horse's behind all the time." He said, "Are you tryin' to say that I am a horse's behind?" I said, "No, Sir, but you can't hardly fool one of them geetchee flies!"

GEORGE "GOOBER" LINDSEY

Born December 17, 1935, Fairfield, Alabama

Although people think "Goober" when they see George Lindsey's name because of his years on the "Andy Griffith Show," "Mayberry, RFD," and "Hee Haw," he studied to be a serious actor at the American Theater Wing at Hunter College in New York. He was a costar in the Broadway musical *All American* and the off-Broadway *Wonderful Town*. In Hollywood, he got parts in television series such as "Alfred Hitchcock Presents," "The Rifleman," "Gunsmoke," and "The Twilight Zone." He also developed a comedy routine that he presented at comedy clubs between theater jobs, playing up his Alabama accent.

George "Goober" Lindsey. Courtesy of Third Coast Talent.

In 1964, after meeting Andy Griffith, he landed the role of Goober on the "Andy Griffith Show" and later "Mayberry, RFD." Lindsey's comedy came into its own with Goober, a somewhat goofy hillbilly mechanic whom he played for seven years. In 1971, he was hired to make appearances on "Hee Haw," leading to a twenty-year run on the network and syndicated show. His comedic character well established, Lindsey was invited to do episodes on "M*A*S*H" and to appear on "Laugh-In," "The Tonight Show," "The Jonathan Winters Show," and the "Wonderful World of Disney." He had roles in the movies *Cannonball Run II* and *Take This Job and Shove It*, and he lent his voice to *The Rescuers* and *The Aristocats*. He starred in the stage production *Hee Haw Live* at Opryland in 1994.

In 1995, he published an autobiography, *Goober in a Nutshell* (with Joe Fann), and in 2001 he published *The Way Back to Mayberry: Lessons from a Simpler Time* (with Ken Beck). He has recorded one comedy album, *Goober Sings*. He does forty or fifty show dates a year to audiences that are familiar with the "Andy Griffith Show" and "Hee Haw" and are already fans. Just in case, though, he usually shows a clip of Goober on the "Andy Griffith Show," and he appears dressed as Goober. He confesses that he used to wear white tie and tails on stage at Las Vegas, but no more. He accepts the fact that his main persona is Goober. As for his material, he looks for clean comedy. He acknowledges his debt to his "Hee Haw" associates, primarily Grandpa Jones and Minnie Pearl. He was impressed by the fact that they could do rural comedy with dignity. He still uses some of the jokes he learned from them.

In recent years, Lindsey has done commercials for the Getty Oil Company and Liberty Overalls, dressed as the mechanic from the "Andy Griffith Show."

Lindsey has used his popularity to promote charitable work. He ran the George Lindsey Celebrity Golf Tournament to raise charitable funds for several years and has raised over a million dollars for Special Olympics in Alabama. He also established the George Lindsey TV and Film Festival in 1997 at the University of Northern Alabama, his alma mater, to educate high school and college students about these industries. He has also helped to establish the George Lindsey Aquatic Center at Alabama State Hospital for the mentally handicapped. His charitable work earned him the 1997 Minnie Pearl Award for significant humanitarian contributions from the TNN Music City News Awards.

One other thing: he was awarded the honorary degree of doctor of humane letters from the University of Northern Alabama and is now Dr. George Lindsey.

> *Goober: An eighty-five-year-old man was walking along, and he saw a frog. He picked it up, and the frog said, "If you'll kiss me on the lips, I'll turn into a beautiful princess." The old man put the frog in his pocket and went on. The frog yelled, "I said if you kiss me I'll turn into a beautiful princess!" The old man said, "At my age, I'd rather have a talking frog."*

LITTLE ELLER LONG. *See Shorty Hobbs and Little Eller*

LONZO AND OSCAR

John Y. "Lonzo" Sullivan, born July 7, 1917,
Edmonton, Kentucky; died June 5, 1967,
Goodlettsville, Tennessee
Rollin "Oscar" Sullivan, born January 19, 1919,
Edmonton, Kentucky
Lloyd L. "Lonzo" George (also Ken Marvin),
born June 27, 1944, Haleyville, Alabama;
died October 16, 1991, Goodlettsville, Tennessee
David "Lonzo" Hooten, born February 4, 1935,
St. Claire, Missouri
Cleo C. "Lonzo" Hogan Sr., born 1925, Park City,
Kentucky; died April 3, 1998, Glasgow, Kentucky
Billy "Lonzo" and "Oscar" Henson, born December
12, 1937, Murfreesboro, Tennessee
Ron "Lonzo" Ryan, born October 17, 1948,
Murfreesboro, Tennessee

The musical and comedy duet of Lonzo and Oscar was a fixture at the "Grand Ole Opry" for many years, first as a part of Eddy Arnold's band and then as members in their own right. Rollin Sullivan was Oscar, but six others have played the part of Lonzo over the years. The duo did regular rube comedy, original humorous songs, and parodies of popular songs of the day.

The Sullivan brothers grew up in a family of ten near Mammoth Cave in Kentucky. Rollin and his brother John were part of a band called the Kentucky Mountaineers, playing for dances while they were still in high school. Rollin states that his first commercial job was with Cliff Gross and His Texas Cowboys at WAVE in Louisville. Then he and John went to WDJS in Jackson, Tennessee, in 1937 and stayed until 1939. It was there that Rollin got his nickname of Oscar from an announcer who couldn't remember his real name. Rollin and John were both drafted into service, but Rollin was discharged because of bad feet. He played USO clubs during the war with Cliff Gross's western band.

Rollin first went to the "Grand Ole Opry" with Paul Howard and His Arkansas Cotton Pickers as a mandolin player. In 1945 he joined Eddy Arnold's band. He remembered, "Eddy said one day, 'Boys, I don't like to come out on stage the first part of the show, so I'd like for a couple of you to open the show with comedy.' He said to the bass player, Lloyd George, who also played guitar, 'You and Oscar do a comedy act.' Well, that's what we did until 1947." At first they were Cicero and Oscar, but then one night in a hotel, Eddy heard an old black man addressed as "Lonzo" and he said, "That's it, Lonzo and Oscar!" By this time John had been discharged and was also part

Lonzo and Oscar (Rollin Sullivan and John Sullivan). Courtesy of the John Lair Collection, Southern Appalachian Archive, Berea College.

of the band. Arnold helped the duo to get a recording contract with RCA Victor, and they cut two numbers, "You Blacked My Blue Eyes Once Too Often" and "I'm My Own Grandpa." The latter was given to and rejected by Arnold, with the comment, "I'm trying to get into the business, not out of it." He handed the song to Lonzo and Oscar, and the recording sold a total of 3,554,000 records.

In 1947, with the success of that recording, the duo became "Opry" regulars and played together until 1950, when Lloyd George decided to go on his own as Ken Marvin. So John Sullivan rejoined his brother, and they were Lonzo and Oscar for the next sixteen years. When John died, David Hooten became Lonzo for the next eighteen years, all at the "Opry." Oscar commented, "We did about fifty-fifty between comedy and music. We'd come on the 'Grand Ole Opry' and shoot a bunch of bull, tell jokes and so forth, and then lead into a song. We always tried to make the song sound good, harmony-wise, always." Also a part of the act from 1952–65 was Clell Summey as Cousin Jody, playing his "biscuit board" electric steel guitar. Lonzo was the nearest thing to a straight man, Oscar said. "Lonzo was the one that tried to keep the wagon going down the road, and Cousin Jody and I were always pushing it off the road." On their comedy, he explained further, "We had a skeleton routine that we went by. We knew about what we were going to do, but our audience played such a big part in our show that when they were getting with it, why we'd work ourselves to death, right along with them. We'd set our cap on about fifteen or twenty people in the audience, getting them to just dying a-laughing, see."

Tommy Ward played bass with the group and also contributed to the comedy. On costume, Oscar commented, "I wore a red wig, a little green Robinson Crusoe hat. The britches were a little bit too big in the waist and came down to about halfway between my knees and my shoetops, with tassels at the bottom. When I'd kick my leg out these tassels would frazzle out, and everybody thought that was funny. I blacked out my teeth. Lonzo dressed about the same way, with a less conspicuous shirt and a cap." In later years, there was less comedy and more music, and they dressed in a more regular fashion, especially when they began playing bluegrass festivals.

Lonzo and Oscar were part of the first "Grand Ole Opry" troupe to play at a state fair (in Missouri). Oscar, with his various partners, has traveled in fifteen foreign countries. Lonzo and Oscar recorded singles for RCA, Capitol, Starday, Columbia, and Decca. They also had their own recording company, Nugget Records. They did a total of eleven albums on various other labels, including *America's Greatest Country Comedians*, *Country Music Time* (Starday, 1960 and 1963), *Country Comedy Time* (Decca, 1961), *Hole in the Bottom of the Sea* (Nugget, 1965), *Mountain Dew* (Columbia, 1968), and *Lonzo and Oscar Old and New Songs* (Hilltop Records, n.d.).

When Sullivan and Hooten retired from the "Opry" in 1985, Sullivan returned to Kentucky and joined Cleo C. Hogan Sr., who ran a Bowling Green television show called "Saturday Night Jubilee," and they played Lonzo and Oscar on the "Jubilee," at bluegrass festivals, and at benefits. They continued to perform occasionally until Hogan's death in 1998. Sullivan, with his second wife Geneva (his first wife, Ruth Evelyn, was killed in an automobile accident in 1959), runs an organization called the Traditional Music Association to promote the old-time music that they cherish. They have had business interests in western Kentucky and now own and operate a campground in Greenbriar, Tennessee. In recent years, Sullivan has performed with Billy Henson, who assumed the role of Lonzo. Rollin Sullivan sold the rights to the Lonzo and Oscar name to Henson, who now plays the role of Oscar with Ron Ryan as Lonzo. They do bluegrass festivals and other events. Henson also has his own band, Summerstar.

The following joke was shared by Geneva Sullivan as one that was part of the repertoire of Lonzo and Oscar:

> *Lonzo and Oscar rented a boat and went out fishing, and they were really having good luck. Oscar said to Lonzo, "I think you'd better mark this spot so we can try it another time. So Lonzo put an X on the bottom of the boat. Oscar said, "Why you stupid thing! What makes you think we're going to get this same boat the next time?"*

LOUVIN BROTHERS

Born Ira Lonnie Loudermilk, April 24, 1924, Section,
*   Alabama; died June 20, 1965, Williamsburg,*
*   Missouri*
Born Charles Elzer Loudermilk, July 7, 1927,
*   Section, Alabama*

The Louvin Brothers are known for their wonderful harmony on gospel songs such as "The Family Who Prays" and such Top Ten secular hits as "When I Stop Dreaming" and "My Baby's Gone," but they also did their share of comedy. Charlie explained, "When you do a two-hour show, you can't just sing the whole two hours. A joke here and a joke there and our Sal Skinner act gave variety. If you got the crowd too serious you could tell a little joke and snap them out of it." He went on to talk about variety: "If you were putting together a balanced show, you would have gospel music, you would have a comedy act, a country act, and a girl singer." He gave credit to Roy Acuff for creating this balance, especially for being first to add a girl singer: "I think that balances a show, and it keeps the language clean. These were family shows. We never did risqué jokes that would offend anybody."

The Loudermilk brothers were born on Sand Mountain in the Appalachian foothills of northern Alabama, where life was hard. Charlie commented that not much of their humor came from these growing-up years. "We didn't find a whole lot amusing in Alabama. There wasn't too much comedy in the cotton fields." The brothers got into show business by winning an amateur talent contest in Chattanooga, "singing silly stuff like 'There's a Hole in the Bottom of the Sea' and 'Johnson's Old Gray Mule,'" and this got them a fifteen-minute spot at 4:30 A.M. on WDEF, a 250-watt station. Ira, already married, had a house in Chattanooga, and Charlie boarded there. Both had day jobs, of course. Soon, however, they got requests to play such venues as PTA meetings for meager pay, but sometimes they made more in a night than they did from working six days in the mill.

Because he was of draft age, Charlie couldn't get a steady day job, and so he volunteered for the army in 1945. In the meantime, Ira got a job playing mandolin and singing bass with Charlie Monroe over WNOX in Knoxville. When Charlie got out of the army, the brothers joined Cas Walker's show on WROL in Knoxville. They changed their name to the Louvin Brothers and eventually went to the "Mid-day Merry-Go-Round" on WNOX. Eddie Hill then invited them to Memphis to join his band playing over WMPS. After two years they returned to WNOX, but their careers were stymied again when Charlie was called back to the army during the Korean War. When he got out, they went to WOVK in Birmingham for a time and then to the "Grand Ole Opry" in 1955.

The Louvin Brothers recorded for Apollo, Decca, MGM, and Capitol. In more recent years, Capitol released several songs from their vaults, and other companies have reissued their material: *Songs That Tell a Story* (Rounder, 1978), *The Best of the Louvin Brothers* (Rebel, 1986), *Radio Favorites* (Country Music Foundation Records, 1987), and *The Louvin Brothers: Close Harmony* (Bear Family box set, 1992). Their big chart songs were "When I Stop Dreaming," "I Don't Believe You've Met My Baby," "Hoping That You're Hoping," and "My Baby's Gone" (log on to charlielouvinbros.com).

Unfortunately, they did not record their comedy. It was done mostly to enliven their personal-appearance shows. Charlie described Ira's adoption of the Sal Skinner character (originally played by the vaudeville team of Boyle and Graham): "Sal Skinner was a great deal like Minnie Pearl, but Ira said she was from Financial Flats. He made most of the humor up, and it was a good act. . . . He sounded so much like Minnie Pearl that once we did a show with her, and when my brother was doing Sal Skinner, Minnie's little poodle actually came on stage—thought he was Minnie Pearl." Charlie served as the straight man. The brothers also wrote and sang comedy and novelty songs such as "Bald Knob Arkansas," "The Red Hen Boogie," and "Ruby's Song."

This brother duet act, although one of the most popular, was not always harmonious, mainly because Ira, a creative talent, was tempestuous and had a drinking problem. The brothers split in 1963 after playing WWVA in Wheeling, West Virginia. Ira quit music for a time but eventually did limited engagements. He and his fourth wife, Anne (Young), were killed in an automobile accident in 1965. He had three children, Gail, Terry, and Kathy. Charlie continues to perform on the "Grand Ole Opry" and to do personal-appearance shows. He is married to the former Betty Harrison, and they have three children: Charlie Jr., Kenneth, and Glenn.

> *Charlie Louvin: One of the old jokes—we used it more than fifty years ago—a guy was going down the road, and a state trooper put the red light on him, but he wouldn't stop. The state trooper chased him down and finally got him stopped. The state trooper was hot because the man had not stopped. He asked him, "Why didn't you stop when I first put the red light on you back yonder?" The guy said, "Officer, I'm sorry about that, but when I seen a state trooper behind me, I remembered that about two or three months ago my wife ran off with a state trooper, and I was afraid that was him bringing her back!"*

LULU BELLE AND SCOTTY

Scott Greene Wiseman, born November 8, 1909,
  Ingalls, North Carolina; died January 31, 1981,
  Gainesville, Florida
Myrtle Eleanor Cooper, born December 24, 1913,
  Boone, North Carolina; died February 8, 1999,
  Spruce Pine, North Carolina

Myrtle Cooper and Scott Wiseman met at the WLS "National Barn Dance" in Chicago when they were thrown together as the comical "Hayloft Sweethearts" who sang a variety of songs in close harmony. John Lair, then the artistic director at WLS, who had a flair for supplying performers with countrified names, changed Cooper's name to Lulu Belle, which she didn't mind because she said it sounded better than Myrtle. Actually, in 1932 Lair had at first teamed her, at age sixteen, with Red Foley as his supposed Kentucky girlfriend who had heard him on the radio and had come to Chicago to get on also, but when Foley got married there was a need to team her with someone else. Scott Wiseman, who had grown up in the Blue Ridge Mountains playing the banjo and guitar and learning and singing the old traditional songs, had been assisted by Bradley Kincaid to land a spot on the "Barn Dance" after he graduated

Lulu Belle and Scotty.
Courtesy of Bill Lightfoot.

from Fairmont College in West Virginia. Lulu Belle and Scotty became a pair in 1932 and were married the same year, although they kept it secret for a time. They became enormously popular at WLS and were on the "Barn Dance" until 1958, except for a short stint at WLW in Cincinnati. As an example of their appeal, Lulu Belle was voted "Radio Queen" of 1936 in a popularity contest sponsored by the *Radio Guide*, winning over a host of popular radio personalities of the day.

For their comedy, John Lair dressed the pair in old-fashioned quaint costumes. Scotty wore pants with suspenders and a checkered shirt, although he had a clean-cut look. Lulu Belle wore pretty but old-fashioned gingham, or what she called "Mother Hubbard," dresses, with pantaloons peeking out below, high-top shoes, and a dimestore braid with a red ribbon. She was the impertinent irrepressible woman, and Scotty was the long-suffering, put-upon boyfriend, and then husband. He was also the straight man. They had several tricks of the trade. Lulu Belle remembered, "I had an old guitar with a mirror on it, and while I was singing a comic song like 'How Can I Sing When

He's Winkin' At Me?' I'd use the mirror to put a spotlight on someone in the audience, like a bald-headed man. That went over real big." She and Scotty sang other comic songs from his traditional repertoire, such as "Madam, I Have Come to Marry You" and "Tildy Johnson."

Lulu Belle and Scotty were good musicians and singers, and they did many serious songs, including Scotty's own compositions that became country standards, "Have I Told You Lately that I Love You?" and "Remember Me (When the Candle Lights Are Gleaming)." These and other compositions, including "Mountain Dew" (with Bascom Lamar Lunsford), "Brown Mountain Lights," and "Homecoming Time in Happy Valley," elevated Scotty into the Nashville songwriters Hall of Fame in 1971.

The folklorist William Lightfoot has pointed out that the popularity of Lulu Belle and Scotty was based on a "musical Appalachian myth" that they created on radio about life in "Happy Valley," Scott's ancestral home place in the Blue Ridge Mountains near Spruce Pine. The myth included "virtuous-but-sunny courtships, harmonious romantic relationships, rural family life, history and traditions, place (home, mountains), close communion with neighbors, fundamental religious beliefs, and simple fun." WLS created a morning show for them, "Breakfast in the Blue Ridge," that included intimate talk of neighbors and local happenings. Fans imagined that the show actually was broadcast from Happy Valley. Their comic songs and comedy included a lot of traditional lore, as well as material from vaudeville and other types of shows, including "battle of the sexes" routines, but as Lightfoot suggests, it was all good, clean fun.

Lulu Belle and Scotty were in seven movies, and they recorded for Bluebird, Conqueror, ARC, Vocalion, Starday, and Vogue. Their material was later released on Old Homestead, Birch, and Castle Germany. Marshall Dial of Mar-Lu Records (700 E. Sixth Street, Portageville, MO 63873) released some of their radio material on six tapes.

When the Wisemans retired to their Spruce Pine home, Scott was approached to run for the North Carolina legislature. With a master's degree, he wanted instead to teach in the local schools and to farm. However, Lulu Belle decided to run as a Democrat in the heavily Republican district and won two terms in the North Carolina House. Scotty and Lulu Belle had two children, Linda Lou Johnson and Steven Scott. After Scotty died of a heart attack on a trip home from Florida, Lulu Belle married Ernest Stamey, an attorney and longtime family friend.

Lulu Belle and Scotty are buried at the Pine Grove Methodist church cemetery near Spruce Pine.

(With credit to Scott G. Wiseman, *Wiseman's View: The Autobiography of Scotty Wiseman*, ed. William E. Lightfoot [Hiddenite: North Carolina Folklore Society, 2000], and Marshall Dial for his interview with Lulu Belle Wiseman, July 1986.)

> Scotty: Anyhow, Gal, when you married me you took me for better or for worse.
> Lulu Belle: Yeah, I know I did, Honey, but sometimes you are a little bit worse than I took you fer!

LUM AND ABNER

Chester Lauck, born February 2, 1902, Aleene,
*   Arkansas; died February 21, 1980, Hot Springs,*
*   Arkansas*
Norris Goff, born May 30, 1906, Cove, Arkansas;
*   died June 12, 1978, Palm Desert, California*

Lauck and Goff, who grew up together in Mena, Arkansas, created one of the most popular pairs of country codgers ever. Their "Lum and Abner Show" was on radio from 1931 to 1954. The pair started out doing "Amos 'n' Andy" imitations as blackface comedy. Perhaps seeing that blackface would not remain popular in a changing world, they hit upon the idea of changing their personas to what a writer called "two old hillbilly characters." Goff and Lauck no doubt were well aware of the image the rest of the country had of Arkansas. They were bright young men and saw an opportunity for themselves, perhaps in vaudeville or in the burgeoning world of radio entertainment, especially in rube-type comedy in association with country music. They hired Grandpa Jones, another young guy who was to become a geezer too, and his sidekick, "Bashful Harmonica Joe Troyan," as part of the Pine Ridge String Band to give an additional country flavor to their show. Before adequate recording equipment was available, they were doing three broadcasts a day (for different time zones) five days a week.

However, Lum Edwards (pronounced, of course, "Eddards") and Abner Peabody were not simply know-nothing rubes; they were country philosophers, given to witty sayings that would have graced Will Rogers. Besides their basic characters, they created

Lum and Abner.

others with their versatile voices: Squire Skemp, Grandpappy Spears, Dick Huddleston, Cedric Weehunt, and others as the need arose. Radio made them immensely popular so that they could also take their routines to stages throughout the country. In 1940, they made their first of many trips to Hollywood to act in seven films: *Dreaming Out Loud, The Bashful Bachelor, Two Weeks to Live, So This Is Washington, Goin' to Town, Partners in Time,* and *Lum and Abner Abroad.*

As a gauge of their enduring popularity, all of the major search engines on the Web have listings of Lum and Abner radio shows, books, and videos of their movies. The Lum and Abner Society held its 2002 meeting in Mena, Arkansas, where Lauck and Goff grew up, featuring actors who appeared in their films. Additionally, Kathy and Lon Stucker operate a Lum and Abner Museum and Jot 'em Down Store in Pine Ridge, Arkansas. If you want more information on this radio pair, available materials, or Kathryn Stucker's book, *Hello, This Is Lum and Abner,* write them at PO Box 38, Pine Ridge, AR 71966.

ROBERT LUNN

Born November 28, 1912, Franklin, Tennessee;
died March 8, 1966

Charles Wolfe called Robert Lunn the "third great Opry comedy act of the 1930s" (after Lasses and Honey and Sarie and Sally). An ex-vaudevillian, Lunn had a fine comedic career based on one song, "The Talking Blues," to which he had fashioned some one hundred verses. Wolfe points out that Lunn adapted his piece from a recording by Chris Bouchillon, who recorded such a song in 1926. Lunn capitalized on this "odd hybrid genre that involved talking in a stylized, sing-song way over a simple guitar riff." Here is one of his best-remembered verses:

> I's out in the wildwood settin' on a tree,
> I set down on a bumblebee.
> Thought it was a snake or a bug, you see,
> On second thought, I knowed it was a bee,
> 'Cause it kept stingin'
> Achin' too,
> No relief.

Lunn grew up in Franklin, Tennessee, and joined a vaudeville troupe as a youth. There he learned showmanship, a left-handed guitar style, and ventriloquism. These skills led him to radio work in the early 1930s at WCHS in Charleston, West Virginia, and KWTO in Springfield, Missouri. However, the Great Depression limited his opportunities, and he returned to Tennessee, where he worked as a bellboy in Nashville's Hermitage Hotel. The hotel sported a low-wattage radio station just for its guests, and Lunn broadcast shows to entertain them. Since the hotel was a stopping place for show-business personalities and executives, he soon came to the notice of officials at the "Grand Ole Opry." George D. Hay, the general manager of the "Opry," liked him and billed him as the "Original Talking Blues Man." He was also popular with audiences, with his ever-expanding verses on topical matters, and he received sacks of mail and was voted the most popular star on the "Opry" for 1936. He also traveled with the "Opry" tent shows until his career was interrupted by service in World War II. After the war, he returned to the "Opry" but eventually took a job with the State of Tennessee.

Lunn recorded his talking blues for Mercury in 1947, and in 1957 he cut *The Original Talking Blues Man* for Starday. Among the entertainers who later used the talking blues style were Woody Guthrie, Curly Fox, the Prairie Ramblers, Tex Williams, Phil Harris, and Bob Dylan.

(With credit to Charles K. Wolfe, *A Good-Natured Riot: The Birth of the Grand Ole Opry* [Nashville: Country Music Foundation Press and Vanderbilt University Press, 1999].)

UNCLE DAVE MACON

Born David Harrison Macon, October 7, 1870,
Warren County, Tennessee; died March 22, 1952,
Rutherford County, Tennessee

Uncle Dave Macon was one of the first performers on what became the "Grand Ole Opry" and was its first real star. He is a legend in country music, as exemplified by a technique devised by the folklorist Charles Wolfe in the making of a movie on Macon. He and the filmmaker drove around middle Tennessee with a huge picture of Macon in the back of a pickup truck recording people as they recognized him and told stories about the old entertainer. There is an annual festival in Murfreesboro named after him. A veteran of the vaudeville stage, Macon, known as "the Dixie Dewdrop," was described as the complete entertainer. He could tell jokes and stories that put people in stitches, pick the banjo in several styles and tunings while doing banjo tricks, sing a great range of songs, dance a bit, and even give a little moral or religious sermon along the way. Beecher Kirby, the longtime comedian in Roy Acuff's band, remembered, "Uncle Dave used to travel with us a lot. Ever' show he did I watched him. He was a one-man show. I got a lot of my stuff from Uncle Dave."

Macon was born near McMinnville, but by the time he was in his teens, his family moved to Nashville, where they operated the Broadway Hotel that lodged vaudeville performers and other entertainers. Charles Wolfe, the foremost authority on Macon, wrote that among the entertainers who influenced young Macon was a comedian and banjo player by the name of Joel Davidson, who did banjo tricks as a part of his act. Macon had acquired his first banjo when he was fifteen and was soon adept with it as well as in telling humorous stories and singing a variety of songs. Wolfe notes also that he had already learned a lot of rural black music, and in Nashville he quickly picked up many vaudeville and minstrel tunes, as well as Tin Pan Alley songs that were part of the popular entertainment of the day.

At first, Macon did not see a career for himself in entertainment. When his father was killed in Nashville, Macon and his mother moved away. He was married at the age of nineteen to Matilda Richardson of Readyville, and apparently they inherited her parents' farm. So Macon became a farmer and later operated a mule and wagon freight company that hauled goods between Murfreesboro and Woodbury. Those who knew him said that he carried his banjo along on his two-day trips and was always willing to entertain people along the way. He was also remembered as a great raconteur, and he was agreeable to performing at any local happening and especially charitable events. For most of his life, he never received any pay for his performing talents.

When he was past fifty, a Loews vaudeville theater scout heard him and imme-diately hired him to perform in Birmingham, where he was so well received that his two-week engagement was extended to five weeks. With this success, he was hired to play numerous other Loews theaters in the country.

Dave Macon had found his niche. He looked around for someone to back him up in his performance and settled on Sid Harkreader, a fiddler who could also play backup guitar, sing, and do comedy as well. In addition to their vaudeville act, Dave and Sid went to New York and recorded two numbers for Vocalion, "Chewing Gum" and "Keep My Skillet Good and Greasy," which became signature numbers for Uncle Dave. These records sold so well that he became a major recording star, waxing more than 180 numbers for various companies, according to Wolfe. In 1925, the great guitarist and banjo picker Sam McGee joined Macon and Harkreader in their act. McGee also had a fine comic bent, and he and Macon could elicit laughs from any group. Macon and McGee were still farmers, and they arranged their vaudeville travels so as to have time for planting and harvesting. It was no wonder that Macon and his group appealed so well to country folks.

Charles Wolfe believed that Uncle Dave Macon and Sid Harkreader performed on a WSM broadcast from the Ryman Auditorium on November 6, 1925, twenty-two days before Uncle Jimmy Thompson played on the barn dance that scholars have called the beginning of the "Grand Ole Opry." At any rate, Macon began performing irregularly on the "Opry," but he mainly continued traveling to better-paying venues. However, he became the most popular "Opry" performer for the next fifteen years and eventually joined the "Opry" tent shows as they traveled to the hinterlands from Nashville. He often traveled with the Delmore Brothers, Bill Monroe, and Roy Acuff. For recording purposes he had a hot string band, with Harkreader, Sam and Kirk

McGee, and Mazy Todd. Bradley Kincaid, who sometimes traveled with Uncle Dave, said that on tent-show trips the old man carried a ham that he himself had cured in a flour sack and that he would take it to the hotel dining room and tell the waitress to ask the cook to cut him two big slices and fry them up with a couple of eggs.

Macon and his fellow musicians continued to record during the 1930s, but because of the deepening Depression, only a few of their recordings were released. Brunswick released none of the numbers he recorded for them in 1930. Macon then went to OKeh for several sides that same year, but the public saw only a few, among them "Tennessee Red Fox Chase" and "Wreck of the Tennessee Gravy Train." He also recorded for Gennett and Victor's Bluebird.

In 1939 Uncle Dave and his son Dorris, who was playing backup guitar with him, were invited to go to Hollywood for the making of the film *The Grand Ole Opry*, with Roy Acuff and others. This film provides the only moving visual record of Uncle Dave's performing talent. He picks the banjo, sings, does his famous banjo tricks, and dances around. A story, no doubt apocryphal, has Uncle Dave sending Dorris to the bank for money to make the Hollywood trip. "How much shall I get?" Dorris asks. Uncle Dave replies, "Oh, I guess you should get a flour sack full."

Uncle Dave continued performing at the "Grand Ole Opry" until shortly before his death in 1952 at age eighty-two. He was elected to the Country Music Hall of Fame in 1966. Several musicians have imitated his style. The best of these currently is LeRoy Troy, a fellow middle Tennessean. Country Records has two Uncle Dave Macon CDs available, *Travelin' Down the Road* and *Go Long Mule*, as well as two cassettes, *Early Recordings, 1925–35* and *Go Long Mule*.

(With credit to Charles Wolfe, especially *A Good-Natured Riot: The Birth of the Grand Ole Opry* [Nashville: Country Music Foundation Press and Vanderbilt University Press, 1999].)

J. E. AND WADE MAINER

*Joseph Emmett Mainer, born July 20, 1898,
   Buncombe County, North Carolina; died June 12,
   1971, Concord, North Carolina
Wade E. Mainer, born April 21, 1907, Buncombe
   County, North Carolina*

Mainer's Mountaineers were one of the premier early country bands, and they set trends in country music in terms of harmony and instrumentation. As several writers, including Bill C. Malone, have pointed out, they were a bridge between the old mountain string bands and the newer hard-driving bluegrass bands. They were lively and at times boisterous, and they played with high good humor.

Wade (R) and J. E. (with fiddle) Mainer with Shelton Brothers and Julian "Greasy" Medlin in blackface. Courtesy of Wade Mainer.

They also emphasized comedy in their personal appearances. Wade remembered, "When we started, we went out and played and maybe told a few jokes. Then I got to thinking maybe we needed more comedy, and in our personal appearances, I'd come in the back door hollering and disturbing the show, telling them they shouldn't have started until I got there." He went on to say that they told a lot of jokes and did routines such as "The Arkansas Traveler." "When I was with J. E., he did the straight man, and I did the comedy. When I formed my own band I got other musicians to do the comedy—Greasy Medlin, who did blackface, and Jeb Hall from Marion, North Carolina." Others, such as Snuffy Jenkins and Pappy Sherrill, no slouches at comedy, were also with the Mainer bands, and a character from Asheville called Pan Handle Pete later performed with Wade, who played a comedian named Corky in whiteface. He commented:

> Back then, they brought their families, and we had to keep our shows clean. The kids would really go for comedy and the old folks too, 'cause there wasn't much of it there during the Depression. I think people really wanted something to entertain them—maybe get their minds off some of the hardships that they went through. Back then they came to see you. They'd walk miles, and sometimes we'd have to put on two shows.
>
> I enjoyed the comedy. Sometimes we'd do jokes on some of the people who were well known. We'd find out when we drove in who the most popular man was, who

the meanest boy was. We'd tell them we wanted to use them, and they'd say "Go ahead." We'd kid them from the stage.

J. E. and Wade grew up on a farm near Weaverville. J. E. left home at the age of twelve and found work in a cotton mill in Concord. He played the banjo and soon learned the fiddle as well, and he and a brother-in-law played for dances. Wade also made his way to Piedmont and the cotton mills, as did many mountain people of the time. He joined J. E.'s band, with his distinctive two-finger style on the banjo. They played on a radio station in Gastonia. In 1934, the band got on the "Crazy Barn Dance" over WBT in Charlotte. The Crazy Water Crystal Company sponsored the show and also sponsored Mainer's Mountaineers at WBT, at WWNC in Asheville, and later at WWL in New Orleans.

Mainer's Mountaineers first recorded for Bluebird, and their 1935 recording of "Maple on the Hill" brought them fame. J. E.'s music was released on King, Arhoolie, Blue Jay, and Rural Rhythm. Wade recorded for RCA, King, Irma, Knob, Old Homestead, and JuneAppal.

After Wade left the band, J. E. continued it with various musicians at several radio stations. His career faded during World War II and afterward, but he continued playing from his home in Concord, eventually with two of his sons. He was rediscovered in the folk revival and appeared at numerous folk and bluegrass festivals. He and his wife Sadie had six children: J. E. Jr., Glenn, Earl, Charles, Carolyn, and Mary. He died of a stroke at the age of seventy-two.

Wade formed another band he called Sons of the Mountaineers. They played at various radio stations, including WWNC in Asheville and WROL in Knoxville. Wade did a concert at the White House in 1942 and was invited to New York to play on a BBC program, "The Chisholm Trail." He left professional music in the early 1950s and worked for General Motors in Flint, Michigan. After he retired, he and his wife Julia, a great traditional singer, continued to sing for religious occasions, and since the folk revival, they have done many festivals. Wade received the National Folk Heritage Award in 1987. In 2004, in his ninety-seventh year, he played the Mountain Dance and Folk Festival in Asheville to a standing ovation. Also in 2004, Wade was interviewed by David Holt for the University of North Carolina archives, and he received the Trailblazer Award from the Board of Uncle Dave Macon Days in Murfreesboro, Tennessee. Wade and Julia reared five children: Frank, Kelly, Leon (deceased), Polly, and Randy. At this writing, Wade is one hundred years old, still sharp, and still getting around, Julia reports.

Here is the Mainer version of the Arkansas Traveler skit.

> *Wade picks the A-part of "Arkansas Traveler."*
> *J. E.: Hello there, Stranger.*
> *Wade: Hello yourself. (picks A-part again)*
> *J. E.: Say, Stranger, how far does this road go?*

Wade: Well, I don't know. If it goes atall, it goes at night, 'cause it's here ever'
mornin' when I get up. (picks)

J. E.: Stranger, you don't understand what I mean. How far is it up here to
the forks?

Wade: Well, I can't tell you that either. When it gets up here to the top of the
hill, it splits all to pieces. (picks)

J. E.: Stranger, how long you been livin' around hyar?

Wade: You see that mountain over yonder?

J. E.: Shore do.

Wade: Well, it was a great big hole in the ground when I come here. (picks)

J. E.: One thing else I want to know, Stranger. How many kids have you got?

Wade: Well, I don't know. Just roll a punkin under the bed and count 'em as
they run out. (picks)

J. E.: Say, Stranger, you got no knives? Do you have any forks?

Wade: No, Sir.

J. E.: Well, then, how do you do?

Wade: Tolerably well, thank you. How are you? (picks)

J. E.: Say, Stranger, you aren't very far from a fool, are you?

Wade: Well, I don't think so. Just this microphone between us. (picks)

J. E.: Don't ye know any more of that there tune?

Wade: Well, I don't reckon there's a man a-livin' that knows the rest of that
tune.

J. E.: Listen, Bud, let me have that there banjo of yours. I'll show you how to
play the rest of it.

Wade.: Well, I've been wantin' to hear it all my life. Here, take it.

(He takes it and plays the B-part of the tune in a lively fashion, and then the
whole band joins in.)

DAPPER DAN MARTIN

Born near Lancaster, Pennsylvania, ca. 1905;
died ca. 1980

Dapper Dan Martin worked for Doc Williams on WWVA and the "Mountaineer Jubilee" in the early 1970s, replacing Smokey Pleacher in Williams's band. He also worked for Bud Messner at WWVA. Doc Williams remembers him as "an upscale music hall comedian." He went on to say that he was entirely different from the rube comedian. "I got a lot of criticism because people loved Smokey [Pleacher], and Dapper Dan was so different." He played a sort of city slicker, dressed in flamboyant checkered clothing. He was somewhere between a Bob Hope and a Smokey Pleacher. He had this hobby horse attached to his belt, and he'd go through the audience on his horse. He also would sing some songs."

Williams remembered that Martin had diabetes and retired shortly after he left his band. Williams believes that he died in a veterans' hospital in the South.

FRANKIE MARVIN

Born Frank James Marvin, January 27, 1904, Butler, Oklahoma Territory; died January 1985, California

Born in Oklahoma Territory, Frankie Marvin followed his older brother Johnny to New York, where the older Marvin was successful as a musician and songwriter of popular music and was also a vaudeville performer. By 1929, when Frankie joined him, Johnny had a radio network show and had recorded for three record companies. However, Frankie had

Dapper Dan Martin. Courtesy of Doc Williams.

a bent for western music and was soon recording such music for Cameo and Melotone. He played the steel guitar and the ukelele and also sang. He and Whitey Ford had a vaudeville comedy act they called "Ralph and Elmer" long before Ford became the Duke of Paducah.

Another Oklahoman named Gene Autry ventured to New York in the 1920s and sought the help of the Marvin Brothers. They gave advice and even tutored the singing cowboy, long before his radio and film career. As Douglas Green has pointed out, Autry was loyal to his friends, and when he hit it big in films, he sent for the Marvins at a time when the Great Depression had put a pall on their careers. Johnny became the producer for "Melody Ranch" and wrote songs for Autry's films and radio shows. Frankie's distinctive steel guitar was a part of the Autry sound for more than twenty years, and he also wrote songs. He, as well as Pat Buttram, did comedy for the radio show, and he had bit parts in most of Autry's films. He retired from the Autry organization in 1955 and lived in retirement in Frazier Park, California until his death in January of 1985 at the age of eighty-one.

(With credit to Douglas B. Green, *Country Roots: The Origins of Country Music* [New York: Hawthorne Books, 1976].)

HAMPER McBEE

Born Walter Henry McBee, 1931, Emory Gap, Roane
County, Tennessee; died May 3, 1998, Monteagle,
Tennessee

Hamper McBee was a powerful singer of ballads and other songs in the old unaccompanied fashion and an extraordinary storyteller and country humorist. He was also a
distiller and imbiber of illegal whiskey. He was never a professional entertainer in the
usual sense, but he was well known in Tennessee for years, and folklorists and others
fascinated with unusual personalities sought him out. Guy Carawan put him on an
album in 1964, and in 1977 Sol Korine and Blaine Dunlap produced a thirty-minute
television documentary on McBee. As a part of the making of this video, Charles
Wolfe and Sol Korine recorded him at an informal singing and storytelling session,
and Rounder released an LP, *Raw Mash: Songs and Stories of Hamper McBee*, in 1978.
He also traveled with the Southern Folk Festival on Tour.

McBee led a colorful life. He dropped out of high school and dug and sold medicinal
roots and herbs before joining the army in 1950. He served in Korea and Germany.
When he was discharged, he began making whiskey and admitted that he drank a lot.
He then did construction jobs, cut timber, worked in a tavern, drove mules, and worked
in carnivals. Through the years he learned the old songs. He loved Bradley Kincaid,
who sang ballads on many radio stations, including Nashville's WSM. He also learned
from the recordings of such people as Almeda Riddle, Woody Guthrie, Burl Ives, and
Vernon Dahlhart.

Hamper's storytelling employed salty language, and thus he was not invited to
appear before general audiences too often. He was truly a "character" in an age of
conformity. Charles Wolfe described his performances as "raw, earthy, direct humor,"
containing "what some radio programmers like to call 'possibly offensive language.'"
Wolfe went on to say that the "stories wouldn't be the same without it." Wolfe compares
McBee to the immortal character Sut Lovingood, created by the Tennessee fiction
writer George Washington Harris: "Sut liked drinking, dancing, singing, yarn-spinning,
and loving; he hated preachers, hypocrites in any form, sheriffs, and middle-class bankers." Wolfe added, "There's a lot of Sut Lovingood surviving in Hamper McBee."

McBee lived most of his life in Monteagle, Tennessee, and died there.

(With credit to Charles K. Wolfe, Liner notes to *Raw Mash: Songs and Stories of
Hamper McBee*, Rounder Records, 0061, 1978.)

Here are a couple of Hamper's stories:

> *This old boy—he was ignorant just like me—he was up there feeling under the river bank*
> *noodling for fish—I used to do that—and he got hold of a muskrat, and it bit him. He said*
> *to his daddy, "Does a catfish have hair on its head?" His daddy said, "No," and he said, "By*
> *God, I'm snakebit then!"*

They had a baptism down here, had twin boys. They baptized one and like to of drowned him, and he come up spittin' up minnows and crawfish and frogs. They baptized his brother, jerked him up, and he said, "I seen Jesus!" His brother said, "You're a damned liar! It was a mud turtle. I seen it myself!"

"DOC" McCONNELL

Born Ernest McConnell, September 20, 1928,
Hawkins County, Tennessee

The nearest post office to where Doc McConnell was born was Surgoinsville, but he claims Tucker's Knob as his home, and many characters and events in his stories originate there. In Tucker's Knob, he says, telling stories and tall tales was a part of ordinary life. "It was not until much later that I realized that storytelling was not as common elsewhere. I've always told stories, and though I've borrowed them from

local tradition, I have told them so long that they are personal to me. They *could* have been part of my personal experience."

He also grew up listening to country radio shows such as Knoxville's "Mid-day Merry-Go-Round" on WNOX, with his favorite comedians Bill Carlisle as Hotshot Elmer and Archie Campbell as Grandpappy. He also listened to the "Grand Ole Opry" and the "Renfro Valley Barn Dance," with its many comedians, and he went to the traveling medicine shows that featured storytellers and comedians.

Doc first entertained before formal audiences as an emcee for local charity or country music shows, where he threw in a funny story now and then. This resulted in his being invited by Jean and Lee Shilling to tell humorous stories at their Festival of the Smokies in Cosby, Tennessee, in 1970. Later, in a discussion about medicine shows at this festival, all mourned the passing of such entertainment. Impressed, Doc went home, borrowed a wagon, found

Doc McConnell. Courtesy of Doc McConnell.

an old long-tailed coat, and brewed up a tonic out of sassafras roots that he named his Rootin' Tootin' Tonic. The next year he re-created an old-time medicine show at the festival with him as the "Doc" telling stories and singing songs to entertain the audience and then whipping out his Rootin' Tootin' Tonic or copper bracelets that cure rheumatism, all the while ranking himself with the medical pioneers Pasteur, Fleming, and Salk. The act went over so well, he was invited to do it elsewhere and has since performed it hundreds of times.

In 1974, Doc was invited to appear at the National Storytelling Festival at Jonesborough, Tennessee, and quickly became a favorite at the event that is credited with reviving storytelling across the United States. Doc helped to found the National Association for the Preservation and Perpetuation of Storytelling (now Storytelling Foundation International) at Jonesborough and served on its first board of directors.

McConnell has a large repertoire of tall tales, fish stories, and anecdotes that allow him to stretch the truth a little bit. One of his favorites is his re-creation of the old folktale about a snake striking a farmer's hoe handle, which swells up so big the farmer takes it to the sawmill and has it sawed for lumber to build a chicken house, but alas, when the swelling goes out of the lumber the coop shrinks and squeezes the chickens to death!

McConnell has appeared on NBC's "Today Show," "Hee Haw," National Public Radio's "Prairie Home Companion," at the 1982 World's Fair, and at national storytelling events. He now entertains all over the country—about 120 dates a year, traveling from his Rogersville home. His venues range from the Opryland Hotel in Nashville and company conventions, including such giants as Coca-Cola, to small church women's and men's groups. He usually tells stories and picks a few tunes on the banjo, but he is still sometimes asked to put on his medicine show as well. He says, "I do all clean humor. People need to get out of their everyday lives now and then, into a sort of fantasy world, so that they can forget their troubles for a little while, and yet not be embarrassed."

From a recording of one of Doc's medicine shows:

> We's coming through Harlan County, Kentucky, about two weeks ago, and all of a sudden out of a laurel thicket jumped an old man of the mountains, about seven foot tall, stepped out in the middle of the road, waved his arms, stopped us, he climbed up in the front seat of the pickup. We went riding down the road there, and about five miles down the road, the old man put his hand over in his coat pocket, pulled out a half-a-gallon fruit jar, unscrewed that Ball Mason lid right off the top of it, shoved that big old jar of moonshine liquor over there to me and said, "Here, boy, have a drink." I said, "No, thank you. I don't believe I want none of that." He said, "Here, boy, have a drink." I said, "No, I'm driving, and I don't think I ought to be drinking." He said, "Here, boy, I said have a drink!" About that time he put his hand down in the other coat pocket, pulled out a big hog-leg gun about two-foot long, had a barrel as big around as a hoe handle. Oh, it was some kind of a gun! He stuck that gun up there in my ribs and pulled the hammer back on it, and he said, "Here, boy, I said have a drink, and I mean have a drink." I submitted to temptation right there. I said, "Get behind me, Satan." I turned that big old drink of moonshine liquor up and took me a great big old snort of that liquid fire, and it burned clean to the bottom of my shoe soles. It took my breath. I died. I went blind, and my heart quit beating. When I finally come around in a few minutes, I said, "Whewww! Man! How in the world can you drink that stuff?" He said, "I can't, hardly. Now here's the gun. Make me take a drink, will you?"

CLAYTON "PAPPY" McMICHEN

Born January 26, 1900, Alatoona, Georgia;
died January 4, 1970, Louisville, Kentucky

One of the most colorful entertainers of all time was Clayton "Pappy" McMichen. He was in fiddle contests as a teenager and at eighteen formed a band called the Hometown Boys that was one of the first groups to play over WSB in Atlanta when it began broadcasting in 1922. McMichen later had a band called the Lick the Skillet Band. In 1926 McMichen joined the Skillet Lickers, which had made recordings in New York for Columbia and were to become the most popular string band of their time on records. Their wildly enthusiastic recordings of "Down Yonder" and "Back Up and Push" are reported to have sold over a million copies, an unheard of number at that time. At first it was Gid Tanner and the Skillet Lickers, but after McMichen joined them, he objected, and his and Riley Puckett's names were added. In addition to their rural North Georgia music, they recorded what were called rural dramas, actually comedy skits that featured the humor of backcountry Georgia mainly having to do with moonshining. The best-known was *A Corn Licker Still in Georgia*, which ran to fourteen sides on 78 rpm records.

Clayton "Pappy" McMichen at WLS, 1933. Courtesy of Juanita McMichen Lynch.

McMichen was considerably younger than the other musicians, and he had little affection for the old rural tunes. He loved jazz and the new pop music. His father, a trained musician, could play any kind of music and did at rural square dances and at ballroom affairs in Atlanta. However, young McMichen was a fantastic breakdown fiddler, a contest winner, and he added greatly to the Skillet Licker sound. Yet, always restless and ambitious, McMichen continued to play and record aside from the Skillet Lickers with his Melody Men, a band that included his brother-in-law Bert Layne on fiddle, Riley Puckett on vocals and guitar, and K. D. Malone on clarinet. He and Bert Layne also formed the McMichen-Layne String Orchestra, adding the progressive guitarist Slim Bryant to replace Malone on clarinet, and later he organized McMichen's Harmony Boys. The first and last groups recorded for Columbia, which released twenty sides of the Melody Men and six of the

Harmony Boys. In 1931, McMichen formed the Georgia Wildcats, who recorded for Columbia and Crown. A later version of the Wildcats recorded for Decca.

In 1932, Jimmie Rodgers invited McMichen to play for recording sessions he was doing in Camden, New Jersey. McMichen took along Slim Bryant, and both played on these and later sessions in New York. McMichen, Bryant, and the Wildcats also went to WLS as part of the World's Fair in Chicago in 1933. They later were in Louisville, playing over both WAVE and WHAS, and then they went to WRVA in Richmond. McMichen, ever restless, went back to Louisville to form a Dixieland band, and he settled in Battletown, an easy drive from Louisville.

During the folk revival, Pappy McMichen appeared at the Newport Folk Festival and did tours of festivals and colleges. He was resentful that the old Skillet Lickers recordings were still popular while his more professional recordings were not. He was indeed one of the most professional of the country musicians of his time and could play pop, jazz, and swing, as well as his usual country music. He was also a composer of songs and tunes, including "Peach Picking Time in Georgia," "Prohibition Blues," and "Pay Me No Mind." In his last years he grew negative about his career and felt that his talents had not been appropriately recognized.

While he never dressed up as a comedian (in fact, he usually wore three-piece tailored suits and spiffy white shirts), he had a comedic demeanor on stage, and he told jokes, served as a straight man to Bert Layne and Slim Bryant, and valued comedy as a part of his entertainment. His daughter, Juanita McMichen Lynch, and Slim Bryant tell great stories of the practical jokes and escapades involving the bands that have kept them laughing affectionately for years beyond Pappy McMichen's death.

(With credit to Norm Cohen, "Clayton McMichen: His Life and Music," *John Edwards Memorial Foundation Quarterly* 11.3 [Autumn 1975]: 117–24, and to Juanita McMichen Lynch for materials provided.)

LARRY MCPEAK. *See VW Boys*

BUTCH MEDFORD. *See Ernest and Elwood*

JULIAN "GREASY" MEDLIN. *See the Hired Hands*

EMMETT MILLER

Born Emmett Dewey Miller, February 2, 1900,
Macon, Georgia; died March 29, 1962, Macon,
Georgia

Emmett Miller was primarily a blackface comedian in minstrel and vaudeville shows, but he was also a remarkable singer whose songs and style through recordings had an influence on country musicians. Emmett was born to John Pink Miller, who worked for the Macon Fire Department, and Lena Christian Miller. After the seventh grade Emmett dropped out of school and worked for a railroad repair shop as an automobile mechanic and as a chauffeur, but all the while he expressed the wish to be a comedian, inspired by the minstrel and vaudeville shows that stopped in Macon. It appears that he got his first minstrel job in 1919 with the Dan Fitch Minstrels and went on to work for O'Brien's Minstrels and the Keith vaudeville circuit. In 1926, he joined the Al G. Field Minstrels that had been founded forty years earlier. Nick Tosches, the principal scholar on Miller, noted, "[T]he irony of Miller's fate was that he had become a minstrel man during minstrelsy's final days. His season of glory with the Al G. Field Minstrels was the last barely successful season that the Field Minstrels would know."

The Field Minstrels, when Miller joined them, were using the same format set by the Christy Minstrels in the 1840s: a parade-around and seating of the minstrels in a half-circle; jokes elicited from the "end men" by the interlocutor; the passing in review; the "olio" with its songs, dances, and comedy; and then the humorous skit or play. Miller excelled in all roles. Since his teens he had been studying black dialect and mannerisms, but from his devotion to traveling minstrel shows, he also learned the stage stereotypes of black people and exhibited them to the extent that he had acquired the nickname of "Nigger" Miller in Macon long before he went into show business. His skills were such that he got rave reviews for his "olio" performances, especially for his unusual vocal abilities, described in several ways but apparently including yodeling, other unusual voice-breaks, falsetto singing, and a powerful delivery.

His vocal abilities led Miller to make several recordings with OKeh in 1924–25 and again from 1928 to 1930 and for Bluebird in 1936, with some thirty numbers released. Among the most influential of his recordings were the "St. Louis Blues," which the Callahan Brothers adopted and copied; "I Ain't Got Nobody," copied by Bob Wills; and "Lovesick Blues," which was number one for Hank Williams for six weeks and elicited six encores at the "Grand Ole Opry." Miller and Roy Cowan also recorded several comic dialogues for OKeh in 1928 as Sam and Bill and joined "Fiddling" John Carson and others in a three-record recording of "The Medicine Show" in 1929.

As minstrel shows faded, so did Emmett Miller's career. He played movie houses and toured as Emmett Miller and His Varieties of 1932. He abandoned blackface for a tour with *The All-Southern Review* in 1937 and 1938, and then with a show called the *Swing Parade*. After a brief tour with Billroy's Comedians, he did his final tour in a show called *Dixiana*. After that, he played nightclubs when he could find such work, and in 1951 he had a brief role in a film, *Yes, Sir, Mr. Bones*.

Nick Tosches recently discovered that Miller married Bernice Valentine Calhoun, a Macon office worker, in 1943 and apparently worked out of their residence in Macon until the couple separated. There were no children. Emmett Miller died in the Macon Hospital in 1962 of throat cancer. He is buried with his parents in Fort Hill Cemetery.

(With credit to Nick Tosches in three magazine articles: "The Strange and Hermetical Case of Emmett Miller," *Journal of Country Music* 17.1 [1994]: 39–47; "Emmett Miller: The Final Chapter," *Journal of Country Music* 18.3 [1996]: 27–37; and "Get Down, Moses," *Oxford American* 16 [Summer 1997]: 128–33.)

HOMER "SLIM" MILLER

Born 1898, Lizton, Indiana; died August 27, 1962,
Lexington, Kentucky

Slim Miller was an early member of John Lair's Cumberland Ridge Runners (including also Karl Davis, Harty Taylor, Doc Hopkins, and Hugh Cross), formed at WLS in Chicago as a part of the "National Barn Dance." Miller followed Lair to Cincinnati and then to Renfro Valley for a long run with the "Renfro Valley Barn Dance." In addition to his fiddling with the band, he was a surefire comedian always able to elicit laughs.

As a child, Miller was adopted by a neighbor, a country fiddler who taught Slim to fiddle at an early age. He was an apt student and developed a unique artistry, playing on the stage in Indianapolis and later going on the road with a stock theater company as a musician. After serving in the army in World War I, he worked in bands in Memphis and at WNOX in Knoxville, where he met Hugh Cross, who was later to join the Cumberland Ridge Runners in Chicago. It was Cross who recommended Slim Miller to John Lair. According to Jim Gaskin, Slim arrived at Lair's house for an audition, "one eye looking to the left, one to the right, a big awkward-looking fellow, who said, 'Are you the feller that wants a fiddler?' Mr. Lair fell back on the bed laughing and said, 'You're hired. I hope you can play the fiddle!'" Another source suggested the audition was at a county fair in Indiana and that Lair heard Miller play at least part of a tune. At any rate, Miller became the fiddler in the Cumberland Ridge Runners and also provided most of the comedy for Lair's shows.

Miller was six foot three and had a morose and forlorn expression that he accentuated with drawn-on clown eyebrows. Lair called him a mime, one of the best in the country, and indeed most of his comedy was in body language, stares, and gestures. Jim Gaskin reported:

Slim Miller. Courtesy of Renfro
Valley Entertainment Center.

He told few jokes—very few words. His comedy was facial expressions and little
mannerisms. He had a trick that he pulled with his hat, with a fishing line and pulley. He'd sail his hat over the audience, and it would come back to him. He was so
funny looking you couldn't look at him without laughing.

Miller could get laughs just by crossing and uncrossing his long legs or by doing his
standard pantomime of looking for a banana he had just peeled. In addition to his
superb fiddling, for many years Slim Miller was the main comedian at the "Renfro
Valley Barn Dance." It was reported that he did not welcome comedic competition.
Pete Stamper writes, in *It All Happened at Renfro Valley*, that when he first came to the
Valley hungry for work, Slim offered him a gig but on the condition that he borrow a
tire off Pete's car to make the trip. Pete dutifully took off the tire and gave it to Slim,
and they agreed on a departure time the next day. Pete waited and waited before learning that Slim and his party had left hours earlier riding on his tire.

Slim Miller was ill with cancer the last two years of his life. He died in 1962 in the
Veteran's Hospital in Lexington. He and his wife Clara (Minter) are buried in Travelers
Rest, Owsley County, Kentucky, Clara's home county. John Lair wrote in a tribute,

"He sleeps the last, long sleep . . . in a remote and beautiful spot hidden away in the Kentucky hills he had learned to love. A lonesome spot, perhaps, for a man who loved crowds . . . but a quiet and peaceful place to rest free from pain and await the summons for the final audition for a place in that greatest of all bands of music makers."

(With credit to Pete Stamper, *It All Happened at Renfro Valley* [Lexington: University Press of Kentucky, 1999], and the *Renfro Valley Bugle* [February 1944, September 1944, June 1954, January 1960, September 1962, October 1972, and January 1977]).

ROGER MILLER

Born January 2, 1936, Fort Worth, Texas;
died October 25, 1992, Los Angeles, California

Bill C. Malone wrote that Roger Miller "emerged from a hard-core country background to become one of the most sophisticated lyricists in country music and a clever and witty singer and comedian." Bill Anderson wrote: "I could fill an entire book with Roger Miller stories. He said more funny things and did more funny things—more crazy off-the-wall things—than just about anybody who ever lived. . . . Roger Miller was the closest thing to a genius I have ever known." Miller went from picking cotton to being a top-notch Nashville songwriter and recording artist, winning eleven Grammy Awards, and capped his career with a Tony award for the music he composed for the Broadway musical *Big River*.

Miller was born poor, and when his father died, he and his brothers were sent to live with various uncles. Roger grew up on his Uncle Elmer's cotton farm at Erick, Oklahoma. Elmer's daughter married the country singer and comedian Sheb Wooley, and he was an influence on young Miller and presented him with his first musical instrument, a fiddle. Miller made it through the eighth grade and then quit to work at various jobs, including ranch hand and rodeo competitor, while also trying to make it as a club singer. He was drafted during the Korean War and became part of a Special Services band at Fort McPherson, Georgia. While there he met Bill Anderson, another aspiring singer-songwriter, and they became lifelong friends. Another person he met in the army was Happy Burns, the brother of Jethro Burns, of Homer and Jethro fame. Happy advised Miller to go to Nashville after his discharge to seek his fortune in music.

In Nashville, Miller resorted to bellhopping at a hotel to keep body and soul together. He auditioned unsuccessfully for Chet Atkins at RCA, wrote some songs, and did a couple of records for Starday that went largely unnoticed. However, he eventually landed a job as fiddler in Minnie Pearl's backup band for road shows. A fellow band member was Mel Tillis, and the work brought Miller into contact with other singers and songwriters, such as George Jones, and he sought out anyone who might be helpful in his career. He later played drums for Faron Young. A songwriting contract with Tree Music brought his songs to the notice of other singers. Ray Price recorded his "Invitation to the Blues," and later so did Patti Page. Ernest Tubb had a hit with his "Half a Mind," and Jim Reeves scored with "Billy Bayou."

Miller signed with RCA in 1960 and had his first Top Forty hit with his single, "You Don't Want My Love," followed by the Top Ten hit "When Two Worlds Collide," a song he had written with Bill Anderson. However, Miller was unhappy in Nashville and went west a couple of times, first to Amarillo, Texas, where he joined Ray Price and His Cherokee Cowboys for a time, and then to Hollywood, where he had appeared on the "Jimmy Dean Show" and the "Tonight Show." On these shows he displayed his wit and flair for comedy. He signed with Smash Records, a subsidiary of Mercury that was more oriented toward pop than country and whose executives were impressed by his comedy and talent for novelty songs. His "Dang Me" was number one on the country and number ten on the pop charts. "Chug-a-Lug" was Top Three country and Top Ten pop. He won five Grammys in 1964 for his songs, recordings, and performances. His other hits on Smash were his landmark song, "King of the Road" (winning six Grammys in 1965), "Chug-a-Lug," "Kansas City Star," and "Husbands and Wives." In 1966, Miller got his own variety show on NBC. However, the bland programming imposed on him, with little emphasis on either country music or comedy, was not aimed at a definite audience, and the show folded in a few months.

On his novelty songs, Miller's dry southwestern accent and distinctive and recognizable voice were great assets. His wit and comedy also were enhanced by his vocal gifts, as well as by his affable and likeable manner. He was witty and inventive with his humor. His friends told many funny and zany stories about him. Bill Anderson, in *I Hope You're Living as High on the Hog as the Pig You Turned Out to Be*, a book about the humorous situations he has encountered in his country music career, told how a simple trip to the Laundromat turned into a five-hundred-mile round trip to Atlanta so that Bill's mother could wash their clothes.

Miller launched a chain of King of the Road motels, which were later to fail, but he continued to record his songs in the 1970s for Mercury and Columbia with considerable success, and he also recorded songs by other writers, including Kris Kristofferson's "Me and Bobby McGee" and Bobby Russell's "Little Green Apples." In 1974 he provided a song and narrated a part in the Disney animated film *Robin Hood*. However, he did not write songs for most of the 1970s and made plans to retire to New Mexico. Then he was offered the opportunity to write the music for *Big River*, based on Mark Twain's *Huckleberry Finn*. The show opened on Broadway in 1985, winning seven Tony awards, including one for Miller's musical score.

Roger Miller's career was cut short by throat cancer, and he died in 1992.

Here are a few Roger Millerisms as reported by Bill Anderson in *I Hope You're Living as High On the Hog as the Pig You Turned Out to Be* (Atlanta: Longstreet Press, 1993), 143–53, with permission:

I once knew a guy who lied so much he had to get someone else to call his dogs.

I caught him in the truth one time, but he lied his way out of it.

When I was a little boy . . . I wanted to be a comedian, but everybody laughed at me.

I once was so hot as a songwriter that I wrote a letter home and it got up to number eight in the charts.

If I ever make any money in this business, first thing I'm gonna do is go home and pave the farm.

Things are so slow for me that buzzards are circling my career.

I once dreamed I died, and my whole life passed in front of my eyes. Trouble is, I wasn't in it.

And looking into the first gleam of daylight after one of his many all-night escapades: Uh-oh! Here comes God with His brights on!

MONK AND SAM

Charles "Monk" Hansen Jr., born Newport, England,
*   birth and death dates unknown*
Sam L. Johnson, born Zanesville, Ohio, birth and
*   death dates unknown*

The Hansen family moved from England to Baltimore when young Charles was six. After two years they moved on to Zanesville, Ohio, where Charles finished his education and became a mechanic until his ability to entertain led him into radio.

Sam Johnson was also educated in Zanesville. He was interested in sports and athletics, and he played in a dance orchestra while he was in high school. After graduation he worked for a dry-cleaning company until he also went into radio work.

Monk and Sam (C. O. Hansen and S. L. Johnson). Courtesy of Charles K. Wolfe.

A "Home-Town" minstrel show brought Hansen and Johnson together as entertainers. Both were musical and both loved the stage. They began entertaining together as singers and humorists at civic clubs, banquets, and other social functions, and later in theaters. Their first appearance together on radio was at WAIU in Columbus, Ohio, probably in 1930. They later worked as Ray and Bob at WKRC and WCKY in Cincinnati before moving on to WHAS in Louisville in 1932, where they became Monk and Sam. Hansen also played a comic female character named Sophronia Apple, and Johnson created a comic character named Silas Tewksberry, owner of the mythical Valley View Farm, where they said "seeds of happiness are sown and which grow into songs of joy, helpfulness, and kindness, mingled with humor and happy harmony." Monk and Sam played guitars and sang as a duet and did a lot of comedy in between.

At WHAS they were on the early-morning show, beginning at 5:45, with other such entertainers as Pee Wee King and the Log Cabin Boys, Asher and Little Jimmie Sizemore, and Clayton McMichen. The announcer was Foster Brooks, later to become nationally famous as a comedian.

In 1933, while they were in Louisville, Hansen and Johnson published *A Trip thru Monk and Sam's Song Farm*, with photos, drawings, songs, comic routines, sentimental and humorous verse, and tongue-twisting recitations.

Monk and Sam left WHAS with Pee Wee King and went to WNOX in Knoxville. There they became two of the first full-time comedians on the "Mid-day Merry-Go-Round" and the "Tennessee Barn Dance." The duo went with Pee Wee King to WSM and the "Grand Ole Opry" with Pee Wee King's band that became the Golden West Cowboys. Eventually Monk and Sam performed separately at the "Opry." No further information on their careers could be found.

(With thanks to Charles K. Wolfe, who loaned his copy of *A Trip thru Monk and Sam's Song Farm*, which contained most of the information for this entry.)

Following is an alliterative tongue twister from the above songbook:

A fly with the flu and a flea with a flaw flew into the flaw in a flue. Said the flea with the flaw in the flaw of the flue to the fly with the flu, Let us flee! Said the fly with the flu to the flea with the flaw in the flue, I'm a firefly! There's fire in the flue, flu in the firefly, a flaw in the flue, leave your flu in the fire in the flue, Let us fly! said the flea with the flaw in the flue from the flaw in the flue to the fly with the flu. So the firefly and flea made the fire fly and flew, and the fly with the flu, the flea with the flaw, both flew with the flu from the flaw in the flue, and both the flea and the fly flew with the flaw from the flue.

MORON BROTHERS

Michael Steven Hammonds, born October 26, 1950,
 Nicholasville, Kentucky
Michael Thomas Carr, born July 1, 1952, Fayette
 County, Kentucky

The two Mikes both grew up in Nicholasville, Kentucky, and even went to the same high school, but they weren't aware of each other until they met at a picking session at a Lexington firehouse in 1996, where Mike Carr was a fireman. Mike Hammonds, a maintenance worker at Lexington Correctional Institute, is a Merle Travis thumb-picking guitar player and singer. Carr mainly plays the five-string banjo and harmonica. Both are writers of mostly comedic songs, and the two got together and worked up an act. They came to the attention of the bluegrass musician Dean Osborne, who invited them to perform at the Lexington Red Mile Bluegrass Festival. Very nervous, the pair held forth, and when they came offstage, a man sitting next to Carr's wife said, "Did you see those two morons that were just on stage?" From that moment on, they were the Moron Brothers with Hammonds as Burley and Carr as Lardo. They have been playing bluegrass festivals and other events ever since.

Carr had a call from Chet Atkins in 1992 about a song he had written about a hog that thought he was a dog, titled "Colby." Atkins published the song and pitched it to Mike Snider, who performed it on "Hee Haw" and on Ralph Emery's "Nashville Now." Later, Carr and Hammonds wrote another song, "If My Nose Was Running Money, Honey, I'd Blow It All on You," and Snider sang it several times on the "Grand Ole Opry" and also recorded it. In June 2001, Snider invited the Moron Brothers to join him on the stage of the "Opry" to help him sing the song. "What a dream come true," said Carr.

The Moron Brothers, Mike Carr and Mike Hammonds. Courtesy of Mike Carr and Mike Hammonds.

Since then, the Moron Brothers have recorded two CDs, *The Moron Brothers: Off the Wall* and *Lardo and Burley on Tour* (Bo-Ann Publishing, 7965 Ridgewood Rd., Goodlettsville, TN 37072). They have performed at the "Renfro Valley Barn Dance" several times, have opened for Merle Haggard at the Kentucky Theater in Lexington, and have played every major bluegrass festival in the state, and others outside, including the South Carolina Bluegrass Festival in Myrtle Beach. Lardo says, "We've already done more and had more fun than we ever thought we would."

Burley is married to the former Pat Shelton. They live in Nicholasville and have three children and two grandchildren. Lardo and his wife, the former Jeanie Taylor, live on the Kentucky River in Mercer County, not far from Nicholasville. They have three children and three grandchildren.

The following story is from a concert at Shepherdsville, Kentucky, with permission:

> *Burley: I got this friend Jim who's a portrait painter, and this lady come to him and said, "Jim, I'll give you five thousand dollars to paint me in the nude." He said, "Noooo," said, "I ain't doin' that." She said, "I'll give you ten thousand dollars to paint me in the nude." He said, "No, I wouldn't feel right doin' that. I ain't never done that. I'm not doin' it!" She said, "I'll give you fifteen thousand dollars to paint me in the nude." He thought about it for a minute and said, "I'll do it, but I'm goin' to leave my socks on, 'cause I got to have somethin' to wipe my brushes on!"*

CLAUDE W. MOYE. *See Pie Plant Pete*

GARY MULE DEER

Born Gary Clark Miller, November 21, 1939,
Deadwood, South Dakota

Gary Mule Deer has been a successful comedian and musician for more than forty years, performing on stages throughout the United States and abroad and making over 350 television appearances, from the Nashville Network to the "Tonight Show" and "Late Night with David Letterman" to co-hosting "Don Kirschner's Rock Concert" on NBC for four years.

Miller, of Cherokee ancestry, grew up in the Black Hills of South Dakota on a cattle ranch. "Mule Deer is a name I adopted in 1968. I always wanted to be an Indian, and I took the name from the Sioux tribe. I grew up near the Sioux Indians." He hunted with a bow and fished and later attended Black Hills State University. He also worked many jobs—fishing guide, painter, bartender, bellman, baker's assistant, and owner-operator of a local movie theater. But somewhere along the way he decided that show business might be the thing for him, so he took a guitar lesson and learned about thirty

Johnny Cash and Buddy Holly songs, all in the key of E, and worked up some humor that he said he fashioned after that of his comedic hero, Jack Benny. This repertoire got him into Black Hills bars. He later formed a rock band called the Vaqueros that was good enough to open for such acts as Jerry Lee Lewis, the Crickets, the Everly Brothers, and the Ventures.

On comedy, he commented:

> My comedy started when I realized that I didn't have the dedication to be a musician. I always had a comedic turn. In school, I really wasn't the class clown, but I fooled around a lot. I didn't take anything very seriously. My humor came from radio. We listened to Jack Benny, Eve Arden, and Edgar Bergen and Charlie McCarthy. It wasn't until later that I began to hear people like Minnie Pearl and Jerry Clower and Grandpa Jones. "Hee Haw" brought me a lot of those comedians, and of course I did the last year and a half of "Hee Haw." I first knew I was funny when I would stop the music and tell jokes and stories. If I hit a wrong chord I'd do it again as if it were intentional. The B7 chord got me out of music and into comedy, because I'd hit it only one out of every four times.

Gary Mule Deer. Courtesy of Nita Mule Deer.

He left the Black Hills for a brief stay in Denver and then ventured on to California, where he roomed with the aspiring comic, actor, and five-string banjo player Steve Martin. The two of them worked up zany off-the-wall comic sketches, combined with their banjo-guitar music, which each has continued to use in their individual acts. Gary soon became a member of the Back Porch Majority, which evolved into the rock group Bandanna. After that, he teamed up with Dennis Flannigan to form the Muledeer and Moondogg Medicine Show, a music and comedy act that appeared on such television shows as the "Midnight Special," the "John Byner Comedy Hour," "David Frost's Madhouse 90," "Jack Paar," and "Merv Griffin," and they did concerts with the Doobie Brothers, the Beach Boys, Chicago, and Earth, Wind, and Fire.

When he and Flannigan parted company in 1976, Gary went solo as Gary Mule Deer. Gary was a regular performer at the Comedy Store and the Improv for more than twenty years. His comedy is offbeat, off-the-wall, and sophisticated, appealing to a wide audience from country music fans to those in Reno, Las Vegas, Lake Tahoe, and Atlantic City. He has appeared with Roger Miller, Merle Haggard, Reba McEntire, Tammy Wynette, Kenny Rogers, Dolly Parton, Vince Gill, and Brooks and Dunn.

He describes his humor as deadpan. "I like to entertain people with clean humor and make people laugh. I like to work for genuine laughter—a long-sustained laugh that almost dies and picks up again. I like to work with people who read, who dress up, and pay a lot of money to come to shows." One of his routines is to execute a rubber chicken with an arrow launched from a guitar string, after blindfolding and offering a last cigarette to the victim. At times he sings "Mama Don't Let Your Babies Grow Up to be Cowboys," and near the end, he says, "Take it, Willie." Willie, of course, is not there, so Mule Deer has him paged over the sound system to report to the stage.

Mule Deer's singing is good, too, for one who indicates that he's not that serious about music. The Colonel Rebel label released his single "Old Glory" for Independence Day 2000. An earlier CD, *Yeah, but the Response Was Great* (Uproar Entertainment, 1997), includes many of his classic routines. His newest CD, *Gary Mule Deer Live*, features his comedy and music. He is currently featured on the DVDs *Jeff Foxworthy's Comedy Classics, Bill Engvall's New All-Stars of Country Comedy*, and *The World's Greatest Stand-Up Comedy Collection*, hosted by Norm Crosby.

As a writer for comedy shows in 1967–68, he and Steve Martin worked on the "Smothers Brothers Show." He wrote later for "Tony Orlando and Dawn" and the "Dinah Shore Show." He also wrote the first "Steve Martin Special" and was a writer/performer for "Hee Haw" and several other shows. He likes to be on the road, however, better than being in an office writing gags.

In 1993, Gary and his wife Nita moved back to Spearfish, South Dakota, and he continues his busy schedule from there. He tours with Johnny Mathis and shares billing with the Smothers Brothers and others at hotels and casinos in Atlantic City, Las Vegas, Lake Tahoe, and Reno. He also entertains for Royal Caribbean Cruise Lines. He is enthusiastic about his comedic work: "Humor, I think, extends your life. I surely believe the happier you are, the more up you are, the more you can laugh, the longer you are going to live. That's the most important thing right there."

Gary Mule Deer in an interview gave these as two of his favorite stories that illustrate his kind of humor:

A doctor is examining three old men for suspected memory loss. He turns to the first guy, says, "What's three times three?" Guy says, "a hundred and fifty-six." He turns to second guy, says, "What's three times three?" Guy says, "Tuesday."

He turns to the third guy, says, "What's three times three?" Guy says, "Nine." Says, "That's right. How did you figure it out?" The guy says, "I just subtracted Tuesday from a hundred-and-fifty-six."

In Alaska this year, they've been warning people about the bear problem. If you wander into the woods away from the main group, it's a good idea to wear bells and carry pepper spray. The way you can tell if you're in a dangerous area, black bear dung is small and round, has seeds and sometimes squirrel fur in it, and grizzly bear dung has bells in it and smells like pepper spray!

HARRY MULLINS. *See A'nt Idy and Little Clifford*

BOB MURPHEY

*Born July 31, 1921, Nacogdoches, Texas; died
November 5, 2004, Nacogdoches, Texas*

Robert W. Murphey grew up in Nacogdoches, a town he claims had to have the first zip code because nobody could spell it, and then every town wanted one. His forebears

Bob Murphey. Courtesy
of Bob Murphey.

were from Tennessee and North Carolina. He spent summers on the ranch of an uncle in the Texas hill country and grew up on Texas stories, mostly from his father, a Nacogdoches businessman and great storyteller. Educated in local schools and at Stephen F. Austin University, Murphey enrolled in the University of Texas Law School in 1942, but World War II interrupted his studies, and he served in the U.S. Merchant Marine from 1943 to 1946 as an officer and bursar. After the war, he continued his studies and got his law degree in 1947.

He said he fell into his career as a humorist and public speaker by accident: "I had an uncle who was governor of Texas [Coke R. Stevenson], and he ran for the Senate against Lyndon Johnson in 1958. I campaigned for him and drove him everywhere. He was a good storyteller. When I was living in Austin and was Sergeant at Arms of the House, I was known around the capitol as a storyteller." Later he became Nacogdoches county attorney and then district attorney. "I cut my teeth there, learned my trade as a speaker at service clubs." Afterward, he was in private law practice. "I started getting so many invitations, started going out of state, and I had to cut down on my law practice. I had to make up my mind whether I wanted to be a traveling humorist or whether I wanted to practice law. And when I weighed the two, it was a lot more fun being a traveling humorist."

Murphey wasn't just a storyteller, however, but always had a message.

I'm not a stand-up comedian. I don't just tell one joke after another. I am a speaker. I make points—how to be happy, how to be successful. I am a motivational-type speaker. What I do is get a good idea, and then I get or make up a story to show what I'm talking about. A lot of the stories were handed down, sitting at the feet of my father. He and his friends would get together to talk about somebody and what they did and what happened. I never forget a good story. I can tell you stories I heard sixty years ago. The Lord gave me the gift, and I sure used it.

Francis Abernethy, a retired folklore professor, author, and president of the Texas Folklore Society, said, "Bob Murphey is the best humorous speaker I've ever heard." He gave an example of Murphey's wit:

> Back in 1968, the Institute of Texas Culture took its show up to the Smithsonian to the American Folklife Festival that featured Texas that year. I took musicians, and Bobby [Murphey] was my emcee. He's just got one arm. When he was a young boy, he was roping out on his uncle's ranch, and he got his arm tangled up some way, and his arm was completely jerked off. We had a whole bunch of children. They all came up to the front of the stage to watch Bobby twirl a rope, and just out of nowhere this little boy said, "Mister, how did you lose your arm?" and I mean, you talk about mothers backing off and sucking in deep air, and even the children got quiet. Bobby looked down at this little boy and said, "I'm going to tell you, but I don't want you to ask me any more questions. Is that all right?" The little boy said, "Yes, Sir." He looked him right in the eye and said, "IT WAS BIT OFF!" He went to twirling his rope again, and I know that kid is still wondering.

Murphey went on to entertain and inform groups in forty-five states, Canada, and Mexico. He mainly spoke at conventions, corporate groups, and national organizations. He appeared on radio and television, including fourteen times on Ralph Emery's "Nashville Now," once on the "Grand Ole Opry," and twice on "Hee Haw." He was a fan of country music, but he has ranged far and wide, from a black-tie dinner honoring members of the Supreme Court to a meeting of the International Chili Appreciation Society, from the Kennedy Center for the Performing Arts to local rodeos. His biographical sheet claims, "Like the country woman who said she didn't enjoy spreading gossip but didn't know what else to do with it, Murphey has passed along his earthy philosophy, sage advice, clean humor, wit, and wisdom to neighbors from coast to coast."

The "Grand Ole Opry" star and humorist Mike Snider, who studied with him, said this about Murphey's type of humor: "Bob Murphey's comedy is clever comedy. You can't be drunk when you're listening to Bob. You have to be *listening* to him. When he's up doing his thing, it's like he is singing a song. He kind of sings through a joke or story."

Bob Murphey was married to Nada Evans Murphey, and they had two daughters, Brenda Hazle and Reba Jane Gayler, and two grandchildren, Hope Hazle and Robert Murphey Gayler.

Bob Murphey made several LP records, 8-track tapes, cassette tapes, and one CD (Delta Records, PO Box 225, Nacogdoches, TX 75961).

Following is one of Murphey's favorite stories:

> *There was an old farmer over here a-plowing his spring garden behind a little old mule, and a feller drove up alongside the wire fence there where he was breaking up his garden and hollered over there, said, "Hey, Old Timer." The old man stopped plowing, whoaed up his mule. The man said, "Where is the road to Houston?" This old man said, "How'd you know my name?" The feller said, "Well, I just guessed it." This old man said, "Well, guess where the road to Houston is."*

BILL NAPIER

*Born William Napier, December 17, 1935, Wise
County, Virginia; died May 2000, Piney Flats,
Tennessee*

Bill C. Malone, in *Country Music, USA*, credits Bill Napier for first introducing flat-picking on the guitar to bluegrass music while he performed with the Stanley Brothers in the late 1950s. Napier also did comedy with the Stanleys, performing as Dad Napier, sometimes with Albert Elliott, who played a character named Towser Murphy. He did his Dad Napier comedy with the other bands in which he played mandolin, guitar, and banjo.

Napier came from a family of eleven children, of which he and a brother were the only ones interested in music. He grew up in a region whose radio stations featured the music that became bluegrass, with such musicians as the Monroe Brothers and the Stanley Brothers. When he was nineteen, Napier, like many other Appalachians, migrated to Detroit in search of employment. There he started playing the mandolin in local bands. He developed his musical skills to the point that in 1957 he was hired by the Stanley Brothers, and he stayed with them for three years and appeared on their influential Mercury and King recordings. Carter Stanley was fond of comedy and knew its value in entertainment, and he encouraged Napier and Elliot to do comedy. Their voices appear on some of the Stanley Brothers' recordings, notably on "Train 45," with Napier sounding like an old man.

For the Mercury recordings, Napier composed a mandolin instrumental, "Daybreak in Dixie," that has become a standard for bluegrass bands. Later Syd Nathan, at King Records, thought that the Stanley Brothers needed a new sound. One day, Carter heard Napier picking "Rawhide" on the guitar, in fact transposing mandolin techniques to the guitar, picking out the melody in a rapid fashion, even doing a tremolo on single strings. Carter had Napier demonstrate his technique for Nathan, who liked it. Thus, Napier pioneered a new sound in bluegrass, that of the lead guitar.

The Stanleys during this period were operating out of Live Oak, Florida, and they were taking advantage of the folk revival to do concerts at colleges and universities. Carter Stanley loved comedy, and they persisted with it even though the college audiences were not as fond of the old rube comedy as they were of the music.

Napier joined up with Charlie Moore and His Dixie Partners in 1960, mostly playing guitar and banjo. He and Moore wrote several songs together, and the band recorded nine albums for King Records. In 1968, they also recorded an album for Old Homestead. His old comedy partner Albert Elliot joined them for the occasion.

Napier left Moore in 1968 and returned to Michigan. There he played with various bands, but because of a drinking problem, he gradually withdrew from music. However, a religious experience helped him to kick his alcohol habit, and he and his wife Karla began singing gospel music in churches and eventually played at bluegrass festivals. In 1994, they moved to East Tennessee to be nearer the center of bluegrass music. There they formed a band called Appalachian Strings.

Bill Napier was described in a tribute by his friend Dennis Cochran as "mischievous," "delightfully artistic," "with a knowing grin, gentle humor, and a warm chuckle." He added, "People loved him for his music and his wit. He always wanted the audience to have at least as good a time as he was having." Bill Napier died in 2000 after a bout with cancer.

(With credit to Ivan Tribe and John Morris, "Bill Napier, Creative Instrumentalist," *Bluegrass Unlimited* 14.7 [January 1980]: 20–23; and Dennis Cochran, "Bill Napier, Not a Perfect Man, Just a Good Man," www.binternet.com/~john.baldry/mando/napier .html).

GRADY NUTT

Born September 2, 1934, Amarillo, Texas; died November 23, 1982, Vinemont, Alabama

Grady Lee Nutt became a licensed southern Baptist preacher at the age of thirteen. He attended local schools and studied at Wayland Baptist College and Baylor University, receiving his B.A. degree from the latter in 1957. He served as a youth minister before enrolling at the Southern Baptist Seminary in Louisville. After receiving his master's degree there, he served churches in Louisville and Graefenburg. He also held the positions of alumni director and assistant to the president at the Southern Baptist Seminary.

But all the while Grady Nutt had an irrepressible sense of humor. He came to the notice of people in need of a humorous and inspirational speaker through his stories aimed at the young people he served as pastor. From local congregations and service clubs, he went on to national Baptist gatherings and other venues. In 1969, McKinney

Associates of Louisville signed him for their speaker and entertainment bureau. He appeared on the Ralph Edwards and Mike Douglas shows and hit the lecture circuit with as many as 250 appearances a year.

In 1979, he was invited to be a regular on "Hee Haw" as the "Prime Minister of Humor." There he regaled his countrified fellow entertainers and a national audience with amusing stories, in his Texas preaching voice, about growing up Baptist in Texas and with observations about religion in general. His "Hee Haw" appearances led to a projected television series, "The Grady Nutt Show," the pilot of which appeared in July 1981. He also recorded six albums, including, *All Day Singin' and Dinner on the Ground, The Gospel According to Pinocchio,* and *Grady Nutt: Prime Minister of Humor.* His books include *Being Me* (1971), *The Gospel According to Norton* (1974), *Agaperos* (1977), and *So Good, So Far* (1979).

His last book was an autobiography, and sadly he was not to live much longer. On November 23, 1982, after a speech to young people in Alabama, his chartered plane crashed. He left his wife of twenty-five years, the former Eleanor Wilson, and two sons: Toby, an investment broker, and Perry Nutt Wilson, who runs a unique educational program in Tennessee located on the Wilson farm in Fayette County, where Grady is buried.

Here is a one-liner from Grady:

You know you're in southern Baptist country when the preacher pronounces "dance" with four syllables, as in "daa-uhn-ce-ah."

TIM O'BRIEN (RED KNUCKLES AND THE TRAILBLAZERS)
Born March 16, 1954, Wheeling, West Virginia

Tim O'Brien is a master musician on the mandolin, fiddle, and guitar and is a gifted singer. He was cofounder of the popular bluegrass band Hot Rize and did sophisticated humor with what has been called Hot Rize's alter-ego band, Red Knuckles and the Trailblazers. He is also a talented songwriter for himself and for such artists as Kathy Mattea ("Walk the Way the Wind Blows") and Garth Brooks ("When No One's Around").

O'Brien grew up in Wheeling, West Virginia, home of WWVA's "Mountaineer Jamboree," a show that influenced him to take up the guitar at an early age. He listened to other kinds of music as well—pop and rock—and was swayed toward bluegrass by the artistry of Doc Watson. As a teenager he played in rock bands but knew staff musicians on the "Jamboree." After a year at Colby College, playing the guitar and ignoring his studies, he headed west to Colorado, mainly because he had been there for a Boy Scout camp and for summer work. In Boulder, he and the banjoist Pete Wernick formed Hot Rize in 1978.

O'Brien's humor was influenced by the Statler Brothers' routine on the fictional Lester "Road Hog" Moran and His Cadillac Cowboys and also by the zany but sophisticated routines of Riders in the Sky. He explained the creation of Red Knuckles and the Trailblazers: "We played bluegrass in bars, and after the second set it would be a little too much bluegrass. So we'd switch instruments and play another kind of music. One time at a concert, after doing this for years, we said, 'Let's change clothes and see what happens.' And all of a sudden we were playing characters. I think the audience liked the idea that you could be somebody else. It was like Halloween every night with the Trailblazers." Tim went on to describe the humor of the group:

> Early on we made a vow that we would never let on that we were the same people. It was a running gag onstage and off. It was the type of humor where you would set up a dual identity thing—a schizophrenia—a situation like on the "Beverly Hillbillies." Milburn Drysdale and Jed Clampett are speaking the same language, but they mean completely different things. All you have to do is establish that as happening, and the gags take care of themselves. With the Trailblazers, we had a different identity, but we are the same people and we claim not to know each other. The Trailblazers come from a town that's been written off. Time has stood still. The jukebox hasn't been restocked since 1960. We don't really understand these modern things, but we're trying to learn. It makes for some funny stuff.

The Trailblazers became the stereotypical honky-tonk band singing all of the old weepy songs from the past but also, as O'Brien explained it, "We'd do 'Red Remembers the Sixties,' with country versions of 'Light My Fire' and 'Purple Haze,' those psychedelic sixties songs with a real twangy guitar and steel." They would also use the canted language of the early performers: "Thank you, thank you so much. Mighty fine. A great big howdy to you," and so on. The musicians assumed other names for the Trailblazers, with O'Brien as "Red Knuckles," Pete Wernick as "Waldo Otto," Charles Sawtelle as "Slade," and Nick Forster as "Wendell Mercantile." Slade, whose name comes from a Mark Twain piece, dresses all in black like so many villains in B-Westerns. "No one has ever seen him eat or sleep, and no photographs of him have ever been successfully developed." The group came from the little town of Wyoming, Montana, except for Slade, who came from Montana, Wyoming, just across the border from Wyoming, Montana. Rounder Records has a CD reissue of the two earlier albums, *Red Knuckles/Hot Rize Live*.

O'Brien has good theories about comedy in musical entertainment: "I think humor is essential. There can be a wall between the audience and you. When you're putting on a show, people want to get to know you, and so you want to reveal something of yourself. It is a mysterious process, but making fun of yourself is easy. You take the music seriously, but you can break the ice with humor." He went on to say that he learned a lot about the power of humor from Jethro Burns, of Homer and Jethro, and from Minnie Pearl and Rod Brasfield. "They always respected the audience's intelligence."

O'Brien now lives in Nashville, where he writes songs and does special projects or tours with some premier instrumentalists—Bela Fleck, Jerry Douglas, Tony Rice, and Peter Rowan—and he also tours with his sister Molly O'Brien, a celebrated folk and blues singer. He has released numerous recordings in recent years, including *Real Time* (Howdy Skies, 2000), *Songs from the Mountains* (Howdy Skies, 1999), *The Crossing* (Alula, 1999), *When No One's Around* (Sugar Hill, 1997), *Red on Blonde* (Sugar Hill, 1996, Grammy nomination), *Rock in My Shoe* (Sugar Hill, 1995), and *Away on the Mountain* (Sugar Hill, 1994). Tim and his wife Kit have two boys, Jackson and Joel. Jackson recently toured Scotland with Tim as his bassist. Joel often clog dances and does a ham-bone routine on his shows. Kit's artwork appears on Tim's recent CDs, *Cornbread Nation* and *Fiddler's Green*, the latter of which won a Grammy in 2006 for Best Traditional Folk Recording.

LUTHER OSSENBRINK.
See Arkie the Arkansas Woodchopper

DOLLY PARTON

Born January 19, 1946, Locust Ridge, Tennessee

Dolly Parton is a talent of great proportions. She has won a multitude of awards as a country singer, pop singer, actress, and songwriter. She is also an astute businesswoman and philanthropist. She grew up hard in the Great Smoky Mountains, the fourth of twelve children. One of her best-known songs, "Coat of Many Colors," is based on the pain of being laughed at because she was poor. Yet Dolly Parton has kept a rare perspective on the successful life she now lives and the poverty of her childhood. This perspective is bolstered by a keen intelligence and confidence in her many talents but also by her sense of humor.

The novelist Lee Smith, a friend of Dolly's, comments on her humor:

I think it is apparent that she has been around a lot of old-style country comedians at the "Opry" and at barn dances. She plays with that tradition in an ironic way. The idea is that it is always funny to be real country. That has given rise to Dolly's persona. She likes to say things that are real country. Everybody in the audience knows that she is just brilliant and a millionaire. It's like she's putting something over on the world, and the audience, particularly if it is a country audience, is in on the joke. The dumber she acts, the more they think that the discrepancy makes for a whole lot of irony. When she says, "It takes a lot of money to look this cheap," all that is wonderful because of the way she is. She's being like us even though she could be living in Italy or anywhere.

She's very shrewd, in the category of the rube who outsmarts the city feller. She looks like a floozy, then is just really funny when she says those things that are so smart. She does a parody of herself. When she's on stage performing, she's just like she is in private, except more so. She enjoys her image.

Hal Crowther, a journalist who has studied Dolly's persona, added other thoughts on Dolly's humor:

She's playing off a number of things. She's kidding herself and parodying her own image. She's playing off the wise rube fooling the city slickers. She's playing off the way she looks, and men's fantasies, the tough woman who can control her whole world very easily, making fun of the sexual images, and she's playing off the lady versus the tramp. She's got a number of these favorite dichotomies that she's working off in her humor, and she's totally aware of it all. She likes to surprise the audience. She doesn't come off at all like the queen, which some country music stars have done. She has this way of making fun of herself and undercutting herself in a way that connects with the audience.

Parton has said that when she was a girl, she wanted to look like the trashy women she saw on the streets of Sevierville and later Knoxville. Therefore, she has worn great blonde wigs and bright and revealing clothing that enhance her unusual figure. At an awards ceremony when her dress split, she said in her acceptance speech that her father had once told her that you couldn't put a hundred pounds of mud into a fifty-pound sack. She makes jokes about her famous bosom, and said bosom has been the object of the humor of several country comedians, as in, "I see Dolly Parton's in the audience," and then, "No, it's just two bald-headed men sitting together."

Her sense of humor is eclipsed by her formidable talents as songwriter, recording artist, actress, and television personality, and yet it enlivens and is integral to whatever she does. Like many southerners who have known hard times, she does not take herself too seriously. For example, an interviewer asked her how long it took to get her hair fixed like she had it, and she replied, "I don't know. I've never been there." This sense of the humorous side of life has endeared her to fans as much as has her other talents.

Dolly has involved members of her family in her shows, and she loves to introduce her parents to audiences when they attend her concerts, sometimes telling a funny anecdote about the family. At a recent concert, she told of growing up in a large family and joked about the reluctance to go to the outhouse on a cold dark night after scary mountain tales such as "Raw Head and Bloody Bones" and someone wetting the bed with several others sleeping in it.

Dolly Parton has won every major music award. She became a member of the "Grand Ole Opry" in 1969, was Female Vocalist of the Year in 1975 and 1976, was named Entertainer of the Year in 1978, and was inducted into the Country Music Hall of Fame in 1999. Dolly has left Nashville for forays to Hollywood, and a West Coast agency manages her career. She got her first big crossover hit with "Here You Come

Again," which was number one on the country and number three on the pop charts. She is best remembered for her major hits "Joshua," "Jolene," "Love Is Like a Butterfly," and "I Will Always Love You." In recent years, Dolly has returned to her mountain roots and released bluegrass-oriented albums: *The Grass Is Blue* (1999), *Little Sparrow* (2001), and *Bridge for Bluegrass* (2002), all on Sugar Hill, winning major awards from the International Bluegrass Music Association.

Dolly also had a major television show on ABC in 1976, which she writes off as a fiasco because the producers and writers did not understand her or the audience who loved her. She gained new fame and success in the movies *9–5*, *Steel Magnolias*, and *The Best Little Whorehouse in Texas*. She is respected as a successful businesswoman, best reflected in her popular theme park Dollywood, in Pigeon Forge, Tennessee. She likes to say, "Many an old boy has found out too late that I look like a woman but think like a man."

Hal Crowther, in John Egerton's book *Nashville*, sums up this entertainer rather nicely: "One of the litmus tests for Southern authenticity would be an ability to appreciate the paradox of Dolly Parton: Beneath a blinding surface of deliberate exaggerated self-satirizing artifice lurks one of the most engagingly authentic individuals in the Nashville pantheon."

In recent years Parton has established the Dollywood Foundation for the benefit of the people of her native Sevier County, emphasizing programs for children.

She is married to Carl Dean, a Nashville contractor.

When Bob Edwards, of NPR's "Morning Edition," asked Dolly what were some of the worst things ever said about her, she responded, "They said I was down in my back because my boobs were so big, that I was pregnant, that I was having an affair with a young boy, that I was having an affair with a young girl. Boy, for a girl who is down in her back, I sure get around!"

CHARLIE PAYNE ("COUZIN ELMER")

Born September 9, 1915, Ashland, Kentucky;
died January 5, 1985, Grayson, Kentucky

Charlie Payne said he "fell" into comedy one night at the Grand Theater in Ashland, Kentucky, working the lights for Gene Autry when 220 volts knocked him onto the stage. It got such a big laugh that Autry asked him to do it again in the next performance, without the shock.

Payne had dropped out of high school at fifteen to work at the Grand Theater as a bill poster, stage manager, and usher. This experience led him to become manager of theaters in Kentucky, Ohio, and Texas. On Friday nights at these theaters he held talent shows, where he served as emcee and developed his comedy act as Couzin Elmer.

Charlie Payne as Couzin Elmer.
Courtesy of Donald Payne.

He also played host to touring celebrities such as Uncle Dave Macon, Tex Ritter, Lash Larue, Roy Rogers (who grew up just down the Ohio River), Hoot Gibson, and Smiley Burnette. These performers also invited him to provide comedy when they did personal appearances at other locations in the area.

With a natural bent for clowning and comedy, he used his Couzin Elmer act as a warmup for such performers. Later, he spent several years providing comedy for traveling "Grand Ole Opry" shows. He also played the "Old Dominion Barn Dance" in Richmond, Virginia, and he traveled with USO shows that entertained troops. He continued working with touring "Opry" stars in his later years whenever they needed comedy. He did shows with Ernest Tubb, Roy Clark, Tom T. Hall, and Kenny Price. He also did radio and TV shows, including guest spots on Cincinnati's "Bob Braun Show," the "Mid-Western Hayride," and the Wheeling "Jamboree." He had his own band, the Kinfolks Show, and he worked with Shannon Gray of Rush, Kentucky, as Couzin Elmer and Couzin Essie. He was a lifetime member of the American Guild of Variety Artists.

Payne was married to Mary Jo Brooks, and they had three children: Richard, Donald, and Carolyn. The couple divorced in the 1950s. He and his second wife, Wilda, were married in 1974 and had two children: Charlie Jr. and Dixie. They lived in Grayson, Kentucky. In his last years he was always available for fund-raisers, professional groups, and civic club events, and he loved playing Santa Claus wherever needed. Charlie Payne once said, "I won't stop entertaining until I die, and even then, I may sit up in my coffin and tell the mourners a joke. When I die, I want to fall off the stage and die right there." He did in fact work even with declining health until his death in 1985.

MINNIE PEARL

Born Sarah Ophelia Colley, October 15, 1912,
Centerville, Tennessee; died March 4, 1996,
Nashville, Tennessee

Sarah Colley, the daughter of a prosperous lumberman, wanted to become an actress. After studying at Nashville's Ward-Belmont College for Girls in voice and drama, she went to work for the Wayne P. Sewell Producing Company helping amateur theater groups in the South to produce plays on which her employer owned copyrights. Working with a group in Cullman, Alabama, Colley boarded with a colorful woman who told stories in an Alabama accent, and she got the idea of doing a monologue based on this country woman. Her creation of the character that became Minnie Pearl was meant at first to stir up interest in plays she was promoting.

After six years with the Sewell Company, she returned home to care for her mother when her father died. In Centerville, she ran a Works Progress Administration children's

Minnie Pearl with Ernest Tubb.
Courtesy of Charles K. Wolfe.

recreation center. She was asked to stage an entertainment show for the Lion's Club, and she devised a play with her performing her country character. This led in 1940 to her being asked by the local banker to perform at a bankers convention that was meeting in Centerville. "They had a speaker," she remembered, "but he wanted me to kill time until the speaker came. So, I performed, never knowing that that night was going to change my life. I've been killing time ever since." A Nashville banker at the convention recommended her to the general manager of the "Grand Ole Opry," and before the week was out she received an invitation to come and do an audition for the show.

During Colley's years in Nashville, she had been involved with the people and institutions that reflected the "Athens of the South" title that the city had long enjoyed, and she knew very little about the "Opry" and country music. However, she performed there on November 30, 1940. She was scheduled for 11:05 PM, allegedly because they were afraid that her comic character might offend rural fans. While she was waiting to go on, she remembered that the "Solemn Old Judge," George D. Hay, commented that she looked nervous. She acknowledged that she was. Hay then gave her the best advice she ever got: "Love them, Honey, and they'll love you right back." Apparently she expressed her love to that first "Opry" audience, for cards and letters rolled in, and Colley became a regular on the show beginning the following Saturday, December 7, 1940.

Minnie Pearl developed as a character during those first years on the "Opry," with coaching help from Hay. Colley created a whole community that she called "Grinder's Switch" and peopled it with such characters as her boyfriend Hezzie, Brother, and Uncle Nabob. Minnie Pearl became the rustic spinster, dressed in print dress, cotton stockings, and a hat with the price tag still dangling, always hopeful for romantic encounters. She purported to be the gossip columnist for the Grinder's Switch newspaper, giving the news of the week, much in the way that the modern humorist Garrison Keillor gives the news from Lake Wobegone on "A Prairie Home Companion." Her monologues included country and vaudeville jokes worked into her narratives as if they had happened to her Grinder's Switch citizens. She also played the piano, sang (usually "Jealous Hearted Me"), and danced a jig. She was effervescent and irrepressible. Soon she was featured on the "Prince Albert Grand Ole Opry," an NBC Red Network thirty-minute primetime spot that by the mid-1940s was heard coast to coast over at least forty stations. Minne Pearl's "How-dee, I'm just so proud to be here," became familiar to millions of listeners.

In 1947, Minnie married Henry Cannon, from Franklin, Tennessee, a veteran of the Army Air Corps who had an air-charter service that served country musicians. He became Minnie's manager and flew her to engagements as well.

For a decade, beginning in 1948, Minnie worked with the veteran ex-vaudeville and ex-tent-rep comedian Rod Brasfield doing "doubles" comedy. Their popular act, including "Opry" tours, was popular throughout the country until Brasfield's death in 1958.

In 1957, Minnie appeared on Ralph Edwards's NBC-TV "This Is Your Life," and in the years to follow she was on the "Tennessee Ernie Ford Show," the "Dinah Shore Show," the "Tonight Show," the "Carol Burnett Show," and the "Jonathan Winters Show." Sam Lovullo was producer of Winters's show, and when he became the producer of "Hee Haw," he made sure that Minnie was on the first show, and she later became a regular playing various roles: schoolteacher, house mother, and editor of the *Grinder's Switch Gazette*. She also appeared for several years on Ralph Emery's "Nashville Now," reading jokes that the audience sent in. She continued to perform at the "Opry," often with Roy Acuff as her straight man.

Minnie recorded several albums and singles—mostly monologues—on Bullet, RCA, King, Everest, and Starday. Her "Giddyup Go—Answer" (to a recitation by Red Sovine) was number ten on the country charts in 1966. Opryland USA also released a video, *Minnie Pearl: Old Times*, in 1988.

In 1965, the Athens of the South embraced Sarah Ophelia Cannon, if not all of country music, by naming her Nashville's Woman of the Year. Minnie was active until she suffered a stroke on June 17, 1991, after a performance in Joliet, Illinois, and she was in a nursing home for five years until her death of additional strokes in 1996. Her illness and death left a gaping hole in the entertainment fabric of the "Grand Ole Opry." In 1999 Kevin Kenworthy published *The Best Jokes Minnie Pearl Ever Told* (Nashville: Rutledge Hill Press). Here is a story from this collection:

> *Well, the big news in Grinder's Switch is that Brother's gone off to college. Somebody asked me what he's studying. I told 'em, "He ain't studyin' anything. They're studying him!"*

HANK PENNY

Born Herbert Clayton Penny, September 18, 1918,
Birmingham, Alabama; died April 17, 1992,
California

Grandpa Jones, who knew a thing or two about comedy, said that while Hank Penny was best known as a bandleader and western swing musician, "he was one of the funniest comics around." He also said that Penny was one of his best sources for comedy. Grandpa and his wife Ramona worked with Penny on the "Boone County Jamboree" over WLW in the early 1940s. Ramona also remembered him as a wonderful comedian: "He dressed like a country bumpkin. We would play county fairs. When we had a big rain and it would be muddy on the track, Hank would jump off the stage and get out there and play around in the mud. He just loved being funny. He'd do anything to be funny."

Young Penny got his start in show business in 1933, at age fifteen, when he joined Happy Hal Burns's radio show on WAPI in Birmingham as a tenor banjoist, although his basic instrument was the guitar. He was with Burns for three years and learned a lot about comedy but also about the whole business of entertainment.

He soon became a fan of the western swing music of Bob Wills and Milton Brown. After a short period at New Orleans's WWL as a solo singer and guitarist, he returned to Birmingham to form his own swing band, the Radio Cowboys. They played various stations in Birmingham and then in 1937 moved on to WDOD in Chattanooga. In 1938, Penny and his band got a contract with the American Record Company, and their first record was produced by Art Satherly, who also produced Bob Wills and Gene Autry. This recording gave his group more exposure, and they soon were invited to join the "Cross Roads Follies" at WSB in Atlanta. There he improved his band with new musicians, including Bordeleaux Bryant and Noel Boggs, and they became popular in a large listening area. Hank received offers to join the bands of Pee Wee King and even Bob Wills, but he declined. His band also had an offer from the "Grand Ole Opry" if he would get rid of Noel Boggs's electric steel guitar. He declined and instead, after more ARC recording sessions, Penny went to WLW in Cincinnati where he formed a new band, the Plantation Boys, and they played the "Boone County Jamboree," working with such other talents as Bradley Kincaid, Grandpa and Ramona Jones, the Delmore Brothers, and Merle Travis.

Hank Penny. Courtesy of Wayne W. Daniel.

Penny and his band took time off from radio in 1944 to travel with USO shows at bases in the United States. After a dispute with management at WLW over a recording contract with King Records, Penny went to California, where his friend Merle Travis had found a more amiable climate and lucrative work. Forming a new band there, Penny began playing the numerous dance halls that catered to factory workers. They also traveled back to Cincinnati for more King recording sessions. According to the writer Rich Kienzle, in spite of their popularity, Penny's band wasn't on the level of those of Bob Wills and Spade Cooley. He wrote, "Hank was leading the best second-level band in Hollywood." Kienzle noted that Hank's success went to his head, and he decided to go back East, where he thought he could capitalize on his California success.

He worked in Atlanta and Nashville before going back to WLW and then to Connie B. Gay's station, WARL, in Arlington, Virginia. He seemed to have difficulty with management wherever he was. Eventually, he went back to Hollywood, where he became a popular disc jockey on KGIL in Sherman Oaks. He soon organized another band and went into partnership to build a six-hundred-capacity dance hall in Los Angeles. In 1948, Spade Cooley invited him to be a guest on his Saturday-night show on KTLA-TV with freedom to do what he wanted to do. He chose comedy that went over well, and he became a regular on this high-rated show. He became "That Plain Ol' Country Boy" from Rimlap, Alabama, who introduced fictional characters, just as Minnie Pearl and Jerry Clower did.

He was at his busiest at the end of the 1940s, with a radio show five days a week and three on Saturdays, a band that performed at dance halls on week nights, a Saturday-night TV show, and comedy engagements at trade shows and banquets.

In 1950, Penny and a business partner opened the Palomino Dance Hall in the San Fernando Valley that hosted primarily country music groups but also jazz, and it continued for some thirty years. He also organized another western swing band called the Penny Seranaders. In 1953, Hank was given a television show, "The Hank Penny Show," but after seven shows the sponsor canceled his contract, and Penny decided to move to Las Vegas, where he played the Golden Nugget for seven years. He had a good band with a jazzy sound, and he mixed in a lot of humor. With first-rate management, he became a sought-after entertainer. He did sessions with RCA and Decca, and he did a jazz LP on the NRC label.

Penny and his band became more country in the early 1960s and played various clubs with the young Roy Clark in the band. Clark was a hot guitarist but aspired to be a comedian. He studied Hank's showmanship and comedy. Thus, Hank was bitter when "Hee Haw" rejected him in favor of Clark. He claimed that Clark had stolen his style and material, although later he apologized for saying so. This "Hee Haw" rejection angered and depressed Penny, and he became a strong critic of the music and entertainment business, and he also quarreled with the musicians' union. He ended his career appearing on television shows as a guest and working as a DJ at WSM, Nashville, and at a station in Wichita, Kansas. Back in Los Angeles, he and his fifth wife, Shari, performed together at such places as Knott's Berry Farm.

Hank Penny was a major talent as a musician, comedian, songwriter, and bandleader, but according to Rich Kienzel, he came along about ten years too early to make it big as a star with his kind of entertainment. No doubt his sometimes confrontational and abrasive manner was a factor in his career. He died of a heart attack in 1992.

(With credit to Rich Kienzle, "The Checkered Career of Hank Penny," *Journal of Country Music* 3.2 [1980]: 43–77.)

Here is one of Hank Penny's best stories. Grandpa Jones learned it from Hank, along with many others, and told it frequently:

> *I took my old aunt to town, and she got in a hotel lobby and came upon a full-length mirror. She never had seen one before, and she didn't know what it was. So she walked up to it and saw her own reflection and said, "Well, poor old thing, you look bad. I believe I'll get you a sweet potato to eat." So she went out and got a sweet potato and walked back into the hotel and over to the mirror, and then said, "Oh, I see you got one already. I'll just eat this one myself."*

IVY PETERSON

Born December 30, 1910, Birmingham, Alabama;
died December 13, 1991, Henry County, Georgia

Ivy Peterson's comedic stage name was Herman Horsehair Buggfuzz, a character he played for many years on the "WSB Barn Dance" in Atlanta. He was also program manager for WSB radio, played with the Peachtree Cowboys, and owned the Covered Wagon, a country-western nightclub in Atlanta.

Peterson started in show business in Birmingham, playing the bass fiddle with pop bands, including Jan Garber's. A three-year stint with the fiddler Curley Fox introduced him to country music, and when Fox lost his regular comedian, he pressed Peterson into service. Peterson later worked with a band called the Ranch Boys at WREC in Memphis for about three years, and then they moved to WMC. The Ranch Boys played western swing along with country and did personal appearances. In 1941, WSB hired Peterson to replace their regular announcer, Cotton Carrier, who had a date with the army. Peterson was in charge of the "Barn Dance" and served as its announcer. In addition, he perfected and performed his character, Herman Horsehair Buggfuzz. Peterson went on to serve in the Marine Corps in World War II but returned to the "Barn Dance." When it closed in 1947, he became the prop and stage manager for

Ivy Peterson (center) with Hank Penny and Chick Stripling. Courtesy of Wayne W. Daniel.

WSB-TV until 1976. At the same time, he played with the Peachtree Cowboys on WSB radio and television, and this group also performed at the Covered Wagon nightclub that he managed for nineteen years.

Ivy Peterson had one son, Richard C. Peterson, of Forest Park, Georgia, and two grandchildren.

(With credit to Wayne W. Daniel, *Pickin' on Peachtree: A History of Country Music in Atlanta, Georgia* [Urbana: University of Illinois Press, 1990], and notes from his interview with Ivy Peterson.)

Following are excerpts from a 1947 routine between Herman Horsehair Buggfuzz and Cotton Carrier on WSB radio, published in *Pickin' on Peachtree*, with permission:

Cotton: Herman . . . Herman, why are you bouncing up and down like that?
Herman: I took me some medicine just now and forgot to shake the bottle. . . .
Cotton: You must be sick all right. . . . What seems to be the trouble?
Herman: Well, you see, ever' time I bend way down, stretch my arms out, and then lift my leg, I get a pain in my chest.
Cotton: But what do you want to do all that for anyway?
Herman: 'Cause that's the only way I can put my britches on. . . .
Cotton: Herman, why do you keep looking down? Have you lost something?
Herman: Huh?
Cotton: I say, have you lost something?
Herman: No, the doctor just told me to watch my stomach. . . .
Cotton: Oh Herman, I wish you'd go away from here. Every time I start talking to you I get a headache.
Herman: Don't worry about a headache, Cotton, I can cure a headache.
Cotton: You can?
Herman: Shore . . . I cured a headache for my cousin Bub once.
Cotton: Well, how did you do it?
Herman: I just gave him two quarts of turpentine.
Cotton: Two quarts of turpentine! Why that would kill me!
Herman: I know! It killed my cousin Bub! So long, Cotton.

PIE PLANT PETE

Born Claude W. Moye, July 9, 1906, Shawneetown,
Illinois; died February 7, 1988, Ridgway, Illinois

Pie Plant Pete joined the WLS "National Barn Dance" at the age of nineteen, singing and playing guitar and harmonica at the same time, using a rack for his harmonica. He reported that he got his unusual stage name from the program director at WLS, who had seen a magazine advertisement for pie plant, a country name for rhubarb. Since he already had the nickname of Pete, he became Pie Plant Pete. He added that it may have come from his music, which at the time was so sour. At any rate, he had a long career in entertainment as a solo artist and in partnership with "Bashful Harmonica Joe" Troyan.

After two years on the "Barn Dance," he worked five years at WTAM in Cleveland, and there he met Troyan, who, with Grandpa Jones, had been playing with Bradley Kincaid over WBZ in Boston. Pete and Joe became a team that would last for most of their careers. They performed for several months over WBZ and then went to WHAM in Rochester, New York, and were back in Cleveland by 1939. Both were drafted into service during World War II. After the war, they performed at radio stations in Cleveland, Rochester, Toledo, and Detroit and toured for personal appearances throughout the Midwest.

Pie Plant Pete did early recordings for Gennett, Decca, and the American Record Corporation, mostly of folk and novelty songs and sentimental numbers. Pete and Joe recorded twenty sides for Process Records in 1947. These recordings were reissued by Cattle Records as *The Old-Time Country Music Collection of Pie Plant Pete and Bashful Harmonica Joe* in 1989.

After Joe retired, Pete worked in children's television and in advertising.

CHONDA PIERCE

Born March 4, 1960, Covington, Kentucky

Chonda Pierce grew up in the South as a sheltered preacher's kid, but she enjoyed an early experience of making people laugh. "I remember when I was a young kid, my mama would rent me out to Sunday School parties." Later she played before larger audiences as a member of the family singing group. Pierce's entry into show business came with a successful audition for a summer job at Opryland USA in 1983, while she was a college student. In the Opryland show, based on the history of country music, she played the part of several country singers, but what changed her life was playing the great country comedienne Minnie Pearl. She was mum about not knowing who Minnie Pearl was when she was asked to read Minnie's part, but the lines were so funny that soon she and the whole cast were laughing. She took herself to the Minnie Pearl Museum, saw the video clips of Minnie's performances, and then began slipping into the "Grand Ole Opry" House to see Minnie perform in person. Later on, Minnie came to the Opryland show and was impressed with Chonda's impersonation. She remembers, "When I met Miss Minnie, I was a college kid, and she was a fan of any kid out there. The thing that impressed me the most was that she was a sweet woman and never had to use filthy language to get a laugh. It encouraged me to know that I could be as funny as the rest of them, without using words or subjects that would [later on] embarrass my own kids." She played Minnie Pearl at Opryland for nearly five years and loved every minute of it.

Her comedic career helped Chonda to heal deep sorrows in her own life, from the loss of two beloved sisters (one in an automobile accident and the other from lymphatic leukemia), a manic depressive father, and the divorce of her parents. She said:

> For me, there was a time when laughter hid some of the pain. As Proverbs says, "Laughter is like a medicine." After a while when you take this medicine, it's just fun. I'd rather live my life in a joyful way than to let all that I went through beat me up, because then, death would have won twice. My sisters wouldn't have wanted me dragging around bitter and disgruntled. I do this in honor of them and my parents.

Chonda Pierce. Photo by Robert M. Ascrof II, courtesy of Chonda Pierce.

Since Pierce had sung with her family gospel group, the Singing Courtneys, it was logical that she would be invited to do comedy with gospel-music tours, and so she has often worked for Bill Gaither and others. In recent years, however, she has had her own tours throughout the United States, doing as many as forty cities in a year, performing in auditoriums, churches, and theaters. Her guest appearances on the "Grand Ole Opry" and the gospel-music tours have assured good audiences for her performances wherever she goes.

When asked why there is so much humor in religion, she said, "When you're working so hard to be serious and something goes wrong, something funny is ten times as funny, like the preacher preaching with his britches unzipped." But she also feels called upon to witness about her Christian faith, explaining, "My personal relationship with God is what enables me to laugh. I can't make somebody believe like I believe, but I'm real quick to tell them that I would love for them to find a balance in their lives. If I'm authentic enough to share a night of crack-up laughter, then I want to be authentic enough to tell them how I have found some peace." When she performs, she also mixes in a few songs "to make a well-rounded program."

Pierce has published six books: *Chonda Pierce on Her Soapbox, It's Always Darkest before the Fun Comes Up, Second Row, Piano Side, I Can See Myself In His Eyeballs: God Is Closer Than You Think,* and *Roadkill on the Highway to Heaven.* She also has several DVDs, videos, and CDs, including *Yes, and Amen, Chonda Pierce on the Soapbox, Havin' a Girl's Night Out! Be Afraid, Be Very Afraid, Have I Got a Great Story for You,* and *A Piece of My Mind.* They are available on her Web site (www.chonda.org).

Chonda finished her 2006 concert tour with the Christmas at the Cove Concert at the Billy Graham Training Center at Black Mountain, North Carolina, near Asheville.

Joining her were George Beverly Shea, Cliff Barrows, and Tom and Teresa Bledsoe. Mr. Graham also made an appearance.

Chonda Pierce lives in Nashville with her husband, David Pierce, and their two children, Chera Kay and Zachary.

Following is a story that illustrates Chonda's ability to see great humor in life's misunderstandings:

> I was on the Opry one night, and I was real excited, 'cause the secretary called before I left the house and said, "Johnny Russell's hosting your segment, and he doesn't want you to leave when you're done. He wants you to go out together." And I was like, wow! It was the same night Mike Snider was on, Jerry Clower was on, and Grandpa Jones. They were highlighting comedians. I was elated! I just couldn't believe it. I thought maybe they were going to make me a member. I was just tickled to death.
>
> And so, when I got to the Opry House, I saw the secretary, and I said, "June, where are we going to eat? Will it be someplace fancy? Am I dressed appropriately?" She said, "What are you talking about?" I said, "Where do you think we'll eat when we go out together?" She said, "Not out to eat—out to take a bow when the show is over!"

"SMOKEY" PLEACHER

Born Charles Eugene Pleacher, September 30, 1918,
Manna Choice, Pennsylvania; died 1971, Altoona,
Pennsylvania

Doc Williams, of the WWVA "Jamboree USA," said that "one of the funniest comedians I ever had was Smokey Pleacher." Pleacher had won an amateur music contest in 1932, with harmonica and washboard, and this emboldened him to seek a job with Harry Flore's Medicine Show, where he learned comedy. In 1938, he got a job on "The Farm Hour" over WCHS in Charleston, West Virginia. He then worked in Pennsylvania with two other groups, the Covered Wagon Boys and the Hawaiianaires, before World War II. He then served three years as a soldier in the European Theater.

After the war, Pleacher worked with Jim and James Klaar in Pennsylvania and then joined Hawkshaw Hawkins on the WWVA "Jamboree" in Wheeling in 1947. He later worked with Wilma Lee and Stoney Cooper at WWVA. After performing in the Niagara Falls area and in Rochester, he came back to WWVA for a tour with Doc William as his comedian in 1952, filling in for Hiram Hayseed when he was ill.

Starting in 1955, Pleacher worked with Hawkshaw Hawkins and Jean Shepherd on the "Grand Ole Opry." He also worked with Lonzo and Oscar as a silent comic partner, but he soon grew tired of that role and went west to join the "Judy Lynn Show" in Las Vegas, Reno, and Lake Tahoe. He also did a USO tour to Greenland and Iceland. In 1960 he rejoined Doc Williams at WWVA for a decade. During this time, he was recorded in various venues and is on two cassettes released by Williams's Wheeling

COUNTRY MUSIC HUMORISTS AND COMEDIANS

Records, *Doc Williams Presents Smokey Pleacher* and *Smokey Pleacher That Handsome Creature* (Box 902, Wheeling, WV 26003).

Pleacher was a gifted singer as well as a comedian. He sang in a smooth tenor voice but could shift into a bullfrog bass à la Smiley Burnett. He did long narratives about such simple acts as going out into the fields and woods with his hound dog, imitating the dog's various tones as he went. According to Doc Williams, Smoky Pleacher died in a veteran's home in Pennsylvania.

The following comes from *Smoky Pleacher That Handsome Creature*, after he has rendered a comic version of "I Never See Maggie Alone," with permission.

Smoky Pleacher. Courtesy of Doc Williams.

I want to tell you about Maggie, 'cause she don't live where she used to. She lived out where she moved to. She lives out on Petticoat Avenue. That's right next to the outskirts. I went out to see her one night, and she was upstairs warshing. I said, "Whatcha doin', Hon?" She said, "Warshing." I said, "Come on down." She said, "Oh, don't be silly. I ain't dressed." I said, "Don't be silly yourself, slip on somethin' and come on down." She slipped on a cake of soap, and there she wuz!

I had my love book with me—showed you how to smooch and make love, you know. So, we went in and set on the davenport. I looked on the first page, and it said we were settin' on the davenport. I's settin' on one end, and she's settin' on the other. I looked on the next page, and it said we's to nudge a little closer. I looked on the next page, and it said to put my arm around her. I looked on the next page, and it said to TURN THE LIGHTS OUT! AND I DID! But I had to turn 'em back on again. I couldn't see what was on the next page!

THE PRESLEYS

Gary Presley, born July 8, 1947, Springfield, Missouri
Eric Presley, born August 10, 1976, Branson, Missouri

Gary Presley, son of Lloyd and Bessie Mae Presley, who head the Presley entertainment dynasty in Branson, Missouri, created a character called Herkimer, the main comedian of their show since 1967. Gary at first used a pair of size fifty overalls from one grandparent and an old-fashioned pair of glasses from another, along with a hat with the brim hanging down to create the ultimate rube character. He now varies his costume but is still the rustic character. He appears not-so-bright but in rube tradition he one-ups the knowing emcee. He is audacious and very energetic, bouncing from

The Presleys. Courtesy of "Presleys' Jubilee."

stage to audience and back with alacrity. At various times his sons, Scott, Greg, and Eric, have followed Herkimer around on stage as Herkimer Jr. More recently, Scott and Greg have joined the band as impressive musicians, and Eric has created his own character of Cecil to do doubles with his dad. Cecil is a country boy trying to dress up in city ways with high pants up near his armpits, a red hat, polka-dot tie, and large white shoes. He is adept as an acrobat and dancer with rubbery legs and gliding steps that would challenge a hip-hop dancer.

The Presleys began their show in a cave outside Branson when Gary was fifteen. In 1967, they constructed a theater on Branson's main drag, Highway 76. They had big sliding doors so that they could convert it into a boat locker if the show didn't go. It did, and now the "Presleys' Mountain Music Jamboree" theater seats 2,100 people and has a cast of twenty-two. In addition to their nightly-except-Sunday shows, the Presleys have been featured on "60 Minutes," "How'd They Do That," and the "Today Show." They have produced several videos (2920 76 Country Blvd., Branson, MO 65616).

KENNY PRICE

Born May 27, 1931, Florence, Kentucky;
died August 4, 1987, Florence, Kentucky

Kenny Price, "The Round Mound of Sound," was best known as a comedian and quartet singer on "Hee Haw," but he was also a solid musician and solo singer who had hits in the Top Ten. Born on a farm in Boone County, Kentucky, near Cincinnati, he learned to play a Sears-Roebuck guitar at an early age and began entertaining local groups. He played over the radio first at fourteen, on WZIP in Cincinnati. As a soldier in Korea, he won an audition for a place in a USO show, and this steered him toward a show-business career when he was discharged.

He enrolled in the Cincinnati Conservatory of Music in 1954 for a serious study of music but soon joined WLW's "Mid-Western Hayride" and went on to the "Home-towners" show on WLW-TV in 1957. He also did comedy and sang on the "Louisiana Hayride." Price had his first Top Ten hit with "Walking on New Grass" in 1966, written by Ray Pennington on the Boone label. "Happy Tracks" also placed in the Top Ten, and he had three other songs in the Top Twenty in 1967. After other singles in the middle of the charts, he had two more Top Tens in 1970 with "Biloxi" and "The Sheriff of Boone County." He also recorded for RCA, MRC, Dimension, Panorama, and with the "Hee Haw" Quartet on the Hee Haw label. His last single, "If I Just Had You," was released on Jewel in 1987.

Price joined the cast of "Hee Haw" in 1976. The producer Sam Lovullo wrote in his book, *Life in the Kornfield: My Twenty-five Years at "Hee Haw,"* "Kenny was such a good comedian that people sometimes had trouble taking him seriously, which impeded the progress of his career." But many people enjoyed the comedy of this lovable oversized (over six feet tall and three hundred pounds) entertainer. His fellow "Hee Haw" cast member Roni Stoneman said, "He was one of my favorite comedians. I loved Kenny. Kenny was the most underrated singer in music."

MARC PRUETT

Born August 19, 1951, Waynesville, North Carolina

Marc Pruett headed the Marc Pruett Band at Bill's Barbecue and Bluegrass in downtown Asheville, North Carolina, for nine years, playing for tourists and coming-through-town celebrities. He has also played banjo in the bands of Jimmy Martin, Ricky Skaggs, and the Whites. He is an understated Appalachian humorist with a lot of droll stories, and his bands always feature humor. In addition, Marc and his wife Anita have issued two tapes of Appalachian humor: *Smoky Mountain Grins and Giggles* and *Smoky Mountain Chuckles* on their Blueground Music label (390 Mosey Mountain Lane, Canton, NC 28716).

Pruett grew up with music. His mother was a singer and accomplished flatfoot dancer, and his father played guitar around home and bass in a combo that performed country as well as swing music. He accompanied his father to the annual Mountain Dance and Folk Festival (founded by Bascom Lamar Lunsford in 1928) and was part of an allied program called the Mountain Youth Jamboree. He got hooked on bluegrass in the following way: "When I was ten years old, I heard Flatt and Scruggs on radio. A local station had 'The Cornbread Matinee.' I'd come home from school and have a snack and listen to this program before doing my homework. One day they brought Flatt and Scruggs on, and it went straight to my heart. I heard how perfect it was even then." He got a banjo and looked around for clues about how to play it. He found them with several musicians: Mike Presley, who had learned from the banjo wizard Raymond Fairchild; French Kirkpatrick, who had a local band and "played wonderful old melodic stuff"; Shorty Eager, who had played in Jimmy Martin's band; and Tom McKinney, who, as Pruett said, "put me deep into the Earl Scruggs thing." Pruett's first band was the Starlight Ramblers, named after his 4-H Club, and he also played in other local bands.

Marc graduated from Pisgah High School in Haywood County and then went on to Western Carolina University for a degree in geology. This prepared him for his day job as director of the Soil and Sediment Program for county government, keeping sediment runoff from building projects out of trout streams, roads, and neighboring lands. He also worked with Jimmy Martin's band for two years, a year with the Whites, and then with Ricky Skaggs's Kentucky Thunder band. He played Lincoln Center once with Jimmy Martin and once with Ricky Skaggs. His present band, Whitewater Bluegrass Company, did 130 performances in 2005. Marc says that this, with his day job, made for a full year, and he reports that he has reached the metallic age: "I've got silver in my hair, gold in my teeth, and lead in my tail."

> We'd ask if there was someone we needed to recognize for a birthday, an anniversary—or celebrating a divorce. That always got a laugh. We'd get notes, and I'd read them off. I'd add to what the notes said. So one might say they were celebrating their thirtieth anniversary, and I'd add, "And they want to wish a happy birthday to their son—who is thirty-one today."
>
> Or we'd make up or add a song title—we'd check to make sure it was all right. If it was an older couple, I'd say such-and-such are having an anniversary, and John wanted us to sing, "The Old Gray Mare Ain't What She Used to Be," and that got a laugh, and then I'd conclude with, "And Mary wanted us to sing 'I'll Be Glad When You're Dead, You Rascal You.'"

Marc also wrote some comical songs, such as "The Bald Spot on the Back of My Head" and "The Payday Friday Grocery Store Blues," a talking blues song about the troubles this country boy had at the grocery store, which he did almost every night. "Oh yeah, comedy is a way to communicate with your audience. We did a mix of dancing tunes, bluegrass numbers, comedy, comedy songs, honky-tonk songs, all in an entertaining way, and it worked."

Marc's wife Anita is a musician as well and played banjo for ten years with the Whitewater Bluegrass Band, the band Marc also played for. Marc and Anita go to local festivals as duet singers with him on banjo and her on guitar. Marc has a daughter, Elizabeth, from a previous marriage, and he and Anita have two children, Zachary (an Eagle Scout) and and Callie.

Here is a Marc Pruett story from *Smoky Mountain Chuckles:*

> *Well, the old man couldn't see lightning, and the old lady couldn't hear thunder. They were driving down the road in a car, and she couldn't hear and he couldn't see. It took both of them to drive, and a patrolman pulled them over, and he walked up to the car. The lady rolled her window down, and he said, "May I see your license, ma'am?" She turned to the old man and said, "WHAT DID HE SAY?" and the old man said, "HE WANTS TO SEE YOUR DRIVER'S LICENSE." So she rambled around in her pocketbook and handed the patrolman her driver's license. He looked at it and said, "Well, I see you're from Asheville, North Carolina." The old lady looked at her husband and said, "WHAT DID HE SAY?" He said, "HE SEES YOU'RE FROM ASHEVILLE, NORTH CAROLINA." The patrolman looked at the license again and said, "I knew a woman from Asheville, North Carolina, one time, and she was absolutely, positively the worst lover I ever had." The old lady looked at the man and said, "WHAT DID HE SAY?" The old man said, "HE THINKS HE KNOWS YOU!"*

RED AND FRED. *See Red Rector and Fred Smith*

RED RECTOR

Born William Eugene Rector, December 15, 1929,
  Marshall, North Carolina; died May 31, 1990,
  Knoxville, Tennessee

Red Rector was born in Madison County, North Carolina, a county that has produced many noted ballad singers, fiddlers, banjo players, and string bands. He grew up in nearby Asheville, where he listened to Wade Mainer's Sons of the Mountaineers and the Morris Brothers on WWNC. He began playing in bands when he was twelve and eventually played at three Asheville stations—WISE, WWNC, and WLOS. In 1943 he got his mother to sign a form, lied about his age, and joined the navy at the age of thirteen. Just as he was set to sail off to war from Portsmouth, Virginia, his true age was discovered, and he was discharged. By then a virtuoso mandolin player and versatile

Red Rector (L), with Fred E. Smith
as Red and Fred. Courtesy of
Manuel Clark.

singer, he went with J. E. and Wade Mainer, Fred Smith, and others to New York to
provide background music for the BBC production "On the Chisholm Trail." There
he met Woody Guthrie, who was also involved in the project.

He subsequently played with Wade Mainer and Johnnie and Jack at WWNC in
Asheville and WPTF in Raleigh. He joined Charlie Monroe and His Kentucky Pardners
in 1949 at WNOX in Knoxville, then went with Monroe to WBOK in Birmingham.
He returned to WNOX to join Carl Story and His Rambling Mountaineers.

Red's wife Ernestine believes that he started doing comedy as a teenager, because
every band had some comedy, and he had studied the repertoires of all the bands that
came through Asheville. He became widely known as a comedian in 1955 when he
teamed up with his fellow Madison native Fred Smith in a music and comedy team,
first as Herman and Thurman and then Red and Fred, on WNOX's "Mid-day Merry-
Go-Round." He and Fred had known one another in Madison County and had played

together in various bands in Asheville. They had also played together with the Mainers and Carl Story, but their comedy act came later in Knoxville. There they did comedy songs and fast-paced comic dialogues with Red as the straight man, using scripts mainly written by the WNOX program director Lowell Blanchard, as well as material created or remembered by Fred Smith.

After playing with Hylo Brown's Timberliners for a year, Red rejoined Fred on the "Merry-Go-Round," where they played until the show closed in 1958, and then they went on Cas Walker's television shows at Knoxville's WROL doing a 7:00 morning show five days a week for five years. During this time they did numerous personal-appearance shows over the listening area.

Red and his mandolin were in demand for recording sessions in Nashville. He also was a regular at bluegrass festivals, playing with Fred Smith, Bill Clifton, Don Stover, Norman Blake, and others, and he was prominent in the 1982 World's Fair in Knoxville.

He recorded with Carl Story's group on RCA and Mercury, with Don Reno and Red Smiley on King, and with Hylo Brown on a Capitol LP entitled *Hylo Brown*, which is celebrated by old-time bluegrass fans. Later, he recorded on Old Homestead *Songs from the Heart* (1973) and *Appaloosa* (1975); on County, *Songs from the Heart of the Country: Red and Fred* (1969), *Norman Blake and Red Rector* (1976), and *Back Home in Madison County* (1981); on Renovah, *Red Rector and Friends* (1978); and on Rebel, with his fellow mandolinist Jethro Burns, *Old Friends* (1983).

(See also the entry on Fred Smith for additional information and a comic dialogue).

DEL REEVES

Born Franklin Delano Reeves, July 14, 1933,
Sparta, North Carolina; died January 1, 2007,
Centerville, Tennessee

Del Reeves was a veteran country singer and songwriter, with hits on such labels as Capitol, Decca, and United Artists, a sometime actor, and star of the "Grand Ole Opry." He was also a gifted mimic of fellow singers as well as others such as Walter Brennan and John Wayne, and he did some stand-up comedy. His impersonation of Johnny Cash was always a hit at the "Opry," and he included impersonations in his concerts around the country. His was an amiable comic persona that went over well with his fans.

Del was the youngest of eleven children in the North Carolina mountain town of Sparta. His mother and four older brothers were musicians on guitars that Del soon learned to play. By the time he was twelve, he was already on the local radio station. He eventually went off to study at Appalachian State University in Boone but dropped out to join the air force and was stationed in California. He made television appearances and did recordings for Capitol while he was still in service. When he was discharged, he stayed in California and married Ellen Schiell, who became his songwriting partner. Their "Sing a Little Song of Heartache" became a hit for Rose Maddox in 1962.

Reeves moved to Nashville in 1962, where he signed with United Artists for a fourteen-year stint, resulting in his best-known country hits, notably "The Girl on the Billboard" (number one), "The Belles of Southern Bell" (Top Five), "Women Do Funny Things to Me" (Top Ten), and "Good Time Charlie" (number three). Reeves also hosted a TV show, "Del Reeves Country Carnival," from 1970 until 1973, and he has appeared in eight movies, including *Sam Whiskey* with Burt Reynolds and Angie Dickenson. After recording with Koala and Gusto/Starday, he did *Greatest Hits and More* with Aria Records in 2001. His work is also available from Bear Family (*Baby, I Love You*) and on Playback (*The Silver Anniversary Album*), as well as on reissues of earlier recordings. In 2001, Aria Records released *Greatest Hits*.

Del Reeves died of emphysema on New Year's Day 2007. He is survived by his wife Ellen and daughters Anne, Karii, and Bethany.

Here's a Del Reeves story:

> *This woman had a fire in her kitchen, and she called the fire department, and said, "I've got a fire down here." The dispatcher asked, "Where is the fire?" She said, "It's in the kitchen." The dispatcher said, "But how do we get to it?" She said, "You can come through the living room or off the back porch, either one." He said, "I mean, how do we get from where we are to where you are?" She said, "Ain't you got one of them red trucks?"*

RENO AND SMILEY

Donald Wesley Reno, born February 26, 1926,
    Spartanburg, South Carolina; died October 16,
    1984, Lynchburg, Virginia
Arthur Lee Smiley Jr., born May 17, 1925, Marshall,
    North Carolina; died January 2, 1972

Reno and Smiley and their Tennessee Cut-Ups rank with Bill Monroe, the Stanley Brothers, and Flatt and Scruggs as trendsetters for bluegrass music. Don Reno worked with the Morris Brothers and Arthur Smith and His Crackerjacks at WSPA in Spartan-burg, and Red Smiley also played with the Morris Brothers and others at WWNC in Asheville before World War II. Both served in the war, Reno in Burma and Smiley in the Italian Campaign, where he was seriously wounded in Sicily, losing one lung. Reno spent a year with Bill Monroe's Bluegrass Boys before he and Smiley came together in Tommy Magness's band at WDBJ in Roanoke in 1949. They began singing as a duet with Magness and later in the band of Toby Stroud. Reno played a three-finger banjo style that he had learned from Snuffy Jenkins in Spartanburg and sang high tenor. Smiley played guitar and sang baritone. In 1951 the duo went to Spartanburg and formed the Tennessee Cut-Ups. They played at radio stations but did few public appearances. Between 1952 and 1954, they recorded forty-four numbers, many written by Reno, for King Studios, including "I'm Using My Bible for a Roadmap," a big seller that became a standard in country and bluegrass music.

During this time, Reno also performed with Arthur Smith in Charlotte. Reno and Smith wrote "Feuding Banjos," that was used many years later in the film *Deliverance* as "Dueling Banjos," and its ownership became the subject of a successful lawsuit filed by Smith and Reno. When he wasn't playing with the Cut-Ups, Smiley worked as a mechanic in Asheville and performed with "Cousin Wilbur" Wesbrooks.

Among the King recordings were two comic songs, "Barefoot Nellie" and "Tally Ho." These songs and the name of the band, Tennessee Cut-Ups, reflect the high good humor of the group. In addition to the comic songs, the entire band dressed up in outlandish costumes, sometimes with Smiley in drag, to do comic routines and stage antics. They also dressed up and clowned around for photos for their album covers.

In 1955, Reno and Smiley were able to get their band back together and keep it going for nine successful years. They played the "Old Dominion Barn Dance" in Richmond and WSVA-TV in Harrisonburg. In 1957, they began their "Top of the Morning" show at WBDJ-TV in Roanoke. In January 1963, they talked their sponsor, Kroger, into doing a couple of pilots of their show for syndication. The first was in January and the second in March of that year, with the Stanley Brothers as their guests. The syndication idea apparently was not successful. However, in the early 1990s, workers at WBDJ discovered the old reel-to-reel black-and-white footage. The major portions of these shows were made into a video by Pinecastle Records, released in 1996 as *Don Reno and Red Smiley and the Tennessee Cut-Ups: The Early Years, with Special Guests the Stanley Brothers* (www.pinecastlerecords.com), narrated by the WSM and "Grand Ole Opry" announcer Ernie Stubbs. The video is a wonderful record of the music of Reno and Smiley and the Stanley Brothers at this time in bluegrass history, including some of their great songs as well as a Tennessee Cut-Ups comedy skit. Strangely, Stubbs affirms in the video what I hope this book denies: that comedy is "no more" in bluegrass music because of the increasing sophistication of its audience.

Among the musicians who played with the Tennessee Cut-Ups and who enthusiastically entered into their comedy were Tommy Faile, Jimmy Lunsford, Red Rector, Mack Magaha, Steve Chapman, John Palmer, and Ronnie Reno.

In 1964, Reno and Smiley ended their partnership. Smiley, who suffered from diabetes as well as from his war wounds, stayed in Roanoke with a daily morning television show. Reno went to Nashville to further his career and eventually teamed up with Bill Harrell. Smiley joined them for several recording sessions. Red Smiley died in 1972; Don Reno survived him by twelve years. His sons, Ronnie, Dale, and

Don Wayne, all superb musicians, continue the bluegrass tradition, playing numerous festivals and other venues.

GILBERT RAY "SPECK" RHODES

Born July 16, 1915, Poplar Bluff, Missouri; died
March 19, 2000, Nashville, Tennessee

Gilbert "Speck" Rhodes's father was a sharecropper who moved the family from farm to farm in Missouri and Arkansas, but he was also a musician who taught his children to play instruments and made his son, little Gilbert, his first banjo. The family group at first played for fun at neighbors' homes but were eventually invited to play at venues where they could make a little money that came in handy in the Great Depression. By 1930, Gilbert, his siblings Perry "Dusty" Rhodes, Ethmer "Slim" Rhodes, and Beatrice "Bea" Rhodes, were good enough to join vaudeville circuits, playing RKO and Orpheum theaters and traveling to thirty states. Speck started doing comedy in 1938, taking a couple of years to develop his character with derby hat, plaid suit, bow tie, and blacked-out teeth. Long before Bob Newhart, he used the technique of doing his comedy as a telephone conversation. For this he developed another character to talk to, Sadie.

Speck Rhodes. Courtesy of Alice J. Rhodes.

From 1938 to 1943 the group played over AWOC in Poplar Bluff, Missouri. For several months in 1943 they entertained over KARK in Little Rock, but their sponsor was seeking a regional network connection and moved them to WMC in Memphis in 1944. The Rhodeses played in Memphis until 1975, including television, beginning in 1947. Bea left the group when she got married in 1943, and Slim died in 1975. Dusty, now in his eighties, has retired twice but is back at work at the White River Hoedown Theater in Branson, Missouri.

While playing WMC, Speck continued to develop his comedy, with Slim as his straight man. He had help from Milton Simon of Simon and Gwynn Advertising agency, who, according to Dusty Rhodes, wrote about 90 percent of Speck's comedy material, including a kind of spinoff of the popular "Lum and Abner Show" called "Skunk Hollow," a skit in the middle of their radio show when Speck and Slim spun yarns. In 1961, Speck was hired as the comedian for the widely syndicated "Porter Wagoner Show." He had known Wagoner when he was a boy in West Plains, Missouri.

Soon the popularity of the show created a full schedule for personal appearances, and audiences expected to see and hear Speck as a popular part of the show. Thus, for the first time he had to leave the family group, which by this time had come to include Dusty's wife and children.

In addition to his travels with Wagoner, Speck played comedy at the "Grand Ole Opry" and the "Renfro Valley Barn Dance," and he also appeared on the "Jimmie Dean Show," Ralph Emery's "Nashville Now," the "Tonight Show," the "Today Show," and Canada's "Ronnie Prophet Show." In 1984, he played a role in the Dolly Parton–Sylvester Stallone movie *Rhinestone*. He made two recordings, *Hello Sadie, This Is Speck* (Picking Post Records) and *Rod's Trip to Chicago* (Hickory Records), both now out of print.

Speck Rhodes continued to perform as a comedian, banjoist, and singer of comedy songs until his death in March 2000. Family and friends talked of his "good clean comedy" and of his sterling character. He is survived by his wife Alice and four children.

The following is an excerpt from one of Speck's monologues at Renfro Valley, Kentucky:

> *I've got a friend in Nashville. He's about five feet tall, and he's going with a girl, and she's six three. Well, they're both a little bit timid and bashful. They were walking down the street, and he was very romantical, and he asked her for a kiss. She said, "I guess it will be all right." So he looked around, said, "We're here in front of this blacksmith shop. You're pretty tall, and I'm short. So I'll hop up on this anvil, and I can do a better job." So he climbed up on that anvil and kissed her good. He got down, and they walked on down the street. He said, "How about another kiss?" She said, "No, I don't think that would be proper right now." He said, "Well, I guess I might as well put this anvil down."*
>
> *I was out at the Opryland park one night. The lights went out, and it was just darker than pitch for fifteen or twenty minutes. One of the guards came walking down through there shining his flashlight on people, and over under a tree there was an old boy standing there with his arm around this girl and kissing her. The policeman said, "Say, Mister, It's against the rules to kiss a woman like that in the park." The guy said, "It's okay, Officer. It's my wife." The policeman said, "Well, excuse me. I didn't know that." The old boy said, "I didn't either until you turned that flashlight on us."*

ORAL "CURLEY" RHODES

Born in Wisconsin, dates of birth and death unknown

Charles Wolfe called Curley Rhodes "the most dexterous bassist on the early Opry" and also the driving force of Pee Wee King's band, the Golden West Cowboys. He also did rube comedy with Pee Wee King as Cicero Sneezeweed, and he and his sister, billed as "Texas Daisy," were a comedic duo, Odie and Jodie.

Rhodes joined Roy Acuff's Smoky Mountain Boys from 1940–42 and did rube comedy with Lonnie Wilson as Odie and Pap. He was in the army during World War II from 1942–46 and was again with Acuff from 1946–55. In addition to playing the bass, he played the guitar and sometimes worked with a washboard equipped with bells and horns. He wore oversized pants with suspenders and a small plug hat.

RIDERS IN THE SKY

> *Douglas Bruce Green (Ranger Doug), born March 20,*
> *1946, Great Lakes, Illinois*
> *Frederick Owen LaBour (Too Slim), born June 3,*
> *1948, Grand Rapids, Michigan*
> *Paul Woodrow Chrisman (Woody Paul), born*
> *August 23, 1949, Nashville, Tennessee*
> *Joey Misculin (the Cowpolka King), born January 6,*
> *1949, Chicago, Illinois*

Riders in the Sky (named for the song by Stan Jones, "Ghost Riders in the Sky") came together in 1977 at Nashville's Herr Harry's Phranks and Steins. The original group included the Country Music Foundation archivist and historian Douglas B. Green, Fred LaBour, and Bill Collins, who left the next year to be replaced eventually by Paul Chrisman, a Ph.D. in theoretical plasma physics. Speaking of Chrisman's doctorate, Green has said, "Riders in the Sky is the most needlessly overeducated band in North America." Green has a master's in literature, and LaBour a master's in wildlife management. These facts may not account much for the quality of their music, but they certainly do account for the sophistication of their comedy. The accordionist Joey Misculin joined the group much later as "Joey the Cowpolka King." He is a session musician who has appeared on many recordings and has produced some of the Riders' later albums.

Doug Green, the son of a Michigan physician, grew up mostly in Bloomfield Hills. He began playing in a bluegrass band in high school, attended Albion College, and graduated from the University of Michigan, where he played in another bluegrass band, by then proficient on the guitar. When visiting Bill Monroe's Bean Blossom Festival, he filled in as a guitarist for Monroe and went on tour with the master. When he moved to Nashville as a graduate student at Vanderbilt University, he played music with several groups. He also became the oral historian and archivist at the Country Music Foundation, where he edited the *Journal of Country Music*. At the Country Music Library, he had access to rare recordings of such groups as the Sons of the Pioneers and the Riders of the Purple Sage. He was enchanted with them and with western music generally and became an authority on it.

Fred LaBour grew up in a Michigan family that loved most kinds of music, and he took piano lessons and learned to play the ukulele and guitar. In high school he

Riders in the Sky. L-R: Joey Misculin, Too Slim, Ranger Doug, and Woody Paul. Courtesy of Doug Green.

joined a rock band. He studied wildlife management at the University of Michigan and also played electric bass in a jazz band. After college, he moved to Nashville to try to make a living writing songs and playing the bass. He learned bluegrass music while performing with the Doug Green Band, and he also played with the bands of Larry Ballard and Ricky Lee. About this time he got hold of an acoustic bass fiddle, and Doug Green introduced him to the songs of Bob Nolan and the Sons of the Pioneers. A cancellation at Herr Harry's Phranks and Steins brought a call from Green asking if he'd like to join him and fill in with a program of western music. He agreed, and this was the beginning of Riders in the Sky.

Paul Woodrow Chrisman describes himself as the authentic hillbilly of the group. Born in a Nashville hospital, he grew up on a farm near Murfreesboro. His father, a schoolteacher, played the banjo, and he and Woody made music with neighbors and even entertained at weekend events. Woody learned to play the fiddle and also banjo and guitar. He listened to old-time country music, especially fiddle tunes, and had little interest in the music his peers were listening to. During the 1960s, he attended the "Grand Ole Opry" and became acquainted with the performers; he even got on stage accompanying Sam McGee and was given a fiddle by Roy Acuff. He enrolled at Vanderbilt University to study engineering and physics but played guitar at local clubs. His advisor, knowing that he played the fiddle, suggested that he take some violin lessons, and he did, not really learning violin but learning techniques. He joined up with Marshall Chapman for gigs around Nashville, playing fiddle, guitar, and banjo. By that time he was listening to the Beatles and other rock and popular musicians. After graduating from Vanderbilt, Woody got a fellowship to the Massachusetts Institute of Technology, where he studied physics. He also got involved in a bluegrass club and found many opportunities to play acoustic music. He learned classical guitar while he was at MIT but later took up the fiddle again and won the New England fiddle championship in 1975. After receiving the Ph.D., he thought of teaching physics, but low pay and some disillusionment with the field led him back to Nashville. He first heard Riders in the Sky at the Old Time Pickin' Parlor, liked them, and became their manager. Eventually he joined the Riders as fiddler and songwriter.

Joey Misculin was born in Chicago; after his parents divorced, he and his mother went to live with her parents, who were of Slovenian origin and listened to all sorts of music, including the "National Barn Dance." His grandfather also played in ethnic bands in the area. Joey's father had brought back an accordion from his service in World War II, and young Joey began at an early age to take music lessons on the instrument. This led to his being asked to play at local functions. He also began listening to recordings of accordion music and sitting in on sessions with Joe Kovich and his Slovenian band. At age twelve, he was playing with a polka band headed by Roman Possedi. Then he joined the band of Frank Yankovic, perhaps the most popular polka band in the country. Yankovic did television shows and traveled widely. On the road the disciplined Joey studied music theory and harmony and practiced on piano and accordion. He played on numerous Columbia, RCA, MCA, and Polygram recordings and produced an album of Yankovic hits that won a Grammy. He later played with a Hawaiian jazz band, and he and his wife opened a nightclub with a dance floor in Cleveland that featured polka and jazz music. In 1986 he moved to Nashville to do studio session work, with the hope of producing records. A fellow musician who admired Joey's musicianship and who also was a fan of Riders in the Sky brought them together. He was asked to back up the Riders on a recording and later to join them for "Riders' Radio Theater." Later he became a regular member of the group.

The Riders' persona and singing style is that of characters in the B-Western movies produced mostly by Hollywood's Columbia and Republic Studios that often featured the superb creative three- and four-part harmonies of the Sons of the Pioneers and later Foy Willing's Riders of the Purple Sage. However, Riders in the Sky have creatively mixed the old Western standards with contemporary numbers, many written by them in the unique Western sound.

Their comedy is a spoof of the B-Westerns, with a gentle poking of fun at the genre even in their monikers: Green as "Ranger Doug, Idol of American Youth"; LaBour as

"Too Slim"; Chrisman as "Woody Paul, King of the Cowboy Fiddlers"; and Misculin as "the Cowpolka King." Their dress, too, is part of the spoof—big sombreros, gaudy shirts with neckerchiefs, fancy boots, and for Too Slim, wooly chaps and a three-dimensional cactus tie ("A Cac-tie"). Their supreme value is in doing everything "in the cowboy way." The movie sidekick, immortalized by such as Smiley Burnett, George "Gabby" Hayes, and Andy Clyde, is a great part of their humor, with Too Slim playing the faithful cook "Sidemeat" as well as other improbable characters. Western movie themes are a large part of their onstage humor, as it was on "Riders' Radio Theater" on National Public Radio.

Humor is a large part of the Riders' high-energy entertainment, with significant looks, knowing smiles (Ranger Doug's and Joey's are dazzlingly toothsome), yodel lessons, Too Slim's imitations of everyone from Louis Armstrong to Lawrence Welk, Western lyrics set to the music of Andrew Lloyd Webber, Sidemeat the sidekick, and much more, all pretty sophisticated for country comedy. The ultimate example of this is a sign next to the horse's skull they include with their stage settings that reads—in Latin—*De Moritius Nil Nisi Bonum* (Nothing good ever comes from dying). Wacky they may be, but rubes they are not.

The Riders' first recordings were on Rounder, beginning in 1979 with *Three on a Trail*. They have eleven recordings on Rounder, five albums on MCA, and three on Columbia. In 1981, they made the first of many appearances on "Austin City Limits," and the next year, they became members of the "Grand Ole Opry." TNN's "Tumble-weed Theater" in 1983 featured them as hosts, running until 1986. Their Rounder *Saddle Pals* was voted Best Independent Children's Album of the Year. In 1987 they switched to MCA to do five albums, three of which received the Wrangler Award from the Cowboy Hall of Fame for best recordings. In 1988, they began "Riders' Radio Theater." In 1993, the Riders were inducted into the Cowboy Hall of Fame. They did three albums for Columbia, before returning to Rounder. "Woody's Roundup" was featured on the soundtrack of Disney's *Toy Story 2* in 2000, the same year the Western Music Association selected them as Group of the Year, and Ranger Doug was a runner-up for Male Vocalist of the Year. The Disney album, *Woody's Roundup Featuring Riders in the Sky*, won a Grammy for Best Musical Album for Children. In accepting, Ranger Doug used a Gene Autry quip to the effect that he didn't deserve it, but he also had tendonitis, which he didn't deserve either.

The Riders' appeal to children confirms their first impression that entertainment based on the folklore of old Western movies featuring good guys winning over bad guys, plenty of sidekick and other humor, and Western musical harmony appeals to an audience of all ages. People young and old and in between have flocked to their two hundred or so live performances a year or faithfully tuned in to "Riders' Radio Theater" over 170 stations and purchased their more than twenty albums, songbooks, and other mementos of Riders in the Sky (www.ridersinthesky.com).

(With credit to Don Cusic, *It's the Cowboy Way! The Amazing True Adventures of Riders in the Sky* [Lexington: University Press of Kentucky, 2003].)

The best advice from Riders in the Sky:

Always drink upstream from the herd.

SPARKY RUCKER

Born James David Rucker Jr., May 7, 1946,
   Knoxville, Tennessee

James "Sparky" Rucker grew up listening to jokes, stories, and songs from members of his family. He soon developed into a gifted musician, as well as a storyteller and humorist. His early education was in segregated schools, and with the rise of the civil rights movement, Rucker sang freedom songs and spoke at rallies and sit-in demonstrations. Early influences were his grandfather and uncles, all Church of God, Sanctified, and preachers with dynamic oral delivery; his parents, aunts, and other relatives; and Bessie Jones, a storyteller from the Georgia Sea Islands.

Rucker graduated from the University of Tennessee and taught art in Chattanooga, but he was also on the road as a festival performer and artist in schools. Eventually he turned to entertainment as a way to make a living, and concerts took him all over the United States and Canada as well as to Europe. He realized early on that he needed variety in performances. As he said:

> You can't just sit there and sing songs all evening. Basically, I find, with my being a big black man, and with everybody [in a white audience] trying to fight off that image, that if I can make them laugh then I've got them for the whole show. Even at a solemn occasion, I use some levity, then give them sad or serious songs. I like to take them from tears to laughter and back again.

Sparky Rucker. Courtesy of
James Rucker.

Many of his narratives are from the black oral tradition, including both Br'er Rabbit stories and those about human tricksters or rebels, such as the folktale character Jack, High John the Conqueror, and those in songs, "Stagolee" and "Wild Bill Jones." His jokes come from his father and other members of his family and from the Appalachian and black humorous traditions.

In recent years, Rucker has performed with his wife Rhonda, who sings and plays various instruments. In addition to their many concerts, they have performed at many major storytelling festivals throughout the United States, including return invitations to the National Storytelling Festival at Jonesborough, Tennessee.

An interest in the Civil War led to a program featuring stories and songs on the subject and an album, *The Blue and the Gray in Black and White* (Flying Fish, 1992). Other albums include *Cold and Lonesome on a Train—Sparky Rucker* (JuneAppal, 1977), *Heroes and Hard Times* (Green Linnet, 1981), and *James "Sparky" Rucker: Patchwork Tales* (Tremont, 1996), and a book of stories, *Sparky and Rhonda Rucker: Done Told the Truth Goodbye* (Tremont, 2006). All are available from www.sparkyandrhonda.com.

Sparky Rucker lives in Maryville, Tennessee, with his wife Rhonda, a physician as well as fellow performer, and their son Jamey.

Sparky learned this story from his father, J. D. Rucker. It is from *Patchwork Tales*), with permission:

> I had a friend—he wanted to be all that he could be, and that was probably all he could be, but he decided he was goin' to join up. He said, "I'm goin' to go all the way—Airborne all the way!" He was ready, man. He was goin' to be a Screamin' Eagle. He was one of those know-it-all guys, can't tell him nothin', "I know it. I know it. I read the manual. I saw John Wayne do it once."
>
> Come the time for his first jump, he was sweatin' like everybody. He said, "I wish I'd a paid attention, man." He was gettin' nervous, there, flyin' in one of 'em big C-130s.
>
> All of a sudden, the jumpmaster got up, and said, "Hook up!" Everybody jumped up and hooked their hooks on the static line there, and they're all shufflin' forward toward the door—red light there, and he was first in line. All of a sudden the green light came on, and he went, "No, I can't remember the name of the Indian I'm supposed to yell, Tecumseh, no that won't work!" And the Jumpmaster, they got orders that if the guy freezes in the door, it can blow the whole stick, and he booted him out the door there. He's fallin' thirty-two feet per second. He said, "I should have been payin' attention. I don't know what to do. Well, seems like you pull the rip-cord." He yanked the chute. He whipped that thing out, "Made in Cherokee, North Carolina, by Japanese." He was really in trouble then. He said, "What am I goin' to do?" He said, "Oh yeah, emergency rip-cord," looked in his hand. It said "Made in Cleveland." "Oh, my God, what am I goin' to do, man?"
>
> About that time, he looked down, and there was a guy floatin' in the sky, comin' up. . . . It was at that point where one was goin' down and one was comin' up, and for a second they were at the same place. He looked over at that guy and said, "Excuse me, do you happen to know anything about parachutes?"
>
> Guy looked at him and said, "No. Do you know anything about gas stoves?"

JOHNNY RUSSELL

Born John Bright Russell, January 23, 1940,
Sunflower County, Mississippi; died July 3, 2001,
Nashville, Tennessee

Johnny Russell, a superb singer and writer of such hit songs as "Act Naturally," "Red-necks, White Socks, and Blue Ribbon Beer," and "Let's Fall to Pieces Together" was also described in publicity material as "a comedian, whose quick wit and rapid-fire humor delights audiences throughout the United States and Europe." He liked the role of comedian and raconteur as much as he did that of singer-songwriter, saying, "I've always loved to laugh, especially at myself. Probably my greatest satisfaction is to see my audiences give off a good belly laugh. It makes me feel great. And that's what entertainment is all about."

Russell lived for a decade in rural Mississippi, listening to the "Grand Ole Opry," and then his family moved to Fresno, California, where he took an active interest in the entertainment industry. After high school, he worked as a radio disc jockey, entered talent contests, and got parts in television dramas. He also recorded one of his own songs, "In a Mansion Stands My Love," that came to the attention of Ralph Emery, who invited him to be on his Nashville radio show. This recording and Johnny also were noticed by Chet Atkins, an executive at RCA's Nashville operation. He persuaded Jim Reeves to record "In a Mansion" on the flip side of "He'll Have to Go," a number-one hit that sold over a million copies.

With this success, Johnny moved to Nashville, but when his recording career didn't take off, he returned to California. After recording with ABC records and continuing to write songs, he sold "Act Naturally" (cowritten with Voni Morrison) to Buck Owens. Owens's 1963 recording went to number one on the country charts, and the song was recorded by the Beatles two years later.

Emboldened, Johnny moved back to Nashville, where he was signed to an RCA contract by Chet Atkins. From 1971 to 1977, he recorded many songs for RCA, includ-ing "Rain Falling on Me" (Top Forty), "Catfish John" (Top Twenty), "The Baptism of Jesse Taylor" (Top Fifteen), and "Hello I Love You" (Top Fifteen). Leaving RCA in 1978, he recorded for Polydor "You'll Be Back Every Night in My Dreams" (Top Twenty-Five, later recorded by the Statler Brothers), and then he recorded a Top Thirty single on Mercury, "How Deep in Love Am I." He also recorded for Sixteenth Avenue, MGM, ABC, Paramount, and OMS.

Among the other artists who recorded Russell's songs were Patti Page, Loretta Lynn, Gene Watson, George Strait, and Dolly Parton, Emmylou Harris, and Linda Ronstadt (with "Making Plans" on their *Trio* album).

Johnny first played comedy with Archie Campbell, and when he had a show of his own, he made comedy an important part. Usually weighing more than 250 pounds, he liked to open his act by inquiring, "Can everybody see me all right?" He was skilled at telling a good joke, and he also did comedy routines with members of his band, in his last years with Charles Lilly, his bass player.

Russell was a guest on many television shows, including "Nashville Now," "Hee Haw," "The Dean Martin Show," "The Dinah Shore Show," "The Phil Donahue Show," "The Bob Braun Show," "NBC Foulups, Bleeps, and Blunders," "Church Street Station," and "Prime Time Country." He continued to perform until he was hospitalized with diabetes-related illnesses. Johnny Russell died on July 3, 2001, in a Nashville hospital after a leg amputation.

Charles Lilly, the son of Everett Lilly (of the Lilly Brothers), related this routine that Johnny Russell liked to do, with Charles as the straight man, at the end of the show when Johnny was pitching his recordings and other things (in this version when they were traveling with Randy Travis):

> *Johnny: Ladies and gentlemen, we've got some products for sale. Randy's selling tapes so he can buy a new horse. He's got thirty-five on his ranch, but he's seen one he really likes, and he has to have it.*
> *Ladies and gentlemen (very solemnly), just before I left Nashville, I stopped by the hospital to see my little brother. Mama was in the room, and she was crying. She was really distraught over the situation. . . . Mama was crying because the doctor says he needs an operation, and without it the chances are he won't make it.*
> *Charles: What's wrong with him, Johnny?*
> *Johnny: His wife has left him and taken his three children with her.*
> *Charles: What's wrong with him, Johnny?*
> *Johnny: We're really not expecting him to make it, so hush.*
> *Charles: What's wrong with him, Johnny?*
> *Johnny: He's sick. Shut up!*
> *Charles: What's wrong with him?*
> *Johnny: He's got a disease. Now shut up!*
> *Charles: What kind of disease?*
> *Johnny: It's the kind that will kill him if they don't buy these pictures and tapes.*
> *Charles: It's got to have a name.*
> *Johnny: It's palsipedia of the punk.*
> *Charles: Palsipedia of the punk? (laughs).*
> *Johnny: Go ahead and laugh. Your brother ain't got it.*
> *Charles: What is it? I never heard of it.*
> *Johnny: Did I tell you it was rare?*
> *Charles: Well, what is it?*
> *Johnny: It's terminal dislocation of the big toe.*
> *Charles: What do you do for that?*
> *Johnny: You call a toe truck!*

RAYE RUTHERFORD

Born July 6, 1934, Clinton, Tennessee

Raye Rutherford became a comedian in 1975, when he joined the Museum of Appalachia Band headed by John Rice Irwin, President of the Museum of Appalachia near Clinton, Tennessee, the site of the annual Tennessee Homecoming. This celebration attracts more than fifty thousand people who enjoy a weekend of music, comedy, art, crafts, and books. Rutherford's comic character is "Cuzin" Raye. He tells jokes between songs when he is emcee for the band. The band does shows for tour and school groups visiting the Museum of Appalachia with its sixty-five acres of historic buildings, artifacts, and the Appalachian Hall of Fame. Rutherford also works for Marshall Andy and His Riders of the Silver Screen Band, and he appears at Knoxville's Bearden Banquet Hall. In addition to comedy, he plays bass and guitar and is a featured singer. The biggest deal for the Museum band was when they performed daily at the World's Fair in Knoxville in 1982.

Raye Rutherford.
Courtesy of Raye Rutherford.

Young Raye took up the fiddle when he was eight but didn't do too well with it, and his mother taught him chords on the guitar. He listened avidly to the "Mid-day Merry-Go-Round" over Knoxville's WNOX as he was growing up and thus heard some of the best musicians and comedians in the business. He played with local bands and went to Nashville in 1966 to play bass with Penny Jay Adams and later with Jimmy Martin and His Sunny Mountain Boys. Then he toured in 1970–71 with Lou Reich's Leatherwood Ramblers out of Cambridge, Ohio, and also played with a country band in California. Returning to Tennessee, he worked in a factory and played at Carl Bean's Big Valley Barn in Clinton. However, it was the Museum of Appalachia Band that gave him his opportunity to do comedy, and he does it with zest.

> *Cuzin Raye: A fellow asked me the other day if I always wake up grumpy. I said, "No, I usually let her sleep."*
>
> *I'm a songwriter, and I usually write in bed. I call it sheet music. The kind of music I play is somewhere between country and rap. I call it Crap. I learned most of my songs at Mother's knee, or some other low joint.*
>
> *David [a band member], him and his wife's got the smartest dog I ever saw. I believe that dog can read. The other day they took him downtown. That dog saw this sign, "Wet Paint," and he did.*

John Rice [Irwin, the owner of the museum] would have been with us this morning, but he fell off his billfold and hurt his back.

FLOYD RAYMOND RUTLEDGE. *See Lennie and Goo Goo*

JUNIOR SAMPLES

Born August 10, 1926, Cumming, Georgia;
died November 13, 1983, Cumming, Georgia

Alvin "Junior" Samples was made famous as a member of the cast of "Hee Haw" beginning in 1969. Before that, with a very limited formal education, Samples had made a living as a sawmill hand and carpenter, and before that, allegedly as a moonshiner. He was a fisherman and a wonderful storyteller and trickster, and he eventually came to the attention of those who appreciate natural talent. This was through a hoax he perpetuated about a giant fish he had caught. Junior's brother had caught a sea bass in the Gulf and brought its head back to Georgia. Junior mounted the head on a board and carried it around in his truck, telling people he had caught a twenty-two-and-a-half-pound bass—the biggest ever landed in Georgia—in a nearby pond. The story spread, and a radio station invited him to tell the story—which had grown through retellings—on the air. There was a huge audience response, and tapes of the radio show were passed around and replayed on other stations. Eventually Chart Records released the recording as "The World's Biggest Whopper," and it reached number fifty-two on the country charts.

Junior was invited by Ralph Emery and Eddie Hill and others for interviews on radio and TV in Nashville, and soon he was known to an even wider audience. Archie Campbell went to Sam Lovullo, the producer of "Hee Haw," and strongly recommended that they hire him forthwith. He arrived for his interview, according to Lovullo in his book, *Life in the Kornfield*, in bib overalls and a different colored sock on each foot, so, he said, he could tell left from right. Lovullo hired him.

On "Hee Haw" he did several spots, the sorry Culhanes, the cornfield sketches, but mainly he shined as the used car salesman with the telephone number BR-549. One of the funniest lines ever on the show was when his secretary, played by the shapely Misty Rowe, showing a customer a car said, "Walk this way," and went swishing off camera. Junior observed, "If I could walk that way, I wouldn't have a car." Part of his humor had to do with his laborious and inaccurate reading of the cue cards. Once in discussing someone having married two women without benefit of divorce, he was told that this was bigamy. He said, somewhat logically, that since there were three people involved, "That's not bigamy; that's trigonometry," except he could never say "trigonometry," and the sketch went on and on with his flubbing of the word. According to Lovullo, it bothered Samples at first that people were laughing *at* him because of his lack of education. But eventually he accepted his role as a country bumpkin.

He did three other recordings on Chart Records: *The World of Junior Samples* (1967), *Bull Session at Bull's Gap* (with Archie Campbell, 1968), and *That's Hee Haw* (1970).

Junior Samples died of a heart attack in 1983. He left his wife Grace and six children.

(With credit to Sam Lovollo with Marc Elliot, *Life in the Kornfield: My Twenty-five Years at "Hee Haw"* [New York: Boulevard Books, 1996].)

SARIE AND SALLY

Edna "Sarie" Wilson, born July 15, 1896;
died June 27, 1994
Margaret "Sally" Waters, born May 2, 1903,
Chattanooga, Tennessee; died November 2, 1967

Long before Minnie Pearl came to the "Grand Ole Opry," Sarie and Sally were doing comedy from its stage as two mountain women, one irascible and disagreeable, the other kinder but scatterbrained. They were actually sisters. Edna Wilson, the older, created the act, and the pair successfully auditioned for a WSM fifteen-minute daytime spot in 1934. On this show they did rural skits created partly out of old vaudeville jokes and sketches. In 1935, they began appearing from time to time on the "Opry," and soon they performed almost every Saturday night. The fan-mail response was good, and they began doing road shows with Pee Wee King, Roy Acuff, Sam and Kirk McGee, and Arthur Smith.

Sarie and Sally. Courtesy of Phillip G. Collins.

Sarie and Sally left the "Opry" in 1939 and went to Hollywood to appear in a movie, *Old Monterey*, with Gene Autry. The sisters split up in 1941, but Edna Wilson continued to perform as a character named Aunt Bunie over WSB in Atlanta and then with Hal Burns and his "Garrett Snuff Varieties" over WMC in Memphis and by transcriptions over radio stations in ten states. Here she did comedy skits with a character named Uncle Ned, played by Milton Simon of the Simon and Gwynne Advertising agency, who wrote scripts for the Garrett Snuff shows. Aunt Bunie was also popular on personal-appearance tours.

(With credit to Charles K. Wolfe, *A Good-Natured Riot: The Birth of the Grand Ole Opry* [Nashville: Country Music Foundation Press and Vanderbilt University Press, 1999].)

TOMMY SCOTT

Born June 24, 1917, near Toccoa, Georgia

Tommy Scott is a musician and singer, a comedian and ventriloquist, and a businessman who got his start in medicine shows and years later revived this form of entertainment with America's Last Real Medicine Show. His stage name during his career was "Ramblin' Tommy Scott," or "Ramblin' Scotty," but in his medicine show he was "Doc" Scott.

Scott learned to play the guitar at an early age, and when Doc M. F. Chamberlain brought his medicine show through upland Georgia in 1936, young Tommy hiked to Toccoa to enter his amateur contest. He won it, and Chamberlain hired him for six dollars a week and a place to sleep in the Dodge truck for which Doc had just traded his mules and wagons. He learned blackface comedy and ventriloquism from Chamberlain. They found some stone carvers who were willing to carve Scott a dummy out of a block of cypress, which they mounted on a Gulf oil can and dressed as a cowboy. He was named Luke McLuke, and he became Scott's lifelong partner in comedy. Doc Chamberlain liked Scott so well that years later when he retired, he gave him the formula for the two patent medicines he was selling—Herb-O-Lac, a laxative, and Snake Oil, a liniment.

When Scott left Chamberlain's show, he sought exposure over radio stations in the Carolinas and Georgia. In 1939, he joined Charlie Monroe's Kentucky Pardners at WHAS in Louisville, and there he met Curley Sechler, who was to become his performing partner for many years. In Louisville he also first met David "Stringbean" Akeman, who also was to be his partner for a while. The Kentucky Pardners went to WWVA's "Mountaineer Jamboree" for a year. Charlie Monroe and his band moved on, but Scott and Sechler stayed at WWVA. He then began playing movie theaters with American United Shows, owned by the Sacks family. Alfred Sacks got Tommy and his band to do some short films that played in theaters before the movie or live

Tommy Scott, with Charles Kuralt. Photo by Frankie Scott, by permission of Tommy Scott, c. 1979, Tommy Scott/Katona Publishing Co./ASCAP.

entertainers came on. This experience got him into a full-length Western movie, *Trail of the Hawk*, based on a novel by James Oliver Curwood with Scott as a coproducer. This led to other short subjects, and in all he did fifty. He also made transcriptions, sponsored by the American Tobacco Company, that were played over several American stations and also the powerful Mexican border stations XEG, XERF, and XERB.

In the early 1940s he did a year and a half on the "Grand Ole Opry." In 1946 he pioneered in making fifty-two shows on film for syndication over the developing medium of television. He and Curley Sechler also did radio shows for the Vim-Herb company of South Carolina as Ramblin' Tommy and Smilin' Bill.

Seeing that the life of most musicians was hard and without great financial reward unless one were a big star, Scott decided to create his own traveling show. At first he had a tent show, but he abandoned it when a big snowfall collapsed his tent. He revived a band he had originated as a youth called the Peanut Band, in which he played a blackface character named Peanut. He also played this same character with Dale Cole as Midnight and Peanut and with David Akeman as Stringbean and Peanut. His show became America's Last Real Medicine Show. By this time, the Food and Drug Administration had put a stop to the practice of herb doctors mixing up their cures in washtubs or bathtubs and bottling them for sale. So Scott arranged for a drug company to supply him with bottles of Herb-O-Lac and Snake Oil. Other changes were that he had to charge admission to make the show a financial success along with the selling of the medicines as a lucrative part of the entertainment. It was reported that purchasers often threw the bottles away at the end of the show, and Doc Scott sent his bandmembers into the bushes to find them for resale. He and his wife Frankie traveled in a modern motor home, more comfortable than Doc Chamberlain's old conveyances. The show was so successful that Scott and his crew stayed on the road as many as 350 days a year up into the 1990s, and part of his success was that he arranged return appearances. He bragged, "I've played every place at least twice." He claims to have played twenty-nine thousand different cities, with twenty-five million tickets sold over more than fifty years on the road.

With the take at the box office he could afford to have more and better talent than the old shows that depended only on medicine sales. He usually had a six-piece band. In addition to his regulars, Frankie did magic tricks and was the comedian Clarabelle; his daughter Sandra did acrobatics; another comedian, Gaines "Old Bleb" Blevins and Blevins's son Scotty Lee, who was born on the show, did comedy and music. Scott called on his other musician buddies, such as Curley Sechler, Clyde Moody, and Stringbean Akeman, to join him when they were free. He also called on the old B-Western stars he met in Hollywood: Colonel Tim McCoy, who was with him for fifteen years; Johnny Mack Brown; Al "Fuzzy" St. John, who died after a performance on Scott's show in Vidalia, Georgia, in 1963; and Sunset Carson. He continued his show with a diminished schedule into this new century. He did thirty shows in 2001, and continued to travel in 2003. He mainly performs now with Randall Franks, Deputy Randy Googe from the TV series "In the Heat of the Night," and Franks has produced a video for PBS about Tommy Scott, "Still Ramblin'," and has made available the entire footage of his film, *The Trail of the Hawk*.

Scott composed over three hundred songs, and he recorded on Bullet, 4-Star, Macy's, and King. In more recent years Cattle Records of Germany, Request, Starday, Old Homestead, Folkways, and others have released his recordings. *At the Medicine Show* (Concorde, 1977) and *Real Medicine Show Songs* (Katona, 1984) give a flavor of entertainment in the old medicine shows. In 1976, Scott's name was placed on the Walkway of Stars at the Country Music Hall of Fame in Nashville.

Tommy's wife Frankie died in 2004. Tommy reports that of the twenty-nine thousand performances he has done over his sixty-year career, Frankie was his performing partner in all but thirty days during their life together. The Scotts had one daughter, Sandra Scott Wentworth, who lives in Toccoa, Georgia. Tommy published the story of his life, *Snake Oil, Superstars, and Me*, in 2007. To order a copy, write Tommy Scott, Box 100, Toccoa, GA 30577.

Here is an excerpt from a routine Ramblin' Tommy and Luke McLuke did on the "Grand Ole Opry":

Tommy: Go ahead now, Luke, say hello to all those good folks out there.

Luke: Hi, folks. How's your liver?

Tommy: Wait a minute! Now stop the smart stuff. How about you singin' all the folks out there a nice song. . . . Tell you what I'll do, I'll give you a dime.

Luke: What-a-ya say?

Tommy: I said I'd give you a dime.

Luke: You owe me thirty cents now!

Tommy: Yeah, I know I owe you thirty cents now. I'll pay you tonight after the show. But my goodness, Luke, you embarrass me up here in front of all these nice people, saying that I owe you thirty cents. Why, the folks will think I don't pay my debts.

Luke: You don't!

Tommy: Go ahead now and tell them the name of your song.

Luke: Name my song, huh, name my song, huh?

Tommy: Yeah, go right ahead now and tell 'em the name of your song.

Luke: Thirty cents!

Tommy: Now listen here, smart alec, now for goodness sakes, let that thirty cents drop, brother!

Luke: You let it drop, brother. I'll pick it up!

Tommy: Now, listen here, you shouldn't talk to me like that, and if you don't stop this smart talk, I'm goin' to carry you back and put you in the box!

Luke: I want my daddy!

Tommy: Daddy or no. . . .

Luke: I want my daddy! Whaa whaa whaa!

Tommy: Wait a minute. Stop your cryin'. Daddy or no daddy, I'm goin' to put you in the box if you don't stop your smart talk!

Luke: Want my daddy, want my daddy, want my daddy!

Tommy: All right, smart alec, will you please tell me who your daddy is?

Luke: What-a-ya say?

Tommy: Will you please tell me who your daddy is?

Luke: Roy Acuff! (Prolonged applause)

BOB SHELTON

Born Robert Attlesey, July 4, 1909, Reilly Springs,
Texas; died 1986

Bob Shelton sang with his brother Joe as the Shelton Brothers (assuming their mother's maiden name), played guitar, fiddle, ukulele, and bass with the Sunshine Boys and the Lone Star Cowboys. He played rube comedy with these groups and on his own after Joe Shelton retired. The Shelton Brothers were one of several popular "brother" duets of the 1930s, and they played mostly over KWKH in Shreveport, WFAA and WAP in Dallas–Fort Worth, and WWL in New Orleans. They sometimes worked with the Tennessee fiddler Curley Fox and the Alabama musician-comedian Lew Childre. Bob led the band of Jimmie Davis during the 1940s, and the brothers traveled and performed with him during his gubernatorial campaign of 1944.

The Sheltons recorded for Bluebird in 1933 as the Lone Star Cowboys (including Leon Chappelear). In 1935 they began recording for Decca as the Shelton Brothers, including some of their most popular numbers, such as "Deep Elem [Elm] Blues" and "Just Because." Their 150 or so sides for Decca were at the top of their bestselling list.

As time went on, their band grew in numbers, electric instruments were added, and their sound reflected the influence of swing and jazz.

After Joe left the entertainment business in the early 1950s, Bob continued with his first love, comedy, into the 1970s, mostly on Dallas's "Big D Jamboree" and Baton Rouge's "Louisiana Hayride." As a comedian, he dressed in overalls and a flop hat.

HOMER LEE "PAPPY" SHERRILL. *See the Hired Hands*

SHOTGUN RED. *See Steve Hall*

THE SKILLET LICKERS

> *James Gideon Tanner, born June 6, 1885, Thomas*
> *Bridge, Georgia; died May 13, 1960, Dacula,*
> *Georgia*
> *Riley Puckett, born May 7, 1884, Alpharetta,*
> *Georgia; died July 13, 1946, East Point, Georgia*
> *Clayton McMichen, born January 26, 1900,*
> *Allatoona, Georgia; died January 3, 1970,*
> *Battletown, Kentucky*
> *(Other musicians played with the Skillet Lickers,*
> *including Fate Norris, Lowe Stokes, Arthur Tanner*
> *[Gid's brother], Gordon Tanner [Gid's son], Bert*
> *Layne, Ted Hawkins, Red Jones, Slim Bryant,*
> *K. D. Malone, and Tom Dorsey.)*

Columbia released eighty-two sides of the Skillet Lickers between 1926 and 1931. Most of their recordings were of their lively fiddle music and songs and ballads, but they also recorded skits about backwoods folks advertised by Columbia as "Entertaining Novelty Records." On these, the Skillet Lickers recorded material much like that in minstrel and medicine shows interspersed with music. Their bestselling skit, "A Corn

Licker Still in Georgia," was on fourteen 78 rpm sides. Other popular skits were "The Medicine Show," "Kickapoo Joy Juice," and "A Bee Hunt on Hell-for-Sartin Creek."

Gid Tanner was the main comedian of the group and loved doing the skits on records as well as comedy in their personal appearances. Clayton McMichen, however, detested the corny rural humor and was not too fond of the old rural tunes. McMichen was considerably younger than other members of the group, and he wanted to play what he called "modern music." He left to form his own bands, but he continued to play and record with the Skillet Lickers from time to time. Even though McMichen went on to play his modern music, including swing, jazz, and big band music, it was the old country sound of the Skillet Lickers that sold the best. Two recordings are available from Rounder: *Gid Tanner and His Skillet Lickers—with Riley Pucket and Clayton McMichen* (1973) and *Gid Tanner and His Skillet Lickers: The Kickapoo Medicine Show* (1977).

ANTHONY SLATER. *See Smilie Sutter*

LARRY SLEDGE

Born 1952, Mount Vernon, Illinois

Larry Sledge got into music at the age of ten when he began playing with a great-uncle's dance band—mandolin, guitar, bass, whatever was left. He grew up on a farm in southern Illinois, finished high school, and did one year of college before he was drafted into the army in 1972. He was stationed at Fort Campbell on the Kentucky-Tennessee border, and a kindly commanding officer allowed him to play music on weekends in Nashville at such places as the Bluegrass Inn and the Old-time Pickin' Parlor. Larry even extended his enlistment for a year to continue playing in Nashville.

While he was still in the army, his cousin, Butch Gregory, began playing at Silver Dollar City in Branson, Missouri, and got Larry a job there. With leave time he left the army early and joined him. It was in Branson that he began doing comedy as well as music. He remembered, "The old country shows in Branson had a lot of comedy mixed in with the music. I'd sing 'The Old Maid's Last Hope' and 'I'm the Man That Rode the Mule around the World.' Used to be they let us do our own thing. Now they're more into productions, with every show being the same." He qualifies this statement, however, saying that in the last few years, they've been encouraged to go back to the old ways of doing their shows, informally with the old songs and comedy in between.

When he was playing in Branson, he spent each winter in Nashville, playing with various groups, including James Monroe's bluegrass band. He also worked on Bill Monroe's farm and helped to construct Monroe's log-cabin home. In 1983, Larry left Branson to travel for two years with Norman Blake, playing mandolin.

When Grandpa and Ramona Jones established their Country Music Dinner Theater in Mountain View, Arkansas, Larry joined them in 1984 as an instrumentalist,
singer, and announcer. This gave him the opportunity to study with the old master,
Grandpa Jones. Ramona put him to telling jokes during his announcing chores, especially when Grandpa was not there. Larry has continued to play at special events with
Ramona and Alisa Jones after Grandpa's death. He has also mastered Grandpa's banjo
style and includes a few rousing numbers in their programs.

Larry is married to the former Brenna Stephens, and they have three girls and a
boy. They live out in the country between Springfield and Highlandville, Missouri.
Larry continues to play and do comedy at Silver Dollar City.

> *Before I sang "I'm the Man That Rode the Mule around the World," I'd say that I rode a
> mule to school when I was a boy, and one night I rode him to a pie supper, and about halfway
> through the program I went out to check on my mule, and somebody had slipped around
> and painted my mule green! I went flyin' back in there and I said, "Would the man who
> painted my mule green stand up?" He stood up, and he was seven feet tall, and his knuckles
> was still draggin' the ground. He said, "I'm the man who painted your mule green. What
> d' you think you're goin' to do about it, you little pipsqueak?" I said, "Well, buddy, the first
> coat's dry, and he's ready for the second one."*

ANDREW JOHN SMIK JR. *See Doc Williams*

RED SMILEY. *See Reno and Smiley*

ARTHUR AND RALPH SMITH

*Arthur Smith, born April 1, 1921, Clinton,
    South Carolina*
*Ralph Smith, born 1924, Camden, South Carolina;
    died 1983, Charlotte, North Carolina*

The Smith brothers grew up in Kershaw, South Carolina, a cotton-mill town where
Arthur learned to play the trumpet in a jazz band headed by his father. Arthur later
formed another jazz band that included Ralph and another brother, Sonny. Arthur
became an accomplished guitarist but also learned to play other instruments, including the fiddle, tenor banjo, and mandolin. The jazz format didn't work for the group
in programs over Spartanburg's WSPA, and so they moved toward a country sound,
eventually becoming the Carolina Crackerjacks. They recorded for Bluebird in 1938,

but they disbanded when members of the band went into service in World War II. Arthur worked for a time at WBT in Charlotte before he joined the navy.

After the war, Arthur returned to Charlotte, where he worked as an instrumentalist with the Briarhoppers and the Tennessee Ramblers on WBT. In 1945, he recorded his signature composition, "Guitar Boogie," for Super Disc. When MGM bought the master and released the tune on its label in 1948, it became a super hit. He also had a Top Ten country hit with "Banjo Boogie" in 1948.

Arthur reformed the Crackerjacks after the war, including Ralph and Sonny Smith. By 1951 the Crackerjacks had a television show over WBT-TV that eventually was syndicated in fifty-six cities. The show featured Arthur's instrumental wizardry, the Crossroads Quartet, Ralph as a musician and comedian, and Tommy Faile as the lead singer, as well as the comedian Cousin Fudd. This show led to traveling package shows over the country as well as abroad.

There was plenty of comedy in the Crackerjack shows. Arthur did comedy songs, such as his 1963 "Tie My Hunting Dog Down, Jed," "Lasses," and "Foolish Questions." Ralph wrote most of the comedy that featured him and Cousin Fudd, including their "Counselors of the Airwaves" program. In this segment, both men dressed in tasseled academic hats and gowns and answered questions sent in by the audience to which they gave comical answers. Arthur commented on humor in entertainment: "Comedy in country music is just something you could not do without. You had to work your concerts around entertaining people. It added variety. A joke or situation that could lighten everything about the show was just a must. It still is, although some of the present superstars don't realize that."

Arthur credited Ralph with being "one of the top country comedians." He went on to say, "We played all over the world, and he was always the guy who kept us going on long-playing trips to the Holy Land or Italy or wherever. His humor was international, and he was the greatest at it. He kept the group alive anticipating what we were going to do."

Arthur and Don Reno composed and recorded "Feuding Banjos" in 1955 for Monument Records, with Arthur on tenor banjo and Reno on five-string. This tune was featured as "Dueling Banjoes" in the movie *Deliverance* without credit to Smith and Reno as the composers. Smith sued and won a credit line for him and Reno and back royalties.

In the 1970s, Arthur Smith set up a recording studio in Charlotte, where he recorded himself and his band and numerous other groups for various labels. He also did six video shows distributed over PBS, using musicians who had been associated with the Crackerjacks and other Charlotte groups through the years. He has other business interests as well. Ralph died in 1983, but Arthur continued to do two or three concerts a month, usually with Tommy Faile as lead singer, until Faile's death in 1998. Smith has done radio and television advertisements for an automobile dealership for over seventeen years. He usually tells a humorous story before giving the sales pitch.

Ralph (in the pose of a revival preacher): Last night I spoke on "What in the World Is Wrong?" and tonight I'm goin' to speak on "What Is Wrong with the World?" I want to tell you this much—what is wrong with the world is these little old shirt-tail girls with them tight skirts on and that head full of teased-up hair! That's exactly the trouble! Their head looks like a stump full of granddaddies [daddy longlegs]! And them skirts—some of 'em cut to the very kneecaps. Oh ho, I'm tellin' you . . . I get on the street sometimes, and here'll come a whole bunch of 'em walking down the street in front of me. I say, "Get you behind me, Satan—AND PUSH!"

FRED E. SMITH

*Born August 31, 1924, Walnut, North Carolina;
died June 4, 2006, Walland, Tennessee*

Fred Smith was born on a farm in Madison County, celebrated for its traditional singers and musicians and also for its storytellers. He was a professional musician but also a comedian, and much of his comedy is based on the humor he learned growing up and from the old medicine shows that set up near his home when he was a boy. He remembered:

They'd sell the Big Chief Tonic and Scalf's Indian River Medicine. The first one I went to was in Mars Hill, in a parking lot. They had good shows. They'd have music, and they did funny stuff. It'd grow every night, and the grand finale would be Saturday, and they'd pack them in. There wasn't no other entertainment back then. Everybody'd come to see it. I learned from them.

He remembered also listening to the radio comedians from the "Grand Ole Opry" and from the WJJD "Suppertime Frolic." "My daddy'd say, 'Now boys, you'd better save your battery if you're going to listen to the "Grand Ole Opry."' Uncle Dave Macon, Rod Brasfield and Kentucky Slim were my favorites."

Fred's family moved to Asheville after he had finished high school. There he was reunited with Red Rector from Madison County. Their fathers had fox-hunted together, and they had grown up together, although Red was five years younger than Fred. They performed in string bands over WISE, WWNC, and WLOS in Asheville and in 1943 went with J. E. and Wade Mainer to New York to play background music for the BBC show "On the Chisholm Trail."

Red and Fred went to Knoxville in 1946 with Carl Story's Rambling Mountaineers. Smith's career as a comedian took off when he and Red Rector teamed up first as Herman and Thurman the Scrub Brothers, and then as Red and Fred on the "Midday Merry-Go-Round" over Knoxville's WNOX. They perfected their comedy act on the "Merry-Go-Round" and the "Tennessee Barn Dance." For a time Red and Fred with a forlorn hound interviewed (on tape) passengers arriving at Knoxville's Greyhound bus station for broadcast. They later worked on the supermarket tycoon

Cas Walker's country shows on WROL-TV and WBIR-TV. Fred would pick up the twelve- or thirteen-year-old Dolly Parton and give her a ride to WBIR when she was beginning to perform.

Red and Fred often went their separate ways. Fred played music and did comedy with Archie Campbell on WROL's "Country Playhouse Show," and then he went back to the "Mid-day Merry-Go-Round." Red followed Carl Story from station to station and also played with Reno and Smiley, but he rejoined Fred at the "Merry-Go-Round," and they stayed there until the show closed in 1958. Then Red left again to play with Hylo Brown, and Fred played for ten years at the Boots Randolph Club in Printer's Alley in Nashville and toured with Randolph.

When Randolph's club closed in 1994, Fred joined Phil Campbell at the "Hee Haw" show that Phil's father Archie had started in Gatlinburg, Tennessee. When that show was sold, Fred played the Comedy Barn in Pigeon Forge for several years, using many of the old "Merry-Go-Round" routines and several of his own, including his "James J. James" routine. In recent years he has occasionally performed with Tim White and his bluegrass band, the VW Boys, over WGOC in Blountville, Tennessee.

Red and Fred recorded an excellent musical album on County, *Songs from the Heart of the Country: Red and Fred* (1969), and the Comedy Barn in Pigeon Forge produced *The Comedy of Fred Smith*.

Fred Smith. Courtesy of Tim Wilshire and Rhonda Harbison.

In 1999, Fat Dog Records (PO Box 750, Blountville, TN 37617-0750) released a CD, *The Comedy of Fred E. Smith: Tales From Spivey Mountain*, and another in 2000, *The Comedy of Fred E. Smith with Guest Archie Campbell*.

The following excerpt was recorded probably in the 1980s at a performance by Red and Fred as an example of a routine they did on the "Mid-day Merry-Go-Round":

> Red: Somebody was askin' before the show tonight about Spivey Mountain. They really want to know if you're from Spivey Mountain.
> Fred: Well, yes, that's where I originated. I was born at an early age. Spivey Mountain, that's a little town in North Carolina, with a population of about five hundred.
> Red: Well, it is small, isn't it?
> Fred: It never gets no smaller, and it never gets no larger, because ever' time a new baby is born, somebody leaves town!

Red: Judging from your hard luck, Fred, you must have come from a large family.

Fred: Yeah, there was nineteen of us, Red.

Red: Nineteen, altogether.

Fred: No, just one at a time.

Red: Oh, I see.

Fred: There was nine boys and nine girls.

Red: Nine boys and nine girls? That only makes eighteen. You said there was nineteen. Where's the nineteenth one?

Fred: That's the stork. See, he liked to live close to his work. . . . And poor! We was poor as whipporwills when I was growin' up. . . . I remember one summer back there in Spivey Mountain, we didn't have nothin' to eat but turnip greens and poke sallet the whole summer long.

Red: That's terrible.

Fred: I eat so many turnip greens and poke sallet that my mama used to take strings and soak 'em in coal oil and tie them around my legs to keep the cutworms from cuttin' me down! They'll work on ye.

Red: You have had your problems.

Fred: Red, we's poor as whipporwills. We'd bite anything that wouldn't bite back.

Red: You was really hungry, then.

Fred: Oh, I'm tellin' you. Many a mornin' I'd eat popcorn for breakfast, drink water for dinner, and swell up for supper!

LEON SMITH

Born March 25, 1922, Roswell, Georgia

Leon Smith, a talented dancer, bass player, featured singer, and comedian, was a member of Pop Eckler's Young'uns on the "Cross Roads Follies" on WSB in Atlanta beginning about 1936. He played a comic character called Little Brother and also danced the buck and wing. In addition, he worked with Uncle Ned (Gene Stripling) and His Texas Rangers on WSB. He won the national buck-and-wing dance contest probably in 1938 at a fiddler's contest set up in the City Auditorium by Pop Eckler.

Smith's career was cut short by World War II. He landed at Normandy and was in an anti-aircraft unit attached to the Ninth Air Force. Apparently he never pursued his musical and comedic career after the war. He was still living in Atlanta in 2000.

RALPH SMITH. *See Arthur and Ralph Smith*

RAYMOND DEWAYNE SMITH. *See Geezinslaw Brothers*

ELWOOD SMOOCH. *See Billy Baker*

MIKE SNIDER

Born May 30, 1960, Gleason, Tennessee

William Michael Snider grew up on the family farm in West Tennessee and has said he might still be there raising hogs and corn if, with his considerable picking talent, he hadn't won the National Banjo Championship in 1983. He admits to being the class clown in high school, but he never aimed to be a comedian. He got his first banjo on his sixteenth birthday, had a real affinity for it, won all the local and regional banjo contests, and then won the National Banjo Championship when he was twenty-two. This led to a guest spot on the "Grand Ole Opry" on January 21, 1984. Being a polite southern boy, he invited his friends and family around Gleason to come hear him, and most of them showed up. The king of country music himself, Roy Acuff, introduced him, and the mayor presented him with the key to the city of Nashville. His performance brought four standing ovations.

Ralph Emery was impressed by this hometown loyalty as well as the Snider talent and invited him on his "Nashville Now" show on TNN. When Snider started talking to Emery, the audience started laughing, at his wit surely, but mostly at his slow West Tennessee drawl. This appearance on "Nashville Now" got him on "Hee Haw" as a guest in 1989 and as a regular in 1990 for seven years. In June 1990, he was inducted as a member of the "Opry," presented by Minnie Pearl. The former Tennessee commissioner of agriculture and a popular humorist himself, L. H. "Cotton" Ivy, sheds some additional light on Mike's beginnings as a humorist. When Ivy ran for the Tennessee legislature, he hired Mike to play the banjo at political meetings:

> I would talk on the back of a pickup truck, and he would play the banjer. He wouldn't say anything. Finally, I said, "Mike, after three songs that bluegrass all sounds alike." He was always funny, and I said, "You need to talk." We were in my pickup when he wrote his first forty-five-minute set. He went out to Texas and worked with Bob Murphey—one of the funniest men I've ever met, one of the true comics in America. I promised Mike a job grading hogs to make it possible for him to come to Nashville, but he never graded any hogs because he went on the "Opry."

Snider has commented that "Hee Haw" was a kind of fantasy land where people are happy all of the time. Like a lot of other performers, he saw comedy as a way to allow people to escape from their daily problems for a little while. He quickly learned what wasn't instinctive about comedy from the other regulars on the show, such as Grandpa Jones, George Lindsey, and Gordy Tapp. Grandpa Jones also taught Snider—a three-finger picker—to frail the banjo in the old style that Grandpa had learned from Cousin Emmy Carver.

Snider now has a wonderful band (that has included Bobby Clark, Charlie Cushman, Blake Williams, and Shad Cobb); they play, and he sings. Doc Watson recently commented, "That's the best old-time band I've heard in a long time." Snider tells a few jokes and just acts natural. He has an authenticity that appeals to his audiences. He says his audience expects him just to be himself.

His enthusiasm for comedy, and his skill, brought him the honor of being one of the Top Five Comedians for twelve years at the TNN Music City News Awards. He hosted TNN's "Fairs and Festivals" in 1989, did regular shows at the Opryland theme park before it closed down, and he logged over 150 performances on "Nashville Now" and "Music City Tonight." Currently he appears regularly on the "Grand Ole Opry," where his comedy is much needed with the death of Minnie Pearl and Jerry Clower, and he does about fifty shows a year around the country. He has recorded a dozen albums, including *Mike Snider String Band*, *Mike Snider Comedy Songs*, *Live at the Station Inn*, *Gospel Harmonica*, *Old Time Favorites*, *Puttin' on the Dog*, and *Live at the Grand Ole Opry* (cassette). He also has a video, *Mike Snider on Stage and Down Home* (all available at PO Box 610, Gleason, TN 38229). He still lives in Gleason with his wife Sabrina and their two children, Katie Lynn and Blake.

ROBBY SPENCER

Born January 2, 1978, St. Petersburg, Florida

Robby Spencer was born outside Tennessee, but his family moved to Bristol before he was a month old, and he's been in the Volunteer State ever since. The local music scene influenced him, and he learned to play the banjo, guitar, and mandolin and learned a lot of the old songs at an early age. At East Tennessee State University, he majored in speech communication. The university had started a program in bluegrass and country music, and he got involved in that. He was a member of the ETSU Bluegrass Band for four years, and in 1998 he was the first recipient of the Benny Sims Memorial Scholarship for Bluegrass and Country Music. When he graduated, he began performing at various venues as a solo artist, but he also organized a band called Robby Spencer and His Grandchildren.

As a solo artist, he has appeared with the VW Boys from nearby Blountville and other groups. He has performed at the Carter Fold in Hiltons, Virginia; the "Renfro Valley Barn Dance" in Kentucky; the Bristol Sessions Seventy-fifth Anniversary Celebration at Mountain Empire Community College, Big Stone Gap, Virginia; "Opry

Star Spotlights" on WSM Radio in Nashville; Seed-Time on the Cumberland Festival in Whitesburg, Kentucky; Dollywood in Pigeon Forge, Tennessee; Uncle Dave Macon Days in Murfreesboro, Tennessee; and the All-American Cities Conference in Philadelphia.

Before all this, Spencer had been a fan of the great musician-comedian Grandpa Jones and learned to play his frailing style of banjo and also learned his songs and routines. He liked Grandpa because he thought he did complete entertainment, singing, playing the banjo and guitar, and doing comedy. "He was my idol, my role model," Robby says. And although he started out doing an imitation of Grandpa Jones, Spencer has evolved his own style of entertainment. He still does a tribute to Grandpa and has even written a touching memorial song about him, "The Old Man from the Mountains Has Gone On," but now he does a more generic "old man" character that he calls Grandpappy Spencer. He tells jokes and stories but usually as he introduces a song, saying something like, "This is a song I learned from an old uncle of mine. He was so mean that when he went down the street, even the sewers backed up." He still performs a lot of Grandpa's jokes and comedy and novelty songs, such as "I'm My Own Grandpa," "Just a Bowl of Butterbeans," "Old Rattler," and "Old Dan Tucker."

Robby Spencer. Courtesy of Robby Spencer.

Robby produced a tribute to Grandpa Jones on video, now out of print, but the CD version is still available, as well as a DVD recording of his own music. He now has his own TV show on local cable, "Robby Spencer's Adventures," and DVDs of his first season are for sale. In addition, he has pioneered in budget-priced five-dollar CDs (PO Box 741, Bluff City, TN 37618, www.robbyspencer.com).

One of Robby's routines on the bass player Teddy Helton:

Teddy Helton called me up this afternoon and said he didn't know if he was going to be able to make the show tonight. I asked him what was wrong, and he said he was constipated. I asked him if he had taken anything for it, and he said, "I've tried everything I know to take, and ain't nothin' worked." I asked him, "Have you tried prunes?" He said, "Yeah, and they didn't work a bit." So I asked him, "How many did you eat?" He got real quiet for a minute, and then he said, "You mean you're supposed to eat them?"

JIM STAFFORD

Born James Wayne Stafford, January 16, 1944,
Eloise, Florida

"Jim Stafford is a great comedian," said John Hartford. "He has a great show in Branson, and he is brilliant. He crosses all the borders. He's country, but he's also just as sophisticated as you want to hear, and he really operates on many different levels."

Jim Stafford descended from Tennessee country musicians, but his parents had migrated south for a warmer climate. Jim early learned the guitar and played in a rock band hopefully called the Legends while he was in high school. This band had the distinction of having three musicians that made a name for themselves: Stafford; Kent

Jim Stafford. Courtesy of
Ann Stafford.

Lavoie, better know as Lobo; and Gram Parsons. After high school, already a good guitar picker—Chet Atkins had become an idol—Stafford moved to Nashville hoping to become a sideman, and he dreamed of being a member of the "Grand Ole Opry." He briefly backed Bill Carlisle on guitar at the "Opry," but noticing that the guy who made the real money was out front, Stafford gave up the idea of being a sideman and moved to Atlanta. There he developed his comedy style and began writing novelty songs. By the early 1970s, his comedy and music had melded into a unique presentation, and he began getting gigs, including sets at Washington's Cellar Door and Chicago's Mr. Kelley's.

His first record was *Swamp Witch* in 1973 on MGM Records, and it made pop Top Forty. In 1974 came *Spiders and Snakes*, which was number three on the pop charts for twenty-six weeks and reached Top Forty on the country charts. Next came *My Girl Bill* (pop Top Three, country Top Seventy); *Wildwood Weed* (pop Top Ten, country Top Sixty), and *Your Bulldog Drinks Champagne* (pop Top Twenty-five). He later recorded for Polydor, Warner Brothers, Town House, and Columbia.

His hits brought Stafford to the attention of people in the entertainment world. The "Jim Stafford Show" ran during the summer of 1975 on ABC-TV. He appeared in numerous music specials and variety and talk shows. He cohosted the ABC-TV show "Those Amazing Animals" with Burgess Meredith and Priscilla Presley, and he also hosted fifty-six episodes of "Nashville on the Road." He has been on the "Tonight Show" a total of twenty-six times. He was producer and head writer as well as a regular performer on "The New Smothers Brothers Comedy Hour" on CBS in 1988–89. He also appeared in the Clint Eastwood movie *Any Which Way But Loose*, for which he wrote "Cow Patti." He received a gold record for his contribution to the Disney film *The Fox and the Hound*, for which he wrote three songs.

After doing nightclubs and comedy clubs all over the country, Stafford opened a theater in Branson, Missouri, in 1990. Since then, he has entertained enthusiastic crowds there year-round. His show is sophisticated and yet with a country flavor (and a dash of the evangelical tone of Brother Dave Gardner) with lights, sound effects, things falling on stage or guitars or what-not being wafted off the stage in a surreal show highlighted by Stafford's comic wit and his pretty amazing guitar licks. He also plays ragtime banjo, piano, organ, harmonica, and fiddle. His signature jokes revolve around his revulsion of Chihuahua dogs. He is a talented singer, also, and his novelty songs, with sound and sight effects, go over very well. He discovered and developed a process for rear-screen 3-D and then produced and wrote a 3-D virtual thrill ride for his show on a fourteen-by-forty-two-foot screen, the only such presentation by a single entertainer. While the show has other talented musicians, Stafford is the main show.

The Jim Stafford Theater of Branson has produced a video of a live performance, *Jim Stafford—Live and Kickin'!* and a live CD (www.jimstafford.com). He can also be heard on *Not Just Another Pretty Foot* (MGM, 1975) and *Jim Stafford* (Polydor, 1987).

Stafford was married for a short time to Bobbie Gentry, and they have one son. He and his second wife Ann and their two children, Sheaffer (who plays five instruments in the show) and Georgia Garland (who is inclined toward comedy), live at Table Rock, outside Branson. Both children have been on stage since they were ten days old, and the whole family is involved in the work of the Jim Stafford Theater. Stafford is also involved in promoting the civic, charitable, and community life of the Branson area. He has twice received the Area Appreciation Award, and he and Ann have also won the Ambassadors Award from the local chamber of commerce. In addition, Stafford has hosted, cowritten, and produced the nationally syndicated radio show "Branson USA."

The following is from the video *Jim Stafford—Live and Kickin'!* (1993), with permission:

> *Stafford: Hey, ladies, do you know what men say? Men say women cannot read a road map. Have you heard that? Fellow the other day asked his wife where they're supposed to be, and she said, "Two inches over and down."*
>
> *Men, on the other hand, will not stop for rest rooms, will they? Will they stop for directions? No. If he's lost and making good time, he's happy. It's true, isn't it? Why is this, ladies? Could it be that us fellows are nothing but momentum with no target? We have no idea what we want. We just want to be in charge of whatever it is. Give us a car, and we'll drive until we drop. Give us a channel changer, and we'll click it until you hide it, won't we, girls?*
>
> *Somebody at intermission the other day told me, she says, "You know, my cat and my husband are about the same, but I think I like my cat a little better." I said, "What do you*

mean?" She said, "Well, neither one of them listens to me when I talk, both lay around on the couch all day, and both of them stay out half the night." I say, "Why do you like the cat better?" She says, "The cat don't miss the litter box!"

PETE STAMPER

Born Wallace Logan Stamper, September 25, 1930,
Dawson Springs, Kentucky

Pete Stamper attended elementary and secondary schools in Charleston, in western Kentucky. When he was fourteen, he and his friends Clarence Williams and Russ Melton formed a band, with two guitars and a mandolin. They wrote to WHOP in Hopkinsville, and without an audition they were given a 6:00 AM daily show. Pete describes their first personal appearance at Walnut Grove at a two-room schoolhouse: "A fellow named James Russell was to be the comedian. We'd listened to [James] Goober Buchanan on WHOP in the early 1940s, so we were well acquainted with his comedy material. Neighbors came from miles around and filled that little place. James looked out through the curtain and positively and tee-totally could not go on as the comic. So out of frustration I said I would. I intended to do the comedy because we were obligated to do the show, and then I'd quit. But it went over so good I wouldn't have given it up for nothing after that."

But Stamper's road to country music and comedy was not easy. He also worked in a sawmill, in a western Kentucky coal mine, and sold insurance. His real chance came after two years in the army in 1948–49. He and Clarence Williams were encouraged to play at the "Renfro Valley Barn Dance," and they performed twice as Waldo and Clarence, a Homer and Jethro type of program with Pete on mandolin and Clarence on guitar. Pete was called back into the army to be sent to Korea in 1950. John Lair promised him a job when he was discharged. In 1952, he and Williams were hired by

Pete Stamper.
Courtesy of Pete Stamper.

Lair. He was by then writing his own comedy material and some songs as well, later to be recorded by such singers as Red Foley, Porter Wagoner, Smiley Burnette, Reno and Smiley, and Bill Anderson. His recording of his composition "Cheva-Kiser-Olds-Mo-Laca-Stude-War-Linco-Baker" (on DOT with Floyd Kramer on piano), about a car made from the parts of cars of several makes, came out before Johnny Cash's better-known similar song but didn't catch on, and when he sang it later people thought he was imitating Cash.

At Renfro Valley he worked as a disc jockey and later manager of their radio station, WRVK. He also wrote for the *Renfro Valley Bugle*. He was encouraged by John Lair to do comedy on the "Barn Dance." He said, "Lair thrived on comedy and novelty. His daughter has a show bill at London [Kentucky] that shows five comedians and one solo artist." Stamper played the bashful country boy in an ill-fitting suit giving the news from back home and directions to where he lived. This routine grew out of one of his articles for the *Bugle*. His comedic manner has been compared to that of Herb Shriner, the late Indiana radio and television humorist.

In 1954, discouraged about the music business and thinking of quitting, Pete learned through Red Foley's daughter, Betty Cummins, that Red was leaving the "Grand Ole Opry" for the "Ozark Jubilee" and that he needed a comedian. Betty took him to Nashville to see Red. Foley told him that he had already hired Ferlin Husky to do his "Simon Crum" character, but he asked Pete to audition anyway. "I was tee-totally scared to death," Pete remembered. "I had a routine that had been going over good at Renfro Valley—the directions to get to my house. When I got through, Red and his wife were down on the floor laughing, and he said we might work something out. He took me on a two-week tour—twenty-five dollars a day out of his pocket. Red was my idol."

Red persuaded the managers of the "Jubilee" to hire Pete, and he did his bashful country-boy humor, first on radio and then on the ABC-TV show when it started in 1955. He was emboldened to call his girlfriend Minnie Lee Taylor back in Kentucky and invite her to come out and "be the wife of a country star," and she did. He stayed with the "Jubilee" until 1957. While on the show, Stamper had been traveling with Porter Wagoner, and when Wagoner left the "Jubilee" for Nashville, Pete joined him there in 1957 and worked for him in road shows. Through Wagoner, he also met Dolly Parton, and he traveled with her in the late 1970s. John Lair's daughter, Ann Lair Henderson, invited Stamper back to Renfro Valley in 1987 for a full-time job. He worked again at WRVK and also put together a vaudeville-type show, inviting in such comedians as Speck Rhodes, Lonzo and Oscar, Jerry Isaacs, Judge Ray Corns, Bun Wilson, and James "Goober" Buchanan, whom he had first heard doing comedy on the radio station WHOP in Hopkinsville.

Pete has been at Renfro Valley ever since, through several owners. He put together the "Renfro Valley Jamboree" in a second barn in 1989, with his and Bun Wilson's comedy running throughout the show. He edited the *Renfro Valley Bugle*, was manager of the radio station, and with the development of the new entertainment complex, he has also been program manager. He serves also as emcee and still does comedy on the "Barn Dance." He, Bun Wilson, and Betty York also do a half-hour of comedy every Saturday afternoon during the Renfro Valley season. His latest accomplishment is the publication of *It All Happened in Renfro Valley* (University Press of Kentucky, 1999), a masterful presentation of the Renfro Valley story with its heavy emphasis on comedy. *My Wife's Driving Lesson and Other Stories from the Country Roadsides* (Renfro Valley Records 3794) reflects his comedy very well.

From a "Renfro Valley Barn Dance" performance:

I thought I'd like to maybe invite some of you all down to my part of the country, if you ever get a chance to come down there. There's a—I don't know the number of it—but there's a road that goes all the way in. So, if you all can get pert-near there by yourselves, I can tell you how to get the rest of the way in.

You'll first hit this little town called Ilsley, and you'll come into it, hit the courthouse, make a right-hand turn, and go all the way around and go back out the same way you come in. That's on account of, I can't recollect right off which road you turn off coming in, but it's the first one on the right coming back out. The next 'un, that'll be my home town, and I guess the only thing there is to tell you is not to go through too fast and miss it. Quite a few people do, unless they just get lucky and hit our traffic light on red. Course that don't usually ever happen. Fact is, if there isn't something coming from the other direction, we don't bother to turn it on. It's a second-hand light, and we had a little trouble out of it at first. It had a sign hanging down that said you could turn right on red. Well, we didn't have a road going that direction. We had a feed store there. Quite a few folks done that.

Once you're up there, you'll be welcome out at our place. We're four miles out there on Route 1. I don't know where you're from. You may call it Root 1, but down there it's Route, actually it's Rut 1. You can't miss our place. Well, there is a fork out there that you want to watch. When you get to it, just remember not to take the left-hand fork, 'cause it peters out there after about a quarter of a mile. It'll fool you. It starts out a good road, but then it turns into a cow path, then to a squirrel trail, up a hickory tree, and into a knothole. But if you get on it, don't worry about it. This is election year, and they've paved it all the way in. I'll tell you how you'll know you're on the right road. When you get around the second curve, you'll see a gate across the road, and the top hinge is broke, and if you look you'll see that the bottom one is fixin' to break. You got to pick it up and pack it around. When you go through there, be sure to shut it back, 'cause Shorty Hewett keeps his cows in there, and if you all happen to let one out, he'll blame it on us. Not long ago, some folks come through there, left the gate open, and he said his best cow got out, got down in the holler there, and got into a little project a feller had goin', and she drunk—I don' know how much she drunk—but she come home and died. Well, she actually just didn't come home and die. She come home giving eggnog, and they milked her to death, is what happened.

Once you git that far, you can't miss our place, just keep looking on the right side of the road, settin' out there about a hundred yards, you'll see a little four-room house, probably be twelve or fourteen young'uns playin' around the yard, more likely playing with a little duck. We don't live there. That's Shorty Hewett's place. That's his young'uns and duck. Actually, it's not a duck. It's a stork with its legs wore off. They'll tell you where we live.

STANLEY BROTHERS

Carter Glen Stanley, born August 27, 1925, Stratton,
  Virginia; died December 1, 1966
Ralph Edmond Stanley, born February 25, 1927,
  Stratton, Virginia

During their time together, the Stanley Brothers were known for their traditional and bluegrass music, but they also appreciated the value of comedy in entertainment. Carter Stanley, the more "forward" of the two, was a great emcee and straight man and hired others for the band who could do comedy, such as Melvin Goins, Albert Elliot, Chick Stripling, and Bill Napier. Also, the fiddler Curley Ray Cline had a comical demeanor that enlivened every program. Carter Stanley had the deeper appreciation for comedy of the two brothers. According to Joe Wilson, he was greatly influenced by the minstrel humor of Tom Ashley. He also appreciated the antics of J. E. Mainer and His Mountaineers. Ralph participated in some of the comedy sketches, but his interest mainly lay in the music, and in recent years he has downplayed the importance of comedy in the Stanley Brothers' performances. However, Ron Thomason, who played mandolin with the Clinch Mountain Boys, talked admiringly of Ralph's wit. Thomason remembered Carter saying that during the hard years, when the band consisted of just Carter and Ralph and George Shuffler, he regretted that they couldn't afford someone who could "lighten up the show."

When they had a full band, various members would do "How Far to Little Rock?" their version of the much-done "Arkansas Traveler" routine. Melvin Goins, in addition to great salesmanship in reviving the fortunes of the Stanley Brothers when bluegrass was in decline, played a boisterous country hick, sometimes dressed in a polka-dot suit and derby. Goins credits Carter Stanley with giving him the name of Big Wilbur: "He liked comedy a lot, and he was a great straight man too. They always used a comedian." Chick Stripling, the fiddler, bassist, and rube comedian who did a fantastic combination of tap and buck dance, was a surefire entertainer with the Stanleys as he was with numerous other groups. Albert Elliott, who played Towser Murphy, was with the Stanleys in the last part of the 1950s when they were centered in Live Oak, Florida. He remembered that he and Bill Napier regularly did a routine. "We'd throw each other jokes, you know, turn about, both dressed up as comedians." The jokes came from a book that Carter had. George Shuffler also filled in with some comedy occasionally.

The Stanley Brothers recorded many albums for Mercury, Starday, King, Columbia, and Rebel. In recent years, Bear Family of Germany has made available the Columbia recordings on CD, and Old Homestead and Copper Creek have released other material. The Copper Creek recordings are of live performances that contain some of their comedy. The Stanley Brothers, along with Cousin Emmy and Chick Stripling, appeared on Pete Seeger's "Rainbow Quest" TV show in 1966 (a video, *Rainbow Quest*

No. 18, is available from Norman Ross Publishing, 330 W. Fifty-eighth St., New York, NY 10019).

After Carter's death in 1966, Ralph took some time before deciding to form another band. He and the Clinch Mountain Boys have been regulars at leading bluegrass festivals around the country for years. They are now one of the most popular bands in the bluegrass world, and Ralph became a member of the "Grand Ole Opry" in 2000. His popularity is due partially to his contributions to *O Brother, Where Art Thou?* the soundtrack of which became Country Album of the Year in 2000, leading to the "Down from the Mountain" concerts around the country, featuring Stanley and the other country stars who appeared in the movie. Numerous other Nashville country-music stars, eager to be associated with such an authentic figure, have enthusiastically joined him for such recordings as *Saturday Night and Sunday Morning* (Freeland Recording Co., 1992) and *Clinch Mountain Country* (Rebel, 2001). However, except for a few oneliners and a joke now and then, Ralph has largely abandoned comedy. In June 2005, Ralph underwent triple bypass surgery, but he was back on the entertainment circuit by the end of the year. While he was laid up, his son, Ralph II, produced a gospel album, *Shine On*. Ralph II is now a regular member of the Clinch Mountain Boys but also writes songs and performs on his own.

Carter Stanley was married to Mary Kiser Stanley, and he left five children: Carter Jr., William, Bobby, Doris, and Jeannie. Ralph Stanley is married to Jimmi Crabtree Stanley, and they have three children: Lisa, Tonya, and Ralph II.

Here Carter and Ralph do the "How Far to Little Rock?" routine, usually called the "Arkansas Traveler" skit.

> *Ralph: Hello, stranger.*
> *Carter: Hello, stranger.*
> *Ralph: Could you tell me how far it is to Little Rock?*
> *Carter: No, Sir, I couldn't, but there's a devil of a big 'un down in Pap's old field. (plays a tune)*
> *Ralph: Hello, stranger.*
> *Carter: Hello, stranger.*
> *Ralph: Your corn looks awful little and yeller.*
> *Carter: I planted the little and yeller kind.*
> *Ralph: You must not be figurin' on but about half a crop.*
> *Carter: That's right, I'm raisin' on the shares—fifty-fifty.*
> *Ralph: You must not be very far from a fool.*
> *Carter: That's right, Son. Just these microphones here between us. (plays a tune)*
> *Ralph: Hello, stranger.*
> *Carter: Hello, stranger.*
> *Ralph: How'd your potatoes turn out?*
> *Carter: Son, you're goin' to have to talk louder. I don't hear too well out of this left ear here.*

Ralph: HOW'D YOUR POTATOES TURN OUT!

Carter: Oh, my taters. They didn't turn out too well atall. My old sow rooted them out. (plays a tune)

Ralph: Would you head that cow for me?

Carter: She's got a head.

Ralph: Turn her, then.

Carter: The hairy side's turned out.

Ralph: Well, would you speak to her?

Carter: GOOD MORNIN', OLD HEIFER! (plays a tune)

Ralph: Hello, stranger.

Carter: Hello there, Booger Mule.

Ralph: Why don't you cover your house?

Carter: Well, when it's a-rainin' I can't, buddy, and when the sun's a-shinin', it don't leak. (plays a tune)

Ralph: How far did you say it was to Little Rock?

Carter: Buddy, ain't you found out yet how far it is?

Ralph: No, I can't find out atall.

Carter: Well, I'd be mighty glad to tell you, Son. It's three lengths of a fool. If you don't believe it, lay down and measure it!

(Note: this routine is usually built around the tune, "Arkansas Traveler." The visitor plays the A part of the tune only, and finally the local fellow teaches him the B part.)

STATLER BROTHERS

Harold Wilson Reid, born August 23, 1939, Staunton, Virginia

Donald Sydney Reid, born June 5, 1945, Staunton, Virginia

Phil Elwood Balsley, born August 8, 1939, Staunton, Virginia

Lewis Calvin Dewitt, born March 8, 1938, Roanoke, Virginia; died August 15, 1990, Haynesboro, Virginia

Lester James Fortune, born March 11, 1955, Williamsburg, Virginia

The Statler Brothers were perhaps the most popular vocal quartet in the country, bridging country, pop, gospel, and nostalgic songs. They also had a lively comic theme running through their performances and television shows. Their most elaborate comedy was their creation of Lester "Road-Hog" Moran and His Cadillac Cowboys, a spoof about a bad country band trying to continue in radio long after radio was the main thing. This spoof was carried primarily by Harold Reid, the bass singer of the

The Statler Brothers. L-R: Don, Phil, Harold, and Jimmy. Courtesy of the Statler Brothers.

four, as Road-Hog, and Reid has also consistently played the dumb rube in their other comedy.

However, none of these boys is dumb. The Statlers mostly write their own songs and have run a complicated business (actually seven companies) in Staunton, Virginia, that included their TV series on TNN, their personal appearances, and recordings and sales of recorded music and other items.

Harold Reid, Lew DeWitt, Phil Balsley, and Joe McDorman first sang together in a high school quartet that became the Kingsmen in 1961, with Don Reid replacing McDorman. By 1964 they were the Statler Brothers, the name coming from a box of tissues in a motel room. By that time, through persistence, Harold talked their way onto a local Johnny Cash appearance and later convinced Cash to allow them to open all of his road shows. They traveled with Cash for some eight years and also appeared on his TV show from 1969 to 1971.

Cash got the Statlers a contract with Columbia Records, and they recorded their first hit in 1965, "Flowers on the Wall" (Top Five in both country and pop). They followed up with two humorous novelty songs in 1967, "Ruthless" and "You Can't Have Your Cake and Edith Too" (country Top Ten). Moving to Mercury in 1970, they recorded "Bed of Roses" (country number nine), a nostalgic album, *Pictures of Moments to Remember*, and two more singles, "Do You Remember These?" (number two) and "Class of '57" (number six). Lester "Road-Hog" Moran began as a segment on "Country

Music Now and Then," and its popularity resulted in a complete album, *Lester "Road-Hog" Moran*, in 1974. In 1994 Mercury released *The Complete Lester "Road-Hog" Moran and the Cadillac Cowboys*. In all honesty, the routine is funny once but does not wear well because Road-Hog is so pathetic and his band is so bad. So the Statlers dropped Road-Hog with the explanation that he was recovering from an autopsy, perhaps the funniest line related to the whole spoof.

In 1981, Lew DeWitt, who suffered from Crohn's Disease, left the band, and he died in 1991. He was replaced by Jimmy Fortune, singing high tenor. Fortune proved to be a versatile singer, guitarist, and composer, writing their hit songs "Elizabeth" and "My Only Love."

The Statlers appear to get along remarkably well together, and all live in and around Staunton. They were known also for their accessibility to their fans and to writers and others. Their amiability showed through in their TNN TV show along with their artistry. They had gone against the odds in making it as a quartet in the world of country music, but they succeeded beyond their own expectations. They believed that the public was still open to a good variety show, and they prevailed on producers to follow their ideas. "The Statler Brothers Show" had a lot of their own music but also comedy and visiting comedians, jugglers, acrobats, and guest singers, and it was the highest-rated show on TNN. Harold Reid wrote most of the humor for the show, and it featured him as the least swift of the group, but his comedy, based on the tried and true rube themes mixed with more sophisticated material, went over well with their audiences. The Statlers were ranked number two in a 1996 Harris Poll to determine the most popular singers, after Frank Sinatra but before Reba McEntire, Garth Brooks, Whitney Houston, Barbra Streisand, the Beatles, and Michael Jackson.

The Statler Brothers retired from concert touring in 2002. Their recorded music and other materials are available from Four-Star Enterprises, PO Box 2703, Staunton, VA 24402-2703; (540) 885-7297; statlerbrothers.com.

RAY STEVENS

Born Harold Ray Ragsdale, January 24, 1939,
  Clarksdale, Georgia

Ray Stevens is one of the all-time great comedy stars, picked second behind Jerry Clower by *Music City News* in their lineup of living comedy stars in 1998 and named Comedian of the Year in 1983 and 1993. He was borne in Clarksdale, a town near Atlanta, and the first music he liked was country—Kitty Wells, Ernest Tubb, and Lefty Frizzell. He started taking piano lessons at the age of six, however, and the family moved first to Albany and then to Atlanta, giving him a chance to hear other regional styles, such as gospel and rhythm and blues, particularly the music of the Coasters and Ray Charles and the Drifters.

In Atlanta, while in high school, he got a job as a part-time DJ and formed a band called the Barons. Later, while he was studying musical composition and theory at Georgia State University, the Atlanta music publisher Bill Lowery recognized his talent and helped him to get a record contract with the Columbia Prep label. Lowery also suggested his name change to Ray Stevens. Prep released "Silver Bracelet" in 1957. At this time, Stevens worked with Lowery doing arrangements for Brenda Lee, Patti Page, and Brook Benton.

Stevens had ambitions to be a straight country songwriter, but he had been a fan of Homer and Jethro and admired their and others' comedy songs. In 1961, Stevens broke into the comedy-song routine with a Mercury recording, "Jeremiah Peabody's Poly Unsaturated Quick Dissolving Fast Acting Pleasant Tasting Green and Purple Pills," that went Top Forty on the pop charts. His single "Ahab the Arab" placed Top Five on the pop charts in 1962 and made him a national star. The comedy song became his forte for the next three decades.

Stevens moved to Nashville in 1962 and became a session musician, arranger, and backup singer, but he soon released "Harry the Hairy Ape," which went Top Twenty. At Monument Records, Stevens did more comedy records and also some serious material: "Mr. Businessman" (1968, pop Top Thirty); "Gitarzan" (1969, pop Top Ten), his first gold record; "Along Came Jones" (1969); and as the first artist to record Kris Kristofferson's "Sunday Morning Comin' Down" (1969), he hit the country charts for the first time. His "Everything Is Beautiful" (Barnaby, 1970) was number one on the pop charts and in the Top Forty on the country charts, and it went gold and won Stevens a Grammy in 1971. Also in 1971, Barnaby released "Turn Your Radio On," which reached the Top Twenty on the country charts, and "Bridget the Midget," a hit in Great Britain. In 1974, "The Streak" went to number one on the pop charts in the United States and Britain and number three on the country charts, selling some five million copies. His biggest country hit was an arrangement of "Misty" that went pop number three and won him another Grammy. Other comedy recordings in this period were: *Shriner's Convention* (RCA Victor, 1970); *Mississippi Squirrel Revival* (1984); *The Haircut Song* (1985); *The Ballad of the Blue Cyclone* (1986); and *Would Jesus Wear a Rolex?* (1987).

For three seasons, from 1991, Stevens performed for a total of more than a million and a half fans in a two-thousand-seat theater in Branson, Missouri, and then he moved back to Nashville to tour off and on and to do a show in the Roy Acuff Theater in the old Opryland Park. He remains popular.

Ray Stevens feels that comedy and novelty songs have not had the proper respect in country music circles. He thinks that doing humorous material is much harder than straight country, and he should know because he is at the top as a comedian and as a serious musician.

Ray Stevens has many CDs available of his music and humor: *Ray Stevens: Greatest Hits* (MCA, 1987); *The Ray Stevens Collections* (MCA, 1993); *Twentieth-Century Masters—*

The Millennium Collection: The Best of Ray Stevens (Hip-Hop Records, 2004); and *Ray Stevens, Box Set* (Curb, 2006). He has four videos available, including *Ray Stevens: Comedy Video Classics* (Curb Video, 1993). Visit www.raystevens.com.

RUTH STEVENS. *See Tillie Thrasher*

CAL STEWART (UNCLE JOSH)

Born ca. 1856, Charlotte County, Virginia;
died December 7, 1919, Chicago, Illinois

The historian Ivan Tribe observed that Cal Stewart was a pioneer in country humor, doing his Uncle Josh character on numerous recordings and setting the stage for the rube comics who were to come, such as Rod Brasfield, Minnie Pearl, and Jerry Clower.

The writer Jim Walsh has pulled together what is known about Stewart's early years and has tried to deal with the contradictory statements from Stewart at various times in his life. In 1903 Stewart published a little book entitled *Punkin Centre Stories* that purported to tell about his life. He said he grew up on a Virginia farm "so poor, we had to fertilize it to make brick," and said that he left home at the age of twelve and had worked as a cook on a river boat, clerk with a surveying crew, tracklayer for a railroad, conductor, brakeman, and fireman on trains, livery stable hand, coal miner, farmworker, schoolteacher, Wells Fargo guard, and salesman. His experience in show business supposedly came after these adventures, including the circus, minstrel shows, farce comedy, burlesque, and dramatic shows. Elsewhere, however, he stated that he first appeared on stage in Baltimore playing a child when he would have been only seven years old. At any rate, he began making cylinder recordings of his "Uncle Josh" monologues and skits in the early 1890s and continued to make recordings the rest of his life. He also wrote and recorded some songs.

Walsh thinks that the Uncle Josh Weatherby character came out of a play, *Way Down East*, about a New England character named Uncle Josh Whitcomb, for which Stewart was the understudy for this main character. Uncle Josh, as Stewart developed him, was a country rustic talking about his hometown of Pun'kin Center, Vermont, in such recordings as *Train Time at Pun'kin Center* and *Uncle Josh Takes the Census*, and also about his problems with change and new inventions as he ventured into cities, as in *Uncle Josh's Arrival in New York* and *Uncle Josh on an Elevator*. Stewart made recordings for Columbia, Edison, and Victor. Some of these recordings featured other persons in skits, such as Ada Jones playing his wife. His voice was that of a country fellow, closer to the accents of New England than to his native Virginia. His presentation on the recordings is more theatrical than simple storytelling, punctuated with hearty laughs, like the modern laugh track, showing the audience where they were expected to laugh. Stewart's recordings were popular, and following his death, other performers used his monologues, usually verbatim, including the laughs.

Jim Walsh produced an album of Stewart's recordings, *Cal Stewart as Uncle Josh* (LP 797), released in 1978 by Mark 56 Records (PO Box 1, Anaheim, CA 92805).

Stewart died of complications of a stroke after a recording session in Chicago in 1919. At the time, he and his wife, Rossinni Waugh Stewart, lived on a farm near Tipton, Indiana.

(Credit to Ivan Tribe and to Jim Walsh and his liner notes to *Cal Stewart as Uncle Josh.*)

Following is an excerpt from *Revival Meeting at Pun'kin Center* (Blue Amberol cylinder No 2009):

> *Uncle Josh: Ha ha, well last winter we had a revival meeting at Pun'kin Center, and pretty nigh the whole town got religion. Some of them have got it yet, and some of them have shed it just like the cat sheddin' its hair. I guess we needed it. Things got so bad in the church we had to have a one-armed brother take up the collection. (Laughs) At the revival some nights we had as many as two hundred come forward to the mourner's bench, and from the testimony they give, it seemed like more than half of Pun'kin Center ought to be in jail. (Laughs) One night the choir had just got through singing, "What Will the Harvest Be?" and they woke up old Jim Lawson, and he stood up and said he thought the harvest was all right. His rye went forty gallons to the acre. (Laughs) We all expected to see Jim get religion, 'cause a couple of weeks before that he got a mighty bad scare. He was comin' home from the drug store carryin' a load of liquor, and he run his old peg leg through a knothole in the sidewalk, and he stood thar and walked around that wooden leg for two hours! (Laughs) And it took three of us to pull him out of that knothole. Deacon Witherspoon reminded him of it and asked him if he wanted to mend his ways. Jim said there aren't but only one knothole in that sidewalk and he knowed whar that was now! (Laughs) We had some mighty interesting things happen at our revival. . . . Obadiah White, the minister from Hickory Corners, was to preach to us that night. I don't think I ever will forget that sermon. He said, "Yeah, verily, Brothers and Sisters, I say unto you Satan has wonderful inducements to offer the sinner! Why, Brothers and Sisters, hell is full of beautiful women, automobiles, fast horses, and champagne," and just then Old Jim Lawson stood up and said, "O death where is thy sting? (Laughs).*

DR. TIM STIVERS

Born November 26, 1934, Louisville, Kentucky

Dr. Tim Stivers is a humorist who was also a podiatrist until he retired after forty years to perform humor full-time. His mother and father were also podiatrists, and thus he has a few jokes about feet, claiming to make house calls in a toe truck. His parents instilled a love of music in their children, and Tim and his brother got a taste of show business in a barbershop quartet, touring the United States and Canada on weekends. Stivers then turned to the art of humor. He has used his profession and his travels around Kentucky to absorb the language, stories, and jokes of rural and small-town people, and what he learned has turned up in routines that highlight the wisdom and humor of country people. Like many other humorists, he has created a bunch of characters to propel his humor. Folks like Buford, Chidley Dunlap, Floyd, Berla May, Otis, Verla Fay, Theryl, Udell, and Cova Mae Smithers populate the scenes that he creates. He is gifted at voice changes to characterize each one.

Even though Stivers wields a country accent and tells country stories, he and his humor are pretty sophisticated. One writer described him as a "differently-tuned humorist who tells devastatingly funny tales of the rural South, but a craftsman who takes a situation, then builds, molds, chops, chisels and lovingly adds a word here, and accent change there, until at the end there is a perfectly timed explosion of laughter." Another commented that "he approaches the everyday, looks at it with stunning clarity, peels off the facade and leaves . . . his audience with a refreshing glimpse at new perspectives."

Tim Stivers. Courtesy of Dr. Tim Stivers.

Stivers performs for all kinds of groups—company conventions, sales meetings, and truck-driver gatherings. In fact, he did six tapes for a truckers' organization on truck-driving safety, using humor to get the principal points across. He appeared on TNN's "Nashville Now" and the "Bob Braun Show" on WLWT in Cincinnati and has done shows in thirty-eight states, including Alaska, and in Ireland and New Zealand. He continues to do about thirty-five dates a year. A pilot, Stivers flew his own Twin Comanche to engagements, and before he retired from podiatry, this made it possible for him to get back to those aching feet waiting in his office the next morning. After a heart attack, he has recently given up flying.

Stivers has produced two three-cassette, or three-CD, collections of his performances. The first contains "This Old Boy," "Terminally Weird," and "Is There Life outside the South?" The second contains "The Other Side of Ugly," "The Future Ain't What It Used to Be," and "A Bubble-and-a-Half off Plumb." Both sets are available from Tim Stivers Enterprises, PO Box 23135, Anchorage, KY 40223-0135; or timstivers.com.

The following is used with permission.

Tim Stivers: Well, I've invented something. Now, y'all have heard of "Dial a Prayer." You know, you dial this number, and you get the prayer for the day. We have "Dial a Prayer for Atheists." We do. You dial this number, and nobody answers.

Now I've invented a new one. I have invented "Dial a Prayer for Agnostics." That's right. You dial this number, and somebody answers, but you don't know who it is. Yeah.

An old boy there at home, on Sunday his mama come in there, said, "Get up. You gotta go to church!" Said, "Don't wanna go." She said, "You got to go to church! You get outta that bed!" He said, "Gimme two good reasons." She said, "I'll give you two good reasons. Number one, you're forty-seven years old! And number two, you're the preacher!"

I had a weird thought the other day. I thought about this for three days, and I don't have an answer yet, but I want to know why it is that the Corinthians never did answer any of Paul's letters.

If you go to a funeral at night, do you leave your lights off?

RONI STONEMAN

Born Veronica Loretta Stoneman, May 5, 1938,
Washington, D.C.

Roni Stoneman is best known as a comedian on "Hee Haw," but she is also an accomplished banjo player and singer. Her father, Ernest "Pop" Stoneman, was one of the first from the southern mountains to record for several companies beginning in 1924. It was he who persuaded Ralph Peer of Victor Studios to do the famous Bristol sessions in 1927 that uncovered the talents of the Carter Family and Jimmie Rodgers, although Pop and Roni's mother Harriett were also part of these recordings. For a short time Ernest and Harriett had income from their recordings, but with the Depression and the closing of some of the record companies, Pop found it necessary to move his already large family where he could find work, and they moved to the Washington, D.C., area, where Roni was born.

Pop started his children on various instruments at an early age, and in the mid-1950s he organized a band with Roni and her brother Van, Zeke Dawson, and Larry King as Pop Stoneman and His Little Pebbles. They won the band contest at the Galax Fiddler's Convention in 1956. Roni also played with other groups before becoming part of the Stonemans, a band made up of Pop Stoneman and his children: Scotty, Donna, Jimmy, Roni, Van, and later Patsy. This group grew out of the earlier Blue Grass Champs that played the Washington area and became a winner on the "Arthur Godfrey Talent Scouts" program in 1956.

After many years of struggling to make a living out of music, in 1965 the family band began playing to enthusiastic audiences at the Black Poodle in Nashville, landed a contract with MGM Records, and started a syndicated television show that played over some fifty stations. They were on the Top Forty country charts with three numbers and won the CMA Vocal Group of the Year in 1966. They did five albums for MGM and then switched to RCA for three albums and several singles.

Roni left the band in 1971 to have a baby and never rejoined, although she came back to Nashville and recorded two singles for Dot Records. In 1973, she joined "Hee Haw" and found her true calling. Her father had cautioned her against playing the silly person on stage, but she credits Mac Wiseman with advising Pop Stoneman to "just let her go because that's what she is—a comic, and people like it." At a party one night she met Sam Lovullo, the producer of "Hee Haw," and got a chance to audition for the show.

She recalled,

> When I got to "Hee Haw," I went all dressed up, fixed my hair, tried to look so pretty, and Bud Wingard said, "You're exactly what we want, because we've got all the pretty girls we need." I said, "Thanks alot." He said they needed a skinny Ma Kettle. I liked Ma Kettle because it reminded me of the Stoneman family and all those children, and I'd learned to mock her, "Paw, git in hyerr!" Years ago I got down on my knees and prayed, "Dear God, make me funny. Give me comedy, give me fun and laughter, the people need it so."

She was especially proud in learning that Minnie Pearl thought she was funny on "Hee Haw." "My God, to be able to make Minnie Pearl laugh. That was the highlight of my life!"

Roni Stoneman as Ida Lee. Courtesy of Roni Stoneman.

She blossomed as a comedian on "Hee Haw," staying with the show through syndication and until it closed in 1992. Her main character was Ida Lee Nagger, the long-suffering wife of the "sorry" Laverne (Gordie Tapp). Ida Lee was handy with the rolling pin and Ma Kettle invective in trying to get Laverne to change his ways. Roni, with five children, coming from a large family, felt a kinship with Ida Lee. "I loved her. That was my life, with the husband I was married to! That wasn't acting. That was real. By golly, I looked and felt that way. I loved Ida Lee, and I still love her because she made people laugh."

Since "Hee Haw," Roni has been involved in several projects, including an all-girl band. She still does solo acts at festivals and concerts, with comedy and also picking the banjo and singing. She has three CDs to her credit—*First Lady of Banjo*, *Stonehouse*, and *Pure and Country*—as well as a gospel album.

(With credit to Ivan M. Tribe, *The Stonemans: An Appalachian Family and the Music That Shaped Their Lives* [Urbana: University of Illinois Press, 1993].)

Roni Stoneman related the following at a Festival of Appalachian Humor at Berea College in 1987:

> *I was the seventeenth of twenty-three children. The reason there were so many of us was because my mother was hard of hearing. Daddy would say to Mama at bedtime every night, "You want to go to sleep or what?" Mama would say, "What?"*
>
> *There was this French lady who used to come by our house from time to time. This lady was concerned with my mother's health because she had so many young'ns. "Mrs. Stoneman," she said one day, "have you ever heard of the rhythm method?" Now all of us picked an instrument, and Mom was so used to musicians around the house. She said, "Well, who would want to get a band together at three o'clock in the morning?"*
>
> *One time I fell through the hole in the outhouse, and Mama pulled me out and got a pan of water to clean me up. Daddy came by and asked her, "Wouldn't it be easier to just have another one than to clean that one up?"*
>
> *I hate to tell you how poor we were, but one time when my brother swallowed a dime, I followed him around for three days with a stick.*

STRINGBEAN. *See David Akeman*

CHICK STRIPLING

Born March 4, 1916, Tifton, Georgia; died November 19, 1970, Alexandria, Virginia

James Wilson "Chick" Stripling was acclaimed by many fellow entertainers as one of the best in the business as a bassist, fiddler, comedian, and buck and tap dancer. Jim McReynolds said of him, "He was one of the funniest guys I believe I've seen on stage. He always had some pretty good jokes, and he'd do the old-time fiddle things, but of course his main attraction was a buck dance he would do. That hardly ever failed." Wayne Daniel added, "Chick's approach to entertaining was to capture the audience one way or another. Before going on stage he knew he could play a fiddle tune, and if that didn't stir up the crowd, he had his comedy routine to fall back on." "And if that don't make 'em laugh," Chick is quoted as saying, "I'll put my feet to work."

Stripling was born in South Georgia not far from the Florida line. His father played banjo, guitar, and fiddle, and Chick and a brother took up the fiddle. The extended family also had musicians, and they formed a band including Chick as a teenager. The family band played for dances in homes and music halls and also played on a local radio station. Chick also liked to dance at an early age and is reported to have worn out the kitchen linoleum in his zeal.

Wayne Daniel has explored Stripling's wandering career from the time he joined Gene Mills's Twilight Playboys in 1937 or 1938 to play at a local radio station and to

Chick Stripling. Courtesy
of Phillip G. Collins.

do tent shows in the area. It was with Mills that he added comedy to his other talents.
Soon he had joined Gene Stripling (no relation), whose stage name was Uncle Ned,
and His Texas Wranglers to play WSB's "Cross Roads Follies," where he performed
for the next eight years until the program was dropped. In 1940 he became a member
of WSB's "Barn Dance" and its midday "Georgia Jubilee." He was one of the most
popular performers on WSB.

During this time, Chick would take leave from WSB and tour with Bill Monroe
and His Bluegrass Boys. When the "Barn Dance" closed in the 1950s, he apparently
played in South Georgia and around Macon for a time. In 1957 or 1958, he showed
up at a concert in Adele, Georgia, by Jim and Jesse and the Virginia Boys, and asked
for a spot on their program. They knew of him and liked his performance so much
that they hired him. He had earlier worked for Flatt and Scruggs, and occasionally he
took leave from Jim and Jesse to travel with Ernest Tubb. He had also worked with
Fiddlin' John Carson in the gubernatorial campaign of Herman Talmadge in 1946. He
was for a time with Red Belcher at WWVA's "Jamboree" in Wheeling, West Virginia,
and also performed with Charlie Monroe, Jimmy Martin, the Stanley Brothers, Don
Reno and Red Smiley, and Alex and Ola Belle Reed and Their New River Boys.

Frank Malloy, who played fiddle with Uncle Ned and His Texas Wranglers, described Stripling as doing a combination of buck and tap dancing. "It was a deal like
Lew Childre used to do. He had a kind of running dialog where he'd be dancing and
talking all at the same time." His fiddling was described as "traditional old-time style,"
but he had been influenced at fiddle contests by Clayton McMichen and others who

played in a more progressive style. As a comedian, Stripling was described as funny on- and offstage, always keeping people laughing.

Little of Stripling's art was recorded. He does a fiddle tune, a dance, and plays the bass on a Stanley Brothers Gusto album *1983 Collector's Edition—Volume 3* (GT-0105) and also appeared on Pete Seeger's "Rainbow Quest" program in 1966, along with the Stanley Brothers, the Clinch Mountain Boys, and Cousin Emmy (a video, *Rainbow Quest No. 18*, is available from Norman Ross Publishing, 330 W. Fifty-eighth St., New York, NY 10019).

Stripling lived in northern Virginia in his last years, where he apparently played with area musicians, probably in local stage and radio shows, but by then he was in bad health and had financial problems. He died in 1970.

(With thanks to Wayne W. Daniel, "Chick Stripling: Dancer, Comedian, and Old-time Fiddler," *Bluegrass Unlimited* 28.5 [November 1993]: 36–39.)

> *Chick: I might could play a little of the "Chicken Reel." Ah, yes, I can't do the "Boogie-Woogie" in these pants. I'll do the "Baggy-Waggy."*

CLELL SUMMEY (COUSIN JODY)

*Born James C. Summey, December 11, 1914, near
Sevierville, Tennessee; died 1976, probably in
Nashville, Tennessee*

Clell Summey, best known as a comedian, started out as a dobro player at WNOX and the "Mid-day Merry-Go-Round" in Knoxville. He soon became a member of Roy Acuff's Crazy Tennesseans. When Acuff auditioned for the "Grand Ole Opry" on February 5, 1938, Summey backed him as he sang "The Great Speckled Bird," the song that made Acuff a permanent member of the "Opry." It was the first time the dobro had been played on the "Opry" stage, and thus Summey helped to establish a distinctive sound in country music. He left Acuff shortly to return to Knoxville to play a more popular kind of music. Before long, however, he was back in Nashville as a member of Pee Wee King's Golden West Cowboys. He started doing comedy with Oral Rhodes as Odie and Jody. Later he joined Lonzo and Oscar as Cousin Jody, a toothless rube comic, playing what he called his "biscuit board," an electric steel guitar that resembled a piece of two-by-four. He became a regular part of Lonzo and Oscar's show, along with the bass player Tommy Ward. For ten years he performed on his own at the "Opry" until cancer slowed him down and caused his death in 1976. He was married to the former Marie Hill.

Summey's antics as Cousin Jody brought him a measure of fame. His music was appreciated also. He recorded eight numbers for Starday, including "Beyond the Next Hilltop," "Blues in Reserve," "Television Set," and "Jody's Chimes." In addition to the "Mid-day Merry-Go-Round" and the "Grand Ole Opry," he played the WWVA "Jamboree" in Wheeling, West Virginia, and appeared as a guest on the "Kate Smith Show," the "Ed Sullivan Show," the "Steve Allen Show," the "Dave Garroway Show," and was on a Camel Caravan tour.

SMILIE SUTTER

Born Anthony Slater, May 11, 1915, East Hartford, Connecticut; died March 19, 1980, Wheeling, West Virginia

Young Slater grew up in New Britain, Connecticut. His father died when he was two, his mother when he was eleven, and he had to support himself at an early age. He grew up listening to the burgeoning radio stations that carried what was to become country music. For a time, he worked as a singing waiter in clubs around New York City. He eventually got into radio himself through an amateur contest. This led to jobs at WMBQ in Brooklyn; WPAY in Portsmouth, Ohio; WLVA in Lynchburg, Virginia; KMOX in St. Louis; WLS in Chicago; and several stations in West Virginia—WCHS in Charleston; WBLK in Clarksburg; WMMN in Fairmont; and finally WWVA in Wheeling. Along the way he became Smilie Sutter. His comedy character was Crazy Elmer, a character he played more and more in the latter part of his career.

Crazy Elmer (Smilie Sutter). Courtesy of Doc Williams.

Sutter was a gifted singer, guitarist, harmonica player, yodeler, and comedian. As Crazy Elmer, he dressed up as a hayseed with a steady stream of stories and jokes. He also sang novelty and comic songs, and he was billed as a "triple" yodeler. He composed his signature yodeling number, "Swiss on Rye." He found a home at the WWVA "Mountaineer Jamboree," where comedy was much favored, and he played there off and on for nearly forty years. He recorded *Inside the Outside of Crazy Elmer* on ARC Canada, and he recorded two of his compositions, "I Heard a Rainbow" and "Swiss on Rye" on Wheeling Records (Box 902, Wheeling, WV 26002).

From a live broadcast:

> *Elmer: I hate women!*
> *Emcee: I know you don't.*

Elmer: Prove it.

Emcee: Listen to me real close. Who brought you into this world?

Elmer: My mother. Do you think I hatched?

Emcee: You listening to me? When you was a little teeny baby, who was it gave you a bath? When you cried 'cause you were hungry, who gave you a nice warm bottle? Who did that?

Elmer: My mother.

Emcee: Then when you was just a little bit bigger than that, your first day in school, a little boy sent you home with a black eye, who was it said, "That's all right. He was a little bit bigger boy than you. Don't feel bad," put a nice little compress on your eye, took all the swelling away. Who was that?

Elmer: My mother.

Emcee: Later on, after you got married, you and your wife had a fight, and you left the house, where did you go? Who did you run home to?

Elmer: (wails) My mother!

Emcee: And after everything is said and done, who do you owe everything in this world to?

Elmer: The finance company!

GORDIE TAPP

Born June 4, 1923, London, Ontario

Gordie Tapp grew up on a farm and is well acquainted with country people, country humor, and country music. He graduated from Lorne Greene's Academy of Radio Arts in Toronto and worked in radio and CBC television for eighteen years. For eleven years he was emcee for the annual national Fiddling Contest in Shelbourne, Ontario. He developed a successful comedy act playing a lovable character named Uncle Clem, a country version of the type played by Frank Fontaine and Foster Brooks. He could sing, and he also did a dozen or so dialects that enhanced his comedy, switching from one to the other to highlight his comic characters. He had written for and appeared in several Canadian television shows and was acquainted with John Aylesworth and Frank Peppiatt, the primary creators of "Hee Haw." This led to his being invited to be a writer and performer on the show, along with Don Harron and Bill Davis, adding up to five Canadians on the show—not surprising, since many Canadians are fond of country music and comedy.

On "Hee Haw," in addition to his writing chores, he was the irascible storekeeper berating his clerk, played by Gailard Sartain, and also the pompous southern gentleman and father of the southern belle, played by Marianne Gordon. In the latter sketches he always had his planter's hat knocked off after a pompous statement. Gordie Tapp wrote most of the sketches in which he appeared. He also was a regular with various artists singing the standard, "Where, O Where, Are You Tonight?" and wrote many of the verses.

Gordie Tapp. Photo by Michael
Dismatsek, courtesy of Gordie Tapp.

Foster Brooks once introduced Tapp as "the world's funniest storyteller." The Toronto critic Blake Kirby commented that the ten or twelve dialects that he uses in comedy "have an authenticity that is uncanny" and that he has "a limitless stock of jokes." He has appeared in three movies and has produced a video of his performances, as well as two audio cassettes. Tapp was recently honored by such colleagues as Anne Murray, Tommy Hunter, Roy Clark, and Foster Brooks for his fifty years in radio and television and was appointed a Member of the Royal Order of Canada by the governor general. He has been involved in many charitable projects to raise money for such causes as muscular dystrophy, Big Brothers, and Shriners' Hospitals. The city of Burlington, Ontario, named Gordie Tapp Crescent in his honor and in appreciation of his many charitable contributions.

Gordie Tapp continues to appear as an entertainer at nightclubs, banquets, and conventions. He and his wife Helen have four children: Barbara, Kathleen, Joan, and Jeffrey.

For videos, CDs, and tapes contact Carl Kees at 519-539-0828.

The following stories were contributed by Gordie Tapp with permission:

A farmer's wife was bending over while he was eating breakfast, and he said, "You're getting as big as my combine," and she didn't say anything. Five nights later they got in bed, and he rolled over and put his arm around her. She said, "What are you doing?" He said, "You know what I'm doing." She said, "Look, if you think I'm starting up a three-hundred-and-fifty-thousand-dollar combine for a little crop like that, you've got another thought coming!

When I was a boy on the farm, we had a cow-calf operation. One year wasn't good—not many calves. I said to Daddy, "I think it's the bull," and he said, "It can't be." I said, "Call the veterinarian." He did, and the vet came out and checked the bull out and said, "The boy's right. It's the bull," and he gave us some pills, and you never have seen anything like it. We were back in the cow-calf business! I said to the vet, "What's in that pill?" He wouldn't tell me. It was just a little blue pill, and it tasted like peppermint.

My mama put the pills up on the window sill in the stable, and us kids got to playing with them and dropped them in the well. Mama phoned the vet five days later and told him what had happened. He said, "Is it making the water taste bad?" She said, "No, but we haven't been able to get the pump handle down for three days!"

BALLARD TAYLOR AND TOMMY TAYLOR

Ballard Taylor, born May 28, 1908, Ashe County,
   North Carolina; died February 20, 1998,
   Covington, Kentucky
Tommy Taylor, born March 17, 1924, Pellyton,
   Kentucky

The Taylor brothers' people were natives of Ashe County, North Carolina, and were musicians dating from their grandfather, a Civil War veteran, who played the banjo and taught their father the song "Tom Dooley." He passed it on to Ballard, who eventually recorded it. Ballard was born in North Carolina, but the family removed to Adair County, Kentucky, and bought a farm, where Tommy was born.

Ballard, a fiddler and banjo picker, joined with his cousin Elmer Rupert in 1928 for a job at WLW, then with five hundred thousand watts. They moved to WCKY in Covington, Kentucky, in 1929. However, the pay was skimpy, so eventually Ballard

Tommy and Ballard Taylor.
Courtesy of Tommy Taylor.

went back to Adair County to raise tobacco on a sharecrop basis, but one year the creek flooded and ruined the crop. In bad financial shape, he auditioned for Henry Warren's Original Kentucky Mountaineers, who were visiting the county, and was hired. At the time, the band was playing over a Rockford, Illinois, radio station and traveling all over the Midwest, primarily as a dance band. Warren liked the way Taylor played the five-string banjo in several styles, and he suggested that he take over the "old man" comedic role that Warren had been playing as "Uncle Henry." Taylor then developed his "Grandpa Nerit" character, the name coming from a question about whether or not he had been married, the answer being, "Near it." After he left the Mountaineers, Ballard went by the name of "Pappy" Taylor.

The group returned to Kentucky in 1936, first at WLAP (in Louisville at that time) and then at WHAS, where they played until 1941. They then moved to Chicago, where they played the "Suppertime Frolic" on WJJD until the program went under from the competition of television a decade later.

Taylor then joined up with the musicians Jim Rains and the Franklin Brothers from West Virginia, and they played for a time in Louisiana and other parts of the South. They got on the "Arthur Godfrey Show" in the early 1950s and won first place, with Pappy playing the five-string banjo and singing "Mountain Dew" and also fiddling "Run, Boy, Run." Part of the deal was that they would be regulars on the Godfrey show for two weeks, but it was near Christmas, and other members of the band decided that they wanted to be home, so they forfeited whatever fame this would have brought them. During this time, Pappy also played with other entertainers, such as Lonzo and Oscar, Roy Clark, and Ernest Tubb, doing country fairs and road shows.

For comedy, he dressed up for Grandpa Nerit with old-fashioned glasses that he looked over, a wig, and a padded vest that made him look humpbacked. His high, piping voice was perfect for his old-man persona. "I said if I ever got into comedy, I'd play an old man. I'd seen vaudeville shows and got some humor from them. I picked up stuff here and there, told jokes that I'd heard or made up, and I ad-libbed. It was all pretty clean back then." He did question-and-answer jokes, for example, "Why did the Indian wear a toupee?" "To keep his wigwam."

In the 1950s, Pappy returned to Kentucky and joined his brother Tommy, who was with Virgil Rice and the Kentucky Ramblers, a seven-piece band that played three nights a week at a nightclub called Gen's Chicken Roost in Kenton County, Kentucky. Tommy was also a fiddler and banjo picker and a fine singer. He had gotten into entertainment after serving in the army in World War II. He played straight man to Pappy's comedy and in the process learned his large repertoire of jokes and routines. He and Pappy had been friends and admirers of Clayton McMichen and Bert Layne and from them had learned twin fiddling and some trick fiddling. Both Taylors were prize-winning fiddlers. The brothers played together for many years, except for five years, when Pappy was in a tuberculosis sanitarium. One of their fondest memories was playing at the Kentucky Center for the Arts in Louisville in a tribute to the Kentuckian and fellow comedian and musician Grandpa Jones. After their performance, Grandpa Jones's guitarist, George McCormick, commented, "Following Pappy Taylor is like following a bulldozer with a teaspoon."

Tommy held down a job as shipping clerk for a company that made prefabricated houses, but he continued to play music and to work at radio stations such as WMOH in Hamilton, Ohio. Eventually, he got religion and quit nightclub work. Since then he has headed an old-time band called the Rabbit Hash String Band and also the Gospelway Bluegrass Singers, the latter doing mostly gospel music. He has also written several gospel songs. Tommy's religion has not dampened his love for the comedy that he performed with Pappy until Pappy went into a Covington nursing home. Tommy continues Pappy's routines with other members of his bands. The Rabbit Hash Band is in demand at festivals and special events in Kentucky and Ohio, and they dish up both music and comedy. They have released *The Rabbit Hash String Band Home Recordings*. Tommy's Gospelway Bluegrass Band has made four recordings, all available from Tommy Taylor, 10231 East Bend Road, Rabbit Hash, KY 41005. In 2001, Tommy won the Appalachian Heritage Award at the Appalachian Festival in Cincinnati.

The following humor was presented at the Celebration of Traditional Music at Berea College:

> *Tommy: We were real poor back home. One night a burglar got in the house, and Daddy said, "Be real quiet. If he finds anything, we'll get up and take it away from him."*
>
> *Pappy: I been trying to get my hair parted. My mother gave me that comb when I was little and said, "Don't never part with it."*
>
> *Do you know why the Indian was here before the white man? The Indian had a reservation. Do you know what a papoose is? That's the consolation prize when you take a chance on an Indian blanket.*
>
> *You know people talk about the hen crossing the road. Everybody has a different version. Some say the hen crosses the road to get on the other side. Some say because there's a rooster over there. That's not it. She was a-layin' for a rooster over there. That ain't all of it. After she laid that egg, she wallered in the dust, and she crossed back to the other side. Now they call that hen a double-crosser.*
>
> *Tommy: Pappy, there's one more reason why she crossed the road. That was to show the 'possum that it could be done.*

MAX TERHUNE

*Born Robert Max Terhune, February 12, 1891,
    Franklin, Indiana; died June 5, 1973, Cottonwood,
    Arizona*

The comedian, ventriloquist, whistler, magician, animal imitator, cowboy sidekick, and character actor Max Terhune was best known for his role as Lullaby Joslin in the Three Mesquiteers series of B-Westerns. He started out in minor-league baseball but went on

Max Terhune with
Elmer Sneezeweed.

to touring shows, appearing with such groups as Ezra Buzzington's Rustic Revellers, the Hoosier Hot Shots, and the Weaver Brothers and Elviry. He joined WLS and the "National Barn Dance" in 1932, where he served as announcer as well as entertainer. There he met Gene Autry, who later encouraged him to come to California to try out for the movies.

He appeared in Autry's 1936 Republic films *Ride Ranger Ride* and *The Big Show*. He then appeared in twenty-one Three Mesquiteers films for Republic, with Bob Livingston, Crash Corrigan, and John Wayne. In them he was Lullaby, providing comic relief mainly with his dummy Elmer Sneezeweed. He moved to Monogram in 1939 to do twenty-four films in a similar series, the Range Busters, with Crash Corrigan. Here he changed his sidekick name to Alibi, but Elmer Sneezeweed remained the same. From 1943 to 1948, he appeared as a character actor in a few other Westerns but thought it best to take the road again. He worked with Tex Ritter, Slim Andrews, and Dub "Cannonball" Taylor (another B-Western sidekick) for a year and then joined Wally Fowler and His Georgia Clodhoppers. During 1944 he was at WNOX and the "Midday Merry-Go-Round" in Knoxville, where he entertained with his expert whistling, bird and animal imitations, and with his old friend Elmer. After a tour with the T. D. Kemp Vaudeville Circuit, he returned to Hollywood in 1948 to make eight more films for Monogram as sidekick Alibi to Johnny Mack Brown.

After the last of these Monogram films in 1949, Terhune went on the road again but returned to play characters in two films, *Rawhide* with Tyrone Power and *Jim Thorpe, All American* with Burt Lancaster. In 1952 he starred in his own children's television show, "Alibi's Tent Show," over KNX-TV in Hollywood. He also had bit parts in other television series, such as "The Lone Ranger" and "I Love Lucy." In 1956 he had a small part in *Giant* with Rock Hudson, and in 1957 he appeared in the *Gunfight at the OK Corral*.

In 1958, Max lost a son, Donald, in a traffic accident, and his wife Maude died in 1966. In 1968, in poor health, he moved to Cottonwood, Arizona. There he died of a heart attack at eighty-one. Two children, Doris and Robert, survived him.

(With credit to David Rothel, *Those Great Cowboy Sidekicks* [Madison, N.C.: Empire Publishing, 2001], 204–13.)

RON THOMASON

Born September 5, 1944, Russell County, Virginia

Ron Thomason is the leader of the Dry Branch Fire Squad, a superb bluegrass band operating out of Ohio. Thomason has done other things as well, such as playing mandolin for Ralph Stanley's Clinch Mountain Boys, teaching English, raising Arabian horses, competing in distance trail rides, working as a cowboy, and, with his wife, putting on three of the largest horse exhibitions in the world. He also skis, climbs mountains, and guides fisherfolk, but no hunters. He is a witty, unpredictable humorist and a social satirist. His band performed at the dedication of the Kentucky Center for the Arts in Louisville, where Charlton Heston was the emcee. Thomason said straightfaced, "We were going to sing a gospel shape-note song about Jesus, but how can you sing about Jesus with Moses standing here?" So they sang something else.

Ron Thomason.
Courtesy of Ron Thomason.

Thomason's father is a Virginian, but his mother is from Ohio. Although he was born near Honaker, Virginia, while his father was serving as an army paratrooper in World War II, the family moved to Ohio to find work after the war. When times got bad, they moved back to the Virginia farm. When Ron was in the eighth grade, the family moved permanently to Ohio, but he retained strong roots in Virginia. He graduated from Ohio University with degrees in English and math and taught English in high school. He took a leave of absence and moved back to Virginia to play with Ralph Stanley for a year.

Thomason started playing music for fun when he was eleven or twelve and professionally when he was thirteen in a rock-and-roll band in a bar with his father as chaperone. He formed the Dry Branch Fire Squad in 1976, and they have played the most prestigious of bluegrass festivals and other music venues, such as the National Council of Traditional Arts and the Smithsonian Institution. The U.S. Information Agency has supported their travel to numerous foreign countries.

Thomason, however, was not satisfied to play good bluegrass music artfully. He felt that the culture out of which the music had come was not there anymore and that the audience knew very little about it. Therefore, as a teacher he wanted to educate his audience, and he knew that a substantial number of fans wanted to deal intellectually as well as emotionally with the music and the way of life it represented. He commented,

> Lecturing is the worst way to teach. Satire is kind of painless, until you hit the mark, but it is a pain most people are willing to endure. I've always assumed that we are performers for people on the right-hand side of the intelligence curve. I say that not out of any kind of arrogance but just to be realistic. People on the other side of the curve are not going out to watch live entertainment any more. They're watching television. What you find is that people who are willing to get up, go out, and pay ten or twelve bucks will give you the benefit of the doubt.
>
> What I'm trying to work from is, let's get rid of these Appalachian stereotypes. It's true, there were a lot of poor people, but that was primarily for political reasons. I want to show what caused people to be poor but show also that we have a wonderful work ethic. Now, only about 3 ½ percent of the people are still part of an agricultural society who are listening to music that came out of a fully agricultural and working ethic culture. That is a lot of information, and I'm just trying to present it in a way that is humorous and light and palatable. But I never, ever make a joke or a comment at the expense of a song. I always try to revere the music. What I am trying to do is to give people the tools they need to enjoy our songs, because they're highly political and beautiful and they're poignant.

Thomason, in effect, has created an alter ego that is the humorist who stands on stage and tells stories and makes satiric comments, and this persona does not always sound like the Ron Thomason who studied literature and satire and who taught English literature. His alter ego sometimes takes liberties with the native tongue and lengthens out a southwestern Virginia accent, but he comes off as a very smart character. Thomason comments, "I want to lay to rest the redneck stereotypes. Just because I'm a hillbilly doesn't mean I can't be educated and smart." He points out also that the hillbilly is the only minority group that you can make fun of without having the politically correct police on your back. He mentions that someone criticized him in a *Bluegrass Unlimited* article for his liberal point of view, saying that a good comedian does not have a point of view. He responds by making some points about satire:

> I think a satirist—no matter what you say about a comedian—has a point of view. It is a classical art starting with Aristophenes, Juvenal, Jonathan Swift, Sam Johnson, Rabelais. All those guys had a real consistent worldview, and a position and an opinion that they wanted to present. They attacked worldviews that were not consistent with theirs. Bill Cosby is a mild satirist. He's said, "I'm not going to do humor about color but talk about people in general." And by being black, he has become a great model.

So I think, "What's wrong with having a 'hillbilly' too, out there saying, 'I'm a hillbilly'?" I would like to model good behavior. I'd like for you to think that I'm not just a rube because of where I come from. You have to judge me with the same criteria you judge yourself.

Thomason directs his satirical comments toward hillbillies as well as toward the other Americans who assume a superiority toward hillbillies. This leads him sometimes to cross the line between enhancing and stereotyping. For example, when the band is up North, he may introduce them as the "single-helix group from the shallow end of the gene pool," or he may ask with a straight and melancholic face, "If two hillbillies get married, and then in a few years they get a divorce, will they still be cousins?" When questioned about such negative quips (and reminded that he has criticized Jeff Foxworthy for his negative redneck jokes), he responds, "I'm allowed to act that way because I'm from Appalachia. I can make fun of my group in the same way that black people can use the N word. My audience knows where my sympathies and affection lie." Dan Hays, the executive director of the International Bluegrass Music Association, supports Ron's view: "When Ron does his comedy, some people may think there's a bumpkin on stage, but he's really very subtle and sophisticated, and if you follow him you'll know that he has an affection for his culture." Bill C. Malone, in a chapter on country humor in *Don't Get above Your Raisin': Country Music and the Southern Working Class*, commented,

> Ron Thomason . . . built his comedic reputation through the seemingly incongruous blending of backcountry and worldly-wise liberal commentary. . . . Thomason grew up with ardent attachments to Appalachian culture and an acute understanding of the larger world that threatened to subsume that culture and its values. Thomason gave well-rehearsed monologues delivered in a dry, hillbilly dialect that were both funny and compassionate.

Ron Thomason in recent years has mostly retired, he says, although he and the band (now consisting of Ron, mandolin, guitar, and lead vocals; Adam McIntosh, guitar and tenor vocals; Danny Russell, banjo and harmony vocals; Mary Jo Leet, rhythm guitar and harmony vocals; and Charlie Leet, acoustic bass and harmony vocals) are doing concerts here and there, and they did a mostly Western tour in 2003. Now divorced, Ron has moved to the Colorado Rockies with five of his Arabian horses. He spends his time working as a cowboy on nearby ranches, mountain climbing, and guiding people to the best trout streams.

For examples of the Dry Branch Fire Squad's music and some of Ron's humor and satire, get ahold of their Rounder recordings *Dry Branch Fire Squad: Live at Last*, *Memories That Bless and Burn* (hymns), and *Hand Hewn*.

Here Ron Thomason makes a little fun of music and musicians in one of his concerts:

> *One of the reasons I tell you the names of the songs is so you can tell 'em apart. I realize you find this hard to believe, but we have the same problem with other kinds of music. A*

lot of music isn't even bluegrass. It's even more primitive music, and it's called old-time music, and in old-time music there's a fine line between playin' it and not bein' able to play at all. . . .

Now where would bluegrass music be without banjos to make it all sound alike? We once went down to Nashville. They'd had a convention of banjo players. They claimed they had 190 banjo players in town that week. I can tell you this, a week later there was still residual pockets of ignorance around town, like if you drove through them, your slate would be wiped clean. You might not believe this, but there's not a lot of creative thinkin' goes on at a banjo convention, but they invented this thing called a banjo joke, which I thought was a redundancy. People were tellin' vicious ones, saying fifty banjo players at the bottom of the Cumberland River was a good start, and what do you have when you have a banjo player up to his neck in concrete? You got a shortage of concrete. And did you hear about this banjo player who was so far out of tune that even the other banjo players started to notice it? And the first three words banjo players' kids learn is, "Attention K-Mart shoppers!"

So we started to say all-constructive things about the banjo—like if you didn't have a banjo player droolin' out of both sides of his mouth, how would you know the stage was level?

TILLIE THRASHER

Born Ruth Stevens, birth date unknown, Dalton,
Georgia; death date and place unknown

Tillie Thrasher was the stage name of Ruth Stevens, known as "the Judy Canova of the South" when she performed with Hal Burns and his "Garrett Snuff Varieties" on WMC in Memphis in the late 1930s and early 1940s. This show was also sold on transcriptions, introduced by local radio personalities, to other radio stations in Alabama, Georgia, West Virginia, North Carolina, Tennessee, Texas, Arkansas, Louisiana, Oklahoma, and Florida. For example, Archie Campbell as "Grandpappy" introduced transcriptions of the show over WNOX in Knoxville and WDOD in Chattanooga. Advertisements for the shows billed Tillie as "Radio's New Comedy Sensation," and in personal appearances she was sometimes called the "Queen of Gully Gulch." A *Memphis Commercial Appeal* headline of March 25, 1940, announced that she was "Near [the] Top of Hillbilly Roles." The article described her act in this way: "Using a distinctive backwoods style of dialog and homespun gags she draws fan mail by the basketfull and sells her sponsor's brand of snuff like hot cakes. Admirers drive long distances to see her perform. Her listeners are legion. She definitely has become a standout Southern radio personality."

Stevens got into radio entertainment by accident. Sitting in a WMC radio show audience, she was invited to read the part of a woman in a radio script. Her delivery and accent impressed Milton Simon, the announcer for the show who was also a partner in the Simon and Gwynne Advertising agency. The agency prepared radio scripts for her performances and, no doubt, coached her in her character. They asked Hal Burns to put her on his show, and he agreed. Burns remembered that "she was really terrific. Oh, she really helped that show."

Tillie sported a high-pitched country voice, sometimes with a dialect that was more black than hillbilly. She often did skits with a fellow performer named Uncle Ned, actually Milton Simon. After the variety show broke up when Hal Burns was called into military service, Tillie's career appears to have declined. She was married to Jackie Boy Pennington, a fiddler from Birmingham, who was also on the variety show.

The following traditional stories come from *Tillie and Uncle Ned's Book of 160 Jokes*, published by the American Snuff Company in 1942 (courtesy of Wayne Daniel). This book was no doubt put together by Simon and Gwynne.

> *Tillie: Uncle Punkin always said that he aimed to live, so when he wanted to get up and move, all he had to do was put out the fire and call the dogs! And I'm a-tellin' you, that man moved so often, the first o' ever' month, by grannies, Uncle Punkin's chickens lined up in front o' him and crossed their feet so's he could tie their legs together.*
>
> *One night, about dark, a flock of wild geese flew overhead, circled, then lit on the pond in our backyard. It wuz fierce cold and the pond froze over so fast, it froze them geese firm by their feet. It got colder durin' the night, and the pond must have a-froze clear to the bottom, for the next mornin', I went out there, and so help me, them geese had flew away and took the pond with them!*

MEL TILLIS

Born Lonnie Melvin Tillis, August 8, 1932,
Tampa, Florida

Mel Tillis is a gifted songwriter, singer, bandleader, and businessman, but he has a handicap that might have stymied his career before it started: he stutters. However, a kindly man to whom Tillis had applied for a job gave him a copy of the "Serenity" prayer about having the courage to change what can be changed, the serenity to accept what can't be changed, and the wisdom to know the difference. This prayer changed his outlook about himself and his handicap. He turned his stuttering into an asset, the cornerstone of his comedy.

The Tillis family moved to Pahokee, on Lake Okeechobee, when Mel was ten, and he grew up there learning to play guitar, but he was also active playing drums in the high school band. One of his teachers told him about the great Greek orator Demosthenes, who was a stutterer and how he overcame it by speaking with pebbles in his mouth. Mel tried it but swallowed half of the pebbles. He was to tell Johnny Carson later that this was the source of his kidney stones. He joined the air force after high school, hoping to become a pilot, but he was rejected because of his handicap. Serving in Okinawa, he formed a band that entertained fellow servicemen.

When he was discharged in 1955, he enrolled at the University of Florida but left after a semester and worked at several jobs. He moved to Nashville in 1957, the year Webb Pierce took Mel's composition "I'm Tired" to number three on the country charts. Tillis got a job with Minnie Pearl's band as a guitar picker and singer (a buddy, Roger Miller, was the fiddler). Minnie noticed that while he sang, he never said a word. He explained that he couldn't because people laughed. Minnie said, "Let 'em laugh. Laughs are hard to get." He reported, "I started talking on stage . . . to introduce my songs. Sometimes I'd make it and sometimes I wouldn't. I began telling little things that had happened to me. Before long I had several routines, and they were almost certain to get laughs." The country soon learned about this gifted songwriter (Bobbie Bare had taken Mel and Danny Dill's "Detroit City" to Top Ten country and Top Twenty pop) who was a good singer but had this funny stuttering act. He was invited to perform on the Johnny Carson, Merv Griffin, Mike Douglas, Dinah Shore, and Phil Donahue television shows.

Tillis has recorded for Columbia, Kapp, MGM, and MCA. He had number one hits with "I Ain't Never," "Good Woman Blues," "Coca-Cola Cow-boy," "Heart Healer," "I Believe in You." and "South-

Mel Tillis.
Courtesy of Mel Tillis.

ern Rains." His songs were major hits for such singers as Webb Pierce, Glenn Campbell, Kenny Rogers and the First Edition, Bobby Bare, Ray Price, and Charley Pride. Tillis has also been in thirteen movies, including *Smokey and the Bandit* and *Every Which Way but Loose.*

Tillis was named Entertainer of the Year by the Country Music Association in 1976 and was installed in the Nashville Songwriters Hall of Fame in 1989. In 1984 he published an autobiography, *Stutterin' Boy.*

Mel Tillis remains active in the entertainment business as a music publisher and a theater owner in Branson, Missouri, where he also performs.

Here is a Mel Tillis story:

This feller took his wife out for their twenty-fifth anniversary dinner. Well, halfway through the meal he got sad and pretty soon started cryin'. His wife said, "What's the matter with you? This is our twenty-fifth anniversary, and you ought to be happy." He said, "Do you remember when your father caught us out in the woods, and he said he if I didn't marry you, he'd see that I went to the penitentiary for twenty-five years?" She said, "Yes, but why are you cryin' now?" He said, "Well, I'd be gittin' out today!"

TOWSER MURPHY. *See Albert Eliot*

JOE TROYAN

Born March 25, 1912, Pleasant City, Ohio; died June 21, 2000, Cleveland, Ohio

When Joe Troyan was asked how big Pleasant City was, he said, "Well, our grandfather lived in the other house." Actually, he was born on a farm with six brothers and one sister, of Slovakian parentage, and even before he could talk he began imitating the farm animals. The first quarter he had went for a harmonica, on which he became proficient, using it also to imitate animals. Joe's father died when he was nine, and

Joe Troyan.
Courtesy of Joe Troyan.

within a few years his mother moved the family to Cleveland. There he entered talent contests with his harmonica and animal imitations, leading to a job on a radio station. When Rudy Vallee came to town and staged a talent show, Joe was one of seven winners out of a thousand contestants. One trick he used was playing the harmonica held behind his back with a beer hose. Another winner in Vallee's contest was a young Kentucky boy, Louis Marshall Jones, as a yodeler.

Shortly thereafter, the "Lum and Abner" radio show, which also performed in personal appearances, advertised for musicians for their Pine Ridge String Band. Troyan and Jones auditioned and were hired, and they stayed with the show for nearly two years, learning a great deal from their fellow entertainers. Then they met Bradley Kincaid, "the Kentucky Mountain Boy," who was then popular on radio. After inquiring about their personal habits (clean), he invited them to get their parents' permission to go with him to WBZ in Boston. Joe remembered, "Bradley was a precious man to me. He took us under his wing and showed us what to do in the world."

It was Kincaid who dubbed him "Bashful Harmonica Joe." Troyan recalled, "I was very bashful when I was young. When I went into comedy, I had to go to the bathroom every few minutes. I had this little bow tie, and when I went on stage I had to swallow, and this bow tie jumped up and down, and people were laughing. So I went out and bought the biggest bow tie I could find." The bobbing tie became part of his act. He also created Mr. Guppy, who talked in a pinched childlike voice and recited monologues or aphorisms that he had written or collected that he called "guppies" (of which he had about a thousand), such as, "The old-fashioned wife darned husband's socks; the modern wife socks darned husband." On WBZ, Jones sounded like an old man and people inquired about his age, and Kincaid started calling him "Grandpa." So Kincaid, with his beautiful singing, and Joe and Grandpa, with their music and comedy, became a great act. They stayed in New England with Kincaid for nearly three years and made personal appearances all over New England.

In 1935, Joe joined up with Pie Plant Pete (Claude Moye), who had played guitar and harmonica and sung over WLS and other midwestern stations. They performed together for nearly a year at WBZ, went to WHAM in Rochester, and then returned to Cleveland in 1939. Their partnership was broken up when both went into service. In the Army Air Corps, Joe was in public relations but also with a Special Service unit that entertained troops, including the first casualties from Guadalcanal. After the war, Joe and Pete teamed up again for some twenty-two years to play mostly over WJR in Detroit, WTAM in Cleveland, and at stations in Schenectady, Rochester, and Syracuse, New York. All the time, they did public appearances in the stations' listening area. After they retired, Joe continued to do shows wherever he was invited and volunteered to entertain at public events and at retirement and nursing homes.

In 1985, Joe and his old friend Bradley Kincaid joined Grandpa Jones when Jones was being honored at the Kentucky Center for the Arts in Louisville. It had been fifty years since they had performed together, but they launched right into their old routines and brought down the house. The writer Ronni Lundy described Harmonica Joe as "purely outrageous. A one-man kinetic sound-effect machine, he created trains, barnyard animals, Fords of many generations, pop bottles, and pumps with his mouth and mouth harp . . . and leapt about the stage like a man possessed." The trio later performed again at a Berea College festival to rousing applause.

Joe Troyan was a fine gentleman who neither drank nor smoked and who never missed a show except for the one when he was stranded in a blizzard. He wrote his mother a postcard every day when he was on the road, and he took care of her until her death at eighty-five. He was married to the former Harriet Neumann, a schoolteacher. Joe was inducted into the Broadcasters' Hall of Fame in Akron in 1991, and he died in 2000 of complications of aplastic anemia. He was eighty-eight.

Joe, with a Mr. Guppy routine, shows his verbal ability:

My dear sir:
In response to your request to send a check for the bill I owe you, I wish to inform you that the present condition of my bank account makes it almost impossible. My shattered financial condition is due to federal laws, state laws, county laws, corporation laws, liquor laws, mothers-in-law, brothers-in-law, sisters-in-law, and outlaws. To these laws I'm compelled

to pay business tax, amusement tax, school tax, gas tax, sales tax, cigarette tax, piggy-back tax, liquor tax, carpet tacks, income tax, food tax, furniture tax, excise tax, yes, even my bunions are taxed. I am required to get a business license, car license, hunting license, fishing license, truck license, not to mention a marriage and a dog license. I am also required to contribute to every society and organization which the genius of man is capable of bringing to life: the unemployment relief and rock-and-roll relief. For my own safety, I am required to carry life insurance, property insurance, liability insurance, accident insurance, business insurance, earthquake insurance, tornado insurance, unemployment insurance, old-age and fire insurance.

My business is so governed that it is no easy matter for me to find out who owns it. I'm inspected, expected, suspected, disrespected, rejected, dejected, examined, reexamined, informed, required, summoned, fined, commanded, and compelled until I supply an inexhaustible supply of money for every known need of the human race. Simply because I refuse to donate to something or other, I am boycotted, talked about, lied about, held up, held down, and robbed until I am almost ruined. I can tell you earnestly that except for the miracle that happened, I could not enclose this check. The wolf that comes to my door nowadays just had pups. I sold them, and here is the money.

Yours faithfully,
Mr. Guppy

UNCLE JOSH. *See Cal Stewart*

DAVE VAUGHT. *See VW Boys*

RACHEL VEACH

Born at Peytonville, Tennessee, date unknown;
died 1981.

Rachel Veach, who grew up on a tenant farm, was the niece of the "Grand Ole Opry" duo of Sam and Kirk McGee, and Sam brought her to the attention of Roy Acuff when he heard he was looking for a girl singer who could pick the banjo. Acuff liked Rachel and hired her in 1939, even though she was too scared to do much picking at her audition. He billed her as "Rachel, Queen of the Hills." Acuff was a great believer in comedy and wanted all of his band members to be able to get a laugh. At first, he gave the impression that dobroist and banjoist Beecher "Pete" Kirby and Lonnie "Pap" Willson, the bass player, were Rachel's country boyfriends. However, as Elizabeth Schlappi reports in her biography of Acuff, fans raised questions about this young girl traveling around with a bunch of men. Therefore, Acuff created the illusion that Rachel was Kirby's sister, and they became "Cousin Rachel" and her "Bashful Brother Oswald." Schlappi quotes Acuff as saying, "So I fooled the public to protect the name of Rachel."

Oswald remembered that the first time they went on stage to do their comedy act dressed as rustics—they just stood there looking at each other and brought the house down. She and Oswald each blacked out a tooth and dressed as rubes, with Rachel making sure that her bloomers showed below her dress. Their act became a central part of Acuff's show. They told jokes, and each developed a loud comic laugh. In addition to their comedy, they did rousing numbers on their banjos and sang songs such as "John Henry."

Veach and Kirby can be seen in the Republic movie *The Grand Ole Opry*, which also featured, in addition to Acuff and band, Lulu Belle and Scotty, the Weaver Brothers and Elviry, and Uncle Dave Macon.

In 1941, Rachel Veach married Bill Wilson, a local farmer, before he went into service. When he returned from the war in 1946, Rachel gradually ceased performing, reportedly because her husband did not want her to continue in show business. They lived in Williamson County, Tennessee, and had four daughters.

VW BOYS

Tim White, born March 13, 1956, Roanoke, Virginia
Dave Vaught, born August 16, 1952, Smith County,
    Virginia
Larry McPeak, born July 13, 1947, Wytheville,
    Virginia (Larry's liver transplant birthday,
    April 13, 2001)

The VW boys, who play out of Blountville, Tennessee, bill their show as "Music, Magic, and Comedy." Each member of the band is gifted in several ways, and they created the band to counter the limited nature of today's entertainment, as compared to the old radio and television variety shows. Tim White says, "Not trying to brag, but we've done a good job creating variety entertainment. We're well received wherever we go." They go to corporate conventions, bluegrass festivals, Tim White's radio show on WGOC-AM in Blountville, and occasionally Dollywood.

Tim White, the leader of the VW Boys, is a bundle of talent, a bluegrass banjo picker for twenty years, promoter of Jim and Jesse McReynolds's bluegrass festivals, a songwriter, radio personality, and a painter (of pictures). He organized the Birthplace of Country Music Alliance (BCMA) in Bristol, Tennessee/Virginia, and he personally painted a thirty-by-eleven-foot mural on State Street in Bristol that commemorates Ralph Peer's famous 1927 Victor recordings in that city. It features a Victor label in the center, with portraits of Peer; A. P., Sara, and Maybelle Carter; Ernest and Hattie

The VW Boys: Tim White, Larry McPeak, and Dave Vaught. Courtesy of Tim White.

Stoneman; and Jimmie Rodgers, whose careers were launched or enhanced by these recordings. The BCMA has promoted concerts, festivals, and educational events to show the importance of the musicians from that part of the country. White also has a daily show on WGOC for three hours each weekday and four hours on Saturday. With the VW Boys, he is adept with music, magic, and comedy.

Dave Vaught has entertained as a musician and magician on cruise ships, at night clubs, conventions, schools, colleges, fairs, and festivals and on HBO and Showtime. He is a fine guitar player and singer with five albums. He has played with Ronnie Milsap, Garry Morris, Silvia, Jerry Reed, and Charlie Pride. With the VW Boys, he contributes magic tricks, harmony singing, and he and White carry most of the comedy.

Larry McPeak grew up in a musical family and began playing and singing early on. He and his brothers played bluegrass and gospel music for thirty years before he joined the VW Boys. He is a well-known bluegrass songwriter whose songs are played by such bluegrass bands as the Lonesome River Band, Seldom Scene, and the Country Gentlemen. He writes most of the comic songs for the VW Boys. He has recorded for RCA, County, Rebel, and Copper Creek. In addition to bluegrass and gospel, McPeak loves to play traditional Appalachian string-band music. In 2001, Larry, near death, received a liver transplant for which fans of the VW Boys raised the money. A part of the VW Boys' shows now encourage members of the audience to take out their driver's licenses and sign the backs for organ donations. They point out that because a young man signed his name years ago, his liver saved Larry for more years of entertaining. Larry tells the audience about his dilapidated condition and the scars resulting from his surgery and then brings down the house by singing Sheb Wooley's "I Just Don't Look Good Naked Anymore."

Comic songs are a great part of the VW Boys' entertainment and are featured on Fat Dog Records (Box 750, Blountville, TN 37617), starting with the *Possum Tapes* with thirteen songs, some written by Tim White, about that lowly but interesting marsupial, including "Five Pounds of Possum," "Mama's Not Dead, She's Just Playin' Possum," "The Possum Blues," and "Possum Promenade." Another album, *VW Boys "Big Fat Earl,"* features the funny title song that is a parody of Jimmy Dean's hit, "Big John." It opens with:

> Ever' mornin' at the diner you'd see him arrive
> He stood five feet five, and weighed three ninety-five.
> He was broad at the shoulders and even broader at the gut,
> And when he bent over, you could see the crack of his butt.

The ballad goes on to relate the climax of the story, when Big Earl's gastric chemistry shuts down a successful business. This CD also has good bluegrass music and their "Man on the Street" interviews. "The VW Boys Radio Show" is done in the style of one of yesteryear's live radio shows, with serious music, comic songs, and comedy. In 2003, they released another CD, *Snappy Lunch*. On this one they are joined by Patsy Stoneman of the famous Stoneman Family, the fiddler Hunter Berry, and the comedian Fred Smith. While Larry McPeak is the most productive writer of comic songs, the trio have collaborated on several songs.

Tim and Dave do magic acts, and these involve a lot of comedy. We learn that since Tim started doing magic tricks, their dove bill has gone up by two-thirds. Tim proceeds to pull a live dove out of a cloth, but then when he's asked to do it again, out comes a cloud of feathers. In a promotional video, all three participate in "Man on the Street" interviews, mainly asking questions about the VW Boys to people who have never heard of them. However, members of the band disguised as people on the street give the band extravagant praise. For some concerts and radio shows, the band also includes the comedy of Fred Smith and sometimes David Browning, who re-creates Barney Fife's role as Mayberry Deputy. In addition to the comedy and comedy songs, the VW Boys present solid, well-performed bluegrass music.

Tim White says of their humor, "We take our comedy very seriously. We try to do it right and make people forget their problems for a little while. People have to have release, an outlet, and we try to provide that. Also, it's good for us. If we have a good time. They definitely have a good time."

> *Tim: Do you know what time it's gettin' to be?*
> *Dave: No, I ain't got a watch.*
> *Tim: I thought you had an expensive watch.*
> *Dave: I did. It was anti-magnetic, self-winding, shock-resistant, water-proof, rust-proof, and dust-proof, but it don't work anymore.*

Tim: Well, what happened to it?
Dave: It caught on fire.

   Tim introduces Dave, who is drinking Windex window cleaner.
Tim: What are you doing? Why are you drinking Windex?
Dave: Uh . . . it's medicine.
Tim: Medicine for what?
Dave: Uh . . . well, I have this strong tendency to take all my clothes off, and
   this keeps me from STREAKING!

FLORA BELL WALTERS. *See Granny Harper*

MARGARET WATERS. *See Sarie and Sally*

THE WEAVER BROTHERS AND ELVIRY

Leon "Abner" Weaver, born April 18, 1886, Ozark,
   Missouri; died 1962
Frank "Cicero" Weaver, born February 2, 1891,
   Ozark, Missouri; died October 29, 1967, Ventura,
   California
June "Elviry" Petrie, born June 23, 1891, Chicago,
   Illinois; died November 27, 1977, Bakersfield,
   California

The Weaver Brothers and Elviry were among several country entertainers who got their start in medicine and vaudeville shows. They saw themselves as the first rube comedians, although the city slicker/country bumpkin theme was older than their act. They were also competent musicians, though specializing in unusual instruments. Leon has been credited with being the first to play the handsaw with a fiddle bow in an entertainment show. He entered show business through the medicine show as early as 1902. His younger brother Frank soon joined him as Cicero. By 1913, they had incorporated Elviry into their act and were touring the vaudeville circuit. By 1920 they were well-paid headline performers with the RKO circuit.

   Elviry initially married Abner, probably in the early 1920s, but then she divorced him and married Cicero in 1928. The act went on in apparent harmony. In fact, they formed a large musical act called "The Home Folks" that was made up of relatives on both sides of the family.

   Abner played various musical instruments—fiddle, mandolin, and guitar, as well as the musical saw. Cicero, who performed as a mute character, also played the saw and a variety of weird inventions, and he did a one-man-band act. Elviry, tall and bony, played a frustrated housewife, beleaguered by the zany brothers. Like many other entertainers, the Weaver Brothers and Elviry were invited to Hollywood to make movies, and they made a total of thirteen, probably the best known of which was *The Grand Ole Opry* (1940), in which they played headline roles along with Roy Acuff, George D. Hay, Uncle Dave Macon, and Lulu Belle and Scotty. For a dozen or so years until Abner died in 1962, they were popular performers over the radio station KWTO in Springfield, Missouri.

LARRY WEBSTER

Born October 2, 1945, Owen County, Kentucky

Larry Webster makes his living as a coalfield lawyer, but for fun and to vent his feelings about various things, he's also been a small-town newspaper publisher and writer, social and political satirist, and leader of the Mule Band, which plays old-time music. In the last role he is known to spin a lot of stories and jokes, most sharpened by his satirical bent. Born in the hills of north-central Kentucky, Webster got hooked on mountain music as a teenager. After graduating from Transylvania University and the University of Kentucky Law School, he was hired by the Republican Governor Louie B. Nunn to investigate conditions in the eastern coalfields. He chose as his base Pikeville, the easternmost county hard up against West Virginia. He helped to write the Black Lung Bill that compensated miners for breathing impairment. He then decided to settle permanently in Pikeville. A major reason was that there were a lot of traditional musicians in the area. Larry himself is a clawhammer banjo player and a singer of considerable ability.

When the Mule Band plays, Larry cracks a lot of jokes, many of them culled from the performances of such as Minnie Pearl, Lonzo and Oscar, and Renfro Valley's Pete Stamper. He also does a lot of Uncle Dave Macon's satirical songs. His political satire is mostly reserved for his weekly column in the local paper, the *Appalachian Express* (that he founded and published for a while) and in monthly columns for the *Lexington Herald-Leader.* Through them, he says, he wants to come off as a country boy who has some smarts. He describes himself as "an anarchist, a Goldwater Republican, a sort of a libertarian anti-state kind of person." He thinks that both major political parties "are racing to see who can get there firstest with the mostest when it comes to government." He says, "It's this foolish idea that it's somebody else's duty to feed us, somebody else's duty to care for our health, somebody else's duty to house or warm us—that it is a common duty, not our own." In his columns he has created two characters, Tie Rod and Slemp, who comment on the sorry mess Webster thinks government has made. In a recent column, for example, he took on the Army Corps of Engineers and hoped that they might find a war somewhere that would get them out of eastern Kentucky.

He takes aim at both the Republicans and the Democrats, especially in the state's legislature that sometimes has a hard time passing a budget, especially when funds are scarce. His two characters comment on the election of 2002 in a December 15 *Lexington Herald-Leader* column:

> Tie Rod took to his bed over the election and won't even take calls from Slemp. Tie Rod is a sort of Jesse Ventura Democrat, and got mad at Slemp when Slemp's Republicans stole the free pills idea from the Democrats.
>
> Payback is hell, is all Slemp will say; and I think he is referring to when Bill Clinton dressed up all the Democrats in all them GOP garments.
>
> He remembers back when pills weren't free in the mountains and you did not get robbed in the parking lot by kids raised on them. He says pharmacy has replaced crafts as the new mountain art.

Another favorite topic for Webster is the perceived elitist attitude of people from Lexington and the Bluegrass section of the state in regard to folks from the mountain portion. He is a combative defendant of the mountain people.

Webster is also the musical director of the annual Shriners-sponsored "Hillbilly Days" in Pikeville, when people dress up and act out outlandish versions of the hillbilly stereotype, as a way to make fun of themselves and those who think they are better than hillbillies. He brings talented musicians to Pikeville and presses the Mule Band into service for the occasion.

Larry Webster is married to the former Cheryl Davidson, and they have two sons, Scott and Mickey, both practicing lawyers like their father.

Webster is radical and unpredictable in his views and comments, but he is a whole lot of fun to be around. Here is one of Larry Webster's favorite jokes at the expense of his bass player:

> *Bill Brooks got real sick and thought he was going to die. He decided he'd better go to church, so he went up to the Free-Will Baptist church and asked the preacher, "What do I have to do to come into this church?" The preacher said, "Well, you gotta go through some purification. For three weeks you don't want to do any drinking, or play any music, or have any sex." So Bill left and came back in three weeks. The preacher said, "How did it go?" Bill said, "Well, I didn't take a drink for three weeks, and I didn't play any music." The preacher said, "What about that other thing?" Bill said, "Well, I did pretty well on that for about two and a half weeks, and then the other morning, the old lady bent over to pick up the corn flakes she'd dropped, and then and there I violated your instructions." The preacher said, "Well, you can't come into this church," and Bill said, "Yeah, and I can't go back to Kroger's either."*

WILLIE EGBERT WESBROOKS (COUSIN WILBUR)

Born March 5, 1911, Gibson County, Tennessee;
died August 13, 1984

Cousin Wilbur Wesbrooks was a popular comedian on the "Grand Ole Opry" with Bill Monroe and the Bluegrass Boys and sometimes with his own band. His work experience included medicine shows, the "kerosene circuit" of county schools, tent shows, and television. He had the distinction of being the first bandleader to hire young Eddy Arnold, back in 1936.

Wesbrooks's first jobs were nonpaying ones at WMPS in Memphis and KLCN in Blytheville, Arkansas, while he picked cotton to keep body and soul together. His first real paying job was at WTJS in Jackson, Tennessee. He did his first comedy while promoting a furniture store in Dyersburg, Tennessee, at a cotton festival. Earlier, with medicine shows, he picked up a lot of jokes and routines. In 1940, he got a job as bass player and comedian with Bill Monroe and stayed with him until he joined the "Opry" in 1944. He was influential in getting Monroe to hire David "Stringbean" Akeman as a banjo player in the pre–Earl Scruggs Bluegrass Boys, and Wilbur and Stringbean did doubles comedy that delighted Monroe and his audiences.

In 1945, Wesbrooks put together a band, Cousin Wilbur and the Tennessee Mountain Boys, and continued playing at the "Grand Ole Opry." Judge Hay loved his comedy and frequently insisted that he sing his hit song, "I'm Saving Up Coupons to Get One of Those," and Hay sometimes became part of the act when he had to come out and get Cousin Wilbur's yodel unstuck. Wesbrooks also followed the trend in Nashville and formed a tent show. His fellow travelers with the show were Stringbean, Uncle Dave Macon, Robert Lunn, Sam and Kirk McGee, Big Howdy Forrester, and Chubby Wise. In 1947, he married Blondie Leatherman, whose stage name was Blondie Brooks, and she became part of his show. Later, they did USO tours for troops.

In the 1950s Wilbur and his group worked at the WWVA "Jamboree" in Wheeling, West Virginia, and then they got into television at WLOS-TV in Asheville, North Carolina. At this time, he had a good band made up of Red Smiley, Buck Trent, Charlie Moore, Ray Crisp, and Blondie. They did seven shows a week, five during the day and two at night. From there they went to Channel 6 in Savannah, before returning to the "Grand Ole Opry" in 1959. He continued to travel widely, even playing casinos in Las Vegas.

Cousin Wilbur was the classic rube comedian on stage, with gaudy shirt, oversized pants torn off at the bottoms, huge safety pin in front, and rubber suspenders that allowed them to bounce up and down, a fringed hat, forelock, round black glasses, and blacked-out teeth. He said he did "just old country boy humor" with "never a vulgar word." He knew how to work the audience, or protect himself from it. He told of being heckled by a fellow who didn't care for rube humor. So Wilbur shouted, "That's my brother's voice. I'd know him anywhere!" It worked. He knew that the way he looked, the heckler would be ashamed to be identified as his kinfolk.

In 1979 Cousin Wilbur published a book with Barbara M. McLean and Sandra S. Grafton, *Everybody's Cousin.* In it he tells his life story, but he also relates some of the tricks and practical jokes that entertainers played on one another to ease the tedium and fatigue of long road trips. For example, he and Big Howdy Forrester devised a scheme to get a drink of Uncle Dave Macon's Jack Daniel's whiskey by convincing the old man that an FBI agent was searching their hotel rooms in the dry county to confiscate illegal whiskey. Uncle Dave gave them the key to his room to rescue his bottle. Another time, Wilbur conspired with two local policemen to have them arrest Kirk McGee and Chubby Wise on a trumped-up charge.

Cousin Wilbur and Blondie continued to perform together and to attend festivals and reunion events into their retirement years.

(With credit to Cousin Wilbur with Barbara M. McLean and Sandra S. Grafton, *Everybody's Cousin* [Rockville Centre, N.Y.: Manor Books, 1979].)

BILLY EDD WHEELER

Born December 9, 1932, Whitesville, West Virginia

Billy Edd Wheeler, from Boone County, West Virginia, is an acclaimed songwriter, performer, poet, playwright, and humorist and was an executive with United Artists in Nashville. His "Ode to the Little Brown Shack out Back," with hilarious imagery about this American institution, was number two on the *Billboard* country chart in 1964. A book, *Outhouse Humor* (August House, 1989), resulted from the jokes fans came up and told him at concerts after he had sung "Ode." He is author of two collections of poems, *Song of a Woods Colt* (Droke House, 1969) and *Travis and Other Poems of the Swannanoa Valley* (Wild Goose, 1977). He is also coauthor (with Loyal Jones) of four other books of Appalachian humor (*Laughter in Appalachia,* 1987; *Curing the Cross-Eyed Mule,* 1989; *Hometown Humor,* 1991; and *More Laughter in Appalachia,* 1995—all published by August House in Atlanta). He and Jones organized four festivals of Appalachian humor at Berea College in Kentucky. Wheeler did another book, *Real Country Humor/Jokes from Country Music Personalities,* in 2002, also published by August House. He is the author of two novels, *Star of Appalachia* (Affinity Publishing, 2003) and (with Ewel Cornett) *Kudzu Covers Manhattan: Chinatown, Knock-Offs, and Contraband* (Book Locker, 2004). He has recorded music with Monitor, United Artists, Kapp, Capitol, and RCA labels, as well as for his own Sagittarius label.

Wheeler's songs have been on over sixty million records, recorded by 150-some artists, including the Kingston Trio, Peter, Paul, and Mary, June Carter and Johnny Cash, Elvis Presley, Nancy Sinatra and Lee Hazelwood, Judy Collins, and Kenny

Rogers. Best-known are "The Reverend Mr. Black," "The Coming of the Roads," "Jackson," "High Flyin' Bird" (his most-recorded song), and "Coward of the County" (with Roger Bowling), but he has written several coal mining–related songs, including "Coal Tattoo" and "They Can't Put It Back," with a harder edge.

Educated at Warren Wilson College, Berea College, and Yale Drama School, Wheeler has written twenty plays, including the long-running *Hatfields and McCoys* in Beckley, West Virginia; *Young Abe Lincoln* in Lincoln City, Indiana; and *Johnny Appleseed*, which opened in Mansfield, Ohio, in the summer of 2004. All of these plays are laced with his original music and humor.

Wheeler and his wife Mary (Bannerman) have two adult children, Lucy and Travis. They live in Swannanoa, North Carolina, and when Billy Edd is not performing, writing songs, plays, or books, he depicts country life in paintings, drawings, and sculpture. The prestigious Blue Spiral Gallery in Asheville, North Carolina, featured Wheeler's work in 2007.

Over the years, Billy Edd has received numerous awards. He was given the Distinguished Alumnus Award from Warren Wilson College and Berea College, and Berea made him an honorary Doctor of Humane Letters in 2004. *Billboard* gave him its Pacesetter Award for Music and Drama in 1970, the Nashville Songwriters Association International inducted him into its Hall of Fame in 2001, Country Music Television voted his song "Jackson" one of the ten greatest love songs of country music in 2005, and his home state inducted him into the West Virginia Music Hall of Fame in 2007. In 2008, *Appalachian Heritage*, a quarterly literary magazine published by Berea College, devoted its winter issue to the art of Billy Edd Wheeler—his musical performances and songwriting (including a retrospective CD), his poetry, his dramatic productions, and his humor.

Billy Edd Wheeler. Courtesy of Billy Edd Wheeler.

Among his available recordings are *The Best of Laughter in Appalachia: Loyal Jones and Billy Edd Wheeler* (Sagittarius Records, 1998); *Billy Edd Wheeler, Songs I Wrote with Chet* (Sagittarius Records, 1994); *Songs and Legends of the Outer Banks*, with Paul Craft (Kitty Hawk Records, 1998); a compilation CD, *Milestones: A Self-Portrait* (Sagittarius, 2002), *A Song of the Cumberland Gap* (2006); and *New Wine from Old Vines: Billy Edd Wheeler Uncorked* (2006). For more information, see www.billyeddwheeler.com.

Billy Edd: This fellow came back home after being away for a spell, saw his neighbor at the edge of town and asked him if there was any news.

"News? Naw, nothing's been happening that I can think of. Hey, wait a minute, there was one thing. Your dog died."

"My dog died? Old Blue? Lordy mercy, how did that happen?"

"Well, I reckon it was that burnt horseflesh that killed him."

"Burnt horseflesh! Where'd he get that?"

"When your barn burned down. Actually, the fire started in your house, then sparks flew over and caught the barn, trapped the horses. The dog ate the horse meat. . . ."

"My house burned down? My gracious, how did that happen?"

"I think it was one of the candles. It must have tilted over during the funeral and set the curtains on fire."

"F-Funeral—at my house? Who died?"

"Your mother-in-law. You see, when your wife ran off with that traveling salesman, it broke her heart, and she died. They had a little funeral service at your house, and that's when the candles by the coffin caught the curtains on fire and then the house and then the barn and them poor horses that Old Blue ate and then died. But other than that, not much has been happening."

LEE ROY "LASSES" WHITE
(see also Lee Davis "Honey" Wilds)

Born 1885, Wills Point, Texas; died December 16, 1949, California

Lasses White had a long career in minstrel, tent, and vaudeville shows, radio, and in films as a B-Western sidekick and character actor. He had an early popular recording called "Nigger Blues" (1912), and his blackface troupers recorded routines for Columbia Records on cylinders prior to the 1920s. George D. Hay hired him and his partner, Lee "Honey" Wilds, in 1932 to start a Friday show at Nashville's WSM based on the act of the vaudeville blackface troupe he had headed. They were so popular that they became regulars on the "Grand Ole Opry" as Lasses and Honey, doing blackface comedy and song parodies.

In 1939 White headed for Hollywood, where he made eight films as the comic sidekick of Tim Holt in 1941 and 1942 and twelve more as sidekick to the singing star Jimmy Wakely from 1944 to 1947. Wakely called him a skilled character actor rather than a slapstick comedian in his role as sidekick and compared him to George "Gabby" Hayes. He also described their travels to theaters to promote their movies and how White would do a comedy routine that was always funny, using his repertoire and experience from vaudeville and radio days.

The films that White did at RKO with Tim Holt had better scripts and were of a higher quality than those he made at Monogram Pictures with Wakely. Since the budgets at Monogram were low, Lasses had to do his own riding stunts, even though by then he was into his sixties and not in good health. Wakely finally decided that he needed a younger sidekick who would also appeal more to the younger set who watched B-Westerns, and he replaced White with Dub Taylor after *Song of the Wasteland* in 1947.

After he left the Wakely series, White got character roles in several feature films, including *The Wistful Widow of Wagon Gap* with Abbott and Costello, *The Dude Goes West* with Eddie Albert, and *In Old Mexico* with Duncan Renaldo. Lee White died in 1949 at the age of sixty-four.

(With credit to David Rothel, *Those Great Cowboy Sidekicks* [Madison, N.C.: Empire Publishing, 2001], 215–24.)

RON WHITE

Born December 18, 1956, Fritch, Texas

Ron White is best known as a member of the Blue Collar Comedy Tour that ran from 2000 to 2003 with Jeff Foxworthy, Bill Engvall, and Larry the Cable Guy. White is known also as "Tater Salad," a title which would seem to enhance his "country" comedian status, although he appears more urbane

Lasses White.

than his fellow comics in the above tour, with his dark suit and props of a glass of scotch and a cigar or cigarette. Although he does not do the slurred speech of earlier comic drunks such as Foster Brooks and Frank Fontaine, he comes across as a hard-drinking bad boy who aspires to some degree of sophistication.

There isn't a lot of information available on White's early life and career. He is reported to have been reared partially by a grandmother in Fritch, Texas, where he says he mostly played in a drainage ditch, catching crawdads and minnows. The family later moved to Houston, where he says he got into some trouble as he grew up, thus buttressing his bad-boy image. He served in the navy during the Vietnam War and saw action. He tells a couple of stories about how he got his "Tater Salad" nickname, but indicates that the true story came out of his naval service. While stateside, his ship had a family day, when relatives of sailors were invited for a picnic on board. He was on watch, and a sailor named Hoskins was to relieve him. Hoskins was late, and he yelled down, "Hey, Hoskins, get up here and relieve me before somebody eats up all the tater salad." So Hoskins started calling him "Tater Salad," and that became his stage nickname. After his tour of duty, he had trouble with drugs and was arrested for public drunkenness. He went through a period of rehabilitation.

He tells of getting a laugh as a child with a knock-knock joke that he himself did not understand. With this and other motivation, he drifted into stand-up comedy. He has mentioned being influenced by such comedians as Richard Pryor, Bob Newhart, Bill Cosby, Cheech and Chong, Andy Griffith, Bill Hicks, and Steve Martin. He has performed on "An Evening at the Improv" and "Caroline's Comedy Hour," on the Arts and Entertainment Network, and also the Just for Laughs Comedy Festival in Montreal. He joined Jeff Foxworthy, Bill Engvall, and Larry the Cable Guy for the Blue Collar Comedy Tour in 2000, which lasted for three years including ninety cities and grossing over fifteen million dollars. Warner Brothers released a full-length film, *The Blue Collar Comedy Tour: The Movie*, in 2003, premiering on Comedy Central and drawing more viewers than any other show on that channel. The DVD version has sold a million and a half copies. A soundtrack CD followed, and WB Cable created a show, "Blue Collar TV," which White declined to be a regular on, reportedly because he didn't want to be typecast as a blue-collar guy. However, he did several guest spots.

Although White's persona is somewhat more sophisticated than his Blue Collar partners, his subject matter is raunchy, and he uses the four-letter words that are now common in stand-up comedy. He gets good marks from critics and fans for his humorous observations on American life. He was voted by comedy-club owners into the top twenty-five comedians in the 2001 American Comedy Awards. Although a Web site states that he refuses to appear in any venue that will not allow him to smoke on stage, when he appeared on "Late Night with David Letterman" in 2002, he did his monologue with neither smoke nor glass of scotch, and his subject matter was rather urbane and clean. He has also appeared twice on "The Tonight Show with Jay Leno."

His first comedy album was *Drunk in Public* (2003), which has been in the Top Ten of *Billboard*'s country charts, selling over 450,000 copies. This album was followed in 2004 with his Drunk in Public tour. In 2004, he released his *Tater Salad: AKA Busted in Des Moines* and *Truckstop Comedy*. *You Can't Fix Stupid* came out in 2006. White also has a 2004 video, *They Call Me Tater Salad*.

Ron White is divorced from his first wife, Barbra. He married Barbara Dobbs in 2004, and they have a son, Marshal.

Advice from Ron White:

> When life gives you lemons, you make lemonade. Then you find someone whose life gives them vodka and have a party.

TIM WHITE. *See VW Boys*

DAN WHITNEY. *See Larry the Cable Guy*

LEE DAVIS "HONEY" WILDS
(see also Lee Roy "Lasses" White)

Born August 23, 1902, Belton, Texas;
died March 29, 1982

Wilds came to Nashville in 1932 with Lee Roy "Lasses" White. They had worked together for many years in minstrel, tent, and vaudeville shows, specializing in blackface humor, calling themselves Lasses and Honey. George D. Hay, the program director at WSM, had seen their act and invited them to do a Friday-night radio show with their comedy routine and song parodies. Soon they were regulars on the "Grand Ole Opry." Wilds liked the name of "Honey" so well that it appeared on his driver's license and on the deed to his house. He was a big man at six feet, two inches, and according to his son, he was not an easy man to deal with, partly because he sometimes drank too much.

In 1939 White was restless and moved to Hollywood to do sidekick comedy in B-Westerns. Wilds also spent time in California and toured with Jim Alexander as Honey and Alexander but returned to the "Opry" in 1940 to do blackface comedy with other partners, Bunny Biggs, Tom Woods, and Harry Levan, as Jamup and Honey. They also did comedy songs and parodies. As an entrepreneur, Wilds was one of the first to invest in equipment and take an "Opry" tent show on the road, staying out from April to October.

In 1954, Wilds took his act to WNOX in Knoxville. By this time, reflecting changing values, he switched from blackface to whiteface comedy but with pretty much the same material. His son David, in an interview, commented on the blackface comedy that his father played but maintained that he was never a racist, citing his friendship with DeFord Bailey, the black harmonica player at the "Opry" who traveled with the tent show in Wilds's car, since Bailey could not drive.

At the end of his career, he tried several business ventures, including a service station. In the early 1960s he had a children's television show in Knoxville, sponsored by Cas Walker's grocery stores. He quit performing around 1967.

(With credit to David Wilds, interviewed by Hank Alden, "The Wilds, the Innocent," *No Depression* 1.4 [Summer 1996]: 48–55.)

WILLIAMS AND REE

Bruce Williams, born April 21, 1950, Nampa, Idaho
Terry Ree, born 1949, Huron, South Dakota

Bruce Williams and Terry Ree met as students at Black Hills State College in South Dakota, where they formed a band in 1969. Their singing repertoire was limited—a dozen or so songs—so they developed their comedy, and it soon became more popular than their music. After college, they moved to Nashville where, as accomplished guitarists and singers, they won the Music City News Award for Best Vocal Duo. However, they are still best known as comedians, doing their politically incorrect "Indian and White Guy" humor. Williams (the white guy) and Ree (the Indian) mine a rich vein of white missionary-to-Indian reservation lore that gives them a chance to comment on wider issues having to do with who's the in-group and who's the out-group in America. They even do a "You might be an Indian if . . ." version of Jeff Foxworthy's redneck routine.

Moving from Nashville to California in the 1970s, the duo honed their comedic skills at the Los Angeles Comedy Store, always on the edge, or sometimes over, with their socially conscious political comments. They build a lot of their comedy around events of the day that highlight our ethnic, class, or social divisions. Ree is quoted as saying, "We don't do jokes. We just comment on what is going on." They also make fun of themselves and single out other groups for good-humored fun.

During the 1980s the duo moved back to Nashville and soon were seen on various TNN shows, including being regular guests on Florence Henderson's "Country Cooking." During 1990–91 they were regulars on "Hee Haw." Williams and Ree do over two hundred gigs a year, including Indian casinos. Even with their Comedy Store experience, they claim to go over better with the older set than with their own age group. One reason is that they don't bother to keep up with what is hip with their own age group—the yuppies—except when they see something to poke fun at. When asked how they keep their humor fresh after performing together for over twenty-five years, Williams says, "There's a little bit of mold on each routine."

Among Williams and Ree recordings are *Live at Seneca Niagra* (DVD, VHS, CD), *Williams and Ree Tongue Studs* (DVD), *Totem Recall* (CD), *Indian Casino Royale* (CD and cassette), and *Williams and Ree Completely Unplugged* (cassette). Visit www.williamsand ree.com.

> *Williams: I've carried you longer than your mother did.*
> *Ree: Yeah, and you've got the stretch marks to show it.*

DOC WILLIAMS

Born Andrew John Smik Jr., June 26, 1914,
Cleveland, Ohio

Doc Williams shied away from telling jokes or being comical himself, but he became a great straight man, and he always had a comedian in his band over the years that he played on the WWVA "Jamboree" from Wheeling, West Virginia, and traveled through the eastern United States and Canada. Among the comedians who were part of his Border Riders were Hamilton "Rawhide" Fincher, James "Froggie" Cortez,

"Crazy Elmer" (Anthony Slater, a.k.a. Smiley Sutter), Hiram Hayseed (Henry "Shorty" Godwin), Charles "Smoky" Pleacher, and Dapper Dan Martin.

Williams did not fit the usual image of the country entertainer. Born of Eastern European parents in Cleveland, he grew up in the coalfields of Pennsylvania. However, his family bought the recordings of the early rural entertainers and listened to the singers on the radio, and young Andrew took up the guitar and began to sing. His brother Cy played the fiddle.

Andrew joined a band called the Kansas Clodhoppers in the early 1930s, and they played over WJAY in Cleveland. He eventually formed his own band, Doc Williams and the Border Riders, which included Cy on fiddle and harmony vocals. Andrew Smik took the name of Doc Williams in 1936 while broadcasting over KQV, WJAS, and WHJB in Pittsburgh. Doc and his band were hired by WWVA in Wheeling in 1937.

Doc married Jessie Wanda Crupe from Bethany, West Virginia, in 1939, and she took the stage name of "Chickie" Williams. Chickie joined Doc's band full-time in 1946. They were to stay with WWVA and the "Jamboree," except for short periods, until they gradually retired in the 1990s. Doc estimates that in addition to their many broadcasts, they did over six thousand two-hour-plus concerts over the United States and Canada. They also established Wheeling Records and released many recordings of Doc and Chickie and the Border Riders and also of the comedians Crazy Elmer, Hiram Hayseed, and Smoky Pleacher (Wheeling Records, Box 902, Wheeling, WV 26003).

Doc Williams.
Courtesy of Doc Williams.

Of the comedy on his show, Doc said, "Humor at that time had a very important function in curing people up and making them feel good. They'd leave those shows and be smiling from ear to ear." He went on to say that his audience knew they'd get three things: a good band, a comedian, and a girl singer. Besides featuring a comedian, he also did skits that involved the whole band. "We did one called 'The Ghost Walks at Midnight.' The kids would be pointing at the ghost and they'd be hysterical. We did another one called 'Pete in the Well,' which had been an old blackface skit. We'd rehearse those things for three or four days before a show."

Doc and Chickie had three children, Barbara, Madeline, and Karen, who were sometimes part of their show. Chickie died on November 18, 2007. Doc, at ninety-three, was still a reliable source on early radio comedy.

The following routine is from *Doc Williams Presents Smoky Pleacher* (Wheeling Records, 1990), with permission:

> *Smoky Pleacher: I was the boss in my family.*
> *Doc Williams: I read an article about that. It said the man has been gradually abdicating his role as the master and head of the family. And you were the boss in your family?*
> *Smoky: I was the boss in my house.*
> *Doc: Bully for you. I'm glad to hear you say it.*
> *Smoky: I used to come home, and when I got tired of telling her off, she'd come crawling to me on her hands and knees.*
> *Doc: That-a-boy, that-a-boy.*
> *Smoky: Then she'd say come out from under that bed, you coward!*
> *Doc: I'm ashamed of you. What are you, a man or a mouse?*
> *Smoky: I'm a man. She was afraid of a mouse!*

ROBIN AND LINDA WILLIAMS

Robin Murphy Williams, born March 16, 1947,
    Charlotte, North Carolina
Linda Hill Williams, born July 7, 1947, Anniston,
    Alabama

Robin and Linda Williams are known to many music fans as regulars on Garrison Keillor's "A Prairie Home Companion" as superb instrumentalists and singers. They have also been members of the Hopeful Gospel Quartet (with Keillor and Kate McKenzie, Molly O'Brien, or Carol Elizabeth Jones). Fans of Keillor's show, as well as those who follow the Williamses at their many concerts and at festivals, also know that Robin and Linda like to loosen up the audience with some humor before performing their music.

Robin Williams talked about their use of comedy: "Our main focus is the music we play, but we use comedy as a way of helping the audience to relax and have a good time. If they're relaxed, that helps us to relax. To see people having a good time frees one up musically. Comedy is really an important part of what we do." They don't do the old rube humor normally associated with country music. They both went to college and are part of the modern world, although they choose to live in a rural area and to sing folk and country music. Their comedy is more akin to other well-educated country and bluegrass musicians such as Riders in the Sky, Tim O'Brien, and Ron Thomason, who tweak the intelligence of their audiences. They are impressive with their music but think of humorous ways to introduce songs that say something about their everyday lives. Robin explains:

> At this point—we're now in our fifties—we say we've stepped over the line into our farthood and what a great point in life it is and how terrible the forties are. There

you have the feeling that you're almost young, and you're dreading turning fifty. When you get to fifty the realization that you are fifty frees you from the shackles and bonds of youth. You don't have to worry about whether you're looking good, whether you're gaining weight, or whether you have your hair and what color it is. Linda says as long as they have color in a bottle, no one's going to know what color it is. You're freed from young people's worries, like making something of yourselves. We're just trying to make it through one more day with our own teeth.

Robin and Linda met at Myrtle Beach, South Carolina, playing individually on the open stage at a bar. Linda was on her way to Nashville, and Robin followed her there. They were married in 1973 and started playing coffee houses, bars, and college convocations. They first appeared on "A Prairie Home Companion" in 1975. Garrison Keillor liked them so much that he invited them to do ten or twelve shows a year until he decided to discontinue the show (temporarily) in the 1980s. Disney videotaped

Robin and Linda Williams.
Courtesy of Robin Williams.

the last few shows from this period and showed them on the Disney Channel. When Keillor did several reunion shows, Disney recorded and showed those also. Two of the shows were in the Radio City Music Hall and Carnegie Hall in New York.

Robin and Linda's band, Their Fine Group, has included Jim Watson and Jimmy Gaudreau, and they have been part of the touring Columbia Arts Program, have played on "Austin City Limits," and have toured England, Scotland, and Denmark. Robin and Linda have been semiregulars on "A Prairie Home Companion" as themselves and as members of the Hopeful Gospel Quartet (with Garrison Keillor and recently Carol Elizabeth Jones). In 2003, Robin and Linda joined with Jimmy Fortune (who was a member of the Statler Brothers) to stage the Fortune-Williams Music Festival, an annual event in Staunton, Virginia.

They are also songwriters as well as playwrights, and their songs have been recorded by Emmylou Harris, Tom T. Hall, and others. Their musical *Stonewall Country* (about Stonewall Jackson) played for twenty years at the Limekiln Theater in Lexington, Virginia, with the Williamses in the cast. Other plays are *Virgil Powers*, *The Black Life*, and *Streets of Gold*, written for New York's Circle Repertory Company.

Robin and Linda have recorded seventeen albums, including *In the Company of Strangers* (Sugar Hill, 2000), *Devil of a Dream* (Sugar Hill, 1998, Gold Star Award for Best Contemporary Folk CD), *Good News: Robin and Linda Williams and Their Fine*

Group (Sugar Hill, 1997), *Climbing Up on the Rough Side*, with the Hopeful Gospel Quartet (High Bridge, 1997), and *Garrison Keillor and the Hopeful Gospel Quartet* (Sony/Epic, 1992). Their latest CD is *The First Christmas Gift* (Red House Records, 2005). See www.robinandlinda.com.

Robin and Linda live in the Shenandoah Valley near Middlebrook, Virginia, in an old house that has been added to over the years. When they're not touring, they write songs, work in their garden, and make art out of natural things.

AUNT JENNIE WILSON

Born Jennie Myrtle Ellid, February 1900, Henlawson,
West Virginia; died March 2, 1992, Logan County,
West Virginia

Aunt Jennie Wilson was a legend in West Virginia as a banjo player and singer and also as a superb storyteller and jokester, appearing at folk festivals, fairs, and college events. She also traveled beyond the borders of her native state at the invitation of West Virginians such as the singer-songwriter-playwright Billy Edd Wheeler, who produced a recording of her music and stories, *Billy Edd Wheeler Presents a Portrait of Aunt Jennie Wilson* (Sagittarius Records, SR 1969), recorded live at Warren Wilson College.

Born on Little Buffalo Creek in Logan County, she knew hard times and sorrow. Her miner husband James Wilson, whom she married in 1918, died in a slate fall in 1939, and she raised her children (Evelyn, Willard, and Virginia) alone on thirty-five dollars a month in compensation money and from what she could earn taking in washing and doing other odd jobs.

Jennie had an indomitable spirit, however, bolstered by her extended family and their love of music, humor, and storytelling. She learned a large repertoire of banjo tunes and songs in the oral tradition, and she followed the practice of collecting handwritten "ballet" sheets of favorite songs. She learned her style of banjo from her father and brothers and from Delpha Maynard, one of her brother's girlfriends. She started playing for square dances when she was about fourteen. Such dances were socially acceptable, but sometimes they got violent. She reported that once "someone fired a pistol, and the shot went through my banjer, and I thought for sure I was shot square through." Another time she told of an altercation where a woman provoked a man with a comment about his wife, and "he come up side of her head, and I swear to goodness, her dresstail popped when she hit the floor!"

Billy Edd Wheeler described Aunt Jennie:

> She was like a little wren. She was perky, soft-spoken—her voice had polka dots in it, ragged—she could come out with some zingers, like when she talked about the Beatles: "Billy Edd, I'd like to get my fingers wound in their hair and pull ever' hair

Aunt Jennie Wilson with Billy Edd
Wheeler. Courtesy of Billy Edd
Wheeler.

in their heads out, 'cause hit's a disgrace what has happened to our young people
on account of them Beatles."

I was driving her down from Peach Creek, and in Beckley, this woman cut right
in front of us, and I nearly hit her. Aunt Jennie said, "Lady, that's a good way to get
your ass in the morgue and your picture in the paper."

In 1955, the West Virginia University folklorist Dr. Patrick Gainer taught a folklore
class in Logan and asked his students to bring someone to class who could talk about
or demonstrate aspects of West Virginia folklore. One of his students brought Jennie.
Professor Gainer was so impressed with her singing and banjo playing that he took her
to Washington to record for the Library of Congress Archive of Folk Song. As a result
of the national folk revival, other festivals and arts and craft fairs were organized in
West Virginia, and Aunt Jennie was invited to perform in them. She became a regular
at the Mountain State Arts and Crafts Fair in Ripley and at the Vandalia Gathering in
Charleston. She was also invited to perform at colleges in West Virginia and elsewhere.
Her superb banjo playing, her singing of the old songs, and her humorous stories from
her life endeared her to thousands of people.

Before she died at the age of ninety-two, Aunt Jennie Wilson received the West
Virginia Department of Culture and History's Lifetime Achievement Award and also

the Vandalia Award. An annual folk festival held at Chief Logan State Park is named in honor of her.

(With credit to Billy Edd Wheeler and to Robert Spence, "Aunt Jennie Wilson: I Grew Up with Music," *Goldenseal* 10.1 [Spring 1984]: 9–15.)

Aunt Jennie: There was a woman that got some birth control pills and got them mixed up with her saccharin tablets. She had the sweetest little baby.

BUN WILSON

*Born Billy Bun Wilson, November 5, 1926,
Puryear, Tennessee*

Bun Wilson was born in West Tennessee, in a family of twelve children, and his middle name came from his father, whose nickname was Bun. He had made fun of a fellow who walked funny and whose wife's name was Bun, and people started calling him "Bun." When his son was born, he passed the name on as a middle name. Wilson remembers why he adopted Bun as his real name: "A teacher called me 'Billy.' She had a West Tennessee accent, and I just hated that. It sounded sissy to me."

Bun Wilson. Photo by Loyal Jones.

"I started out as a musician playing fiddle, then guitar. We were doing a show, and the comedian showed up drunk. I told him to leave but to give me his bag of clothes. So I did comedy that night. I had so much fun, I've done it ever since." When asked what it is like to make an audience laugh, he said, "There's no way to describe it. I just know that it does something to you." Fellow performers testify that he is also funny offstage. "Some comedians don't do comedy until they are on stage. I play it from the time I get up until I go to bed."

In 1957, Wilson was chosen for the Philip Morris Country Music Show that traveled out of Nashville giving free shows to promote the company's tobacco products. The shows were staged by the Jim Denny Artist Bureau and were billed as the "largest individual package sale in country music history." The cast included, from time to time, Carl Smith and His Tunesmiths, Goldie Hill, Red Sovine, Little Jimmy Dickens, Gordon Terry, George Morgan, and Bobby Lord, with Bun Wilson as the comedian. The first show opened in Richmond, Virginia, in January 1957 and then played to full houses in West Virginia,

Kentucky, Tennessee, Mississippi, and Louisiana. Extended to a sixteen-week tour, it eventually played to some four million people from one end of the country to the other. The Friday-evening performances were broadcast over the Mutual and then the CBS networks from whatever theater they were playing. This free show brought country music and Bun Wilson's comedy to new audiences and is judged to have spurred the growth of the industry. In between the concerts, the cast also entertained at military bases, at veteran's and other hospitals, and at manufacturing plants.

"When we started the show," Bun remembers, "they had me down for two minutes. So I'd throw in something extra, and they'd say, 'Leave that in.' When we finished that show—Red Sovine was my straight man—we had over thirty minutes of comedy in it."

During 1966–68, when a group of Nashville investors, including Hal Smith, Ray Price, Willie Nelson, and Hank Cochran, took an option on the "Renfro Valley Barn Dance," Bun Wilson was invited to do occasional shows there. Years later, when John Lair took over the shows again, Lair's daughter Ann Henderson asked Pete Stamper to put together a special show, and he and Bun Wilson came up with an all-comedy show to be called "Renfro Valley Comedy Daze," which included, in addition to Wilson and Stamper, James "Goober" Buchanan, Speck Rhodes, and several of the Renfro Valley musicians. In between shows, Bun had a camper-sales business in Clarksville, Tennessee. However, with things picking up in Renfro Valley, he became a regular on the "Barn Dance" and the "Jubilee," and he continues playing there every weekend. In addition to providing comedy for the evening shows, he, Pete Stamper, and Betty York do a Saturday-afternoon comedy show.

Bun's main comedy routine is doing a well-inebriated country fellow who would not be on anyone's social list and who usually comes in and interrupts the singing of the emcee, Jim Gaskin. His repertoire of jokes seems endless, reinforced by a wealth of material given to him by the old vaudevillian James "Goober" Buchanan. At the end of his act, however, Bun, a religious person, will straighten himself up, take off his askew hat, take up his guitar, and sing a hymn in a melodious bass voice.

The following recording is available: *Bun Wilson: Up Close and Personal* (RVEC BWO199, Renfro Valley Entertainment, Renfro Valley, KY 40473).

From a live performance at the "Renfro Valley Barn Dance":

> *Jim Gaskin: I told you that this Renfro Valley audience is a family-type show. I don't want none of them traveling salesman jokes that you've been telling the boys back there in the dressing room.*
> *Bun: This is a different traveling salesman.*
> *Jim: All right, it better be.*
> *Bun: He's traveling down this country road, graveled road. It was mighty rainy, and he had a flat tire. He got out and opened up his trunk, and he didn't have no jack. He didn't know what he was going to do.*
> *Jim: It was a mess, wasn't it?*

Bun: He looked across the field and seen this light at a farmer's house. . . .
Jim: Whoa, now, this sounds like this traveling salesman–farmer joke.
Bun: This was different farmer.
Jim: All right.
*Bun: He seen this light, see, and he clumb the fence and started walking across
    the field, stepping over the cow tracks, mud and stuff, got up and knocked on
    the door, and this farmer come to the door. The traveling salesman said, "I've
    had car trouble, and I need someplace to stay. Could you put me up tonight?"
    And the farmer said, "I ain't got but two beds. Me and my wife sleeps in one
    bed, and the redheaded schoolteacher sleeps in the other. . . ."*
Jim: Whoa! Now this sounds like that. . . .
Bun: Different schoolteacher.
Jim: All right.
*Bun: I said, "I don't mind sleeping with the redheaded schoolteacher, 'cause
    I'm a perfect gentleman." And the farmer said, "Well, I don't imagine the
    redheaded schoolteacher would care neither, 'cause he's a perfect gentleman
    too."*
Jim: Awwww!

EDNA WILSON. *See Sarie and Sally*

JUSTIN WILSON

*Born April 24, 1914, Roseland, Louisiana; died
September 5, 2000, Baton Rouge, Louisiana*

Justin Wilson's ticket to fame was Cajun humor and cuisine. The Louisiana Public Broadcasting shows that he hosted—"Cookin' Cajun," "Louisiana Cookin'," and "Easy Cookin'"—were carried over numerous other PBS stations, and his humorous stories and assertion "I ga-ron-tee" were known to millions. These shows led to five cookbooks, twenty-seven albums of Cajun humor, and one of Christmas songs, some of which he had composed, and he did after-dinner speeches and public appearances, some connected to country music shows.

Some Cajuns, including folklorists, took exception to Wilson's characterization of Cajun people and their dialect, but Wilson, who called himself a humorist rather than a comedian, responded that they were taking themselves too seriously and that he was laughing *with* rather than *at* Cajun people. He stressed further that he really admired Cajun wit, humor, and way of life. He said he was not Cajun but that his mother was of French extraction and that he had grown up in Cajun country. He also pointed out that he has done human-relations workshops helping groups, including police departments, to deal with diversity.

The son of a Louisiana Department of Agriculture commissioner, Wilson went to college for a while and then worked at whatever job he could get during the Depression. He eventually became a safety engineer inspecting warehouses in Louisiana. A student of Cajun dialect, stories, and food, he became a good cook, calling himself more of a gourmand than a gourmet, and when he landed his first cooking show he began telling Cajun stories. His first album of stories sold over a million copies. It was followed by others that sold well too (on Paula Records, a division of Jewel and Tower Records), and these led to five cookbooks published by Pelican Press and two others published by McMillan and William Morrow. Pelican also published three storybooks of Cajun humor. Justin Wilson Enterprises (Box 40446, Baton Rouge, LA 70835), in addition to his albums and books, sells several Cajun sauces.

Justin Wilson was married four times and had three daughters. In later years he made his home in Summit, Mississippi, forty-one miles from where he was born. He worked for numerous causes relating to preservation of wildlife and the natural environment, human relations, and patriotism. He is buried in St. William Cemetery, Port Vincent, Louisiana.

Justin Wilson. Courtesy of Justin Wilson Enterprises, Inc.

The following Justin Wilson story, "Sure Cure for a Sick Mule," is used with permission:

Not long ago I was down at Johnny Guitereau's, run by Peggy Berceguey. He's a wonderful man. That's a place where you can go at a quarter of five any mornin'. That's 4:45, I'm talkin' 'bout AM o'clock. And I's sittin' at the bar with a whole bunch, and you can get drunk if you want to! Dey're dere. You go back at ten o'clock and dey still dere too! At ten o'clock you ax one, "How 'bout a beer?" He say, "I maht try onnnne."

Well, I was in dere one day 'bout just a few week ago, talkin' to a Cajun friend of me, and another Cajun walked up to this Cajun what was a friend of me, and he say, "My friend, maybe you can help me. My old mule, my plow mule, what I got to make my garden and they hard to get now, he sick like hell. I don't know what's wrong with him. He got the colic or something, I don' know, maybe either one. Maybe you can tell me what to do."

The other'n said, "My old mule got sick like dat, and I give him a quart of turpentine." He say thanks. He went to the hardware store and picked up a quart of turpentine and went to his house and gave dat mule a quart of turpentine—killed him deader'n hell!

About four or three days he's back at Johnny Guitereau's, and I happened to be dere too—drinkin' buttermilk. He walked up to this other Cajun, said, "Didn't you say you gave your mule a quart of turpentine?" He say, "Dat's raht." He say, "I gave my mule a quart of turpentine, and it killed him deader'n hell!" Dat other Cajun said, "It killed mine too!"

LONNIE "PAP" WILSON

Born September 24, 1914, Comal, Texas;
died October 14, 1994, Tennessee

It is not clear how Lonnie Wilson got to Knoxville, Tennessee, but he already had show-business experience and used the title of "the Playboy Farmer." Shortly after Roy Acuff left Doc Hauer's Medicine Show in 1932, Roy and Lonnie played for square dances in the Knoxville area. He was a member of Roy's Tennessee Crackerjacks, later to become the Crazy Tennesseans, but he left to work in a shoe store. According to Elizabeth Schlappi, in her biography of Acuff, when Roy became a member of the "Grand Ole Opry" in 1939, he asked Wilson to look up Beecher "Pete" Kirby to see if they could play together. They could, and so Acuff offered them jobs with his "Opry" band, soon to become the Smoky Mountain Boys.

According to Schlappi, he perfected his "Pap" character shortly thereafter, based on an uncle who was described as a real character. Wilson usually wore chin whiskers, old-fashioned eyeglasses, a checkered shirt, suspenders, boots, and an old battered hat with the brim turned up in front. He was adept on guitar and also sometimes played the bass and sang baritone on duets. He did what Schlappi called "jovial slapstick" comedy and could balance the bass fiddle on his nose or chin, in imitation of Acuff's trick of balancing his fiddle in this way. He also led the jug band with the humorous pretense that they were going to depart from hillbilly music and render a classical number.

The war interrupted Wilson's career, and he served in the navy as a radar technician assigned to marine units that participated in island landings in the South Pacific. When he returned to the Smoky Mountain Boys, Joe Zinkan was playing the role of Pap. Wilson reassumed the old role, with Zinkan remaining as a member of the band. Apparently Acuff and Wilson did not tolerate each other too well, and the latter frequently left the band for other endeavors, but when he was there he played Pap, and he was in all of Acuff's movies. Schlappi reported Wilson as saying, "Roy and I go along together just so long, and then we drift apart." So he played off and on with Acuff between 1946 and 1960, when he left for good. He was a member of the Smoky Mountain Boys and supported Roy Acuff when he ran for governor in 1948. In 1963, Wilson did an LP for Starday, *Jokes, Laffs, Songs, and Gags about the Funny Side of Life, or How to Have Fun Even If You're Married* (SLP 219).

Lonnie Wilson and his wife Dixie had a daughter, Gail, born in the late 1930s. He died in 1994.

(With credit to Charles K. Wolfe; and Elizabeth Schlappi, *Roy Acuff: The Smoky Mountain Boy* [Gretna, La.: Pelican Publishing Co., 1978.])

Here are two stories from Pap about school days:

There was a second-grade teacher trying to teach spelling and arithmetic, and she was working on the word "feet." Agatha was having trouble. The teacher said, "Now, Agatha, what do I have two of that cows have four of?" And Agatha told her!

The teacher asked Johnnie which of his parents he favored, and he couldn't answer, so he came home and asked his mother. She replied, "You just tell her that you have your father's features but your eyes are like mine." Little Johnnie was hardly in the school when he made himself heard, "I can answer your question now, Teacher. My eyes are like my mother's, but I have my father's fixtures."

TIM WILSON

Born August 5, 1961, Columbus, Georgia

Tim Wilson writes and performs comedy songs, such as "Garth Brooks Has Ruined My Life" and "He's My Brother-in-Law." As a stand-up comedian he comes up with biting satire about everything from Abraham Lincoln to Al Gore, with a lot about the foibles of American life in between. He has appeared on "Evening at the Improv," "Caroline's Comedy Hour," "Comedy on the Road," Showtime's "Comedy Club Network," "Nashville Now," "The Tonight Show," "The Grand Ole Opry," and he performs at comedy clubs all over the nation. He has also played a character in the sitcom "Grace under Fire."

Besides his funny songs, Wilson does good stand-up comedy. He has an aggressive, in-your-face manner and a shouting country voice. He's good at imitating others, such as Strother Martin as the prison warden in *Cool Hand Luke*, and he can do a wonderfully irritating secretary on the telephone. His humor has a political bite to it, with liberals getting the worst of it. One of his funniest routines is "White Guys," like plumbers that won't come and fix anything because, "We're all covered up. We've got all we can do. We can't get to you today." Wilson figures that they're all covered up in Hispanics doing all the work. He concludes, "A Mexican is a great American!" Wilson isn't too concerned about political correctness.

Wilson admits that he was "always the ham growing up. I loved being the center of attention." After high school, he attended Presbyterian College in South Carolina, intending to be an English major, but he dropped out and supported himself with odd jobs before he thought about being a stand-up comedian. He started performing at a small theater in Atlanta, and then tried out for and won a contest sponsored by HBO and Cinemax. He won, and the prize was a chance to perform at Catch a Rising Star in New York City. This opened the way for television appearances, such as on "The Tonight Show with Jay Leno." In 1988 he won the southeastern Johnny Walker Red comedy competition. He released LPs on Southern Tracks and then signed with Capitol for the following cassettes and CDs: *Tim Wilson: Gettin' My Mind Right* (1999), *It's a*

Sorry World (1999), *I Should've Married My Father-in-Law* (2001), *Certified Aluminum: His Greatest Recycled Hits* (2002), *Hillbilly Homeboy* (2003), and *Super-Bad Sounds of the '70s* (2003).

Wilson has been the opening act for other entertainers such as Ricky Van Shelton, Clint Black, and the Beach Boys.

SCOTT AND MYRTLE WISEMAN.
See Lulu Belle and Scotty

SHEB WOOLEY

Born Shelby F. Wooley, April 10, 1921, Erick, Oklahoma; died September 16, 2003, Nashville, Tennessee

Sheb Wooley was a country-western singer, songwriter, actor, and comedian. He was known far and wide for his big hit "Purple People Eater" (number one pop) but also for his roles as an actor in such films as *High Noon* (with Gary Cooper and Grace Kelley), *Rocky Mountain* (with Errol Flynn), and *War Wagon* (with John Wayne). He was also a writer and cast member of the first twelve episodes of "Hee Haw" and wrote the theme song for the show.

Wooley is almost as well known for his comic character Ben Colder as he is by his real name. Wooley had a real talent for writing parodies of well-known songs as well as funny original ones, and he recorded a bunch of them as Ben Colder, including "Purple People Eater," which sold some three million copies. Colder is an alcoholic character on the order of Frank Fontaine, Foster Brooks, and Bun Wilson. His fictitious biography states that he was born "a little north of Nome, Alaska, where he tried to join the 'Alaska Club,' which has the requirements of drinking a quart of whiskey straight down and then shooting a polar bear and rubbing noses with an Eskimo woman." Ben, however, after gulping the whiskey, gets confused and rubs noses with the bear, which leaves him in a sorry shape. Wooley, as Ben Colder, won the Country Music Association's Comedian of the Year Award in 1968.

Wooley grew up on a farm, so he was familiar with animals and while a teenager began competing in rodeos in Oklahoma. His father swapped a shotgun for a guitar, and this sparked his interest in music. He started a band while he was still in high school. He went to Nashville in 1945 and sang over WLAC and recorded a few numbers for Bullet Records that didn't exactly take off. He moved to Fort Worth, Texas, in 1946, where he did radio work before moving on to Hollywood to try to get into the movies. In California he wrote songs and got a contract with MGM Records, a company he remained with for two decades. In his spare time, he took acting lessons and was successful as a character actor. In addition to the movies mentioned above, he had roles in *Little Big Horn*, *The Man without a Star*, *Rio Bravo*, *Giant*, and *How the West Was Won*. In 1958 he landed a role in the long-running television western "Rawhide" as Pete Nolan. In all, Wooley appeared in more than sixty films and fifty television shows.

Most of Ben Colder's fame comes from his comic recordings of Wooley's parody songs, such as "I Walk the Line No. 2," "Detroit City No. 2," "Runnin Bare," "Almost Persuaded No. 2," "Green, Green Grass of Home No. 2," "D-I-V-O-R-C-E No. 2," and of course "Purple People Eater," "Help Me Fake It through the Night," and "I Just Don't Look Good Naked Anymore."

Sheb Wooley settled in Nashville and made personal appearances as himself and Ben Colder until shortly before his death. His recordings are available on MGM and Bear Family.

HERMAN YARBOROUGH

Born August 14, 1930, Winston-Salem,
North Carolina

Herman Yarborough, a steel guitarist who played with several groups, created a comic character named Roscoe Swerps. Yarborough got into radio in Sanford, North Carolina, about 1947 with Smokey Graves and the Blue Star Boys. He played with them in Bristol, later in Burlington, North Carolina, and then in Roanoke and Lynchburg, Virginia. In Lynchburg they did their first television work on WLVA-TV. Before creating his Roscoe Swerps character, Yarborough and Jody Rainwater were a comedy duo with the Blue Star Boys beginning in 1949. Yarborough did Roscoe Swerps with the group until they disbanded in Stanton, and Yarborough found work at a mental hospital. In 1958, Buddy Starcher, who had left the entertainment business for a while, was putting together a band to play TV and radio in Harrisonburg, Virginia, and he hired Yarborough as a comedian. Yarborough described Buddy Starcher as "one of those rare people who knew how to program a show. He did not feature himself but built up the talented people around him. He was the straight man. We had a lot of fun working together." After a couple of years they moved to Channel 13 in Huntington, West Virginia, for a Saturday-night show sponsored by a mobile-home dealership. Then they moved to WCHS-TV in Charleston, where Yarborough spent the rest of his career.

Roscoe wore a ball cap turned sideways and Bermuda shorts until, he said, "the TV people didn't want to look at those bony legs anymore, and I had to change over to longer pants." He went on, "The latest thing I did, I had a handmade shirt with psychedelic lines on it somebody had sent me that I would slip into, which was handy for television. I wore one of those old state trooper's hats, with the brim turned up in front." He told jokes and did routines with others in the band, but, he said, "My main stay was songs, kind of nutty things, like 'Onions, Onions,' and 'If Texas Told What Arkansaw, What Did Tennessee?' old Lonzo and Oscar songs. I never resorted to anything that anyone in the family couldn't hear. If it wasn't funny enough clean, then I didn't use it."

Herman Yarborough retired to Elkview, near Charleston, and before heart surgery and a procedure to clear a carotid artery, he played the electric steel guitar and did comedy at the Elkview Community Center. He hopes to do so again.

> *Roscoe Swerps: Our old cow wouldn't give any milk, so we sold him.*
> *Our old cow fell through the bridge and strained her milk.*
> *(Sometimes given as mock song titles.)*

BETTY LOU YORK

Born February 20, 1938, Williamsburg, Kentucky

This popular comedienne at the "Renfro Valley Barn Dance" was born Betty Lou Davis in Williamsburg in southeastern Kentucky. Her family, like many other Appalachian migrants, moved north for employment, and she grew up in Richmond, Indiana. Her husband-to-be, George York, born in Conway, Kentucky, also migrated to Richmond, and there they met and were married. York got into comedy by doing a skit for her TOPS weight loss club. Her act, including diet jokes, went over so well that she was invited to entertain at other clubs. Then George pressed her into service for his Lions Club variety show, and she made such a hit that program directors from other clubs and from companies began calling. People who saw her perform encouraged her to go to Nashville or to get on television, but she held back because of a regular job and two children to rear. In fact, she hung up her dress and Minnie Pearl-type hat and tried to quit comedy entirely.

But she continued doing shows in and around Carlisle, Ohio, where the York family lived, and eventually Chubby Howard, the pedal steel player at the "Renfro Valley Barn Dance," taped her act and took it to Pete Stamper, the show's entertainment director, and the next week Pete called and invited her to be a guest. She was already familiar with the "Barn Dance," since her family had attended it frequently on visits to Kentucky. Stamper remembers, "She was not what we would call a professional entertainer, but right away I recognized a delivery and a knowledge of comedy material that is seldom seen in performers with her limited experience. For some time we had been making an effort to find a female comedian. I knew our search was over." After two trial shows, she was invited to become a regular in 1991 and has been at Renfro Valley ever since, delighted to be back in Kentucky. She was gratified too by her ability to make people laugh.

York believes that everybody needs humor in their lives and talks of the health-ful effects of laughter. Her comedy reflects a woman's point of view, in her case, the never ending struggle to keep from gaining weight, but she also gathers bits and pieces of conversation that can be worked into her act, and she makes up comedy that reveals the inconsistencies of human nature. "I don't do any ethnic jokes," she says, "or about any particular people. I only do jokes on me, my family, my husband. If I make fun of anybody being fat, it's me. That way I don't hurt anybody's feelings. I don't like humor at the expense of some-one else. People like to be incorporated into the humor and to know that you see that they're there, that you recognize them, but not to be made fun of." She goes on to talk about her father enjoying jokes and his love of laughter. She emphasizes the influence of comedians on radio, especially on the "Grand Ole Opry" and the "Renfro Valley Barn Dance." "Never in my wildest dream did I think I'd ever be on that stage," she said.

Betty Lou York. Courtesy of Betty Lou York.

York has made five comedy tapes that are avail-able through the General Store (Renfro Valley Entertainment Center, Renfro Valley, KY 40473). She has a daily radio program on WRVK in Renfro Valley. She and George live in Renfro Valley, and they have two sons, Steve and Scott.

Betty Lou: You know, I have noticed that thin people and fat people even think different. For instance, you stop on the street and ask a thin person for directions, and they'll think for a couple of minutes, and they'll say, "Well, you go down to the first intersection, turn left on Lincoln Avenue, go through three traffic lights, and it's a brown building in the middle of the block."

Now, you stop and ask a heavy person for the same directions, and I would say, "You go down here to Arby's, turn left, go past McDonald's, Wendy's, Hardee's, Pizza Hut. It's the chocolate-colored building right across from Kentucky Fried Chicken."

You see my dress? I figure, with a shape like mine, if you can't hide it, decorate it!

Did you see my first husband, Old George, when you came in tonight? Ain't he some-thing!? . . . He's aged a little bit, and now he thinks he's Peter Pan of the prune juice set. . . . He has taken up jogging now, though. I said to him, "George, why on earth wait till your senior days to take up jogging?" He said, "I just wanted to hear some heavy breathing again." . . . He went down to our local department store to buy me a new bra, went in the lingerie section, got that part right, told the sales lady he wanted a size seven and a half. She said, "Sir, how did you come to that size?" and George said, "With my hat." He came home, and he said, "Betty, I bought you a cowboy bra." I said, "Honey, what on earth is a cowboy bra?" He said, "It rounds 'em up and heads 'em out!"

JOE ZINKAN

Born 1918, place unknown; died January 15, 2003,
Nashville, Tennessee

Joe Zinkan played a rube known as "Cowboy Joe" with Pee Wee King and His Golden West Cowboys in 1937 and afterward. In 1943 he joined Roy Acuff's Smoky Mountain Boys when Lonnie "Pap" Wilson went into the navy. He played "Pap" with chin whiskers and rube costume, but when Wilson returned, he stayed on as a musician with the Smoky Mountain Boys until 1956. Zinkan retained his rube costume, but in deference to Wilson he took off his whiskers. Wilson, who had an on-and-off relationship with Acuff, often left the band, and Zinkan played "Pap" when he was not there. Zinkan also played "Smilin' Joseph," a character who never smiled.

Elizabeth Schlappi, author of *Roy Acuff: The Smoky Mounain Boy*, described Zinkan as a good showman with the bass fiddle—with "dry humor, but silent, reliable." He eventually became a studio musician in Nashville. A serious bassist, he played on the recordings of dozens of country music stars.

(With credit to Elizabeth Schlappi, *Roy Acuff, The Smoky Mountain Boy* [Gretna, La.: Pelican Publishing Co., 1978].)

SOURCES

BOOKS AND ARTICLES

Adler, Thomas A. "The Uses of Humor by Bluegrass Musicians." *Mid-American Folklore* 10.2 (Fall/Winter 1982): 17–26.

Alvey, R. Gerald. *Dulcimer Maker: The Craft of Homer Ledford.* 1984; reprint, Lexington: University Press of Kentucky, 2003.

Anderson, Bill. *I Hope You're Living as High on the Hog as the Pig You Turned out to Be.* Atlanta: Longstreet Press, 1993.

Artis, Bob. *Bluegrass.* New York: Hawthorne Books, 1975.

Blount, Roy, Jr. "Tennis-Shoe Tongue in His Head: How Brother Dave's Political Incorrectness Boomeranged." *Oxford American* 40 (Fifth Annual Music Issue, n.d. [ca. 2001]): 205–7.

Campbell, Archie, with Ben Byrd. *Archie Campbell: An Autobiography.* Memphis: Memphis State University Press, 1981.

Carlin, Richard. *The Big Book of Country Music: A Biographical Encyclopedia.* New York: Penguin, 1995.

Center for Folklife Programs and Cultural Studies Archive. Smithsonian Institution, Washington, D.C. Audio holdings on selections with Medicine Show in all fields, 1998.

Choate, Billy. *Born in a Trunk . . . Just Outside the Center Door Fancy.* Kearney, Neb.: Morris Publishing, 1994.

Cogswell, Robert G. "Jokes in Blackface: A Discographic Folklore Study." Ph.D. dissertation, Indiana University, 1984.

Cohen, Norm. Liner notes to *Minstrels and Tunesmiths: The Commercial Roots of Early Country Music* (LP-109). Los Angeles: John Edwards Memorial Foundation, 1981.

———. "The Skillet Lickers: A Study Of A Hillbilly String Band and Its Repertoire." *Journal of American Folklore* 78 (1965): 229–44.

The Complete U.S. Country Music Encyclopedia. London: Boxtree, 1995.

Cusic, Don. "Comedy and Humor in Country Music." *Journal of American Culture* 16.2 (Summer 1993): 45–50.

———. *It's the Cowboy Way! The Amazing True Adventures of Riders in the Sky.* Lexington: University Press of Kentucky, 2003.

Daniel, Wayne W. "'Are You Ready, Hezzie?' and Other Harmonious High Jinks of Those

Hilarious Hoosier Hot Shots." *Nostalgia Digest and Radio Guide* (October–November 1996): 26–30.

———. "Chick Stripling: Dancer, Comedian, and Old-Time Fiddler." *Bluegrass Unlimited* 28.5 (November 1993): 36–39.

———. "Cousin Emmy: A Popular Entertainer Country Music History Almost Forgot." *Bluegrass Unlimited* 20.4 (October 1985): 64–68.

———. "Goober Buchanan: The Favorite Nut of the South." *Old Time Country* (Fall/Winter 1993–94): 12–17.

———. "Good Old Songs, Good Old Jokes, Good Old Boys." *Bluegrass Unlimited* 23.10 (April 1989): 32–86.

———. *Pickin' on Peachtree: A History of Country Music in Atlanta, Georgia.* Urbana: University of Illinois Press, 1990.

———. "Tex Forman and Curley Collins Remember Pop Eckler and His Young'uns." *John Edwards Memorial Foundation Quarterly* 16.59 (Fall 1980): 133–39.

Faulk, John Henry. *Fear on Trial.* Austin: University of Texas Press, 1983.

Fredriksson, Kristine. "Minnie Pearl and Southern Humor in Country Entertainment." In *Country Music 2000 Annual.* Ed. Charles K. Wolfe and James E. Akenson. Lexington: University Press of Kentucky, 2000. 75–88.

Fulcher, Bobby. *The Cumberland Music Tour.* Nashville: Tennessee Arts Commission, 1988.

Gentry, Linnell, ed. *A History and Encyclopedia of Country, Western, and Gospel Music.* 2d ed. Nashville: Clairmont Corp., 1969.

Green, Douglas B. *Country Roots: The Origins of Country Music.* New York: Hawthorn Books, 1976.

Hagan, Chet. *Grand Ole Opry.* New York: Owl Books, 1989.

Hall, Wade. *Hell-Bent for Music: The Life of Pee Wee King.* Lexington: University Press of Kentucky, 1996.

Hall, Wade, and Greg Swem. *A Song in Native Pastures: Randy Atcher's Life in Country Music.* Louisville: Harmony House Publishers, 2002.

Haynes, Henry "Homer," and Kenneth "Jethro" Burns. "From Moonshine to Martinis." *Journal of Country Music* 15.2 (1993): 4–5; 15.3 (1993): 3–4; and 16.1 (1993): 3–5.

Henderson, Ann Lair. *On the Air . . . with John Lair.* Mount Vernon, Ky.: Polly House Publications, 1998.

Henry, Murphy. "Joe Forrester: Forgotten Blue Grass Boy." *Bluegrass Unlimited* 37.2 (August 2002): 44–50.

Holland, Ted. *B Western Encyclopedia.* Jefferson, N.C.: McFarland and Co., 1989.

Hull, Kenneth C. *Lily May and the Legendary Coon Creek Girls.* Lexington, Ky.: N.p., 1985.

Jones, Louis M. "Grandpa," with Charles K. Wolfe. *Everybody's Grandpa: Fifty Years behind the Mike.* Knoxville: University of Tennessee Press, 1984.

Jones, Loyal. *Radio's 'Kentucky Mountain Boy,' Bradley Kincaid.* Berea, Ky.: Berea College Appalachian Center, 1980.

Kienzle, Rich. "The Checkered Career of Hank Penny." *Journal of Country Music* 3.2 (1980): 43–77.

Kinsgbury, Paul, ed. *The Encyclopedia of Country Music.* New York: Oxford University Press, 1998.

Lee, Judith Yaross, *Garrison Keillor: A Voice of America.* Oxford: University of Mississippi Press, 1991.

Lightfoot, William. "Brother Dave Gardner." *Southern Quarterly* 4.3 (Spring 1996): 81–93.

———. "Esoteric and Exoteric Dimensions of Appalachian Folk Humor." In *Curing the Cross-Eyed Mule: Appalachian Mountain Humor.* Ed. Loyal Jones and Billy Edd Wheeler. Little Rock, Ark.: August House, 1989. 187–203.

Lornell, Kip. *Virginia's Blues, Country, and Gospel Records, 1902–1943: An Annotated Discography.* Lexington: University Press of Kentucky, 1989.

Lovullo, Sam, and Marc Eliot. *Life in the Kornfield: My Twenty-five Years at Hee Haw.* New York: Boulevard Books, 1996.

Malone, Bill C. *Country Music, USA.* Rev. ed. Austin: University of Texas Press, 1989.

———. *Don't Get above Your Raisin': Country Music and the Southern Working Class.* Urbana: University of Illinois Press, 2002.

McCloud, Barry, ed. *Definitive Country: The Ultimate Encyclopedia of Country Music and Its Performers.* New York: Perigree, 1995.

McLean, Albert F. Jr. *American Vaudeville as Ritual.* Lexington: University Press of Kentucky, 1965.

McNamara, Brooks. "The Medicine Show." *Festival of American Folklife Program Book.* Washington, D.C.: Smithsonian Institution, 1979. 15–16.

Parton, Dolly. *Dolly: My Life and Other Unfinished Business.* New York: Harper Collins, 1994.

Rice, Harry S. "Renfro Valley on the Radio." *Journal of Country Music* 19.2 (1997): 16–25.

———. "Traveling Shows." In *Encyclopedia of Appalachia.* Ed. Rudy Abramson and Jean Haskell. Knoxville: University of Tennessee Press, 2006. 494–95.

Rosenbaum, Art. *Folk Visions and Voices: Traditional Music and Song in North Georgia.* Athens: University of Georgia Press, 1985.

Rosenberg, Neil V. *Bluegrass: A History.* Urbana: University of Illinois Press, 1985.

———. "Folklore in a Frame: Bluegrass Comedy Routines." Paper presented at the Annual Meeting of the American Folklore Society, Baltimore, October 23, 1986.

Rothel, David. *Those Great Cowboy Sidekicks.* Madison, N.C.: Empire Publishing, 2001.

Rouark, Constance. *American Humor: A Study of the National Character.* Garden City, N.Y.: Doubleday, 1953.

Schlappi, Elizabeth. *Roy Acuff: The Smoky Mountain Boy.* Gretna, La.: Pelican, 1978.

Shelby, Anne. "The R Word: What's So Funny (and Not So Funny) about Redneck Jokes." In *Confronting Appalachian Stereotypes: Back Talk from an American Region.* Ed. Dwight B. Billings, Gurney Norman, and Katherine Ledford. Lexington: University Press of Kentucky, 1999. 153–60.

Shelton, Robert, and Burt Goldblatt. *The Country Music Story: A Picture History of Country and Western Music.* Secaucus, N.J.: Castle Books, 1966.

Smyth, William Jensen. "Early Knoxville Radio (1921–41): WNOX and the 'Mid-day Merry-Go-Round.'" *John Edwards Memorial Foundation Quarterly* 67–68 (Fall/Winter 1982): 109–15.

———. *Traditional Humor on Knoxville Radio Entertainment Shows.* Ann Arbor, Mich.: UMI Dissertation Services, 1987.

Spears-Stewart, Reta. *Remembering the Ozark Jubilee.* Springfield, Mo.: Stewart, Dilbeck, and White Productions, 1993.

Stamper, Pete. *It All Happened in Renfro Valley.* Lexington: University Press of Kentucky, 1999.

"Top Ten Living Country Comedians." *Music City News* 35.9 (March 1998): 28–41.

Tosches, Nick. "Emmett Miller: The Final Chapter." *Journal of Country Music* 18.3 (1996): 27–37.

———. "Get Down, Moses." *Oxford American* 16 (Summer 1997): 128–33.

———. "The Strange and Hermetical Case of Emmett Miller." *Journal of Country Music* 17.1 (1994): 39–47.

Tribe, Ivan M. "Kentucky Slim: Comedian in Medicine Shows, Old-Time, and Bluegrass Music." *Bluegrass Unlimited* 16.5 (November 1981): 20–22.

———. *Mountaineer Jamboree: Country Music in West Virginia.* Lexington: University Press of Kentucky, 1984.

———. *The Stonemans: An Appalachian Family and the Music That Shaped Their Lives.* Urbana: University of Illinois Press, 1993.

Tribe, Ivan M., and John W. Morris. "Bill Napier: Creative Instrumentalist." *Bluegrass Unlimited* 14.7 (January 1980): 20–23.

Wesbrooks, Cousin Wilbur, with Barbara M. McLean and Sandra S. Grafton. *Everybody's Cousin.* Rockville Centre, N.Y.: Manor Books, 1979.

Wilds, David, interviewed by Grant Alden. "Hank, Honey, and History." *No Depression* 1.4 (Summer 1996): 48–55.

Williamson, J. W. *Hillbillyland: What the Movies Did to the Mountains and What the Mountains Did to the Movies.* Chapel Hill: University of North Carolina Press, 1995.

Wolfe, Charles K. *A Good-Natured Riot: The Birth of the Grand Ole Opry.* Nashville: Country Music Foundation and Vanderbilt University Press, 1999.

———. *In Close Harmony: The Story of the Louvin Brothers.* Jackson: University of Mississippi Press, 1996.

———. *Kentucky Country: Folk and Country Music of Kentucky.* Lexington: University Press of Kentucky, 1982.

———. *Tennessee Strings: The Story of Country Music in Tennessee.* Knoxville: University of Tennessee Press, 1977.

Zwonitzer, Mark, and Charles Hirshberg. *Will You Miss Me When I'm Gone? The Carter Family and Their Legacy in American Music.* New York: Simon and Schuster, 2002.

SELECTED RECORDINGS

Blue Sky Boys, Bill and Earl Bolick, on Radio. Vol. 1: *Rare Radio Transcriptions in Atlanta, Georgia, in 1946 and 1947.* Liner notes by Bill Bolick (Copper Creek Recordings, 1993).

Carl Hurley: Might as Well Laugh! Cassette (Louisville: McKinney Associates, 1996).

Chonda Pierce on Her Soapbox. Cassette (Franklin, Tenn.: Michael Smith and Associates, 2000).

Comedy for the Road. Vol. 2. Cassette (King Records, 1996).

The Comedy of Fred Smith. Cassette (Pigeon Forge, Tenn.: Comedy Barn, n.d.).

Comedy Songs of Lulu Belle and Scotty. Vol. 3. Cassette (Portagevile, Mo.: Mar-Lu Records, n.d.).

Cotton-Pickin' Good! The Comedy of Cotton Ivy. Cassette (Louisville: McKinney Associates, 1997).

Dry Branch Fire Squad. Cassette (Rounder Records, 1996).

Hee Haw Laffs. Vol. 1. Video (Nashville: Hee Haw Video, 1996).

The Hired Hands with Snuffy Jenkins and Homer Sherrill: Something Special. Cassette (Brighton, Mich.: Old Homestead Records, 1989).

Jerry Clower's Greatest Hits. Cassette (Universal City, Calif.: MCA, 1979).

Jim Stafford: Live and Kickin'! Video (Branson, Mo.: Jim Stafford Theater, 1993).

Landry, Bill. *The Heartland Series*. Vol. 14. Video (Knoxville: WBIR-TV).

Live from the Mel Tillis Theater. Video (Branson, Mo.: Mel Tillis Theater, 1994).

Louisiana Hayride, Classic Comedy Radio. Cassette (Music Mill Entertainment, 2000).

Memories of the Legends. 24 vols. Video (Orlando, Fla.: Gannaway Productions, 1999).

Minnie Pearl: Old Times. Video (Nashville: Opryland Home Video, 1988).

Presleys' Jubilee. Vol. 5. Video (Branson, Mo.: Presleys' Jubilee, n.d.).

Rainbow Quest. Number 18: *Pete Seeger, Clinch Mountain Boys, and Cousin Emmy* (New York: Norman Ross Publishing, n.d.).

Randall Franks with "Doc" Tommy Scott: Comedy Down Home (Tunnel Hill, Ga.: Randall Franks Fan Club, 1999).

Still Ramblin': The Tommy Scott Show. Video (Toccoa, Ga.: Katona Productions and Peach Picked Productions, 2001).

Tribute: Grand Ole Opry Stars of the Fifties. 12 vols. Video (Orlando, Fla.: Gannaway Productions, 1996).

Uncle Dave Macon: Early Recordings, 1925–35. Cassette (Floyd, Va.: County Records, n.d.).

Virgil Anderson . . . on the Tennessee Line. LP 777 (Floyd, Va.: County Records, 1980).

The VW Boys Radio Show. Cassette (Blountville, Tenn.: n.d.).

What a Crowd! What a Night!: Ralph Emery and the Geezinslaw Brothers. Video (Nashville: Shadetree Productions, 1993).

Will the Real Shotgun Red Please Stand Up! Video (Nashville: Shotgun Red Merchandise, 1991).

INTERVIEWS

Francis Abernethy (telephone), Nacogdoches, Tex., April 4, 2002.

Shelia Kay Adams (telephone), Mars Hill, N.C., July 9, 2002.

Sammy Allred (telephone), Austin, Tex., December 16, 1997; February 4, 2003.

Virgil Anderson, Wayne County, Ky., assisted by John Harrod, July 20, 1984.

Randy Atcher (telephone), Louisville, Ky., December 15, 1999; February 4, 2002.

Billy Baker (telephone), Pigeon Forge, Tenn., May 23, 2002.

Terryl Bechtol (telephone), Pensacola Beach, Fla., December 11, 2002.

Bill Bolick (telephone), Hickory, N.C., December 16, 1996; July 17, 1998.

Bruce Bollerud (telephone), Madison, Wisc., January 1, 2003; January 21, 2003.

Claude Boone (telephone), Strawberry Plains, Tenn., November 12, 1999.

Rick Bragg (telephone), Jacksonville, Ala., October 14, 2003.

Thomas Hoyt "Slim" Bryant (telephone), Pittsburgh, Pa., May 16, 2001.

James G. Buchanan (telephone), Bowling Green, Ky., September 11, 1996.

Phil Campbell (telephone), Powell, Tenn., October 30, 1996; January 20, 1997.

Bill Carlisle, Norris, Tenn., October 12, 1996.

Joe Carter, Hiltons, Va., August 28, 1976; (telephone) May 16, 2003.

Bobby Cheek, Norris, Tenn., October 13, 1996; (telephone) October 31, 2001.

Billy Choate (telephone), Wayne City, Ill., September 4, 2002.

Manuel "Old Joe" Clark, Richmond, Ky., October 30, 1996.

Clarence C. "Slim" Clere (telephone), Charleston, W.Va., October 4, 1999.

Jerry Clower (telephone), Yazoo City, Miss., February 10, 1998.

Roby Cogswell (telephone), Nashville, Tenn., March 22, 1997.

John Cohen (telephone), Putnam Valley, N.Y., December 8, 1999.

SOURCES

Charlie Collins, Norris, Tenn., October 12, 1996.

Hal Crowther (telephone), Hillsborough, N.C., October 4, 2002.

Leora Day (telephone), Falls of Rough, Ky., November 3, 2005; February 21, 2008.

Richard Day (telephone), Waterloo, Iowa, November 7, 2005, February 21, 2008.

William Day (telephone), Waterloo, Iowa, March 28, 2006.

Ronald DeMoor (telephone), August 13 and 14, 2002.

Rodney Dillard, Lexington, Ky., June 12, 1999.

Albert Elliott (telephone), Big Stone, Va., February 15, 2001.

Wayne Erbson (telephone), Swannanoa, N.C., October 12, 1996.

Etta May (telephone), Lexington, Ky., May 29, 2002; June 6, 2002.

Tommy Faile (telephone), Gastonia, N.C., December 9, 1996.

Tex Forman (telephone), Douglasville, Ga., February 26, 2000.

Joe Forrester (telephone), Hermitage, Tenn., February 7, 2003.

Bill Foster (telephone), Florence, Ala., June 11, 2002.

Tom Fouts (telephone), Young America, Ind., November 20, 1996.

Randall Franks (telephone and e-mail), Ringgold, Ga., December 2006 and January 2007.

Kinky Friedman, interview by Bill Malone and Bobbie Malone, New York, N.Y., September 3, 1999.

Al Gannaway and Allen Messer (telephone), Nashville, Tenn., February 15, 2000.

Jim Gaskin, Renfro Valley, Ky., November 16, 1996; (telephone) June 16, 2000.

George Gilbertson (telephone), Madison, Wisc., January 21, 2003; February 21, 2008.

Freddie Lee Goble (telephone), Prestonsburg, Ky., October 6, 2001.

Melvin Goins, Stanton, Ky., October 21, 1996; (telephone) May 5, 2000.

Roy "Whitey" Grant (telephone), Charlotte, N.C., December 7, 1996; July 16 and 17, 1998.

Douglas B. Green (telephone), Nashville, Tenn., October 9, 2001.

Rayna Green (telephone), Washington, D.C., January 3, 2000.

Archie Greene (telephone), San Francisco, Calif., March 12, 2001; April 25, 2003.

James Gregory (telephone), Marietta, Ga., May 15, 2003.

Steve Hall (telephone), Nashville, Tenn., February 24, 2003.

Rodney Harris (telephone), Centerville, Tenn., February 23, 1998.

John Hartford, Norris, Tenn., October 12, 1996; (telephone) October 15, 1996.

Ann Lair Henderson (telephone), Mount Vernon, Ky., February 3, 2003; February 10, 2008.

Dick Hill (telephone), Hastings, Neb., October 15, 2000.

Glenn Hinson (telephone), Chapel Hill, N.C., September 5, 2001.

Arvol Hogan (telephone), Charlotte, N.C., December 6, 1996.

David Holt (telephone), Fairdale, N.C., December 2, 1996.

Carl Hurley, Richmond, Ky., January 22, 1997.

Jerry Isaacs (telephone), Somerset, Ky., April 28, 1998.

L. H. "Cotton" Ivy (telephone), Decaturville, Tenn., August 8, 2002.

Mitch Jayne, Lexington, Ky., June 12, 1999.

Louis Marshall "Grandpa" Jones, Norris, Tenn., October 12, 1996.

Ramona Jones, Norris, Tenn., October 12, 1996.

Carl Keys (telephone), Woodstock, Ont., March 13, 2003.

Beecher Kirby (telephone), Madison, Tenn., October 16, 1996.

Fred LaBour, Frankfort, Ky., November 8, 2003.

John Lair, Renfro Valley, Ky., April 30, 1974; April 15, 1975.

Doyle Lawson, Norris, Tenn., October 13, 1996; October 14, 2001.

Homer C. Ledford (telephone), Winchester, Ky., December 13, 2002.

Charles Lilly (telephone), Nashville, Tenn., January 5, 1998.
Dan Lilly (telephone), Beckley, W.Va., December 24, 1997.
Everette Lilly (telephone), Beckley, W.Va., November 1, 1996.
Charlie Louvin (telephone), Nashville, Tenn., November 15, 1996.
Wade Mainer (telephone), Flint, Mich., November 9, 1996.
Bill C. Malone (telephone), Madison, Wisc., April 20, 2001; August 5, 2002; September 5, 2002; May 16, 2003.
Juanita McMichen Lynch (telephone), Battletown, Ky., November 14, 2000; May 21, 2001.
Jim McReynolds (telephone), Nashville, Tenn., November 11, 1996.
Butch Medford, Norris, Tenn., October 13, 1996.
Bonnie Lou Moore (telephone), Morristown, Tenn., March 30, 2000.
Dorothy Morford (telephone), Gastonia, N.C., November 20, 2000.
Gary "Mule Deer" Morris (telephone), Spearfish, S.Dak., September 7, 2000.
Bob Murphey (telephone), Nacogdoches, Tex., April 5, 2002.
Tim O'Brien (telephone), Nashville, Tenn., January 6, 1998.
Donald Payne (telephone), Ashland, Ky., April 17, 2001.
Chonda Pierce (telephone), Nashville, Tenn., September 14, 2000.
Anita Pruett (telephone), Asheville, N.C., March 8, 2003.
Marc Pruett (telephone), Asheville, N.C., January 15, 2003.
Ernestine Rector, Norris, Tenn., October 12, 1996.
Perry "Dusty" Rhodes (telephone), Dickson, Tenn., November 9, 2000.
George Riddle, Norris, Tenn., October 12, 1996.
James Roberts (telephone), Lexington, Ky., August 28, 2001.
James "Sparky" Rucker, Norris, Tenn., October 12, 1996.
Raye Rutherford, Norris, Tenn., October 13, 1996; (telephone) October 17, 2001.
Homer Sherrill (telephone), Chapin, S.C., November 8, 1996; August 29, 2001.
Larry Sledge, Norris, Tenn., October 12, 1996.
Joe Smiddy, Norris, Tenn., October 12, 1996; (telephone) May 6, 1998.
Fred E. Smith, Pigeon Forge, Tenn., September 15, 1996; (telephone) November 16, 1999.
Lee Smith (telephone), Hillsborough, N.C., October 4, 2002.
Mike Snider, Norris, Tenn., October 11, 2002; Gleason, Tenn. (telephone), December 17, 1996; November 11, 2002.
Robby Spencer (telephone), Bluff City, Tenn., April 19, 2003.
Ann Stafford (telephone), Branson, Mo., August 24, 2001.
Pete Stamper, Renfro Valley, Ky., April 16, 1998.
Ralph Stanley, Norris, Tenn., October 11, 2002; McClure, Va. (telephone), January 12, 1997.
Bill Stewart, Norris, Tenn., October 11, 1998.
Tim Stivers (telephone), Anchorage, Ky., December 20, 2001.
Roni Stoneman (telephone), Nashville, Tenn., February 5, 1997.
Rollin Sullivan and Geneva Sullivan (telephone), November 15, 1996.
Slim Sweet, Norris, Tenn., October 12, 1996.
Gordie Tapp (telephone), Woodstock, Ont., March 13, 2003.
Ballard Taylor, Covington, Ky., November 13, 1996.
Tommy Taylor, Rabbitt Hash, Ky., November 13, 1996; (telephone) October 11, 2001.
Ron Thomason, Lexington, Ky., summer 1999; (telephone) January 14, 1997; and January 29, 2003.
Ivan Tribe (telephone), McArthur, Ohio, March 22, 2004.
Harriet Neumann Troyan (telephone), Cleveland, Ohio, January 30, 2002.

SOURCES

Joe Troyan (telephone), Cleveland, Ohio, January 2, 1997.

Sam Venable, Norris, Tenn., October 11, 1998.

Larry Webster (telephone), Pikeville, Ky., December 14, 2002.

Billy Edd Wheeler (telephone), Swannanoa, N.C., June 12, 2001; December 11, 2002; January 18, 2003.

Don White (Whitsell) (telephone), Charlotte, N.C., December 7, 1996.

Tim White (telephone), Blountville, Tenn., April 4, 2003.

Doc Williams (telephone), Wheeling, W.Va., December 20, 1996; March 22, 2002.

Robin Williams (telephone), Middlebrook, Va., April 12, 2001.

Bun Wilson, Renfro Valley, Ky., November 16, 1998; (telephone) May 26, 2000.

Lulu Belle Wiseman, interview by Marshall Dial, Spruce Pine, N.C., July 1986.

Betty Lou York (telephone), Renfro Valley, Ky., November 21, 1996.

INDEX

LOYAL JONES is author, coauthor, or editor of ten books and dozens of articles on Appalachian culture, including *Appalachian Values, Faith and Meaning in the Southern Uplands*, and *Laughter in Appalachia: A Festival of Southern Mountain Humor*. After twenty-three years directing the Appalachian Center and teaching Appalachian studies at Berea College in Kentucky, he retired in 1993.

Music in American Life